Flags commemorating 100 years of Canadian Confederation line the walk leading to the Peace Tower of the Houses of Parliament. A "mountie", a member of Canada's famed RCMP, is in the foreground.

The name "Canada", believed to have been derived from the Huron-Iroquois Indian word *kanata*, meaning a village or community, first appears in a narrative of Jacques Cartier (1535) and a century later in Robert's Merchants' Map of Canada, 1638. Thereafter, the name became the popular designation for the colony of New France and ultimately for the whole country.

# CANADA

## ONE HUNDRED

# 1867-1967

*Prepared in the*
Canada Year Book
Handbook and Library Division
Dominion Bureau of Statistics
Ottawa

*Published under the authority of*
*The Honourable Robert H. Winters*
*Minister of Trade and Commerce*

# Contents

# Contents (Continued)

# Foreword

The production of this book, *Canada One Hundred 1867-1967*, is the special contribution of the Dominion Bureau of Statistics to the publishing program of the Government of Canada in commemoration of its first hundred years of Confederation. It is the latest in a series of illustrated Official Canada Handbooks launched on the occasion of Canada's Diamond Jubilee of Confederation in 1927 and published annually since 1930, depicting *recent progress* in the economic, social and cultural development of the nation.

This enlarged Centennial volume, published instead of a standard Official Handbook "Canada 1967", portrays the changing 'Face of Canada' during a *century of progress;* the land and its people, the Canadian manner of nation-building, the spread of settlement, and the development of the pioneer colonial community into a modern industrial state. It covers Canada's social institutions and cultural milieu, its emergence as a 'middle power' in international affairs, and concludes with examples of Canadian plans for the 1967 Centennial celebrations and a selected list of books about Canada.

I join with the Editor in expressing gratitude to the contributing writers from within the Public Service of Canada and the Universities (brief biographical notes on whom appear near the close of this volume), and to our colleagues in the Bureau of Statistics. Particular recognition is due to members of the staff of the Canada Year Book, Handbook and Library Division of the Bureau of Statistics for their work in checking statistical data, typing drafts and final copy, and in the proof-reading and indexing of the book. I wish to acknowledge the extensive assistance of the Queen's Printer and his Publications Production Branch, and the encouragement received from the Centennial Commission and the Interdepartmental Committee on the 1967 Program throughout the production of this Centennial volume; and finally to record our appreciation of the fine craftsmanship of the commercial typographic, photographic, lithographing and book-binding firms associated in the final stages of its production.

*Canada One Hundred 1867-1967* was planned, edited and produced by Dr. C. C. Lingard, Director of the Canada Year Book, Handbook and Library Division, assisted by Miss Helen Champion.

Walter E. Duffett.

Dominion Statistician

Dominion Bureau of Statistics,
Ottawa, November 1, 1966.

(Above) St. John's, Newfoundland, one of the oldest settlements in North America, is Canada's most easterly city. Here Marconi received the first transatlantic wireless message (1901); and Alcock and Brown began the first non-stop flight across the Atlantic (1919).

(Right) Vancouver, British Columbia, is Canada's largest seaport on the west coast. Incorporated in 1886, it is now the third largest city in Canada.

CANADA, 1867-1967

# Introducing Canada

*The wholesome Sea is at her gates*
*Her gates both East and West,*
*Then is it strange that we should love*
*This land, our Land, the best?*
*—J. A. Ritchie*

# The Land and People

*"In geographical area, this Confederation of the British North American Provinces is even now large—it may become one day second only in extent to the vast territories of Russia . . . ."*

—*Earl of Carnarvon, 1867*

It was a prescient observation—all the more remarkable since the land of which the Earl spoke so eloquently was sparsely populated, embraced only a minuscule proportion of the vast domain that is Canada today, and was beset by economic and financial difficulties.

Less than a century later, however, the nation had fulfilled the promises of 1867. Today Canada *is* "second only in extent to the vast territories of Russia". It has an area of 3,851,809 square miles, is bounded by three oceans, the Atlantic, Pacific and Arctic, and on the fourth side shares an unfortified frontier of almost 4,000 miles with the United States. Despite its giant size, Canada's population is only some 20,000,000 —a modest increase from its 3,500,000 at Confederation.

Canada's geological history may be traced back more than two billion years, but its recorded story is brief, indeed. Peopled by Indian and Eskimo nomads some thousands of years ago, and subsequently explored by other adventurers, Canada defied "official" discovery until a Venetian, John Cabot, sailing under a British flag in 1497 found a vast continent in the western world. His report of the region induced maritime nations of Europe to exploit the rich natural resources of the area. Then came Jacques Cartier in 1534 to plant the flag of France on a Gaspé promontory. Colonization soon followed. A fellow countryman, Samuel de Champlain, erected a settlement at Port Royal in 1605 and at Quebec in 1608. British settlements, too, soon appeared. Though thousands of peoples of other nationalities have since found on this continent a haven of economic opportunity—and of freedom—the original British-French composition still predominates in the ethnic composition of Canada.

Nowhere has time changed the industrial and social milieu more swiftly, more dramatically, than in Canada during the past hundred years. Where there were only four provinces in 1867, there are now ten, with two vast northern territories hovering on the brink of provincial status. An economy dependent on staple products in 1867 has been supplemented by a bustling manufacturing complex; social security measures, undreamed of a century ago, have become the prerogative of a nation; cities and towns have expanded into a multiplicity of metropolitan areas; communication and transportation facilities have surmounted difficulties of terrain and distance to provide the most modern services; hydro and thermal electric power, nuclear installations, and vast mineral discoveries have provided the sinews of immense industrial power. Millions of dollars, too, are being spent on the advancement of education in Canada, and the arts are flourishing.

It is impossible to define Canada—or Canadians. The area is too vast, too diverse; its people too varied in outlook and origin to earn the designation, "typical". Actually, there are many Canadas—the historic Atlantic area where ceaseless tides beat their rhythm on the shores and headlands of four provinces; the French-Canadian province of Quebec, the newly-awakened giant of the industrial world; Ontario, for so long

Reminiscent of the lochs and glens of old Scotland are the highlands of Nova Scotia's beautiful Island of Cape Breton, site of the only Gaelic College in Canada.

the magnet of industry and immigrant; the three prairie provinces where lofty oil rigs tower over vast wheat fields; the Pacific coast province with its abundant forests and mountainous terrain; and, finally, the Yukon and Northwest Territories—an area once dismissed as a romantic "Land of the midnight sun"—which is now producing minerals and oil, and founding communities in the high Arctic.

This year Canada celebrates its one hundredth birthday as a federal state and has invited many peoples to share in its natal festivities. While the nation turns now towards its bicentenary, it is not surprising that it casts an appraising—almost nostalgic—glance at the past century. The years between 1867 and 1967 provide, in a very real sense, an historic measuring rod.

The Confederation of 1867 had evoked little applause—even in Canada—a century ago. A few peoples, concerned with their own problems, wondered idly how the new nation would fare—whether it would surmount its difficulties or be overcome by its new and awesome responsibilities.

The answer was not long forthcoming. Within a century Canada passed from a limited federation to a continental confederation, from a junior nation to one of the leading industrial powers of the world.

The Fathers of Confederation, meeting in solemn conclave in Charlottetown and Quebec, indeed "builded better than they knew".                    (HELEN CHAMPION)

THE LAND AND PEOPLE                                                            3

Over 28,000,000 acres of prairie lands are devoted to wheat production. Average farm receipts are approximately $900,000,000 annually.

## Canada in 1867*

```
Nova Scotia............................. 21,731 sq. mi.
New Brunswick.......................... 27,322  "   "
Quebec..................................193,355  "   "
Ontario................................107,780  "   "
Total land and freshwater area............350,188  "   "
```

*Census of 1871.

## Canada in 1967

### Approximate Land and Freshwater Areas, by Province or Territory

| Province or Territory | Land | Freshwater | Total | Percentage of Total Area |
|---|---|---|---|---|
| | sq. miles | sq. miles | sq. miles | |
| Newfoundland........................... | 143,045 | 13,140 | 156,185 | 4.1 |
| Island of Newfoundland........................... | 41,164 | 2,195 | 43,359 | 1.1 |
| Labrador........................... | 101,881 | 10,945 | 112,826 | 3.0 |
| Prince Edward Island........................... | 2,184 | — | 2,184 | 0.1 |
| Nova Scotia........................... | 20,402 | 1,023 | 21,425 | 0.6 |
| New Brunswick........................... | 27,835 | 519 | 28,354 | 0.7 |
| Quebec........................... | 523,860 | 71,000 | 594,860 | 15.4 |
| Ontario........................... | 344,092 | 68,490 | 412,582 | 10.7 |
| Manitoba........................... | 211,775 | 39,225 | 251,000 | 6.5 |
| Saskatchewan........................... | 220,182 | 31,518 | 251,700 | 6.5 |
| Alberta........................... | 248,800 | 6,485 | 255,285 | 6.6 |
| British Columbia........................... | 359,279 | 6,976 | 366,255 | 9.5 |
| Yukon Territory........................... | 205,346 | 1,730 | 207,076 | 5.4 |
| Northwest Territories........................... | 1,253,438 | 51,465 | 1,304,903 | 33.9 |
| Franklin........................... | 541,753 | 7,500 | 549,253 | 14.3 |
| Keewatin........................... | 218,460 | 9,700 | 228,160 | 5.9 |
| Mackenzie........................... | 493,225 | 34,265 | 527,490 | 13.7 |
| Canada........................... | 3,560,238 | 291,571 | 3,851,809 | 100.0 |

# Canadian
# Nation-Building

# "British North America" in the 1860's

Canadians today probably find "British North America" a rather old-fashioned term: in the century that has elapsed since Confederation, "British North America" has become "Canada".

In the 1860's, just before Confederation, the three words, "British North American", represented much of what the scattered colonies had in common: they were all in North America and they were all "British". All their citizens owed allegiance to the British crown, and from Great Britain had been derived both their institutional life and the origins, traditions and language of most of their citizens. French-speaking British subjects themselves fully accepted the designation, though determined then, as now, to preserve their own identity.

The 1860's mark the half-way house in the evolution of British colonies into present-day Canada. It was in the 1760's that there occurred the change in regimes from old "New France" to "British North America". This half-way mark, the 1860's, should not seem overly remote. Many now living may have heard from their own parents anecdotes and incidents from those days for it is not hard to bridge 100 years by human memory. Yet oral tradition is not enough and resort must be had to the written record.

The newspapers of those days, for example, are nearly all still available. If we were to turn to them, we would find much space devoted to news from abroad, especially to British politics and the European wars of the period. There would also be the usual collection of trivia. Local politics would be reported with a fullness not found today: parliamentary debates would often be reported virtually in full. Nor were these neglected by readers. The speeches of the great men of the day were read aloud in the families of their supporters, their arguments noted and their crushing replies to party opponents duly applauded.

In the first year of the decade, 1860, Edward, Prince of Wales, paid the first Royal state visit to British North America. The occasion filled the newspapers. Scarcely was it over before the American Civil War broke out and, for the next four years, the spectacle of this volcano in eruption just over the garden fence, so to speak, gave journalists all the copy they could use. As interest lessened with the defeat of the South, it was regained by the murder of Lincoln.

Meanwhile, events that were to lead to the building of a new country "north of the line" were capturing the headlines: the squabbles in the provincial parliament of Canada, the increasing instability of its ministries, the Charlottetown Conference, the Quebec Conference, the various uncertainties of the years 1864-66 and, at last, the culmination in Confederation. The remaining three years of the decade were anti-climax. Even so, they were marked by a great event, the extension of the new Dominion to include "Rupert's Land and the North-Western Territory".

In the 1860's the various colonies already stretched from Newfoundland to Lake Huron and beyond to include the two dots of people at Red River and on the Pacific coast. Each colony had grown up by itself; nearly all were in separate stages of development; and some contained every stage at the same time. It is therefore difficult to make general statements about them.

Montreal harbour, 1880. Time has changed the design of ships and the facilities of the harbour but not the popularity of Montreal. Geography and history have combined to make it the largest city in Canada, a crossroads of the continent, and a capital of industry, commerce, and culture.

**Newfoundland**—Newfoundland was a staple product colony, the staple being codfish. Those of its people with fishlines in their hands, the mass, depended upon the local fishbuyers, "the merchants", who kept them in a state of semi-servitude comparable to the fur companies' relations with their Indians. The fishbuyers, in turn, depended upon the St. John's exporters, and the St. John's exporters depended upon the foreign markets. The consequence was an unstable economy, with poverty for most of the fishermen and an uncertain opulence for the St. John's exporters. The society that resulted was similar to all societies dependent on an inadequate staple, precarious and poor. But it appears to have had enough common will to resent vigorously any suggestion of going into the new Confederation:

> *"Men, hurrah, for our own native isle, Newfoundland,*
> *Not a stranger shall hold one inch of her strand;*
> *Her face turns to Britain, her back to the Gulf.*
> *Come near at your peril, Canadian wolf!"*

**Nova Scotia**—Across the Cabot Strait lay Nova Scotia, which was already a relatively mature society. It had had representative institutions for over a century and its resources were varied enough to sustain a number of types of activity. Down to the Confederation period, the province—it was a "colony" no longer—experienced reasonable growth and within the easily comprehensible boundaries of peninsula and island-adjunct (Cape Breton), this had produced a corporate consciousness and pride which amounted to an incipient nationalism. It found its voices in men like Haliburton and Howe. Who can forget Howe's description of the proud old mother showing him the picture of her "boys"? "These are not boys," Howe had said, "but stalwart men." "And each one the captain of his own fine ship," the old lady had replied. It was to be the misfortune of Nova Scotia and Canada that the change in technology which substituted iron ships for wooden, steam for sail, was almost to coincide with the decade in which the province entered Confederation.

**New Brunswick**—Across the Bay of Fundy, New Brunswick had also developed a certain provincial life of its own, which renders the term "colony" inappropriate. But it was cut up by its river valleys, was not as close-knit as Nova Scotia and if not as dependent on a single staple—wood, in New Brunswick's case—as was Newfoundland, yet it was too dependent for a healthy economy. Even so, New Brunswick, too, had taken a few tentative steps beyond the mere economic aspects of life and there was in its little capital the group that later on was to give to Canada one of its leading poetic voices, Charles G. D. Roberts.

**Lower Canada**—In Lower Canada, or Quebec, the same difficulty faces the inquirer as today: he is not dealing with one community but two, French and English, with the English further subdivided into Protestant and Catholic. French-speaking people (1961) numbered some 87 per cent of the total population of the province. In 1871, they numbered 78 per cent. They have always formed a homogeneous group, whereas the "English" have become more and more split up into different cultural, religious and racial groups. The position of the French thus has strengthened to a degree greater than their numerical increase would indicate. In the Confederation decade, as in the 1960's or the 1760's, there could be no doubt of the nature of the French group: here was a *people* in a sense that the English could neither rival nor understand, a unified human community throughout which sentiments, emotions, responses, intuitive understanding, went like an electric current. "Nous autres" was far more than a mere phrase. "English" Canada, itself so woefully lacking in knowledge of such matters, has difficulty in understanding this.

In the 1860's this homogeneous group—what modern "francophones" mean by the word "nation"—was in control of nearly every aspect of its life except the economic and the military. It had produced its leaders in church and state. It was expanding its traditional system of education, which was that of the aristocratic France of the Old Regime. The population of Ontario was a third as large again as that of Quebec, the number of Quebec's illiterates three times that of Ontario, but the students in "classical colleges" in Quebec were three times as numerous as college students in Ontario. These students and the class they represented were the "élite", the officers, as it were, of the army that followed them. These different conceptions of society were to prove, indeed still prove, a major stumbling block to mutual comprehension between the races. Democratic schooling, that is, universal compulsory education, reflects that traditional liberal empiricism of the entire English world which goes back to Protestantism and the great revolutionary upheavals of the 17th century, whereas the French Old Regime, by no means overturned in French Canada by the Conquest, rests firmly on the principle of authority. It is the challenge to the Old Regime which is the source of Quebec's "quiet revolution" of the 1960's.

The challenge of today is not the first. Stimulated by the waves of liberal thought sweeping out of France, many mid-19th century French Canadian intellectuals found themselves in revolt against a too rigorous orthodoxy. These were the men who, as a political party, were known as *les rouges*. They included the young Wilfrid Laurier. The battle of *les rouges* against things as they were in Quebec was bitter and prolonged. They received a surprising amount of support, but the Quebec of the 1860's was not ready to throw over its old orthodoxies in favour of something that looked like blasphemous free thought in both church and state, and since the reactionary spirit, termed ultra-montanism, had been vastly strengthened by the actions and proclamations of Rome itself (such as Pio Nono's "Syllabus of Errors")*, it proved an easy victor over *rougeisme*, though the latter lingered on, and in another generation was to contribute appreciably to Laurier's victory in 1896.

French Canada's corporate sense was producing its natural fruit, an incipient literary culture. Garneau's *History* had already appeared. There had been some poets and some novelists. True to the genius of that strain of aristocracy prominent in its society, French Canada in this field was probably already ahead of English—which is not to say that either had gone very far.

With some exceptions, the English-speaking community in Lower Canada stood in strong contrast to the French: here was the classical Canadian exemplification of the two ways of life. For the most part the English were gathered in Montreal, Quebec, and in some regions of the countryside. The agricultural way of life followed by the people of these rural areas did not differ greatly from that of their French neighbours, but their ethos was distinct. Like the mercantile communities of the cities, the rural English were possessed by the "gospel of getting on". As a result, today their communities are skeletons or graveyards.

The urban English were large enough and concentrated enough to persist as linguistic units, though they never succeeded in making themselves into complete communities, with all ranks present from common labourer to grandee. They have maintained themselves—where they have maintained themselves, which is mainly Montreal—largely on immigration from the Maritimes and Ontario. As they had been from the Conquest so, in the 1860's, they were in control of the economic life of the province and of much of the rest of British North America. They were also still influential in political life. Some had become patrons of art, but of any original artistic or literary culture among them, there was not a glimmer.

**Upper Canada**—Ontario's variety and the different times at which its parts were settled make it hard to describe briefly. One statement at least can be made: in contrast to Quebec, there was never at any time a movement or a group that stood for something like total rejection of the general values of the community. There were plenty of reformers, but no "root-and-branch" radicals against either church or state. The reason is plain: in Ontario, as in the other non-French provinces, there was no rock-ribbed superstructure of authority, and explosions could take place in the open air. Denominational jealousies, however, accompanied by scrambles for "the loaves and fishes", were of a bitterness unknown to us today. These, in part, reflected class rivalries.

Ontario's advantages of soil and climate easily account for its relatively rapid movement forward. But, within the province, these factors vary greatly. The western peninsula is better for an agricultural-based settlement than the eastern or St. Lawrence section, and both are infinitely superior to the rock and sand of the Canadian Shield. Settlement naturally followed the great inland waterway of the St. Lawrence and the lower lakes—"The Front"—so that even before the war of 1812 travellers were com-

---

*Pope Pius IX: "Syllabus complectens praecipuos nostrae aetatis errores", 1864.

menting on the well-cultivated districts with their comfortable farmsteads. But it was not until after 1850 that settlement made much impression on the upland soils of the Georgian Bay counties. Muskoka had hardly been touched in the 1860's, and the other "districts" (the term used in contrast to "the counties") were wilderness. As the railways were built backward from "The Front", through to the Ottawa River, Lake Nipissing, Georgian Bay and Lake Huron, they opened up the remaining good lands for settlement (especially in the Lake Huron counties), or supplied the province with a vast acceleration to its lumber industry. But at Confederation, Ontario was still essentially the St. Lawrence and the lower lakes, a spur up the Ottawa valley, the southern part of the western peninsula, with some bridges over to the first row of inland lakes, such as Simcoe.

Despite the speeches of George Brown, there is little to induce one to believe that there was much provincial sense of identity in Upper Canada (Ontario). The farmers of the western peninsula might elect "Clear Grits", but they did so for good, practical reasons tied in directly to their own local circumstances. Upper Canada never became a racial and religious unit of the same type, though opposite complexion, as occurred in Lower Canada. If it had done so, George Brown might have remained its premier for more than four days.

Upper Canada's progress was the kind that the whole continent understood. It consisted in growth, development, increase of wealth and of well-being. Minor lip-service might be paid to "culture" in isolated groups in the larger towns, but there could have been few topics which would have interested the general run of people less. Everybody could see a building going up and, however repulsive architecturally, it would be commendable because new, but few, indeed, would have taken any interest in a picture shaping itself and almost as few in a book. The wonder is that among a population to whom philistinism came as naturally as breathing, so much good work could be accomplished in buildings: the Kingston City Hall and Court House (1840's), Osgoode Hall, Toronto (1820's, 1850's), University College, Toronto (1850's) have never been surpassed. There are plenty of bigger buildings today, but none better.

Such buildings were not built for their own sakes: something went on inside them. That something was mainly talk: political talk in the Parliament Buildings; talk of every description in such buildings as University College, or its rivals in Cobourg and Kingston; religious talk in the big new churches (everyone went to church!). A people civilizes itself by talk. From this point of view the process is limitless and never-ending. In the 1860's in British North America schools were multiplying, colleges growing though slowly, newspapers increasing in numbers and thickness and even libraries were to be found. No question but that what we were doing then was exactly what we are doing now—civilizing ourselves, building our community, through talk.

The 1850's had been the most prosperous decade in British North America's history. Population had increased by 33 per cent. The city of Montreal was more than half as large again by 1861 as it had been in 1851, forming a tidy little metropolis of 90,000 people. Toronto, already claiming to be "the Queen City of the West", had grown nearly 46 per cent to 44,000. The ancient capital, Quebec, had increased almost as much. "Improved land" and land under crop had increased proportionately to the population growth. Major factors in this growth are easily discernible: the markets created by the Reciprocity Treaty of 1854, the Crimean War and the big splurge of railway building. All this applied to large tracts of virgin land and forest.

At Upper Canada Village, a project of the 1950's to preserve historic buildings and furnishings from sites to be flooded by the St. Lawrence Seaway development, visitors are reminded of bygone days.

The 1860's told a different story. Population increased by 14 per cent and this was reflected in the cities, whose growth sharply slackened—to 19 per cent in the case of Montreal, and 25 per cent in that of Toronto. Quebec actually decreased. "Improved land" and land under crop, however, continued in rapid expansion. It is interesting to note what was being raised. Milk cattle went up from 730,000 in 1851, to 960,000 in 1861, and 1,252,000 in 1871, an increase disproportionately greater than that of the people. Wheat seems to have increased to a peak of some 27,000,000 bushels in 1861. The peak had been reached in Lower Canada in 1851 but Upper Canada was the big wheat province and its wheat crop did not decline until 1871. The same applies to oats, which doubled 1851-61 and then remained stationary. The big jumps, however, were in—potatoes and turnips! What were the people of British North America doing with the 51,000,000 bushels of potatoes they raised in 1871, over 15 bushels per head, 900 pounds for each and every one?

Due allowance for error must be made in these early statistics but, however we look at them, we must conclude that a plentiful supply of food was available in those years, even allowing for generous exports. By 1871 there was, in fact, far more food than there were people to eat it. The situation is puzzling until we recall one fact: by 1861 nearly all the good Crown land had been alienated to private ownership but by no means all the land thus alienated had been put under cultivation. The decade of the 1860's was one wherein gaps were filled. Those who in an earlier day had managed to secure grants to vast acreages could now dispose of them to settlers. Farmers could buy farms for their sons. In this way "the clearings"—the "holes in the bush"—of pioneer days were rapidly turning into the countryside of contiguous farms and settlement. Naturally all this new land was productive: hence, presumably, the vast increase in returns during the 1860's.

The birth rate of a pioneer rural people and plentiful food produced many human beings in the 1860's as in the 1850's. In 1871, there were in Quebec about 33 children under one year of age to 1,000 of the population and in Ontario nearly 29. (*Ontario*, 1851, 39.4; 1861, 38.1; 1871, 28.9; *Quebec*, 1851, 44.6; 1861, 36.7; 1871, 33.9). Quebec had a small increase in numbers between 1851 and 1861; Ontario, a substantial increase. Both suffered a decrease between 1861 and 1871.

## Emigration to "the States"

What became of all these people? The answer is simple: they emigrated. And every Canadian knows where they went: from 1860 to 1870, the numbers of Canadian-born in the United States increased to nearly half a million. To get a more correct idea of the emigration southward, this figure would have to be increased by the numbers of those persons who had come from abroad to British North America, lived there for some time and then gone southward, taking their British North American children with them, and by the total of deaths among the Canadian-born residents of the United States.

Further corroboration of the mass drain southward during the 1860's comes from the experience of Lower Canada (Quebec). The population of that province increased during the whole decade by only 80,000 people. In the 1860's so fertile a people as the French increased in Quebec by only 82,000 (from 847,615 to 929,817), while their non-French fellow Roman Catholics actually decreased by some 6,000. This was the period during which boarded-up farm-houses began to line the country roads and large settlements of French Canadians began to appear in the mill towns of New England. "La Fièvre aux États-Unis", French-speaking writers have termed it. How much it had to do with a willingness to accept the experiment of 1867 has not been ascertained, but it is reasonable to assume that faced with the virtual depopulation of the countryside, the authorities of Quebec, especially the religious authorities, would be willing "to try anything once".

It is clear that the demographic behaviour of British North Americans had a much weaker pulse in the 1860's than it had in the 1850's. For this, as noted above, one major explanation lies ready to hand: the closing of the agricultural frontier. For the next 20 years, the people of Canada were to find their frontier of expansion in the New England states or in the homestead lands of the American middle west. Not until a way to the Canadian West could be found could the country once more experience vigorous growth.

## Increasing Urbanization

There is more, however, to the genesis of a society than mere expansion in numbers and area. A community is not a collection of separated atoms but a corporate personality wherein all are "members one of another". There are various signals to

A barouche leaves Crysler Hall, Upper Canada Village.

indicate that British North America by 1860 had turned from the atomism of pioneering and was beginning to build up its corporate life. Of these, Confederation itself was the most prominent, but there were others. By 1860, for example, various institutions of higher learning had been established, in addition to the grammar schools and common schools that already served most localities. If there were no great cities, there were a number of flourishing towns.

In the countryside, visual evidences of the beginnings were diminishing: for example, in 1851 there were in Upper Canada some 17,000 dwellings listed as "shanties", but by 1871 these had decreased to just over 1,000. Their places were being taken by the substantial farm-houses that still dot the countryside and provide us with one of our most original cultural products, a local domestic architecture of merit. Other institutions, not visible to the eye, were also springing up or increasing in numbers, such as banks, insurance companies, stock exchanges, agricultural and other societies. Among the miscellaneous societies, temperance organizations were becoming particularly prominent, for pioneer drinking had been hard, frequent and ugly, and movements to check it were a natural reaction. The "temperance movement", later to become the "prohibition movement", was just gathering strength in the 1860's. During the remainder of the century it was to become the most strongly marked of all Canadian movements looking to social reform.

"Temperance" may in part be correlated with the shift in the centre of social gravity that can be sensed in the 1860's. With the receding of the frontier and the growth of towns—in 1851, there were only nine places in British North America having over 5,000 inhabitants; in 1871, there were 21—an amelioration of manners can be discerned. Apart from the larger cities, every town was primarily a market town, dominated by shopkeepers. Such men were typically lower middle class, which meant that to them respectability was all in all. No solid citizen could afford to be caught up in bar-room fights or picked out of the gutter on a Saturday night: his place was with his family in the family pew on Sunday morning.

The gateway of Upper Fort Garry in downtown Winnipeg, Manitoba, is all that remains of the historic fur trading post. The name is commemorated in the Fort Garry Hotel in the background.

In the provincial capitals and Montreal something approaching an upper middle class could be found, but even in Toronto, third largest of the cities, the typical figures of the 1860's were no longer Family Compact grandees like Sir John Beverley Robinson but new men such as William McMaster, the Baptist banker, his co-religionist William Davies, butcher and meat packer, the Masseys and, a little later, Timothy Eaton. Smaller editions of such men, whatever their denominational connections, dominated the secondary rising towns. Many seem to have been old-country men, but townsmen in origin and not of the peasantry that had come in its thousands to British North America in the generation after the Napoleonic wars.

Such folk brought with them a decorum and a code of conduct of which many accounts contend that the country was much in need. As small businessmen in close contact with the country people, their influence would radiate. In non-French Canada, both town and countryside were dominantly in the Protestant tradition, so that when once the settler began to see himself as on the way up, "the Protestant ethic" came to him as naturally as to the townsman—not that "the Protestant ethic" of drive, accomplishment, "getting on", was confined to Protestants for Catholics found that, with modifications, it fitted their circumstances, too.

In the 1860's, the consequences of this rising urbanism were visible. It was becoming more difficult to stage large-scale drunken public brawls, though they still went on in such lumber towns as Ottawa. There was more emphasis on cleanliness (first private baths, 1840's). It became not entirely impossible to be polite in manner and speech and remain a man. There was more insistence on schooling and very "advanced" people were coming to believe that a girl could stand some grammar school attendance even if she were not destined to become a "lady".

The growth of a national civilization, of course, is a gradual and complex process but it seems relatively safe to regard the decade of the 1860's in British North America as marking a fairly distinct movement forward towards that goal.

(A. R. M. Lower)

# Factors in Confederation

If there is one political operation more difficult than another, it is putting two or more communities together into one. It is difficult enough at the municipal level. It becomes more and more difficult the nearer the communities approach the status of independent states. There are plenty of examples in history of the more usual way of accomplishing the feat, that is, through conquest, but of union by consent there are few, and most of these have been provided by the English-speaking world.

The question is, how did this most difficult of operations come to be performed in British North America and in the 1860's? The difficulty lies not in the details but in the underlying factors without which no political action would have been forthcoming.

## Two Major Forces

There were two major predisposing forces towards union. One of these was common allegiance: the British North American provinces were *British*. They might be connected with their American neighbours by powerful associations of language, trade, and family relationship, but between them and the Americans there still yawned the gulf of revolution. The States had severed the ancient ties, the Provinces had not. The descendants of the Loyalists had long memories and the second layer of population which had come into British North America from the British Isles after 1820 shared the prejudices of their predecessors. Moreover, every one was afraid of "the big bad wolf" which daily grew stronger, larger and apparently more ravenous. "I have a tremendous swaller for territory," General Cass of Michigan is reported to have exclaimed. Who wants to be "swallered"? Those who remember the violent reaction caused by careless American words in the 1911 Reciprocity Election campaign— words like "adjunct"—will not be surprised that in the 1860's similar words, such as "manifest destiny", forced the British North Americans closer together.

This sense of difference from the American neighbour was by no means merely negative. Every "reasonably well-informed person" could point to "the blessings of British government" and could contrast them with the shortcomings of American rule. American shortcomings at the time were emphasized by the "War between the States". Why be attracted to a country which was dissolving in civil war and many of whose components enshrined that institution odious to all right-thinking Britons, slavery?

The other major predisposing factor was the extension of communication. The electric telegraph was being extended throughout the provinces so that not only messages but news could go from one end to the other. Steamship communication had become easy. While there was no direct railway communication between the St. Lawrence and Maritimes as yet, still it was possible to go down the St. Lawrence as far as Rivière du Loup by rail, or to cross from Montreal to Portland, Maine, overnight, thence by steamer to Saint John.

Beyond these tangibles lay intangibles. Probably one of these was the steady improvement in schooling which was leading ordinary people to extend their vision of the world, thus increasing the sense of common interests and destinies. Another intangible was the sheer logic of the idea: this would not by itself have secured action but it was an ever-present incentive to action.

The Charlottetown Conference (above) which opened on September 1, 1864, with five delegates from each of the Maritime Provinces had been convened to discuss a political union. The Government of the united provinces of Upper and Lower Canada sent a delegation of eight politicians to discuss a still larger union. The result was a further conference at Quebec the following month.

The Quebec Conference (below) opened on October 10, 1864. It was attended by delegates from Newfoundland, Nova Scotia, Prince Edward Island, New Brunswick and Canada. These 33 representatives have since been described as the Fathers of Confederation—even though Prince Edward Island did not enter the Union until 1873 nor Newfoundland until 1949.

16

In 1866 representatives of Canada, Nova Scotia and New Brunswick met in London to discuss terms of union with representatives of the Colonial Office. The result was the British North America Act, which received Royal Assent in 1867, and under which three provinces were united in a federation called Canada.

## Immediate Factors

Such were the large background factors. The more immediate are not hard to discern. It is not to be overestimated, but the first official Royal visit to British North America, that of the Prince of Wales in 1860, probably heightened the collective sense of loyalty. Then there was the well-being of the 1850's which, particularly in Canada, made men feel that the time was becoming ripe for some heightened status. In 1860, John A. Macdonald could exclaim that Canada was too large to be considered a colony any longer but was an associate of Great Britain, not a mere dependency. Yet an official survey of 1858 had shown that practically all the good land of "the Canadas" had been granted away from the Crown and that in future young men would have little option but to emigrate. Simultaneously, there was a revival of interest in the land beyond the lakes, the ancient *pays d'en haut*. In the late 1850's several exploring expeditions penetrated the Red River country and the prairies. Upper Canadian politicians, especially William McDougall and George Brown, began to catch a vision of westward expansion which would build a still greater country. That vision grew slowly, but when the British North America Act had become law, there was in it provision for the inclusion within the new country, Canada, of "Rupert's Land and the North-Western Territory" (Section 146). The vision of expansion—almost solely an Upper Canadian vision—must then be included in the "factors".

FACTORS IN CONFEDERATION

Proposals for some kind of common government for the colonies remaining in the British allegiance had begun to appear almost as soon as the Americans had gone their way. They had continued to be made from time to time, but had been before their age. The only vestige of reality in the legal idea of unity had lain in the Queen's representative, the "Governor-in-Chief" at Quebec, who throughout retained vice-regal status, if not function. This slender link of union was not without its importance in maintaining a reminder to every colonist that he was part of a greater whole.

Practical proposals for union, however, could hardly have taken shape much before they did, that is, in the late 1850's. A. T. Galt's union proposals of 1858 were among the first of these: Galt would not enter the Cabinet of the day unless it accepted his dream "in principle". A mere "principle", however, it remained until other circumstances began to clothe it with greater reality. It would take much more space than is available to enumerate these in detail. Let a few be briefly noted:

The fear of the great neighbour and what it might do with its unemployed army after its Civil War had ended. During the War, there was ample evidence of the hostility entertained by the North against the provinces. A little spark might easily have brought armed invasion.

The probable termination by the United States of the Reciprocity Treaty of 1854 and the commercial distress that might then ensue.

The paralysis of government in the Province of Canada, 1862-64, election after election bringing no party a majority sufficient to enable the Cabinet of the day to carry on and get necessary legislation enacted.

The age-old spectre of racial discord, joined to religious discord. This convinced many people in both halves of the province—the "Separatistes" of the day—that the union of 1840 must be dissolved.

The inability to devise a substitute if the union were dissolved.

The "behind-the-scenes" influence of the British financial groups connected with the Grand Trunk Railway and the Hudson's Bay Company.

The gradual conversion of the "home" authorities to the idea of the larger union, and their eventual, powerful support for it.

In the later stages of the Confederation movement from 1866 on, the United States-based Fenian invasions and the need of the Provinces for mutual protection to which they pointed.

Finally, as with a flash of light, the obvious solution coming—bury the local differences of the old provincialisms in a greater union, make flesh the union of the British Provinces that had been hovering about for eighty years as a kind of ghost!

And, lastly, the men. It is impossible to measure a man's size with the calipers of the engineer, but it may be asked whether we have ever had since in Canadian life such a galaxy of talent as stood on the political stages of the 1860's, and all of them men in the prime of middle life. To name only a few: in Canada, Macdonald, Cartier, Brown, Mowat, Dorion, Galt, McGee. In Nova Scotia, Howe, Tupper. In New Brunswick, Tilley. The colonial stages had grown too small for such men. If Howe, for example, had been brought up in England, he could conceivably have become a great imperial statesman. No wonder that they were in a continuous state of explosion against each other.

## A Political Miracle

It must have been hard for these individualist *prima donnas* to work with each other, still harder for them to put off their antagonisms and "convictions", shake hands with their opponents and subordinate themselves to each other. Yet when Macdonald and Brown stepped into the middle of the Assembly chamber, that fateful day in Quebec in 1864, to patch up their differences and start over again, that is what happened: a resolution of animosities, an agreement on objectives, an attempt to realize a vision.

There was to be much hard work, many obstacles to surmount, before the vision was realized. The intricate, complex terms of union had to be worked out, colonial governors such as Gordon in New Brunswick had to be outmanoeuvred or won over, jealous and narrow-minded colonial assemblies had to be convinced or outflanked. All this was done. The stages in the path are marked by such events as the original Macdonald-Cartier-Brown coalition, the Charlottetown Conference, the Quebec Conference, the reverse in the New Brunswick elections of 1865, anti-Confederationism in Nova Scotia, involving the alienation of Joseph Howe, the withdrawal of Newfoundland and Prince Edward Island, the regaining of the position in New Brunswick through Tilley's electoral victory of 1866, the Westminster Palace Hotel Conference in London and finally the easy enactment of the British North America Act.

It may not have been "the consecration and the poet's dream": that would be language far too grandiose. But for us, humble British North Americans, henceforth all to be Canadians, it was, nevertheless, something like a miracle, a political miracle, whose result was, July 1st, 1867, the first Dominion Day, and the long procession of its successors! (A. R. M. LOWER)

The recently-erected Macdonald-Cartier Bridge joining downtown Ottawa and the eastern limits of Hull commemorates two Fathers of Confederation: Sir John A. Macdonald, the first Prime Minister of Canada and Sir Georges-Étienne Cartier, a member of the first Cabinet.

# Expansion "...from sea to sea...."

Though representatives from (the united province of Upper and Lower) Canada, New Brunswick, Nova Scotia, Prince Edward Island and Newfoundland attended the historic Quebec conference of 1864, only Canada (divided into Ontario and Quebec), Nova Scotia and New Brunswick entered into union in 1867. Economic persuasion was the principal factor in bringing the remaining two—and others—into the Canadian fold.

## Manitoba

In 1870 the vast Hudson's Bay Company territories of Rupert's Land and the North-Western Territory, were transferred to the new Dominion. Out of this tremendous acquisition was carved the province of Manitoba. The arrangements were anticipatory. By Act of May 12, 1870, the Federal Government made provision for the new province. However, it was not until July 15 that the area was legally transferred. The "postage stamp province", as it was soon nicknamed, was only about half the size of New Brunswick. In 1881 its boundaries were extended west and north; in 1912, to their present limits.

## British Columbia

Out on the west coast where Vancouver Island had rejoined the mainland in 1866, British Columbia was considering union with Canada. Cut off by hundreds of miles from the settled areas of the Dominion, and with population fast increasing south of its border, the possibility of maintaining a separate identity appeared remote.

The promise of a transcontinental railway, among other considerations, induced the province to enter Confederation in 1871. The line involved the building of more than two thousand miles of track, much of it through wilderness territory. "If the railway scheme is utopian," a Canadian newspaper ventured, "so is Confederation. The two must stand or fall together." Fourteen years later—in 1885—the promise was fulfilled: British Columbia was linked with the eastern provinces when the last spike in the Canadian Pacific Railway system was pounded in at Craigellachie.

## Prince Edward Island

In 1865, Thomas D'Arcy McGee, one of the Fathers of Confederation, had remarked facetiously: "Prince Edward Island will have to come in, for if she does not we will have to tow her into the St. Lawrence". But the Island, which had been the site of the first Confederation conference, maintained its independence until 1873. Then, on the promise of "continuous communication" with the mainland, of assistance with its land and railway problems, Prince Edward Island also joined the Dominion. With the bridge-tunnel-causeway complex between New Brunswick and Prince Edward Island now under construction, the Island will soon have that "continuous communication" envisaged so many years ago.

Ten years after the North-Western Territory and Rupert's Land were added to Canada, other British territory within the Arctic archipelago were ceded by Imperial Order in Council.

# Canada 1867 and 1967

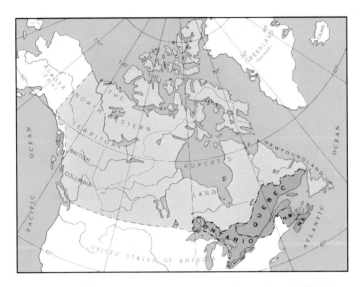

**1867** On July 1, 1867, the united province of Upper and Lower Canada (which there-upon became the separate provinces of Ontario and Quebec) joined with Nova Scotia and New Brunswick to form a federal state called "Canada".

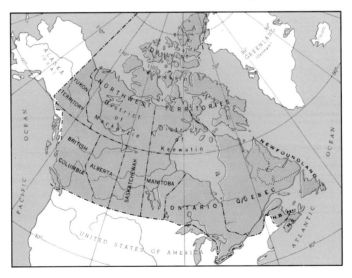

**1967** A century after Confederation, the number of provinces had increased from four to ten. Yukon has territorial status and the Northwest Territories are divided into three districts: Mackenzie, Keewatin, and Franklin.

EXPANSION "... FROM SEA TO SEA...."

# Territorial and Political Evolution of Canada since Confederation

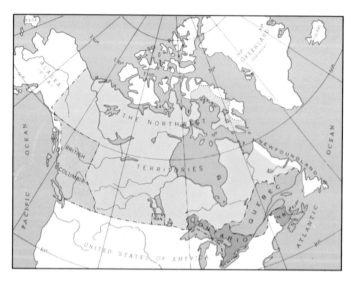

**1870-1873**  In 1870, Manitoba became a province of Canada; in 1871, British Columbia joined the union; and, in 1873, Prince Edward Island.

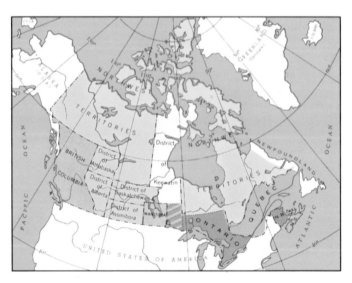

**1874-1882**  In 1874, provisional boundaries were established for Ontario; in 1876 the district of Keewatin was formed. In 1880 the Arctic Archipelago passed under the suzerainty of Canada; in 1881 the boundaries of Manitoba were extended. In 1882, the districts of Assiniboia, Saskatchewan, Alberta and Athabasca were created.

# Territorial and Political Evolution of Canada since Confederation

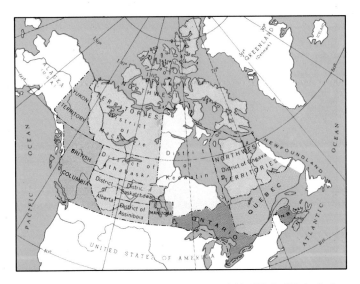

**1884-1898** Ontario's boundary with Manitoba was settled in 1889. In 1895 the districts of Ungava, Franklin, Mackenzie and Yukon were created. In 1898 Quebec's boundary was extended northward, the district of Keewatin was enlarged, and the district of Yukon organized as a separate territory.

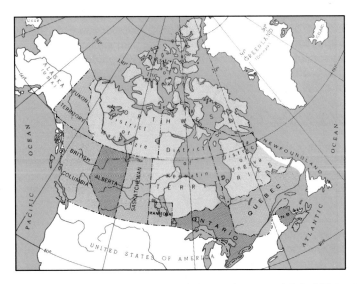

**1903-1905** In 1903 the British Columbia-Alaska boundary was settled; in 1905 the provinces of Alberta and Saskatchewan were created and the district of Keewatin was transferred to the newly-defined Northwest Territories.

EXPANSION "...FROM SEA TO SEA...."

# Canada's Federal System of Government

The Canadian experiment in nation-building, launched on July 1, 1867, was both bold and unique. Its boldness is evident in the courageous spirit and manner in which the Fathers of Confederation surmounted the diverse and formidable geographical, cultural and economic obstacles which confronted them 100 years ago; its uniqueness lies in the political solution they devised through a combination of the British parliamentary system of Cabinet government with a distinctly Canadian adaptation of the principles of federalism then operating in the United States.

Face to face with the facts of history and environment as they knew them in North America and strengthened by the vision of a great new political nationality, the pragmatic Founding Fathers believed that only a federal union possessing a strong, central government could safeguard the isolated provinces from economic collapse and political absorption by their powerful southern neighbour; that only a broad transcontinental confederation could provide or secure the resources essential to extensive railway construction that would link the Maritimes with the St. Lawrence Lowlands, bridge the geographical barriers of the Canadian Shield and the Western Cordillera, open the intervening western plains as a new frontier of settlement and source of a new strategic staple of trade.

Only a federal union would permit the logical division of legislative powers whereby the central government would be competent to deal with all matters of common interest to the whole country and the provincial governments severally to enact legislation of local concern and befitting their peculiar regional circumstances. Only a federal union could hope to satisfy the demands of cultural dualism, of local loyalties and of diversely endowed regions and still provide the organizational structure and common arena within which a sense of community and national identity might slowly develop and mature. Indeed, only federalism would leave unimpaired, in both the national and the provincial arenas, the practice of the unwritten conventions of responsible government recently won by the colonial legislatures—the responsibility of prime minister and cabinet to the legislature and the close integration of legislative and executive functions at both levels of government.

## The Constitution—the Terms of Confederation

Such were the visions, concepts and practical observations—some rooted in British institutions and traditions, some deduced from the immediate experience of the neighbouring United States, and some shaped by local history and constitutional convention or practice—which dictated the essential terms of Confederation, drafted and agreed upon by the Founding Fathers and enacted by the United Kingdom Parliament in the imperial statute known as the British North America Act, 1867.

The paramount British influence was proclaimed in the preamble to the Act as an expressed desire of the federating provinces for "a Constitution similar in Principle to that of the United Kingdom". Hence, the "One Parliament of Canada" embraces the Queen (the executive head and the Governor General, her representative), an appointed Senate with life tenure (amended June 2, 1965 to provide for retirement on reaching 75 years of age) and an elected House of Commons. The executive and

The cornerstone of the original Houses of Parliament was laid in 1860. Sittings of the legislature of the united province of Canada were held here from 1866 until Ottawa became the federal capital of the new dominion. The building (with the exception of the Gothic library) was destroyed by fire in 1916. Above is shown the first sitting of Parliament. Present are representatives from Nova Scotia, New Brunswick, Quebec and Ontario.

legislative powers are in close identification through the control of the administration by leaders of the parliamentary majority. Financial measures are initiated by the Crown and in practice introduced into the House of Commons by a Cabinet Minister. An appointed judiciary is virtually independent of control by either the executive or legislative branches of government and holds office during good behaviour. Also characteristically British is the lack of specific "bill of rights" clauses in the Act and of any legal definition of the principles of responsible government—such fundamental features of parliamentary government being considered deeply entrenched in British common law, in the customs and usage, and in convention already operative in the federating provinces.

A hardly less significant feature of the British North America Act is the part dealing with the distribution of legislative power between the Parliament of Canada and the legislatures of the provinces, and here the Founding Fathers saw in the experience of the United States much both to encourage and to dissuade. Endeavouring to profit by the experience of the United States where exaggerated states' rights appeared to have produced dissension and civil war, the Canadians adopted a unique form of federalism that initially leaned strongly toward the centralized unitary state. This is especially evident in the balance of authority between the central government and the provinces, the distribution of legislative jurisdiction, and the placing of the residual power with Ottawa as noted immediately below.

The Parliament of Canada was endowed with authority (Section 91 of the BNA Act) "to make laws for the peace, order and good government of Canada, in relation to all matters not coming within the classes of subjects by this Act assigned exclusively to the legislatures of the provinces". For greater certainty, 29 specific powers were enumerated as being within the exclusive legislative authority of the Parliament of Canada, including, among others, the control of the Armed Forces, the regulation of trade and commerce, banking, credit, currency and bankruptcy, criminal law, postal services, patents and copyrights, fisheries, the Indians and lands reserved for them, the census and statistics, navigation and shipping, railways and canals and telegraphs, and the raising of money by any mode of taxation.

On the other hand, the provincial legislatures received (under Section 92) exclusive jurisdiction over 16 subject groups embracing mainly such matters of local or private nature in the province as property and civil rights, direct taxation within the province for provincial purposes, borrowing money on provincial credit, hospitals and asylums, administration of justice in the province including the constitution, maintenance and organization of provincial courts, municipal government, the incorporation of companies with provincial purposes, management and sale of public lands, and amendment of the constitution of the province except with regard to the office of Lieutenant-Governor.

Concurrent legislative powers were granted, by Section 95, to the Parliament of Canada and to the provincial legislatures in respect of agriculture and immigration, with the federal law having overriding authority in the event of conflict.

Among the most distinctively Canadian sections of the Act were those that reflect the duality of culture which has since been so characteristic of Canadian federalism. Acknowledging over 200 years of Roman Catholic religion and civil law in the compact French community on the banks of the St. Lawrence, well entrenched by the Quebec Act of 1774, and conscious of the Quebec fear of the English majority in the new federation, the Fathers wrote cultural guarantees into the Constitution. The provincial legislatures were endowed, by Section 93, with exclusive authority in relation to education, subject to certain safeguards for any legal right or privilege in denominational schools possessed by any class of persons in the province at the Union. Likewise, the use of the English and French languages was safeguarded (Section 133), it being specifically provided that either language *might* be used in the debates of the Parliament of Canada and of the Legislature of Quebec and in the courts of Canada and of Quebec; and that both languages *should* be used in the respective records and journals and in the printed Acts of the Parliament of Canada and of the Legislature of Quebec.

Of particular interest to Quebec were two guarantees of minority rights: Section 98 required that judges of the courts of Quebec be selected from the Quebec Bar in order to safeguard the French Civil Law of the Province; and the exclusion of that province from the provision (Section 94) permitting the legislatures of the original three common-law provinces to delegate to Ottawa, if they wished, some or all of their jurisdiction over "property and civil rights".

Another distinctively Canadian influence was the provision (Section 146) for the realization of the ambition of the Fathers of Confederation to build a vast, transcontinental union stretching westward to the Pacific. Within four years, upon the acquisition of the vast interior of Rupert's Land and the North-western Territory (July 15, 1870), the creation of Manitoba as a province (1870) and the admission of the far western province of British Columbia (1871), the new Dominion, in an unparalleled westward expansion, was extended to the Pacific. The Province of Prince Edward Island entered the Union two years later, followed by the spacious Canadian off-shore Arctic archipelago in 1880 and the transformation by federal statutes of a large block of western territory into the prairie provinces of Alberta and Saskatchewan (1905), and Britain's oldest colony of Newfoundland rounded out the nation's territorial expanse through union with Canada as a province, by British and Canadian statutes, as recently as March 31, 1949.

The British North America Act 1867, with its score or more of amendment Acts*, is popularly held to be the Constitution of Canada. However, in its broadest sense, the Constitution comprises certain other British statutes (such as the Statute of Westminster, 1931), Statutes and Orders in Council of the Parliament of Canada and the provincial legislatures relating to their respective constitutional institutions and government matters, judicial interpretation of their statutory law, substantial sections of the common law and, perhaps even more important, well-established though unwritten constitutional usages, conventions and principles of democratic government which have long been thriving in the Canadian environment through the evolutionary processes of historical growth. Among the most significant are those concerning the executive power mentioned briefly at pages 38 and 42.

## Methods of Continual Adaptation

During the past hundred years the diversified, multi-component character of Canada's constitution has been continually changing and adapting to new problems and con-

---

*The important BNA Amendment Acts bear the dates: 1871, 1875, 1886, 1889, 1907, 1915, 1930, 1940, 1946, 1949 (Nos. 1 and 2), 1951, 1952, 1960, 1962, 1964.

ditions, both national and international, in several ways*:

(a) by formal constitutional amendment of the fundamental British North America Act;
(b) by legal amendment authorized by the British North America Act;
(c) by Acts of Parliament and Orders-in-Council;
(d) by strict judicial interpretation of the constitution; and
(e) by the more flexible elements of convention, usage, and informal executive and administrative practice.

**Formal Amendment**—The omission from the British North America Act of any mention of formal amending procedures *and* the failure of the people of Canada to decide which method of amendment should be applied have meant that throughout Canada's first hundred years as a federal state the British Parliament has remained the agent used by the Canadian people for achieving formal amendment of a substantial portion of their Constitution entrenched in certain fundamental parts of the Act. The joint address of the Canadian House of Commons and the Senate has been the *method* of approaching the British Parliament to request the passage of the 16 formal British North America Act amendments listed above (see footnote p. 29) and such amendments have, on the initiative of the Canadian Parliament, been made automatically and without question by the British Parliament.

Outstanding examples of such substantive amendments include: the *1930* Act confirming the agreements transferring to the Prairie Provinces the administration of their natural resources which had been retained by the Federal Government in a quasi-imperial relationship since their admission to the federation; the *1940* Act giving to Parliament jurisdiction over unemployment insurance by adding a new subsection 2(a) to Section 91; the *1949* (*No. 1*) Act admitting Newfoundland to the Canadian federation; the *1949* (*No. 2*) Act significantly enlarging the legislative powers of the Parliament of Canada respecting wholly federal matters; and the *1951* and *1964* Acts giving to the Parliament of Canada (through a new Section, 94A) the power to make laws in relation to old age pensions (1951) and supplementary benefits, including survivors' and disability benefits (1964), without affecting the operation of any existing or future law of a provincial legislature in relation to any such matter.

However, as implied in the Amendment Act of 1949 (No. 2), there still remains the problem of devising an acceptable procedure for amending in Canada, in the national interest, those provisions of the Constitution which concern *both* federal and provincial legislatures and which may be among those either most cherished and rigidly guarded or requiring urgent adaptation to altered circumstances. A series of constitutional conferences of federal and provincial Prime Ministers, Premiers, Ministers and government officials, held in the years 1935-36, 1950, 1960-61 and 1964, have generally striven to find a solution to this problem that would provide different methods of amendment for different kinds of constitutional clauses or subjects affecting the provinces individually and collectively. Proceedings had advanced sufficiently far by late 1961 to have the eleven governments agree that the amending power should rest in Canada but they were still unable to reach unanimous agreement on how to bring it to Canada or how to amend the Act once it was domiciled here.

---

*See *infra* pages 48-50, for significant mile-posts in the attainment of national sovereignty, and Part VI for the gradual development of Canada's external relations.

CANADA, 1867-1967

As a result of consultations and conferences of Attorneys General in 1960-61 (chaired by the Hon. E. D. Fulton), and in 1964 (chaired by the Hon. Guy Favreau), a "Fulton-Favreau amendment formula", subsequently accepted by the Conference of Prime Minister and Premiers in October 1964, was set forth in a draft Bill "to provide for the amendment in Canada of the Constitution of Canada",* bearing the date of October 30, 1964. In the spring of 1966, the Government of Canada was still awaiting the acceptance of the "Fulton-Favreau formula" by all ten provincial governments as an essential prerequisite to the introduction of the Bill to the Parliament of Canada for enactment. If and when enacted, the "formula" will have terminated all authority now vested in the Parliament of the United Kingdom to enact statutes forming part of Canadian law, by transferring to Canadian federal and provincial legislative authorities—acting either singly or in combination—complete and exclusive power of amendment over the whole of the Constitution of Canada.†

**Legal Amendment**—Although most parts of the British North America Act during the past 100 years could be amended only by the British Parliament, some could be altered by the Parliament of Canada and some by the provincial legislatures through legal amendment authorized by the Act of 1867 or one of its Amendments. For example, provision existed for the Parliament of Canada and the legislatures of the provinces to pass representation Acts changing the electoral districts for the House of Commons and the legislatures, respectively, and for the provinces to amend their own constitutions except the office of Lieutenant-Governor.

As a result of the passage by the British Parliament of the BNA Amendment Act of 1949 (No. 2), the legislative powers of the Parliament of Canada were significantly enlarged with respect to all matters of concern only to the Federal Government (through a new subsection 1 to Section 91) giving it the right to amend from time to time the "Constitution of Canada", *except* for matters assigned by the British North America Act of 1867 exclusively to the legislatures of the provinces, or rights and privileges already secured to the provincial governments and legislatures, or constitutional guarantees regarding education and the use of the English and French languages, and the parliamentary annual session and maximum five-year term, with provision, however, for continuation of the term by Act of Parliament in time of real or apprehended war, invasion or insurrection, if such extension is not opposed by the votes of more than one third of the members of the House of Commons.

The most recent application of this enlarged amending power of the Parliament of Canada was the passage in 1965, with provincial concurrence, of an Act (SC 1965, c.4) providing for the retirement at 75 years of age of any Senator appointed after the coming into force of the Act.

**Acts of Parliament and Orders in Council**—Many statutes and orders in council of the Federal Government and the provincial legislatures are constitutional in character and therefore form part of the Canadian Constitution. Significant among these are Acts and/or Orders in Council admitting new provinces into the Union, adjusting provincial subsidies, altering boundaries, creating new departments of government, and adapting the offices and functions of government to the emergencies of wartime.

---

*Text of this draft Bill appears at pages 110-121 of *The Amendment of the Constitution of Canada*, Queen's Printer, Ottawa, February 1965.    †*Ibid.*, p. 10.

**Judicial Interpretation**—Although all the above forms of amendment are being used constantly, the major part of constitutional development has occurred gradually through judicial interpretation and through constitutional convention, executive and administrative co-ordination at federal and provincial levels of government.

Beginning in the 1880's, at a time of decline in federal leadership, and continuing intermittently through a series of reference cases arising out of the Federal Government's "new deal" legislation during the depression of the early 1930's, the interpretations of the Judicial Committee of the (Imperial) Privy Council, led by Lords Watson and Haldane, so *restricted* such heads of federal jurisdiction as the regulation of trade and commerce, of fisheries, of agriculture, and of international treaties, and so *reduced* the federal residuary clause of "peace, order and good government" to that of a wartime emergency power, while *extending* provincial control over "property and civil rights" so as to include such matters as the regulation of wages and hours of labour, agricultural marketing, unemployment insurance and welfare legislation, that many Canadian constitutional authorities argued that the Judicial Committee had in effect divorced the Constitution from the well-known intentions of the Founding Fathers to maintain a strong federal state.

Thus, these judicial interpretations had so increased the stature and social responsibilities of the provinces that they lacked the financial resources to protect the people against the widespread unemployment that accompanied the world economic depression of the 1930's. The Federal Government, on the other hand, possessed the financial means but insufficient legislative authority to deal promptly on a national level with the social problems of the time.

The need for a re-examination of the distribution of legislative powers under the BNA Act in the light of the economic and social developments within the Canadian Confederation was most urgent but World War II intervened before the Report of the Rowell-Sirois Royal Commission on Dominion-Provincial Relations, which provided this re-examination in 1940, could receive thorough study. Fortunately, the outbreak of hostilities temporarily solved the constitutional problem by bringing into play both federal *emergency* and *defence* powers, thereby enabling Ottawa to handle effectively the manifold problems involved in mobilizing the nation's resources for war and subsequently in easing the return to a thriving peacetime economy.

Although such federal-provincial fiscal contractual arrangements as the five-year Taxation Agreements of 1947, 1952, 1957 and 1962, as well as equalization grants, conditional grants and shared-cost programs were initiated, these constitutional arrangements did not evolve from any change in the BNA Act or, indeed, from any new interpretations of either the Judicial Committee of the Privy Council, or (after the abolition in 1949 of appeals to the Committee) of the Supreme Court of Canada in its role as final arbiter of the BNA Act.

Rather, they were brought about by substantial constitutional innovations effected through the somewhat informal executive and administrative practice of continuous consultation between the two levels of government and interaction at federal-provincial conferences where the business of reconciliation of conflicting social interests—the very characterizing core and *raison d'être* of Canadian federalism—could make an ally of time and allow compromise to emerge on a basis of mutual give-and-take. The problems concerned with the regulation of competitive industry, with the immense size and complexity of modern economic institutions, and with the provision of various social services often could not be adequately dealt with at the provincial level, nor was it desirable to have 10 or 11 separate and often conflicting policies striving to cope with problems that were nation-wide and called for a "synthesis of action".

A quiet revolution has therefore been taking place since World War II in the structure of Canadian federalism and these new institutional arrangements and refined techniques for dealing with federal-provincial economic relations have evolved under the new-coined phrase of American origin, "co-operative federalism"—which, in practice, permits the central and regional legislatures through a truly common effort of co-operation to retain their separate jurisdictions over different aspects of the same subject, while facilitating close contact and discussion between ministers and civil servants at both levels of government so that even legislative enactments may be made as the result of joint decisions. These new techniques for dealing with problems arising from the somewhat formal division of powers between the federal and provincial authorities have been operating as informal agencies of developing constitutional convention or custom—in legal terminology—"by way of a gloss" on the constitution as written, and they may be said to be "already part of the constitutional law-in-action" now functioning in Canada.

It seemed clear in 1966 that the reasoned pragmatic approach and techniques of "co-operative federalism", which constitute a continual re-examination of the distribution of powers and the sharing of policy-making in the light of ever-changing conditions, were well suited to provide room both for political manoeuvre and for the safeguarding in Canada of a rich and desirable diversity within a frame of unity. Indeed, it appeared that only in such an approach would Canada achieve an accommodation that gives fair assurance to the aspirations of Quebec and of the other provinces without disrupting the highly productive and integrated national structure of the Canadian transcontinental federation. Through this "unemotional rationality", this pragmatic development of "functionalism in politics", Canada may well find its best hope for a "workable concept of federalism" befitting the challenges of its second century as a federal state.

## Machinery of Government

The British North America Act, 1867 provided for the establishment and functioning of political institutions at three levels of representative government in the Canadian Federation—the national, provincial and local or municipal.

**The National or Federal Government**—Modelled on the British parliamentary system, Canada's institutions of government at the federal or national level consist of three branches—the executive, the legislative, and the judicial. Yet, there is no separation of branches, that is, "checks and balances" in Canada. Rather, the Crown is the unifying *symbol* in all three spheres of power and is the legal point of reference for state authority, and the unifying federal legislative *authority* is vested in "One Parliament for Canada, consisting of the Queen, an Upper House styled the Senate, and the House of Commons".

**Her Majesty Queen Elizabeth II**

**The Queen**—Her Majesty Queen Elizabeth II is Queen of Canada, symbolizing the continuity in the Canadian Constitution of the traditions of the British constitutional monarchy and the free association of member countries of the Commonwealth of which she is Head. The Royal Style and Title approved by the Parliament of Canada and formally proclaimed at Ottawa on May 29, 1953, is "Elizabeth the Second, by the Grace of God of the United Kingdom, Canada and Her other Realms and Territories Queen, Head of the Commonwealth, Defender of the Faith". Her personal participation in the functions of the Crown for Canada is necessarily reserved to such occasions as a royal visit or the periodic appointment of her personal representative on the advice of the Prime Minister of Canada.

## Sovereigns of Canada since Confederation in 1867

| Sovereign | Dynasty | Year of Birth | Date of Accession |
|---|---|---|---|
| Victoria | House of Hanover | 1819 | June 20, 1837 |
| Edward VII | House of Saxe-Coburg and Gotha | 1841 | Jan. 22, 1901 |
| George V | House of Windsor | 1865 | May 6, 1910 |
| Edward VIII | House of Windsor | 1894 | Jan. 20, 1936 |
| George VI | House of Windsor | 1895 | Dec. 11, 1936 |
| Elizabeth II | House of Windsor | 1926 | Feb. 6, 1952 |

**The Governor General**—The personal representative of the Queen in Canada is the Governor General, appointed by Her Majesty on the advice of her Canadian Prime Minister for an unfixed term of customarily five years. Under new Letters Patent issued under the Great Seal of Canada, effective October 1, 1947, he is empowered to exercise, on the advice of the Queen's Privy Council for Canada, (a committee of which constitutes the Ministry or Cabinet), all royal powers and executive authority of the Crown in relation to Canada. He receives no instructions from Westminster and makes no reports thereto but rather exercises such formal authority as summoning, proroguing and dissolving Parliament and assenting to Bills in the Queen's name. Since 1952, distinguished Canadians have served as Governors General of Canada.

## Governors General of Canada since Confederation

| Name | Date of Taking Office | Name | Date of Taking Office |
|---|---|---|---|
| Viscount Monck | July 1, 1867 | The Duke of Devonshire | Nov. 11, 1916 |
| Lord Lisgar | Feb. 2, 1869 | Lord Byng of Vimy | Aug. 11, 1921 |
| The Earl of Dufferin | June 25, 1872 | Viscount Willingdon | Oct. 2, 1926 |
| The Marquis of Lorne | Nov. 25, 1878 | The Earl of Bessborough | Apr. 4, 1931 |
| The Marquis of Lansdowne | Oct. 23, 1883 | Lord Tweedsmuir | Nov. 2, 1935 |
| Lord Stanley of Preston | June 11, 1888 | The Earl of Athlone | June 21, 1940 |
| The Earl of Aberdeen | Sept. 18, 1893 | Viscount Alexander of Tunis | Apr. 12, 1946 |
| The Earl of Minto | Nov. 12, 1898 | The Rt. Hon. Vincent Massey | Feb. 28, 1952 |
| The Earl Grey | Dec. 10, 1904 | Gen. The Rt. Hon. Georges P. Vanier | Sept. 15, 1959 |
| H.R.H. The Duke of Connaught | Oct. 13, 1911 | | |

**The Privy Council**—The Queen's Privy Council for Canada is composed of about 100 members appointed for life by the Governor General on the advice of the Prime Minister. The Council consists chiefly of present and former Ministers of the Crown but occasionally membership in the Privy Council is conferred on former speakers of the Commons and Senate, on distinguished public servants, and on distinguished visitors such as H.R.H. The Duke of Windsor, H.R.H. The Prince Philip, The Duke of Edinburgh, and Earl Alexander of Tunis. The Council does not meet as a functioning body and its constitutional responsibilities as adviser to the Crown are performed exclusively by a select committee composed of the Ministers who actually constitute the Cabinet of the day.

**The House of Commons and the Cabinet**—A new House of Commons is chosen in a general election usually held subsequent to the normal dissolution of Parliament by the Governor General on the advice of the Prime Minister at any time within five years after the last election. Occasionally, (indeed, only in 1926 and 1963 in this century), a general election may be called following a dissolution subsequent to defeat of a government measure or passage of a vote of want of confidence by the House in the government of the day.

Sir John A. Macdonald

Hon. Alexander Mackenzie

Sir John J. J. C. Abbott

Sir John S. D. Thompson

Sir Mackenzie Bowell

Sir Charles Tupper

Sir Wilfrid Laurier

Sir Robert L. Borden

Rt. Hon. Arthur Meighen

CANADA, 1867-1967

# Prime Ministers

# since Confederation

Rt. Hon. William L. Mackenzie King

Rt. Hon. Richard B. Bennett

Rt. Hon. Louis S. St. Laurent

Rt. Hon. John G. Diefenbaker

Rt. Hon. Lester B. Pearson

The franchise or right to vote is conferred upon all Canadian citizens or British subjects, male or female, of the age of 21 or over, who have been resident in Canada for 12 months prior to polling day, with certain exceptions such as persons confined in penal institutions or mental hospitals, federally-appointed judges and returning officers for electoral districts. Seats in the House are distributed by provinces and territories as follows:

| | | | |
|---|---|---|---|
| Newfoundland | 7 | Saskatchewan | 17 |
| Prince Edward Island | 4 | Alberta | 17 |
| Nova Scotia | 12 | British Columbia | 22 |
| New Brunswick | 10 | Yukon Territory | 1 |
| Quebec | 75 | Northwest Territories | 1 |
| Ontario | 85 | | |
| Manitoba | 14 | **Total** | **265** |

Readjustment of representation in the Commons through revision of electoral boundaries, by provinces, was in an advanced stage of completion in the early summer of 1966.

The current Parliament of Canada, the 27th since 1867, was elected in the General Election of November 8, 1965. Party standing in the House of Commons as of *July 15, 1966*, with party leadership in brackets, was as follows: Liberals, 131 (Rt. Hon. Lester Bowles Pearson); Progressive Conservatives, 96 (Rt. Hon John George Diefenbaker); New Democratic Party, 21 (T. C. Douglas); Social Credit Party, 5 (R. N. Thompson); Social Credit Rally, 9 (Réal Caouette); Independent, 1; Others, 2. Four members of the House were women.

Constitutional convention under the parliamentary system of representation requires that the leader of the party that has won the largest number of seats in the newly-elected House of Commons shall be asked by the Governor General, as representative of the Queen, to form the Government. He becomes the Prime Minister and generally chooses party colleagues from among the elected members to form the Cabinet. If he wishes to have in his Cabinet someone who is not a member of the House of Commons, that person must, through a by-election, secure a seat in the House within a short time or receive appointment to the Senate by the Governor General upon the nomination of the Prime Minister. Almost all Cabinet Ministers are also heads of executive departments of the government, for the work of which they are responsible to the House of Commons.

The Cabinet is responsible for determining all important policies of government and securing the passage of such legislation, financial measures and administrative provisions as their supporters may approve. The Ministers of the Crown, as the members of the Cabinet are called, are chosen generally to represent all regions of the country and its principal cultural, religious and social interests.

The Prime Minister, the Cabinet, its composition, and the requirements that all its members have seats in the Commons or in the Senate and that most be heads of executive departments and, above all, that the Prime Minister and his Cabinet have the support of a majority of the House of Commons—all these references to the executive power are *not* mentioned in the BNA Act but rather are essential elements of the unwritten, but none the less cherished, conventional constitution.

# Governor General

## of

## Canada

General Georges P. Vanier, 1959-

Georges Philias Vanier, who has been Governor General of Canada since 1959, is a graduate in law of Laval University. During World War I, he won the Military Cross with bar and the D.S.O. He served as A.D.C. to the Governor General, represented Canada at the London Naval Conference, at the General Assembly of the League of Nations and, as Canadian minister to France, remained at his post until the fall of France in World War II. In 1944 he returned to Paris with the rank of ambassador and held that appointment until his retirement in 1953. Below, Governor General Vanier is shown with Madame Vanier en route to Parliament.

FEDERAL SYSTEM OF GOVERNMENT

39

Viscount Monck, 1867-1868

Baron Lisgar, 1868-1872

Earl of Dufferin, 1872-1878

Marquis of Lorne, 1878-1883

Marquis of Lansdowne, 1883-1888

Baron Stanley of Preston, 1888-1893

Earl of Aberdeen, 1893-1898

Earl of Minto, 1898-1904

Earl Grey, 1904-1911

CANADA, 1867-1967

# Governors General

## since Confederation

Duke of Connaught, 1911-1916

Duke of Devonshire, 1916-1921

Baron Byng of Vimy, 1921-1926

Viscount Willingdon, 1926-1931

Earl of Bessborough, 1931-1935

Baron Tweedsmuir, 1935-1940

Earl of Athlone, 1940-1946

Viscount Alexander, 1946-1952

Rt. Hon. Vincent Massey, 1952-1959

The First Ministry of the Canadian Confederation, as sworn in on July 1, 1867 and headed by Canada's first Prime Minister, Sir John A. Macdonald, is listed below:

| | |
|---|---|
| Hon. Sir John Alexander Macdonald | Prime Minister, Minister of Justice and Attorney General. |
| Hon. Sir George Etienne Cartier | Minister of Militia and Defence. |
| Hon. Samuel Leonard Tilley | Minister of Customs. |
| Hon. Alexander Tilloch Galt | Minister of Finance. |
| Hon. William McDougall | Minister of Public Works. |
| Hon. William Pearce Howland | Minister of Inland Revenue. |
| Hon. Adams George Archibald | Secretary of State for the Provinces. |
| Hon. Adam Johnston Fergusson Blair | President of the Privy Council. |
| Hon. Peter Mitchell | Minister of Marine and Fisheries. |
| Hon. Alexander Campbell | Postmaster General. |
| Hon. Jean Charles Chapais | Minister of Agriculture. |
| Hon. Hector Louis Langevin | Secretary of State of Canada and Superintendent General of Indian Affairs. |
| Hon. Edward Kenny | Receiver General. |

The membership of the federal Ministry or Cabinet, as of *October 3, 1966*, and their respective portfolios are listed below according to precedence:

| | |
|---|---|
| Rt. Hon. Lester Bowles Pearson | Prime Minister. |
| Hon. Paul Joseph James Martin | Secretary of State for External Affairs. |
| Hon. Robert Henry Winters | Minister of Trade and Commerce. |
| Hon. John Whitney Pickersgill | Minister of Transport. |
| Hon. Paul Theodore Hellyer | Minister of National Defence. |
| Hon. Mitchell Sharp | Minister of Finance and Receiver General of Canada. |
| Hon. George James McIlraith | Minister of Public Works. |
| Hon. Arthur Laing | Minister of Indian Affairs and Northern Development. |
| Hon. Lucien Cardin | Minister of Justice and Attorney General of Canada. |
| Hon. Allan Joseph MacEachen | Minister of National Health and Welfare. |
| Hon. Hédard Robichaud | Minister of Fisheries. |
| Hon. Roger Teillet | Minister of Veterans Affairs. |
| Hon. Judy LaMarsh | Secretary of State of Canada. |
| Hon. Charles Mills Drury | Minister of Industry and Minister of Defence Production. |
| Hon. Guy Favreau | President of the Queen's Privy Council for Canada and Registrar General of Canada. |
| Hon. John Robert Nicholson | Minister of Labour. |
| Hon. John Joseph Connolly | Member of the Administration. |
| Hon. Maurice Sauvé | Minister of Forestry and Rural Development. |
| Hon. Edgar John Benson | Minister of National Revenue and President of the Treasury Board. |
| Hon. Léo-Alphonse Joseph Cadieux | Associate Minister of National Defence. |
| Hon. Lawrence T. Pennell | Solicitor General of Canada. |
| Hon. Jean-Luc Pépin | Minister of Energy, Mines and Resources. |
| Hon. Jean Marchand | Minister of Manpower and Immigration |
| Hon. John James Greene | Minister of Agriculture. |
| Hon. Joseph Julien Jean-Pierre Côté | Postmaster General. |
| Hon. John Napier Turner | Member of the Administration. |

The choice of the Canadian electorate at the time of a general election not only determines who will form the Government of Canada but, by deciding which party receives the second largest number of seats in the House of Commons, it designates which of the major parties becomes the Official Opposition.

While the Ministers of the Crown carry the political responsibilities of their respective departments, the federal civil service forms the staffs of the 20 departments and of various boards, commissions, corporations, bureaus and other agencies of the government. The day-to-day administration of a department is handled by a permanent head, usually known as deputy minister. As of Jan. 1, 1966 there were 344,674 federal civilian employees.

**The Senate**—The Senate or Upper House of the Parliament of Canada shares with the House of Commons the responsibility for the enactment of all federal legislation in

The Parliament Building which overlooks the Ottawa River, is built on the site of the edifice destroyed by fire in 1916. The building was opened in 1920. The cornerstone of the tower was laid in 1919 and the edifice was completed for dedication at the Diamond Jubilee ceremonies in 1927. Ottawa had a population of some 18,000 in 1867 and was derisively termed the "Westminster of the Wilderness". Its metropolitan population is now close to half a million.

Confederation Hall at the entrance to the Parliament Building eloquently symbolizes the federal union of the provinces. Sculptors have much detailed ornamental display work to execute before their task is completed.

that Bills must pass both Houses before receiving Royal Assent through the Governor General. Yet the influence of the Senate on legislation is immeasurably less than that of the Commons in which most public Bills are introduced by the Administration and to which the latter is responsible. Indeed, the BNA Act reserves to the elected House and to the Government of the day the origination of any Bill for the expenditure of

As loca
there a
variatio
in area
the pow
legislatı
known
villages,
politan
provide

Munic
and resp
elected
the othe
councillo
associate

The Can
the law.
and supr
and to t
magistrat
and of n
Council a
ment of
inces adı
civil and

The Su
under th
Court an
by the G
attaining
the Senat
cises gene
It is also
Council.
the Privy
(1949), th
conclusiv
and its ju
the right

The House of Commons Chamber, caught by the cameraman in an interlude of solemnity is generally the scene of lively discussion and verbal brickbats. Of Tyndall limestone, Canadian oak, gold leaf cornices and painted Irish linen ceiling, this Green Chamber has a grandeur all its own.

any public money or the imposition of any tax. None the less, the Senate has the power to perform a valuable service to the nation in amending and delaying the passage of measures that might result from sudden shifts in public opinion or party strength. Moreover, it may initiate measures overlooked by a busy Commons and carry on significant committee work on various matters of state.

Senators are appointed by the Governor General on the nomination, by constitutional usage, of the Prime Minister. In June 1965, life appointment was reduced by legislation providing for the retirement of Senators on reaching the age of 75 years. Representation in the Senate is as follows:

| | | | | |
|---|---|---|---|---|
| Ontario | 24 | Western Provinces | | 24 |
| Quebec | 24 | Manitoba | 6 | |
| Atlantic Provinces | 30 | British Columbia | 6 | |
| Nova Scotia | 10 | Alberta | 6 | |
| New Brunswick | 10 | Saskatchewan | 6 | |
| Prince Edward Island | 4 | | | |
| Newfoundland | 6 | Total | | 102 |

# Attainment of National Sovereignty

Canada acquired the foundations of national sovereignty both peacefully and piece-meal throughout the eighty years 1867-1947, during which the Canadian Government gradually threw off the Imperial restraints on its autonomy in both internal and external affairs.

The nation progressively expanded the scope of responsible cabinet government from its initial pre-Confederation application to purely local and internal issues (1848), including the legislature's right to control the trade tariff (1859), until the Federal Government, through a series of adaptations, prior to World War I, not only extended its powers over the negotiation of Canadian commercial agreements but won for Canada exclusion from the automatic application of new trade agreements made by the British Government.

Down to 1914 in respect of political treaties, however, the diplomatic unity of the British Empire was maintained and, in the vital matters of declaring war, making peace, appointing diplomatic agents and participating in international conferences, Canada (as well as the other dominions) had no share. Hence Canada, on August 4, 1914, found itself automatically at war through the action of the British Government. Thereafter, a rapid and far-reaching chain reaction was set in motion, linking a conspicuous war effort with a strong national consciousness, a new awareness of maturity with a determination to win greater control of its own destinies, extending to Canadian participation at the Paris Peace Conference (1918), original membership in the League of Nations (1919), and a succession of constitutional issues including the Chanak incident (1922), and culminating in the Balfour declaration of the Imperial Conference of 1926 proclaiming the complete *equality in status* of Britain and the dominions "in no way subordinate one to another in any aspect of their domestic or external affairs, though united by a common allegiance to the Crown, and freely associated as members of the British Commonwealth of nations . . . ."

Five years later, the Statute of Westminster confirmed and augmented the autonomy of the dominions, proclamed in 1926, although on the initiative of Premier Ferguson of Ontario and with the approval of Prime Minister Bennett following the convening of a Dominion-Provincial Conference, a reservation respecting Canada (Sect. 7, subsect. 1) was inserted in the said statute stating that:

"Nothing in this Act shall be deemed to apply to the repeal, amendment, or alteration of the British North America Acts 1867 to 1930, or any order, rule or regulation made thereunder".

Thus, although Canada had become a fully sovereign state by its own volition, it chose, as recently as 1930-31, to leave the British Parliament as the instrument of amendment. While this "instrument of amendment" passed an amending statute in 1949 giving the Parliament of Canada power to amend the British North America Act in purely federal matters, the federal and provincial governments have failed, despite lengthy negotiations reaching into 1966 (noted above at pages 30-1), to agree to a method of amendment in Canada by Canadians which would cover matters involving both the federal and provincial governments.

Despite this, and one or two other anomalies, Canada's role in world affairs since 1939 has been that of a fully independent sovereign nation. Canada entered World

The Queen of Canada greets veterans of the nation's wars.

War II on the decision of its own Parliament seven days after Britain declared war and, through its tremendous industrial and military war effort during 1939-1945 and its subsequent activities in the United Nations and the various Specialized Agencies, has been recognized as a "middle power" among the nations, willing and able to participate in international conferences considered appropriate to Canada's interests and to accept international responsibilities undreamed of prior to 1939*

Additional signs that Canada outwardly and inwardly had come of age are evident in the passage (1946) of the Canadian Citizenship Act, the appointment by the Queen of distinguished Canadians, The Right Honourable Vincent Massey (1952-59) and General The Right Honourable Georges P. Vanier (1959-  ) as Governors General on the advice of the Prime Minister of Canada, and finally in the proclamation (February 15, 1965) of the National Flag of Canada.

## Canadian Citizenship†

Despite Confederation in 1867, eighty years were to elapse before the people of Canada, of diverse ethnic origins, possessed the recognized legal status of "Canadian". In the interval between the two world wars and particularly during and immediately subsequent to the war years 1939-45, a strong sense of national consciousness and pride developed among Canadians from their awareness of having, during these years of conflict, matched the highest international standards of scientific, engineering, industrial, military and political endeavour.

Motivated by the desire to gratify this national pride and to provide a precise definition of 'Canadian citizen' which would end the long-standing source of irritation often felt by Canadians when reminded that there was no such thing as a 'Canadian', the Parliament of Canada passed the Canadian Citizenship Act in 1946. Proclaimed effective January 1, 1947, the Act defined 'Canadian citizen', whether natural-born or naturalized, as distinct from the category of 'British subject' and declared that while the "basic national status" was to be "Canadian citizen", all Canadian citizens were "British subjects".

---

*See *infra*, Part VI, for a succinct account of Canada's relations with the outside world during its first hundred years as a federal state.

† See also pages 100-102.

More than half a million newcomers have taken out Canadian citizenship papers since World War II.

## National Flag of Canada

The most recent indication of Canada's attainment of complete national sovereignty has been the proclamation by Her Majesty the Queen on February 15, 1965 of the National Flag of Canada as adopted by the Canadian Parliament on the preceding December 15, after prolonged debate. Canada's new maple leaf flag—"a red flag of the proportions two by length and one by width, containing in its centre a white square the width of the flag, with a single red maple leaf centered therein"—replaced the Canadian Red Ensign which an order in council of September 5, 1945 had authorized might be flown on Federal buildings inside and outside Canada "until such time as action is taken by Parliament for the formal adoption of a National Flag". Three days after the "formal adoption" of the 'National Flag of Canada', Parliament approved resolutions recognizing the continued use of the Union Jack to symbolize "Canada's membership in the Commonwealth of Nations and . . . her allegiance to the Crown".

Thus, two symbols may fly side by side in Canadian skies—one that flies as "a symbol of Canada alone . . . that will say one word and that word is 'Canada'"*; the other, our symbol of "a Commonwealth of Nations of which an independent Canada is a part"†.

Speaking on behalf of all Canadians, who are becoming increasingly conscious of the proud achievements, bountiful resources and unmatched potential of this, their native land, or land of adoption, the Rt. Hon. Lester B. Pearson, Prime Minister of Canada, enunciated the fervent prayer at the National Flag ceremony on Parliament Hill (noon, Feb. 15, 1965) that:

"Under this Flag may our youth find new inspiration for loyalty to Canada; for a patriotism based not on any mean or narrow nationalism, but on the deep and equal pride that all Canadians will feel for every part of this good land".

(C. Cecil Lingard)

*The Prime Minister of Canada, House of Commons Debates, December 11, 1964, p. 11038.
†*Ibid*, p. 11031.

Sir Edmund Head, Governor-in-Chief of Canada, 1854-61, advised Queen Victoria to choose Ottawa as the capital of the province of Canada. The provincial capital later became the federal capital.

# The National Capital

As a capital reflects the soul of its people, Ottawa mirrors the aspirations, the industry and the politics of the Canadian people. From this centre in the Ontario-Quebec area radiate the guidelines of economic and cultural pursuits; here nation meets nation in the diplomatic representatives of many lands.

Ottawa is a beautiful city. Nature provided a magnificent site at the junction of the Ottawa and Rideau Rivers with the glistening curtain of the Rideau Falls on the Ottawa bank complemented by the Gatineau River on the Hull side. The community was first known as Bytown in honour of Colonel John By, a military engineer, who built the Rideau canal system. It developed from a military settlement into a prosperous lumbering centre. When a capital was sought for the united province of Upper and Lower Canada, the Governor, Sir Edmund Head, drew the attention of Queen Victoria to the attractions and strategic advantages of this then-small settlement.

Described as "Ottawa, the proposed new seat of the Canadian government", this sketch was reproduced in the London Illustrated News, April 25, 1857.

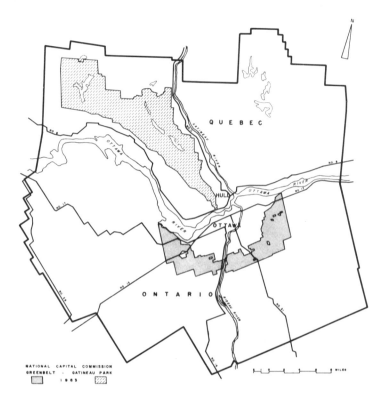

NATIONAL CAPITAL COMMISSION
GREENBELT · GATINEAU PARK
1965

## Ottawa, the Nation's Capital

Thousands of blossoms
have made Ottawa
the tulip capital
of Canada.

Rideau Falls. Its
curtain of mist earned it
its French designation.

The heart of Ottawa, a jewel in the night.

Queen Victoria has a place of honour in the capital she chose.

Rideau Hall, Residence of the Governor General.

Gatineau Park with its thousands of acres of woods and lakes is only a few minutes' drive from Parliament Hill.

"Ottawa," Sir Edmund pointed out, "is the only place which will be accepted by the majority of Upper and Lower Canada as a fair compromise. With the exception of Ottawa, every one of the cities proposed is an object of jealousy to each of the others. Ottawa is, in fact, neither in Upper nor Lower Canada. Literally it is in the former; but a bridge alone divides it from the latter . . . " The Queen chose Ottawa over its rivals—Kingston, Montreal, Toronto and Quebec, and when Confederation was consummated in 1867, Ottawa became the national capital of the new dominion. Slowly the city changed from a roistering pioneer centre into a sedate centre of parliamentary discussion and initiative. The transformation of the capital and its environs into an even more beautiful metropolitan area has been, since 1959, the responsibility of the National Capital Commission, a Crown agency of the Federal Government. Replacing the Federal District Commission (1927-59) which, on its part, was the lineal descendant of the Ottawa Improvement Commission (1899-1927), the NCC has, during the 1960's, been engaged in implementing the National Capital Plan (1945-51) of France-born Jacques Gréber and his Canadian colleagues. This has been for "the development, conservation and improvement of the National Capital Region" of 1,800 square miles surrounding the Ottawa-Hull metropolitan area on both sides of the Ottawa River, "so that the nature and character of the seat of Government may be in accordance with its national significance".

The five key recommendations of the National Capital Plan are concerned with: the increase of open green space in Ottawa, establishment of a greenbelt around Ottawa, relocation of railway station and lines, planned siting of Federal Government buildings, and the development of Gatineau Park which embraces 75,000 acres of the Laurentian Shield on the Quebec side of the Ottawa River. The park is only a few minutes by bus from the centre of the National Capital and is justly famous for the majesty of its forests, the limpidity of its lakes and the magnitude of its vistas.

Landscaped grounds of Federal Government buildings add to the green areas in the capital as do the many scenic parks and driveways. The Ottawa River Parkway which skirts the Ottawa River for some six miles, provides a magnificent entrance to the heart of the city. To relieve parking problems and provide spacious settings for modern public structures, many new Federal Government buildings have been erected on the outskirts of the city, particularly at Tunney's Pasture where the Dominion Bureau of Statistics and the National Health and Welfare departments are located, and at Confederation Heights where the Department of Public Works, the Department of Fisheries, and the headquarters of the Canadian Broadcasting Corporation are now situated. Since the Second World War, an accelerated expansion of industrial and residential construction has also taken place in Ottawa. The Capital's metropolitan population, which was some 226,000 in 1941, had soared to approximately half a million in 1966.

In the great international world of today the name Ottawa has become the symbol of a God-fearing people whose national policies are founded on the democratic traditions of freedom, justice and individual initiative, whose foreign commitments have involved the nation in countless enterprises for the common good of mankind. A country with a high standard of living, an expanding economy, and a tremendous industrial potential is Canada's heritage. May its Capital reflect continued wise use of its resources.

(J. M. LANDRY)

and the United States. The area they cover is immense, but the numbers of Eskimos in the world may be fewer than 60,000. Some 13,000 of these live in Canada where their natural increase (three to four per cent a year) indicates that their numbers will double in about 20 years. They are the only native people who live in both Asia and America.

Rasmussen describes an early morning on the summit of East Cape, the steep headland that forms the eastern extremity of Siberia when the first snow had already settled on the heights. "The landscape has a calm grandeur of its own; far away in the sun-haze of the horizon lies Great Diomede Island, here forming the boundary between America and Asia."

It was Parry's second expedition in 1821-23 that seems to have aroused popular interest in the Eskimos. Parry spent two winters in Foxe Basin in the heart of the Eskimo country and both he and Lyon, his second-in-command, left excellent accounts which were widely read.

Canada's efforts since 1903 to bring the Eskimos more within the framework of the nation are described in Diamond Jenness' *Eskimo Administration in Canada*, a study prepared for the Arctic Institute of North America with support from the Department of Northern Affairs and National Resources. It takes a scholarly, often troubled look at a situation whose built-in problems were immense, and attempts to deal with them often desultory, uncoordinated, hobbled by poor communications and lack of northern policy.

As the century opened, the Inuit must have seemed a long way from the rest of Canada. So, too, must many of those who were working in Eskimo country—missionaries, whalers, traders, the police. The Eskimos' impression of the white man's culture, customs, and motivations must have been a curiously blurred image of heroic devotion, shrewd paternalism and hard-nosed drive for gain.

## Department Created

In the intervening years Eskimo affairs reflected the labours of many dedicated public servants, but it was not until December 8, 1953, that the enormous question of what to do about the north was finally wheeled below the national spotlight. In a lengthy statement in the House of Commons, Prime Minister Louis St. Laurent moved second reading of a Bill to create the Department of Northern Affairs and National Resources, now the Department of Indian Affairs and Northern Development.

"We must leave no doubt about active occupation and exercise our sovereignty in these northern lands right up to the pole," the Prime Minister declared. It had surprised him to note on the map that the Northwest and Yukon Territories jointly comprised 39.3 per cent of Canada. "Apparently," he observed, "we have administered these vast territories of the north in an almost continuous state of absence of mind."

Whatever the past, notice had been served that from now on action was to be the word and there was an exhilarating feeling that new opportunities were to be offered to the venturesome. "The north" had a romantic ring about it and no one could doubt that its development was of first-class importance to Canada.

After so long a period of on-and-off administrative effort it was perhaps not surprising that one of the hard facts to confront the planners was Canada's lack of any substantial body of Arctic research to draw on. Only a handful of Canadians outside the north were fluent in Eskimo; no real reserve existed of qualified men and women with Arctic experience who could be tapped for northern service.

Partly, at least, this was the price paid by a nation larger in area than any except Russia and with a population less than 15,000,000—a nation that had taken two wars and a depression in stride and concentrated its economic and social energies on developing opportunities closer to home.

Engineers already seasoned at building on muskeg and permafrost, at rock-blasting and working at below zero temperatures elsewhere in Canada, were set new and complex problems to adapt cold weather experience to Arctic town-planning. In all areas of the northern program, pressure was heavy to show results; to do even faster whatever could be done in a hurry. In the Arctic not much can.

Canadians who had not seriously looked at their maps in years discovered that the distance between Alert and Point Pelee was almost as great as between Newfoundland and British Columbia. Polar projection maps that showed Canada in relation to other Arctic powers were in great demand.

But it was not the maps of engineers; nor was it the teachers, doctors, nurses, Northern Service Officers and many others who went to serve on the frontier that made the north seem real to the rest of Canada.

It was the Eskimos. So remote, so legendary, it was almost as though they inhabited outer space. It was the Inuit who gripped the imagination and aroused the concern of thousands of Canadians who might never visit "the beautiful land", might never even see an Eskimo.

What sort of land was it to be—this new north?

In a few short words Gordon Robertson, then Deputy Minister of Northern Affairs and National Resources and Commissioner of the Northwest Territories, described the north he and his men were working to build: "A region where race lines are unknown, and where the north will be run by its own people, standing on their own feet, and doing the job better than we in the south can do it". Whatever their racial origin, northerners were to be tomorrow's men.

The opportunities for Eskimo leadership appeared never so great. But the process of calling it forth, reviving it, creating it, were slow. The bridge between Eskimo past and contemporary Canada was only beginning to be built. It would take a long time to finish and be the work of many hands. Then would come the task of keeping it in repair. It would be a work never finished. The letter of Akeeko is part of that bridge.

## Akeeko of the Old Arctic

Akeeko was a very old man living in a small settlement in the Keewatin, land of the terrible winds. He had seen much change come to his land and of late years when he could no longer hunt, had had much time to think. And some of his thoughts troubled him. So, in 1957 he began a great labour, which was to write a letter to the Department of Northern Affairs and National Resources (now the Department of Indian Affairs and Northern Development).

Akeeko's letter spoke of the good and bad things in the days before the kabloona came—family joys, hunger, blizzards, the pleasures of hunting, and life lived always in

Eskimos call it "the beautiful land".

the shadow of sickness and of sudden or lingering death. Akeeko was a child when the first white men came—whalers from Scotland and America, and his father used to go with them in their boats. Sometimes they would stay away a whole year, locked in by ice. There were no schools then but plenty of game until, without explanation, the game went away.

Akeeko recalls one bitter winter when his father was away and he was still a child, too young to hunt. He, his mother and his baby sister remained alone in the igloo.

"The weather was bad and there were blizzards. Our food would not last us and there I was not knowing how to kill fox. My sister would be crying all day because my mother did not have milk at her breast. You cannot tell whether a child knows emptiness but it does, and that is why my sister cried most of the time—not knowing yet sort of knowing."

In August the ice broke up, seals were plentiful and one day his father returned in the middle of a storm. "I could not believe he was alive . . . I just started to cry."

When Akeeko married, he and his wife were at first happy and well, but even in the good times reverses came. The caribou went away. "We were living in huts made of earth . . . everything seemed to come at once . . . no proper home, people sick, no money." Many Eskimos died that winter. He himself spent three years in hospital.

But now, Akeeko writes, many things have changed. The Government has provided schools for the children, care for the sick, welfare services for families who cannot care for themselves, boats and nets for the Eskimos to increase their sea harvests of fish, whales and walrus meat. Eskimos have learned from the kabloona how to organize their own co-operative to market Arctic char and salmon. The West Baffin Eskimo Co-operative at Cape Dorset, has become famous for the quality of its sculpture and graphic art, and other communities, too, are producing good art and fine crafts. There is some kind of learning and training for all ages.

Akeeko did not suppose the kabloona could make these things work alone. They had to have the support and understanding of the Inuit, and the hard work, too. But a lifetime had taught him that people are people everywhere and there is no magic to make all sensible or honest or hard working. They are simply people—mixed-up, good and bad. The opinions of Akeeko are full of sense, the views of a man who knows his own people. "Some Eskimos hunt well and some do not. Some work very hard, some do not. Some have sense and help each other, and some do not. This is the way it is in our country." He might have added, "Some Eskimos get drunk now and some don't". Learning how to handle liquor is all part of the warm houses and a bit of money in the bank; part of the years of trial. (As some kabloona have not yet learned how to stop falling on their own faces they have not much yet to teach the Inuit.)

The views of old men are listened to politely but seldom regarded. Akeeko knew this but it did not stop him writing about what was on his mind. The new things that had come into the lives of the people—the teaching now offered to Eskimos of all ages, the better harvests, the wages for those prepared to work white men's hours—many of these were good. But much of it was confusing because it was coming too fast and in a way to shake the pride of men confident and efficient in the old skills of the land. He thought some kabloona were too concerned pressing on with their own day's work to seek the advice of the Eskimos.

"It would be better," Akeeko wrote, "if they talked to us more . . . the written explanations we get are hard to follow. That is why the things we are asked to do never get done. It would be better if we were told by tongue. Eskimos do not pay attention to written things—not even myself."

But he knew the white man well enough to know that the only way to get these things through the heads of those who talked with paper was to put it all down in writing. "This is Akeeko writing," he reminded Ottawa halfway through the letter, "Other Eskimos know much more than I do but they do not write." A humble man with a firm mind, he had no wish to turn back the clock but to remind the kabloona that it takes time to learn many new things and that if they are not learned right, there is danger a man may lose his self confidence and even forget he is an Eskimo.

Akeeko's is the voice of an old man who lived all his life in the wind-torn Keewatin, drove his dogs across the sea ice in winter and in his youth was an excellent hunter. His was the voice of the old Arctic; of Yesterday's men.

## Okpik of the New Arctic

Now listen to the voice of Abraham Okpik who works in the area of public responsibility, of getting things done. He is one of the North's new men.

Tall, heavy-set, with an air of purpose, Mr. Okpik is the first Eskimo to be appointed a member of the Council of the Northwest Territories. He has never been ruffled by publicity, of which he has received a good deal since becoming a civil servant some years ago. At the time of his appointment to Council on October 19, 1965, he was

An Eskimo carved chess set—a fine example of the sculptor's art.

Abraham Okpik, the first Eskimo member of the Council of the Northwest Territories, attends a meeting of the Council in Ottawa.

working in Yellowknife helping Eskimo hardrock miners from Rankin Inlet in the Keewatin adjust to urban life. Before that he had been program director and, later, acting director of the Eskimo Rehabilitation Centre at Frobisher Bay.

Speaking English with a slight Scottish burr from first having learned English from a Scottish teacher, he wasted no words in letting Council know where he stood. "I want no favours because of my origin," he declared, "I will express my convictions and be ready to criticize what I think should be criticized." To a reporter who asked if he ever planned to go back to a life on the land he replied, "I've no desire to go back to trapping and living in an igloo but if I had to, I could".

What does it mean to be an Eskimo? Some years ago, in an eloquent plea to his own people, Mr. Okpik wrote in the Eskimo language magazine, *Inuktituk*, "We are living in the present times without observing what we are losing, and that is our own Eskimo Inuk culture, which our great-great-grandfathers have passed on to us generation after generation . . . . We should learn as much as we can from this new culture but we must not forget our own culture . . . . Keep our language alive. Tell the old stories, sing the songs, dance the old dances, make jokes, enjoy this great power for thought developed from long ago by our ancestors . . . . There are only very few Eskimos but there are millions of whites, just like mosquitoes. It is something very special and wonderful to be an Eskimo—they are like the snow geese. If an Eskimo forgets his language and Eskimo ways, he will be nothing but just another mosquito. It is up to the Eskimos of today to use their Eskimo strength of word and thought. It is up to the young people".

Mr. Okpik was writing in 1962. Since then he has become progressively more involved in the broader context of the north. As a member of the Northwest Territories Council he is dealing with legislation and planning that include Eskimo affairs but go beyond them; in his full-time job he is continuing to work directly with and for the Eskimo people.

Segments of the Government's northern program directly affect the future of the Eskimos, and in other areas the Inuit share equally in such programs with all residents of the Northwest Territories. In October 1965, Northern Affairs Minister Arthur Laing announced a $12,000,000 program to provide 1,600 new Eskimo homes, in addition to the 1,000 basic housing units already built. The problems in this area of Eskimo affairs are as large as they are human. The rising birth rate, good in itself, has created acute over-crowding and a type of squalor that scars the face of too many Arctic communities.

## Educational Program

In the north, children of all races go to school together. An education program that has built more than 60 schools will, by 1971, provide northerners with a pre-university education as good as any in Canada. Vocational education and training, and job placement services are an essential part of this, to forestall the human disaster of well-educated young northerners with no place in which to apply their skills and knowledge.

Major questions beset the education program and in some instances there are no clear-cut answers yet. School training must be adapted to be of value to the Eskimo child who will choose to live on the land; equally it must serve the abilities of those who continue their academic work and may one day become leaders in their own regions or in the rest of Canada. From the beginning of school it takes 12 to 14 years to train the kind of skilled technician required by modern industry. The children who started school in the autumn of 1965 are the workers and leaders of 1980. All this cannot be accomplished overnight.

Evidence of the government's resolve to push ahead with political development of the north was contained in an announcement by the Minister, May 11, 1965, regarding the setting up of an Advisory Commission on the Development of Government in the Northwest Territories.

Political development, he pointed out, must keep pace with the remarkable changes occurring in the north. Territorial governments with powers commensurate to their present capacity for self-government and their ability to assume the financial and other responsibilities entailed, are essential if policies and programs responsive to the needs of the people of the Northwest Territories are to be achieved.

All this is part of the changing north.

Akeeko of the old Arctic was a man without schooling who knew the beauty of his land when the sun returns in the springtime, and knew its dark, ferocious winds. In his youth he had fought back sickness and weather but when he laid his thoughts before the far-off kabloona he wrote as a humble man not realising that though the men he was writing to were different, they were no better than he. Okpik, the first time he spoke before the Council of the Northwest Territories, used the tone of a man addressing equals, neither better nor worse than himself.

62

High in the Arctic, at Cambridge Bay on Victoria Island, Eskimos shop at a Hudson Bay Company store. According to estimates (1966) Canadian Eskimos number some 13,000.

## Between the Old and the New

Between these two men of the old and new Arctic, lies a valley where many Eskimos still dwell not knowing which kind of men they are or where they are going. Some see clearly, but others drift left and right like blind men. They know *inuktitut*, the Eskimo way, but not yet how to walk a middle path between ways that are both new and old. This kind of walking cannot be learned in a day.

Let a thoughtful white man have the last word, "We cannot push the Eskimos and we dare not hold them back. Progress is a very delicate operation. They are tough and able on their own ground and about things they understand. But on our ground they are less sure and this is where the trouble starts. They do not always see through us as we see through one another." He paused, frowned at a plane growing larger in the sky and added, "The day the Eskimo can easily and often say No to the white man, when he believes he is right and the rest of us wrong, then—and only then—will we be brothers. For brothers we must be. Neither they nor we can carry the future alone".

(IRENE BAIRD)

THE ESKIMOS IN CANADA

# Indians in Transition

The hundred years of Confederation have been years of transition, growth and expansion in all areas of Canadian life. For the Indians, most of whom still lived the nomadic hunting and fishing life of their ancestors at the time of Confederation, the transition has often been particularly difficult. None the less, there has been a valuable interchange of cultures and much of Indian culture has become an integral part of the Canadian scene. More and more Indians are being drawn into the main stream of Canadian economic and social life with an attendant increase of mutual understanding and appreciation.

Indians have a right to be proud of their contributions in the making of the nation. It was they who guided explorers and showed them how to survive in a little-known land. They formed the backbone of the fur trade, the country's first major industry. Indian foods like corn, beans and squash are now common fare. The toboggan, canoe and snow-shoes, unchanged in basic design, are still important means of transportation in isolated areas, and elsewhere are enjoyed as means of recreation. The Indian motif constantly appears in murals, designs, patterns and other media of artistic expression. Through the American Revolutionary War, the War of 1812, and the two World Wars, the Indians joined other Canadians and fought with valour and distinction.

**Ten Linguistic Groups**—An estimated 200,000 Indians inhabited the vast territories now known as Canada when the Europeans first landed on this continent. They were scattered across the whole country in distinctive culture groups and were also divided into ten linguistic groups, namely, from east to west, the Algonkian, Iroquoian, Siouan, Athapaskan, Kootenayan, Salishan, Wakashan, Tsimshian, Haida and Tlingit. Except for the Kootenayan and Tlingit each linguistic group was divided into a number of sub-groups speaking related languages or dialects.

By the time of Confederation, the Indian population had dwindled gradually through epidemics introduced from Europe, internecine strife aggravated by competition in the fur trade, and increasing scarcity of natural food supplies. After Confederation, there was little change in the total Indian population until the 1930's, when it began to increase. Today there are more than 225,000 Indians in Canada with an annual increase rate of over three per cent, the greatest of any ethnic group in the country.

The Indians in different regions of Canada showed great diversity in language, culture and economic pursuits. The Iroquoian Indians of southern Ontario and Quebec were skilled in agriculture, lived in stable communities, and had evolved complex social and political organizations before their first contact with the Europeans. The Indians on the Pacific coast, whose economy was based largely on the products of the sea and the giant cedar trees which grew in profusion throughout the area, also had sufficient leisure time in which to develop a rich social life, a strong social structure, and highly sophisticated art forms. Nevertheless, at the time of Confederation the majority of Indians who inhabited the hinterlands of the north and west still followed the nomadic way of life, securing their livelihood from hunting, trapping and fishing.

By this time, however, there were modifications of the traditional culture in even the most remote regions. Lonely explorers, fishermen and fur traders, far from home and enjoying the solace of wilderness hospitality, left their imprint on the new country. Large numbers of metis, proud of their mixed heritage and exerting great influence over the Indians, established liaison between the new settlers and the original inhabitants of the country.

From the early years of settlement of this country special consideration was given to the relationship with the Indians and a separate administration was established by the government to deal with Indian affairs. At the time of Confederation, it was recognized that Indian affairs were of national rather than provincial concern and, consequently, a special provision was included in the British North America Act which placed Indians under the legislative jurisdiction of the Parliament of Canada. Since then a special branch of government has been responsible for carrying out the policy of Parliament with regard to Indians.

## Under Federal Jurisdiction

The new Federal Government absorbed the administrative machinery of the several provinces which had stressed the protection of the Indian people, first from unscrupulous merchants and traders and later from land speculators. Federal legislation in 1868, and a new Indian Act in 1876, consolidated existing federal and provincial legislation relating to Indians. While providing certain powers of self-government, the Indian Act of 1876, which formed the basis of Indian policy until the passing of a new Indian Act in 1951, was mainly oriented towards paternalism and protection. It provided for government control over the management and sale of Indian lands and the expenditure of band funds. As a protective measure, Indians were prohibited from consuming intoxicating liquors and severe penalties were imposed for sale of liquor to them. Trespassing on Indian reserves was forbidden. Indian lands were not subject to taxation and Indian presents and annuities could not be claimed for payment of debts.

**Reserves Established**—In the five older provinces, the Indians were, for the most part, settled on reserves at the time of Confederation. The newly-established Federal Government was confronted with the problem of assisting the Indians to adjust to and participate in a nation-wide transition from a frontier economy to a stable agricultural livelihood, and ultimately to become a self-sustaining, self-governing and progressive segment of the population.

With this goal in view, the Federal Government endeavoured to persuade wandering groups of Indians to settle in permanent locations and give up their migratory habits, particularly since the steadily-advancing tide of settlement in the southern and central areas was driving fur and game farther north. Indian agents attempted to introduce more advanced methods of farming, building and stock raising. Government assistance was provided for seed, grain and implements in an effort to establish Indians in agriculture. However, these measures generally met with failure (or limited success) as agricultural pursuits were at variance with traditional Indian patterns of life.

In 1870 the Hudson's Bay Company, which had held sway over the vast regions known as Rupert's Land and the North-Western Territory for nearly two hundred years, ceded its territorial rights to the Crown for a cash compensation to be paid by

Canada. Great Britain then transferred these lands to Canada, thus opening the way to a great western expansion of the new nation.

The Hudson's Bay Company had always maintained friendly relations with the Indians, who were disturbed when the old regime came to an end. The Indians also feared the encroachments of an agricultural society as the frontier moved steadily westward. Traders poured into the prairies, dispensing "fire-water" for the furs and horses of the Indians, and left the people impoverished. In addition, the buffalo herds were visibly diminishing. The Government of Canada was faced with the dual problem of gaining the co-operation of the Indians and maintaining their goodwill, before the country could be opened for settlement.

In the evolution of the colonial period the Crown had soon recognized that the Indians had special rights in the soil and had made agreements, or treaties as they were afterwards called, with various Indian tribes for the extinguishment of these rights. A Royal Proclamation issued in 1763, often referred to as the Magna Charta of the Indians, had reserved to the Indians all the lands west of a line along the heads of the rivers running into the Atlantic, in which the resident tribes were to be left undisturbed in the possession of their hunting grounds. Land required for settlement was to be purchased from the Indians. In accordance with the principles of the Royal Proclamation, agreements or treaties were made with the Indians in southern Ontario as settlement advanced.

## Formal Treaties Concluded

The Government of Canada, to prepare the way for expansion westward, negotiated formal treaties with the Indians of Manitoba and the North-West Territories. The Indians also were eager to conclude treaties because they feared for their future. Between the years 1871 and 1877 the Government of Canada concluded seven treaties with the Indians of the west and northwest. In return for certain considerations the Indians relinquished their rights to the lands from Lake Superior to the foot of the Rocky Mountains.

The treaties, in general, gave the Indians the right to hunt and fish in the ceded territory as long as it remained the property of the Crown. Lands were allotted to the Indians, to be set aside as reserves for homes and agricultural purposes, with the proviso that these lands could not be sold or alienated without the consent of the Indians concerned and for their benefit. Annuities were promised in perpetuity to each Indian man, woman and child who came under treaty. Provision was made for the establishment of schools on reserves for the instruction of Indian children, and agricultural implements, oxen and cattle to form the nuclei of herds were given to Indian bands on a once-for-all basis to help them make the transition to an agricultural way of life.

Some twenty years later and continuing down to the early 1920's other treaties were made with Indians, covering northern Ontario, Saskatchewan, Alberta, the Peace River block and the Mackenzie River district.

In addition to the plains Indians with whom treaties were made, a large number of American Sioux Indians took refuge in Canada in the 1860's and 1870's and reserves were set apart for them.

Akaya-ni-Muka (Many Guns) is the Blackfoot name of James Gladstone, first Canadian of Indian ethnic origin to sit in the Senate. He is shown here dressed in street clothes, also in the ceremonial attire of a Blood Indian.

The Indians, faced with a total disruption of their economy, soon realized they would have to find some new means of subsistence. The only alternative was agriculture. Crowfoot, head chief of the Blackfoot nation, a man of outstanding sagacity and influence, saw the need for adopting a new mode of life. He and his people co-operated with the government and the Indians willingly received instructions in farming. Even so, rations had to be issued for many years although, when possible, the Indians were expected to work in return for the food so that they would not become entirely dependent on the government for their subsistence.

There were no Indian wars in northwestern Canada such as occurred elsewhere in America because law and order, personified by the famed North West Mounted Police, preceded settlement. However, in 1885 a tragic and unnecessary episode marred the otherwise peaceable history of the Canadian northwest. Many of the metis residents in the territories already owned their homes and farms. Others had lived by hunting buffalo and other game. A third group was identified with the Indians, living with them and speaking their language.

The construction of a transcontinental railway was well under way by the early 1880's and a stream of settlers in search of good farming land followed the railway.

Surveyors came in the vanguard of the railroads. These developments, combined with the disappearance of the buffalo and threatened loss of their hunting grounds and farm lands, caused fear and apprehension among the metis. They made representations to the Federal Government requesting that the surveyors respect the boundaries of their lands, and that their claims to scrip, that is certificates which could be exchanged for land, be granted. Unfortunately, means of communication were slow and inadequate from a frontier area. In addition the official reports did not present an accurate picture of the situation, and the petitions of the metis appeared to be ignored.

**Invitation to Riel**—Fearful and disillusioned, the metis sent an invitation to Louis Riel, then resident in Montana, to lead them. Continued representations to the Federal Government were made without avail and it appeared to the metis that their claims would remain unheeded. In the spring of 1885 violence erupted in the northwest.

Some wandering bands of Indians, still reluctant to settle on reserves, and certain of the settled bands, joined in the uprising. Many Indian leaders remained neutral and, in fact, did much to influence their followers not to take part.

Canadian troops were brought into the country to put down the uprising and the leaders were apprehended and sentenced according to the law. This was the last episode in the retreat of the plains Indians before the advance of agricultural settlement. Attempts were made by the government to resolve the problems of the metis and there were no further outbreaks of violence in the northwest.

On the Pacific coast there was little settlement until the 1850's but the colonial governments provided some special measures, including reserves, for the Indian people. When British Columbia entered Confederation in 1871, the Terms of Union provided that Indian affairs and the management of Indian lands should come under Federal jurisdiction, which would continue a policy "as liberal as that hitherto pursued by the British Columbia Government". In order to carry out this policy, provision was made for the conveyance of tracts of land from the provincial to the Federal Government to be held in trust for the use and benefit of the Indians as required. Both governments entered into an agreement in 1875-76 under which a joint commission was constituted to allot the reserves, the number, extent and location of reserves to be determined for each "nation" separately. A reserve might be enlarged or diminished in proportion to the number of band members occupying it, the extra land being allotted from Crown lands, and land no longer needed reverting to the province.

The reversionary interest, which set up a sort of dual ownership of these Indian reserves, caused many administrative difficulties and led to numerous disputes and appeals regarding land. To settle these claims an agreement between the federal and provincial governments was negotiated in 1912, which provided for the appointment of a Royal Commission to adjust the acreage of Indian reserves in British Columbia and to set aside new reserves. The reserves finally fixed by the Commission were to be conveyed to the Federal Government free of any reversionary interest except in the case of a band becoming extinct. The report of the Commission, which was adopted in 1924 by both governments, was considered by them to be the final settlement of all Indian land questions between the Federal Government and that of the Province of British Columbia. This was not acceptable to the Indians as they had claimed over the years that their aboriginal rights had not been extinguished.

Wherever high structural steel is being erected, Mohawks from the Caughnawaga Reserve near Montreal are found among the workers. Here, the last steel beam in the 56-storey tower of the Toronto-Dominion Centre has been bolted into place, and workers celebrate.

## Indian Education

As the frontier extended and larger numbers of people were established in stable communities, increasing emphasis was placed on education for both Indians and non-Indians. Indian education had been carried on for the most part by the various religious denominations prior to Confederation The Federal Government continued this policy, subsidizing mission schools already in operation with grants corresponding to the attendance and type of school. During the 1870's a system of government grants to Indian day schools was inaugurated on a per capita basis, but difficulty was experienced in securing sufficient pupils as there was no way of enforcing attendance.

Four Indian residential schools had been established in Ontario before 1867, and industrial schools were established in the western provinces as a means of overcoming indifference and other problems encountered by the day schools. The residential schools received per capita grants from the government and were operated under religious auspices.

Pupils at the residential schools divided their time between the classroom and the performance of menial tasks together with some agricultural instruction which would be helpful to them when they returned to the reserves. A policy was inaugurated of apprenticing graduate pupils to settlers for further training in agriculture and the trades. Thousands of Indian children, particularly those living a nomadic life in the isolated areas where livelihood depended on hunting, trapping and fishing, were not in school at all.

Relief and medical services were provided to the Indians in the Yukon (created in 1898), through the North West Mounted Police and educational assistance was granted in a few settlements. Beginning in 1900 land for residential sites and woodlots was reserved for the Yukon Indians.

The Federal Government took steps to assist in maintaining the fur industry in the Northwest Territories by the establishment of Native Game Preserves, in which trapping is confined to Indians, Eskimos, metis living the life of natives, and white trappers already living in the area. Five of these reserves were established between 1923 and 1938.

By the turn of the century many influences were changing and moulding the Canadian community as a whole and affecting the Indian population. The industrial revolution of Canada was gaining impetus and there was a shift of population from the isolated farms and villages to rapidly-growing industrial centres. The self-sufficient farmer who produced his own food and many necessities of life was being replaced by specialized farms. Technological developments in all areas of industry called for governmental regulation of economic life. There were many social problems as well, which called for increasing government intervention in the fields of education, public health, social security and social welfare services. The *laissez-faire* or negative attitudes to the role of government which had prevailed at the time of Confederation gave way to the positive state. While Indians were affected by these changes, many were left behind. The fact that during the 1940's the Indian population, which had remained relatively static for many years, started to increase rapidly, intensified the need for a re-examination of governmental policies with regard to Indians.

## In Armed Forces

Indians from all parts of Canada were well represented in the Armed Forces in the World Wars of 1914 and 1939 and demonstrated their abilities and resourcefulness. There were important and far-reaching results. Young men, who had seen little beyond the limits of the reserves or the peripheral hunting grounds, lived in daily close contact with other young men from very different environments over a period of months and years, shared mutual interests and pursued a common goal. They became world travellers and encountered peoples and customs of which they had no previous knowledge. Many of those remaining in Canada left the reserves and joined in the main stream of the Canadian economy making an industrial contribution to the war effort. These peoples thereby acquired a broader concept of the world and their own relation to it. For their non-Indian comrades of the firing line or the factory, the image of Indians changed from the legendary creations of romantic fiction and western movies to persons like themselves with qualities and abilities that commanded admiration and respect.

## Policy Reviewed

The depression of the 1930's and then World War II had postponed any critical examination of Indian policy. After the Second World War Canadian Indian administration came under searching public review. For the first time an exhaustive parliamentary inquiry into Indian affairs was undertaken. All interested organizations and groups, including Indians, made their views known. The parliamentary committee recommended a complete revision of Indian legislation aimed at giving Indians greater control in the conduct of their affairs and removing restrictive and protective provisions on a gradual basis.

The policy in the early years of Confederation had been designed to protect the Indians from unscrupulous persons, and to assist them by the provision of rations and agricultural needs until they became self-sustaining. The whole policy was oriented towards dependence upon a few primary industries with emphasis on agriculture. At this period the economy of Canada as a whole was based on the primary industries and the reserve system was designed to provide natural resources for the use of the Indians. In the intervening years Canada had been changing with accelerated speed into an industrial urban society, with little place for the subsistence farmer. The policy of paternalism, too, tended to foster dependency rather than to develop initiative and self-reliance. Other factors such as differences in language, continuance of traditional customs and isolation on reserves combined to leave the Indians far behind the main current of national development.

In recent years Canadian Indian policy, simply stated, is to assist the Indians to participate fully in the general social and economic life of the country both as individuals and communities. A great deal of social legislation has been inaugurated such as family allowances, old age assistance and pensions, blind persons' allowances, and other welfare measures and these have been extended to Indians. They are also being encouraged to take control of the administration of their own affairs at the local level along the lines of municipal government.

Under the Indian Act, Indian band councils have powers and duties similar to those of municipal councils. They make by-laws about health, traffic, disorderly conduct, game and fish management, public works and other matters pertaining to their reserves. Band councils may also be granted the power to raise funds through taxation or licensing for band purposes. All band councils were encouraged to take the lead in planning for band fund expenditures and many were given authority to control their own revenue funds. In Ontario, band councils administer their own public assistance program under provincial legislation in the same way as municipalities. In these and other ways the band councils have been demonstrating local initiative and self-government.

Increasing emphasis has been given to education. At the end of World War II there was an enormous backlog of educational underprivilege—children out of school, high drop-out rates, uncertified teachers, and inadequate and run-down buildings, and this problem was greatly exaggerated by the remarkable upsurge in population which had taken place. Today, virtually all school-age children are in school. New schools have been built, unqualified teachers have been replaced and the one-time apathy of parents to education is being overcome. More Indian children are staying longer in school and achieving higher levels of academic training than ever before. The drop-out rate remains a problem, because of a lack of motivation arising from language difficulties, home background, isolation and attitudes toward an increasingly acquisitive society.

Indians are encouraged to attend provincial schools with other children whenever this can be arranged, the Government paying tuition fees and contributions towards the cost of facilities as required.

An Indian student with ability can go through his entire schooling, including university if he wishes, with full assistance from the Federal Government if this is necessary.

**Indian Leaders Trained**—The Department of Indian Affairs and Northern Development recognizes that the quality of Indian leadership is a major factor in Indian advancement and that leadership is most effectively exerted through the band council and other local organizations. The Department has, therefore, made arrangements with universities and other educational institutions for the provision of leadership training courses designed to train Indian leaders in the knowledge and techniques that will best equip them to be of service to their own people.

Another program conducted by the Department is the Indian employment placement program which aims at assisting Indians to find jobs. The program includes development of work skills, vocational training and on-the-job training. Arrangements for job and social counselling services are made with local agencies. In many urban communities friendship centres have been established with government assistance to help Indians make the transition from a rural to an urban society, and to provide a friendly atmosphere when it is most needed.

The rapid expansion of industrialization has provided employment for an increasing number of Indians. However, a large number live in northern and outlying districts where wage employment is scarce and seasonal, and they must depend on game, fish and fur for much of their livelihood. Joint programs for the development of fur and other renewable resources have been undertaken by agreement with the provinces concerned. The Branch co-operates in programs for the conservation of fur-bearing animals and the management of game, and participates with other federal and provincial agencies in sponsoring fur exhibits for the promotion of wild fur sales at home and abroad.

**Health Services**—Indians share, with the Eskimos, in special medical services provided by the Department of National Health and Welfare through annual appropriations. Medical care and public health services are thus made available to all band members who cannot otherwise provide for themselves.

There is general agreement that the widest range of federal, provincial and municipal services currently provided to non-Indians should be extended to Indians. Federal services available to other citizens in the fields of health and welfare and elsewhere are available to Indians. Provincial services have already been extended to Indians and Indian communities in a number of fields, including welfare assistance, child welfare, rehabilitation, community development, road construction and natural

Indian artist.

Indian nurse

resources conservation. In the vital field of education, agreements have been made with provincial or municipal school authorities across the country under which Indian children attend school with other children.

In working toward the development of Indian communities the involvement of the Indians themselves is considered of primary importance. New consultative processes have been developed to provide for joint participation and discussion by means of Regional Indian Advisory Councils and a National Indian Advisory Board.

The cultural dimension must not be overlooked. Indians are striving for cultural identification, and are justly proud of their traditional handicrafts, dancing and other ancient skills. A special unit has been created to help preserve and encourage Indian expression and maintain pride of race and community spirit.

As Canada crosses the threshold of a new century of nationhood, the Indians, along with other Canadians, diversified as to race, language and culture, can look forward with justifiable hope to the attainment of common objectives and to the fulfilment of individual aspirations. (R. F. Battle)

While Toronto symbolizes British tradition, its growing ethnic population has made it a vital cosmopolitan centre. Successor to "muddy York", and second largest city in Canada, it is a major financial, commercial, manufacturing and cultural centre.

# The Two Founding Peoples

It has become common in the past decade to refer to the English and the French in Canada as "the two founding *races*". This designation is obviously misleading in that the French and the English both belong to the same Caucasian race. It is misleading also in that the first inhabitants of the geographical area now known as Canada were Indians. The area, prior to European discovery, was occupied by countless bands of Indians and Eskimos each regarding a certain portion of the country as their own. The term, "the two founding *peoples*", seems more appropriate and is slowly replacing the

74                                                                 CANADA, 1867-1967

former designation. These reservations made, the phrase, "the two founding peoples or races", constitutes suitable reference to the attempts by English and French-speaking inhabitants in the northern half of British North America to solve their differences. After more than two and a half centuries of quarrels and open conflicts, they chose to adopt a political constitution designed to safeguard the aspirations of both groups.

As Canadians are preparing to celebrate the one hundredth anniversary of this accommodation, it seems timely to review the history of these two peoples from their first landing on North American soil to the present day, and to analyze the historical developments which, having brought them together, led them to seek a compromise allowing each other a certain freedom to maintain their institutions, languages and cultures within a single state.

No attempt will be made to identify the great men—and there were many—who led the two language groups, or their roles in each of the main developments that eventually resulted in Confederation in 1867. More often than they perhaps realized, these men were the product of their times. It is difficult to say to what extent they led the events or were led by them, to what extent they produced new structures in Canadian society, or were the product of structures that preceded them, and to what extent they gave orientation to history or received their own personal orientation from that which history itself had already given to the two language groups into which they were born.

Historic port on the St. Lawrence, Quebec City long has been the bastion of French culture in Canada. It was founded by Champlain in 1608, and has a large import-export trade.

THE TWO FOUNDING PEOPLES 75

By the Treaty of Paris in 1763, France irrevocably ceded Canada to Great Britain. With the exception of Louisiana, all the former French possessions on continental North America west to the Mississippi became part of a single British Empire stretching without interruption from Hudson Strait to the Gulf of Mexico. In order to understand the Act of Confederation, which was passed slightly more than a hundred years later, and the socio-political realities of present day Canada, it would be necessary to review the history of French and English occupations of the entire geographical area north of the Rio Grande from the first landings to present day immigration. It would also be necessary to refer occasionally to the relations of these two great nations in Europe as the successes and defeats of the military and the diplomat in France and England frequently had their repercussions in North America.

On the eve of the Centennial of its Confederation, Canada appears to be facing a crisis in that considerable attention is being given to French-English relations and more particularly to the place of French-speaking Canadians within Confederation. The dramatic way in which this question is discussed tends to make one forget that at no other time since Cabot and Cartier respectively claimed part of Canada for the Kings of England and France, have French-English relations been more cordial and harmonious.

Indeed, history placed together on the North American continent two great peoples who, while alike in so many ways, or perhaps because they were so much alike, already had a long history of competition and conflict before crossing the Atlantic.

The years have mellowed both the people and the issues. The progressive adjustments that led to the current improved relations can be traced through three main periods which could be called, for illustrative purposes, the struggle for a continent (discovery to Treaty of Paris in 1763), a period of accommodation (1763 to Confederation in 1867), the building of the Canadian community (1867 to the present day). Each period has contributed to the emergence in each national group of a set of mental and emotional concepts which are still the main determinants of French-English relations and frequently exercise a strong influence in the government of the country.

## The Struggle for a Continent

The first French contacts with North America occurred well before Jacques Cartier planted his cross on the Gaspé Peninsula. French fishing vessels knew the shallow Newfoundland waters teeming with cod. Jacques Cartier, however, sailed past the northeastern tip of Newfoundland into the Gulf of St. Lawrence, claiming, on July 24, 1534, the new land for the King of France.

As significant as this act was, the French presence in North America remained focused for some years upon the traditional fishing grounds and the new waters visited by Cartier. Progressively, in the next fifty years, the fur trade led to the establishment of inland positions. In order to protect their monopoly, traders sought to interest colonists to settle near their posts. The first such settlement recorded under French rule took place in 1598 on Sable Island nearly a hundred miles east of Nova Scotia where the Marquis de la Roche established some 50 colonists.

Later, Champlain developed a stable form of colonization. His personal qualities as an explorer and colonizer, as well as the lessons learned in the 75 years since the planting of the cross in Gaspé, set patterns of French occupation which, in the next century, led to a great expansion of French interest in North America and resulted in the establishment of a French Empire up the St. Lawrence and the Great Lakes to the western prairies, and down the Mississippi River to the Gulf of Mexico.

Meanwhile, Britain was also laying foundations in America. In 1497, only five years after Columbus' discovery of America, John Cabot, sailing under an English charter, also reached the continent of North America. No permanent settlement resulted from this first contact. The first serious attempt at English colonization was made in 1578 with Gilbert and Raleigh. After a number of rather ill-fated trips to the eastern seaboard, Gilbert reached the harbour of St. John's, Newfoundland, and took permanent possession of that country in the name of the Queen of England. While this first attempt ended in disaster, his experience did assist other expeditions. Soon, thirteen colonies were established along the Atlantic coast while elsewhere in New-foundland, at Hudson Bay and on the Pacific coast, small pockets of English occupation increased that country's interest in America.

Having established their footholds in North America, France and England each tried to expand as fast as possible. Thus started what was to be close to 150 years of strife for the possession of the broad continent. Each power, though occupying only a few acres of an almost boundless domain, was jealous of a single foot of it held by the other. The first phase of this struggle ended in 1763 with the Treaty of Paris and the transfer of French interest in Canada to England.

## The Period of Accommodation

After the Fall of Quebec and Montreal and the signing of the Treaty of Paris, Britain had complete control of the entire eastern half of North America. On the surface all seemed well. Already, however, the newly-acquired colony was "pas comme les autres", "not like the others". After military defeat, the French Canadians immediately set out to retain as many of their institutions as possible. No less than eight of the 55 articles in the Capitulation of Montreal concerned the preservation of as much of the cultural heritage of the colonists as possible under the circumstances.

On the one hand, the French Canadians were anxious to negotiate for as complete a restoration of French institutions as possible while, on the other hand, Governor Carleton was personally convinced that the new colony would become loyal to the British Crown only if it won the confidence of its inhabitants. The Quebec Act in 1774 re-established the French civil law and confirmed the right to freedom of worship. This soft approach did retain French Canadian loyalties and, in 1775, they refused the invitation of the 13 colonies to join them in the War of Independence.

One of the unintended consequences of the American revolution was the introduction of a new dimension in French-English relations in the newly acquired colony. The migration of Loyalists changed the composition of the Canadian people from one that was predominantly French to one that became predominantly Anglo-Saxon. The sudden increase of population led to the creation of two new provinces, namely, New Brunswick and Upper Canada. More important still, these men and women whose strong convictions had led them to prefer British rule brought with them a set of emotional and mental concepts which have since characterized the English-speaking people of Canada as the colonists of Champlain and Talon had made their profound impression on the French a full century before.

Quite naturally, the Loyalists, upon settling in Canada, were not pleased with the compromise that had been reached with the French-Canadians through the Quebec Act. They did not like the French civil law and were anxious to have an elected assembly similar to that which they had been enjoying in the colonies. The Constitutional Act in 1791 marked a new step in English-French relations. Upper Canada was given the English system of law while the French civil law continued to prevail in Lower Canada. In giving the English provinces the rights to an elected assembly, the Act also gave the French the same privilege. Thus started the second step towards self government and provincial autonomy for the French-Canadians.

The ratio between French- and English-speaking Canadians changed at an even faster rate in the 50 years that followed as steps were taken to encourage immigration from the British Isles. Between 1815 and 1850, approximately 800,000 persons left Britain for British North America—almost twice the 1815 population of the Maritimes and Canadas combined.

As had happened in the 13 colonies some 50 years earlier, the inhabitants of the British colonies grew restless. They longed for more home rule. In both Upper and Lower Canada, there were short-lived attempts at armed rebellions. Lord Durham was sent to investigate. One of his recommendations was the reunion of the two Canadas. Even though there had been uprisings in both Canadas, Lord Durham felt that in the case of Lower Canada the predominance of French Canadians was a key factor and gave a different dimension to the problem. Union, he felt, would help to solve the difficulty by eventually reducing the French to a minority in the new government. He proposed, moreover, that the French should be made like English Canadians as rapidly as possible by discouraging the use of their language and changing their laws. In short, Lord Durham was recommending the full assimilation of the French.

His recommendations on this question were not fully accepted. On the contrary, even though some kind of assimilation was, in fact, an aim of the Union Act the reunion of the two Canadas produced a model of co-operation between the French and the English which has often been imitated. As soon as the first Cabinet was formed, Robert Baldwin and Louis H. Lafontaine, became convinced that the only way they could promote successfully their progressive views was by pooling the support which each was receiving from his own ethnic community. A generation before, such reunion would have seemed most indecent but, by the mid-nineteenth century, after more than 200 years of coexistence on North American soil, the Canadians of French expression and the Canadians of English expression, British subjects all, were at last prepared to accept each other as "here to stay" and were willing to devise principles of co-operation. Far from the assimilation recommended by Lord Durham, the two political and social reformers favored co-operative coexistence, a formula which later was to be adopted again by the partnership of Sir John A. Macdonald and Sir Georges E. Cartier. Stephen Leacock summarized the work of Baldwin and Lafontaine in these words:

"To find a real basis of political union between French and British Canada, to substitute for the strife of unreconciled races, the fellow-citizenship of two great people, and set up in the foremost of British colonies an example of self-government that should prove the lasting basis of empire—this was the completed work by which they have amply earned the rest of eventide after the day of toil".

Some 600 Quebec exchange students, after spending a month in English-speaking homes of Ontario promoting bilingualism and biculturalism, exchange experiences in Ottawa's railway station.

Canada's growing international commitments have spurred the teaching of foreign languages.

While the social and political life of the country was evolving more and more into what it is today, events to the south were again to have a strong impact on Canadian history. As the American Civil War was coming to an end, it became obvious that the British provinces to the North were weak compared with a united American state. A union of the five British provinces into a single state and its westward expansion became urgent considerations. The Quebec resolutions in 1864 became the basis for the federal union of the provinces outlined in the British North America Act of 1867.

The Fathers of Confederation accepted the principle that a number of safeguarding clauses should be put into the BNA Act to protect minority rights without sacrificing national unity. The Protestant and Catholic religions were given certain guarantees in respect to separate schools. French and English languages were both to be used in the Acts and official records of the Parliament of Canada, and the Legislature of Quebec. Either language was allowed in the Debates of those bodies or in pleading before the Courts of Quebec and of the Dominion. Finally, the Civil Code of Quebec was protected from alteration except by the provincial Legislature.

These precautions illustrate well the concern of the Fathers of Confederation. While they were reuniting several geographical areas, they sought also to unite two peoples within a broad framework of cultural tolerance and goodwill. "We are of different races", said Cartier, "not for the purpose of warring against each other, but in order to compete and emulate for the general welfare".

Needless to say, the high ideals of mutual respect and tolerance expressed by the Fathers of Confederation proved difficult to adapt to all the spheres of social, political and economic realities. The world has not yet discovered, it would seem, a perfect framework for completely harmonious relations between ethnic, racial, religious, or national groups.

## Building the Canadian Community

If travellers of modern spacecraft were to converse about the situation in the human relations field, as they circled planet Earth, they would most likely identify, within the boundaries of every state below, some minority groups who aspired to greater self-expression than is now possible given the socio-political realities under which they live. In some areas, they would witness open hostilities and ruthless repressions; in others, silent sufferings and patient endurance; elsewhere, improved conditions through positive dialogue, leading to more tolerable intergroup relations. Upon landing, the space travellers would no doubt reflect with humility that even their own country was not free from problems and that it was indeed most unfortunate that each nation, on its day of confession, would have to acknowledge some difficulties.

Canada also has had to face the challenge of a multi-ethnic state. Yet the very problems that Canada has had to overcome because of its bi-national nature have been productive of distinctive Canadian characteristics which are developing into strong ligaments, binding the Canadian community strongly together and enriching its national heritage.

After the Treaty of Paris of 1763, the Quebec Act of 1774, the Constitutional Act of

Music bridges the cultural gap between English and French peoples as youth such as Les Petits Chanteurs de Granby entertain in Montreal.

1791, the Union Act of 1840, the British North America Act of 1867, and the Statute of Westminster of 1931, Canada appears on the verge of new amendments to the politico-social framework within which its people relate to each other and seek to achieve their own goals on the North American continent.

It is in the nature of social changes that they are often quite imperceptible except when observed at distinct intervals. Many improvements have taken place in French-English relations in Canada since Confederation. Though much progress was made, the period of accommodation which followed the Peace of Paris had not yet completely succeeded in eliminating all misunderstandings and hostilities by the enactment of the British North America Act. Relations have continued to improve. The fact that each major improvement may have been preceded by a period of uneasiness may have led superficial observers to place too much emphasis on the conflicts and not enough on the progress. Many of the more acute crises were, in retrospect, nothing more than "growing pains" which eventually contributed to the strengthening of the nation.

The progress made since the end of World War II in French-English relations has produced a new set of conditions within which hopefully it will be possible to make lasting changes. The present situation is all the more promising in that the appointment of a Royal Commission on Bilingualism and Biculturalism has given Canadians the opportunity to explore the many formulas which can be applied when two peoples come together to form a single state.

The French-English question has now achieved new dimensions. Immigration has introduced in the Canadian context a large population which is neither French nor English. While immigration is usually a personal or a family matter, the presence of a certain number of former nationals of any particular state does create a new social phenomenon. Within the Canadian traditions of mutual respect and tolerance, these new ethnic groups have developed a rich cultural life of their own while integrating at the same time in either of the two main national streams.

There are many indications that the recent crisis is being resolved much as the others have been in former years. While the final report of the Royal Commission is not yet published, there are signs which justify much optimism. More and more Canadian communities now expect their schools to teach both official languages to their children. Consistent with this trend, the Federal Government, for several years, has been taking practical steps to encourage bilingualism in the public service, as part of its fundamental objective of promoting and strengthening national unity on the basis of equality of rights and opportunities for both English-speaking and French-speaking citizens. A special secretariat was established for the implementation of the government's policy in this field.

Elsewhere in the social and commercial sectors of Canadian society, similar trends towards bilingualism are being observed. This is not to say that all is well in the best of worlds. New problems will undoubtedly arise and new generations of Canadians may again have to face the challenge which their forefathers thought they had resolved. However, the patterns set for the solution of these questions should provide good guidelines for the continued coexistence within a single state of two great peoples sharing the righ endowment of a boundless domain with representatives of the main nations of the world and bearing witness, daily, by their spirit of compromise and brotherhood to the highest ideals of world fellowship. (JEAN H. LAGASSE)

# The Canadian Mosaic

At Confederation, the population was some 3,500,000. The first census (1871) following the union indicated that the cultural and ethnic pattern which characterizes Canada today had already been established to a striking degree.

The *French* were the largest single group with a total of 1,082,940. Settlement began in 1605 at Port Royal, Nova Scotia, and in 1608 with the founding of Quebec by Champlain. Now, more than 250 years later, settlement has spread into neighbouring provinces. Group settlements are to be found at such scattered locations as Windsor, Ontario, settled in the mid-1700's, and at St. Boniface, Manitoba, where settlers took up land in 1818.

At the time of Confederation, the *Irish* were the second largest group, with some 846,000 listed in the census of 1871. By 1753, about one third of the population of 13,000 in Newfoundland was of Irish descent. In Halifax, Nova Scotia, there were 1,000 Irish in a total population of some 3,000. A succession of crop failures brought many thousands to Upper Canada in the first two or three decades of the nineteenth century. By 1826 some 20,000 had settled in the Lake Erie district. Between 1823 and 1825, large groups of Irish settlers took up land in the Peterborough district of Ontario as well as in the counties of Lanark, Renfrew and Carleton. Others came from Northern Ireland to Prescott, Kingston, Cobourg, York (Toronto), and London. Still others were found in the Eastern Townships of Lower Canada and in the Rice Lake district of Northumberland county, Upper Canada.

The *English* numbered some 706,000 at the time of the 1871 census. While English groups had been involved in the settlement of Newfoundland, it was not until after the capture of Quebec in 1759 that English merchants, traders and settlers showed an interest in the new colony. The American Revolution, however, sent thousands of United Empire Loyalists of English stock to new homes in Nova Scotia, New Brunswick, the Eastern Townships of Quebec, and along the north shore of the St. Lawrence River and Lake Ontario. Depressed conditions in the British Isles after 1875 led to many assisted emigration schemes. Among the most important were the crofter settlements at Killarney, Manitoba, and Saltcoats, Saskatchewan, which were settled by English and Scottish pioneers.

The *Scots*, who numbered 549,946 in 1871, had been involved in many attempts at early settlement. Following the acquisition of the colonies by the British in 1759, the settlement of Scots in Canada was almost continuous. In 1763 the Fraser Highlanders were disbanded and given grants of land. Further settlements were established in Prince Edward Island, Nova Scotia and New Brunswick. In Upper Canada numerous Scottish settlements appeared between 1783 and 1850. Notable were the Glengarry settlement, and the establishment of significant numbers of Scottish families at Perth, Lanark County; in MacNab Township; at Guelph and Talbot; and in Middlesex, Huron and Bruce counties. In 1811, a group of Scottish pioneers arrived at York Factory en route to the Red River, Manitoba.

In addition to the French and British groups, those of *German* origin were the most numerous at Confederation. The census of 1871 sets the figure at 202,000. Some 2,000 arrived in Nova Scotia in 1750-52. In the following year, a group arrived in Lunenburg and established the community which was to become famous in the Atlantic fisheries. The American Revolution brought many Loyalist settlers of German origin into the

Maritime Provinces and Upper Canada, notably into the eastern counties along the St. Lawrence, and into what is now southwestern Ontario.

**Other Groups**—There were, of course, other ethnic groups represented in the population. For example, Dutch (29,000), Negroes, or as they were listed in the census, "Africans" (21,000), as well as Welsh, Swiss, Italians, Spanish and Portuguese. Ukrainians, who were to become the fourth largest group in Canada were not listed in the census of 1871. They came later. Mention was made, however, of a Russian Polish group.

The Chinese, too, were already here in considerable numbers, concentrated in British Columbia. However, though the province entered Confederation in 1871 it was too late for inclusion in census figures. Between 1870 and the turn of the century, the prairies burst into life with the arrival of thousands of settlers, mainly from Europe. Soon, prairie towns made their appearance with all of the characteristics of the frontier community. Such settlements as Esterhazy, Steinbach, Lettonia and Dnieper, reflected the origins of the settlers and their desire to retain some attachment to their former homelands.

The first distinguishable group to take advantage of the favourable conditions for settlement in the West were the *Icelanders*. In 1871, as a result of unfavourable economic prospects at home, four young Icelanders settled in Wisconsin. Hundreds of others followed, including a group of 365 that arrived in Nova Scotia, en route to Wisconsin, and were persuaded to settle in Eastern Canada instead. After a short period, the majority migrated in 1875 to the western shore of Lake Winnipeg in

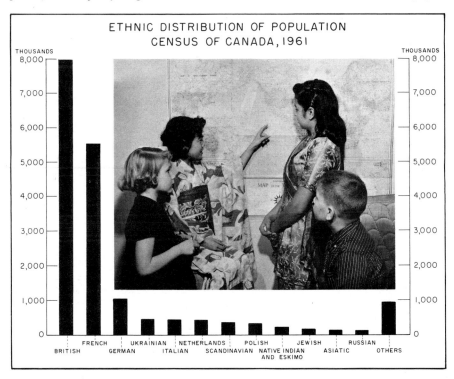

ETHNIC DISTRIBUTION OF POPULATION
CENSUS OF CANADA, 1961

Manitoba where they founded the town of Gimli, meaning "the great hall of Heaven". Gimli was the first of a series of settlements making up the colony of New Iceland which, in turn, became the source of new waves of migration to other areas.

In the true spirit of the pioneer, the Icelanders spread out across the west. Settlements were founded at Wynyard, Foam Lake, Quill Lake, Calder and Churchbridge in Saskatchewan and at Markerville in Alberta. There were Icelandic families living in Vancouver and Victoria even before the Canadian Pacific Railway was completed through the mountains in 1885. Most of the Icelanders settled on farms, although significant numbers engaged in commercial fishing on Lake Winnipeg where their descendants still fish today.

From 1880, Canada received thousands of destitute *Jews* who were fleeing from persecution and pogroms in many European countries. The majority came from small villages in Russia, Lithuania, Russian Poland, and parts of White Russia and the Ukraine; others from Roumania and Galicia. With the help of the Jewish Colonization Association, many settled on farms in the West. Although many Jews had had no agricultural experience, and gave up farming after a desperate struggle, others remained, their second and third generations today operating the original farms. A number of Jewish immigrants settled on farms in Eastern Canada as well. The majority, however, found themselves more at home in towns and cities, especially Montreal and Toronto, where they soon proved themselves in virtually every walk of life. The first Jewish Member of Parliament was Henry Nathan, who was elected in 1871 to represent Victoria after British Columbia entered Confederation.

In the 1870's settlers from Scandinavian countries first made their appearance in Canada in considerable numbers. The oldest colony of *Danes* was established at New Denmark, in the St. John River Valley, New Brunswick, in 1872. They consisted of seven families and ten single men. Other early settlers were established in Ontario near London and at Pass Lake in the Port Arthur district.

*Swedish* immigrants first came to the North-Western Territory in 1811 as part of the Red River colony. After 1870, considerable numbers reached the prairies, mainly through the United States. A large-scale movement of Norwegians began in the 1890's largely via the United States. Joined by significant numbers of Norwegian-Americans they spread across the Canadian prairies and into the fishing harbours of the West Coast, so reminiscent of their native fiords.

In 1874 a large group of Russian *Mennonites*, seeking religious freedom, arrived in southern Manitoba where eight townships were provided for settlement. The newcomers created a prosperous farming region with Russian-named Steinbach as its centre. Between 1874 and 1880, about 6,000 Mennonites settled in the new province. Many were German-speaking.

A common method of travel throughout the west at this time was by Red River cart, which was first mentioned in Alexander Henry's 1801 journal: ". . . men now go for buffalo meat with small, low carts, the wheels of which are one solid piece sawed from the ends of trees whose diameter is three feet. These carriages are more convenient and advantageous than horses and the country being so smooth and level, we can use them to go in all directions".

The journey to reach the western plains was long and arduous. Many of the early settlers reached the area via the United States. In 1868, the government undertook the construction of the Dawson road from Prince Arthur's Landing (now Port Arthur) to Fort Garry (now Winnipeg). By 1869 the trail was blazed for a distance of 48 miles and by 1870 had been pushed seven miles farther. The entire route covered a distance of 433 miles of which only 137 were on land. The remainder was navigable water. However, in the first year some 600 immigrants travelled over the trail on their way to the prairies.

The construction of the Canadian Pacific Railway led to the vast influx of immigrants which was to characterize the last two decades of the century. Begun in 1881, the railway was pushed rapidly westward, largely through the efforts of immigrants who toiled relentlessly to lay an average of two and one-half miles of track a day. In describing the Port Arthur-Winnipeg section, Sanford Fleming observed that it was not without sacrifice and tragedy that the work was finally completed. "A few rude graves on a hillside," he said, "mark the violent death of the poor workmen who suffered from the careless handling of that dangerous explosive, nitro-glycerine. . . . In the fifty miles we have passed over, upwards of thirty poor fellows have lost their lives by its use."

Many thousands of *Italians* came to Canada after 1880 to do railway construction work. At first, the majority were transitory immigrants from both Italy and the United States who worked on construction projects in the summer, returned to Montreal, or moved south across the border, in winter. A considerable number of *Finns* also came to Canada to work on the C.P.R. While many of them arrived in the West from Michigan and Minnesota in the United States, a few came directly from Finland.

The first *Chinese* reached Canada from California in 1858 when gold was discovered on the Fraser River. The Chinese, like other miners, enjoyed mixed success in their search for gold and by 1866 many had given up the effort and either left the country or turned to other pursuits. When construction of the C.P.R. through the mountains began, the contractors brought in some 17,000 Chinese coolies from the province of Kwangtung in south China. They came by sailing ship and steamer to the port of Esquimalt. There they were transferred by river boats to Yale, Boston Bar, China Bar and other places in the Fraser canyon where they were immediately given jobs.

The work was brutally hard, but the coolies saw in it the possibility of quick riches and a life of luxurious ease back in China. They left home with no intention of remaining away permanently. They saw no reason to alter their ways or to adjust to life in this strange land which they would be leaving in due course. Meanwhile the work went on and it is no exaggeration to say that the railway would not have been completed in 1885 had it not been for the tremendous effort of the Chinese workers.

The completion of the Canadian Pacific opened vast new regions of the West to settlement. In 1886, largely due to the personal initiative of Count Paul d'Esterhazy, an organized group of *Hungarian* immigrants arrived in the West from Pennsylvania. Many had worked on the land in the old country and they readily set about the task of establishing farms. The first colony of 35 families was located at Kaposovar in what became known as the Esterhazy district of southeast Saskatchewan. The colony was reinforced by a further group direct from Hungary in the spring of 1888.

About the same time, the first Hungarian settlement in Manitoba was established at Hun's Valley in the Riding Mountains. Coming mainly from the United States, the group was soon engaged in grain farming, cattle raising and market gardening.

By 1913, Hungarian settlements had spread throughout much of Saskatchewan with the largest concentration in the Qu'Appelle Valley, north and southeast of Regina and further north in the Prince Albert district.

In 1884, four *Czech* farmers and their families settled at the hamlet of Kolen in the Esterhazy district. Others followed in 1896-98. A further four families came to Edmonton in 1900 and were soon settled on the land.

The first *Polish* community in Canada was established at Wilno, Renfrew County, Ontario, in 1860. While immigration was sporadic, the flow was renewed in the 1890's when economic conditions in the homeland brought substantial numbers of farmers to the west, mainly from Galicia.

*Slovak* miners, first employed in the coalfields of Pennsylvania, came to Canada in 1885-86. A further group from Montana settled in the Lethbridge area of Alberta while others were attracted by the new coal mines of Crow's Nest Pass.

The great majority of immigrants arriving in Canada throughout these years were farmers in search of economic security. The *Mormons* of Utah and Idaho had a different motivation. For some time they had been engaged in a political controversy in the United States over the question of polygamy.

The dispute finally precipitated migration of the group in 1887 to the southwest corner of Alberta. In June of that year, forty-one colonists took up land on the site of the present town of Cardston. Within four years a community store, sawmill, flour mill and cheese factory were in operation. A well-organized religious and social life had also lent stability to the settlement. (Within three years of the migration, the Mormon Church discontinued polygamy as a form of marriage.) Aside from their industry and enterprise the Mormons made a distinctive contribution to agriculture in Western Canada through the development of irrigation projects. Such projects were soon followed by the sugar-beet industry which added much to the economy of the region.

An event that was the forerunner of a substantial movement of homesteaders into the Canadian West was the arrival in Canada, in 1891, of two adventurous peasants from the Western Ukraine. They were followed three years later by another nine families that settled near Star, Alberta. Thus began a migration of *Ukrainians* to Canada, as a result of over-population, economic and political instability in the homeland. By 1901 the number exceeded 5,000 and became a veritable flood in the next ten years when it reached 75,000. They quickly adapted themselves to life on the broad prairies from southeast Manitoba to the region of Edmonton, Alberta. The "Men in Sheepskin Coats," as they came to be known, were soon building communities characterized by sod-covered dwellings and imposing churches with domed spires.

A few *Dutch* settlers had entered Canada in the late 18th and early 19th centuries as part of the flow of United Empire Loyalists from the United States. It was not until the opening of the West, however, that a group movement of Dutch farmers began. The first 80 immigrants arrived in 1894. By 1901 the number had exceeded 33,000, many of whom took up land in the West. Dutch farmers are said to have introduced strip farming to southern Alberta. Soon, the appearance of such communities as Edam and Amsterdam were evidence of the origins of the pioneer settlers.

The year 1896 was a milestone in the history of Canadian settlement. In that year the Laurier Government came into power with Clifford Sifton as Minister of the Interior. He set about energetically to induce immigrants to come to Canada. Arrange-

Halifax, capital of Nova Scotia, is one of Canada's ice-free east coast ports, and has one of the finest natural harbours in the world. The city has had a rapid industrial expansion since World War II.

ments were made with shipping companies to obtain immigrants from such countries as Holland, the Scandinavian countries, Germany, Russia, Austria-Hungary, Finland, Luxembourg and Switzerland. The companies were paid a set sum for each farmer or domestic settled in Canada.

Within three years the plan began to achieve results. In 1899, after considerable negotiation, a group of over 7,000 *Doukhobors* reached that part of the North West Territories which later became the province of Saskatchewan. There they settled near Yorkton, Thunder Hill and Prince Albert on land set aside for them under the Homestead Act. By the end of the year, the majority of families were housed and the first crops harvested.

Differences of opinion between the leaders of the group and the government over such matters as land holdings and basic schooling became evident almost at once. These differences were to plague both government and Doukhobors alike over ensuing years. The first nude parade was staged in 1903 when a group of extremists gathered in their village to march to Yorkton. By 1908, some 6,000 of the more community-minded Doukhobors had moved to British Columbia.

From 1899 until 1903 the number of immigrants from continental Europe was approximately double the number from the British Isles. In 1903, Austria, Hungary, Germany and the Scandinavian countries each contributed more than 12,000 immigrants for settlement in Western Canada. Nor were the opportunities available here of interest only to immigrants from Europe.

By 1900, there were over 4,000 *Japanese* immigrants settled in British Columbia. The first arrivals, like the Chinese, came to Canada to meet an acute labour shortage and were largely drawn from farming, fishing and labouring classes. At first welcomed because of their contribution to the rapidly-expanding economy, the concentration of Japanese in British Columbia soon led to the so-called "Japanese problem," as their competition was felt in the local labour markets. Industrious and enterprising, the Japanese were soon well established in fishing and agriculture.

In addition to the impressive influx of European, British and Oriental immigrants in the early years of this century, there was a substantial flow of settlers from the United States. In fact, during the years 1899 to 1904 the number of immigrants from the United States (159,565) was considerably greater than that from the British Isles (137,036). The *American* immigrants were mainly experienced farmers with capital and equipment, who soon became producers of more wealth and the owners of substantial farms.

The advantages to be found in Canada were not recognized only by outsiders. Many native-born Canadians in the eastern provinces sought greater opportunities "out west". In fact, many western cities were populated in considerable measure by migrating Canadians from the east. In 1906, for example, the town of Gravelbourg, Saskatchewan, was settled by French-speaking farmers from Quebec who migrated west under the guidance of Father Louis Pierre Gravel, after whom the community was named. Some idea of the growth of western settlement is conveyed by the fact that two new provinces, Alberta and Saskatchewan, came into being in 1905. Towns and cities grew at a spectacular rate. In 1884, Winnipeg had a population of 16,694. By 1911 it had grown to a city of 136,035. In the same year, Vancouver reached 120,847 inhabitants.

Still the flood continued. The decade 1904 to 1914 witnessed the greatest movement of people to Canada from other countries that had ever taken place. It was during this period that the cultural diversity of the country became clearly defined. While much of the settlement took place in the western provinces, there was also a spectacular increase in immigrant population in the urban centres throughout Eastern Canada.

The appearance of *Austrians* coincided with the dissolution of the Austro-Hungarian Empire. Many individuals from the farming class migrated to Canada after 1900. By 1911 the census of that year recorded over 44,000 persons of Austrian origin. Many settled in the west, but sizable numbers preferred life in the large cities.

A new feature in the pattern of settlement was introduced in the period 1907-1909 when some 4,700 East Indians, almost all of whom were *Sikhs*, arrived in British Columbia from the Far East. The group consisted of unskilled labourers who found employment in the many industries then developing on the west coast, notably lumbering.

The first decade of the century was also marked by the appearance, in significant numbers, of immigrants from Southern European and Mediterranean countries, including Armenians, Bulgarians, Croatians, Greeks, Lebanese, Maltese, Roumanians, Serbians, Syrians and Turks. Attracted by the prospects offered by a New World, most of the new arrivals sought employment in the larger centres.

The bulk of the immigration flow, however, continued to come, throughout the years before the First World War, from Britain and the United States. Between 1910 and 1914 over 1,200,000 immigrants reached Canada from these two sources, compared with some 440,000 from all other countries.

Austria, China, Germany, Italy, Poland, Russia, the Scandinavian countries and the Ukraine all contributed substantially to the steady stream of immigrants arriving in Canadian ports. The record for admissions was set in 1913 with 400,870 immigrants —a figure never approached again in a single year.

The outbreak of war in 1914 brought about a dramatic reduction in the immigrant flow. By 1916 the number of admissions was scarcely more than 10 per cent of the 1913 figure, some three quarters of whom were from the United States. In fact, a certain reverse flow took place as many immigrants, especially from the British Isles, returned to Europe to take part in the fighting.

## Post-World War I Migration

The return of peace in 1918 brought about a renewal of the immigrant stream. However, it never again reached the proportions of the pre-war days. It is interesting to note that Chinese immigrants numbered 4,333 in 1919, the highest figure for any group except the British and Americans. In 1923 the Chinese Immigration Act was passed. It reduced the number of eligible categories to the point where only 15 merchants, clergymen and students were able to enter Canada during the next 18 years.

Immigration from Belgium and France had been slight before 1918. The picture changed for a time after the war, as many Canadian soldiers returned to Canada with Belgian and French brides. The unsettled conditions in Europe also led some Belgian and French farmers and artisans to emigrate to Canada.

One of the last group movements to Canada based upon religious grounds occurred after the war when some 50 families of Hutterites migrated to western Canada from South Dakota as a result of alleged persecutions suffered as conscientious objectors during the war. Virtually all of the Hutterites settled in Alberta and Manitoba where their communal way of life subsequently brought them into conflict with government and people alike.

Periods of conflict and tension have always been reflected in the migrations and movements of peoples. This statement holds true for the period following World War I. Between 1920 and 1929, many thousands of people came to Canada from countries recently purged by war, or torn by internal conflict or economic instability. During those years over 30,000 Finns came to this country, the majority settling in the cities of Ontario, British Columbia and Quebec or they found employment in the mining or lumbering industries.

Many Jewish people, notably from Russia and Poland, also sought relief from wars and persecutions through migration to North America. The majority were city dwellers who found their way into various occupations notably as workers in the garment, textile and fur industries. In time, substantial numbers established businesses of their own and were active in many fields of public interest. There was also a substantial movement of Ukrainian and Polish immigrants many of whom remained in the larger urban centres and found employment in trades and industry.

The boom of the 1920's also brought considerable numbers of Italian labourers who found ready employment in construction and heavy industry. It has been said, without too much exaggeration, that there was scarcely a major construction project, a mile of sewer or roadway, undertaken during this period that was not built or laid largely by Italian workers. Many German artisans also migrated to Canada at this time where their industrial and technical experience found ready use. Other groups participating prominently in the immigration flow at this time were the Hungarians, Slovaks, Yugoslavs and, for the first time in significant numbers, the Lithuanians, nearly 2,000 of whom entered the country in 1929-30. During these same years, some 20,000 immigrants arrived from Denmark, Norway and Sweden with the proportions about equally divided among the three countries.

When the world was caught in the throes of economic depression in 1930, the number of immigrants admitted to Canada dropped in spectacular fashion. By 1935 the figure reached a low of 11,277 from all countries, due to the effects of an Order in Council passed in August 1930 which restricted immigrants entering the country to wives and children of heads of families already established in Canada and agriculturalists with sufficient money to commence farming at once.

At the same time, events were transpiring in Europe that were to lead to the Second World War. Adolf Hitler was talking of a "master race" and was striking dread into the hearts of millions. After 1935 there was a steady flow of Jewish refugees from Nazi Germany and adjoining areas to other countries, including Canada. Many were educators, scientists, engineers, industrialists and other leaders whose assets were appropriated by the state or who feared for the lives of their families or themselves. In 1939 alone, some 1,700 Jewish immigrants arrived in Canada, a large proportion of whom were refugees. They settled almost exclusively in the cities and other urban centres where a significant number became attached to universities and other seats of learning.

The outbreak of war in 1939 again brought the flow of immigrants to Canada virtually to a halt. It was not to be renewed in any significant numbers until the war came to an end in 1945. Then it was characterized by the arrival of thousands of persons who had been uprooted by the war, scattered throughout Europe and who were unable or unwilling to return to their former homelands.

## Post-World War II Migration

The first group movement of the postwar period took place during the winter of 1946-47 when some 4,600 Polish war veterans arrived to take up a new life in Canada. The majority had served with the Polish Division of the First Canadian Army.

Soon the stream of so-called "displaced persons" became a veritable flood as thousands sought to leave an unsettled and uncertain Europe. Prominent among these groups were refugees from Estonia, Latvia and Lithuania. An important

Between 1946 and 1965 more than 2,500,000 immigrants were landed in Canada. The banner year was 1957 when 282,164 newcomers arrived.

Thousands of postwar immigrants came by air. This family of ten children, arriving in Montreal, is typical of the many thousands of such newcomers who enrich Canada with their skills and cultural attainments.

THE CANADIAN MOSAIC                                                                 91 characteristic of this refugee movement was the high percentage of people who had occupied positions of prominence in their respective fields of endeavour. There were business leaders and industrialists, educators and scientists, professional men and women, and outstanding representatives of all arts and skills.

Meanwhile, the main stream of immigration again built up from Britain and continental Europe generally. Additional numbers of Chinese also began to arrive as the admission of immediate relatives of Chinese in Canada was approved. New sources of immigration also became evident as significant numbers of Spanish and Portuguese, mainly from the Azores, made an appearance in Canadian cities and towns throughout the country. There was also a considerable upsurge in the number of Dutch, Italian and Greek arrivals. While the Dutch maintained their traditional inclination towards land settlement, the other immigrant groups in the postwar flow demonstrated a marked tendency to congregate in the cities, where they found ready employment in construction, commerce and industry.

After 1951, the number of Germans entering Canada increased substantially. Between that date and 1960, some 250,000 German immigrants arrived—a figure exceeded only by Italians and British. Many newcomers were highly-trained workers attracted to Canada by the opportunities available in the expanding industries.

The Hungarian revolt in 1956-57 led to a dramatic rise in the number of Hungarian immigrants entering Canada. In one year following the revolt, some 35,000 refugees were admitted, including the entire faculty and student body of the Department of Forestry, Sopron University. The faculty promptly became affiliated with the University of British Columbia where the students continued their studies.

There has been a marked increase over the past ten years in the number of immigrants entering Canada from the British West Indies. While the majority consist of young Negro women who enter domestic service in Canada, or are registered students at Canadian universities, an increasing number, since 1960, have obtained positions in other fields of employment.

A notable characteristic of the immigration flow in recent years has been the decline in the number of persons from countries now lying within the Soviet sphere of influence. For many years, such countries as the Ukraine and Poland provided substantial numbers of people who contributed much to the development of this country. Today, the number of new arrivals from eastern European countries grows constantly smaller as the national groups now residing in Western Europe continue to shrink in size. A striking example is provided in the Ukrainian figures. In 1912 there were 19,222 Ukrainians admitted to Canada; 50 years later the number had dwindled to 128.

Since 1945 well over 2,500,000 immigrants have taken up a new life in Canada. They represent some 60 ethnic groups, and are found throughout all of the provinces and territories, although the main concentrations are in the large cities, notably Toronto and Montreal.

Today, some 27 per cent of the population of Canada is of neither English nor French origin. More than 180 foreign-language publications are produced regularly in Canada in 27 different languages.

Immigrants have established thousands of new businesses including that of glass making. For the first time in half a century decorative handmade glassware is being produced. The new industry started in 1963 when glass workers from the island of Murano, the centre of the Venetian glass industry, were encouraged to settle in Canada.

## Ethnic Contributions

The contributions of Indian peoples, both to life and culture, have continued throughout the century since Confederation and have been acknowledged by successive generations of people who have benefited from the insight, skills, artistry and experience of Indians, the influence of which far exceed the effect of their numbers.

At the time of Confederation, the French group had 250 years of Canadian history behind them. They developed skills in sculpture, architecture, crafts, music and other fields that were unique in North America. How well they succeeded in building a French-Canadian society is evident in the prominent place that was occupied by French-Canadian leaders in the deliberations that took place prior to the union of the provinces in 1867.

Those of British stock had, like the French, long been associated with the early history of North America. They had brought to the New World their strong attachment to democratic parliamentary institutions, their knowledge and skills in trade, commerce and industry; their ability to organize and develop vast engineering and other construction projects. By 1867 there were few fields of endeavour that did not include representatives from among the English, Irish and Scottish groups.

While little mention was heard of the Eskimo people prior to Confederation, this group was ultimately to have an impact upon the development of Canada. As interest in northern regions grew, it was the Eskimo who taught the techniques of survival in Arctic regions, which made life possible for others. In more recent years, the Eskimo people have enriched the cultural life of Canada through the production of sculptures and prints.

**Industry**—In the early years after Confederation, there were two major fields in which newly arrived immigrants made outstanding contributions to the expansion and development of Canada. These were the fields of settlement and heavy construction. While a few skilled workers or tradesmen were found among the European immigrants arriving in Canada at that time, the overwhelming majority were from the farming or labouring classes in their former homelands. They accepted with determination, and even enthusiasm, the privations, isolation, and sacrifices necessary to acquire a piece of land that, for the first time in their lives, they could really call their own. In the West the most spectacular developments took place. Here, settlers from virtually all countries of Europe turned their energies to the establishment of new villages and towns, the building of roads, the development of great stretches of fertile prairie lands.

Many found work in heavy construction, notably railway building. Within a few short years, Canada was linked by steel from coast to coast. This achievement was due in no small measure to the combined efforts of thousands of immigrant workers.

As Canada advanced into the twentieth century there was a growing need for workers to build and man factories. Roads, canals, harbours, dams, and industrial plants, have also been constructed and expanded. A great reservoir of manpower was available to meet these needs. Italians, Germans, Poles, Czechs and Slovaks, Finns, Dutch, Ukrainians, Hungarians, etc., have contributed to the huge projects that have characterized the emergence of Canada as a great industrial and trading nation.

Since 1946 over 2,500,000 immigrants from all parts of the world have entered Canada. Postwar immigrants now represent over 12 per cent of the Canadian labour force. Many possess skills that are urgently needed in a growing industrial economy. This fact is reflected in the concentration of immigrant males in manufacturing, which is about 40 per cent higher than that of other Canadian workers. The figure for female immigrant workers is even more impressive at 64 per cent above that for other workers in Canada. A high percentage of immigrant workers are craftsmen with skills and experience oriented towards the mechanical trades and manufacturing industries. In these fields their concentration is more than 50 per cent higher than the national average. Even more impressive is their concentration in the construction trades, which is about 66 per cent higher than for other Canadian workers. An illustration is the highly specialized skills of tile setting and mosaic work that Italian craftsmen have brought with them from Italy.

Following World War II there was a sharp increase in the number of professionals emigrating to Canada. Many were, in fact, refugees who preferred to start again in a new country rather than to live in, or return to, a homeland under totalitarian rule. Large numbers of such professionally-trained immigrants have found their places in research institutions, universities, hospitals, industry, government and other public and private institutions throughout the country. One has but to mention Dr. Hans Selye, now head of the Institute of Experimental Medicine and Surgery at the University of Montreal, who has won world-wide recognition for his studies in the field of human stress, or Dr. Gerhard Herzberg, director of the Pure Physics Division of the National Research Council, who is an international authority on spectroscopy, dealing with the structure of atoms and molecules, in order to emphasize the point. There are, of course, many other professionals, representing an imposing array of scientific and other fields, who now bring honour and prestige to Canada.

Children of Ukrainian origin rehearse their roles as flowers in an Ottawa play.

The enterprise and resourcefulness of many immigrants is seen in the number who have established their own businesses in Canada. From 1950 to 1964 more than 14,000 newcomers had acquired their own businesses for which they had paid some $170,000,000. These business ventures had, in turn, provided employment for almost 59,000 workers. Nor do these figures include large business enterprises such as Alaska Pine and Cellulose of Vancouver, which was established by Leon Koerner, a refugee from Czechoslovakia. The firm is now the largest producer of wood pulp for use in the manufacture of textiles in the province and employs nearly 5,000 workers. The Bata Shoe Company of Batawa, Ontario, and Bick's of Canada Ltd. (pickle-makers), are other examples of large-scale enterprises that owe their existence to far-sighted business men who came to Canada in search of opportunity and who have contributed substantially to Canadian industrial development.

Mention should also be made of the important drainage projects that have resulted in bringing into production thousands of acres of waste land. The development of Holland Marsh near Toronto by Dutch and other immigrants has received wide publicity. Less well known, perhaps, are the drainage schemes at Grand Bend, Ontario, organized by a Belgian immigrant, Gerhard Vanden Bussche, and at Pitt Polder in the lower Fraser Valley of British Columbia, where an industrious group of Dutch engineers and farmers has reclaimed about 8,000 acres of marshland.

**Culture**—Newcomers to Canada have played an equally important role in the cultural life of the country. They have contributed generously of their talents, experience and creative ideas to virtually all branches of the arts. The internationally famous photographer, Yousuf Karsh, for example, has, for many years, made a distinctive contribution towards sustaining the name of Canada in the top rank of his chosen field of portraiture. His outstanding portrait of the late Sir Winston Churchill is known and admired throughout the world. Born in Armenia, Mr. Karsh came to Canada with his family as a young man.

All three of the leading professional ballet companies today owe their origin and subsequent development to the inspiration and direction provided by dancers from other lands. The Royal Winnipeg Ballet was founded by Gweneth Lloyd, while Celia Franca was the first artistic director of the National Ballet Company. Both of these artists came from Britain. Ludmilla Chiarieff, the founder of the youngest ballet company, les Grands ballets canadiens, is of Russian origin.

Celia Franca was also the founder of the first ballet school in Canada which teaches academic subjects as well as dancing. The National Ballet School, located in Toronto, was the first of its kind in North America to be directly affiliated with a professional company, and young Canadian dancers are now beginning to graduate from its classes.

The appearance in Canada of experienced directors and singers has contributed much to the growth and development of opera in Canada. The Canadian Opera Company owes its origin to the efforts of Dr. Arnold Walter who came to Canada from Austria in 1937. The present general director is the energetic, German-born Herman Geiger-Torel who has made opera a lively and respected part of the Canadian artistic scene. The same story could be told in other branches of music. Orchestra conductors, individual musicians and composers, who have emigrated to Canada in significant numbers, have exerted an important influence upon the expanding musical scene, especially as teachers of young Canadians interested in furthering their training and knowledge.

The Canadian theatre, including radio and television drama, has been greatly enriched by the contribution of experienced actors, directors and set designers. This is especially true of English- and French-speaking newcomers. The National Theatre School, which has produced a number of outstanding young actors, has had André Muller and his predecessor Jean-Pierre Ronford, both from France, as artistic director of the French section and Welsh-born Powys Thomas as director of the corresponding English section.

Canadian stage design has benefited greatly from the fresh originality brought to it by such newcomers as Rudi Dorn from Austria and Russian-born Nicolai Soloviov. The list could be augmented by a dozen or more other names. The same situation is true in other branches of the arts. Painters, sculptors, architects have established themselves in Canada in impressive numbers and their work is giving great stimulus to the artistic life of the country. An example is to be found in the establishment in Montreal in 1965 of the Loyola Bonsecours Art Centre, under the auspices of Loyola College, with Michael Millman, a recent arrival in Canada, as resident painter. Although born in Britain, Millman has painted as an accredited United Nations war artist in Korea, in a monastery in Avignon, France, served as professor of art and design at

**Ethnic distribution of population,
Census of Canada, 1961**

| | | | |
|---|---|---|---|
| British | 7,996,669 | Polish | 323,517 |
| French | 5,540,346 | Native Indian and Eskimo | 220,121 |
| German | 1,049,599 | Jewish | 173,344 |
| Ukrainian | 473,337 | Asiatic | 121,753 |
| Italian | 450,351 | Russian | 119,168 |
| Netherlands | 429,679 | Others | 953,829 |
| Scandinavian | 386,534 | | |

THE CANADIAN MOSAIC                                                97 the University of Tokyo and acted as a consultant in art to the government of Malta.

Handicrafts are flourishing in Canada today, largely as a result of the influx of expert craftsmen from abroad in recent years. When the first National Fine Arts Crafts Exhibition was held at the National Gallery in Ottawa in 1957, many of the entries bore the names of immigrants—now an integral part of the Canadian cultural community. Many of the craftsmen have become teachers of young Canadians, thus adding greatly to the enrichment of Canadian life.

**Sports**—Brief mention should also be made of the contributions of ethnic groups to sports in Canada. The Italians, Poles, and Ukrainians are among those who have done much to popularize soccer with Canadians—especially in the major urban centres where professional leagues now draw substantial crowds of supporters. Local amateur teams are numerous, with many enjoying the benefit of expert coaching from seasoned European players now living in Canada.

The influence of immigrants upon other sports is also noticeable. The Toronto Water Polo Club is composed mainly of Hungarian athletes now living here. The Club, which is the strongest in Canada, has won several international competitions. In table tennis, Max Marinko, former central European champion, has won virtually every title in Canada and the United States including the U.S. Senior Championships. Newcomers from Germany, Finland, Czechoslovakia and Sweden have done much to elevate the standard of gymnastics. Willie Weiler, a gymnast from Germany, won three gold medals for Canada at the 1963 Pan-American Games. Austrian and Hungarian fencers have been largely responsible for the growing interest of Canadians in this sport. Volleyball has gained a new impetus as a result of the efforts of Ukrainians and Baltic groups to popularize the sport.

**Foods**—A very agreeable field in which the ethnic communities are exerting a strong influence is the preparation of foods. In recent years Canadians have developed a cosmopolitan taste for foods as a result of the establishment of many fine Italian, Hungarian, Greek, German, Chinese, Austrian, Japanese and other ethnic restaurants serving an array of exotic dishes to please the most discriminating taste. Coffee houses and delicatessen shops have introduced the people to a great variety of raw and prepared foods and ingredients which lend zest to meals and add to the general enjoyment of living.

**Traditions and Customs**—The ethnic communities have also brought to Canada many religious and cultural traditions and customs that are now finding a place in our pluralistic society. Examples are found in the Ukrainian Christmas, which follows the Julian calendar, and is observed on the twelfth day after December 25th; St. Nicholas Day, that falls on December 6th and which is dear to the hearts of the Dutch and other groups, and the Chinese New Year which usually occurs in February and which is a major festival for the Chinese community.

Throughout its history as a nation, Canada has appealed to the imagination of peoples from all parts of the world as a land of opportunity and security. Of the millions of immigrants who have reached its shores, many sought economic security. Others were in search of religious freedom. Still others looked mainly for adventure in the New World. Whatever the reason of their coming, they have contributed their talents, skill, knowledge and experience to make Canada today a nation that is an example to, and the envy of, much of the world. (W. H. AGNEW)

## Immigration to Canada by Calendar Year 1867-1965

| Year | Arrivals | Year | Arrivals | Year | Arrivals |
|------|---------:|------|---------:|------|---------:|
|      | No. |      | No. |      | No. |
| 1867 | 14,666 | 1900 | 41,681 | 1933 | 14,382 |
| 1868 | 12,765 | 1901 | 55,747 | 1934 | 12,476 |
| 1869 | 18,630 | 1902 | 89,102 | 1035 | 11,277 |
| 1870 | 24,706 | 1903 | 138,660 | 1936 | 11,643 |
| 1871 | 27,773 | 1904 | 131,252 | 1937 | 15,101 |
| 1872 | 36,578 | 1905 | 141,465 | 1938 | 17,244 |
| 1873 | 50,050 | 1906 | 211,653 | 1939 | 16,994 |
| 1874 | 39,373 | 1907 | 272,409 | 1940 | 11,324 |
| 1875 | 27,382 | 1908 | 143,326 | 1941 | 9,329 |
| 1876 | 25,633 | 1909 | 173,694 | 1942 | 7,576 |
| 1877 | 27,082 | 1910 | 286,839 | 1943 | 8,504 |
| 1878 | 29,807 | 1911 | 331,288 | 1944 | 12,801 |
| 1879 | 40,492 | 1912 | 375,756 | 1945 | 22,722 |
| 1880 | 38,505 | 1913 | 400,870 | 1946 | 71,719 |
| 1881 | 47,991 | 1914 | 150,484 | 1947 | 64,127 |
| 1882 | 112,458 | 1915 | 36,665 | 1948 | 125,414 |
| 1883 | 133,624 | 1916 | 55,914 | 1949 | 95,217 |
| 1884 | 103,824 | 1917 | 72,910 | 1950 | 73,912 |
| 1885 | 79,169 | 1918 | 41,845 | 1951 | 194,391 |
| 1886 | 69,152 | 1919 | 107,698 | 1952 | 164,498 |
| 1887 | 84,526 | 1920 | 138,824 | 1953 | 168,868 |
| 1888 | 88,766 | 1921 | 91,728 | 1954 | 154,227 |
| 1889 | 91,600 | 1922 | 64,224 | 1955 | 109,946 |
| 1890 | 75,067 | 1923 | 133,729 | 1956 | 164,857 |
| 1891 | 82,165 | 1924 | 124,164 | 1957 | 282,164 |
| 1892 | 30,996 | 1925 | 84,907 | 1958 | 124,851 |
| 1893 | 29,633 | 1926 | 135,892 | 1959 | 106,928 |
| 1894 | 20,829 | 1927 | 158,886 | 1960 | 104,111 |
| 1895 | 18,790 | 1928 | 166,783 | 1961 | 71,689 |
| 1896 | 16,835 | 1929 | 164,993 | 1962 | 74,586 |
| 1897 | 21,716 | 1930 | 104,806 | 1963 | 93,151 |
| 1898 | 31,900 | 1931 | 27,530 | 1964 | 112,606 |
| 1899 | 44,543 | 1932 | 20,591 | 1965 | 146,758 |

## Immigrant Population, by Period of Immigration and by Province, Census 1961

| Province or Territory | Before 1930 | 1931–40 | 1941–45 | 1946–50 | 1951–55 | 1956–61 |
|------|---------:|---------:|---------:|---------:|---------:|---------:|
|      | No. | No. | No. | No. | No. | No. |
| Newfoundland | 1,356 | 339 | 338 | 1,317 | 1,230 | 2,310 |
| Prince Edward Island | 1,170 | 217 | 117 | 439 | 452 | 567 |
| Nova Scotia | 14,752 | 2,165 | 1,079 | 4,434 | 5,281 | 9,412 |
| New Brunswick | 10,496 | 1,451 | 886 | 3,184 | 2,887 | 5,601 |
| Quebec | 121,164 | 14,202 | 5,321 | 38,452 | 87,873 | 180,422 |
| Ontario | 462,705 | 41,959 | 15,190 | 169,044 | 323,528 | 448,597 |
| Manitoba | 101,758 | 4,259 | 1,483 | 15,925 | 21,134 | 32,616 |
| Saskatchewan | 116,192 | 3,170 | 1,034 | 8,124 | 9,497 | 14,459 |
| Alberta | 156,324 | 8,446 | 2,420 | 25,326 | 48,263 | 58,714 |
| British Columbia | 229,790 | 11,300 | 4,498 | 37,296 | 65,947 | 97,186 |
| Yukon and Northwest Territories | 1,292 | 195 | 79 | 443 | 1,098 | 833 |
| **Canada** | **1,216,999** | **87,703** | **32,445** | **303,984** | **567,190** | **854,600[1]** |

[1] Including 3,883 not specified.

THE CANADIAN MOSAIC

# Canadian Citizenship

Twenty years ago, Canada's search for a national identity found expression in a significant piece of legislation—the Canadian Citizenship Act. This Act, which came into effect on January 1, 1947, ended the confusion regarding the status of citizens of Canada.

Prior to the enactment of this legislation, there had been considerable uncertainty over the proper designation of "Canadians". From 1831, when legislation of the British Parliament gave the status of British subjects to the people of Canada, until 1947 when Canadians received the right to call themselves Canadians, several acts had confused, rather than clarified, the situation. The fact that Canada could legislate on naturalization matters within its borders but not beyond meant that aliens granted naturalization under Canadian law were not recognized as British subjects in foreign countries. Shortly after Confederation, Canada passed a naturalization Act.

As a result of Imperial Conferences immediately before and after the turn of the century, it was agreed that the Dominions were competent to grant British naturalization which would be recognized throughout the world. This led to the passage in Britain and in Canada of what are called Imperial Naturalization Acts, the other Dominions quickly following suit. The appropriate Canadian legislation is "*An Act respecting British Nationality, Naturalization and Aliens*".

The intensification of nationalism during, and after, World War I, and the confusion over national status resulted in the passage of an Act in 1921 which gave Canadians (either natural-born or naturalized) the right to call themselves "Canadian Nationals", thus distinguishing them from other British subjects. The passage of this Act meant that there were then on the statute books three Acts dealing with the status of Canadians—the Immigration Act, the Naturalization Act and the Canadian Nationals Act. Until 1947 these three Acts regulated the national status of residents of Canada and Canadians living abroad.

In 1947 the Canadian Citizenship Act defined Canadian citizens in two categories: the natural born and the non-natural born. A natural born Canadian is a person who was born in Canada or is the child born outside Canada to such person. The non-natural born Canadian is the person who was naturalized in Canada or granted Canadian Citizenship. Because there was a large number of British subjects residing in Canada, the definition was enlarged to confer Canadian citizenship automatically upon those British subjects who on January 1, 1947, had Canadian domicile; or who on that date had been residing in Canada for a period of 20 years; and women married to Canadian citizens who came to Canada before 1947. Subsequent amendments clarified legal "loopholes". Citizens also retain the status of British subjects. By a 1950 amendment, the term, "Commonwealth citizens", was introduced and was accorded the same meaning.

To process the unprecedented number of post-World War II applications for citizenship and to give greater uniformity to citizenship procedure, special arrangements were made. In 1955 Courts of Canadian Citizenship were opened in Toronto and Montreal; subsequently, in Hamilton, London, Vancouver, Edmonton, Winnipeg, Moncton, Ottawa, Calgary, Halifax, Regina and Sudbury, with offices in a number of other communities. In addition, in remote areas such persons as RCMP officers or

A Court of Canadian Citizenship (Ottawa). Here applicants swear allegiance and receive their certificates.

magistrates have been appointed "courts" for the purposes of the Canadian Citizenship Act; and overseas, certain Deputy Judge Advocates of Armed Forces act in similar capacity.

In general, an applicant for Canadian citizenship must be 21 years of age or more, have had his place of domicile in Canada for at least five years after legal admission to Canada (with the last year being one of continuous residence), and must also satisfy a Court of Canadian Citizenship, that he, or she, has complied with the requirements of the Canadian Citizenship Act, is of good character, has an adequate knowledge of the duties and responsibilities of Canadian citizenship, intends to comply with the Oath of Allegiance, and to remain permanently in Canada. Between 1947 and 1965 inclusive, Canadian Citizenship certificates were granted to 114,236 British subjects and to 737,789 aliens.

Every year Citizenship Day is observed on the Friday immediately preceding the legal observance of Victoria Day. It is not a statutory holiday; Citizenship Day was instituted in 1950 as a day on which private citizens, public bodies and voluntary organizations could stress by proper ceremonies the value, privileges and responsibilities of Canadian citizenship. As a former Minister of Citizenship and Immigration remarked: "Canadian citizenship has much to offer. . . . We are a nation which has an honourable record of resistance to aggression, which has used its vast resources to aid underdeveloped countries, which has menaced no other land but, instead, has been both good neighbour and friend to large and small countries. We recall how Canada opened its doors to succor refugees, and we know that we have room still in our hearts and our vast territories for many, many more people. We can be proud of a nation which is founded on a bulwark of freedom, which has an orderly and stable form of government, great economic opportunities for its people, and an even more enviable future . . . ."

"What actually constitutes good citizenship?" the Minister asked and continued: "It is the observance of the laws of the nation . . . an active partnership in community and national projects . . . courage of a high order . . . support of worthy causes . . . unselfishness in business and social relationships . . . little every day kindnesses, thoughtfulness in deed and word . . . avoidance of discrimination and prejudice".

Human rights and fundamental freedoms, regardless of race, national origin, colour, religion or sex, are enshrined in Canada's Bill of Rights which received Royal Assent in 1960. These include the following:

(a) the right of the individual to life, liberty, security of the person and enjoyment of property, and the right not to be deprived thereof except by due process of law;

(b) the right of the individual to equality before the law and the protection of the law;

(c) freedom of religion;

(d) freedom of speech;

(e) freedom of assembly and association; and

(f) freedom of the press.

Reflective of the nationalism of Canadians, and closely identified with the union which is now being hailed across the broad reaches of the Dominion, are two popular songs: *The Maple Leaf Forever*, and *O, Canada*. Coincidence links them with previous celebrations.

*The Maple Leaf Forever* appeared in 1867, the inspiration of Alexander Muir, a Scottish-born immigrant. While walking, a maple leaf fell onto his sleeve and stuck fast. It provided the inspiration for his poem—which his wife suggested should be put to music. Unable to find a suitable tune, Muir composed the accompaniment. The song found ready acceptance with the public—and remains a link with Confederation year.

The words of *O, Canada* were composed by the Hon. Sir Adolphe Routhier, the music by Calixa Lavallée. They were written in 1880 to mark the official visit to Quebec of the Governor General, the Marquis of Lorne, and H.R.H. Princess Louise. Some twenty versions of this song have since been published. The most popular English translation, made by the Hon. R. Stanley Weir for the tercentenary of Quebec (1908), was published in official form for the Diamond Jubilee of Canadian Confederation in 1927. As Canadians celebrate the centennial of Confederation, *O, Canada* is both officially and popularly regarded as a national anthem.[*]     (HELEN CHAMPION)

---

[*]On January 31, 1966, the Prime Minister placed on the order paper in the House of Commons a Government notice of motion: that the government be authorized to take such steps as may be necessary to provide that *O, Canada* shall be the National Anthem of Canada while *God Save the Queen* shall be the Royal Anthem in Canada.

# The Canadian

# Economy

# Agriculture

At the time of Confederation the farmers of Canada were still relatively independent and were concerned mainly with production for family needs. Today they function as part of a highly integrated economic and social structure in which 33 persons are supplied with foodstuffs and fibre by the production of one farm worker.

The developments leading to this change, together with the status of Canadian agriculture in 1967, are the subject of this chapter.

At the time of Confederation more Canadians were concerned with farming than with any other occupation. The Census of 1871 classified the population as 80 per cent rural and 20 per cent urban. In Ontario, farmers made up 49 per cent of the gainfully-employed workers; in Quebec, the percentage was 47. In both provinces and in Nova Scotia and New Brunswick the numbers engaged in agriculture greatly exceeded those of any other occupational grouping.

There were 367,862 farms in 1871 with 36,046,401 acres, of which 17,335,818 were improved land. Field crops valued at $111,116,606 were produced. Wheat, oats, barley, corn, potatoes, hay and clover were the principal crops. Horses numbered 836,743, milk cows 1,251,209, other cattle 1,373,081, sheep 3,155,509 and swine 1,366,083.

Flour and grist mills to the number of 951 in Ontario and 810 in Quebec were operating in 1871. The decline of self-sufficiency was earlier indicated by 44 tanneries in Nova Scotia in 1861 and in the same year by the production of leather, saddlery, and boots and shoes valued at $750,015 in New Brunswick; also by 20 boot and shoe factories and 122 woollen mills in the province of Canada in 1867. In the British Columbia interior in 1870 some 11 small flour mills were in operation.

The beginnings of a dairy processing industry date from 1864 when cheese factories in Ontario and Quebec—the first a co-operative in Ontario—were established. By 1866 there were 60 factories in what is now Ontario and 12 in Quebec. In 1867 there was one in New Brunswick. Butter, too, came under factory production about the same time when the farm-produced product could not compete in the British market with oleomargarine. There were 22 creameries in Canada in 1871.

Chief items of export in 1871 were: wheat 1,748,977 bushels; wheat flour 306,339 barrels; oats 542,386 bushels; hay 23,487 tons; bacon, ham, shoulders and sides 103,444 cwt.; butter 15,439,266 pounds; cheese 8,271,439 pounds.

The decade of the 1870's witnessed the commencement of an export trade in cattle to Britain via the St. Lawrence in the summer and through the port of Halifax in winter. In the same period apples from the Annapolis Valley were exported to Britain and potatoes from all three Maritime Provinces found their way to the American market.

## Land and Development

The total area of occupied agricultural land in Canada in 1961 was 172,551,051 acres, just under eight per cent of the total land area of 2,278,552,320 acres. The area in farms was made up of 103,403,426 acres of improved land and 69,147,625 acres of unimproved land. The improved land included 62,435,534 acres under crops, 10,247,896 acres in pasture, 28,243,386 acres in summer fallow and 2,476,610 acres in other uses.

The new headquarters building of the Canada Department of Agriculture, Ottawa, commemorates Sir John Carling, Minister of Agriculture, 1885-92, who was responsible for the founding of the Dominion Experimental Farms system. Nearby is Carling Avenue also named in the late Minister's honour.

The area in farms in 1961 was just under five times the acreage reported in 1871. Canada's largest area in farms, 174,046,654 acres, was reported in the Census of 1951.

In addition to the present area in farms, some 40,000,000 acres of virgin land could be used for arable crops if the need arises; also, 55,000,000 to 60,000,000 acres suitable for unimproved pasture could be added to the present arable land and potential reserves.

The area in farms, in relation to the total land area, varies greatly by provinces. The range is from 68.7 per cent in Prince Edward Island to two per cent in British Columbia. Saskatchewan with 45.7 per cent in farms is in second place.

**Eastern Canada and British Columbia**—Agriculture in the Maritime Provinces and central Canada was well advanced at the time of Confederation. There were 8,859,000 acres in farms in Nova Scotia and New Brunswick in 1871 and 11,766,000 in 1891,* with Prince Edward Island included. In the three provinces combined, the acreage was 9,645,000 in 1931.

In Quebec the area in farms in 1871 was 11,026,000 acres. It increased to 14,444,000 in 1901 and to 18,063,000 acres in 1941. The acreage in Ontario in 1871 was 16,163,000. It rose to 21,350,000 in 1901 and to a maximum of 22,841,000 acres in 1931.

On entering Confederation in 1871 British Columbia retained control of its land resources. In 1881, the area in farms was 441,000 acres. This increased to 3,542,000 acres in 1931 and to 4,702,000 in 1951.

---

*Census data relating to numbers of farms in 1891, 1901 and 1911, as used herein, have been adjusted to eliminate plots of less than one acre in order to make such data comparable with those of later censuses.

**The Prairie Provinces**—The addition of 136,500,000 acres to the area in farms since 1867 is one of the achievements of Canadian development. Most of the increase occurred between 1870 and 1931, as a result of the opening of the prairie region. In a very real sense this was a result of Confederation and was made possible by the transfer of the lands held by the Hudson's Bay Company under Royal Charter—roughly all of the land comprising the agricultural area of the present Prairie Provinces—to the Dominion of Canada, June 8, 1870.

This development included the formation of the province of Manitoba and its inclusion in the Dominion in 1870; the addition of British Columbia in 1871; the construction of the Canadian Pacific Railway in the 1880's and other railways later. But its fulfillment required the settlement of the area to establish its agricultural potential.

In 1872 legislation was enacted by Parliament providing for "free" homesteads—a quarter section of land, 160 acres—on payment of a $10 entry fee and completion of certain residence and cultivation requirements. Provision was later made for the acquisition of additional land, e.g., a "purchased homestead" of 640 acres, a "pre-emption" of a quarter section adjoining the homestead (1874) and the granting of "scrip" to war veterans.

There were restrictions on settlement. An area of 7,031,257 acres in the "fertile belt" was set aside for the Hudson's Bay Company as partial payment for the surrender of its Charter lands. The railroads would receive as subsidies 31,784,610 acres of the most conveniently-located lands and some 9,353,250 acres would be acquired for school purposes.

In the period of Dominion Lands Administration, 1870-1930, some 59,777,460 acres of land were disposed of as homesteads. Pre-emptions, scrip and purchased homesteads amounted to 16,116,563 acres; 48,169,117 acres went to settlers through sales of railroad company, Hudson's Bay Company and school lands; a total of 124,063,140 acres.

Net entries for homesteads, 200,428, and sales of land by railway companies and the Hudson's Bay Company, 14,615,948 acres, were both heaviest in the decade 1902 to 1911. Settlement of such an area could not have been achieved at the rate desired by natural increase of the population at the time of Confederation. It required the addition of millions of immigrants and emphasis on settlement needs. Immigrant arrivals in the period 1902-1911 totalled 1,919,688 persons.

The settlement of the Prairie Provinces was not accomplished without heavy cost. Records indicate that 98,997,800 acres of land were represented in original homestead entries up to 1927; yet the total land actually disposed of in this manner by the Dominion to 1930 was 59,777,460 acres. The difference represents cancellations involving loss of financial investment and human effort.

In the process of large-scale settlement and the rush to obtain land it was perhaps inevitable that some areas would be opened for homesteading that were unsuited to farming, for there was little information on soil and climatic conditions to serve as a basis for decisions. It was necessary later to return some of this land to range use.

The settlement of the Prairie Provinces, including related immigration policies, was a function of the Government of Canada until 1930. In that year the land remaining for disposition was turned over to the three provinces concerned. Since then each province has formulated its own settlement program. Land is now inspected for agricultural suitability. Although settlement is limited, Crown lands are disposed of in Manitoba by sale, in Saskatchewan by lease, and in Alberta by lease or sale. Units of 320 acres are now generally permitted. Rental rates in Saskatchewan are based on soil productivity.

In the period under review the expansion of settlement in the Prairie Provinces was from 2,698,000 acres in farms in 1881, to 109,738,000 in 1931. In 1961 the area stood at 129,814,122. The increase between 1931 and 1961 indicates the development under provincial lands administration.

**Land Tenure: Quebec**—The seigniorial system of land tenure was introduced into New France, now Quebec, by the French in the 17th century. It provided for grants of land to seigneurs with the requirement that sub-grants be made to others for settlement purposes. The system was, in effect, a form of permanent rental with certain rights and obligations. Numbers of seigneurs sold their properties after 1760 but the system remained in diminished numbers and with modifications until 1935.

With the advent of British authority in Acadia after 1713 and in New France after 1763 ownership, or something approaching it, came into effect and became the dominant and desired form of tenure. In 1871 there were 326,160 farms operated by owners, 39,583 by tenants and 2,119 by managers or employers. Since then the percentage of tenancy has varied from about six to thirteen per cent. The high was experienced in 1941, the low in 1961.

The most significant change in tenure status has occurred in the part owner-part tenant classification. There an increase of from 4.4 per cent in 1901 to 20.8 in 1961 took place. In the latter year 42.0 per cent of the total area in farms was operated on that basis. The percentage varied greatly between provinces, being 52.2 per cent in Saskatchewan, 12.5 in Newfoundland and only 9.4 per cent in Quebec.

The shift to a part owner-part tenant basis would seem to reflect economic pressure calling for large-scale, low-cost operations. The variation between provinces and areas suggests that certain types of farms have difficulty in adapting to the equipment and techniques necessary to such operations. Farms operated by managers or employees have never represented a significant proportion of the total farms in Canada. There were 2,396 such farms in 1961.

## Sizes of Farms

The average area per farm in 1871 was 97.9 acres, which included 47.1 acres of improved land. In 1931 the area had increased to 223.9 acres per farm with 117.6 acres improved. In 1961 the areas were 358.8 and 215.0 respectively. Today's farm is more than three and a half times the area of the Confederation farm and larger still in terms of improved land.

Sizes vary greatly between provinces. In Newfoundland in 1961 almost 90 per cent of the farms had an area of less than 70 acres per farm. In the other three Atlantic Provinces and in Ontario and Quebec there were more farms in the 70 to 129 acre range than in any other. In all three Prairie Provinces more farms were in the 240 to 399 acre grouping than in any other. In British Columbia two thirds were of less than 70 acres.

Perhaps the most meaningful classification system is one based on value of products sold. In the Census of 1961, all farms that produced commodities to the value of

The Prairie Provinces, the great grain-producing area of Canada, harvested an estimated 820,000,000 bushels of wheat in 1966. Modern combines enable farmers to harvest a maximum of acres with a minimum of labour.

The community of Riceton in the Great Regina Plains is an oasis of habitation among thousands of acres of cultivated fields. In 1966 Saskatchewan produced an estimated 540,000,000 bushels of wheat.

Grain fields etch a pattern of prosperity around the community of Gray, Saskatchewan.

$1,200 or more in the preceding 12 months were classified as commercial farms. The number of such farms was 353,293, just under three quarters of the 480,903 farms enumerated. Of these, 140,260 each had an output valued at $5,000 or more.

Over a third of all farms in Ontario, Saskatchewan and Alberta were in this $5,000 or more category. Manitoba and British Columbia were next in descending order with 28 and 26 per cent respectively. Quebec and the four Atlantic Provinces each had less than 20 per cent of their farms producing a return of $5,000 or more.

CANADA, 1867-1967

At opposite extremes in this classification were 9,507 farms, half of them in Ontario, each of which had an output valued at $25,000 or more and at the other end of the scale 127,610 small-scale, part-time and residential farms each of which contributed less than $1,200 worth of products.

## Capital Structure and Credit Facilities

The census taken in 1901 indicated that the capital value of all Canadian farms at that time was $1,787,102,630. In 1961 the value reported was $13,171,221,700. The capital value per farm in 1901 was $3,497; that for 1961 was $27,388. In 1961 there were 185,519 farms—more than a third of all farms—with a capital value in excess of $24,950 per farm. The average capital value of 353,293 commercial farms, i.e., farms that sold products to the value of $1,200 or more that year, was $32,907.

Operating costs, too, have risen appreciably. In 1931 expenditures for rent, taxes, labour, feed and seed averaged $314 per farm; in 1961 they were $1,624. Total operating and depreciation charges in 1961 were estimated at $1,979,757,000, about $4,100 per farm.

Prior to Confederation the capital requirements of agriculture were met largely by farmers themselves, but with some assistance from others in the community, including merchants. Loan companies entered the field shortly before Confederation, followed by trust and insurance companies. They operated on an extensive scale, particularly in Western Canada, until the 1930's. At that time drought, depression, moratoria and debt adjustment legislation caused the virtual withdrawal of these companies from the field of farm credit. Mortgages and agreements for sale amounting to $159,222,961 were held by these bodies in 1936.

In an effort to increase loanable funds and to reduce interest rates that many thought excessive, particularly in Western Canada, most provincial governments established a farm credit agency during the period 1912 to 1922. These, too, experienced the effects of drought and depression. Some ceased lending operations in the 1920's; others withdrew when the Federal Government entered the field. Loans to the amount of $92,620,233 were made during their period of operations.

In 1929 the Federal Government established the Canadian Farm Loan Board which, in due course, functioned in all provinces. First mortgage loans were made at five per cent and the Board extended credit to the amount of $168,905,335 over a period of 30 years.

## Developments since World War II

The settlement of veterans of the Second World War and Korean Force has been a substantial undertaking. Some 29,951 veterans have been placed on farms and 53,153 on small holdings. Expenditures to the end of 1963 totalled $546,582,978. Reflecting the changing conditions in farming, the maximum loan has been raised to $40,000 to encourage the development of economic family farm units.

The need for intermediate term credit to finance new farm buildings, electrification, fencing, drainage, new equipment and livestock brought the Farm Improvement Loans Act in 1945. It authorized the Federal Government to guarantee banks against loss on loans made to farmers for such purposes and under certain limitations. In recent years loans in excess of $100,000,000 annually at five per cent interest have been made under this legislation.

In the 1950's provincial governments re-entered the farm credit field or revised existing legislation. The establishment of sons of farmers on land, expansion of existing farms to economic units, land clearing and the development of livestock herds are among the purposes served.

In 1959 new federal legislation established a Farm Credit Corporation to succeed the Canadian Farm Loan Board. The Corporation may lend up to 75 per cent of the appraised value of a farm, including buildings, or $40,000, whichever is lesser. Under a second provision, when the borrower agrees to accept supervision of his operations for a time, the loan may be 75 per cent of the appraised value of land, buildings, equipment and livestock or $55,000, whichever is lesser. Loans disbursed annually increased from $35,840,882 in 1959-60 to $139,750,639 in 1964-65.

Credit requirements of short duration, mainly to finance current operations, have traditionally been provided by chartered banks, local merchants, farm machinery, feed and fertilizer companies, credit unions and oil companies.

Estimates put the amount of farm credit outstanding in 1961 at $1,802,500,000. This represented an indebtedness of 13.7 per cent on the $13,171,221,700 capital value of farms reported by the 1961 Census. Long-term indebtedness made up 45.7 per cent of the total, intermediate-term 14.4 per cent, and short-term, 39.9 per cent.

## Land and Water Conservation

The Prairie Provinces between 1891 and the late 1930's experienced several periods of sub-normal precipitation. Notable among these were the years 1917-20 and 1929-38. Drought, grasshoppers and soil-drifting during these periods had a severe effect on prairie agriculture, the results of which were felt in the whole Canadian economy.

**Prairie Farm Rehabilitation**—Among the steps taken to deal with the situation was the enactment by Parliament of the Prairie Farm Rehabilitation Act in 1935. The Act originally provided for assistance in the conservation and reclamation of land and water resources in Manitoba, Saskatchewan and Alberta. Operations were later extended to British Columbia.

PFRA has completed 76,732 dugouts, 9,416 dams and 4,732 irrigation projects. It has developed and operates 75 community pastures and administers 20 major irrigation reclamation and water storage projects. One of its undertakings, the South Saskatchewan River project, sponsored jointly by the federal and Saskatchewan governments, will irrigate 500,000 acres and provide a power potential of 475,000 kwh. Much of this program is conducted with the co-operation of provincial departments of agriculture. This applies particularly to community pastures in Saskatchewan, irrigation development and flood control in Alberta, river and flood control in Manitoba, and irrigation in British Columbia.

In addition to PFRA, other services of the federal and provincial governments and universities have conducted research and experimental effort on land use and water conservation. Industry, too, has helped by providing more suitable farm equipment.

As a result of all this effort a good deal has been learned about dry-land farming. Many now believe that with the application of recommended practices, farmers will be able to maintain production at levels above those of earlier years, even under drought conditions.

**Marshland Rehabilitation**—The reclamation program was extended to the tidal marshlands of the Maritime Provinces in 1948. Dyked lands, mainly in the area of the Bay of Fundy—some of them tracing their development to the 17th century French regime—were in need of restoration. Other lands needed dyking. The program is a joint federal-provincial undertaking. Some 81,000 acres in 123 areas have been protected by 250 miles of dykes and 437 aboiteaux or tidal dams.

**Irrigation**—Irrigation in Alberta traces its origin to the 1890's when some private projects were launched. Corporate irrigation began in 1901. The Federal Government encouraged irrigation but did not become involved financially until the passage of the Prairie Farm Rehabilitation Act in 1935. At that time the irrigated area in Alberta was in excess of 400,000 acres. The province allocates water to irrigation projects and administers construction work on several projects. Much of the work is carried out in co-operation with PFRA. In 1960 there were 14 Irrigation Districts with 545,348 acres actually irrigated. Gross cash returns from the irrigable area were estimated at $30,000,000.

In the same year British Columbia reported 44 major projects with 218,000 acres of irrigated land and an additional potential of 400,000 acres. Three quarters of the irrigated area was made up of individual projects, the other quarter being served by the larger projects. In Saskatchewan 46 water users districts had been organized up to 1961, comprising 203,749 acres. Some 54 irrigation projects had been initiated on which topographical surveys had been conducted on 440,289 acres.

**Other Aspects of Conservation**—In addition to PFRA and the programs already mentioned, land and water conservation has been encouraged in all provinces. Land drainage, reclamation, soil improvement and other projects have received provincial financial support. Extensive soil and economic classification of land has contributed to these programs and to better land use.

Multiple purpose projects combining land and water conservation with power development, flood control, reforestation and recreation have received considerable attention. An extensive program is in effect in Ontario, several projects of which have qualified for federal assistance under the Canada Water Conservation Assistance Act.

## Marketing of Products

As population increased in the decades following Confederation and as transportation, communications and refrigeration became available, agriculture broadened its mixed farming base and pushed out with some vigour into areas where climatic and soil conditions favoured specialized types of farming. Emphasis for a time was on wheat and cattle on the western plains but in due course existing areas of specialization were expanded and many new areas developed. As this occurred, private enterprise and co-operative endeavour concentrated on the provision of marketing services—assembly and shipping facilities; warehousing, processing and manufacturing plants; stockyards, grain and livestock exchanges; terminal and harbour facilities. These were provided at hundreds of centres throughout Canada, including ports on the Great Lakes, Hudson Bay, St. Lawrence Seaway and on the Atlantic and Pacific coasts.

Indicative of this development is the existence of 5,226 licensed country grain elevators with a capacity of 367,000,000 bushels and 101 terminal, mill and eastern elevators with a combined capacity of 277,000,000 bushels. For the marketing of livestock there are 10 public stockyards and 67 sales agencies and dealers operating under federal supervision; also an estimated 200 auction centres; 317 meat processing plants under federal inspection and about 1,200 other processing plants.

There are hundreds of fruit and vegetable packing plants, dairy processing plants and facilities for marketing wool, tobacco, oil seeds and other products. For the handling of perishable foods there were 3,114 commercial warehouses with 148,000,000 cubic feet of refrigerated storage in 1963.

**Co-operative Marketing**—At the time of Confederation co-operative cheese factories were being organized in Ontario, Quebec, New Brunswick and Nova Scotia. Co-operative butter factories came soon thereafter.

In 1899 there were 26 local co-operative elevators west of Winnipeg. They were followed on the prairies by several line-elevator type grain handling co-operatives and, there and elsewhere, by associations for the marketing of livestock, poultry, fruits and vegetables and other products. Co-operative purchasing of farm supplies was also undertaken.

The 1920's brought the wheat pool movement with producers' associations in the Prairie Provinces and Ontario; also a central selling agency and extensive local and terminal elevator facilities.

In 1963 sales of farm products and supplies by 1,583 co-operatives totalled $1,589,200,000. Saskatchewan with $454,300,000 was the largest contributor; Quebec and Alberta were next in order. By commodities, associations marketing grain, with a volume of $525,100,000, were the largest handlers. Dairy and livestock co-operatives were next in line.

The number of co-operative associations reporting to the government reached a peak in 1950, with 2,495. In 1962 the number was 1,877. The reduction is attributable in some measure to consolidations. The volume of business was up from $1,015,264,000 in 1950 to $1,372,605,000 in 1962.

**Control of Marketing**—A third stage in the development of agricultural marketing traces back to World War I. At that time, for three years, the marketing of wheat was controlled by boards established by the Federal Government. Efforts by farmers and provincial legislatures to restore such control when prices declined drastically in 1920-21, were unsuccessful.

Between 1927 and 1936 several Acts of the British Columbia legislature and of the Parliament of Canada led to the establishment of marketing boards which functioned for some time, but were found to be *ultra vires*. In 1936, a British Columbia marketing Act was declared *intra vires*. It then became the model for marketing board legislation that evolved in all ten provinces.

Subsequently, legislation permitting the Federal Government to extend to provincially-authorized producer marketing boards power to engage in interprovincial and export trade was enacted by Parliament.

In 1963, eighty such boards, functioning in nine provinces, reported sales for 218,637 producers totalling $460,138,000. Quebec with 49 boards had the largest but Ontario led in volume of sales with $362,964,000.

**Milk Control Legislation**—The control of fluid milk marketing was first undertaken in Manitoba during the depression period of the 1930's. By 1940, most provinces had such legislation. The control bodies established are financed from public funds, licence fees or assessments on the fluid milk industry. They set minimum prices that distributors may pay for milk sold for fluid consumption and most of them also set either minimum or fixed wholesale and retail prices for fluid milk.

**The Canadian Wheat Board**—The Canadian Wheat Board has functioned since 1935. It has authority over the marketing of wheat, oats and barley produced in Manitoba, Saskatchewan, Alberta and the Peace River area of British Columbia. It is concerned with interprovincial and export trade but uses its authority through regulation and agreement. It owns no grain handling facilities but negotiates for the use of such. In selling wheat it uses the services of shippers and exporters. It regulates the rate of grain delivery and flow through country and terminal elevators.

Western Canadian farmers receive the price for their grain that the Wheat Board receives, less its operating cost, which includes certain carrying charges. The general level of prices received by the Board is determined by competitive conditions in world markets.

# Exports of Products

The value of agricultural exports amounted to $1,702,017,000 in 1964, the highest on record. In the period 1960-64 they averaged $1,264,000,000, about 20 per cent of total exports, and were 25 per cent above the level of the 1950's. Compared with the late 1930's there has been an increase of 300 per cent. Prices meanwhile have risen about 130 per cent.

Grain and grain products made up two thirds of the value of agricultural exports. Animals and animal products were the next largest contributors, followed by oil seeds, dairy products and tobacco.

The destination of agricultural exports has changed appreciably since 1935-39. In that period, with the value averaging $307,000,000 annually, 62 per cent went to Britain, 21 per cent to the United States and 17 per cent to all other countries. In the years 1960-64, Britain took 24 per cent, United States 16 per cent, and other countries 60 per cent. In the last-named group, major purchasers in 1964 were the U.S.S.R., Japan, China (Communist) and the European Economic Community.

Total cash receipts from farming operations in 1964, excluding Newfoundland, were estimated at $3,455,582,000, the highest ever recorded. Crops contributed $1,569,825,000 and livestock $1,852,983,000 to that total. Grains as a group represented more than two thirds of the total for crops, with wheat alone at $940,748,000. Other important contributors were potatoes $55,114,000, fruits $71,131,000, vegetables $86,036,000 and tobacco $96,723,000.

Sales of cattle and calves totalled $645,487,000; hogs $325,526,000 and dairy products $530,983,000. Poultry and eggs added $305,721,000.

Prince Edward Island has long been famous for the quality of its seed potatoes. In 1966 the Island produced an estimated 8,850,000 cwt. of potatoes.

Saskatchewan, with its heavy production of wheat, led the provinces in the crops section with sales valued at $670,764,000 but Ontario with emphasis on livestock and dairy products had the largest combined sales amounting to $996,596,000. Quebec was fourth with total sales of $456,635,000, featuring dairy products.

Total net income of farm operators from farming operations in 1964, excluding Newfoundland, was $1,432,019,000, nearly 14 per cent below that of 1963 but 4 per cent above the average for the years 1959-63. A substantial decline in grain inventories contributed to the reduction compared with 1963. Saskatchewan with $378,031,000 led the provinces. Ontario was second with $345,280,000, and Alberta third with $286,804,000. Quebec produced $154,521,000. New Brunswick with $15,177,000 was highest in the Maritimes.

The average farm net income for all farm families in Canada was obtained in 1958 by means of a comprehensive survey. It revealed an average of $1,026 per farm in the Maritime Provinces, $1,803 in Quebec, $2,532 for Ontario, $2,816 for the Prairies and $2,017 in British Columbia. The national average was $2,344. The amounts have increased since 1958 but the relationship between provinces probably has not changed appreciably.

The survey indicated above also revealed that for all farm holdings in Canada one third of total farm family income in 1958 came from sources other than the farm. The average from this source was $1,262. Off-farm income in the Maritimes and British Columbia exceeded income from farming operations. Off-farm income came mainly from wages and salaries earned through non-farm work. Second in importance were government pensions and allowances. Off-farm wages and salaries decreased as farm sales increased, but the converse was true of investment income.

114

Developed by Atomic Energy of Canada Limited, this mobile irradiator inhibits sprouting in such vegetables as onions and potatoes, allowing vegetables to be stored at normal temperatures for long periods.

(Left) Potatoes treated by irradiation from gamma rays—and those without such treatment—provide a vivid contrast.

## Federal Government Agricultural Services

The British North America Act provides for concurrent federal and provincial jurisdiction in the field of agriculture but gives the Dominion overriding authority in case of conflict. The consequence of that duality is that we have a federal Department of Agriculture and ten provincial departments concerned with agriculture. Fitting services together to minimize duplication and overlapping has been a challenge; but it has been achieved with considerable success.

The present services, federal and provincial, stem from the development of agricultural societies, the first of which were formed at Quebec and Halifax in 1789. Agricultural fairs, efforts to improve farm husbandry, and grants in aid of such activity led to supervision and provincial boards, from which bureaus and Departments of Agriculture emerged in the several provinces prior to 1867.

The federal Department of Agriculture was established in 1867. Early activities of the Department were concerned with the control of contagious diseases of livestock, protection of field crops against disease and insects, the expansion of grading and inspection services and the establishment of the Dominion Experimental Farms system.

The Canada Department of Agriculture today has four main branches—Research, Health of Animals, Production and Marketing, and Economics. It also has the Information Division, the Agricultural Stabilization Board, the Agricultural Products Board, the Prairie Farm Rehabilitation Administration and Crop Insurance. The Farm Credit Corporation and the Board of Grain Commissioners also report to the Minister of Agriculture.

**Research Branch**—The Branch's program is tailored to contribute toward the solution of problems in the production, protection, harvesting, processing, and storing of the country's agricultural commodities. Thus, the program is problem-oriented with a balanced effort in terms of basic studies to understand problems, and short-time investigations where the results are of immediate practical value. The Branch carries out its program through a central group of institutes and services in Ottawa and a chain of research stations, experimental farms, and sub-stations located from coast to coast to support the various segments of the agricultural industry. Its efforts are co-ordinated with those of the universities, provincial Departments of Agriculture, and other agencies involved in research, education, and extension.

**Health of Animals Branch**—The Branch administers legislation providing for the control of contagious diseases of animals through preventive measures, inspection and quarantine. It also conducts eradication programs, notably of bovine tuberculosis, brucellosis and Johne's disease. It conducts a regular inspection service at packing plants engaged in interprovincial trade. The Branch also operates animal pathology laboratories across Canada for the study of animal diseases. It manufactures diagnostic reagents and biological products at its central laboratory.

**Production and Marketing Branch**—Important among the functions of this Branch is the inspection and grading of farm products, a service that traces its origin to the pre-Confederation period and is now conducted in co-operation with provincial Departments of Agriculture. Six Divisions administer legislation and policies relating to the production and marketing of farm products. Markets information, consumer interests and storage facilities are the responsibility of three Sections.

Registration of livestock pedigrees, performance testing and recording of cattle, hogs and poultry, supervision of race track betting and maintenance of quality standards for seeds, fertilizers and pesticides are other functions of this Branch.

**Economics Branch**—The Economics Branch is concerned with the collection, analysis and interpretation of information useful in the formulation and administration of departmental policies and programs. It also conducts studies looking to the improvement of production, marketing and living conditions on farms. International aspects of agriculture are a concern of the Branch. Close working arrangements are maintained with universities and provincial Departments of Agriculture through Ottawa and five regional offices.

**Services of Other Departments**—The Canada Department of Agriculture has been responsible for the development and administration of most federal policies and services relating to agriculture but other departments have also made important contributions. These include the extensive statistical services provided by the Dominion Bureau of Statistics on every phase of agriculture and the role played by the Department of Trade and Commerce in export marketing and agricultural representation abroad. The Departments of Labour, Forestry and Rural Development, Indian Affairs and Northern Development, and several others also serve agriculture in various ways.

## Agricultural Assistance Programs

**Prairie Farm Assistance Act**—In 1939 Parliament provided through the Prairie Farm Assistance Act for direct money payments to farmers in areas of low crop yields in the Prairie Provinces and in the Peace River area of British Columbia. Payments are made on an acreage and yield basis and are intended to assist in dealing with a relief program which the provinces and municipalities could not handle alone; and to enable farmers to put in a crop the following year.

Farmers themselves contribute to the fund from which payments are made, the amount being one per cent of the value of grain sales. Additional funds required are provided from the federal treasury. Payments to 1965 totalled $353,016,572, of which farmers contributed just under one half. Farmers are not required to pay the one per cent levy under P.F.A.A., nor are they eligible for payments, if they are insured under the Crop Insurance Act.

**Feed Grain Assistance**—In 1941 a program was inaugurated under which the Federal Government would contribute to the cost of moving feed grains from the Prairies to British Columbia and to Eastern Canada. Intended as a means of increasing the volume of livestock products for the wartime food program, it also provided an outlet for western feed grains and helped to eliminate complaints that export rail rates to Canadian ports were such as to give producers in other countries, who purchased Canadian grain, a competitive advantage over Canadian farmers in the production of livestock products.

The program has been continued since the war. In its present form it provides for most of the strictly transportation costs to central points in all zones leaving at the most a balance of $2.00 per ton to be paid by livestock producers. Expenditures under the program in 1964 totalled $14,975,000 in the five eastern provinces.

**Agricultural Stabilization**—The Agricultural Stabilization Act, 1958, replaced a 1944 statute under which price support programs were conducted in the adjustment period following World War II. The Board provided for by the Act is required to support, at not less than 80 per cent of the previous ten-year market or base price, the prices of nine commodities (cattle, hogs, sheep, butter, cheese and eggs; and wheat, oats and barley outside the prairie areas as defined in the Canadian Wheat Board Act). Other products may be supported at such percentage of the base price as may be approved by the Governor in Council. Honey, potatoes, soybeans, sunflower seeds, sugar beets, tobacco, turkeys, apples, peaches, apricots, raspberries, asparagus, tomatoes, milk for manufacturing and skim milk powder have been supported at one time or another. The Board may use an offer to purchase, a deficiency payment or such other payment as may be authorized, as the means of stabilizing a price.

The Board operates on a revolving fund of $250,000,000. The cost of the program to 1965 averaged $57,000,000 per year. An advisory committee named by the Minister of Agriculture assists the Board in its operations.

**Crop Insurance**—In 1959 Parliament enacted crop insurance legislation. The Act permits the Federal Government to assist provinces in providing insurance but the initiative rests with the provinces. Insurance schemes may be based on specific crops or areas within provinces. Federal assistance may run to 50 per cent of the administrative costs incurred by a province and 20 per cent of the amount of premiums paid in any one year. The Federal Government may also lend money to a province under certain limitations when indemnities exceed premiums. In 1964, programs were in effect in Manitoba, Saskatchewan and Prince Edward Island involving 8,600 farmers and providing $18,800,000 insurance coverage. In 1965 a scheme was introduced in Alberta.

**Rural Rehabilitation and Development**—The Agricultural and Rural Development Act, known as ARDA, was proclaimed June 22, 1961. It is intended to help rural people adjust to economic, social and technological changes. It provides for programs involving: (a) more effective land use, especially for marginal and sub-marginal farm lands; (b) the conservation and improvement of lands suitable for agriculture; (c) the development and preservation of rural water supplies; (d) the development of employment opportunities in rural areas; (e) the conduct of research necessary to these purposes. The ARDA program is intended to correlate and supplement existing federal and provincial programs; and to fill gaps. It is also intended to stimulate community interest in the development of economic and social programs to be implemented co-operatively by all levels of government and private organizations.

A 1964 Federal-Provincial Conference resulted in the acceptance of a general agreement covering ARDA operations until 1970, involving a federal contribution of $125,000,000. Up to 1965 a total of 729 projects involving a sharable cost of $60,979,517 had been agreed upon; the federal contribution amounting to $34,517,573.

## Provincial Government Services

All provinces have a Department of Agriculture, or one including agriculture. In New-foundland agriculture is represented by a Division in the Department of Mines, Agriculture and Resources; in Quebec by the Department of Agriculture and Coloni-zation; and in Manitoba by the Department of Agriculture and Conservation. In the larger provinces agricultural services are numerous and are grouped in Branches or Divisions. In smaller provinces service may be provided by a corps of specialists. All departments have an agricultural representative service with one or more officers in each county or district. Most have home economists and a 4-H club or junior farmer service. The majority provide specialist services for field crops, horticulture, livestock and poultry, dairying, agricultural engineering, economics, statistics and co-operative associations. Some departments provide farm credit and operate experi-mental or demonstration farms. Subsidies for land clearing and use of limestone and assistance in marketing, rural planning, fur farming, soil and water conservation are other services provided.

An unusual design in farm buildings was introduced to Canada in 1964. This grain-storage shed, designed by an Alberta farmer, is of plywood construction, is post-free, easy to erect, inexpensive and holds 60,000 bushels.

## Output and Efficiency

In the years 1960-64 inclusive, the physical volume of agricultural production in Canada averaged 66 per cent above the output of the period 1935-39. During the interval, the agricultural labour force declined from 1,186,000 persons in 1946 to 630,000 in 1964.

The increase in agricultural output is attributable to several factors. The area in farms was up 9,000,000 acres from 1931, but of more significance, improved land increased by almost 18,000,000 acres, thus indicating more intensive use of land. Inputs other than land were also important.

This greater intensity of land use reflects the trend toward specialization and commercial development. The individually owned and operated farm still predominates, but it is more specialized. The 1961 Census revealed a significant decrease in the proportion of farms found to be in the "mixed farming" classification as compared with 1951 results.

Commercialization is being achieved by substituting capital for labour and by increasing the size of business. In 1951 only a third of all Canadian farms had a capital investment in real estate, machinery and livestock of $10,000 or more, but in 1961 four fifths of all farms were in that category. In 1951, only 5 per cent had a capital investment of $25,000 or more, while almost 40 per cent were in that grouping in 1961. Even after allowing for increased prices and land values, the extent of this trend is significant and is an indication of rapid commercialized development. These larger farms produce the greater proportion of total output. In 1951, farms with sales of $5,000 or more constituted 14 per cent of all farms and produced 47 per cent of all sales; but in 1961 the corresponding proportions were 29 per cent and 71 per cent. In the latter year 10 per cent of all farms with an average of 810 acres per farm accounted for 45 per cent of all sales.

In the period 1960-63 agricultural productivity was 75 per cent higher than in the late 1930's. The average increase was 3 per cent annually. Total inputs were down slightly due to the reduced labour content but capital inputs in the form of machinery, feeds, livestock, fertilizers, pesticides and the like were up 134 per cent.

The use of these inputs together with the products of research—new plant varieties, improved breeding and feeding practices and new technology—have contributed substantially to over-all efficiency and output. They have pointed the way to higher yields of grains, fruits and vegetables; raised milk production per cow more than 60 per cent to an annual average of 6,000 pounds; and increased the average rate of lay for all poultry flocks from 140 eggs per layer to almost 200. They have enabled efficient operators to make a pound of gain in poultry meat production from 2.5 pounds of feed instead of 6 pounds as in 1941. They have made it possible for one farm worker in the 1960's to produce sufficient food and fibre for 33 people, compared with 11 in the 1935-39 period. These factors have made possible an average annual increase in Gross Domestic Product per man in agriculture of 4.3 per cent since 1935, compared with just over 2.2 per cent in the manufacturing industries.

Because of these advances, consumers can now purchase larger quantities of farm products with an hour's wage than formerly. Consumers also benefit because the rise in agricultural productivity has released resources, particularly labour, for the production of other goods and services.

Increases in agricultural efficiency have also created adjustment problems for many farmers. Those who have not been able to increase the scale of their operations, or adapt to changing conditions, have had to seek part-time or full-time employment off the farm. Problems of this nature will continue to confront farmers, and particularly the children of farmers, as agriculture becomes even more closely integrated with non-farm businesses and urban life.

Increased productivity has, however, benefited those who could make the necessary adjustments to keep abreast of developments. Between 1946 and 1961 real income per worker in agriculture increased by 2.5 per cent annually—slightly slower than those of employed factory workers whose earnings increased 2.7 per cent, but faster than the rate of increase for the non-farm labour force as a whole, which was 1.5 per cent annually.

One of the by-products of increased agricultural efficiency, particularly the contribution of mechanization, is a decline in the number of farms. Mechanical power and related equipment—represented in 1961 by 659,963 automobiles and motor trucks, 549,789 tractors, 155,611 grain combines and 89,522 hay balers on Canadian farms—has had that effect. It has enabled a farm family to handle a larger acreage of land. As a result farms have increased in size from an average of 237 acres in 1941 to 359 acres in 1961 and farm numbers have declined from 732,832 to 480,903.

Such results are not new. The introduction of the grain binder in the 1870's and other implements about that time contributed to the enlargement of farms and the development of Western Canada, but led also to consolidation and some abandonment in Eastern Canada. Farm numbers declined in Ontario and Quebec in the decade 1891-1901 and again after 1911. The decline in the Maritimes after 1891 was more or less continuous.

All areas have shared in the decline since 1941 but the greatest percentage loss in numbers has been experienced by the Maritime Provinces as a group. In the same period, 1941-1961, the value of machinery and equipment on farms increased from $596,046,300 to $2,568,631,500.

**Changing Status**—There are fewer people living on farms and fewer farms and farm workers in Canada today than a quarter century ago. By these standards the relative status of agriculture has declined. In other respects, however, agriculture is a much bigger industry; bigger in terms of capital employed, volume of business and acreage of improved land, as already indicated. It also has extensive relationships with other groups and industries.

Agriculture at the farm level provides employment for 630,000 persons—more than three times as many workers as all other primary industries combined—and many more people are involved with the processing and marketing of farm products. Roughly 314,000 persons are employed in the manufacturing industries using products of farm origin, both domestic and imported, and they make up about a quarter of all employees in such industries. Manufacturing plants using products of farm origin constitute 27 per cent of all plants and include firms making bakery products, preserving fruits and vegetables, making dairy products, milling flour, preparing feed and operating meat packing and tobacco processing establishments. The retailing of food through independent and chain stores provides employment for 77,000 persons.

On the other hand, the farming community is a large consumer of industrial products and services, the provision of which means employment for a steadily increasing number of urban workers. For instance, farm operating costs in 1964 represented an outlay of $1,956,882,000, two thirds of which involved expenditures for equipment, commodities and services acquired from the industrial sector of the Canadian economy. Included were costs of operating tractors, trucks and automobiles amounting to $416,796,000; payments for machinery parts and repairs, $104,406,000; purchases of fertilizer and lime, $126,356,000; building materials and repairs, $118,591,000; and miscellaneous commodities and services costing $165,635,000. Electric power which is in use on 85 per cent of Canadian farms cost $24,455,000.

Sales of new farm implements and equipment have exceeded $200,000,000 annually at wholesale prices. The industry has 69 factories and employs 11,000 people. There are 45 fertilizer plants in Canada producing mixed fertilizers and scores of other establishments located in towns and cities throughout the country catering to the production and family needs of farmers.

The movement of farm products to markets, domestic and export, provides revenue to transportation agencies amounting to upwards of $370,000,000 annually. Some 200,000 workers are employed by such bodies. Farm products represented 35 per cent of the tonnage carried on the St. Lawrence Seaway in 1962; wheat alone made up 15 per cent of the total volume.

The fact that agriculture today is a bigger industry than ever before in terms of investment and physical output is important. The emphasis on factors of production other than land and labour that has contributed to this development has also created a multitude of new urban industries and services on which agriculture itself is now dependent.

In short, agriculture's greater output has become a boon, not only to urban consumers, but also to processors, manufacturers, and distributors; and to urban employment. In reaching this position agriculture in turn has become more highly commercialized and more closely linked with the urban community. It seems likely that this trend will continue and that agriculture will find in the resulting relationship a new and significant status.                                                                  (J. F. Booth)

# Fisheries

Off more than 30,000 miles of Atlantic, Pacific and Arctic coastlines, and in more than 290,000 square miles of freshwater lakes and rivers, Canadian fishermen find an unusually rich fishery resource awaiting harvest. Over 150 species of fish and shellfish are caught. The inventory of many stocks is still incomplete and several species known to be available in large quantities, for example the capelin, have yet to be exploited commercially for human food. Yet, in a world where starvation is a swallow away for tens of millions of people, the importance of the ocean and freshwater fishery resources in and around Canada grows with each passing year.

## Historical Review

With Confederation, the new nation of Canada inherited a problem that had existed for more than 90 years and for which no immediate solution was in sight—that of the disputed Atlantic coast fisheries. Bitter were the arguments between Canadian and American fishermen over the right of New England vessels to fish the bays, gulfs and inshore waters of the Atlantic provinces and frequent acts of violence and vandalism against persons and equipment emphasized the intensity of the dispute.

Until the War of Independence in 1775, fishermen from the American colonies and from what are now the Canadian Atlantic provinces enjoyed equal privileges in prosecuting the fishery along the coast and in the inlets of Nova Scotia, New Brunswick and Prince Edward Island. With the coming of peace, the question of the nature and extent of fishing privileges to be enjoyed by the fishermen of the new republic was raised. The Treaty of Paris, 1783, contained a compromise agreement which allowed Americans to take fish on the coast, bays and creeks of British North America and to dry and cure fish on unsettled bays, harbours and creeks of Nova Scotia, the Magdalen Islands and Labrador. These rights were automatically terminated with the outbreak of the War of 1812 between Great Britain and the United States.

In the negotiations which brought peace in 1814, and in the Treaty of Ghent of the same year which formally ended the War, the question of the fisheries was not included, largely because of a basic difference of opinion between the British and Americans on the status of the fishing privileges conferred by the Treaty of Paris, and not from any mutual agreement that the fisheries problem no longer existed. The British held the view that the Americans no longer enjoyed the privilege of participating in the inshore fisheries along the coast of British North America by virtue of the rule that treaties between nations are annulled by subsequent wars. On the other hand, the Americans maintained that "since the division of territory survived the war, so the division of fisheries survived". These diametrically opposed views were not reconcilable and there was an early confrontation between the New England fishing boats and the British naval vessels patrolling the inshore fishing grounds of British North America. In all, twenty American fishing vessels were seized for trespass before a satisfactory agreement was reached to end the dispute. After many months of negotiation, the Convention of 1818 was signed which granted the United States certain specific fishing rights in perpetuity in exchange for a much more restricted area in which commercial fishing operations by American vessels could be conducted. Furthermore, the British suc-

The original Bluenose brought renown to Canada throughout the 1920's and 1930's in international schooner races, and her likeness is on Canadian ten cent pieces. Bluenose II, a replica of the original ship, was launched in 1963.

Islington, Newfoundland. Famed for her fisheries, the charm of her coastal ports, her immense power resources, mines and minerals, the newest province is attracting an increasing number of visitors—and industries.

ceeded in having the Americans renounce claim to areas in which they had previously prosecuted an inshore fishery. However, the wording of this renunciatory clause gave rise, in later years, to a serious difference of opinion which was not entirely resolved by 1867.

The first two decades of Confederation were marked by conflicts and clashes between Canadian and American fishermen, particularly along the Nova Scotian coast, resulting in part from a disagreement over the extent of American privileges under the Convention of 1818 as well as insistence by Nova Scotian commercial interests that American vessels be prevented from trading directly with Canadian fishermen and fish curers. Tension was relieved by the Treaty of Washington of 1873*. Following its termination in 1885, statesmen in Canada and the United States, weary of the long-standing fisheries dispute and anxious to avoid further strife, negotiated a *modus vivendi* under which, on payment of a licence fee, Canadian harbours could be entered and used by American fishermen for the purpose of purchasing supplies, trans-shipping fish and other specified privileges. This arrangement, which began in 1888,

---

* Signed, 1871; ratified, 1873.

CANADA, 1867-1967

was intended to be temporary until a treaty satisfactory to both sides could be concluded. Such a treaty has not yet been written and other statutory arrangements have been made over the years to replace the *modus vivendi* privileges.

In recent years, there has developed a desire on the part of many nations to protect their valuable inshore marine resources against exploitation by foreign fishing vessels through defining boundaries of national sovereignty over fisheries beyond the traditional three-mile territorial limit. Although Canada has formally adopted a twelve-mile fishing limit, boundary lines have not yet been drawn to delineate those waters over which sovereignty with respect to fisheries is claimed.

The British North America Act gives the Federal Government full legislative jurisdiction over the coastal and inland fisheries of Canada. For the first few decades after Confederation, complete administrative control of the fisheries also was exercised by the federal authority. However, as a result of various judicial decisions and agreements with the provinces, the pattern of administration has been remodelled so that today the Federal Government administers all tidal and sea fisheries, except in Quebec, and the freshwater fisheries of the Atlantic Provinces and the Yukon and Northwest Territories. British Columbia, Ontario and the Prairie Provinces administer their freshwater fisheries and Quebec administers all fisheries.

## Development of the Resource

**Pacific**—Prior to 1867, the fishing industry of British Columbia centred almost entirely on salmon, had few export outlets, and was confined to the supplying of fresh fish to the local market. In 1869, the first salmon cannery began operations on the Fraser River. The ready availability of fish from the great spawning migrations encouraged a rapid expansion in the industry and attracted canners from the Atlantic provinces and the United States.

By 1901, the pack of canned Pacific salmon had increased to 1,247,212 cases from 67,387 cases in 1877, but significant advances in the technology of harvesting and processing the catch were soon to change the tempo of the industry. Purse-seining was introduced, making possible larger catches with fewer fishermen, and the "iron chink" was installed in canneries to head and gut the fish mechanically and so increase production. With mechanization came the amalgamation of small canning firms with larger, more centralized organizations. The industry gradually moved to the north to exploit the salmon runs of the Nass, the Skeena and the Babine and those other noble and turbulent rivers of British Columbia which thread their way through the mountain passes to the sea. The completion of the transcontinental railway in 1915 to Prince Rupert, and the building of a cold storage plant, further encouraged the industry shift.

The trend toward more amalgamation and continued modernization in the catching and processing sectors of the industry was accelerated in the post-World War I period by high labour costs and the need for large-scale capital input. The high price of the two major products, canned salmon and frozen halibut, and the highly competitive nature of the export market motivated integration of sales effort.

World War II gave a tremendous impetus to the commercial fisheries of Canada and created a most favourable environment for industry expansion which continued well into the postwar period. Larger fishing craft equipped with the latest and most sophisticated electronic devices for finding fish and the mechanization of fish catching and handling has resulted in more than doubling the investment per man in the primary fishing operations in British Columbia since 1945. The fish processing industry has, in general, continued to consolidate and to concentrate its facilities in Vancouver and Prince Rupert.

Statistics inadequately describe the dramatic development of the rich fishery resources of British Columbia over the past 90 years. In 1876, with a capital investment of $49,000, the industry marketed $123,000 worth of fish products caught by 444 fishermen. By 1964, the B.C. fishery was exploited by 13,300 fishermen whose catches had a value of over $48,000,000. The total capital invested in the catching and processing industry had grown to $87,000,000.

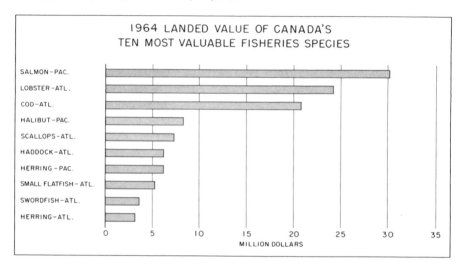

**Atlantic**—In 1867, the cod was the mainstay of the fisheries of the Maritime Provinces and Quebec, although mackerel and herring assumed considerable local importance in the Gaspe region of Quebec and in the Magdalen Islands. Salted, dried and pickled fish were the staple products for the export markets. In the early 1880's, dried salted cod reached its maximum level of production but the gradual disappearance of the wooden ships and changing market conditions and requirements caused a steady decline which, with few exceptions, has continued to the present day. By 1900, the historical cod-fishery which contributed so directly and so greatly to the early settlement and economic development of the Atlantic provinces had begun to give way to lobster.

At the turn of the century, new methods, processes and techniques began to appear which were, in time, to have far-reaching effects on the inshore and offshore fisheries of the Atlantic provinces. Sails gave way to the gasoline engine permitting much greater mobility and wider-ranging operations. The dragger or otter-trawler was introduced in 1908, but the use of this highly-efficient means of catching fish was soon shackled by the restrictions imposed by Government at the strong insistence of small-boat, handline fishermen, who feared for the stability of their markets and the security of their livelihood. While the purpose of the restrictive law may have been to ensure

126

More salmon is processed in British Columbia than in any other province. In 1965 total landed value was approximately $25,000,000.

that the greatest number of fishermen would continue in the fishery, the actual effect was to limit individual incomes through retarding the growth of productivity.

The growth of the urban populations in Canada and the improving of transportation and refrigeration facilities created new and important markets for fresh and frozen fish and resulted in a change in the pattern of production, particularly of salted fish. One of the most important incentives to the industry to give more attention to the Canadian market was a federal subsidy on shipments of fish by refrigerated freight from the Atlantic and Pacific coasts to inland centres. The subsidy was paid for ten years, from 1909 to 1919.

In the history of the frozen fish trade of the twentieth century there have been two major technological developments, each of which revolutionized the industry at the time and kept fish competitive with other food products. The first, in 1923, was the technique of filleting and the quick-freezing of the fillets. Thirty years later came fishsticks and other fish portions of uniform weight made by sawing small, rectangular pieces of fish flesh from frozen blocks of fillets, dipping them in batter and breading material and cooking them prior to freezing and packing.

FISHERIES

Filleting and quick-freezing opened a new and challenging market for the Atlantic fishing industry but the challenge was not fully met for many years. The caution and conservatism which characterized the industry during the inter-war period, and political opposition to more efficient methods of large-scale harvesting of fish populations, acted as effective brakes on rapid reorientation and expansion. Despite these obstacles, progress was made in developing the domestic market and, in the 1930's, in establishing a valuable, new market in the central United States, particularly with chilled fresh fillets of cod and sole. Concurrently began the trend toward amalgamation of small processors and centralization of the industry in the larger ports, notably Halifax and Lunenburg.

Because of the vastly-increased demand for fish products generated by World War II, the moribund salt-fish industry was revitalized and the frozen fish processors expanded their facilities. The long-standing restrictions on draggers were relaxed by the exigencies of war and the modernization of the fishing fleets began. In a few years, that graceful workhorse of the Atlantic fishery, immortalized by the *Bluenose*, became a nostalgic memory as the schooner with her deckload of dories gave way to the sturdy, un-romantic but efficient, draggers and trawlers.

In the past decade, the considerable increase of capital investment and rapid advances in the technology of food-processing have resulted in a remarkable growth of the fish catching and processing capacity of the Atlantic provinces and an accompanying spectacular rise in output. In 1876, the products of the Atlantic fishery, excluding Newfoundland, had a marketed value of $10,500,000 and nearly 48,000 fishermen were employed. Nearly 90 years later, in 1964, the number of fishermen had dropped to 26,000 but the value of the processed production had risen to $142,000,000.

**Newfoundland**—On April 1, 1949, Newfoundland joined the Canadian Confederation bringing with it a rich and colourful history which began nearly 100 years before the first permanent European settlement on the North American mainland at Port Royal, Nova Scotia. The telling of the events and deeds which have woven the proud mantle of Newfoundland fisheries tradition is beyond the scope of this article yet a brief background is necessary to give perspective to problems which existed in the industry at Confederation.

From its beginning centuries ago, the cod-fishery of Newfoundland had provided the raw material for the famous dried, light-salted fish so prized by traditional Mediterranean markets, as well as for the more heavily salted cod well known to world trade. As may be expected with an economy largely based on a single resource and relying entirely on export markets, the fortunes of Newfoundlanders were subject to extreme uncertainty and seldom through the years did a year of good catches coincide with a seller's market.

During World War I, Newfoundland benefited from a sharply increased demand for salted cod and there was considerable expansion in the industry. Following the War, traditional markets contracted and new outlets were sought by the Newfoundland trade in the West Indies which precipitated a price war with Nova Scotian exporters who normally supplied that market. Beginning in 1926 and continuing over the next decade, the price of fish fell by more than 50 per cent. The earnings of Newfoundland

Salt cod, for centuries a Newfoundland staple, is still exported from the province, each country preferring a slightly different cure. This shipment is for the West Indies where smaller, harder-dried cod is preferred.

British Columbia salmon is sold frozen, canned or fresh. Approximately 60,000,000 pounds are canned yearly on the Pacific coast.

His boat loaded with traps, a Prince Edward Island fisherman hustles out of his harbour. Lobsters provide the most valuable returns to Island fishermen.

FISHERIES

129

fishermen were so reduced that an acute economic depression resulted which contributed to the failure of responsible government in 1933.

For centuries the salt fish trade of Newfoundland had been organized on the merchant system based on a structure of credit. Merchants in the outports supplied fishermen with food, clothing and other necessities of life as well as with fishing equipment. In return, the fisherman delivered his cured and dried fish to the merchant to be credited against his debts. The merchant was not usually a direct exporter and so delivered his fish purchases to the trading organization in St. John's which had originally provided him with the resources in money and goods to outfit the fishermen.

In 1936, the Commission of Government established the Newfoundland Fisheries Board with wide powers over production and marketing of fish. The Board instituted a system of licensing exports and merchant groups were formed to sell in particular markets. This move effectively reduced internal competition between Newfoundland exporters and strengthened their export marketing position against a growing tendency of foreign governments to develop their fishing industry and to protect its production through tariffs and other economic measures.

World War II caused an advance in prices for salted fish which continued until 1947. However, memories of the market slump of the 1930's remained vivid in the minds of Newfoundlanders and there were some fears for the continued prosperity of the industry once the abnormal pressures of wartime requirements disappeared. Having seen the value of group action under the export licensing system which began in 1936, the industry formed the Newfoundland Association of Fish Exporters Limited (NAFEL), in 1947, which was given exclusive right of export for all salted codfish produced in Newfoundland. In part, it was felt that such a marketing monopoly would stabilize export prices and give the highest possible returns to fishermen. The agency was prevented by law from buying fish from fishermen and from setting prices paid to fishermen. These functions rested solely with the 30 or more exporters who provided the agency with supplies of salt fish to meet allocations issued to fill export contracts. At Confederation in 1949, NAFEL had gained control over nearly 25 per cent of the world trade in salted fish and, in the Caribbean markets, it held a dominant position.

As had been expected, the postwar period saw a decline in demand and lower prices for salted fish and the earnings of fishermen were again depressed despite the efforts of NAFEL to maintain a satisfactory level of returns. Shortly after 1949, federal assistance to fishermen became necessary through the Fisheries Prices Support Board.

There were other more serious problems facing the Newfoundland fishing industry which placed immediate demands on governments and the trade. In thousands of small settlements in the new province, the way of life of the fisherman and his family had remained relatively unchanged for over 200 years. Complete dependence on the local merchant for credit and supplies, coupled with the physical limitation on his productivity of salt fish because of traditional and obsolete catching and curing techniques, condemned fishermen to a lifetime of unremitting and unrewarding labour. The lack of alternate employment opportunity further restricted and bound him to his little world of poverty and toil.

Recognizing that a partial solution lay in increased efficiency in all phases of the industry, a program of development for the Atlantic fisheries in general was put in motion in 1950 and some of its most dramatic results are seen in Newfoundland.

Fishing ranks second among the primary industries in Nova Scotia, and a constant check is maintained at the Fish Inspection Laboratory, Halifax, on the quality of the produce.

New harbour works have been built to provide better landing facilities, community stages have been constructed to aid the fishermen in improving the quality of his production, improved equipment and techniques have been introduced to increase productivity, technical training facilities have been developed for fishermen, special programs to rehabilitate depressed communities have been devised, and loans and grants have been made available for fishing vessel construction. In 1964, a Federal-Provincial Ministerial Conference on Fisheries Development was held in Ottawa in an attempt to formulate a national policy for fisheries of Canada, particularly with respect to economic development. Among the decisions reached were the setting up of a special Commission to study the Atlantic salt fish trade and a program of relocating and retaining Newfoundland fishermen living in disadvantageous settlements.

Since the end of World War II, there has been a spectacular development of facilities for filleting and freezing fish in Newfoundland which has encouraged substantial foreign investment. Improved roads have made it increasingly possible for inshore fishermen to divert their catch to this new industry and thus to free themselves from the limitations of producing salted fish. Yet in many instances, the real income of these fishermen has not improved because of their continued dependence on small boats and ineffective catching methods. In 1964, the marketed value of the Newfoundland production of all types of fish was $46,600,000. About 22,600 fishermen were employed.

## Freshwater Fisheries

Seventeenth and eighteenth century explorers of the unknown country lying to the west of Montreal make almost daily reference in their diaries to the importance of fresh fish in their diets. While the lakes and rivers formed, in truth, the highway to the heart of the new continent the several species of fish which could be so readily caught from their waters provided the food for extended forays to the great northwest.

Although the early settlers along the St. Lawrence and the lower Great Lakes placed heavy reliance on the beasts and birds of the forest and field for their food supply, lake fish were an important source of animal protein. Because of their tendency to school during spawning thus making capture easier, large quantities of trout and whitefish were taken in the fall and salted for winter use. In 1867, about 1,700 commercial fishermen took nearly 3,500,000 pounds of fish from the Great Lakes and connecting waterways, the St. Lawrence River and Lake Simcoe.

Following the purchase of Rupert's Land from the Hudson's Bay Company in 1869, the great settlement of the west began. Many families emigrated from Iceland to the inter-lake region immediately to the north of Winnipeg and pioneered the Lake Winnipeg pickerel and whitefish fishery. Markets were gradually developed in the American midwest. Because of its high fat content, whitefish from Lake Winnipeg was highly desirable for smoking for the delicatessen trade and became internationally known as "Selkirks" from the name of the port on the Red River where the major fish-exporting firms first made their operating headquarters.

As early as 1905, small-scale commercial fishing was carried on in Saskatchewan and Alberta with the catches being sent to Winnipeg for export to the United States. As was the case in the coastal fisheries, World War I sparked a rapid increase in the production of freshwater fish and many prairie lakes were fished for the first time in order to meet the demand.

Because of a continued growth of urban populations there was little contraction in demand during the postwar period. Almost from its beginning, the freshwater commercial fishery has exported nearly 90 per cent of its output to the wholesale markets of Chicago, Detroit and New York where a fairly constant demand for whole and dressed fish has existed. Nevertheless, the freshwater fisheries did not escape the effects of severely-depressed prices during the 1931-39 period. Yet, in an enterprise where fishing is often an off-season venture by farmers and loggers, the returns from the fishery provided a small but important supplementary income during the depression.

Due in part to the relatively high price of the raw material, filleting as a form of processing has been slow in developing. Saskatchewan has led the way in this field as a means to improve markets for whitefish from more remote lakes.

Once again war intervened in 1939 and the demand and prices for lake fish increased. It became profitable to fish lakes in northern Ontario and the Prairie Provinces which were remote from the railway and bring the frozen catch overland in the winter months to railhead. As the industry moved farther north, new techniques in transportation were born, including the tractor train and the snowmobile. With few exceptions, the export market for freshwater fish has remained buoyant since 1945 and industry continues its northward progress. Great Slave Lake began production in 1945 and today accounts for nearly 80 per cent of all lake trout exports.

The production from the Great Lakes has changed in nature and amount over the post-World War II period because of the depredations of the sea lamprey which virtually annihilated the lake trout populations. Of even greater gravity, the cumulative effects of industrial and residential pollution are changing the ecology of the lakes. Whitefish, pickerel and cisco have almost disappeared from Lakes Erie and Ontario and have been replaced by smelt, shad and other less valuable species.

By 1964, Canada produced 105,000,000 pounds of freshwater fish with a market value of $18,300,000. Over 17,000 fishermen, using gillnets almost exclusively, operated over a 3,000-mile range from the mouth of the Mackenzie River in the Northwest Territories to Lake St. John, in Quebec.                    (H. V. DEMPSEY)

# Forestry

Three and a half centuries ago the first European settlers in Canada found a land covered by forests. From the shores of the rivers to the crests of the distant hills the stands of pines and spruces, maples and birch, seemed to be limitless. To the new-comers the forest was, perhaps, more of a hindrance than an asset because of the immense labour involved in clearing land for farms; on the other hand, it provided wood for buildings and stockades and fuel for cooking and heating. Use of wood for industrial purposes developed very slowly.

In the second half of the eighteenth century a modest trade grew up between eastern Canada and the British colonies in the Caribbean Islands, in which planks and boards and barrel staves were exchanged for sugar, molasses and rum. This trade increased considerably after the American Revolutionary War because of British restrictions on colonial trade by foreign countries. Some of the finest white pine trees were reserved for use as masts and spars, first in French and later in British ships. In contrast, many splendid stands of hardwoods along the upper St. Lawrence River were burned by Loyalist settlers who cleared the land and found in the ashes their first cash crop. Lye was leached from these ashes for the manufacture of soap.

## Square Timber Trade

Demand for Canadian forest products, on a larger scale, arose suddenly following Napoleon's blockade of the Baltic ports which had formerly supplied timber to Britain. Almost overnight, the production of large timbers of white and red pine, squared in the forest with the broad-axe, became a flourishing industry which was to endure long after peace returned to Europe. The industry grew so rapidly that Quebec City became for a time the largest timber-exporting port in the world.

Production of these timbers, under conditions then existing, was a rugged and demanding business. The finest pineries were to be found along the Ottawa River and here an operator might discover a suitable stand of trees, engage a crew of lumberjacks with their horses, arrange for supplies for the winter, build camps and haulage sleighs and primitive roads, and supervise the felling, timber-making and transportation of the timbers to the river bank. After the ice ran out in the spring he had the timbers fastened together in sections or cribs and the cribs assembled into rafts on which crude living quarters were erected. Then he would embark with his men on the long and hazardous voyage downstream to Quebec, to sell his wood to the representatives of British importers.

## Sawmill Industry

Important as the square timber trade became, it had a rapidly growing rival in the sawmill industry. The earlier mills relied upon waterpower and their rate of output was small. Introduction of the steam-engine in the 1820's made possible the location of mills wherever timber was plentiful and provided the energy needed for faster production. At about the same time the opening of a series of canals, soon to be followed by the construction of railroads, gave access to the almost insatiable demand for lumber which developed in the United States as its population expanded westward. Here the demand was for planks and boards, and species other than pine—chiefly the spruces—found ready acceptance. In Britain, also, the demand for sawn deals was growing.

By 1867, logging and sawmilling were firmly established as Canada's major industries and some of the larger mills were of a size which would be considered respectable even today. But, in the year preceding Confederation, a new competitor for the raw materials of the forest appeared on the scene with the erection of two wood pulp mills in Lower Canada. This new departure marked the first step towards Canada's present position as the world's largest producer of newsprint paper.

**Logging in British Columbia**—During the years following Confederation the logging industry on the west coast of British Columbia developed slowly but steadily, although the difficulty of moving the huge logs of Douglas fir, hemlock and cedar with primitive equipment restricted operations to the vicinity of tidewater. Introduction of the steam-driven donkey engine in the 1890's marked the beginning of mechanized logging

Timber slides permitted the passage of "cribs" which held 16 to 20 pieces and were steered down the slides by men with long sweeps. This slide was on the Hull side of the river.

One of the last rafts of square timber passes Parliament Hill. The timber trade and immigration were closely connected in the 19th century. Bulky commodities such as timber provided return space for immigrants.

FORESTRY

and, later on, the opening of the Panama Canal gave access to the markets of the eastern American seaboard and of Europe and enabled Canada's westernmost province to take full advantage of its magnificent forest resources.

Compilation of comprehensive statistics relating to production and trade in forest products was not undertaken until the present century. The total average annual exports of forest products between 1880 and 1882 inclusive amounted to $23,270,000. Of this amount logs brought in $263,000; square timber, $4,621,000; sawn timber, $16,794,000; other products and ashes, $1,592,000. Fifty per cent of the revenue thus derived came from Britain; approximately 39 per cent from the United States.

The majority of Canadians now live in cities and towns and, for them, close contact with the forest has been lost. It is true that thousands of families spend their brief vacations in wooded areas and that fishermen and hunters still follow the pursuits of their forbears for a few days each year; but, to most of the population, the forests are almost unknown. Above all, very few persons are able to grasp the sheer immensity of the forest estate. One could fly from eastern Quebec due west for 1,700 miles to Lake Winnipeg and then, after a 300-mile offset to the north, continue for another 1,300 miles to the west coast and pass over almost continuous forest cover all the way. In the east the stands of conifers and hardwoods are broken by innumerable lakes and in the west by the barren peaks of the mountains; otherwise, the land beneath the line of flight is occupied by countless millions of trees.

## Forest Regions

The nature of the forests in any country is influenced by many factors, including climate, geology and topography. In Canada different combinations of these factors and the post-glacial migration of tree species from the south have resulted in eight distinct forest regions, which may be further subdivided into 90 sections, each with its own ecological characteristics.

The largest of these regions is known as the Boreal Forest and extends across the country from the Atlantic Ocean northwestward to the Alaska boundary. Its principal tree species are spruces, balsam fir and jack pine, accompanied by poplars and white birch. In the Acadian and Great Lakes-St. Lawrence regions, white and red pines, spruces, balsam and hemlock are the most important conifers, and maples, yellow birch and other hardwoods are widespread. In the southern part of the Ontario peninsula the small Deciduous region contains hardwoods not found elsewhere in Canada. In the Subalpine, Montane and Columbia regions of western Alberta and the interior of British Columbia lodgepole pine, Engelmann spruce, and several true firs are found along with Douglas fir and other coast species. Finally, the Coast region is characterized by stands of Douglas fir, western red cedar and western hemlock.

Good management of the forest resources must be based on accurate knowledge of their extent and nature but preparation of forest inventories in a country as large as Canada presents formidable difficulties. Fortunately, two relatively recent developments in forest survey techniques, aerial photography and modern methods of sampling, have made possible the mapping and description of most of the forests. Recent estimates indicate a total forest area of nearly 1,100,000,000 acres. Within the boundaries of the ten provinces, taken together, four out of every five acres of land are forested.

A log boom under tow on the St. John River, New Brunswick, is a reminder of the important role which the forests still play in the province's economy. Of its total land area, 86 per cent is classed as productive forest.

Some 619,000,000 acres are classified as productive forest, capable of producing successive crops of timber suitable for industrial use. Four fifths of this area bears coniferous or softwood species growing in pure stands or in mixture with hardwoods. It is estimated that nine per cent of the productive forest land is not bearing trees at the moment because of recent fellings, forest fires or windfall; but there are 241,000,000 acres of young growth, restocked by nature, which demonstrate the powers of recovery of the forests after such disturbances.

The total volume of merchantable timber is estimated to be 752,000,000,000 cubic feet, of which 611,000,000,000 cubic feet are of softwood species. These enormous figures, by themselves, mean little to most people; but when they are compared with the quantities of wood harvested annually—about 3,400,000,000 cubic feet—they give assurance that Canada's forest industries, large though they are, can be still further expanded.

**Ownership and Administration**—Nine tenths of all the productive forest land in Canada is publicly owned but the harvesting of timber is carried out entirely by private industry, an arrangement believed to be unique among the major wood-producing countries. Some 57,000,000 acres of forest have passed into private ownership through early grants to individuals, or governmental grants to corporations, to encourage the construction of railways, or through their inclusion in farms—the so-called farm woodlots.

In the early days of the square timber trade and the small, primitive sawmill, the forests were thought to be limitless and the idea that forest lands could produce perpetual crops of timber did not exist. On the contrary, the lumberman was thought to be performing a public service by clearing the land for agricultural use. Under these circumstances the operator was concerned solely with obtaining rights to cut the trees he wanted on a "cut out and get out" basis. Later on, competition for the best stands and the investment of considerable sums in larger mills made necessary more positive arrangements for ensuring timber supplies—a tendency which has culminated in the large timber limits now held by pulp and paper companies to supply raw materials on a sustained yield basis to their costly and immovable mills. To meet the needs of various large and small operators a system of leases, licences and timber sales was gradually developed through which corporations or individuals can obtain rights to cut Crown timber on defined areas and during specified periods of time.

The British North America Act of 1867 assigned certain matters to the exclusive jurisdiction of the legislatures of the Provinces, and included the following subsection: "5. The Management and Sale of the Public Lands belonging to the Province and of the Timber and Wood thereon". This subsection applied equally to provinces which joined the Confederation at later dates although, for reasons of convenience, the Federal Government continued to administer the forests of the three Prairie Provinces and the railway belt in British Columbia until 1930. Since that date, its administrative responsibility has been limited to the forests of the northern territories, national parks, Indian reserves and a few other small areas. With 11 different forest authorities in Canada a great diversity of policies and forest laws might have been expected to develop; in fact, the similarities are far more significant than the differences.

Competition for choice stands of timber and for rights to use and improve streams and rivers for floating logs to mill or market led to most of the earliest forest legislation. Later on, governments insisted on the public interest in the forests and required payment for each unit of timber cut, at rates which are adjusted from time to time.

Until the beginning of the present century there was little public concern about the welfare of the forests but, in 1906, a turning point was reached when a Forestry Convention was held at Ottawa under the presidency of the then Prime Minister, Sir Wilfrid Laurier. Public interest was aroused and results followed swiftly. During the eight years preceding the outbreak of World War I, faculties of forestry were established at three Canadian universities; a fourth was to follow in 1921. Most of the governments concerned established forest services and commenced to employ professional foresters. Special attention was given to protection against forest fires.

The War checked progress for a time but, shortly after it ended, the larger forest industries also commenced to employ professional men in the management of their woods operations. Governments required the occupants of large timber limits to make detailed inventory surveys as a basis for long- and short-term working plans to

In world production of pulp, Canada is in second place. This pulp and paper mill is in Newfoundland.

ensure that fellings would be carried out in an orderly manner; also, the volumes cut were to be restricted to the estimated productive capacity of the forest lands. Both government and industry increased their efforts to control losses from fire, insects and tree diseases.

Following the transfer of control of their national resources to the Prairie Provinces in 1930, the Federal Government concentrated its forestry efforts on research. Forest products laboratories had been established by the Forestry Branch of the Department of the Interior during the war years and a number of forest experiment stations were opened during the 1930's. Research leading to the control of forest insects and tree diseases was carried on by the Department of Agriculture. The Canada Forestry Act of 1949 authorized the federal authorities to enter into agreements with the provinces whereby financial assistance is given to specified provincial programs such as forest inventory surveys. All these federal activities were brought together on the establishment of the federal Department of Forestry in 1960.

## Forest Industries

National statistics relating to the forest industries recognize five principal groups— operations in the woods, sawmills, pulp and paper mills, wood-using industries and

Log loaders at Fort William, Ontario, speed the operations of the lumber industry.

paper-using industries. Great changes in logging methods and in working conditions in the woods have taken place during the past hundred years. The crude log shanty, where men were expected to spend six or seven months subsisting on a diet of salt pork, beans, molasses and tea, has been replaced by modern camps with recreational facilities, excellent food, and transportation services.

The axe and the cross-cut saw have given way to the power saw; oxen and horses have been replaced by motor trucks travelling at high speed along roads built by the diesel tractor and modern road-building equipment. There is an urgent demand by management for new and better techniques and equipment in the drive for lower costs and more efficient production. In Eastern Canada efforts have been made to extend the traditional winter logging season and to provide year-round employment for more people. On the west coast year-round logging has always been possible and employs a body of highly-skilled professional loggers.

In 1962 the total production of wood in Canada amounted to 3,400,000,000 cubic feet, of which nearly 54 per cent was accepted by the sawmilling and wood-using industries and 34 per cent by the pulp and paper industry. Fuelwood, formerly an important product, accounted for less than seven per cent. Most of the roundwood produced was processed or used in Canada, only 3.3 per cent being exported.

It has been shown that the sawmill industry was firmly established and widely distributed in Canada at the time of Confederation, but national statistics describing its make-up and production are not available prior to 1908. In 1911 the output of sawn lumber totalled 4,900,000,000 board feet, of which 27 per cent was produced in British Columbia. The principal species cut were spruces and balsam fir, white and red pines, and Douglas fir. Ninety-four per cent of the lumber was of softwood species and only six per cent was hardwood, chiefly maple and yellow birch. This volume of production was not equalled during the following 30 years, but by 1961 the national

140

lumber output exceeded 8,200,000,000 board feet. British Columbia provided 74 per cent of all lumber shipped during the year. Spruce continued to be the principal species, followed by Douglas fir and western hemlock. Output of hardwood lumber showed little change.

The Dominion Bureau of Statistics received reports from 3,260 sawmills but some 2,600 of these were small establishments of the portable or semi-portable types. Among the bigger mills were 13 very large plants, each of which produced sawn lumber and other products valued at $5,000,000 or more annually.

The total value of shipments of sawn lumber for the year 1963 exceeded $450,000,000 and the sale of other products brought the industry total up to $535,000,000. Most important among the by-products were pulp chips, manufactured from slabs and edgings resulting from the sawing of logs into lumber. Sales closely approached 2,500,000 tons valued at $36,000,000. This use of material of types formerly consumed in refuse burners is a relatively new development which is profitable to the lumber industry and helps to reduce the drain upon the forests.

Paper was first made from rags in Canada in 1803 but the modern industry, based on wood fibre, was only one year old at Confederation. The growth of the industry in modern times can be measured by the increase in its consumption of wood. In 1922 about 3,000,000 cords were converted into mechanical and chemical wood pulps; 40 years later the industry required nearly 15,000,000 cords of roundwood plus 2,500,000 cords of pulp chips and other wood residues from sawmills, giving a total consumption of nearly 17,500,000 cords; a sixfold increase during the period. Production of wood pulp increased from 2,100,000 tons in 1922 to 12,100,000 tons in 1962 and the output of newsprint increased from 1,100,000 tons to nearly 6,700,000 tons.

Shipments of all kinds of paper and paperboard from 125 producing mills totalled nearly 8,700,000 tons in 1962, with a value of $1,190,000,000. Export shipments of wood pulp amounted to 3,000,000 tons valued at $370,000,000. In addition, shipments of building boards and converted paper products were worth $98,000,000.

The latest available summary (1961) for all the forest-based industries shows a total employment equivalent to 301,000 man-years. In fact, a considerably larger number of people obtained work because many operations in the woods in Eastern Canada are of a seasonal nature. Net value of production by the whole group of industries was $2,400,000,000.

## External Trade

At the time of Confederation, Canada's forest industries were already dependent on export markets for the sale of much of their output. At present about two thirds of the sawn lumber produced, more than nine tenths of the newsprint paper, and sizable proportions of many other products of the forest industries, are sold to other countries. During the ten-year period ending in 1964 lumber exports increased from 4,600,000,000 to 6,500,000,000 board feet; wood pulp exports rose from 2,400,000 to 3,600,000 tons, and newsprint exports from 5,800,000 to 6,800,000 tons.

The values of exports are high while the values of imports of products made from wood are relatively low. This relationship has existed for many years and seems likely to continue. Thus Canada can rely on the forest industries as a reliable source of large amounts of foreign funds with which to pay for many of the imports essential to her high standard of living. From the point of view of the average Canadian it is well that the forest is a renewable natural resource.

### External Trade in Selected Forest Products, 1964
(Millions of Dollars)

| Products | Exports | Imports | Favourable Balance |
|---|---|---|---|
| Roundwood | 34 | 21 | 13 |
| Lumber | 515 | 38 | 477 |
| Wood pulp | 461 | 10 | 451 |
| Newsprint paper | 835 | — | 835 |
| Other paper and paperboard | 58 | 51 | 7 |
| Plywoods and veneers | 67 | 19 | 48 |
| **Totals** | **1,970** | **139** | **1,831** |

# Future Outlook

A report by the Royal Commission on Canada's Economic Prospects, published in 1957, forecast an over-all growth in industrial consumption of wood from 3,100,000,000 cubic feet in 1954 to 4,900,000,000 cubic feet in 1980; an increase of 60 per cent in 26 years. In 1959 a committee of experts assembled in Rome by the Food and Agriculture Organization of the United Nations (FAO) forecast an increase in world demand for paper and paper products from 56,000,000 metric tons in 1955 to 134,000,000 metric tons in 1975; an increase of 139 per cent in 20 years. World statistics for 1963 indicate that the anticipated rate of increase was reached during the first eight years.

These estimates encourage optimism. Recent studies leave no room for doubt about the potential capacity of Canada's productive forest lands to yield far more wood, annually, and in perpetuity, than they have ever been called upon to supply in the past; always provided that protective measures and forest management practices continue to improve. Forty years ago there was some alarm about the capacity of the forests to sustain the then current rate of depletion; in future the problem may be one of finding ways to use profitably all the wood they can grow.

Achievement in full measure of the economic and other benefits that the forests can provide will involve great efforts. Canadian manufacturers must continue to offer goods of high quality to the domestic and foreign markets, at acceptable prices; forest managers must be able to adjust their methods as new techniques in the harvesting and transportation of wood develop; flexibility will be essential in the face of changing demands, and more research by government services, industrial organizations, and individual companies will be needed to enable Canada to consolidate its position as one of the chief suppliers of wood products to the world.

Fortunately, Canada has the means to meet the requirements of the future. The faculties of forestry of its universities and the more recently established schools for forest rangers and technicians provide men trained to guide the conservation, or wise use, of its forest resources. Alert industrial organizations encourage the development of new and better processes and methods, and Canadian trade commissioners stationed in other countries are constantly on the look-out for new markets. With these assets the future of the forest-based industries should be bright indeed.

(J.D.B. HARRISON)

Canada is one of the major producers of elemental sulphur, almost all of it as a by-product from natural gas processing plants in Western Canada.

# Mines and Minerals

## Pre-Confederation Period

The first inkling that Canada was rich in mineral wealth was revealed more than 400 years ago to the French explorer, Jacques Cartier. In 1534, Cartier returned to France with two red-skinned natives of the New World who told of a legendary Kingdom of the Saguenay where gold and precious stones could be found in great quantities. The surge of interest in the new continent was due in no small measure to these and other stories of great riches that awaited the venturesome individual.

On Cartier's second voyage the following year, the natives at Hochelaga (Montreal), confirmed the story of the Kingdom of the Saguenay and indicated that it was along the Ottawa River. Five years later Cartier returned once again and made an unsuccessful bid to establish a colony at Charlesbourg, where the Cap Rouge River empties into the St. Lawrence River. These early settlers found iron deposits and flakes of gold in the sand along the river banks. They also found stones which they thought to be diamonds. Following a severe winter during which many died of scurvy, Cartier abandoned Charlesbourg and returned to France. What he thought were gold and diamonds turned out to be iron pyrite, with just a trace of gold and quartz.

Martin Frobisher experienced similar disappointment in the more northern latitudes. He made three voyages between 1576 and 1578 in an attempt to find a sea route to Cathay and the Indies and returned from Baffin Island to England with rock rumoured to be gold ore. On the promise of great mineral wealth, Frobisher obtained support for additional expeditions. He shipped back many tons of rock, all of which proved worthless.

Little else appears in recorded history concerning Canada's mineral potential during the 16th century. Indeed, from 1497 through the 16th century, Canada's wealth was almost solely from the sea. However, the 17th century brought renewed interest in the New World. The name most famous in this era was that of Samuel de Champlain who, in 1603, was a member of a successful two-ship expedition to Tadoussac on the north shore of the St. Lawrence River. This expedition returned to France with a rich load of furs. On his second voyage the following year Champlain was accompanied by a mining engineer, Master Simon, who was to investigate mineral occurrences and to develop them. Discoveries of silver were made at St. Mary's Bay, and native copper at Cap d'Or in what is now Nova Scotia. Although these discoveries were of little significance, perhaps they provided some incentive to Champlain who went on to establish a permanent French settlement at Port Royal in 1605 and at Quebec in 1608.

One of the surprising things about this era is the fact that the coal deposits of Cape Breton went virtually unnoticed. From the discovery of that island to 1672, numerous voyages were made to the coast by intelligent, enterprising navigators, but there is no mention in their narratives of the existence of the coal seams which were plainly visible in the cliffs of almost every bay or headland. The first printed notice of the existence of coal in Cape Breton is met with in the *Description géographique et historique des Costes de l'Amérique Septentrionale*, by Nicholas Denys, published in Paris in 1672. Denys was appointed governor of all the eastern part of Acadia, including Cape Breton, in the year 1637. In 1654 he obtained a concession from Louis XIV of the whole island, with full powers to search for and work mines of gold, silver, copper and other minerals, paying to the king one tenth of the profit. In his preface, he says: "There are mines of coal through the whole extent of my concession, near the sea-coast, of a quality equal to the Scotch, which I have proved at various times on the spot, and also in France, where I brought them for trial". Denys also noted the existence of gypsum or "plaister". Being almost exclusively engaged in the fisheries and fur trade, Denys, during his long residence in Cape Breton, made no attempt to work the coal seams, probably for want of a market.

The first attempt at systematic coal mining was made upon the 10-foot seam on the north side of Cow Bay in 1720, when it was found necessary to obtain a supply of fuel for the officers, soldiers, mechanics, traders, and labourers who went out to lay the foundations of the celebrated fortress of Louisbourg. Cargoes of coal were, about this time, exported from Cow Bay to Boston. Although direct trade between French and English colonists was forbidden by the treaty of neutrality, the New England traders carried on an active clandestine trade with Louisbourg, receiving French products in exchange for bricks, lumber and provisions.

Elsewhere in New France gradual progress was being made in other mineral fields. The first examination of bog iron deposits at Baie St. Paul and in the St. Maurice Valley, Quebec, was made by Sieur de la Portardière who came out from France in 1667. A rich lead-silver deposit was discovered on the eastern shore of Lake Timiskaming in 1686. However, this deposit did not attract the French, presumably because of its inaccessibility and the consequent difficulties of mining, smelting and transportation. La Compagnie des Forges commenced the first smelting of bog iron deposits in the St. Maurice district of Quebec in 1737. The St. Maurice forges operated there until the 1880's. Iron smelting operations were also carried on in Bagot, Nicolet and Drummond counties. All were of considerable importance in the early history of Quebec.

After New France was ceded to England in 1763, English interests carried on the mining activities started by the French. Large quantities of coal were mined in Cape Breton to supply the needs of the militia at Halifax, while iron was still smelted at St. Maurice and elsewhere for use in the manufacture of pots, stoves, ploughs, and other necessities.

As settlement spread westward, iron deposits were found in Upper Canada early in the 19th century and an iron furnace was erected in 1800 in Leeds County. A number of industrial mineral deposits were worked, one of the earliest being gypsum near Paris in 1822. Industrial mineral materials were mined at a number of localities throughout the colonies for local construction purposes and, although there is no record of quantities used, various types of building stone as well as clays, sand and gravel began to have widespread use. The first portland cement made in Canada was produced in 1840 at Hull, Quebec.

At first, extensive operation remained in the hands of a few large companies, mainly the General Mining Company which was given a monopoly of mining rights in Nova Scotia in 1836, and the Montreal Mining Company, which was established in 1845. Prospectors, however, continued to roam throughout the trackless regions of central Canada in search of mineral wealth. By the middle of the 19th century, there had been sufficient mineral industrial activity to promise a major resource. The time had come to begin its development on a large scale.

## Mid-19th Century Period

A considerable impetus was given to mining and prospecting by the formation of the Geological Survey of Canada in 1842. The reports of geologists and surveyors employed by the Survey were invaluable in creating interest in regions that had been wholly unexplored by private mining companies. Keen interest was shown in the area lying about Lake Superior inasmuch as copper had been known from early times to exist there. In 1847 a substantial deposit of the mineral was discovered at Bruce Mines on the North Channel of Lake Huron and mining operations were begun the following year. It was necessary to ship the ore to England for refining which made profitable development of the mines very difficult; yet, in 1863, over 4,500 tons of copper ore were exported. Some idea of the extent of operations may be gained from the fact that when the Canada West Mining Company bought the property in 1864 they were employing nearly 400 men.

Meanwhile, the development of industry, the building of railways, and the expansion of steam navigation resulted in a great increase in the demand for coal. In 1856 the monopoly of the General Mining Company in Nova Scotia was broken and increased exports from Cape Breton mines, especially to American seaports, took place. Shipments were facilitated by the construction of the Intercolonial Railway which enabled coal from Cape Breton to pass through Halifax. However, markets were difficult to maintain since Nova Scotian coal was required to compete with English coal which was brought in as ship's ballast.

A different situation existed on the Pacific coast where coal had been discovered on Vancouver Island in 1835. The California "gold rush" of 1849 brought thousands of settlers into the western regions. This, in turn, led to a demand for coal from Vancouver Island and the rapid development of the mines there. In 1852 the export trade in coal from the west coast began with a shipment of 2,000 tons from Nanaimo to San Francisco. By 1869 over 200 men were employed in coal mining in the Nanaimo district. Although steady progress had been made in the development of the coal mines on the Pacific coast, Nova Scotia continued to be the main coal-producing region. In the decade 1861-70 over 5,000,000 tons were produced in that province.

In Newfoundland, which was not destined to join Canada until 1949, a lead-mining venture at La Manche commenced in 1857 and continued for about 16 years. The profits from this mine are said to have helped finance the laying of the first transatlantic cables at a point near La Manche in 1858 and 1866. Other developments in Newfoundland during this era included the opening up of a copper mine at Tilt Cove in 1864, followed by discovery of the Betts Cove copper deposit in 1874, and Little Bay copper mine in 1878. Subsequently, several other notable copper deposits were developed and, in the decade 1871-80, Newfoundland attained 14th place among the copper-producing countries of the world.

**Gold and Oil Discoveries**—Meanwhile, in Canada, two major developments had occurred that were to exercise a profound effect upon the mineral industry. In 1852 gold was discovered on Queen Charlotte Islands followed by several other finds on the mainland and then the famous discovery of placer gold in the lower reaches of the Fraser River in 1858. In the same year the first oil well on the North American continent was dug at Oil Springs, Ontario.

Development of the western Ontario oil fields was rapid. Surface wells were dug at Oil Springs while drilling operations resulted in the first flowing well being struck in Black Creek Valley in 1862. By the autumn of that year, 35 flowing wells and 200 wells using pumps were in production. The rise of Petrolia after 1865 led to the construction of a number of small refineries in that area, while the completion of pipelines and large storage tanks about 1867 further hastened the concentration of the oil refining industry in that district. By 1870 production of oil reached about 5,000 barrels a week, much of which was exported to Europe. Incidental to oil exploration, salt was discovered at Goderich in 1865, and the salt industry based on a very large resource has continued to grow over the years. As is often the case in mineral discoveries, the importance of this salt resource was not realized for many years.

The discovery of gold along the Fraser and Thompson Rivers in 1858, and in the Cariboo district in 1861, led to the first of the "gold rushes" which characterized the industry during the last half of the 19th century. Thousands of miners were attracted from the gold fields of California where the boom had subsided. Placer gold production reached its peak in the mid-1860's and then the miners began to move northward to the upper waters of the North Saskatchewan, the Peace, the Liard and the Yukon Rivers.

# The 1860's and 1870's

**Mineral Diversification Begins**—Discovery of gold in Eastern Canada followed closely in the wake of British Columbia's first gold rush. In 1861 quartz gold was found in the Eastern Townships of Quebec near Sherbrooke, while placer gold was discovered near Tangier Harbour in Nova Scotia about the same time. A small gold rush took place in the Chaudière River region of Quebec in 1864, and during the next 20 years nearly $3,000,000 worth of gold was to come from the mines of that district. A gold discovery at Madoc, Ontario, in 1866 was the first gold discovery in the Canadian Shield.

Agricultural expansion, railroad construction, more widespread settlement and growing industrialism were closely linked with the increasing pace of mining development which followed Confederation. Within a decade, several important projects got under way. Silver veins on Silver Islet in Lake Superior were discovered in 1868 and worked profitably to produce $3,000,000 worth of silver from 1870 to 1884 when the mine was flooded in a storm. The mineral apatite, a source of phosphate, was mined as early as 1870 from a number of localities in Ontario and Quebec to meet the European demand for fertilizer following the exhaustion of the Chilean and Peruvian guano beds. Apatite mining led to production of the closely associated mica deposits. As population grew, stone quarries were opened up, and brick and tile plants based on the extensive clay deposits near Toronto were established. Asbestos was discovered in 1877 during the building of the Quebec Central Railway and production commenced the following year. Within 10 years, production in the Eastern Townships exceeded 4,500 tons of fibre annually. The asbestos industry has remained one of the most important in the mineral economy. Copper has been known in the Eastern Townships since 1841 and a number of mines have been operated intermittently since that time. The Eustis mine was the most important producer; it started production shortly after its discovery in 1865 and was closed in 1939.

Iron mining came to be of major importance in the years following Confederation as the industry expanded. Much of the ore from eastern Ontario mines was exported to the United States, although some iron was smelted in 1868 on the Gatineau River near Hull. In 1870-71 over 14,000 tons of ore were shipped to the United States through the port of Kingston, from mines in Frontenac, Leeds and Lanark counties.

# The 1880's

**Sudbury and Other Mineral Developments**—In 1883, while blasting operations were in progress for the Canadian Pacific Railway, a huge deposit of nickel-copper ore—at first mistaken for copper—was unearthed in the Sudbury region of Ontario. With this discovery, the foundation of Canada's nickel industry was laid, although the importance of the find was not fully recognized at the time since world consumption of the metal was small. Metallurgical research leading to the development in 1892 of processes for separating copper and nickel made possible the opening up of the Sudbury deposits on a large scale. In 1902 most Sudbury workings were merged into the newly-formed International Nickel Company. In subsequent years the Sudbury district was to become one of the most valuable mining regions of the world.

The nickel and other mineral developments of the day led the *Statistical Record* of

1886 to state: "Minerals of almost every kind are known to exist in Canada and their development in the future will constitute one of the chief sources of wealth for the country". While the future importance of Canada's mineral wealth was thus accurately forecast, the lack of capital in the 1880's was a great handicap to mining development. Speculative enterprises had thrown suspicion on genuine mining projects and Canadian investors were anxious to place their savings in some other type of enterprise. As a result, early development of the Sudbury nickel deposits was based largely on United States capital.

In 1887, the first year of complete mineral production statistics, coal was the most important mineral product in Canada, with the output of the mines being 2,429,000 tons. Practically the entire output came from the provinces of Nova Scotia and British Columbia, although large deposits in the then "North-West Territories" (province of Alberta) had been uncovered and extensive development was being planned. Next in importance was gold. In British Columbia, according to the *Statistical Record*, there was "scarcely a stream of any importance in which the colour of gold cannot be found, and paying mines exist in localities extending through ten degrees of latitude". In Nova Scotia, 58 mines were producing gold while considerable value was attached to discoveries of that mineral in the provinces of Ontario and Quebec.

Iron ore had been discovered in many areas, but lack of capital and enterprise held up any extensive development. Even in Nova Scotia, where the ore was of relatively high grade, production was limited largely to the Acadia Mines at Londonderry. In Ontario, iron mining was confined to the mines of the Kingston and Pembroke Mining Company and some mines in the district of Hastings. In Quebec, operations were mainly carried on in the vicinity of Drummondville and Trois-Rivières. The

This was the main street of Porcupine, Ontario, in 1910 with the mine recorder's office on the right. Since the first claim was staked in 1909, the area has developed into a great gold mining centre.

The first discovery of rock salt in the Maritimes and the first in Canada to be discovered at a depth sufficiently shallow for economic mining was found at Malagash, Nova Scotia. Work was undertaken in 1917.

Construction of the Canadian Pacific Railway across the Sudbury Basin in northern Ontario revealed a rich deposit of nickel-copper ore in 1883. The district produces about half of the world's output of nickel. This is the site of the Murray Mine in 1892.

MINES AND MINERALS

total production of iron in Canada in 1887 was slightly over 76,000 tons.

Copper constituted one of the main mineral resources of the country, the ores being found over wide areas in Ontario, Quebec, Nova Scotia, British Columbia, and New Brunswick. Again, the lack of capital held up development, and since there was no smelting works in Canada, all of the copper ore was exported for treatment elsewhere. Production in 1887 was limited to mines near Sherbrooke, Quebec; Sudbury, Ontario; and the Goodfellow Mine in Albert County, New Brunswick, the quantity being almost 3,300,000 pounds of copper. In that year plans were under consideration for the construction of a smelting works at Sudbury in Ontario near the site of which were "perhaps the largest deposits of copper ore in the world". By 1890 two furnaces were in operation.

Ontario continued to be the only producer of petroleum, although oil occurrences had been found in Quebec, Nova Scotia, New Brunswick, and in the North-West Territories. The output of crude oil was nearly 25,000,000 gallons in 1887. The occurrence of oil in the North-West Territories was creating considerable interest about this time. The *Statistical Record* for 1888 stated that "the most extensive petroleum field in America, if not in the world, is believed to exist in the Athabasca and Mackenzie vallies in the North-West". In that year a committee of the Senate was appointed to inquire into the resources of that area, and the report contained the observation that "it is probable that this great petroleum field will assume an enormous value in the near future, and will rank among the chief assets comprised in the Crown domain of the Dominion". The Athabasca oil sands, one of the world's great oil resources, are only now being brought into production, some 80 years after this pronouncement.

Phosphates for use as fertilizer were increasing in importance throughout this period. In 1887 two main sources of supply were being worked: Ottawa County, Quebec, and the area north of Kingston, Ontario. Production from these two mines totalled nearly 25,000 tons, the bulk of which was exported to the United States, Great Britain, and Germany. Asbestos was the only mineral being worked in the Eastern Townships of Quebec. Production had steadily increased and by 1887 more than 4,000 tons were being shipped annually from Canadian mines.

In 1888 the Ontario Provincial Government appointed a Commission to inquire into the mineral resources of that province. The Commission Report, published in 1890, gave the following description in part of the mineral wealth of the province:

> "In the Sudbury district copper and nickel mines are being worked on a large scale. In the township of Denison, gold-bearing quartz and extensive deposits of copper and nickel are found. Along the north shore of Lake Huron, gold and silver-bearing mines, iron, copper and galena, and many varieties of marble have been discovered. North of the Height of Land and extending toward James Bay, prospectors report a promising mineral region. North of Lake Superior localities of gold, silver, copper, iron, galena, plumbago, and zinc ores have been taken out. West of Port Arthur is a silver district which, judging from explorations already made, promises to be an argentiferous region of great richness. Beyond this region to the northwest are found veins of gold-bearing quartz and extensive ranges of magnetic iron ore, believed to be a continuation of the Vermillion iron range of northern Minnesota. In the region adjacent to the Lake of the Woods gold-bearing veins of great promise have been discovered".

Subsequent events were to prove that this Commission was justified in its optimistic appraisal of mining developments and of Ontario's mineral resource potential.

# The 1890's

**Mining Boom in British Columbia and the Yukon**—Completion of the Canadian Pacific Railway to the west coast in 1885 and of the Dewdney Trail from Hope to Nelson was followed by an influx of prospectors from Montana and Idaho into the country between the United States boundary and the railway line in British Columbia, with some silver-lead discoveries being made in the 1880's. In 1889 the initial copper-gold discovery of the famous Rossland mining camp was made and this was followed in the 1890's by a number of gold, silver and base metal discoveries in a region stretching from Cranbrook westward to the Similkameen country. At this time, too, the Bridge River gold district was discovered but it was a number of years before production commenced.

The Slocan mining area between the Slocan and Kootenay Lakes became noted for its silver-lead-zinc production. To the east, near Cranbrook, the world-famous Sullivan mine commenced shipments in 1895, although large-scale production had to await the development of the flotation process for the treatment of its complex silver-lead-zinc ore. The copper discoveries of southern British Columbia led to a copper mining boom centered on the new town of Rossland and soon a smelter was built at Trail. The CPR bought the Trail smelter which became a market for the coal and coke transported over the railway's new Crow's Nest Pass line. As a number of copper mines came into production in the southern part of the province, smelting of copper ores at Rossland commenced in 1896 and at Grand Forks and Greenwood in 1900. As a result of this mineral activity in the southern part of British Columbia, the province by 1900 was accounting for one quarter of Canada's total mineral production.

By far the most important of these mining developments in British Columbia was the opening up of the Sullivan mine but it was many years after the 1890's before a scale of production appropriate to this huge mineral deposit was achieved. The first shipments were made in 1895 but the mine was closed down in 1907 because of financial difficulties with a smelter. In 1909 The Consolidated Mining and Smelting Company took an option on the property, began shipments of ore to Trail, and commenced metallurgical studies to separate the complex ore. The first real break-through came with the successful use of the flotation process in 1920. A large concentrator was built at Kimberley in 1923 and shipments of lead and zinc concentrates to the Trail smelter were commenced. Thus it took over 30 years to bring the mine into large-scale production. The accomplishments of this early period, and of subsequent years, that resulted in the huge metallurgical complex now at Trail are illustrative of the progress that has been made in chemistry and metallurgy in support of Canada's mineral resource development.

The 1890's probably achieved their greatest mining fame with the discovery of placer gold in the Klondike, Yukon Territory, in 1896, followed by one of the world's most spectacular gold rushes. From 1898 to 1905 more than $111,000,000 worth of gold was mined from the gravels of creeks near Dawson but the boom quickly faded and by 1907 the small high-grade placers were depleted. Like the Fraser River and Cariboo gold rushes of the 1850's and 1860's, this great epic of early mining history was of greatest importance in that it attracted attention to the mineral possibilities of British Columbia and the north, and as the mines of the southern part of the province were established settlement soon followed, and gradually spread north.

## The Turn of the Century

**The Ontario Boom and World War I**—Mention has already been made of the nickel-copper deposits discovered in 1883 in the Sudbury district. This discovery stimulated mining activity in the region of the Canadian Shield although it was not until after 1900 that the main discoveries were made. Shortly after the turn of the century, the Ontario Government undertook to run a railway line north to the clay belt surrounding Hudson Bay. In the construction of this railway line, blasting operations at Long Lake (later Cobalt Lake) in 1903 uncovered a fabulously rich deposit of silver ore. This was the beginning of the famous Cobalt silver camp which through the years has made an important contribution to the mineral wealth of Canada.

The discovery of silver at Cobalt provided a strong incentive to mining corporations and prospectors, and the rocky areas of the Canadian Shield of northern Ontario began to reveal their great mining possibilities. Gold was discovered at Larder Lake in 1906. In 1907 silver was discovered near Gowganda, northwest of Cobalt. In the following year gold was discovered at Porcupine, and in 1909 ground was staked leading to the development of Ontario's three great gold mines—Dome, Hollinger and McIntyre. Porcupine subsequently became Canada's leading gold producing area. Kirkland Lake, which became Canada's second largest gold mining camp, got under way in 1911. Fortunately these gold discoveries had been preceded by the development of the cyanide process for treating gold ores. This metallurgical advance, plus the technical improvements in mining and ore concentrating, prepared the way for the fast growth of a great gold industry. With these gold and silver discoveries, Ontario quickly assumed mineral production leadership and by 1910 was accounting for two fifths of Canada's mineral output. It has remained the leading producer since that time.

At the turn of the century, Canada's steel industry, as we know it today, came into being. American capital and skill, the availability of iron ore from the Mesabi range south of Lake Superior, and the accessibility of coal from areas south of Lake Erie and Lake Ontario led to the strengthening of steel enterprises in the 1890's, and the establishment of the Algoma Steel Company in 1901 and the Steel Company of Canada in 1910.

In the west, much interest was being taken in oil development in Alberta. Drilling operations had resulted in the discovery of large supplies of natural gas and some oil even before the turn of the century. However, it was not until 1913 that the first major discovery was made with the recovery of gas from the Turner Valley field near Calgary. Oil was discovered in this large field in 1924.

The period of World War I was a time of important new base-metal mining and smelting developments. In 1914 the Anyox copper smelter in northern British Columbia was blown in to process the production from copper deposits in the Portland Canal district. In the same year the Flin Flon copper-zinc deposit on the Saskatchewan-Manitoba border was discovered. In 1916 the Falconbridge nickel deposits in the Sudbury district were found and an important metallurgical milestone was reached

The proven resources of Alberta include huge volumes of crude oil, natural gas, sulphur and coal. This Fort Saskatchewan refinery, which receives its nickel concentrate from Lynn Lake, Manitoba, uses natural gas as an energy source and in chemical processes.

with the initial production of electrolytic refined copper and zinc at the Trail, B.C. smelter. In 1918 refined nickel production began at Port Colborne, Ontario, and preparations commenced to bring the rich Premier mine near Stewart in northern British Columbia into production as a silver-gold producer. In the late 1940's this famous mine also became a lead-zinc producer.

The time involved in overcoming major financial, metallurgical and transportation problems in Canadian mining is again well illustrated in the history of the Flin Flon development. Although discovered in 1914, the complex ore presented major metallurgical problems. It was not until 1927 that the necessary financing could be arranged and the processing problems solved. Arrangements were also successfully completed by that time for a railway to this northern location, for a large electric power development and for a copper smelter and zinc refinery. The first blister copper and refined zinc were produced in 1930.

## The 1920's

**Noranda, Flin Flon and Red Lake**—Mining activities proceeded at a rapid pace in the northwestern region of Quebec in the 1920's. In 1921 the discovery of gold and copper in the Rouyn district, at the site which was later to become the Noranda mine, eventually brought thousands of people into the area. The Noranda mine and smelter went into production in 1927 and, since that time, the Noranda-Rouyn area has been one of Canada's most important sources of copper and gold. Noranda was to be the forerunner of many other mines in northwestern Quebec.

Prospecting activity also spread westward and, in 1925, gold was discovered in the Red Lake district of northwestern Ontario. In Manitoba and Saskatchewan, at the time that efforts were being made to get the Flin Flon deposit into production, a copper deposit 75 miles north of The Pas was also under development. As the Sherritt Gordon mine, it reached the production stage in 1931 but had to be closed till 1937 because of low copper prices. The 1920's was an active period in northern British Columbia and the Yukon, with the Premier gold mine near Stewart and the silver-lead properties in the Mayo district in full production.

In 1929 Canada stood first in the world in the production of asbestos and nickel, third in gold and silver, fourth in copper, fifth in lead, sixth in zinc, eleventh in pig iron and twelfth in coal. During that year Canada produced 90 per cent of the world's nickel, 70 per cent of the world's asbestos, one third of the world's cobalt, 10 per cent of the gold, 9 per cent of the silver, 8 per cent of the lead, and 6 per cent of the zinc and of the copper. More than 2,300 mining firms, employing over 95,000 men, were engaged in the industry and the value of minerals shipped from the mines reached the substantial total of $311,000,000.

The period of expansion in the 1920's saw the first use of the aeroplane in mineral exploration. The use of planes in western Quebec and the Red Lake area of Ontario introduced airborne exploration and prospecting ventures throughout Northern Canada. Following the reduced exploration activity of the World War I period, the 1920's marked the start of a new era in mineral exploration in Canada. Accompanying the major mineral property developments of this period was the equally important development of the flotation method for the extraction of metals from sulphide ores. As a result, the Sullivan mine in British Columbia went into large-scale continuous production in 1923. The Britannia mine on Howe Sound, the Sherritt Gordon mine in northern Manitoba, and other properties, were able to go into production as a result of this development.

## The 1930's

**Depression Followed by New Mining Growth**—The economic depression, which embraced Canada as well as the rest of the world in the early 1930's, led to a substantial decrease in the volume and value of mineral production in Canada. Only the gold mining industry remained active. Although the prices of base metals were at all-time lows, the gold price was increased in 1934 to $35 (U.S.) an ounce and many gold mines were brought into production in Ontario, Quebec, British Columbia and Manitoba. By 1936, general economic conditions were again beginning to show improvement, metal prices began to increase and prospecting again went forward with increasing impetus in both old and new areas.

In Nova Scotia emphasis was, of course, on coal production, with Cape Breton, Cumberland and Pictou coal fields the main producers. Gold mining was being revived, while shipments of silver, lead, and zinc were resumed from the Sterling mine. Other mineral products included gypsum, salt, quartz, and silica brick.

In New Brunswick mineral production was confined almost entirely to non-metallic minerals, the most important being coal, which was being mined in the Minto-Chipman district. Petroleum and natural gas were also being produced in some quantity, while gypsum was mined in the Hillsborough area. Important deposits of clay, stone, and structural materials were also being worked, and small intermittent shipments were made from manganese deposits.

In Quebec, metal mining was largely centred in the northwest section of the province, the products being mainly copper, gold and silver. In 1936 one of the most spectacular deposits of native gold ever encountered in Canadian mining was unearthed in the O'Brien mine. At Noranda, copper-gold-silver ore was being continuously smelted, while steady operations were being maintained in the Eastern Townships at the Eustis copper and pyrites mine. Silver-lead-zinc ores were produced at the Tetreault mine, Montaubain-Les-Mines. Conditions in the non-metal mining sector had improved throughout the province. Asbestos production was up, as well as the value of clay products. Cement production had also increased.

In Ontario, prospecting had extended over a wide area and gold had been discovered at Red Lake, Woman Lake, and Central Patricia. New gold production records were being set. Considerable progress was made in the mining and refining of nickel and copper through the introduction of improved plants and equipment and the construction of copper refineries at Copper Cliff and Montreal East. A new non-metallic mine product, nepheline syenite, a mineral employed chiefly in the glass and pottery trades, was produced commercially in Ontario for the first time. The leading position Ontario had taken in Canadian mining soon after the turn of the century was maintained with the province accounting for approximately half the dollar value of total mineral output in the 1930's.

In Manitoba, the principal interest was in mining operations at Flin Flon, where silver, copper, gold, zinc, and other metals were being produced in quantity. A new producer, the Gunnar gold mine, began operations in 1936 in the God's Lake area. Other minerals produced included feldspar, gypsum, quartz, salt, clay products, and cement.

In Saskatchewan, considerable interest was displayed in the mid-1930's in the new gold field at Lake Athabasca, although the province's production was largely confined to that part of the Flin Flon mine lying west of the Saskatchewan-Manitoba boundary. The province produced important quantities of lignite coal. Other minerals produced included quartz, clay products, and sodium sulphate which was used extensively in the pulp and paper and nickel smelting industries.

Coal continued to be the most important mineral product in Alberta. At the same time, the province was achieving prominence as a producer of petroleum and natural gas, principally from the Turner Valley field. The first big crude oil well in the field was brought into production in 1936. Other minerals produced in Alberta included brick, cement, and lime, while a small quantity of alluvial gold was being recovered annually from Alberta streams.

By the mid-1930's, British Columbia had become one of the world's greatest sources of lead and zinc. Mining operations of silver, copper, and gold were also being expanded. Production of coal and other minerals including gypsum, magnesium sulphate and sulphur were showing substantial increases.

At Great Bear Lake in the Northwest Territories, Eldorado Gold Mines found high-grade silver ore with pitchblende. In 1932, ores mined in this region were shipped to Port Hope, Ontario, for the recovery of silver, radium and uranium products. Alluvial gold mining was being carried on extensively by well-established companies in the Yukon, while a great deal of prospecting was in progress in the Northwest Territories leading to the opening of the Yellowknife gold mining camp.

Thus, the decade of the 1930's was a period of considerable upsurge in mineral activity following the 1929 crash. Notwithstanding the progress made, including a doubling in the value of production, it was not nearly as great as that of the 1950's or the 1960's.

## The 1940's

**World War II and Mineral Resources**—The outbreak of World War II placed a heavy strain upon the Canadian mining industry. The lack of manpower as a result of enlistment in the Armed Forces, together with a shortage of mining machinery and equipment, caused many difficulties for the industry. In spite of these handicaps, Canada supplied 80 to 85 per cent of the Allied nickel requirements, making up for the deficiencies from the loss of refining facilities in Norway and France. From the mines of the Eastern Townships of Quebec came most of the asbestos used by the Allied countries. Sufficient aluminum was produced from imported bauxite ore to supply close to 40 per cent of the Allied needs for that metal.

Production of nickel, copper, lead, and zinc during the six war years had a value of more than a billion dollars. In terms of output, Canada's mines produced 810,000 tons of nickel, 1,800,000 tons of copper, 1,600,000 tons of zinc, and 1,300,000 tons of lead. Over three quarters of this was exported. Smelting and refining facilities at Sudbury, Noranda, Montreal East, Trail, and Flin Flon were expanded to meet these large wartime requirements.

In the early part of the War, every effort was made to encourage the production of gold. In 1940, Canada gained second place among nations of the world as a gold producer with 12.6 per cent of the total world production. Subsequently, a much greater need developed for other metals, and miners working in gold mines were diverted to other branches of the industry. It is noteworthy, however, that Canada produced approximately $953,000,000 worth of gold during the war years, 1940-45.

## 1947 to 1967

**The Greatest Period of Mineral Industry Expansion**—The post-World War II growth of the Canadian mineral industry has been the greatest in the history of the industry. Rapid advances have been made in all phases of mineral exploration, notable among these being the adaption of the airborne magnetometer, as developed during the War, to mineral exploration. Coupled with advances in technology was the launching of an unprecedented mineral exploration and development program by all sectors of the industry from coast to coast and into the Arctic regions.

CANADA, 1867-1967

Canada is the world's leading supplier of nickel, accounting for about 60 per cent of the world production. This is the Thompson mine in Manitoba, with part of the townsite in the foreground.

This activity has resulted in vast expansion in each of the sectors of the mineral industry—metals, industrial minerals and fuels. In the metals sector, development of Quebec-Labrador iron ore resources commenced in the early 1950's, resulting in the establishment of the new mining towns of Schefferville, Labrador City and Gagnon, new railway and dock facilities, and many service industries. The iron ore industries of Ontario and British Columbia also progressed so that Canada's total iron ore production, which had been nil in the period 1924-39, rose from 1,100,000 tons in 1945 to 16,300,000 tons in 1955 and 39,800,000 tons in 1965. The uranium industry grew spectacularly in the 1950's with the opening up of the Elliot Lake and Lake Athabasca areas, reaching a peak of some 16,000 tons of uranium oxide in 1959 then swiftly declining but ready for new markets expected to develop in the 1970's. Non-ferrous mineral production facilities have been greatly expanded in postwar years by such mines as the Thompson nickel mine in northern Manitoba; the Chibougamau area copper mines, 200 miles north of Noranda, Quebec; the copper-zinc mines of the Lake Manitouwadge area, 40 miles north of Lake Superior; the Craigmont and Bethlehem copper mines of central British Columbia; the Gaspe copper mine at Murdochville; the Bathurst area lead-zinc mines in New Brunswick; reactivated copper mines in the Notre Dame Bay region of Newfoundland; the newly-discovered zinc-silver-copper deposit near Timmins, Ontario, slated for production in 1967; and the large Pine Point lead-zinc deposits in the south shore of Great Slave Lake, known since 1899 and brought into production in 1965. The important molybdenum discoveries in British Columbia and a tungsten operation in the Northwest Territories have further diversified the mineral industry. Among the metals, only gold production has failed to expand; a gradual contraction of the industry has taken place under a condition of rising costs and fixed price, and a large Federal Government subsidy has been necessary to prevent its rapid decline.

In the industrial minerals sector, expansion in the asbestos industry included the opening up of the Cassiar asbestos mine in northern British Columbia, and Advocate asbestos mine at Baie Verte, Newfoundland. Potash and elemental sulphur operations have been established on a large scale in Western Canada and the country is now capable of producing 15 per cent of the world's requirements of potash and sulphur. The mining of rock salt was commenced at Pugwash, Nova Scotia.

In the fuels sector, coal has lost out to other fuels, and the coal industry has become uneconomic in the Maritimes and dependent on government subsidies. The oil and gas industry in Western Canada has gone ahead rapidly since the Leduc, Alberta, oil discovery of 1947. Many oil and gas fields have since been discovered, and oil and gas pipeline transportation facilities have been built across Canada and to export points on the Canada-United States border. Crude oil production increased from 7,000,000 barrels in 1946 to 294,000,000 barrels in 1965. Natural gas production increased from 48,000,000,000 to well over 1,400,000,000,000 cubic feet a year in the same period.

The extent of mineral industry expansion in the period 1947-1967 is indicated by the production value increase as compared with output growth in previous periods. In 1886, the value of Canada's mineral production was $10,000,000; in 1910 it was $107,000,000; in 1945, $500,000,000; in 1950, $1,045,000,000; and in 1967, an estimated $4,200,000,000. A major resource industry, with a long history of development, the mineral industry is now firmly established in all regions of Canada and is a leading component of the Canadian economy.

## The Mid-1960's

Mineral industry progress since Confederation may be appraised by examination of some highlights of the production and mineral activity record for the year 1965. Some 60 mineral commodities valued at $3,700,000,000 were produced with the leaders being crude petroleum, $718,000,000; nickel, $435,000,000; iron ore, $419,000,000; copper, $388,000,000 and zinc, $251,000,000.

Canada in the mid-1960's led the western world in the production of nickel, zinc, platinum-group metals, asbestos and nepheline syenite; was in second place in the production of uranium, cobalt, titanium (ilmenite), gold, cadmium, molybdenum, sulphur and gypsum; and stood high in the production of many other minerals including iron ore, copper, lead, silver, and magnesium. Canada was among the first five producing countries of the world for 19 minerals and only the United States and the U.S.S.R. had a greater diversified mineral production.

World nickel consumption, excluding Communist–bloc countries, in 1965 was estimated at 660,000,000 pounds with Canada accounting for 522,000,000 pounds. In Canada, the expansion under way in the mid-1960's was certain to ensure Canada's leading position for many years. The increase in nickel production from mines in Ontario and Manitoba, particularly the former, was being accompanied by an increase in copper production. Canada's production at 517,000 tons in 1965 was an all-time high. Seven new copper mines commenced production and five others were being prepared for early operation. Of particular significance was the intensive exploration being conducted on the large low-grade, porphyry-type deposits in British Columbia and the development of a large zinc-copper-silver deposit in the Porcupine district of northern Ontario.

Iron ore shipments totalled 39,800,000 net tons. Three new mining projects, two of which involved pelletizing plants, were completed in 1965. Pellet capacity at the end of 1965 was over 15,000,000 tons a year. By 1970, Canada's iron ore productive capacity was expected to be about 55,000,000 tons a year. Exports to the United States were approximately 80 per cent of production with the balance being about equally divided between domestic and offshore markets.

Canada's output of zinc rose to a record 832,000 tons in 1965, approximately 147,000 tons more than in 1964. World production was an estimated 4,000,000 tons. Lead mine production in Canada, which for years averaged about 200,000 tons a year, increased in 1965 to nearly 287,000 tons. The start of regular lead-zinc ore shipments from extensive high-grade deposits on the south shore of Great Slave Lake in the Northwest Territories, the completion of the first full year's operation of a large mining enterprise in the Bathurst area of New Brunswick, and higher output of zinc and lead by established producers all contributed to the greatly increased shipments of lead and zinc. Canada's mine production of silver was nearly 33,000,000 troy ounces, only slightly less than the record high of 34,000,000 ounces in 1960. The increase in recent years has been due largely to higher output of base metals from which about 80 per cent of Canada's production of silver is obtained as a by-product.

Canada became one of the world's top-ranking producers of molybdenum in 1965 with production exceeding 9,000,000 pounds compared with the previous all-time high of 1,225,000 pounds in 1964. The shortage of molybdenum that developed early in 1963 sparked an intensive and widespread search for molybdenum deposits in British Columbia, Quebec and Ontario. This search was successful, particularly in British Columbia, and at the end of 1965 eight mines were in production. Capacity by 1968 was expected to be at least 23,000,000 pounds a year.

Production of gold and uranium ($U_3O_8$) continued to decline. Several gold mines that had been large producers were approaching the end of their ore reserves. The few gold mines scheduled to commence production will not offset the losses incurred through some mine closures and reduced production from other mines. Shipments of uranium oxide were 8,615,000 pounds in 1965 compared with 14,570,307 pounds the previous year. Deliveries to the United States under a purchase contract at prices averaging about $10.50 a pound were completed in 1964; deliveries to Britain at a base price of $5.03 a pound commenced in 1964 and will continue until 1970; deliveries to the Canadian uranium stockpiling program commenced on July 1,1965, at $4.80 a pound of $U_3O_8$. A resurgence in uranium demand for the generation of electricity in nuclear power plants is expected in the early 1970's. Canada has the world's largest developed reserves and there remains much ground in known areas that is favourable for the extension of these reserves.

At Fort McMurray on the Athabasca River, Alberta, 270 miles northeast of Edmonton, is a $230,000,000 tar sands separation plant, which will extract oil from 100,000 tons of sand per day. By late 1967 the plant is expected to employ some 700 persons and to produce daily 45,000 barrels of synthetic crude, 2,900 tons of coke and 300 tons of elemental sulphur.

Production gains and announced mine development plans for potash in Saskatchewan highlighted progress in the industrial minerals sector in the mid-1960's. Three companies contributed to the 1965 output of 1,400,000 tons and development programs were under way to add six new producers by 1968 and to raise production to at least 6,000,000 tons by 1970 when Canada will be the world's leading producer. Potash reserves in Western Canada, particularly those in Saskatchewan, are the largest and highest grade in the world and by far the most economically attractive of all known deposits. Recovery of elemental sulphur from the processing of natural gas also made marked gains in a period of world shortage. By the mid-1960's, Canada's production of sulphur from natural gas, smelter gas and pyrites was second only to that of the United States in world output. Following five successive years of production records, asbestos output declined slightly in 1965, but development plans for production announced for the Clinton Creek deposit in Yukon Territory and for the Asbestos Hill deposit in far northern Ungava in Quebec were indicative of continuing resource expansion. Canada and the Soviet Union are the world leaders in asbestos output. Production of most other non-metallic minerals was at record or near-record levels in the mid-1960's.

The fuels group of crude petroleum, natural gas, natural gas liquids, and coal continued to set production records, the aggregate value in 1965 being $1,080,000,000.

Crude petroleum accounted for two thirds of this value. Coal production has been fairly stable in the 1960's following a decline from 19,000,000 to 10,000,000 tons in the 1950's; the 1965 output value accounted for less than 7 per cent of the fuel sector total compared with 55 per cent in 1950. The fivefold increase in fuel production value in the period 1950-65 was due entirely to the dynamic growth of the oil and natural gas industry in Western Canada.

## Minerals and Transportation

Throughout the history of the Canadian mineral industry the factor of transportation has been a major determinant in the nature and rate of mineral development. With an area of 3,850,000 square miles—almost seven per cent of the land surface of the globe—and with only about one half of one per cent of the world's population, Canada has had many transportation problems to overcome. Many of these have been associated directly or indirectly with the mineral industry.

Several examples in reference to the history of the mineral industry may be cited to illustrate the relationship of mineral industry activity to the nation's over-all development as determined by transportation. In the mid-19th century, the needs of Nova Scotia for markets for its coal, and the limits which inadequate transportation facilities placed on the industrial expansion of Quebec and Ontario, were important factors in bringing about Confederation so that railway construction could be financed. The Intercolonial Railway and the Canadian Pacific Railway provided the necessary connecting transportation links for the development of an iron and steel industry and associated manufacturing industries in a country much too completely dependent on staples such as fur, timber, and agriculture. The gold mining industry in British Columbia of the 1850's and 1860's had attracted large numbers of people to the province and completion of a transcontinental railway link became a condition of British Columbia's entry into Confederation. Thus there were forces related to mineral industry growth in Eastern, Central and Western Canada which led to the key transportation developments associated with Confederation.

The gold rush to the Yukon after 1896 brought about an influx of people into Western Canada and thereby hastened the building of two more transcontinental railways north of the Canadian Pacific Railway line. As in the case of the CPR, mineral developments were part of the circumstances which led to the building of these railways. At the same time there were many mineral discoveries, in effect accidents of geography, that were made during or shortly after these early railway construction projects. Discoveries related to the construction of the CPR included the Sudbury nickel deposits at the time of construction and the finding of many base-metal deposits in southern British Columbia within ten years of the completion of the railway through to the Pacific coast. The construction of the Timiskaming and Northern Ontario Railway northward in Ontario to the clay belt led to the discovery of the rich silver deposits of the Cobalt area in 1903, and this initial discovery in turn triggered an extensive search in northern Ontario and northwestern Quebec leading to the Porcupine, Kirkland Lake, Noranda and other discoveries.

Important transportation developments have also come about as a result of the need to service mineral projects after discovery and development. There are many important examples of this type of transportation relationship with the mineral industry, particularly in the period since 1945 when the majority of new railway construction was undertaken primarily to service the mineral industry. Leading examples are the Quebec-Labrador railway built in the early 1950's to the new iron ore development at Schefferville and the subsequent lateral extension to Labrador City; the railway in northern Quebec to the Chibougamau copper mining area built in the late 1950's; a line into the Thompson nickel mine and smelter site in northern Manitoba in 1960 from the railway running to Churchill, and the extension of the line northward from The Pas to Lynn Lake in 1951; and the line north from the Peace River area to Pine Point on Great Slave Lake in 1965 to serve the new lead-zinc development there. These and other northern railway systems built to serve mineral developments are having a far-reaching effect in extending the boundaries of settlement and economic activity northward.

Transportation in the north by air, which commenced with the airborne mineral exploration programs of the 1920's, is also strongly linked with mineral resource development. The Yellowknife gold mining area on the north shore of Great Slave Lake opened up in the 1940's and the uranium mining area on the north shore of Lake Athabasca which went into production in the mid-1950's were almost completely dependent on air service for moving freight into the mines and transporting products of the mines to market. The air transport system in the North is being continually extended to meet many needs but owes its existence in the main to mineral development.

Pipeline transportation has become a major component of Canadian transportation during the past 20 years. Capital investment in oil and gas pipelines now amounts to almost $2,000,000,000, and oil and gas pipelines systems serve all provinces except the Atlantic area. The tonnage of crude oil received by pipeline for delivery from oil fields to refineries is now almost as great as the total mineral tonnage of freight car loadings. Unlike rail, road and air transport systems, pipelines are used only for the transportation of oil and gas although other commodities may eventually be moved by pipelines. However, the financing and building of pipelines have posed the same types of national and economic problems as other transportation systems, as was evident in the 'pipeline debate' in the House of Commons in 1957.

The establishment of a vast road transportation network system in Canada has involved the mineral industry in the supply of huge quantities of road-building materials. In addition, many pioneer roads that later became main transportation arteries were built in the first instance to serve a mineral operation.

Reference to any form of transportation reveals a significant relationship between mineral and transportation developments during the past 100 years. Some mineral developments were the sole or principal event leading to the establishment of a transportation system; still others have been the mainstay of a system which, in turn, provides invaluable service to other sectors of the economy. Because of the remote location of many mineral resources in a country of vast area, the availability of economic transportation has been a principal determinant in the timing of most new mineral enterprises. In this respect, the mineral industry is characteristic of the economy at large: growth of the economy has depended greatly on transportation. Through its impact on transportation growth, the mineral industry in the past 100 years has had a much greater effect on the country's economic development than would be evident from mineral production statistics alone.

The Department of Energy, Mines and Resources studies the bacterial decomposition of sulphide-bearing uranium ore to determine the factors involved in order to increase the efficiency of bacterial leaching at uranium mines.

The prosperity of Alberta is symbolized by drilling rigs, working night and day. Since the famous 1947 Leduc discovery in Alberta, Canadian oil production has reached a million barrels a day.

## Growth Indicators of Mineral Economy

The mineral industry of the 1960's has an importance for all sectors of the Canadian economy. Never in its four centuries of history has the industry made such an impact on the economy of the country as a whole as it does today. The industry's relative importance in the national economy has been growing in the 100 years since Confederation but the period of the past 20 years has been outstanding. A measure of the industry's present importance can therefore be obtained by examining certain growth indicators for this recent period. These indicators are an expression of the actual growth of the mineral industry itself. They also reflect the direct or indirect impact its growth has had on the economy as a whole through other resource industries, the secondary industries which make up the manufacturing and construction groups, and the various tertiary activities in the economy such as transportation, communications, trade, finance and other service industries.

In 1945 the value of mineral production was $500,000,000, equivalent to 4.2 per cent of the country's gross national product. In 1966 mineral output approached the $4,000,000,000 level, eight times the value in current dollars of the production of 1945, and 7.2 per cent of the gross national product of 1966. In terms of indexes of physical volume of production, the mineral industry also led the economy with the 1966 index of mineral production at the primary stage being 380 (est.), on a 1949 base of 100, while the index for Canadian industry as a whole was 275 (est.). These indicators show the mineral industry to be a pace setter in economic development, a role that has been maintained since Confederation.

Net value added in the production process is a measure of the contribution of various sectors of the economy to economic growth and, therefore, an indicator of the relative importance of each industry. The net value added in mining production and in mineral

MINES AND MINERALS                                                               163 processing constituted about 10 per cent of the net value of production of all primary and secondary industries in the late 1940's; by the mid-1960's it was almost 15 per cent. Mining and mineral processing net value (est.) as a percentage of resource industry net value, increased from 30 to 40 per cent in the same period. This indicator thus points to a growing importance of mineral industry activity in the Canadian economy, particularly in relation to the other resource industries. The mineral industry is also a leader in cyclical upturns in the economy. In three production cycles in the 1950's and 1960's, the per cent gain in mining output was exceeded only by the gain made by electric power and gas utilities, and the growth in that industry grouping was based in considerable part on mineral industry expansion.

These indicators evaluate production progress; others concerned with the facilities for production and with marketing also are useful in measuring the importance of the mineral industry in the economy. In the mid-1960's capital investment in mining, smelting and refining, petroleum refining, non-metallic mineral processing, and primary iron and steel making was accounting for close to ten per cent of all capital investment in Canada. This percentage considerably understates the mineral industry role as it does not account for capital investment in facilities which the transportation, communication, utilities and other service industries establish as the result of the development of mineral industry enterprises. Such enterprises as the Quebec-Labrador iron ore mining operations, the northern Manitoba nickel mining and smelting activities, the Pine Point lead-zinc mine development, the oil and gas producing activities of Western Canada and Saskatchewan's potash mining have all brought into being a host of service industries and greatly multiplied the employment opportunities beyond those provided directly in mining and oil production operations.

The mineral industry's importance is also evident from export trade data. Mineral exports in crude and fabricated forms account for almost one third of Canada's merchandise exports in the 1960's compared with less than one fifth in the late 1940's. The minerals group thus leads the other groups of commodity exports: farm and fish products, forest products, and manufactured goods. It gained the position of leadership from the forest products group in the late 1950's. The mineral industry's leading role in the country's export trade is apparent from a listing of the country's 20 leading exports, one half of which are minerals and mineral products. Thus, in addition to its prominent position in the domestic economy, the mineral industry is an important factor in Canada's balance of trade position and in maintaining Canada's position as fifth largest exporter in world trade.

In celebrating Canada's Centennial of Confederation, Canadians can find satisfaction in the fact that the country's economic growth is in considerable part based on vast mineral resources which are being efficiently developed. They can also take pride in the fact that only the United States and the Soviet Union have greater mineral industries and, in terms of per capita mineral output, Canada leads in diversified mineral production. Canada has had an important role in world mineral supply in the past 100 years; it will have a much more important role in the future in helping to meet the mineral requirements associated with the rising living standards of a fast-growing world population. The Canadian mineral industry's prominence in the world mineral industry today gives perspective to the importance it has achieved in the Canadian economy during the period 1867-1967.

(R. B. Toombs and K. J. Stewart)

The Flin Flon mining-smelting complex on the Manitoba-Saskatchewan border. Discovered in 1915, the mine only commenced production in 1930 owing to remoteness and metallurgical problems. It marked the start of the base-metal industry in the western Canadian Shield.

## Mineral Production of Canada by Provinces and Territories, 1900-1965

| Area | 1900 | | 1910 | | 1920 | | 1930 | |
|---|---|---|---|---|---|---|---|---|
| | $'000 | % | $'000 | % | $'000 | % | $'000 | % |
| Newfoundland . . . . . | a. | | a. | | a. | | a. | |
| Prince Edward Island | — | — | — | — | — | — | — | — |
| Nova Scotia . . . . . . . | 9,299 | 14.4 | 14,196 | 13.3 | 34,130 | 14.9 | 27,019 | 9.7 |
| New Brunswick . . . . . | 439 | 0.7 | 582 | 0.5 | 2,492 | 1.1 | 2,384 | 0.8 |
| Quebec . . . . . . . . . . . | 3,292 | 5.1 | 8,270 | 7.7 | 28,886 | 12.7 | 41,215 | 14.7 |
| Ontario . . . . . . . . . . | 11,258 | 17.5 | 43,538 | 40.8 | 81,716 | 35.9 | 113,531 | 40.6 |
| Manitoba . . . . . . . . } | | | 1,500 | 1.4 | 4,224 | 1.9 | 5,453 | 1.9 |
| Saskatchewan . . . . . . } | 23,452 | 36.4 | 498 | 0.5 | 1,837 | 0.8 | 2,369 | 0.8 |
| Alberta . . . . . . . . . . } | | | 8,996 | 8.4 | 33,586 | 14.7 | 30,428 | 10.9 |
| British Columbia . . . . | 16,681 | 25.9 | 24,479 | 22.9 | 39,412 | 17.3 | 54,953 | 19.7 |
| Yukon . . . . . . . . . . . . | — | — | 4,765 | 4.5 | 1,577 | 0.7 | 2,522 | 0.9 |
| Northwest Territories | — | — | — | — | — | — | — | — |
| **Canada Total . . . .** | **64,421** | **100.0** | **106,824** | **100.0** | **227,860** | **100.0** | **279,874** | **100.0** |

| Area | 1940 | | 1950 | | 1960 | | 1965 ᵖ | |
|---|---|---|---|---|---|---|---|---|
| Newfoundland . . . . . | a. | | 25,824 | 2.5 | 86,637 | 3.5 | 220,483 | 5.9 |
| Prince Edward Island | — | | — | | 1,173 | 0.05 | 985 | 0.03 |
| Nova Scotia . . . . . . . | 33,319 | 6.3 | 59,482 | 5.7 | 65,453 | 2.6 | 66,634 | 1.8 |
| New Brunswick . . . . . | 3,436 | 0.6 | 12,757 | 1.2 | 17,073 | 0.7 | 83,944 | 2.2 |
| Quebec . . . . . . . . . . . | 86,314 | 16.3 | 220,176 | 21.1 | 446,203 | 17.9 | 704,704 | 18.8 |
| Ontario . . . . . . . . . . | 261,483 | 49.3 | 366,802 | 35.0 | 983,104 | 39.4 | 986,183 | 26.3 |
| Manitoba . . . . . . . . | 17,829 | 3.4 | 32,691 | 3.1 | 58,703 | 2.4 | 182,011 | 4.9 |
| Saskatchewan . . . . . . | 11,506 | 2.2 | 35,984 | 3.4 | 212,093 | 8.5 | 327,326 | 8.7 |
| Alberta . . . . . . . . . . | 35,092 | 6.6 | 135,759 | 13.0 | 395,344 | 15.9 | 799,345 | 21.4 |
| British Columbia . . . . | 74,134 | 14.0 | 138,888 | 13.3 | 186,262 | 7.5 | 286,162 | 7.6 |
| Yukon . . . . . . . . . . . . | 4,118 | 0.8 | 8,051 | 0.8 | 13,330 | 0.5 | 13,341 | 0.4 |
| Northwest Territories | 2,594 | 0.5 | 9,036 | 0.9 | 27,135 | 1.1 | 72,863 | 1.9 |
| **Canada Total . . . .** | **529,825** | **100.0** | **1,045,450** | **100.0** | **2,492,510** | **100.0** | **3,743,981** | **100.0** |

Note: Provincial distribution of total Canadian mineral production is not possible from available data prior to 1899.
a. Newfoundland mineral production is not shown prior to Confederation in 1949. — nil.

## Mineral Production of Canada—Ten Leading Minerals, 1890-1965

| Item | 1890 $'000 | % | Item | 1900 $'000 | % |
|---|---|---|---|---|---|
| Coal | 5,676 | 34.0 | Gold | 27,908 | 43.3 |
| Clay products | 2,041 | 12.2 | Coal | 13,742 | 21.3 |
| Asbestos | 1,260 | 7.6 | Nickel | 3,327 | 5.1 |
| Stone | 1,162 | 7.0 | Clay products | 3,195 | 5.0 |
| Gold | 1,150 | 6.9 | Copper | 3,066 | 4.8 |
| Copper | 947 | 5.7 | Lead | 2,761 | 4.3 |
| Nickel | 933 | 5.6 | Silver | 2,740 | 4.3 |
| Petroleum | 903 | 5.4 | Stone | 1,657 | 2.6 |
| Silver | 419 | 2.5 | Petroleum | 1,151 | 1.8 |
| Lime | 412 | 2.5 | Lime | 800 | 1.2 |
| **Total** | **14,903** | **89.4** | **Total** | **60,347** | **93.7** |
| Other minerals | 1,860 | 10.6 | Other minerals | 4,074 | 6.3 |
| **Total all minerals** | **16,763** | **100.0** | **Total all minerals** | **64,421** | **100.0** |

| | 1910 $'000 | % | | 1920 $'000 | % |
|---|---|---|---|---|---|
| Coal | 30,910 | 28.9 | Coal | 82,497 | 36.2 |
| Silver | 17,580 | 16.5 | Nickel | 24,534 | 10.8 |
| Nickel | 11,181 | 10.5 | Gold | 15,814 | 6.9 |
| Gold | 10,206 | 9.6 | Cement | 14,798 | 6.5 |
| Clay products | 7,630 | 7.1 | Asbestos | 14,792 | 6.5 |
| Copper | 7,094 | 6.6 | Copper | 14,244 | 6.3 |
| Cement | 6,412 | 6.0 | Silver | 13,450 | 5.9 |
| Stone | 3,669 | 3.4 | Clay products | 10,665 | 4.6 |
| Asbestos | 2,574 | 2.4 | Stone | 7,594 | 3.3 |
| Natural gas | 1,346 | 1.3 | Natural gas | 4,233 | 1.9 |
| **Total** | **98,602** | **92.3** | **Total** | **202,621** | **88.9** |
| Other minerals | 8,222 | 7.7 | Other minerals | 25,239 | 11.1 |
| **Total all minerals** | **106,824** | **100.0** | **Total all minerals** | **227,860** | **100.0** |

| | 1930 $'000 | % | | 1940 $'000 | % |
|---|---|---|---|---|---|
| Coal | 52,850 | 18.9 | Gold | 204,479 | 38.6 |
| Gold | 43,454 | 15.5 | Copper | 65,773 | 12.4 |
| Copper | 37,948 | 13.6 | Nickel | 59,823 | 11.3 |
| Nickel | 24,455 | 8.7 | Coal | 54,676 | 10.3 |
| Cement | 17,713 | 6.3 | Lead | 15,864 | 3.0 |
| Lead | 13,103 | 4.7 | Asbestos | 15,620 | 2.9 |
| Clay products | 10,594 | 3.8 | Zinc | 14,464 | 2.7 |
| Natural gas | 10,290 | 3.7 | Natural gas | 13,000 | 2.5 |
| Silver | 10,089 | 3.6 | Cement | 11,775 | 2.2 |
| Zinc | 9,635 | 3.4 | Sand and gravel | 11,759 | 2.2 |
| **Total** | **230,131** | **82.2** | **Total** | **467,233** | **88.1** |
| Other minerals | 49,743 | 17.8 | Other minerals | 62,592 | 11.9 |
| **Total all minerals** | **279,874** | **100.0** | **Total all minerals** | **529,825** | **100.0** |

| Item | 1950 $'000 | % | | 1960 $'000 | % |
|---|---|---|---|---|---|
| Gold | 168,989 | 16.2 | Nickel | 295,640 | 11.9 |
| Copper | 123,211 | 11.8 | Uranium | 269,938 | 10.8 |
| Nickel | 112,105 | 10.7 | Copper | 264,847 | 10.6 |
| Coal | 110,140 | 10.5 | Iron ore | 175,083 | 7.0 |

| | $'000 | % | | $'000 | % |
|---|---|---|---|---|---|
| Zinc | 98,040 | 9.4 | Gold | 157,152 | 6.3 |
| Petroleum | 84,619 | 8.1 | Asbestos | 121,400 | 4.9 |
| Asbestos | 65,855 | 6.3 | Sand and gravel | 111,164 | 4.5 |
| Lead | 47,886 | 4.6 | Zinc | 108,635 | 4.4 |
| Sand and gravel | 36,435 | 3.5 | Cement | 93,261 | 3.7 |
| Cement | 35,894 | 3.4 | Stone | 60,641 | 2.4 |
| **Total** | **883,174** | **84.5** | **Total** | **1,657,761** | **66.5** |
| Other minerals | 162,276 | 15.5 | Other minerals | 834,749 | 33.5 |
| **Total all minerals** | **1,045,450** | **100.0** | **Total all minerals** | **2,492,510** | **100.0** |

| | 1965p | |
|---|---|---|
| | $'000 | % |
| Petroleum | 718,248 | 19.2 |
| Nickel | 435,332 | 11.6 |
| Iron ore | 419,393 | 11.2 |
| Copper | 388,005 | 10.4 |
| Zinc | 251,234 | 6.7 |
| Natural gas | 197,297 | 5.3 |
| Cement | 144,582 | 3.9 |
| Asbestos | 139,805 | 3.7 |
| Gold | 136,143 | 3.6 |
| Sand and gravel | 129,330 | 3.4 |
| **Total** | **2,959,369** | **79.0** |
| Other minerals | 784,612 | 21.0 |
| **Total all minerals** | **3,743,981** | **100.0** |

Open-pit operations at the Gagnon mine in northern Quebec, Canada's second largest producer of high-grade iron ore concentrates.

Labrador City on the remote Labrador-Quebec border serves the giant iron ore mining projects of Wabush Mines and Carol Lake.

MINES AND MINERALS

The Shipshaw hydro development on the Saguenay River, Quebec, was started in 1926 but because of the depression was not completed until 1943. The power is chiefly used for the nearby smelter at Arvida.

# Energy Resources

The most prominent characteristic of an industrial society is the utilization of energy in the production of goods and services. It was the abundance of this energy which was a major factor enabling a sparse population, scattered across millions of square miles, to develop into a modern industrial nation. Canada's place in the discovery, development, and utilization of energy resources has been one of leadership from which the entire world has greatly benefited.

In 1672 coal was first discovered in Canada in Cape Breton, Nova Scotia. Although oil seeps were first noted in Canada in 1793, it was not until 1858 that the first oil well in North America was completed at Oil Springs, Ontario. Natural gas was discovered in the 1870's. One of the first electric power stations was put into commercial service in 1882 and electric energy was derived from nuclear power in 1962.

Without this abundance of energy, Canada could never have developed a national identity, for it would not have been possible to build and sustain the vast transportation and communication networks, to produce the heat for homes in a country of long and cold winters, and to have the power for its machines on farms, in mines, and in factories.

## Three Distinct Periods

Energy has developed in three distinct periods and has had a profound impact on the national economy. The original economy of Canada was based upon animal and water power, with coal and wood resources mainly used for heating. From the 1800's to the 1930's, coal was the dominant source of energy. By the mid 1930's this coal-based energy economy had been supplanted by petroleum which, with electric power, allowed Canada to industrialize and to develop its huge lumber, mining and smelting resources. These developments culminated in the 1950's with the development of large new oil fields in Western Canada, of hydro-electric sites on the St. Lawrence Seaway, at Kitimat and other parts of Canada. By the 1960's, however, Canada had entered its third stage, that of an energy economy characterized not by predominance of one energy form but by a multiplicity of energy types.

Petroleum still accounts for some 70 per cent of energy consumed followed by coal and gas with 15 per cent each. Transformation of energy to electric power produced from coal, oil, gas and nuclear power is rapidly assuming a new importance. The future holds promise of dramatic new developments in all these energy fields. The indicated rate of increase of energy use will require such new sources as nuclear power, will involve the rich and virtually-untapped tar sands of Alberta, and the large but remote hydro projects now in the planning stages. These new sources will allow Canada to continue its rapid growth rate and to maintain its high standard of living.

**Electric Power**—Although the electric power industry began in the early 1880's, its foundations were established late in the 19th century when major generating stations were built at Montmorency Falls, Quebec and at Niagara Falls, Ontario. These two stations were the forerunners of Canada's modern electric industry. The history of the electric power industry in Canada has always been closely related to the economic advancement of the country. Such power developments as the Sir Adam Beck generating station at Niagara Falls, Ontario; Beauharnois and Saguenay River, Quebec; and Kitimat, British Columbia, are world-famous feats of engineering triumph. Major hydro-electric projects now being developed include the Peace River and Columbia River projects, the Manicouagan and Outardes installations, and the current Churchill Falls project.

Although electric energy in Canada has been closely related to the development of its hydro resources, important technological developments are creating a new look in the industry. Thermal fossil fuel stations, first developed for remote areas and as standby stations, have now become an important part of central electric power systems. In 1930, eight per cent of all capacity was in fossil fuel stations, accounting for about two per cent of all generation, while in 1965 their capacity was 25 per cent and accounted for 18 per cent of the generation.

Electric power is now used in virtually all of the nation's 4,853,000 households; in 1920 only some 40 per cent of the households were served by electricity, and 60 per cent in 1940. In 1940 households used only 8 per cent of all electricity; in 1960 they had increased their consumption to 20 per cent while average consumption per householder increased to 6,360 kwh. from 1,445 kwh. The most important users of Canada's electric energy are the pulp and paper, smelting, refinery and chemical industries which, in 1964, consumed about 45 per cent of all electric energy produced.

The Canadian electrical industry is truly a giant. It employs over 40,000 people, has revenues of $800,000,000 a year and has investments in fixed assets of almost $10,000,000,000.

**Petroleum and Natural Gas**—The petroleum and natural gas industry in 1965 was one of the largest contributors to the economy. In 1965 it spent some $1,000,000,000 exploring, developing and producing crude petroleum and natural gas. In 1964 it operated almost 20,000 oil and gas wells, 45,000 miles of oil and gas pipelines, 93 gas processing plants, and 40 refineries. It also produced $847,000,000 worth of crude oil, natural gas and by-products, and sold 365,000,000 barrels of refined products.

This is a much changed industry from 1867 when crude petroleum was known only from surface seeps and pits, in several small fields in southwestern Ontario. In these early days Canadian technology was exported abroad with Canadian drillers prominent in the Middle East, Venezuela and the United States. It was not until 1936 that significant discoveries of oil gave Canada major status as a producer. In that year Turner Valley was discovered. There followed 11 years of relatively little success; then, in 1947, Leduc oilfield was discovered, signalling an oil boom that has never stopped. Redwater 1948, Pembina 1953, Swan Hills 1957, Rainbow 1964, are all major discoveries that have resulted in nearly 200 fields, containing over 7,000,000,000 barrels of oil reserves and 43,000,000,000,000 cubic feet of natural gas.

Natural gas discovered in the 1870's was never more than of local importance until 1957-58 when the "big inch" pipelines of Westcoast Transmission Company Limited and Trans Canada Pipelines Limited were built from the interior plains of Alberta and British Columbia, to the southwest coast of British Columbia, and to the Great Lakes and St. Lawrence Valley of Eastern Canada.

Waste of energy resources has always been of major concern, particularly in the petroleum and natural gas industry. As far back as the 1860's oil was produced in such excess quantities that it flowed down the Black Creek "to a depth of four or more feet". In the 1930's the excess gas produced from Turner Valley was flared; the light could be used to read a newspaper in Calgary, 20 miles away. In this one field 1,000,000,000,000 cubic feet of gas was wasted, an amount sufficient to handle all of Canada's present day needs for almost two years. The industry and public, however, no longer permit this type of waste and several important measures, such as regulated production, secondary recovery, etc., administered by the Provincial Governments, minimized .the imprudent use of this valuable resource.

In 1961, Canada produced 221,000,000 barrels of oil of which 65,000,000 were exported. In addition, Canada imported 133,000,000 barrels of crude oil and 30,000,000 barrels of products. Sales from this oil supply amounted to 103,000,000 barrels of gasoline, 112,000,000 barrels of middle distillate fuel oils, 51,000,000 barrels of heavy fuel oils and 32,000,000 barrels of lubricating oils and grease, asphalt and other products.

Ontario Hydro's thermal-electric Lakeview Generating Station, under construction on the western outskirts of Toronto, has four 300,000 kw. generators installed at the $268,000,000 plant. By 1968 when eight units are completed, this station will have a capacity of 2,400,000 kw.

The Nuclear Power Demonstration Unit on the Ottawa River at Rolphton went into operation in 1962 and is a prototype for much larger stations. Canada is prominent in the science devoted to the productive uses of atomic energy.

New Brunswick's $113,000,000 Mactaquac hydro-electric development, now under construction, is situated 14 miles west of Fredericton, the provincial capital.

ENERGY RESOURCES

Natural gas produced in 1961 amounted to 657,000,000 Mcf. of which 169,000,000 Mcf. were exported, 120,000,000 Mcf. were sold to residential consumers, 195,000,000 Mcf. to industrial consumers, and 56,000,000 Mcf. to commercial consumers. The remaining amounts were used, or lost, in the fields, processing plants or pipelines.

By 1965 the total production of natural gas had increased to 1,440,000,000 Mcf. worth some $192,000,000. In addition, natural gas processing plants through which much of Canada's natural gas is processed to remove natural gas liquids and sulphur, produced an additional $92,000,000 in condensate propane and butane.

**Coal**—Coal, although currently not as important as petroleum, has been, during the last 100 years, the outstanding source of energy for Canadians. Its production increased from 631,000 tons in 1867 to 15,012,000 tons in 1913. The stimulus came primarily from extensive railway building and the accompanying development of the iron and steel industry. Not only was there an ever-increasing supply of coal needed for transportation, but the expanding output of steel also required an increasing input of coal. However, the most significant occurrence was its replacement of fuel wood for space heating. Coal production during this period was primarily confined to the east, with the greatest expansion in output taking place in Nova Scotia. This was the coal industry's most prosperous period.

During war years the industry suffered a decline in output, due to high transportation costs, and a shortage of labour. However, the War proved only a temporary influence. One must look at the underlying factors which prevented the coal industry from expanding at its previous pace during the period from 1920-1939. These factors included the slowdown of railway expansion which, in turn, forced the iron and steel industry to look for new markets. The market for coal in these two areas thus remained stable. Another factor contributing to the levelling off of demand was the increased efficiency in the use of coal as a source of energy. Technological advances made it

A gas pipeline snakes its way through the Rocky Mountains to British Columbia. By 1958 Canadian natural gas was used in all provinces west of Quebec. By the end of 1964 there was a total of more than 41,800 miles of gas pipelines in Canada.

Canada is fortunate to have ocean communication with inland ports. The St. Lawrence River and Great Lakes provide a marine highway. Here, traffic is shown on Lake Superior, largest of the Great Lakes.

possible to provide the same output of goods with a much smaller input of coal. Although this increased the competitive position of coal, it also meant that a smaller quantity was required to do the same job. Due to the slow increase in productivity of coal per man-hour, the coal industry has experienced ever-increasing difficulty in competing with petroleum, gas and hydro-electric power, particularly in Quebec, Ontario and Western Canada. The government, therefore, implemented subsidy payments to assist coal in this difficult transitional period.

Subsequent to World War II, coal production declined absolutely because of the conversion of railroads to oil, and the replacement of coal in domestic heating. During this period, industrial requirements for coal and coke remained remarkably stable. As an example, industrial consumption of coal and coke increased only 3,000,000 tons from 12,400,000 tons to 15,500,000 in the 14 years from 1949 to 1963. In contrast to this, consumption of coal and coke by railroads declined from 12,400,000 tons in 1948 to virtually zero in 1963; domestic consumption fell from 14,200,000 tons in 1949 to 3,800,000 tons during the same period. Regionally, the major declines in output of coal occurred in Alberta and British Columbia, due to the importance of

A Manitoba company which commenced operations in 1950 is now in the forefront of manufacturers producing nuclear detection equipment in North America. Its principal market is the United States.

railroad and domestic consumption in these areas. Although there was some decline in output in Nova Scotia, increased subvention payments kept this to a minimum, thus enabling Nova Scotia to make inroads into the Ontario and Quebec markets.

### Selected Energy Statistics, 1867-1961

| Item | Units of measurement | 1867 | 1891 | 1911 | 1921 | 1931 | 1941 | 1951 | 1961 |
|---|---|---|---|---|---|---|---|---|---|
| Coal production.... | '000 tons | 631 | 3,578 | 11,323 | 15,057 | 12,243 | 18,226 | 18,587 | 10,398 |
| | '000 $ | 1,057 | 7,019 | 26,468 | 72,452 | 41,207 | 58,060 | 109,039 | 70,053 |
| Oil production..... | '000 bbl. | 190 | 755 | 291 | 188 | 1,542 | 10,134 | 47,616 | 220,848 |
| | '000 $ | ... | 1,010 | 357 | 641 | 4,212 | 14,415 | 116,655 | 487,560 |
| Gas production.... | '000 Mcf. | — | 1,800* | 11,644 | 14,077 | 25,875 | 43,495 | 79,461 | 655,738 |
| | '000 $ | — | 150 | 1,918 | 4,594 | 9,026 | 12,665 | 7,159 | 68,422 |
| Electric power production...... | '000 Kwh. | — | ... | ... | 6,000(E) | 17,620 | 36,479 | 61,447 | 113,714 |
| | '000 $ | — | ... | ... | ... | ... | 186,000 | 374,000 | 868,000 |
| Oil and gas pipelines........ | '000 miles | — | — | ... | ... | ... | ... | 7 | 45 |
| Electric power transmission lines..... | '000 miles | — | — | ... | ... | 20 | ... | ... | 169 |
| Electric power stations capacity. | '000 kw. | ... | 20 | ... | 1,526 | ... | 6,021 | 10,781 | 24,091 |

* Estimated.

Canada is the second largest per capita user of energy in the world. Its demand for commodities to provide this consumption has increased 8.2 times since the turn of the century as dependence on energy has increased and changed the nation's entire social and economic structure. The future indicates an ever-increasing demand for energy and will require great expansion of the nation's financial, physical, and human resources to meet these needs. The first hundred years of Canada's history have been devoted to the development and extraction of energy resources. The next hundred will be spent in developing new technologies, promoting efficiency, minimizing waste and pollution—thus wisely using the country's heritage.

(R. L. Borden)

# Manufacturing

The growth of manufacturing is often considered to be a measure of economic development, but it can be a misleading indicator. For a country with a relatively small or widely-dispersed population and a rich endowment of natural resources, manufacturing is likely to be of comparatively less importance than for more densely-populated countries. A wealth of natural resources ensures a greater role for resource industries and technological advances which favour larger units of production tend to concentrate manufacturing activities in densely-populated areas. The kinds of manufacturing which were in the past likely to develop in a country such as Canada were those that could be economically located near the sources of the raw materials they use, and those that could be economically carried on in small units located in the communities or regions they serve. The validity of this generalization is dependent, of course, on the extent to which Canadian secondary industries have been cut off from world markets by barriers to trade. Thus, it is not surprising that in Canada, even in recent years, manufacturing output per capita has been only about two thirds that in the United States.

What is important is not the size of Canadian manufacturing but whether it reflects an effective use of Canadian resources and skills and whether, therefore, the potential for efficient manufacturing activity is being realized. The aim of this chapter is to describe the pace of development of manufacturing since Confederation, to indicate the relative importance of the various industrial groups, and to refer to the problems which have affected the capacity of the industry to realize its potential.

Long-term comparisons are made more difficult by the absence of estimates for Gross National Product (and other aggregates) in which one can have full confidence. Following are some of the available comparisons* which seem most relevant:

### Related Indicators of Growth, 1870 and 1956

| Item | Unit | 1870 | 1956 |
|------|------|------|------|
| Population.......................................... | '000,000 | 3.6 | 16.1 |
| Urban........,.................................. | " | 0.7 | 9.3 |
| Ontario and Quebec.............................. | " | 2.8 | 10.0 |
| Exports (value)................................... | $ '000,000 | 59.0 | 4,789.7 |
| Index of Volume.............................. | | 100 | 2100 |
| Primary Products (value)........................... | $ '000,000 | 206.0 | 3,729.0 |
| Manufacturing (value added)....................... | " | 93.9 | 9,612.2 |
| Index of Volume.............................. | | 100 | 4400 |
| Manufacturing (gross value)........................ | $ '000,000 | 216.4 | 21,969.3 (1957) |
| Index of Volume.............................. | | 100 | 3600 |
| Primary Manufacturing............................ | $ '000,000 | 80.4 | 6,572.2 |
| Index of Volume................................ | | 100 | 2900 |
| Secondary Manufacturing......................... | $ '000,000 | 136.0 | 15,397.0 |
| Index of Volume................................. | | 100 | 4000 |

These figures indicate the growth and some of the features of the Canadian economy which are most closely related to manufacturing activity. The year 1956 is used as a

---

*Based on *Historical Statistics of Canada* (Toronto: Macmillan Co. of Canada, Ltd., 1965) except for gross value figures, which are from Gordon W. Bertram, "Historical Statistics on Growth and Structure in Manufacturing in Canada, 1870-1957", in *Conferences on Statistics, 1962-1963 Papers* (University of Toronto Press, 1964). Volume indexes for manufacturing are calculated by deflating value figures with import price indexes.

A carpet plant in Truro, Nova Scotia, which sells its products all across Canada is a United States-British joint venture. A combination of federal, provincial and municipal incentives is attracting a growing number of companies to locate in the province.

terminal year because it is the latest year of peak prosperity for which all the aggregates required for comparison are available. For reasons which will be clarified later in the text, the choice of 1956 understates the growth of manufacturing in Canada's first century because of substantial changes which have since occurred in this sector. The population has grown to almost five times its size at the time of Confederation; and the urban population in 1956 was over 60 per cent of the total, whereas it was only 20 per cent a century ago. Since manufacturing is by far the most important goods-producing activity in the cities, this is an impressive indication of a dramatic shift in the nature of the Canadian economy.

## Concentrated Market

In view of the importance of a concentrated market for the development of manufacturing, the population of Quebec and Ontario is singled out in the above statistics. While these provinces now contain a smaller proportion of the total Canadian population, primarily as a result of the addition of three new provinces since 1900 (Alberta, Saskatchewan and Newfoundland), the growth of the central region from 2,800,000 in 1870 to over 10,000,000 in 1956 (and more than 12,000,000 in 1966) is probably one of the most important facts affecting the present new status and prospects of Canadian manufacturing, since it represents a substantial home market base for a wide range of manufacturing activity. It is no longer reasonable to view Canada's manufacturing activity as beyond the fringe of the great central production and marketing heartland of the North American continent. It is the northern section of the world's richest economic region, divided from the rest by an easily crossed river system and by the consequences of an international boundary.

The implications of the economic growth of North America for Canadian manufacturing are reflected in the remaining figures. While Canadian exports have increased by 21 times, and the value of production of primary industries by about the same proportion, manufacturing activity measured by the "value added" in the manufacturing process has grown by 100 times, and probably nearly 44 times in volume. Parallel development is indicated in the gross value of manufacturing. However, it is notable that the growth of the primary group of manufacturing industries, which is most closely based on Canada's resource endowment, has been outstripped by the growth of secondary manufacturing.

(The primary manufacturing industries include those which are engaged in processing natural products—part of the food and beverages and wood products groups [sawmills but not furniture factories], most of the paper and non-ferrous metals products groups and a small part of non-metallic minerals and chemicals products.) In volume terms it has been estimated that the primary group has multiplied 29 times in size while secondary manufacturing was by the mid-1950's about 40 times larger than in 1870.

A United States company established in 1964 in Nova Scotia a plant for the production of cans. After only a year of operations demand from local and central Canadian companies was so great that the plant had to be doubled in size.

## Manufactures, by Rank of Industrial Groups

| 1870 | | Value Added by Manufacture | 1956 | | Value Added by Manufacture |
|---|---|---|---|---|---|
| Rank | Industrial Group | | Rank | Industrial Group | |
| | | $ '000,000 | | | $ '000,000 |
| 1 | Wood products | 19.5 | 1 | Iron and steel products | 1,444.5 |
| 2 | Iron and steel products | 15.7 | 2 | Food and beverages | 1,299.5 |
| 3 | Food and beverages | 15.2 | 3 | Paper products | 908.7 |
| 4 | Leather products | 13.1 | 4 | Transportation equipment | 906.2 |
| 5 | Clothing | 6.4 | 5 | Non-ferrous metals | 672.1 |
| 6 | Transportation equipment | 6.4 | 6 | Wood products | 646.2 |
| 7 | Textile products (ex. clothing) | 3.4 | 7 | Electrical apparatus | 577.4 |
| 8 | Non-metallic mineral products | 3.0 | 8 | Chemicals and allied products | 556.2 |
| 9 | Printing and publishing | 2.6 | 9 | Petroleum and coal products | 489.3 |
| 10 | Petroleum and coal products | 2.1 | 10 | Printing and publishing | 459.2 |
| 11 | Chemicals and allied products | 2.0 | 11 | Clothing | 438.4 |
| 12 | Tobacco and products | 1.2 | 12 | Textile products (ex. clothing) | 323.8 |
| 13 | Paper products | .9 | 13 | Non-metallic mineral products | 322.8 |
| 14 | Non-ferrous metals | .9 | 14 | Rubber and products | 198.6 |
| 15 | Electrical apparatus | .5 | 15 | Leather products | 112.9 |
| 16 | Rubber and products | .1 | 16 | Tobacco and products | 88.3 |
| 17 | Miscellaneous | 1.3 | 17 | Miscellaneous | 188.0 |

## Structural Changes

The structure of manufacturing has been completely transformed in Canada's first century. In 1870 Canada's greatest processing industry was that producing lumber,

The first passenger car plant in Quebec began operations in 1965 at Ste-Thérèse Ouest. When capacity production is reached, employment at the plant is expected to total 2,500.

which comprises four fifths of the wood products group and accounts for over one sixth of the net value of all manufacturing. When the food and beverage-processing industries and leather industries are added, the three industries, based almost entirely on Canadian farm, fishery and forest products, accounted for nearly half of Canadian manufacturing. Now these three account for less than 20 per cent. One of the greatest changes has been in the forest-based industries. Paper is now more important than wood and accounts for nearly 10 per cent of the net value of manufacturing. Mine-based industries (excluding iron) have grown from about six per cent to about 15 per cent of the total. The most spectacular rise has occurred in non-ferrous metals and petroleum, both based primarily on resource discoveries, though technological adaptations in mining and smelting have also played an important part.

The major remaining industry groups—chemicals and allied products, iron and steel products, transportation equipment, electrical apparatus, textile products and clothing —are those which dominate modern industrial society and are least resource-based. In 1870 they accounted for a little more than one quarter of the net value of Canadian manufacturing, the bulk of this comprising simple agricultural implements and household hardware. By the mid-1950's they accounted for nearly 45 per cent and continue to increase in relative importance.

It is apparent that three factors have contributed to the changing pattern of Canadian manufacturing: (1) the uncovering and fuller exploitation of Canadian resources, most notably of minerals and water power, which were virtually untouched at the time of Confederation; (2) the advance of industrial technology, especially that which has made economic the exploitation, complex processing and diversification of the products of Canadian mines, rivers and forests; and (3) the growth of the Canadian market, so that in spite of the fact that Canada's natural wealth still marks it as a great net exporter of food and industrial materials, the Canadian economy is now remarkably diversified.

But the impact of these forces and of others, such as the National Policy, which are not so self-evident can better be assessed by an examination of successive periods of development in federal Canada's first century. This will be treated under three headings: A Protected Infancy, 1870-1910; A Troubled Adolescence, 1910-1953; Maturity and Opportunity since 1953.

**A Protected Infancy, 1870-1910**—Between 1870 and 1910 the percentage of the Canadian population engaged in manufacturing rose from five per cent to some seven per cent. The value added by manufacture increased by between five and six times in the same period, and the significance of this change is accentuated by the indications that prices were lower in 1910 than in 1870. The rate of growth in real output over the first two decades of this period averaged 4.2 per cent per year, then dropped to an average growth of only 2.4 per cent during the last decade of the century but rose with the wheat boom in the first ten years of the new century to an average growth rate approaching 6 per cent per annum.

The pattern of manufacturing had already begun to shift by 1910. Lumbering had declined in relative importance, especially since 1890, and primary food processing had risen to a higher rank. In the 1890's the primary paper products industry showed a marked gain in importance while between 1900 and 1910 the mineral processing industries for the first time achieved a notable role in the Canadian economy. As a group the primary manufacturing industries grew slightly in relative importance, accounting for 28.9 per cent of total value added in manufacturing in 1910, as compared with 26 per cent in 1870. Among secondary industries non-ferrous metal products and electrical apparatus and supplies showed marked gains in the first decade, moving from just over 2 per cent to 4.5 per cent of the net value of manufacturing. Other industries which showed substantial gains in relative importance were tobacco and transportation equipment, the latter due to the building of the railroads. Clothing had made a marked gain in relative importance in the first decade after Confederation but levelled off thereafter. Leather products and petroleum and coal products fell off, reflecting in all probability a deterioration in Canada's relative position as a supplier of these commodities at that time.

In general, there was increased diversification in Canadian manufacturing, oriented to a growing domestic market. Except for primary iron and steel, railway rolling-stock, and primary textiles, the bulk of industry was designed to supply only local or sparsely-populated regional markets; and the technology of both production and transport of that period were such that small-scale operations could operate with little fear of low-cost competition from distant, more populous areas.

Much has been said about the importance of the National Policy after 1879 in contributing to the development of Canadian manufacturing. The role of public tariff and transportation policies remains a subject of debate. In fact, there is very little evidence that the National Policy played the strategic role sometimes assigned to it, except perhaps for the indirect effect of the completion of the CPR. Both production of manufactures and imports in those categories such as textile and iron and steel products, in which highly manufactured items predominate, show the greatest growth in the period after 1896. There is little evidence that 1879 represented a turning point in the course of Canadian development. The refinement of available statistics points to a conclusion that "manufacturing growth proceeded at a much greater pace prior to 1890 than is generally recognized", that it paused in its advance in the early 1890's but went on to take advantage of the growing domestic market thereafter.

The regional distribution of manufacturing warrants a final word on this early period. This was a period of growth of cities and more rapid growth of urban manufacturing. At those places where the commercial needs of the resource industries could best be served, manufacturing centres emerged. During the entire period, 1870-1910, just over half of the manufacturing output came from Ontario, while with the shift from lumber to wheat the relative importance of the Maritimes dropped from 13.4 per cent to 7.7 per cent and of Quebec from 34.5 per cent to 29.3 per cent. On the other hand, all the western provinces benefited—the Winnipeg region from wheat and British Columbia from both wheat and lumber. By 1910 the gross value of manufacturing per capita of British Columbia's population was about equal to that of Quebec, while the figure for Ontario was over 40 per cent higher.

**A Troubled Adolescence, 1910-1953**—The adolescence of Canadian manufacturing was troubled not only by the usual problems of growth but also by the circumstances of the times. It was coming of age at a time of world wars and recession, events which in turn provided artificial stimulants and severe depressants to industries striving for maturity. The value added in manufacturing in Canada increased from $500,000,000

Typical industries of Manitoba are (right) Pioneer Electric and (left) Doris Hosiery.

Though the majority of clothing industries are found in the Central Provinces, such establishments are also widely scattered throughout the other provinces. This is a shirt factory in Edmundston, New Brunswick.

A garment factory, Alberta.                    Nuclear Enterprises, Manitoba.

to more than $9,500,000,000 in the period, with perhaps little more than half of the increase being attributable to increased prices. Persons employed in manufacturing almost tripled between 1910 and 1956, while the Canadian population as a whole grew from some 7,000,000 to more than 16,000,000. However, the rates of growth in terms of value added by manufacture varied widely during the period, as shown in the following annual average rates:

| | | |
|---|---|---|
| 1910-1919................... 1.9% | | 1939-1946................... 7.4% |
| 1919-1929................... 5.6% | | 1946-1957................... 4.8% |
| 1929-1939................... 1.2% | | |

The stimulating effect of World War I would seem to have been felt largely in the postwar decade, while that of World War II was more immediate. Part of the contrast may be explained by the statistical problem of comparing the 1910 estimate with the more consistent postwar figures. But other factors include the stimulus to manufacturing arising out of the much greater equipment demands of World War II, and the greater capacity of the Canadian economy to meet the needs of defence production. By contrast, the Armed Services made much greater demands on the smaller Canadian labour force in World War I. In the inter-war years the period 1926-29 saw a record average rate of growth in real product—over nine per cent—but even this period witnessed some distortion of manufacturing activity as a consequence of the boom psychology of those years. Then came the stagnation of the 1930's, the forced draft growth of the defence industries in World War II and a period of reconstruction and Korean crisis which postponed the return of relatively normal peacetime conditions until 1953. For this reason the long-term changes in Canadian manufacturing can, perhaps, be best identified by comparing 1910 with 1926-29 and the years of the mid-fifties.

### Value Added in Selected Canadian Manufacturing Industries as Percentages of Total

| | 1910 | 1926-29 | 1957 |
|---|---|---|---|
| **I. Direct resource-based manufactures.**................ | **28.9** | **25.7** | **23.9** |
| a) Food and beverages................................ | 9.2 | 7.8 | 6.2 |
| b) Wood products (mainly lumber)...................... | 13.2 | 5.4 | 3.9 |
| c) Pulp and paper..................................... | 2.3 | 7.6 | 6.9 |
| d) Non-ferrous metals................................. | 3.1 | 2.8 | 4.6 |
| e) Primary chemicals.................................. | 0.1 | 1.1 | 1.4 |
| f) Non-metallic minerals............................... | 1.0 | 0.9 | 0.9 |
| **II. Traditional secondary industries**................... | **56.0** | **53.5** | **46.5** |
| a) Textiles: | | | |
|    i) Clothing....................................... | 8.6 | 5.2 | 3.6 |
|    ii) Other........................................ | 4.1 | 6.1 | 4.3 |
| b) Iron and steel products............................. | 14.0 | 12.9 | 15.1 |
| c) Other*............................................. | 29.3 | 29.3 | 23.5 |
| **III. Newer secondary industries**....................... | **14.3** | **19.5** | **27.7** |
| a) Electrical apparatus................................ | 1.6 | 3.3 | 5.8 |
| b) Transportation equipment........................... | 7.4 | 7.7 | 9.8 |
| c) Petroleum and coal products........................ | 1.8 | 2.3 | 5.5 |
| d) Chemical products.................................. | 2.9 | 3.4 | 4.8 |
| e) Rubber............................................ | 0.6 | 2.8 | 1.8 |

*Includes such industries as tobacco, food processing (other than that under I), furniture, paper products, publishing, leather products, non-metallic minerals, and non-ferrous metal products.

The changes in the pattern of manufacturing during the past 50 years are better revealed by identifying three types of manufacturing activity—direct resource-based manufactures, traditional secondary industries, and newer secondary industries. The decline in the relative importance of resource processing activity has not been balanced by a growth in the traditional secondary industries, but rather by the development of new manufacturing activity. Most of these latter activities involve complex technology and product design and frequently important economies of scale. The size of the Canadian domestic market has justified a marked growth not only in the absolute but also in the relative importance of these industries, especially since the late 1920's.

After World War I, certain processing industries led the way, notably pulp and paper, but all the newer secondary industries showed marked gains—electric apparatus, petroleum and coal products, and chemicals. The aggregation of transportation equipment masks the shift from railway rolling-stock to passenger automobiles and trucks. The numbers of railroad cars produced dropped by half in the first postwar decade while passenger car production doubled. The latter development is also reflected in the percentages of rubber products.

Among the textile industries the clothing category decreased in relative importance while industrial textile production grew. However, apart from the pulp and paper and automobile industries, the 1920's were years only of beginnings among the most dynamic of Canada's modern manufacturing industries. It was in the late 1920's that smelting began of varied non-ferrous metals, and that the electric apparatus and chemical industries gained a foothold. The first washing machines, electric stoves, refrigerators, and radios were produced and sold in the 1920's. Although those branches of chemical production which grew out of the explosives production of World War I were already well established, the soaps, paints, and pharmaceuticals were new in the late 1920's. The 1930's saw the development of non-ferrous metals production buoyed up by the presence of gold in base-metal ores at a time when, due to monetary tradition, gold prices were among the few to be maintained.

Between the late 1920's and the postwar period, three changes with important consequences for manufacturing occurred—the discovery of large new deposits of minerals, especially iron ore and petroleum; the stimulus to metal products production and industrial technology during the War; and the growth of the Canadian domestic market. The first of these provided the petroleum and primary iron and steel industries with larger supplies of raw materials close at hand. This and the nature of war demand gave rise to new industrial activity such as the Sarnia petrochemical complex. Wartime contracts and postwar defence needs ensured forced draft growth of the aircraft, machine tool, and electrical and electronic industries as well as that of chemicals. Later reconstruction needs, the renewal of defence contracts after the Korean outbreak and the delay in returning to peacetime competitive conditions in international trade helped to maintain hothouse conditions until 1953. During the 1953-57 boom, Canadian industry again experienced competition from the United States and, for the first time since the late 1920's, returned to normal peacetime prosperity.

**Maturity and Opportunity Since 1953**—Comparison of Canadian manufacturing activity in the mid-1950's with that of the late 1920's indicates that secondary industry kept pace with the great postwar boom in the resource industries and that the newer manufacturing industries, in which the problems of firm and plant scale are most important, have made great gains in relative importance. The key to the explanation of postwar growth in manufacturing would appear to be the great increase in the size of the

A continuous butt-welding pipe mill at the Steel Company of Canada, Limited, McMaster works, Contrecoeur, Quebec.

Thickening the mechanical pulp at the Rothesay Paper Corporation, Saint John, New Brunswick. The pulp and paper industry is first in Canada in net value of shipments, exports, total wages paid and in capital invested.

Canadian domestic market. There were 10,000,000 people in Ontario and Quebec by the mid-1950's, a substantial market base in which the developing industries could sell a substantial share of their production. Access to Commonwealth markets, which had provided the incentive for the establishment of many United States subsidiaries in Canada in the 1920's and 1930's, was no longer required as a motive for the expansion of manufacturing.

However, Canadian manufacturing is not yet able to take full advantage of its potential. Broadly speaking, two problems remain. These relate to the particular circumstances of the two principal groups of industries—those processing Canada's natural resources and those which are primarily market- and technology-oriented. The former group has been able to convert typically Canadian resources into partly processed forms but has been barred from further processing by foreign tariffs which make it impossible to export more highly processed products. Some countries bar or severely restrict the import of flour and canned fish or even frozen fish, while levying little or no duties on the natural products. Among pulp and paper products, only pulp and newsprint easily move abroad. More highly processed non-ferrous metals must also surmount higher trade barriers.

It is by no means inevitable that highly processed forms would necessarily be supplied to world markets most economically by Canada, even in the absence of trade barriers. In those instances in which advanced manufacture nearer the origin of raw materials would reduce transportation cost, or in which lower Canadian wage costs would give Canadian producers an advantage over Americans, more Canadian processing could be expected. Where the Canadian market is insufficient to absorb a substantial part of a more specialized product, the net advantage may continue to be closer to the centre of the market. Some of the less widely used non-ferrous metal and paper products are examples. On balance, it is expected that the removal of foreign trade barriers would result in more rational and larger manufacturing sectors in those secondary industries using Canadian raw materials.

The other problem relates primarily, though not exclusively, to those industries which do not depend primarily on Canada's natural resources. Such industries have served mainly the domestic market though, as mentioned above, they have also supplied Commonwealth markets made accessible by the preferential tariff treatment accorded by some parts of the Commonwealth. Whereas this was a more important consideration before World War II, the growth of the Canadian market and the closing of the Australian and other markets to some of the products Canada exported to them in inter-war years means that now only Britain itself is relatively freely accessible to Canadian manufactured exports.

Canadian manufacturing industries have generally grown up under the tariff protection which dates from the National Policy of 1879. This fact should not be taken to signify that such protection is essential for the survival of manufacturing in Canada, or, indeed, that a somewhat different but possibly substantial manufacturing sector would not have existed in any event. The device of tariff protection was chosen at a time when United States industry had a considerable head start, due to the rapid settlement of the West and the artificial stimuli of its civil war.

The Canadian Government has not attempted to determine whether or when Canadian protection policies should be phased out. This is the sort of long-term policy decision which is rarely given explicit attention. What has happened instead is that the demands of the export-oriented resource industries have gradually eroded protection. Agriculture succeeded in getting tariffs wiped out entirely on agricultural machinery and chemical fertilizers. The fishing and mining industries have induced successive governments to write into the tariff schedule numerous "end use" items which permit producers of primary and related processed products to avoid duties on imports of specialized materials and equipment which are available only at higher costs and prices in Canada. This compromise position was more acceptable when the more complex manufactures could not in any event be produced at internationally competitive costs. But now that there are many indications that Canadian manufacturers could be competitive internationally, the effect of permitting some Canadian buyers (the resource industries) to obtain low cost imports while others must pay for higher cost domestic goods is merely to reduce the market available in Canada to those manufacturers who must compete with imports. If such producers could become efficient suppliers of manufactures in the international markets, they might well be better off if their obsolete Canadian protection could be relinquished in exchange for the elimination of duties on similar goods by the United States and other countries.

There have been numerous indications of a new competitive strength, or potential strength, in Canadian manufacturing in the last decade of Canada's first century as a federal state. When vigorous United States competition was again felt by Canadian manufacturers in the mid-1950's, many of them held at first that this represented new evidence of a fundamental inability to compete with their United States counterparts. During the years up to 1961, while the Canadian dollar was at a premium, many of them continued to lack confidence in their capacity to meet foreign competition, which was now accentuated by the restoration of European competition and by such unique events as the influx of European automobiles. In retrospect, the over-valuation of the

Canadian dollar during those years, though by no means an appropriate means of encouraging more efficient manufacturing, effectively removed perhaps 10 per cent of the tariff protection sheltering Canadian producers and thus promoted efforts at cost reduction and increased managerial efficiency. Unfortunately it also, in effect, raised the export prices of Canadian goods and thus added to the barriers to export development as a means of achieving more specialized and efficient manufacturing.

None the less, many industries achieved positions of great strength. The most notable success story was in primary iron and steel in which Canada moved from a substantial net importer to a position of virtual balance; and Canadian prices became equal to, and even lower than, American prices. The more specialized rolled products continue to be imported, but a substantial range of the more commonly used flat and square shapes are now produced at prices which are fully competitive with United States prices and are even, on occasion, exported over foreign tariffs. While other industries did not experience such striking changes, many did improve their competitive strength. The traditional textile industries were modernized, with larger and more specialized firms gaining strength while some smaller ones dropped out.

In those industries which produce goods primarily for other industries—industrial machinery and equipment and industrial chemicals—both the general improvement in demand, as resource processing and other manufacturing industries grew, and specific opportunities for exports contributed to growth. Certain sections benefited from lower levels of foreign tariffs. Particularly in those sectors in which the Canadian tariff was not especially high and the Canadian market was not large enough to support an efficient production unit, specialized exports have been developed. Some basic petrochemicals may be cited as examples. But for many other lines of producer goods, the United States and other markets have not been accessible enough to permit this kind of development.

For consumer durables such as automobiles and electrical appliances, there have tended to be several producers of each line, many of them subsidiaries of large foreign (especially United States) firms. The Canadian tariff has permitted each to maintain rather diversified assembly operations plus some component manufacture. Little tendency has been evident for these firms to rationalize their positions by selecting longer runs of more specialized products. Apparently the reason has related, at least in part, to the desire to maintain relative shares of the Canadian market which roughly reflects in some cases the sharing of the United States market among parent United States firms. Clearly this structure of industry depends upon the Canadian tariff, which permits individual firms to earn a respectable rate of return on operation of relatively small-scale plants. This same small-scale and diversified production also makes it difficult to justify fixed investment in research and design facilities to develop distinctively Canadian products.

Much attention has been paid to the solution of the problem. It is increasingly recognized that, especially given the number of firms already firmly established in Canada, the most effective way of achieving internationally competitive manufacturing may be to remove those barriers to international trade which prevent Canadian manufacturers from achieving long runs of more specialized products. But the question remains as to the kind of transitional arrangements required to ensure a more effective integration of Canadian manufacturing in the world economy. It is sometimes claimed that the prevalence of United States ownership would make it difficult to develop exports from Canadian branch plants to the United States. But it is difficult to support the view that parent firms would resist such integration or adaptation of their Canadian operations if that were the means of achieving greater efficiency and of maintaining their returns on branch plant investment. In those industries or product lines in which it has been possible to export without a substantial foreign tariff handicap, many foreign-controlled firms have already responded to the opportunity. At any event, as has been demonstrated in the case of the automobile industry, it is possible to devise methods of encouraging firms to undertake the kind of specialization and export required. In the automobile case, for a variety of reasons, the method adopted has been rather direct and specific agreement between the Canadian Government and the manufacturers.

There are reasons why such a system would not be appropriate for the majority of other industries. Where one or more important Canadian-owned firms are operating in an industry, the opportunity to develop an export business would probably require a transition period in which such firms could develop their distributive facilities in the export market, thus putting them on an even competitive basis with foreign subsidiaries which would often have, through the parent firms, ready-made facilities for distribution in the parent firm's home market.

A similar argument applies to research and product development. Both the Canadian-owned and foreign subsidiary would have a better opportunity to develop specialized research facilities when the market to which the resulting product can gain access can be extended beyond Canada. The advantages of an established international company in providing the technical know-how and in sharing research facilities might mean that firms which had customarily depended on the domestic market would require some assistance in achieving competitive position in research and development.

## Transitional Problems

Clearly many transitional problems beset Canadian manufacturing while it moves to take full advantage of its opportunities for efficient production in this tenth decade of Canadian Confederation. Imaginative adjustment policies are being devised, but it is clear that the effect of such policies will depend very much upon the kind of commercial policy with which they are combined. If adjustment policies enable the Canadian economy to adapt to the opportunities afforded by fuller access to world markets, then Canadians can be confident that their industries are meeting the test of competitiveness and are thus making their best contribution to Canadian economic welfare. If, on the other hand, policies for adjusting or rationalizing Canadian manufacturing take place without reference to the application of the criterion of international competitiveness, then they become means of varying the form, and perhaps the degree, of subsidy which is embodied in the system of protection generally afforded to an infant or adolescent manufacturing sector. There is a very real question whether, in a world of vast free trade areas like the United States, the European Economic Community and the European Free Trade Association, (EEC and EFTA), Canada could remain competitive in manufacturing with a protected economy dependent almost exclusively on a market of 20,000,000 or 30,000,000 people. The early years of the second century of Canadian Confederation offer the opportunity to realize the full manufacturing potentials implicit in the circumstances of 1967.        (H. E. ENGLISH)

Winnipeg, Manitoba, is called the gateway city of the keystone province. Midway between the east and west coasts, it is a major railway and airways junction. There were about 1,000 manufacturing establishments in the metropolitan area at the time of the 1961 Census.

# Construction and Capital Investment

Construction activity and output are evident in every sector of the economy—in homes, on streets and highways, in factories, repair shops, offices and stores, in air, water and rail transport, in schools, hospitals and other institutions. All the gas, electric, water and sewage disposal systems servicing these structures are part of construction output.

In 1965 there were, on the average, some 600,000 persons employed continuously in building such structures—exclusive of employment in the production of machinery and equipment housed or used within the completed structures. Average expenditures on new construction alone accounted for 15 per cent of Gross National Product throughout the 20-year period from 1943 to 1963.

Many factors or forces influencing economic conditions, or business or market prospects, are reflected sooner or later in variations in the level of construction activity. Both the over-all level of construction and shifts in the regional or industrial pattern are significant. Substantial changes in either may effect the livelihood of many thousands of workers, not only those engaged in construction and the industries directly associated with it, but, as well, those in the many other industry and service areas dependent on construction output for expansion, modernization and repair. Because of these far-reaching effects of changes in the construction cycle and their relationship to general levels of economic activity, a careful watch is kept on construction output.

## 1867-1897

The great emphasis in the period following Confederation was on the development of transportation and, in particular, the extension of the railroad systems, some of which had already been started before Confederation.

**Canals**—Prior to 1867 the canal system in Canada had developed in part as the result of a challenge from the United States which had started its system with the opening of the Erie canal in 1825. Upper Canada responded by building the Lachine Canal in 1825, and the Welland in 1829, but both were too shallow to be effective. After the union of Upper and Lower Canada in 1841 new efforts were put forth and the system was greatly improved, but the American West did not respond to the bid made for its trade, and little further development took place for some years. After 1867, however, the new Federal Government became responsible for the continuation of these projects and, in 1870, appointed a Royal Commission to consider the adequacy of the existing canals and the desirability of constructing certain new ones. The Commission issued a majority report in 1871. As a result, the canals along the St. Lawrence River were enlarged and deepened and new canals were built at Lachine Rapids, Soulanges and Cornwall. Major improvements were also made to the Welland Canal, and a new canal, the largest built in Canada up to that time, was constructed at Sault Ste. Marie. The three canals on the lower Ottawa River were also enlarged.

**Railways**—However, the building of these additional canals failed to give the expected traffic advantage and the colonies of North America turned their attention to the building of railways. Several small systems had been established prior to 1867 and over the next 20 years the prolific issue of railway charters in Canada resulted in the construction of nearly 100 separate railroad lines, some of which were subsidiaries of the larger companies. Two of the main characteristics on which railway development was based prior to Confederation were: dependence on English capital and the continental plan, i.e., the idea that the railways built in the British North American colonies should serve the whole continent not just their own areas. After 1867 there was a gradual transition from English to Canadian control and from continental to national economy in keeping with the over-all philosophy of the "National Policy".* Up to 1867, approximately $155,000,000 had been spent in building about 2,500 miles of railway lines in British North America. By 1881, this total had risen to about 7,400 miles and by the end of the century it had increased to nearly 18,000 miles. Thus, in the 30 odd years following Confederation, about 15,000 miles of railway lines were brought into operation. The two most important railway lines constructed in this period were the Canadian Pacific Railway and the Intercolonial Railway. In addition, the Grand Trunk Railway instituted a very large network within the province of Ontario.

The Intercolonial may be described as the first real "political" railway in Canada.

---

*See page 208.

Prefabricating of housing units, as in this plant at Buctouche, New Brunswick, provides for faster on-site construction.

It was part and parcel of Confederation as far as the provinces of New Brunswick and Nova Scotia were concerned and they insisted on having it written into the British North America Act as part of the terms of union. Negotiations for its construction began as early as 1850 and continued intermittently until final ratification in 1867. Apart from its route, the main debate was whether it was to be a private or a public railroad system. This was finally settled in 1874 when it was placed under the control of the Department of Public Works. The route was from Halifax to Rivière du Loup, 562 miles, later extended to Montreal, another 275 miles, with final completion in 1879.

The Canadian Pacific Railway, like the Intercolonial, was a "political" railway in the sense that it fulfilled a pledge made to British Columbia on its entry into Confederation. It was a natural request for, without some means of direct communication, there was little for British Columbia to gain from the union. Other considerations were the need to save the Western Plains from being drawn into the American orbit and to supply a means of opening the West for new Canadian settlers. By the terms of agreement in 1870 the Federal Government was committed to a beginning within two years, and completion in ten years, of the proposed railway line. The negotiations for the contract were both complex and confusing with two companies competing for ownership of the line. The rival companies represented American capital vs. Canadian capital, and the commercial interests of Montreal vs. those of Toronto. The first negotiations having failed, a new charter was awarded in February 1873 to a new company called the Canadian Pacific Railway Company. This company went through several financial

Buses are an important means of transportation in Canada and motor coach industries such as this Manitoba plant provide opportunities for the employment of skilled workers.

crises including the "Pacific Scandal" of 1873 which overthrew the Conservative government of Sir John A. Macdonald. Between 1873 and 1879 little progress was made so that by 1879 British Columbia was threatening to withdraw from Confederation. With the return of Sir John A. Macdonald to power in 1878 a reorganized Canadian Pacific Railway Company was established, under the dynamic leadership of W. C. Van Horne as general manager, which pushed the line to completion by October 1885. From Montreal to Port Moody the line ran 2,893 miles.

**Electric Railways**—Probably because of the emphasis on railway construction, scant attention was paid to improving roads and highways, which were the responsibility of the provincial and municipal governments. It was in this era, however, that electric railways were introduced to Canada. The first was built in St. Catharines, Ontario, in 1887, and was followed by others in Vancouver, Ottawa, Montreal and Toronto. These electric railways were soon extended beyond the cities into the suburban areas as a convenient means of transportation. By 1893 the over-all mileage for all such lines totalled 256.

Adequate data are not available to show either the kind or value of all construction projects between 1867 and 1897. However, population had increased from 3,500,000 to over 5,000,000 in this 30-year period and it has been estimated that, in addition to the projects mentioned, approximately 500,000 housing units were constructed between those years, including many in rural areas.

## 1898-1918

This period really begins with the election victory of the Liberal Government under the leadership of Sir Wilfrid Laurier. It was to be characterized by Sir Wilfrid's slogan: "the twentieth century belongs to Canada". It was an era when large-scale immigration was encouraged as the West was opened up and mineral and other natural resources were exploited. The basic needs were for labour, equipment and capital. The labour problems were eased through an open-door policy on immigration and, consequently, during this 20-year period, more than 3,000,000 immigrants arrived in Canada and the population increased from some 5,000,000 to 8,000,000. The capital required to finance such expansion could have been obtained at home only very slowly. However, an important factor contributing to this rapid growth was the ease with which money could be borrowed abroad. A substantial increase in investment took place prior to the outbreak of war in 1914, and it has been estimated that between $4,500,000,000 and $5,000,000,000 was invested in capital goods during 1900-1914, much of it in the latter part of this period. During the 1914-1918 War, construction in general was at a low ebb, except for the building of munition plants.

From 1900 to 1914 capital investment covered a wide range of industries and activities but was noticeably directed toward the further development of transportation such as railways, canals and harbours since these were essential for furthering both internal and external trade. The opening of Western Canada as a prime agricultural area also involved heavy investment of capital for buildings as well as for livestock and equipment. In Central Canada, the development of hydro-electric power, for export as well as for domestic consumption, and the beginning of the pulp and paper industry required heavy investment in fixed capital to construct the required facilities.

As in the earlier period, 1867-1897, the largest share of the heavy investment in transportation facilities between 1900 and 1914 went toward the extension of existing, and the construction of new, railway lines. The last two major railroad systems to be established in Canada occurred as a result of the policy of the Liberal government. The Canadian Pacific Railway, running from Montreal to the West Coast by 1885, had been granted a virtual monopoly in the West in order to protect its investment in its early stages of operation. This aroused protests from the western farmers and, with the opening of the West and the wheat boom, the Liberal government sought to alleviate the situation by permitting two new transcontinental lines to be built.

The first of these was the Canadian Northern Railway Company, a private enterprise project guided by Messrs. Mackenzie and Mann. The Canadian Northern started as a local line in Manitoba in 1896, but by 1915 possessed 9,362 miles of track which extended from Quebec to Vancouver. The second and last line to be established was the National Transcontinental. It was the result of pressures from both East and West. Both New Brunswick and Quebec were seeking extra railway coverage and the Liberal government fitted their demands into an elaborate transcontinental system. A line was to be built from Moncton, New Brunswick to Winnipeg, Manitoba, 1,810 miles, (the National Transcontinental) by the government and then leased to the Grand Trunk Pacific, a subsidiary of the Grand Trunk Railway. The latter was to establish

A vast construction boom which has affected every province of Canada is symbolized by this massive girder.

CONSTRUCTION AND CAPITAL INVESTMENT

the Grand Trunk Pacific as a transcontinental railway by building a line from Winnipeg to Prince Rupert, via Edmonton, an over-all distance of 1,964 miles. Both parts of this line were completed by 1914, but the cost of the National Transcontinental section built by the government had been so enormous that the Grand Trunk Pacific could not possibly take over the government lease since it was close to a state of bankruptcy itself. Both the Canadian Northern and both sections of the National Transcontinental were built in an era of rising costs. When war broke out in 1914 and brought the boom in the West to a close, the financial resources of the two lines were too small to support the overextended systems.

By 1916, the construction of railway facilities in Canada had become such a complex problem, particularly in the method of financing new lines, that the Federal Government established a Royal Commission to study the whole question. The Report revealed that as of June 30, 1916, the six major railway companies covered a total of 25,398 miles of track with a book value of nearly $2,000,000,000. Toward the construction of all these railway lines, the Federal Government had contributed either directly or indirectly nearly $970,000,000. The interests of the Canadian Northern, the National Transcontinental and the Grand Trunk were merged to form the Canadian National Railway system in 1923.

Improvements also continued to be made to Canada's inland waterways and deep-sea port facilities. All tolls on Canada's canals were abolished in 1903. From 1901-18 total investment in canals was $47,700,000 and in harbour and river work, $158,400,000.

**Roads**—In this period, as in the previous one, road construction continued to be given a low priority. Roads were built and maintained either by the townships or by toll companies. Statute labour was used extensively and the cost of construction, over and above the statute labour, was met by provincial grants. Following the Yukon gold rush of 1896, the Federal Government became directly involved in the building of roads in the Yukon Territory, where it constructed over 500 miles of good wagon roads including the main highway from Whitehorse to Dawson. As the number of motor cars increased, provincial governments were forced to repair and maintain old roads as well as to build a few new highways. After 1914 the first hard-surfaced roads were built in Canada, the Toronto-Hamilton highway being among the first. Total investments in provincial highways and bridges, 1901-18, was $66,400,000.

Although complete data are not available for this period, it has been estimated that between 1898 and 1918 the Federal Government invested in new construction a total sum of $533,800,000 of which $244,600,000 was in railway construction, $214,800,000 in other forms of transportation, and $74,700,000 in buildings and other types of construction. The figures for provincial governments are available only from 1901-18 and show an estimated investment in new construction of $131,700,000. It has also been estimated that from 1898 to 1918 slightly more than 900,000 housing units were constructed.

# 1919-45

The years 1919 to 1945 probably represent the most complex period in the economic development of Canada. As in earlier periods external forces were largely responsible for the trend of development. At the beginning of the 1920's in the change from a wartime to a peacetime economy the country was caught up in a slight recession. This was followed by an unparalleled period of economic prosperity from 1922 to 1929. Then, in late 1929, the world-wide stock market crash ushered in the most prolonged period of economic depression in the nation's history. This was finally alleviated with the outbreak of World War II in 1939.

When World War I ended and the armistice was signed in November 1918, there was great apprehension that a depression was imminent. Accordingly, the Federal Government inaugurated a ship-building program to help provide employment for returning servicemen and those released with the closing down of the munition plants. When the actual depression did occur in 1921, the "good roads" programs of the provincial governments also contributed much needed additional employment.

With the acceleration of the economy after 1922, construction in general moved forward at a rapid pace to meet the backlog resulting from the suspension of many construction projects during the 1914-18 war. The peak of this new cycle was reached in 1929 when for that year the value of construction (at 1949 prices) reached approximately $2,000,000,000. The vulnerability of construction to recession and depression was vividly revealed during the period that followed. By 1933, the total value of construction for that year (at 1949 prices) had declined to $900,000,000, less than half the level reached in 1929. There was some recovery made between 1933 and 1939, but the 1929 level was not reached again until 1943.

In World War I the most pressing need had been for men, in World War II, for machines. To produce such machines, many hundreds of new plants had to be constructed and enormous quantities of new equipment manufactured. After the initial rush, and the high levels of building in 1942 and 1943, there was some decline in construction activity in 1944 and 1945 as more workers were absorbed into the Armed Services and in the actual production of war equipment. To relieve housing pressure in congested areas, the Federal Government in 1941 created Wartime Housing Limited, a Crown company, and charged it with the duty of finding accommodation for war workers and their families.

The great building era of the railroads which had been proceeding at a feverish pace for over half a century came to an end around 1919. It was replaced by an era of consolidation and abandonment of unnecessary track and equipment. This new period was bolstered by the development of the electric railway which reached its peak by 1925 and then went into a steady decline. The electric railways had been designed while roads were in a poor state of development and before automobiles were produced on a mass scale. Increasing motor traffic forced highway improvements and created serious competition for electric railways. Furthermore, the flexibility of the motor car over the fixed route of trams gave added impetus to the greater use of motor cars and motor buses, thereby seriously reducing the number of passengers using the electric railways.

The increased use of the motor car forced governments to pay attention to road conditions. A great deal of construction work was carried out in improving old roads and in building new highways. Construction expenditures for rural highways, bridges and ferries for the period 1919-45 amounted to $1,700,000,000.

**Civil Aviation**—Before 1914 aviation was in a purely experimental stage. When the War ended in 1918 Canada possessed a large number of military aeroplanes, pilots and technicians. These readily available assets formed the base on which a new program

Gravel pit at Portage Mountain, British Columbia. With the completion of the Portage Mountain Project in the Peace River, the province will have one of the largest power plants in the western world. This, combined with the mighty Columbia River development, also under way, will provide a sound basis for industrial expansion far into the future.

of civil aviation was founded. As a new means of transportation, aviation expanded quite rapidly and played a major role in the development of the northern areas. By the end of 1945, Canada had constructed a total of 146 civil airports of which 45 were for water use only.

A major project carried out in this period was the construction of the Shipshaw hydro development on the Saguenay River in Quebec as part of the complex of the Aluminum Company of Canada. The project was started in 1926 but because of the great depression was not completed until 1943. The total generating capacity of this hydro plant is 717,000 kw. The power is chiefly used for the smelter located nearby at Arvida. Since 1943, considerable additions have been made to the power complex.

One of the most critical shortages which developed during World War I was in the field of housing. Despite high building costs and a severe shortage of materials, a considerable building program was undertaken throughout the 1920's. Supply, however, never quite caught up with demand so that when construction activity was cut back following the depression of the 1930's, a great deficiency in housing was apparent. In order to facilitate and encourage the building of houses, and to stimulate construction in general, the Federal Government passed the Dominion Housing Act in 1935. It had a two-fold purpose: (1) to assist in the improvement of housing conditions, and (2) to assist in the absorption of unemployment by the stimulation of the construction and building material industries. The Government also passed the "Government Home Improvement Plan" in 1937, the National Housing Act in 1938, and a new National Housing Act in 1944. In 1945 Central Mortgage and Housing Corporation was established as a Crown agency to administer federal housing policy. From 1919 to 1945, when population increased from 8,300,000 to 12,100,000, approximately 1,100,000 houses were completed.

A multi-million dollar cement plant was opened at Brookfield, Nova Scotia, in 1965.

The outbreak of war in 1939 stimulated construction activity and, in reality, forced Canada to become a highly industrialized nation. The following brief summary of the construction activity during the war years is taken from the 1945 Canada Year Book:

"Since the beginning of the war, more than 701 hangars and hangar-type buildings have been erected. In all, 195 airfields have been built. Paved runways on these fields equal a highway extending from the Atlantic to the Pacific and back as far east as the Rocky Mountains. The construction work for the British Commonwealth Air Training Plan, alone, involved the erection of more than 5,506 buildings. Aircraft plants, employing over 100,000 men and women, have been built up almost from nothing. Shipbuilding and munition plants, dry docks, and other ship-repair facilities, and coastal defence batteries have sprung up. Millions of dollars have been spent on power development and transmission lines. A $51,000,000 plant, capable of turning out sufficient synthetic rubber to meet all Canada's wartime requirements, has been erected. More than 17,300 dwellings for war workers have been built in areas where congestion was acute, as well as 1,075 houses for families of men in the Armed Services."

Three major wartime construction projects which should be mentioned are the Alaska Highway, the Canol Project, and the Polymer Corporation. The Alaska Highway was originally built for military purposes under a joint agreement with the United States

Government. It is a 1,600 mile roadway extending from Fort St. John, British Columbia, through Whitehorse, Yukon, to Fairbanks, Alaska. Started in the spring of 1942, it was opened for wheeled traffic six months later, on November 20, 1942. About 10,000 United States engineer troops, and 4,000 civilians, of whom half were Canadian, completed this difficult task in the incredibly short span of only six months. An equally difficult task was the building of the Canol Project during 1943-44 across virgin mountainous terrain, the largest defence undertaking authorized by the Government of Canada. Built under wartime conditions when speed was essential and cost secondary, it is estimated to have cost between $130,000,000 and $140,000,000. It was a joint defence undertaking authorized by exchanges of notes between the Governments of Canada and the United States involving: (1) a program of development designed to increase the production of oil in the Northwest Territories to supply the requirements of the Armed Forces in Canada and Alaska and for use along Alaska highways; (2) the construction of a pipeline to convey crude oil from Norman Wells to Whitehorse, plus product pipelines from Whitehorse to Skagway, Carcross to Watson Lake, and Whitehorse to Fairbanks for an over-all total of about 1,500 miles for the four pipelines, and (3) the erection of an oil refinery at Whitehorse. The construction of the Polymer synthetic rubber plant at Sarnia was one of the major engineering feats of the War as far as Canadian engineers were concerned. The plant, built on American plans, was completed ahead of similar plants which were being constructed in the United States at the same time.

The projects listed above are intended to illustrate only a few of the major construction projects carried out during the war years when it might be said that the construction industry in Canada succeeded in the biggest job it ever faced.

Complete statistics are not available for the whole period of 1919 to 1945 but data are available from 1926 to 1945 and show a total investment of $11,937,000,000 for new construction, a total of $6,178,000,000 for repair construction and a grand total of $18,115,000,000.

## 1946-67

Since the end of World War II the population of Canada has increased from 12,300,000 to 20,000,000 and the country has been undergoing an almost unprecedented economic boom. Consequently, each year since 1946, except for the three years 1954, 1959 and 1960, capital expenditures on new construction have exceeded the total for the previous year. Total capital expenditures on new construction for the years 1946 to 1965 should exceed $87,000,000,000. Construction now accounts for about two thirds of the total capital expenditures each year, with machinery and equipment accounting for the other third. On an annual average basis, for the period 1954 to 1963, new construction expenditures as a percentage of the Gross National Product have averaged just slightly below 16 per cent. When expenditures on machinery and equipment are added, the annual average increases to over 22 per cent, a rate of investment in capital assets higher than that recorded by any other industrialized private enterprise economy. As in the case of the early boom of 1909-1913, the high rate of expansion has been maintained by a substantial inflow of funds from abroad; in the present boom, chiefly from the United States.

One of the major areas of expansion in the postwar period has been in the utilities sector. It became clear shortly after the War ended that the facilities in this field were

Wilderness holds no terrors for this mighty transporter wending its way through bush and swamp of the Northwest Territories.

inadequate to support the level of activity to which the economy was moving. As a result, utilities have absorbed a greater share of over-all expenditures in more recent years than in earlier postwar years. Within the utilities sector, the major share of expenditures has gone into the construction of electric power facilities, particularly new hydro facilities. Since 1946, a total of 21 major power projects have been started, all of which will be completed by 1970. The nation's output of electric power has expanded from 43,425,000,000 kwh. in 1947 to 143,200,000,000 kwh. in 1965.

The 21 new major projects referred to include the Peace River development but not the Columbia River development because, in the early stages of the latter, all of the new electric power will be generated in the United States. Of particular interest is the development of the hydro project at the headwaters of the Manicouagan and Outardes Rivers in Quebec which will result in adding 5,600,000 kilowatts of new capacity.

Further development has also taken place in the Saguenay complex of the Aluminum Company of Canada since 1946. Three new powerhouses have been added to the hydro plants previously built so that the total generating capacity available in the district is now just under 2,000,000 kw. The total investment in this huge complex by 1965 had reached nearly $600,000,000, and possessed the capacity to produce more than 976,000,000 pounds, or 488,000 short tons, of aluminum annually.

A second major development of the Aluminum Company of Canada, and one of the largest and most imaginative construction projects, was undertaken by Canadian engineers near the Nechako-Kemano-Kitimat development in British Columbia. The Kenney dam across the Nechako River is the largest, sloping, rock-filled, clay-core dam in the world. The power for the smelter at Kitimat is transmitted across 51 miles of mountainous terrain from the underground powerhouse at Kemano. The entire plant was built in the wilderness about 500 miles from a supply base and with only limited transportation facilities. The smelter was built with an initial capacity of 91,500 metric tons but has since been expanded to add another 60,000 metric tons. The over-all cost of the complex has been estimated at about $450,000,000.

As in the earlier periods, there have been some major construction projects carried out by the railways as new lines have been built to link newly-developing areas with established settlements. Since 1946 at least five new lines, totalling nearly 1,200 miles, have been built. The two longest were: (1) the Quebec North Shore and Labrador Railway, originating at Sept Îles, Quebec, and running 358 miles almost due north, passing through the western part of Labrador to Schefferville, Quebec, and (2) the Great Slave Lake Railway which extends 430 miles northwards from Roma, Alberta, to Hay River and Pine Point on Great Slave Lake.

One of the most exciting projects carried out since 1946 was the St. Lawrence Seaway. Construction of this waterway has been aptly described as the "master project of the North Atlantic Continent". As a major artery of transportation, providing low-cost water transportation, it can offer more economic advantages to the mid-continental region that it serves than any other specific factor affecting the economic prosperity of this large region. As a major construction project, it provided at one time or another employment for nearly 61,000 persons. The total cost amounted to $470,000,000 of which Canada's share was $330,000,000. The project also included the development of a new hydro-electric station with a total capacity of 1,640,000 kw. of which Canada's share is 912,000 kw.

The heavy manufacturing industries also contributed substantially to the construction boom in this period, particularly the iron and steel industry, the pulp and paper industry, the automobile industry which carried out a major rebuilding program in 1953, and the chemical industry through the development of synthetic plants.

The discovery of the Leduc oil field in Alberta in 1947 touched off a boom which has not yet subsided. In 1946, annual domestic oil production was only 7,600,000 bbls., but by 1957 it had risen to 182,000,000 barrels and by 1964 to 275,000,000 barrels, thereby supplying the country with about 58 per cent of its total refinery crude oil receipts. Associated with the discovery and production of crude oil has been the discovery and production of natural gas. In 1946, about 48,000,000,000 cubic feet of natural gas were produced but in 1964 just over 1,407,000,000,000 cubic feet were produced. In order to produce, refine and distribute these oil and gas products a large network of transmission pipelines, oil refineries, and natural gas processing plants were constructed.

The passing of the Trans-Canada Highway Act on December 10, 1949, started a major construction project which required the building of a new or improved highway 4,860 miles in length. The highway was officially opened on September 3, 1962. The total cost of the project up to March 31, 1965, was $924,000,000 of which the Federal Government contributed $587,000,000.

Housing, as one of the nation's most valuable assets, has certainly played a major role in the whole field of construction, and house building is one of the largest industries.

High temperature thermal insulation tests are performed on premoulded pipe sections at the Department of Public Works Testing Laboratory, Ottawa.

Since 1960, house construction has represented on an annual average basis slightly over 27 per cent of all new construction, and about 18 per cent of all new capital expenditures, i.e., construction plus machinery and equipment. One of the factors revealed in the housing censuses of 1941, 1951 and 1961 has been the high percentage of total dwellings which were reported as owner-occupied for each of the census years, as follows: 56.7, 65.6 and 66.0. This trend in percentage increase is likely to show a decline in the 1971 census as a result of the construction in recent years of numerous large apartment blocks in preference to single unit housing. The percentage of all housing starts classified as single-housing units has been declining steadily from over 60 per cent during 1950-57 to 51 per cent in 1962, and to 47 per cent and 42 per cent in 1963 and 1964 respectively.

The volume of house-building in Canada since 1935 has been spectacular and this must be attributed in a very large measure to the assistance that the Federal Government has given through various housing Acts. The National Housing Act of 1954 is the latest piece of legislation in this field. It has been estimated that close to half the country's present stock of approximately 5,000,000 houses have been built since the first legislation was passed in 1935. From 1935 to 1964, a total of 2,641,811 houses of all types have been started and, of these, 846,279, or 32 per cent, have been financed by mortgage loans under the various housing Acts, including starts in Federal-Provincial projects.

Since 1946 the investment in new and repair construction in public and private institutions has been of major significance. From 1946 to 1960, a total of $8,587,000,000 has been invested in constructing and repairing institutions thereby representing nearly 8 per cent of total investment in construction for those years. About 45 per cent of this $8,587,000,000 has gone toward building schools, another 28 per cent has been absorbed in building hospitals, with 7 and 5 per cent being invested in churches and universities respectively. The remaining 15 per cent has been used to construct or repair other types of institutions.

Helicopters prove their worth in hydro line construction. Where the terrain is particularly formidable, the whirly birds fly in pre-assembled sections of aluminum towers and perform other heavy lifting chores. They are also used for line maintenance.

The period 1946 to 1967 is the only one for which complete statistics are available to show the pattern of investment in construction between the public and private sectors of the economy. For the period 1946 to 1965, total investment in new and repair construction amounted to an estimated $110,599,000,000 of which $70,509,000,000, or 63.7 per cent, was invested by the private sector, and $40,090,000,000, or 36.3 per cent, by the public sector. When the public sector is broken down into government levels, it is found that the federal, provincial and municipal governments invested 9.5, 15.6 and 11.1 per cent respectively of the total public and private investment.

## Technical Changes

Technical changes in the field of construction over the past 100 years might be considered in three broad categories: (1) changes in on-site construction methods, (2) changes in off-site techniques, and (3) changes in the use and form of conventional building materials and the introduction of new materials.

Changes in on-site construction methods have come about mainly through the greater use of power equipment of all kinds from bulldozers, power shovels and cranes down to small tools. The mobility and flexibility of this new equipment has added immeasurably to the ability of contractors to complete their projects more efficiently and more quickly than ever before. Another feature of the new equipment is that it is available on a rental basis and, therefore, available to the whole industry. Although the use of power equipment increases the output per man-hour, it has also necessitated a higher level of capital investment and equipment per dollar of construction put in place.

Changes in off-site techniques are centred largely in the development of prefabrication methods. Certain small parts of any construction projects, e.g., windows, doors, etc., have always been prefabricated, but now whole units are built off-site and then through the use of heavy machinery brought to the site and erected. This technique which was, perhaps, at first more generally used for residential construction is now used extensively also for non-residential and engineering construction. Closely associated with these off-site techniques has been the development of specialized construction companies which carry out either one phase of a large-scale project or act as a co-ordinator for the whole project.

Casting reinforced concrete girders, Saint John, New Brunswick. At the end of 1964, the mileage of highways and rural roads in Canada (exclusive of those in centres of more than 1,000 population) was 438,866.

The development has introduced a degree of specialization in the construction field that was completely unknown fifty years ago. This specialization is mostly confined to large construction projects although large-scale builders in the house-building industry have also developed the use of sub-contractors to a very high degree.

Perhaps the most profound changes in the construction field are to be found in the new uses being made of conventional materials and the introduction of new materials many of which have been developed only in recent times. While the importance of some conventional materials has declined, others have grown substantially within the past few years. Lumber which was used so widely for frame construction over the years has declined considerably in use although other wood products such as veneer and plywood are in big demand for various types of construction. The production of aluminum siding for houses has also decreased the use of such wood products as shingles and clapboard. Cement and quarry products are also in big demand but the greatest increase of all is the demand for concrete products. The development of ready-mix plants and pre-stressed concrete beams and slabs has placed a big demand on the manufacturers of concrete products. The diversification of the steel industry has also speeded up the production of structural materials many of which had previously been imported. Of particular significance here has been the manufacture, in Canada, in recent years, of both large and small diameter steel pipe for use in the transmission of crude oil, natural gas and other petroleum and chemical products. The development of the petrochemical industry has in turn resulted in the manufacture of many new building and industrial products such as floor and acoustic tile, new insulating materials and paint solutions.

Due to the over-all rapid growth of industry in Canada and the development of many new industrial products, the Canadian construction materials industry has been for some time relatively self-sufficient. From an historical viewpoint, it means that Canada since 1867 has changed from the traditional building technique of wood and stone, largely put in place by manual labour, to the twentieth century symbol of steel and concrete, much of it prefabricated, and put in place by the massive use of power equipment. (W. A. MONAGHAN)

CONSTRUCTION AND CAPITAL INVESTMENT

All first class mail goes by air in Canada. Two major airlines form the nucleus of freight and passenger service. In addition there are four domestic air carriers licensed to operate scheduled commercial air services in Canada.

# Transportation

Canada is the second largest country in the world; it extends, continent-wide, 4,000 miles encompassing an area of nearly four million square miles. As the main topographic barriers extend in a north-south direction, whole sections of the country are separated from one another: water barriers on the east coast; rough, rocky terrain between the Atlantic Provinces and Quebec; vast stretches of rock, water and barren muskeg, north of Lakes Huron and Superior, nearly 800 miles wide, between Eastern Canada and the Prairies, and a rugged mountain range between the Prairies and the Pacific Coast.

The task of tying together a number of colonies widely dispersed over this great territory a hundred years ago was one of the major problems of Confederation. Political union in 1867 was heavily dependent upon the provision of transportation facilities; indeed, without them there would probably have been no Confederation.

## Political and Economic Background

In the years immediately preceding Confederation, the Maritime colonies, Upper and Lower Canada, the Prairie settlements and the colony on the Pacific Coast were all undergoing changes. In the Maritimes, the "Golden Age" was fast coming to an end. The Maritimes had early established a highly unified and integrated economy based on resources of forest and sea, the products of which, carried in their own wooden ships, exploited world markets under the benefits of the old British Commercial System and the Reciprocity Treaty with the United States. The adoption of free trade by Britain

The "Lady Elgin", the first locomotive in Ontario, had a dignity all its own.

in the 1850's, the abrogation of the Reciprocity Treaty in 1866 and the gradual replacement of sail by steam, severely undermined this closely-knit economy. Not only were the region's markets lost, but in the process, the carrying and shipbuilding trades dried up. The coming of the railway, however, held out the possibility of a new era of economic expansion and development in relation to the markets in the Upper Colonies.

The Upper Colonies faced similar problems of industrial change, loss of markets, finance and transportation. Competition from the Erie Canal and the later development of railways in the United States rendered the St. Lawrence Canal System—completed at a cost of $20,000,000—largely obsolete. In addition, the hope that American grain and other products might be tempted to use the Canadian route in order to gain the advantage and preference in British markets was nullified by Britain's adoption of free trade.

The Upper Colonies faced an additional problem of defence arising out of the growth of the United States as a strong military power following the close of the Civil War; for this reason the Upper Colonies were also interested in the construction of a railway to the Maritimes. An additional consideration was the fear that New Brunswick's railway might be extended to the American boundary. Construction of an all British route, therefore, was essential.

Trade, transportation and defence were equally serious problems in the settlements on the Prairies and the Pacific coast. Great distances separated them from the central colonies and with sparse population there was fear of annexation by the United States. The slow rate of settlement was another problem. The broad and fertile lands of the American mid-west proved more attractive and were more accessible to prospective immigrants.

The tide of migration of United States citizens to British Columbia following the gold strikes of the 1850's gave rise to the fear that the colony would join or be annexed by the United States. This led to an increasing concern on the part of the central colonies to have the Pacific colony join the proposed national federation. As a result, Canada's interest in the Prairies was extended to the Pacific coast.

## Rail Construction and the National Policy

In 1850 there were 66 miles of railway in all the British North American colonies; ten years later there were over 2,000 miles; most of this comprised the Grand Trunk Railway which extended from Sarnia, through Toronto and Montreal, eastward to Rivière du Loup, Quebec. A transcontinental railway, joining the rail lines in the Maritimes to the Grand Trunk and the extension of the Grand Trunk westward to the Pacific coast now became an important part of the Confederation dream.

For some time the Maritimes had spent heavily on building railways in the hope of eventually linking up with the Grand Trunk; two previous attempts having failed, the Maritimes saw in Confederation the opportunity to obtain an intercolonial railway. Promise of its construction was to be a prerequisite to their entry.

British Columbia similarly desired a connecting link with Central Canada. The rapid extension of American railways, particularly the Northern Pacific, threatened to reach into Canada and divert the trade and interests of the west towards the United States. Accordingly the construction of a railway to the Pacific coast on Canadian soil became an essential condition for the creation both of political unity and of a truly national Canadian economy.

**The Intercolonial Railway**—The promised construction of an Intercolonial Railway from Central Canada to the Maritimes formed an integral part of the Terms of Union and was written into the British North America Act of 1867:

> Section 145. "Inasmuch as the Provinces of Canada, Nova Scotia, and New Brunswick have joined in a Declaration that the construction of the Intercolonial Railway is essential to the Consolidation of the Union of British North America, and to the Assent thereto of Nova Scotia and New Brunswick, and have consequently agreed that Provision should be made for its immediate Construction by the Government of Canada: Therefore, in order to give effect to that Agreement, it shall be the Duty of the Government and Parliament of Canada to provide for the Commencement within Six Months after the Union, of a Railway connecting the River St. Lawrence with the City of Halifax in Nova Scotia and for the Construction thereof without Intermission, and the Completion thereof with all practicable Speed".

Based on this promise, Nova Scotia and New Brunswick joined Confederation; however, Prince Edward Island delayed entry until 1873 when the Dominion Government agreed to absorb its railway debt and guarantee year round ferry service.

The Intercolonial Railway was completed in 1876; its cost—over $34,000,000— brought total public indebtedness for railway construction to well in excess of $100,000,000.

The Canadian Pacific Railway's first through transcontinental scheduled train arrives at Port Moody, British Columbia, July 4, 1886.

**The Pacific Railway**—One of the conditions of British Columbia's joining Confederation was that:

> "The Government of the Dominion undertake to secure the commencement simultaneously, within two years from the date of the Union, of the construction of a railway from the Pacific towards the Rocky Mountains, and from such point as may be selected, east of the Rocky Mountains, towards the Pacific, to connect the seaboard of British Columbia with the railway system of Canada; and further, to secure the completion of such railway within ten years from the date of the Union".

British Columbia's entry into Confederation in 1871 occurred during a period of economic expansion. Exports, manufacturing and immigration were rapidly increasing. The Dominion Government took over huge tracts of western land from the Hudson's Bay Company out of which were subsequently carved the provinces of Manitoba, Saskatchewan and Alberta. All of these factors contributed to a rising spirit of national prosperity.

This optimism was short-lived, however, as a world-wide depression in 1873 turned prosperity into slump. A declining rate of expansion coupled with political upheavals and government turnovers slowed construction of the transcontinental railroad. By 1880 near the time committed to British Columbia for its completion only about 700 miles had been built and the province on the Pacific was threatening to secede from Confederation.

Construction of the Pacific Railway constitutes an epic in Canadian transportation history and a challenge both to nature and to fortune. The line was to run for nearly 2,000 miles from Central Canada, 400 miles of which was barren muskeg and rock, 1,200 miles Prairie flatland and 500 miles of unexplored passes and mountain ranges. It was a daring project with an uncertain economic future. In its initial conception private capital was uninterested in the project. Its construction and completion was to become an integral part of the National Policy.

**The National Policy**—In an effort to restore prosperity, the Government, in 1879, announced the National Policy. A logical consequence of Confederation, the National Policy was, in effect, a series of policies designed to develop a truly transcontinental economy. Briefly, it was a three-pronged plan to settle the West, join it to the East through completion of the Pacific Railway and erect tariffs on manufactured goods to protect and encourage the development of secondary industry strengthening the flow of east-west trade. It thus rounded out a broad, consistent and comprehensive program of national development for the young country.

**Completion of the Pacific Railway**—As part of the National Policy, the Government in 1880, contracted with a syndicate, later known as the Canadian Pacific Railway Company, to complete the transcontinental railway. In return for a cash subsidy of $25,000,000 and land grants of 25,000,000 selected acres and other benefits, including a monopoly clause which practically freed the company from competition, north of the American border, the Company undertook to complete the railway. Despite the many difficulties, however, construction proceeded rapidly; the link from Port Arthur to Winnipeg was completed in 1883; the following year construction commenced on the difficult section through the wilderness north of Lake Superior, with costs running as high as $700,000 per mile of track in many sections. Meanwhile a line was being pushed through the mountains of British Columbia and the final gap was closed when the last spike was driven at Craigellachie in the Eagle Pass, November 7, 1885. The longest railway in the world was now open from coast to coast as East and West were finally linked by steel.

## Canals and Shipping

While railway construction played the dominant role in Canadian transportation policy after Confederation, continued efforts were made to improve the waterways system, the objective being to provide cheap transportation for the export grain of the rapidly-expanding area west of the Great Lakes. By the close of the century, the Canal system had been enlarged from nine feet to a minimum depth of 14 feet at a cost to the Dominion Government of $100,000,000. Despite these improvements, however, the tremendous volume of freight moving through the canals soon became too large for their limited depth. In addition, the limited navigation season, the constantly increasing size of vessels with deeper drafts, competition from the railways and other factors, further handicapped the growth of inland shipping with the result that the system failed to become the main artery of trade and commerce.

Canada's ocean shipping and shipbuilding industries also declined during this period. In 1878 Canada was the fourth largest ship-owning nation in the world with over 7,000 vessels totalling one and a third million tons. The depression, competition from foreign flag vessels and particularly the advent of iron and steel ships saw

The tonnage and traffic of the St. Lawrence Seaway has steadily increased in its eight years of operation. Freight traffic through Canadian canals in 1965 was almost three times greater than it was in 1955. All Canadian canals, with the exception of two on Cape Breton Island, are in the Central Provinces.

Canadian shipbuilding and vessel ownership fall behind that of Britain and the United States. By 1900, ocean shipping tonnage had decreased by nearly half and continued to decline until World War I.

## The Turn of the Century—Railway Crisis

The end of the depression in 1896 was followed by a period of rapid economic development with a great increase in population and capital investment. By 1913, the net value of manufacturing production increased by more than two and a half times, textile production more than doubled, production of iron and steel products increased more than threefold. Exports of timber and wood pulp, minerals such as nickel and copper, meats and dairy products all showed important increases. Most spectacular of all was the development of Prairie wheat and the rise of Canada to a leading position in the wheat markets of the world.

All of these changes, of course, had important effects on transportation, notably a feverish expansion of railway mileage during the closing years of the nineteenth

In four-score years, freight traffic on the railways has changed considerably. Canada's chief secondary industries now include chemicals, textiles, automobiles, electrical equipment and furniture.

century. A second transcontinental railway, the National Transcontinental, was built at government expense from Moncton, New Brunswick to Winnipeg, Manitoba, while the Grand Trunk Pacific Railway was extended from Winnipeg to the Pacific coast; concurrently, the Canadian Northern Railway was authorized to continue its line westerly from Edmonton to the Pacific coast and easterly from Port Arthur to Quebec. It was during this period that the so-called "railway problem" was born when three railway lines spanned the Dominion: there were three lines through the Rocky Mountains, two of them parallel, and three connections between Central Canada and the Maritimes, two of them through Canadian territory. Between 1903 and 1917, railway mileage almost doubled compared with a population increase of 40 per cent. Canada enjoyed the dubious distinction of having the highest per capita railway mileage in the world. It was a luxury the young country could ill afford.

## The Canadian National Railway System

The situation called for government help. A Railway Inquiry Commission in 1916 recommended that the government absorb several of the bankrupt lines, together with certain government-owned lines, including the Grand Trunk and the Intercolonial. Thus the nucleus of the Canadian National Railway system was formed in 1923.

More by accident than by design, the Government of Canada became the owner of what is today one of the largest railway systems in the world. Its establishment meant that this new system and the Canadian Pacific now owned or controlled some 95 per cent of all the railway mileage in Canada. In 1923 the Canadian National had 20,573 miles of track, while the Canadian Pacific had 13,563 miles.

The situation in 1967 with respect to railways in Canada is unique in history—the country owns and operates the Canadian National Railways in competition with the privately-owned Canadian Pacific, almost as large. These two rail systems offer a country-wide service extending from the Atlantic to the Pacific, covering some 41,000 miles of track. Together they represent a combined investment of over $5,000,000,000.

The effort to create an adequate national transportation system proved an expensive proposition for Canada. From Confederation to the formation of the Canadian National Railways, the Federal Government spent or pledged over $2,000,000,000 on railways; Canada's national unity and economic development depended upon them to a very large extent, however, and geography exacted a heavy price as the cost of national unity.

No sooner was this period of Canada's transportation development closing out than another was in the making as two new forms of transportation made their appearance, the motor vehicle and the aeroplane. By 1920, Federal Government controls had been established to regulate air transportation and to provide for the construction of airports and related facilities; it would be some years, however, before the true commercial significance of air transportation would be revealed. In the meantime the motor vehicle was well on its way to becoming an important factor in Canadian transportation.

## The Age of the Motor Vehicle

Prior to the turn of the century, intercity highways were few in number. Constructed for the most part of earth and gravel, they were designed for the purpose of colonization, defence, and as feeders to the rail and water transport systems. Most of the road building was concentrated in and around cities and towns to facilitate the local economy.

After 1900 the number of motor vehicles increased rapidly. Ontario started licensing automobiles in 1903 and by 1913 all provinces had registration systems. By 1915, registrations had risen to 95,000, almost one half in Ontario. There was a rapid development during the next 15 years and by 1930 registrations had increased to 1,232,489. Although the majority of these were passenger cars, the proportion of commercial vehicles had grown significantly from less than one per cent of the total in 1915 to 13 per cent in 1930.

This rapid increase in the number of motor vehicles gave rise to urgent demands for more and better roads. As the Federal Government was mainly concerned with the financing of canals and railways, the provinces and the municipalities assumed responsibility for roads and streets. Following World War I most provinces undertook major road and street building programs. Between 1921 and 1930 capital investment in streets, highways, bridges and ferries increased from $364,000,000 to $743,000,000. The new sources of tax revenue which the motor vehicle provided enabled the provinces to finance these large expenditures. During this same period, provincial revenues from motor vehicle licenses increased by $11,000,000 and gasoline taxes which had not yet been imposed in 1921, yielded more than $23,000,000 in 1930.

As registrations continued to increase, expenditures on roads and streets rose accordingly. By 1936 the provinces and municipalities had spent more than $875,000,000 on roads and bridges. The road and street network grew considerably. In 1922 there were only 49,000 miles of surfaced highways; in 1939 surfaced mileage increased to 135,000, including 9,000 miles of urban streets. Total road and street mileage amounted to 375,000.

In the Canadian Automotive Museum, Oshawa, automobiles of an earlier era remind the passer-by of the narrow, treacherous, gumbo roads that many such vehicles had to navigate, and of the horses that shied so violently at sight of these noisy contraptions.

## Air Transportation

Following World War I, the ability of the aircraft to penetrate areas inaccessible to other forms of transport found increasing use in mining development and exploration in the opening up of the Canadian North. The first air service for the regular conveyance of passengers, mail and freight commenced in 1924 in the opening up of the Rouyn-Quebec gold mines. Over 1,000 passengers, nearly 80,000 pounds of freight and some 15,000 pieces of mail were carried that year by air.

In the late 1920's, flying operations continued to expand in Canada as routes were opened up to new resource developments and the beginnings of an east-west pattern emerged as flying services began between major urban centres for the transport of mail. This period witnessed the first regular intercity airmail delivery established, flying clubs organized, government interest in trans-oceanic and long distance air transport, and the establishment of a trans-Canada airway.

The depression years of the early 1930's curtailed the development of the national system in Canada, though bush flying continued to expand. Between 1931 and 1937, freight carried in northern operations increased tenfold—to over 24,000,000 pounds— far more than in any other country in the world. It was during this time that the feats of Canada's bush pilots became legendary throughout the world.

For the general advancement of civil aviation in Canada, the Government in 1937 established Trans-Canada Air Lines (renamed Air Canada in 1964) as a national airline, thereby marking the beginning of airline operations in Canada in the modern sense. By the close of the 1930's Air Canada had inaugurated regular passenger services between Montreal, Toronto and Vancouver, between Montreal, Ottawa and Toronto, and between Lethbridge and Edmonton with a mail and express service to the Maritimes.

# Water Transportation

As mentioned previously, the Canadian shipping and shipbuilding industries had deteriorated close to the point of extinction by 1914. World War I, however, gave new life to the industry and Canada emerged from the War with one of the largest merchant fleets and shipbuilding capacities in the world. The depression of the early 1920's and the great depression of the 1930's, plus growing competition from other maritime nations, however, brought about a serious decline in Canada's international sea-borne shipping which continued to the outbreak of World War II in 1939. During and after the War, this pattern of rapid expansion and decline in the industry was once again repeated.

Inland shipping, particularly on the St. Lawrence-Great Lakes system also experienced difficulties between the two World Wars. Technological change, the appearance of larger vessels, depression, drought, a succession of poor crops on the Prairies, the development of Vancouver and Churchill for grain exports were all factors which combined to place inland shipping companies in financial difficulty. Though government expenditures to improve the waterways system and harbour facilities were extensive, shipping activity declined with the result that full utilization of the waterway was not realized. Proposals further to enlarge and deepen the waterway were advanced but no definite agreements or commitments could be realized at that time.

A modern car ferry links the provinces of Nova Scotia and Newfoundland.

# National Transportation System prior to World War II

As the 1930's closed, a fairly extensive national system of transportation facilities existed in Canada. An inventory taken at this time revealed that fixed plant consisted of nearly 1,900 miles of navigable inland waterways, leading from the Atlantic Ocean to the heart of the continent; nearly 43,000 miles of railway comprising two transcontinental systems; 375,000 miles of roads and streets with an almost completed route from coast to coast within Canada; and transcontinental airway routes under development.

Much of this had been completed at government expense. The extensive railway network had been constructed largely by the governments of Canada and the provinces; virtually the whole of the waterway system was developed at public expense. Total federal investment in both areas amounted to $3,400,000,000 in 1936, an investment of over $300 per capita. Reported outlays on roads and streets exceeded $1,000,000,000 between 1919 and 1936 alone, most of which had been expended by provincial and municipal governments; the transcontinental airway system was the responsibility of the Federal Government although a number of feeder and mining lines were privately owned. Combined, the provision of all these transportation facilities aggregated a public investment at nearly three quarters of the non-self-supporting debt of all levels of government in Canada by the end of 1937.

# A Revolution in Transportation

The outbreak of war in 1939 greatly affected all forms of transport. Construction of defence plants, conversion and expansion of existing industrial capacity in steel making, aircraft, ship and motor vehicle production and terminal facilities of all kinds brought about heavy capital investment in transportation facilities and intensive utilization of the national transportation system.

With the return to peace in 1945, Canada's economy continued to expand due to the backlog of demand for all types of consumer and industrial goods and a great increase in world demand for raw materials. The rapid growth of the economy during these early years was accompanied by significant changes in the transportation industry. New forms of transport appeared on the scene and new concepts and techniques utilizing different forms of transport were introduced.

Railroads and water carriers dominated the Canadian intercity freight transportation scene for over three quarters of a century, from Confederation to the end of the Second World War. In 1945 rail and water carriers accounted for 97 per cent of the volume of intercity ton-miles, 72 per cent of which was carried by the railways. By 1953 their combined share had dropped to 86 per cent while that of the railways alone decreased from 72 to 57 per cent. Trucks by this time had more than tripled their share of intercity ton-miles to nearly 10,000,000,000, while airlines recorded a sevenfold increase to 21,000,000 ton-miles.

As a result of the discovery of oil in Western Canada in 1947, pipelines emerged as a major form of transport, accounting for 6 per cent of intercity freight ton-miles in 1953. The net result was the growth of a competitive system of transportation that for all practical purposes eliminated the monopoly element which characterized this segment of the economy up to this time.

As stated in the MacPherson Royal Commission Report on Transportation (1961):

> "Since the end of World War II, the transportation environment in Canada has been transformed from a monopolistic one, very much dominated by the railways, into a highly competitive one in which a number of different modes of transport are vying for the available traffic. This fundamental change in environment has been accompanied by the development of a transportation system responsive to the greatly increased and changing demands of an expanding Canadian economy".

The story of postwar transportation developments in Canada, therefore, is to be told largely in terms of the growth of the newer forms of transportation and the efforts of the older carriers, particularly the railways, to adapt to the changed environment.

## Competition in Freight Transportation

A comparison of the work performed by each form of transport in terms of ton-miles, the standard unit measurement of transportation performance, reveals the nature of the change which has taken place in freight transportation.

**Intercity Ton-Miles Performed in Canada by Mode of Transport, 1938-64**
(000,000)

| Year | Rail | % | Water | % | Road | % | Air | % | Pipe-line | % | Total |
|---|---|---|---|---|---|---|---|---|---|---|---|
| 1938........ | 26,835 | 51.0 | 24,267 | 46.1 | 1,515 | 2.9 | 1 | .. | — | — | 52,618 |
| 1945........ | 63,349 | 71.7 | 21,994 | 25.0 | 2,995 | 3.3 | 3 | .. | — | — | 88,341 |
| 1950........ | 55,538 | 61.2 | 27,017 | 29.7 | 7,597 | 8.4 | 8 | .. | 610 | 0.7 | 90,770 |
| 1953........ | 65,267 | 56.9 | 32,845 | 28.6 | 9,778 | 8.5 | 21 | .. | 6,817 | 6.0 | 114,728 |
| 1955........ | 66,176 | 53.8 | 34,348 | 27.9 | 10,248 | 8.3 | 31 | .. | 12,302 | 10.0 | 123,105 |
| 1960........ | 65,445 | 46.8 | 36,869 | 26.4 | 13,841 | 9.9 | 43 | .. | 23,640 | 16.9 | 139,838 |
| 1961........ | 65,828 | 43.3 | 39,169 | 25.8 | 16,099 | 10.6 | 45 | .. | 30,791 | 20.3 | 151,932 |
| 1962........ | 67,937 | 41.6 | 42,720 | 26.2 | 16,585 | 10.1 | 49 | .. | 36,005 | 22.1 | 163,296 |
| 1963........ | 75,796 | 42.4 | 46,559 | 26.0 | 16,704 | 9.3 | 54 | .. | 39,880 | 22.3 | 178,993 |
| 1964........ | 85,033 | 42.4 | 54,164 | 27.0 | 18,181 | 9.0 | 64 | .. | 43,334 | 21.6 | 200,776 |

.. Less than one per cent.
— Nil.

## The Trucking Industry

The growth of the trucking industry since World War II has been one of the most significant developments in Canadian transportation history.

In the Report, *Transportation in Canada*, prepared for the Royal Commission on Canada's Economic Prospects, 1956, some of the more important reasons for the growth of trucking in Canada are set out— the development of secondary manufacturing, decentralization of industry, the growth of metropolitan areas, technological improvements in truck design and more and better roads. The development of light manufacturing industry following World War II created a demand for transportation which trucks were ideally suited to provide.

The main advantages of truck transport are flexibility and adaptability and these add up to economy and speed. Of the two, speed—the time elapsed from initiation of the shipment to delivery at the destination—is the more important to shippers in many instances due to savings in transit times. Another advantage of trucks is their ability to adapt the vehicle to the size of the shipment, enabling economical handling of less-than-carload freight. Door-to-door service, less warehousing and handling of goods, lower packing costs, are additional advantages of truck transport.

Technological improvements in the design of motor vehicle equipment have also been important. Trucks are larger and, with light-weight bodies and trailers, can carry heavier loads over longer distances, thus improving operating efficiency. The growing use of diesel engines has added further economies in fuel consumption, greater mileage between major repairs and overhauls.

Expansion and improvements in roads and streets have also been major factors in the growth of the trucking industry. Such major road programs as the Trans-Canada Highway, for example, have been of inestimable benefit to the trucking industry. Begun in 1949, the Trans-Canada Highway now stretches across Canada from coast to coast. This and other related major highway projects have greatly increased the economical length of truck operations: by 1966 truck hauls of over 2,000 miles were by no means uncommon and highway operations over distances of even 3,000 miles were being successfully undertaken.

### Road and Street Mileage

| Year | Highways and Rural Roads | | | Urban Streets | | |
|---|---|---|---|---|---|---|
| | Paved | Other | Total | Paved | Other | Total |
| 1945............ | 17,339 | 340,192 | 357,531 | 6,256 | 7,988 | 14,244 |
| 1950............ | 24,820 | 351,281 | 376,101 | 7,364 | 7,168 | 14,532 |
| 1955............ | 34,164 | 366,195 | 400,359 | 10,831 | 11,195 | 22,026 |
| 1960............ | 50,617 | 373,498 | 424,115 | 19,843 | 15,805 | 35,648 |
| 1963............ | 59,631 | 381,787 | 441,418 | 25,942 | 17,144 | 43,086 |
| 1964............ | 61,677 | 377,189 | 438,866 | 26,061 | 16,116 | 42,177 |

### Road and Street Expenditures

| Year | Highways and Rural Roads | Urban Streets | Total: All Roads and Streets |
|---|---|---|---|
| | $ | $ | $ |
| 1945...................... | 84,164,757 | 19,430,465 | 103,595,222 |
| 1950...................... | 277,913,759 | 53,116,916 | 331,030,675 |
| 1955...................... | 513,852,270 | 111,014,007 | 624,866,277 |
| 1960...................... | 794,873,201 | 272,388,000 | 1,067,261,201 |
| 1963...................... | 921,228,956 | 291,407,000 | 1,212,635,956 |
| 1964...................... | 1,100,628,717 | 283,015,000 | 1,383,643,717 |

Comprehensive statistics on the growth, nature and make-up of the trucking industry in Canada first became available in 1957. At that time the estimated truck population, excluding trucks not engaged in transportation service, was 832,055. Private urban trucks and farm trucks each accounted for approximately a third of these; private intercity trucks, a quarter, while intercity for-hire or public vehicles amounted to less than six per cent. This relationship was practically the same in 1966.

Not all of these trucks, of course, are necessarily competitive with other forms of transport; trucking within cities and most farm trucking is not competitive. The real significance of trucking is in the competitive segment of the industry—intercity trucking by both for-hire and private carriers: between 1957 and 1963 for-hire and private intercity ton-miles doubled to 16,000,000,000 or 85 per cent of total truck ton-miles.

# Pipelines

An equally significant postwar development in Canadian freight transportation has been the increasing number of ton-miles performed by pipelines in Canada. Development started on a large scale in the early 1950's following the construction of a number of important pipelines. By the mid-1950's, oil trunk pipelines accounted for over 10 per cent of total intercity ton-miles. A decade later with a number of important gas pipelines in operation, the pipelines' share more than doubled to over 21 per cent of the total, more than 43,000,000,000 ton-miles, which was well over twice that for trucks and nearly equal to water ton-miles.

This remarkable growth in such a short period of time was brought about by the discovery and exploitation of vast quantities of oil in Western Canada early in the postwar period. Up to 1947, crude oil production was small and confined mainly to the Turner Valley field in southwestern Alberta. The Leduc discovery in that year marked the beginning of a whole series of finds in Western Canada. Production of crude oil increased from less than 8,000,000 barrels in 1947 to 275,000,000 barrels in 1964. At the beginning of this period Canada's production met only about 10 per cent of domestic requirements; in 1964 it met approximately 60 per cent. This is particularly significant considering consumption rose over 400 per cent during the same period.

This tremendous growth in the production of oil brought about a spectacular increase in pipeline mileage in Canada with an important impact on other energy-producing industries and on transportation. In the ten years following Leduc, a network of over 5,000 miles of crude oil pipelines had been laid, including 3,200 miles of trunk lines carrying oil from the prairies to Central Canada and the Pacific Coast. By 1959 as production continued to increase, nearly 5,500 miles of oil trunk pipelines and an extensive network of gathering lines had been constructed; that year the railways carried only about a third of the volume of crude oil handled ten years earlier, despite the large increases in Canadian production and consumption during this period. By the end of 1964, there were nearly 8,000 miles of oil trunk pipeline in Canada.

The exploration for crude oil in Western Canada led to the discovery of major reserves of natural gas. In 1953 natural gas supplied roughly three per cent of the nation's energy needs. Ten years later production had multiplied tenfold to over one trillion cubic feet. During the period 1956-1962 the natural gas industry in Canada developed at a pace rivalling that of the oil industry in the early 1950's. Nearly twice as much gas was produced, transported and consumed in this period as in the previous 50 years.

Here again, successful marketing of these huge reserves in eastern and western Canada and the United States was dependent upon the construction of pipelines, the sole economic means of transporting natural gas. By the end of 1958 the 650-mile West Coast line from the Peace River district to Vancouver and the United States border was in operation and the following year the Trans-Canada pipeline extending 2,290 miles from Alberta to Toronto and Montreal was completed. By that time, natural gas transmission pipelines totalled over 4,100 miles. By the end of 1964, this had increased to nearly 6,000 miles.

## Crude Oil and Natural Gas Production and Pipeline Mileage, 1947-64

| Year | Crude Oil Production ('000 Barrels) | Pipeline Mileage Gathering | Pipeline Mileage Trunk | Pipeline Mileage Total | Natural Gas Production ('000 Mcf.) | Pipeline Mileage Gathering | Pipeline Mileage Transmission | Pipeline Mileage Total |
|------|------|------|------|------|------|------|------|------|
| 1947........ | 7,692 | | | | | | | |
| 1948........ | 12,287 | | | | | | | |
| 1949........ | 21,305 | | | | | | | |
| 1950........ | 29,044 | 265 | 1,158 | 1,423 | | | | |
| 1951........ | 47,616 | 333 | 1,244 | 1,577 | | | | |
| 1952........ | 61,237 | 380 | 2,120 | 2,500 | | | | |
| 1953........ | 80,899 | 436 | 3,358 | 3,794 | | | | |
| 1954........ | 96,080 | 569 | 4,087 | 4,656 | | | | |
| 1955........ | 129,440 | 887 | 4,193 | 5,080 | not available | | | |
| 1956........ | 171,981 | 1,405 | 4,646 | 6,051 | | | | |
| 1957........ | 181,848 | 1,778 | 5,095 | 6,873 | 220,007 | 167 | 2,707 | 2,874 |
| 1958........ | 165,496 | 2,000 | 5,147 | 7,147 | 337,804 | 257 | 3,850 | 4,107 |
| 1959........ | 184,778 | 2,382 | 5,426 | 7,808 | 417,335 | 298 | 4,110 | 4,408 |
| 1960........ | 189,534 | 2,776 | 5,661 | 8,437 | 522,972 | 306 | 4,365 | 4,671 |
| 1961........ | 220,848 | 3,164 | 6,390 | 9,554 | 655,738 | 393 | 5,077 | 5,470 |
| 1962........ | 244,115 | 3,494 | 6,543 | 10,037 | 946,703 | 405 | 5,190 | 5,595 |
| 1963........ | 257,662 | 3,681 | 6,926 | 10,607 | 1,117,425 | 405 | 5,505 | 5,910 |
| 1964........ | 274,626 | 3,792 | 7,952 | 11,744 | 1,407,098 | 464 | 5,917 | 6,381 |
| 1965........ | 293,572 | n.a. | n.a. | n.a. | 1,470,083 | n.a. | n.a. | n.a. |

# The St. Lawrence Seaway

As previously seen, improvements and enlargements in the St. Lawrence Canals system were undertaken periodically over a period of many years in an attempt to utilize the economical water route which the system offered for the transportation of goods in and out of the industrial heart of North America.

Negotiations between Canada and the United States to construct the Seaway began towards the end of the last century. In 1895, a Deep Waterways Commission was created by the governments of the two countries to report on the feasibility of a deep channel from the Great Lakes to the Atlantic. By the early years of the present century, the scheme was clearly conceived on the broad lines along which it now stands accomplished—as a joint undertaking of the two countries and with the joint purposes of a ship channel and a hydro-electric power source.

By 1900, the canal system had been deepened to 14 feet as the controlling depth. In 1912 the Canadian Government proceeded to improve the Welland Canal to provide 27-foot depths with locks 800 feet long and 80 feet wide. Work began the following year, was suspended during the War, but was finally completed in 1932 at a cost of $132,000,000. This was the first decisive step in the construction of the present St. Lawrence Seaway.

Negotiations continued between the two countries during the intervening years, punctuated by a series of plans and proposals and of chronic delays in reaching firm decisions. The growing needs of commerce increasingly pointed to the desirability of building the Seaway and in 1954 agreement was reached between the two countries to proceed with its construction. Opened in 1959, the 400-year dream of a deep waterway extending some 2,300 miles from the Atlantic Ocean to the head of the Great Lakes finally became a reality.

Like pipelines, the decision to build the Seaway was associated with resource development, notably iron ore, following the opening up of the Quebec-Labrador iron ore deposits. The increased demand for iron and steel in the United States coupled with declining sources of supply prompted the Materials Policy Commission in the U.S., set up to examine the outlook for domestic supplies and imports, to report:

> "Construction of the proposed St. Lawrence Seaway is necessary if ore is to move in quantity from Labrador to mills in the Midwest. The Seaway, with its 27-foot channel, would make it possible to transport ore in large carriers directly from Seven Islands to lower lake ports. It would reduce the cost of the all-water route by more than 25 per cent, permit a fourfold expansion of these shipments, and exercise pressure on rail rates from Montreal and Baltimore to Pittsburgh and points west".

From Canada's point of view, the important power and resource development associated with the Seaway, together with savings in transportation costs, principally on grain from the Lakehead to Lower St. Lawrence ports, were advanced as the major arguments supporting construction of the Seaway; in addition, the Seaway held promise of more efficient use of shipping in the upbound movement of iron ore and coal. These were the three main commodities expected to benefit from the Seaway.

**Traffic.** Following its completion, the annual volume of traffic expected to use the Seaway was estimated at 20,000,000 tons of iron ore, up to 10,000,000 tons of grain and grain products and 4,000,000 tons of coal. Other volume movements were estimated at around 1,500,000 tons of paper, pulpwood and wood pulp, and possibly 8,000,000 tons of miscellaneous cargo. In 1957, traffic on the St. Lawrence Canals averaged 10,000,000 tons a year. An estimated $45,000,000 to $50,000,000 in transportation savings were expected annually by the avoidance of costly trans-shipment enabling continuous carriage through the Seaway by large bulk carriers which provide one of the cheapest methods of transportation in the world.

The St. Lawrence Seaway, a network of navigable waters comprised of the St. Lawrence River and the five Great Lakes, enables vessels up to 730 feet in length to sail directly from the Atlantic Ocean to the westernmost reaches of the Great Lakes, a distance of some 2,300 miles.

These anticipated savings were, of course, dependent upon the level of tolls. The St. Lawrence Seaway Authority Act stipulated that tolls should be sufficient to cover the cost of maintaining and operating the Seaway, of paying interest at current rates on the funds borrowed, and of amortizing the investment over a period of fifty years, estimated at approximately $20,000,000 a year.

The Tolls Committee estimated that traffic through the new portion of the Seaway in the first year would approximate 25,000,000 tons, doubling to 50,000,000 by 1968. For the Welland Canal, tonnage was estimated at 40,000,000 tons in 1959, increasing to 60,000,000 in 1968.

### St. Lawrence Seaway Traffic and Revenue
### Forecast and Actual, 1959-64

| Year | St. Lawrence Canals | | | |
| | Volume of Cargo | | Toll Revenue | |
| | Forecast | Actual | Forecast[1] | Actual |
| | ('000 tons) | | ($ '000) | |
|---|---|---|---|---|
| 1959 | 25,000 | 21,221 | 9,301 | 7,400 |
| 1960 | 29,000 | 20,752 | 10,789 | 7,300 |
| 1961 | 33,000 | 23,673 | 12,277 | 8,200 |
| 1962 | 37,000 | 25,748 | 13,765 | 9,200 |
| 1963 | 41,000 | 31,164 | 15,254 | 11,200 |
| 1964 | 44,000 | 39,440 | 16,370 | 14,200 |
| | Welland Ship Canal | | | |
| 1959 | 40,000 | 27,506 | 2,060 | 1,800 |
| 1960 | 43,000 | 29,281 | 2,215 | 2,000 |
| 1961 | 46,000 | 31,404 | 2,369 | 2,200 |
| 1962 | 50,000 | 35,511 | 2,575 | 1,400[2] |
| 1963 | 53,000 | 41,325 | 2,730 | 800 |
| 1964 | 55,000 | 51,416 | 2,833 | 900 |

[1]Report of St. Lawrence Seaway Authority Canadian Tolls Committee June 12, 1958.
[2]Tolls suspended July 18, 1962.

Data for the first six years of operation show that while traffic has not been up to predictions, it has been increasing each year at a growing rate. Evidence of this can be seen in the fact that in 1964 there was an increase of 27 per cent in tonnage through the Seaway. If this trend continues, the ultimate objective of 50,000,000 tons may be reached and exceeded.

Traffic in the Welland Canal also increased substantially in 1964, passing the 50,000,000-ton mark for the first time. A modernization program in this section is expected to result in a substantial increase in potential cargo tonnage beyond the 60,000,000 ton-mark.

The St. Lawrence Seaway has been of great economic benefit to Canada. It made it possible for Canada to become a world leader in the export of grain, provided low-cost transportation for the raw materials needed for the industrialization of the country, and has been of inestimable benefit to other modes of transport as every pound of goods carried on the Seaway has to be carried to or from it by some other mode. Indeed, the Seaway has proved one of the principal means by which Canada has achieved its present position of long-sustained prosperity.

# Air Freight

Compared to other modes of transport, the amount of freight transported by air in Canada is relatively insignificant, less than one tenth of one per cent of total intercity ton-miles. In terms of rates of growth, however, air freight has far outdistanced all other carriers, with the exception of pipelines. From less than 12,000,000 pounds in 1945 the tonnage of freight moved by air rose to 222,000,000 pounds in 1964 while air ton-miles increased from 3,000,000 to 64,000,000 during the same period.

The major growth in air freight occurred in the early 1950's as a result of resource developments and the building of defence projects in the Canadian North. Between 1951 and 1956 air freight increased from 50,000,000 pounds to 300,000,000 pounds— an all-time high. It is unlikely that the Knob Lake, the Kitimat and the DEW line projects would ever have been completed so quickly without the availability of air transport. Indeed, in this respect, the airplane is playing as important a role in the development of the North as did the railways in opening up the West.

In more recent years, the growth of air freight has been mainly in the field of inter-city operations. Between 1960 and 1964 the volume of freight (excluding express) transported by Canadian scheduled carriers rose from 54,000,000 pounds to 93,000,000. Air freight ton-miles doubled to 57,000,000 during this period. Both Air Canada and Canadian Pacific Airlines equalled this performance. Air Canada increased its volume to 67,000,000 pounds and Canadian Pacific to 8,500,000.

This growth in air freight has resulted largely from the advantages of air transport over other carriers, mainly speed, particularly significant for perishables or style-dated commodities. Other important advantages of air freight are elimination or reduction of inventory and the elimination of costly packaging. With the introduction of larger and more economic aircraft, service and capacity have been greatly increased with corresponding reduction in costs; indeed, in recent years there has been a downward trend in air freight rates and various class and commodity rates have been put into effect to develop particular markets.

The rapid rate of expansion of air freight shows no sign of slackening as airlines of almost every nation are carrying larger payloads of revenue-producing freight. The International Air Transport Association recently reported that shipments over the Atlantic routes increased by almost two thirds during the first quarter of 1965 compared with those in the previous year. Loads on the all-cargo planes were 84 per cent higher, while mixed flights (passengers and air cargo) improved by about 50 per cent. An example of the mixed aircraft is Air Canada's DC-8 jets which carry 69 passengers and seven cargo pallets, each capable of holding 7,000 pounds.

What started out as a high cost premium service for special shipments has now become an important means of transport for the fast movement of freight to distant points. Virtually anything can be carried by plane and the range of goods going by air is constantly growing. The growth of air freight in Canada, though impressive, is only in its infancy. Indeed, it has been estimated that by 1970 the volume of air freight will double to more than 1,250,000 tons of goods annually.

## Railway Transportation

The years following World War II were difficult ones for Canada's railways. With the removal of price and wage controls, they were immediately faced with substantial increases in wage costs. Coupled with this was the growing problem of truck competition. In 1949 a Royal Commission was appointed to study the whole problem of railway transportation in Canada. The railways reported to the Commission that truck competition was costing them millions of dollars annually in lost traffic; as a partial solution, they requested equal regulation of the trucking industry and greater freedom in pricing policy.

A nine-day railway strike in 1950 forced shippers to turn to trucks, many of them for the first time; the trucking industry met the challenge and much traffic was irretrievably lost to the railways. The Royal Commission which reported in 1951 stated:

> "Truck competition in Central Canada has grown to such a size as to eat into the railways' revenues by capturing a great portion of their most profitable traffic and by making it necessary for them to reduce their rates to what looks like a dangerously low point in order to retain some of it".

Despite the Commission's recommendations, no immediate solution to the railways' problems was forthcoming. To meet truck competition, the railways turned to the wide-scale use of "agreed charges", which are competitive rates tied to a traffic volume guarantee, and were highly successful in their efforts. Revenues earned from agreed charges doubled between 1950 and 1954 to $20,000,000, representing about 6 per cent of total railway freight earnings. By the end of 1963, over 1,200 agreed charges were in effect accounting for more than 21 per cent of total railway freight revenue.

Another significant change in railway pricing policy has been the substitution of competitive for class rates. In 1951, for example, 8.4 per cent of railway traffic measured in ton-miles moved under class rates; by 1962 this had decreased to 2 per cent. Revenue from this traffic declined from 21 per cent to 5.5 per cent. Traffic under competitive rates, on the other hand, again measured in ton-miles, doubled during the same period to 16 per cent, while revenue nearly tripled to 25.5 per cent.

During the past 15 years, the railways have undertaken large-scale programs of plant and equipment modernization. Much of the old equipment was replaced in an effort to improve service and reduce costs. The most dramatic example of this was the conversion to dieselization and by 1963 the railways in Canada had become completely dieselized. The greater pulling power of the diesel locomotive over the older steam engine is indicated by the fact that in 1964 with 29 per cent fewer units the railways achieved 50 per cent more gross ton-miles than in 1950.

Other major innovations and technological improvements in plant have been the extension of centralized traffic control, expediting train operations and increasing main-track capacity, construction of electronically-controlled classification yards, replacing obsolete and scattered flatyards; mechanization of maintenance-of-way procedures and many other important technological innovations such as welded rail, improved communications and control devices.

Significant improvements and innovations have been made in rolling-stock with new and improved freight cars of various designs featuring heavier load and cubic capacity, special tank cars for hauling bulk liquids; automobile triple-deck transporter cars, and a vast variety of other types tailored to specific commodity movements.

The railways also attempted to meet truck competition directly through the operation of their own trucking fleets. The two major railways are among the largest truck operators in the country operating entire trucking fleets as wholly-owned subsidiaries and by direct purchase of truck lines. An important related aspect of this has been the growth of railway piggyback operations. This service of carrying highway trailers on railway flat cars was first started in 1957 and since that time has grown from 77,000 trailers in 1958 to nearly 232,000 in 1964. In the latter year Canadian National Railways reported a 30 per cent increase in trailers loaded on flat cars and ordered an additional 400 piggyback cars to add to the existing fleet of 800. The Canadian Pacific Railway Company has over 1,500 cars in piggyback service with more on order. This equipment and 59 piggyback terminals make Canadian Pacific one of the largest plan 1 (common carrier's trailers on railway owned flat cars) piggyback operators in North America.

Other innovations, both technological and administrative have been introduced by the railways in recent years as part of a concerted effort to regain lost traffic and to strengthen their competitive position. Both major railways have introduced new types of service for handling less-than-carload traffic and express, offering co-ordinated service by road and rail and in some cases by air and water. They have also invested heavily in specialized containers designed to achieve intermodal flexibility. Thus on these two broad fronts all the major railways have attempted to adapt to the changed transportation environment.

Though in relative terms the railways' share of intercity freight traffic has decreased, they are carrying substantially increased volumes of traffic each year. From 1961 to 1964 rail traffic increased from 174,500,000 tons to 211,500,000 tons, and ton-miles increased almost a third during the same period from 66,000,000,000 to over 85,000,000,000.

The important pioneering role played by railways in the early history of the country is being repeated today in the North. While first main or single track mileage in Canada shows a gain of only about 1,000 miles since the end of World War II, new lines opened to traffic during that period have increased by more than 2,300 miles. Branch line abandonments of some 1,300 miles account for the smaller net gain.

The general direction of much of this main line increase has been northward to Canada's hinterland, stimulated by resource developments. To mention a few of the more significant: a 114-mile line was completed in 1953 between Sherridon and Lynn Lake in northern Manitoba opening up a rich new source of base metal wealth; in 1954 the Iron Ore Company of Canada constructed a 358-mile railway line between Sept Îles and Schefferville to tap the rich iron ore deposits of Ungava, near the Quebec-Labrador Boundary. In 1957, the 161-mile Beattyville-Chibougamau line was constructed; in 1959 a 133-mile line from St. Félicien to Chibougamau completed a 294-mile arc of rail cutting through the lumber and mineral-rich Quebec northland. In 1957 the Pacific Great Eastern Railway extended its line from Prince George to Fort St. John, British Columbia, a distance of 252 miles; in 1962 the 190-mile Cartier Railway was completed from Port Cartier to iron ore areas at Lac Jeannine and Mount Wright in the province of Quebec; and in 1964, 430 miles of railway between Roma, Alberta, Hay River, N.W.T. and Pine Point were built to carry lead and zinc concentrates from the Pine Point mining area on the south shore of Great Slave Lake to smelters at Trail, British Columbia and to help develop the north Peace River country. The last-named is the first railway to operate in the Northwest Territories and the second Canadian Railway to cross the 60th parallel; the first being the White Pass and Yukon Route between Skagway, Alaska and Whitehorse, Yukon.

Changes in the pattern of passenger travel have been equally significant. According to the Report, *Transportation in Canada*, the passenger car had established itself as the principal means of intercity travel in Canada as far back as 1928, accounting for nearly 60 per cent of total intercity passenger-miles. Railways were in second place with 38.3 per cent, while intercity buses had 2.2 per cent.

The situation changed significantly during the 1930's. By the middle of the decade the passenger car had increased its share of passenger-miles to nearly three quarters of total passenger-miles and intercity buses doubled their share to nearly five per cent. Much of this increase had been at the expense of railway passenger traffic which dropped by almost half to just over a fifth of the total. During the War, passenger car travel was necessarily restricted and railways once again became the leading mode of transport, accounting for nearly half of all passenger-miles in 1945. Following the War, the great increase in the number of motor vehicles and the growth of air travel changed the relative situation dramatically.

### Intercity Passenger-Miles by Mode of Transport, 1949-64

| Year | Automobile | | Rail | | Bus | | Air | | Total | |
|---|---|---|---|---|---|---|---|---|---|---|
| | '000,000 | % | '000,000 | % | '000,000 | % | '000,000 | % | '000,000 | % |
| 1949......... | 15,695 | 69.5 | 3,193 | 14.1 | 3,327 | 14.7 | 385 | 1.7 | 22,600 | 100.0 |
| 1950......... | 17,364 | 72.3 | 2,816 | 11.7 | 3,386 | 14.1 | 445 | 1.9 | 24,011 | 100.0 |
| 1955......... | 30,227 | 81.9 | 2,892 | 7.8 | 2,801 | 7.6 | 995 | 2.7 | 36,915 | 100.0 |
| 1960......... | 41,351 | 85.5 | 2,264 | 4.7 | 2,593 | 5.4 | 2,143 | 4.4 | 48,351 | 100.0 |
| 1961......... | 42,990 | 85.8 | 1,961 | 3.9 | 2,654 | 5.3 | 2,519 | 5.0 | 50,124 | 100.0 |
| 1962......... | 44,845 | 85.8 | 2,019 | 3.8 | 2,713 | 5.2 | 2,708 | 5.2 | 52,285 | 100.0 |
| 1963......... | 47,180 | 85.9 | 2,070 | 3.8 | 2,862 | 5.2 | 2,826 | 5.1 | 54,938 | 100.0 |
| 1964......... | 49,679 | 85.1 | 2,681 | 4.6 | 2,886 | 5.0 | 3,109 | 5.3 | 58,355 | 100.0 |

### Intercity Passenger-Miles by Mode of Transport
### Public Carriers only, 1949-64

| Year | Rail | | Bus | | Air | | Total | |
|---|---|---|---|---|---|---|---|---|
| | '000,000 | % | '000,000 | % | '000,000 | % | '000,000 | % |
| 1949.................. | 3,193 | 46.2 | 3,327 | 48.2 | 385 | 5.6 | 6,905 | 100.0 |
| 1950.................. | 2,816 | 42.4 | 3,386 | 50.9 | 445 | 6.7 | 6,647 | 100.0 |
| 1955.................. | 2,892 | 43.2 | 2,801 | 41.9 | 995 | 14.9 | 6,688 | 100.0 |
| 1960.................. | 2,264 | 32.4 | 2,593 | 37.0 | 2,143 | 30.6 | 7,000 | 100.0 |
| 1961.................. | 1,961 | 27.5 | 2,654 | 37.2 | 2,519 | 35.3 | 7,134 | 100.0 |
| 1962.................. | 2,019 | 26.4 | 2,713 | 38.1 | 2,708 | 35.5 | 7,440 | 100.0 |
| 1963.................. | 2,070 | 26.7 | 2,862 | 36.9 | 2,826 | 36.4 | 7,758 | 100.0 |
| 1964.................. | 2,681 | 30.9 | 2,886 | 33.3 | 3,109 | 35.8 | 8,676 | 100.0 |

### Intercity Passengers Carried by Mode of Transport, 1941-64

| Year | Rail | | Bus | | Air | | Total | |
|---|---|---|---|---|---|---|---|---|
| | '000 | % | '000 | % | '000 | % | '000 | % |
| 1941.............. | 29,779 | 45.7 | 35,276 | 54.1 | 138 | 0.2 | 65,193 | 100.0 |
| 1944.............. | 60,336 | 37.6 | 99,640 | 62.2 | 285 | 0.2 | 160,261 | 100.0 |
| 1949.............. | 34,884 | 19.2 | 145,404 | 80.1 | 1,259 | 0.7 | 181,547 | 100.0 |
| 1950.............. | 31,139 | 18.6 | 134,487 | 80.5 | 1,500 | 0.9 | 167,126 | 100.0 |
| 1955.............. | 27,230 | 22.2 | 92,158 | 75.1 | 3,249 | 2.7 | 122,637 | 100.0 |
| 1960.............. | 19,497 | 20.9 | 68,580 | 73.3 | 5,452 | 5.8 | 93,529 | 100.0 |
| 1961.............. | 18,784 | 21.1 | 64,288 | 72.4 | 5,741 | 6.5 | 88,813 | 100.0 |
| 1962.............. | 19,258 | 22.4 | 60,695 | 70.6 | 6,064 | 7.0 | 86,017 | 100.0 |
| 1963.............. | 20,636 | 23.7 | 60,040 | 69.1 | 6,278 | 7.2 | 86,954 | 100.0 |
| 1964.............. | 22,915 | 26.3 | 57,370 | 65.9 | 6,772 | 7.8 | 87,057 | 100.0 |

## The Passenger Car

The number of cars has increased, on the average, by well over 200,000 a year since 1949; in that year there were less than 1,700,000 passenger cars in Canada, one for every eight persons; in 1964 there were over 6,000,000, one for every four persons. Canada has more cars per person than any other country in the world, except the United States, which has one for every 2.8 people. In 1964, Canadians drove over 50,000,000,000 miles, an increase of 150 per cent over 1949 mileage.

Once considered a luxury, the automobile has become a virtual necessity for most Canadians—for driving to work, for shopping, and for the annual vacation. Higher incomes, relatively easier financing, have brought ownership within the reach of most families. Indeed, Canada now has more cars than households with many families owning more than one car. In 1959 about 7.2 per cent of Canadian households had two or more cars while in 1965 12.4 per cent had more than one car. The automobile is also used extensively for business purposes, particularly by commercial travellers.

Though owning and operating an automobile is considerably more expensive than travelling by either rail or bus, the convenience, privacy and ready availability of the family car make comparative cost virtually meaningless. The passenger car now accounts for well over four fifths of all intercity passenger travel and its predominance in this field, for the above reasons, seems unlikely to change.

## Air Travel

Though the number of passengers carried by air is relatively small compared with carriage by railways and buses, air passenger-miles exceed both rail and bus passenger-miles. Between 1945 and 1955 air passenger-miles increased from 132,000,000 to 1,000,000,000. By 1964 domestic air passenger-miles exceeded 3,000,000,000. At this time the airlines' share of intercity passenger-miles performed by public carriers had risen to 36 per cent, whereas the rail and bus shares declined to 31 per cent and 33 per cent respectively.

This great increase in commercial air travel in the past 20 years is another of the outstanding developments in Canadian transportation history. The War, of course, had a tremendous effect on the development of aviation in Canada. The construction of new airports, improvements and expansion of existing airports, radio and navigational facilities, the training of personnel, the development of domestic and international routes, the advent of larger and faster aircraft were important factors bearing on the postwar growth of commercial aviation in Canada. An important event in the field of civil aviation occurred in 1942 when a number of independently-owned airlines were amalgamated to form Canadian Pacific Airlines. In the first year of operation, this new airline carried a total of 60,000 passengers and 10,000,000 pounds of freight, express and mail.

Air Canada also expanded during the War and by the end of 1943 was operating nearly 5,000 miles of routes. Another significant wartime development was the establishment of the Canadian Government Transatlantic Air Service in 1943 using Air Canada personnel and equipment. With the return to peace in 1945, commercial flying developed rapidly. A number of regional carriers were established mainly by returning air force personnel, greatly expanding domestic operations.

The two major airlines undertook substantial programs of development by the acquisition of new aircraft and the establishment of additional services. In 1947 Air Canada formally took over the Government's transatlantic service on a full commercial basis in competition with other commercial airlines over the transatlantic route. The Canadian-designed and Canadian-built North Star was introduced on this service as well as on domestic transcontinental service and was also used in the extension of transborder and southern services to the United States and the Caribbean.

In 1949 Canadian Pacific Airlines inaugurated service to Australia, New Zealand and the Orient. During the 1950's as continued route expansion took place, new equipment was introduced. Super Constellations and DC6's were first used in international service and were subsequently replaced by Viscounts, Vanguards and Britannias. Air Canada established service to continental Europe and Canadian Pacific Airlines to Mexico, South America and Europe via the southern transatlantic route. During this time both Air Canada and Canadian Pacific became world airlines, Air Canada ranking among the world's top ten.

Early in the 1960's the jet age was inaugurated and air travel continued to grow at an impressive rate. The number of passengers carried increased over a million in just four years from 5,500,000 in 1960 to 6,800,000 in 1964. Much of this increase was in international traffic. Air passenger travel now accounts for well over a third of intercity passenger-miles performed by public carriers.

The relatively small number of passengers travelling by air indicates that the air travel market has great potential. Lower fares, increasing personal incomes, longer vacations and increased leisure time have all made air travel the most desirable means of travelling long distances. As faster, larger, more luxurious aircraft are introduced, air travel can be expected to continue to expand.

## The Intercity Bus

Bus travel has declined steadily since World War II. In 1949, 145,000,000 passengers were carried by bus; by 1964 the total had fallen to 57,000,000, less than half. While in terms of total intercity passenger-miles, the relative importance of bus travel has declined, from 15 per cent of the total to 5 per cent; comparing only public carriers, the decline has been much less pronounced—from roughly half of the total to a third. The great increase in airline passenger-miles, moreover, accounts for much of this apparent decline. Compared to the postwar trend in rail travel, bus passenger-miles have maintained a close relationship. In 1964, buses performed 2,900,000,000 passenger-miles compared to 2,700,000,000 railway passenger-miles. In terms of passengers, however, buses carried more than 2½ times as many as the railways.

Undoubtedly, the main reason for the decline in bus passenger travel has been the growing use of the automobile. The advantages of the private car over the bus are many and, though more expensive, cost is seldom reckoned on a comparative basis. As mentioned previously, the private car is used principally for short trips, but an increasing proportion of longer trips are also being made by car for business and recreational purposes.

Railway competition has also been a factor partially responsible for the decline in bus travel but not to the same extent. Passengers carried and passenger-miles performed by rail and bus indicate that bus travel has been most heavily used for short and medium hauls since rail and bus passenger-miles are nearly equal, despite the wide disparity in numbers of passengers carried. The introduction of new equipment and facilities, better scheduling and improved service has enabled the industry to

The Seaway is now in its ninth season of operation. Today a "laker", fully loaded to a maximum permissible draft of 25½ feet, can carry 1,000,000 bushels of grain and on the journey back transport a full load of iron ore from the rich Quebec-Labrador fields to the blast furnaces of the heavily industrialized middle west.

maintain this position in the face of competition from both the automobile and the railways.

## Rail Travel

Like bus traffic, railway passenger traffic has declined steadily since World War II. From the peak year 1944 when 60,000,000 passengers were carried, the number dropped to less than 20,000,000 in 1961, the lowest point ever. Only in very recent years has this trend been reversed. Rail travel has been hard hit by the passenger car and bus in the short and medium haul fields and by air carriers in the medium and long haul fields. Comparing all modes of transport the railways' share of intercity passenger-miles has decreased from 14 per cent of the total in 1949 to less than 5 per cent in 1964. Compared with public carriers, however, the railways' share has dropped from roughly half of the total in 1949 to less than a third in 1964. Increases in automobile and air passenger-miles largely explain this trend.

As noted previously, the trend has been reversed. The number of passengers carried has increased from nearly 19,000,000 in 1961 to almost 23,000,000 in 1964, due largely to new rail passenger fares. The Canadian National pioneered this in North America with its unique "red, white and blue" fare plan and, with the addition of much new equipment, is making an intensive effort to attract passengers back to the railways. The success of the railway's attempts will largely determine whether the current upward trend in rail passenger travel will continue.

## Highlights of a Century

The construction of the St. Lawrence Canals system prior to Confederation; the stitching together of the scattered colonies with railways; the building of the Canadian Pacific Railway in the 1880's; the railway crisis of World War I and the establishment of the Canadian National Railway system; the coming of the motor vehicle; early bush flying and the founding of the national airlines in the 1930's; and, following World War II, the growth of trucking; the building of pipelines; and the construction of the St. Lawrence Seaway, constitute the highlights of a century of transportation development and progress in Canada.

Canada is, perhaps, unique among modern nations in that, possessing no formal national transportation policy, it has developed one of the finest transportation systems in the world. Its two major railways are among the world's greatest; indeed, the Canadian National is the continent's largest railway system and the Canadian Pacific, the world's largest privately-owned railway, and the two vigorously compete with each other with the fortunes of the privately-owned railway strongly influencing those of the government-owned system.

The two major airlines, one of which is publicly and the other privately owned, provide a standard of service unexcelled by any other major nation and in serving virtually all have become truly world airlines in the modern sense.

The St. Lawrence Seaway, extending from the Atlantic to the heart of the North American continent, has fulfilled the dreams of its early planners by tapping much of the trade of the entire continent thereby enabling Canada to maintain its role as one of the world's leading trading nations.

Pipelines have played a major role in making it possible for Canada to exploit economically its virtually limitless resources of oil and natural gas, and thus have added substantially to the nation's total productive wealth.

The motor vehicle has affected the lives of all Canadians by bringing about fundamental changes in the way they live, in the way they move, and in the way they ship their goods.

None of this came about by accident, or at small cost. Canada's transportation system developed largely as a result of political expediency, economics playing a secondary role. Great in size and small in population, with vast resources of raw materials but with a limited domestic market, this was and is, perhaps, in the nature of things.

(A. L. BROWN and E. T. STEEVES)

# Retail Trade

The retail store is familiar to every Canadian of practically every age. To the average Canadian, it reflects, to some extent, the economic conditions in his country, for over 60 per cent of his available income is usually spent in such establishments.

## 1867-1920

The economy of Canada in the early years of Confederation was distinctly resource-oriented. The majority of the population was employed in farming or in other primary activities such as mining, forestry, fishing and hunting. The manufacturing concerns which existed at this time were engaged, for the most part, in such activities as flour-milling, saw-milling and tanning. Flourishing businesses also existed for the manufacture of boots and shoes, alcoholic beverages, bread and other important staples.

The retailing sector of the economy clearly reflected the rural character of Canada. Most transactions between retailer and consumer, outside the larger cities, were consummated through negotiations. The price paid for a particular item invariably represented a consensus between the merchant and consumer, and the time required to achieve this consensus could vary from a few moments to a few hours.

**Business by Barter**—In rural areas, barter was the most common method of doing business. Farmers brought in their produce, such as eggs and butter, hides and wool, in order to pay for proposed purchases. Merchants were required to be familiar not only with the goods they sold but with the value of the bartered produce as well. For most merchants, the exchange of goods was by no means the end of their responsibilities. Delivery of commodities was not commonplace except for such large items as sugar, flour and salt. Most of these items were delivered in bulk and one of the functions of the shopkeeper was to package them in varying quantities to suit individual purchasers.

Merchants were required to travel to the various wholesalers, who were usually located in the larger cities, in order to purchase smaller-sized items. Goods received by merchants in barter were either sold to buyers who regularly came through the country collecting these goods or were carried by the merchants to the cities on their own buying trips. In some rare instances, the farm produce was transported to wholesalers by rail.

Pedlars were a common sight during the early years of Confederation. These "mobile merchants" were eagerly awaited by most families in rural areas. This was also the age when the wholesaler was to reach his pinnacle of power and influence in the distribution of goods. Both the manufacturer and the retailer conducted their activities on a small scale and therefore had to rely on the merchant-wholesaler not only for the distribution of their goods but also, in many instances, financial assistance. Direct selling and/or buying, common practices today, were practically non-existent for most manufactured commodities. All imported commodities flowed through wholesalers' hands and most exports were sold to wholesale exporters.

**The Department Store**—It was during this time, however, that a new development in merchandising was taking place which was to disturb greatly the old order—the birth of the department store. On December 8, 1869, Timothy Eaton opened a store in Toronto at 178 Yonge Street. This, in itself, was not an earth-shaking occurrence.

The attractive displays of downtown and suburban stores lure their quota of customers. Between 1956 and 1965 the value of retail sales in Canada increased 50 per cent.

What set the winds of change in motion through the then traditional methods of merchandising goods was Timothy Eaton's philosophy. This young merchant, who had operated a general store in St. Mary's, prior to his move to Toronto, had become acutely aware of the limitations imposed on a merchant doing business in the usual manner, especially in rural areas. He was eager to rid himself of the functions imposed on the storekeepers of his day under the system of barter and merchant-customer price negotiations. By locating in Toronto, he was able to rid himself of the onerous barter system, since in urban areas most purchases were made for cash. Even in urban areas, however, long-term credit and "bargaining" or "dickering" were still in vogue.

In his new store, Timothy Eaton decided to eliminate entirely the practice of bargaining. All goods were clearly marked as to price and were not subject to change. In addition, the store granted no credit; all transactions were on a cash basis only, at least until 1926, when the Deferred Payment Plan was introduced. Another radical departure from the normal business practices of the day was the Eaton slogan: "Goods satisfactory or money refunded". In most other establishments, the merchant's responsibility for the goods sold ceased as soon as the goods changed hands.

Although most merchants scoffed at such radical innovations, their success is evidenced by the fact that in both 1876 and 1877 the Eaton store was enlarged in size and new commodity lines were added. In August 1883, the store was moved to even larger premises on Yonge Street, and thereafter the growth of Eaton's was phenomenal. In 1884, the first Eaton Catalogue was printed—a booklet six by nine inches, containing 32 pages of store values and lacking illustrations except on the front cover.

The T. Eaton Company was also in the forefront of retailing in the vertical integration of its activities. In 1890, this company moved into manufacturing—in this instance, the manufacture of white-wear. In 1893, a buying office was opened in London, England. The T. Eaton Company also initiated many other merchandising innovations which

230

were to become commonly accepted in the future—bargain days, Saturday half-day holidays during the summer months and, possibly even more important, the opening of a mail-order office in 1916—the first of its type in North America. The slow decline of the wholesaler from his position of power can be traced, in some measure, to the policy utilized by the Eaton Company of buying direct from manufacturers or manufacturing the goods itself.

Although no sales statistics are available, one measure of the growth of the T. Eaton Company is the number of its employees. In 1886, there were 150 employees; by 1919, the number of persons engaged in the Toronto store only, the mail-order department and the factory, numbered over 16,000.

The success of the department store concept is all the more surprising when it is realized that the period between 1867 and 1900 was not a particularly favourable one, either in terms of population expansion or economic development. In 1873, due largely to outside influences, Canada entered a period of depression which was to last for at least six years. Many retailers as well as wholesalers were forced into bankruptcy, especially those in the dry goods, general, hardware, lumber and grocery trades. Although conditions were somewhat alleviated by the completion of the Canadian Pacific Railway, business remained depressed until the early 1890's.

It is within the present century, however, that the spectacular expansion of the population and the economy has taken place. The "opening of the West" attracted hundreds of thousands of immigrants to Canada, thereby creating new markets for both foreign and domestic manufactured goods. Between 1903 and 1913, over 2,500,000 persons entered Canada. Foreign capital flowed into the country in ever-increasing volume, mostly from Great Britain and the United States. The War of 1914-1918, and a subsequent period of depression between 1920 and 1923, dampened to some extent the rapid expansionary pressures evident in Canada's economy. There is no doubt, however, that the period 1867-1920 was the era of the department store. The T. Eaton Company, together with Simpson's, which was to become its major competitor in the department store field, were the principal forces in revolutionizing retail trade in Canada. By the early 1920's, the era of the mass merchandiser had dawned.

## 1920-1930

The period between 1925 and 1929 was one of economic expansion and general optimism. Construction activity was being carried on at fever-pitch and employment had reached previously-unequalled levels. By 1929, retail sales in current dollars had risen to just over the $3,000,000,000 mark and the gross national product had surpassed $6,000,000,000.

Chain Stores—This decade may be described as the "chain store era" in Canada, although there was mention of chain store development prior to that time. Chain store retailing took place in Canada as early as 1670, with the establishment of the first of a chain of Hudson's Bay Company trading posts in the northern regions of the country. These trading posts, however, were far-removed from the modern concept of a chain store organization; selling was not an end in itself, but served rather as a method of securing various goods, usually furs, at the most favourable terms.

In more recent times, reference has been made to a chain of variety stores which began operations in Toronto during 1897 under Seymour H. Knox and to another variety chain, operated by E. P. Charleton and Company, which opened stores in Montreal and Vancouver around 1900. In 1912, these two firms became part of the spreading United States variety chain—the Woolworth Company.

In the field of food retailing, T. P. Loblaw is generally recognized as "the father of chain store groceteria operations in Canada". Loblaw and an unnamed partner, after first discarding a chain of nineteen full-service corner-store groceterias, opened their first in a new chain of self-service "Loblaw" stores in 1920.

By the end of 1926, there were approximately 4,000 chain outlets operating through-out Canada with sales of possibly $100,000,000, which represented about 4 per cent of total retail trade. The food retailing group had the largest representation in the chain field—approximately 900 outlets.

Between 1926 and 1930, there was an enormous increase in the number of chain outlets operating in Canada. Over 4,000 new chain outlets were established after 1925, with the most significant increase taking place in the food trade. By 1930, chain store units registered sales of over $503,000,000 or 18 per cent of total Canadian retail sales.

Numerous reasons have been advanced to explain the success of the chain store movement during this period. Certainly one of the more significant underlying factors was the rapid urbanization of the Canadian population. This concentration of popula-tion enabled chain store organizations to locate relatively large numbers of outlets in close proximity to one another. This, in turn, made it possible for chain stores to achieve certain economies of scale. The costs of advertising, management personnel and warehouse operations, for example, could be spread over a large number of stores. The greater use of automobiles also helped materially in the growth of chain stores. Consumers were prepared to experience some inconvenience in travelling, in return for the lower prices offered by chain stores. The availability of the automobile also led to a more rapid acceptance of the "cash and carry" technique used by most Canadian food chains.

Possibly the most important single factor which led to the success of the chain store was "price". There is no doubt that chain stores were able, in most instances, to charge less for their goods. Many chains became engaged in the manufacture of private-brand goods for sale in their own stores, but even more, largeness itself allowed chain stores to by-pass wholesalers and deal directly with manufacturers. The placement of large orders enabled chains to extract from their suppliers, additional price and other concessions, which in turn could be passed on to consumers in the form of lower prices.

The growth of large-scale retailing, especially in the food field, led to another development which was to attain widespread popularity within a few short decades—the voluntary chain. It is not surprising that the voluntary chain movement had its greatest growth in the food field. This trade group, composed initially of small entre-preneurs, was the first to face the onslaught of the chain store. In 1923, it is estimated that only 8 per cent of the total sales in this field went to chain food stores; by 1930, only seven years later, chain stores had captured over 29 per cent of the available market.

It did not take long for food wholesalers and independent retailers to realize that the only way open for self-preservation was the adoption of many of the chain store's own practices. Since, however, neither the wholesaler nor the independent retailer could adopt separately the positive characteristics of the chain store organization—quantity discounts, advertising allowances, the expertise of specialists—there was no

Manitoba's clothing industry is one of the province's biggest employers. A wide range of clothing is produced and export markets are expanding.

Retail inspection of agricultural produce ensures high quality merchandise.

Winnipeg is one of Western Canada's largest meat packing centres.

Produce from the inland fisheries of Alberta is prepared for the retail trade.

RETAIL TRADE

other choice than joint co-operation between the two. There is every reason to believe that the 1920's (in particular 1924-1929) witnessed a rapid growth in the number of retail outlets affiliated in various forms of voluntary association. For the year 1930, estimates of the membership have ranged from 4,485 to 4,802 with aggregate sales of approximately $121,000,000.

Department store sales also kept pace with the upturn in the total retail market between 1925 and 1929, rising 40.7 per cent during this period compared with 44.9 per cent for total retail trade. The golden era of the 1920's in merchandising came to a jarring end in October 1929, with the stock market collapse in the United States— the "Great Depression" had been ushered in.

## 1930-1941

The early 1930's were marked by heavy unemployment and declining prices. When the trough of the Depression was reached in 1933, the number of persons unemployed had risen to a staggering 19.3 per cent of the labour force and the gross national product had declined by 42.8 per cent. During this same period of time (1930-1933), the total value of retail sales declined even more rapidly—43.5 per cent in current dollars.

By 1934, the Canadian economy had begun a cautious recovery. Increases in personal income provided the basis for a significant advance in consumer expenditure, notably in the purchase of durable goods. From 1934 onwards, retail sales began the long upward climb to pre-Depression levels. It was only in 1941, however, that the value of retail sales finally surpassed the sales figure registered in 1930.

Not all segments of the retailing sector suffered to the same extent during the Depression years. In general, retail chain stores weathered the storm in somewhat better fashion than independent retailers. This statement, however, must be qualified. Had it not been for the food and variety chains, and their much greater degree of stability during this period, the results for the chain store system as a whole would have been much worse. Chains in these two trades were able to limit their decline in sales, during the worst period of the Depression (1930-1933), to less than 20 per cent, whereas the decline in sales for all other chains was over 40 per cent during the same period. By 1937 and 1939 respectively, the variety and food chains had surpassed their 1930 sales levels—but it was not until 1941, on the other hand, that chains in other trades were able to reach their 1930 sales levels.

The stability of the chain food stores during the Depression era is of particular interest. These chains were apparently very successful in exploiting the enormous flexibility of the chain store system of operation—closing and opening outlets whenever and wherever actual sales or potential sales indicated that a change was necessary. In the early 1930's, the food chains were opening more new outlets than closing old ones. The tide turned, however, around the middle of the decade, when the frequency of new store openings fell below the rate of closings. The stores closed were, for the most part, low-volume units, while the new outlets were of the supermarket variety.

The variety chains, on the other hand, continued to expand the number of outlets in operation throughout the whole period of the Depression. The success of the variety chains may be attributable to the broad range of commodities sold through such outlets as well as to their lower price structure. In contrast, as might be expected, chain specialty stores were the ones to feel the full brunt of the Depression years.

234

At the many outdoor markets that abound in Canada farmers sell directly to consumers. The fresh produce and easy camaraderie attract many customers to such centres.

Although very little statistical data are available on the voluntary chain movement during the 1930's, it would appear that the Depression seriously affected the previously rapid growth of this movement, especially during the latter part of the decade. The voluntary movement had undergone expansion during the early 1930's; by 1933, approximately 6,500 retailers had joined the trend to voluntary affiliation. The Census of 1941, on the other hand, showed 5,080 retail outlets as members of voluntary groups. This decrease, however, may have been due in part to statistical or conceptual difficulties encountered in the completion of the 1941 Census of Merchandising and Service Establishments. Nevertheless, this decade witnessed a rapid increase in the number of affiliated pharmacies. By 1941, 753 drug stores, with a total sales of approximately $20,500,000, had joined the voluntary movement.

The department stores were also seriously affected by the Depression. Although the decline in sales between 1930 and 1933 was less than for total retail trade—31.9 per cent as compared to 35.2 per cent—the rate of recovery to the 1930 sales level was slower than for total retail trade. It was not until 1941 that sales registered by department stores exceeded the sales volume of 1930.

During this period (1930-1941), the growth-rates of retail outlets and population were roughly on par. In 1930, there were 125,003 retail outlets serving a population of 10,208,000, which represented one store for every 81.7 persons. These stores were, for the most part, small in terms of annual sales—approximately 75 per cent of all the outlets had sales of less than $20,000 annually. By 1941, there was one retail store for every 83.8 persons. There was, as well, a slight decrease in the percentage of retail establishments doing business in the under-$20,000 category—71.9 per cent compared to 74.8 per cent in 1930.

In summary, the 1930's saw very little change in the retailing industry of Canada. The early years of the decade witnessed a substantial decline in retailing activities—

followed, during the latter years of the decade, by a slow recovery back to pre-Depression levels.

## 1941-1951

Canada's entrance into World War II, in 1939, touched off a tremendous expansion in personal consumption—the result of major increases in government expenditures, employment and personal, disposable income. In the first two years of the War, the gross national product rose from $5,636,000,000 to $8,328,000,000, an increase of 47.8 per cent. At the same time, retail sales jumped from $2,578,000,000 to $3,415,000,000, a gain of 32.5 per cent. Even though approximately one half the gain in retail sales was due simply to higher prices for consumer goods there was also a sizable net increase in the "real" consumption of goods. Consumer expenditures continued to rise during the 1942-1944 period, although purchases of durable goods dropped off sharply because of war-time scarcities and the resultant rationing of many essential commodities.

It was not, however, until the War ended in September 1945, that the greatest acceleration in retail sales took place. This is partially accounted for by the fact that a vast accumulation of savings and a backlog of demand on the part of both the civilian population and business had built up during the period of war-time shortages and rationing. In addition, the rapid demobilization of thousands of troops brought a sudden large influx into the consumer market. As a result, the first great postwar buying spree between 1945 and 1946 produced a spectacular 26.6 per cent increase in retail sales. All segments of retail trade shared in this upsurge in sales. The food chains, which had been particularly hard-hit during the War because of capital restrictions and rationing, blossomed forth. Between 1941 and 1951, sales in food chains increased by 253.9 per cent—far exceeding the rate of growth of total retail trade (209.6 per cent) and chain stores in general (176.2 per cent).

The principal reason for the inability of the chains, with the exception of the food group, to keep pace with the tremendous growth in total retail trade was the strong upsurge of sales in trades in which independent retailing flourished and chains were relatively insignificant. The largest of these was the automotive trade group. Between 1941 and 1951, sales by motor vehicle dealers climbed an amazing 423.3 per cent, with most of this increase occurring during the latter half of the decade. A measure of the significance of this growth—and the impact it made on the independent sector— is indicated by the fact that, in 1951, the value of sales made by this trade group ($1,884,627,800) accounted for nearly one quarter (23.3 per cent) of all independent store sales.

Starting in 1946, this decade also saw an over-all reversal of the trend towards net decreases in the number of chain store outlets in operation, although in the food field it was not until much later that the chains were once again opening more new stores than closing old ones. During this decade, the number of voluntary chain members continued the decline which had started in the mid-1930's, although sales generated by member firms began to increase significantly. It is likely that the increase in average sales per member firm was due, in part, to a greater degree of selectivity by wholesalers in offering membership to—or retaining as members—only the largest and most efficiently-operated retail outlets.

The department stores, during this decade, witnessed a further decline in their share of the total retail market. In 1930, over 12 per cent of all retail sales was generated in department stores; by 1941, the proportion had dropped to 11.0 per cent and this decline was to continue until 1951, when the department stores' share of the market had declined to 8.5 per cent. This decrease may be attributable to a number of trends which were affecting many other retail businesses as well: the increasing disinclination of shoppers to visit downtown stores; the spread of pre-retailing; and the shift in consumer spending away from apparel, furniture, home furnishings and food. As the trickle of population moving into the suburbs developed into flood proportions after World War II, the department stores, located for the most part in the central core, found themselves more and more cut off from a growing and unusually-prosperous segment of the market.

A second development which raised difficult problems for department store organizations was the increased tendency for manufacturers to pre-retail their lines. Because pre-retailing tends to shift control of several marketing functions, especially the selling function, from retailers to suppliers, the shoppers' loyalty, so important to department stores, tended to diminish.

The third development was the strong competition faced by department stores in the sale of their most important commodities. About three quarters of department store sales are derived from five major commodity groups—clothing and footwear, furniture, house furnishings, food and major appliances. In each of the first three categories, the share of the total market going to department store organizations had declined steadily and substantially since 1930. This decade (1941-1951) also saw the growth of population far exceed the growth in number of retail stores—to the extent that, by 1951, there was one store for every 92.4 persons. It would appear that this was due to the relatively slower growth in smaller stores having few or no employees, since larger stores with numerous employees had a growth-rate exceeding the population increase.

# 1951-1961

During this decade, the economic growth of Canada, as measured by the Gross National Product, advanced rapidly—but there were periods of economic dislocation as well. The outbreak of hostilities in Korea, in mid-1950, brought inflationary pressures on the economy which resulted in Federal Government adoption of tighter credit restrictions to combat rising prices. Although retail sales rose by over 12 per cent between 1950 and 1951, this rise was due entirely to increased prices—in actual value, the volume of retail sales actually declined.

The year 1952, however, ushered in a period of sustained growth. The two-year period which followed, however, was one of recession in both Canada and the United States. Generally-declining prices had a minor dampening effect on the growth of retail trade, which resulted in an increase of only 0.4 per cent in real terms between 1953 and 1954. By mid-1955, the economy was again on the upswing. At year-end, GNP stood at $27,070,000,000, up 9.0 per cent over 1954, and retail sales had surpassed the $13,000,000,000 mark, for a sizable gain of 8.7 per cent.

The period from 1956 to 1961 was characterized by a slow but steady increase in the growth of retail trade—marred, however, by two further recessions, one in the latter part of 1957 and the other in 1960. In both cases, the effect on consumer spending was minimal and retail sales volume was soon once more on the rise. A growing population, especially in the younger age groups, accounted for a marked rise in the purchase of durable goods, including automobiles, during this period. As a result, retail trade had, by 1961, increased a further 17.3 per cent in current dollars and 8.3 per cent in volume. A number of dramatic changes in the distributional pattern took place during this decade. Among the most important was the development of shopping centres in Canada.

**Shopping Centres**—Although the basic concept of the shopping centre may be traced back to the Roman Empire and medieval Europe, the shopping centre—as it is known today—was a distinctly twentieth-century, North American retailing innovation. In Canada, the first planned shopping centre—the Park Royal in Vancouver, B.C.—was established in 1950, approximately forty years after the opening of the first shopping centre in the United States. By 1961, 281 shopping centres were in operation throughout most regions of Canada.

The development and rapid growth of shopping centres during the 1950's were attributable to a number of interrelated changes which had gradually been taking place in Canada's economic and social structure, such as the growth in population and its effect upon the changing pattern of urban-rural settlement, increased ownership and use of automobiles and the growing affluence of a majority of the population.

In 1931, the population of Canada was divided almost evenly between urban and rural—53.7 per cent urban as compared to 46.3 per cent classified as rural. By 1961, the percentage of urban dwellers had risen to approximately 70 per cent. A large percentage of the growth in urban settlement has occurred in the areas surrounding the core cities of Canada's metropolitan areas. The rate of growth in the fringes since 1931 has consistently exceeded that of the core cities by a wide margin. The most spectacular increase in fringe-area population growth took place during the period from 1951 to 1961. During this period, the suburbs of seventeen metropolitan areas experienced an average increase of 96.8 per cent while the cities proper rose only 19.1 per cent.

The boom in residential home construction, rising per capita incomes and the increased ownership of automobiles, had repercussions on all sectors of retailing. Demand for furniture and appliances increased significantly during this period, and many retailers, especially the chains, foresaw the benefits which could be derived by following these new markets into the suburbs. That shopping centres have been successful is evidenced by the fact that retail sales generated through shopping centres have risen from approximately 0.2 per cent of total retail sales in 1951 to 5.5 per cent in 1961. Another development which was to symbolize the changes in the distributive system was the creation of a vending machine industry.

**Vending Machines**—Prior to World War II there were only a very few small operators who supplied relatively primitive gum, candy and chocolate bar machines. By the mid-50's it is estimated that approximately $8,000,000-$10,000,000 were injected by consumers into vending machines. Even at this time, Canadian vending was still characterized by a heavy incidence of small "fly-by-nighters" who used inferior machines and products and gave the legitimate operators an unsavoury reputation.

A number of unrelated developments, however, were acting together to create a favourable climate for the growth of the vending industry. First, certain technological

This typical shopping centre is in Hamilton, Ontario. More and more suburbanites find it easier to shop in nearby centres rather than to journey into the downtown area where parking is more of a problem.

developments perfected during the war years—particularly in refrigeration, electronic cooling and packaging—were channeled into the production of an entirely new variety of vending machine, making possible previously undreamed-of usages for the new postwar consumer. Second, it was an era of fast-developing industrialization, especially in secondary industries, and two noticeable trends soon emerged: a shorter work-week and consequently a greater frequency of shift-work. Lastly, the "coffee-break" became universal and workers in both plants and offices found it convenient to have coffee and cigarettes close to their job locations. By 1961, sales through vending machines had increased to approximately $45,000,000, an increase of 350 per cent over the estimated figure of $10,000,000 in 1953.

This decade also witnessed rapid chain store growth in both number and sales. It was during this decade (1951-1961) that the trend towards fewer chain outlets in the food field underwent a dramatic reversal. Sales of chain stores increased by 109.4 per cent between 1951 and 1961, almost double the rate of growth for sales of independent retailers—61.1 per cent. Not unexpectedly, the rate of increase was highest in the grocery and combination field, which rose by 179.3 per cent over 1951. The importance of the grocery and combination trade in the chain store field can hardly be over-stated. By 1961, nearly one-half of all chain store sales were made in this trade. With only 5 per cent of all grocery and combination stores (chain and independent), the chains had captured over 46 per cent of the sales volume generated by this group.

There is no doubt that the development of the supermarket was one of the important factors in the great rise in the chains' share of the food field. The trend to supermarket retailing, which was in evidence as early as 1941, came into full prominence during this decade.

There were a number of factors which were conducive to the further growth of the corporate chain system and the increased popularity of the supermarket concept.

Briefly, these factors were as follows: (1) the movement of population to the suburbs and the resulting development of planned shopping centres in many of which a giant food store served as a focal point. It may be interesting to note that in Canada the food chains were in the forefront in the development of shopping centres. In fact, at one time one of the major lessors of shopping centres was a leading chain food organization; (2) the increasing demand—and the ability to pay—for a much wider selection of commodity lines and products, particularly in the field of "convenience" foods, which consumers were unable to find in smaller corner-grocery stores; and (3) the desire on the part of modern-day buyers to shop less frequently and do as much of their shopping as possible in one place—all of which made necessary the construction of larger stores, with more shelf space, a broad commodity mix including both food and non-food items (the latter being one of the more important innovations in super-market merchandising in recent years), and with ample parking facilities.

It was also during this decade that the voluntary chain movement steam-rollered to a position of importance within the distributional system. The rapid growth of corporate chains after 1945, especially in the food field, again raised the spectre of doom for the unaffiliated retail store-keeper. The small independents began to feel the full brunt of the chain supermarket and turned, in ever-increasing numbers, to the wholesaler for assistance in the fight for survival. In terms of members and aggregate sales, the voluntary chain made its greatest impact on the distribution of food; sales generated by affiliated food stores had, by 1961, increased by more than 700 per cent over 1951—and these stores accounted for over 21 per cent of the total grocery and combination store market by the close of the decade.

The 1951-1961 decade was also a period of growth for department stores in Canada. Retail sales jumped from $910,000,000 in 1951 to $1,550,000,000 in 1961, a gain of over 58 per cent. This increase compared favourably with the increase of 58.8 per cent for total retail trade. One trend which was noticeable during this decade was the increased utilization of shopping centres by department stores for the establishment of branch outlets. In 1956, there were only 10 department store outlets located in shopping centres. These branch stores accounted for 4.4 per cent of the total retail volume produced by all department stores in Canada. By 1961, 37 department store branches were generating 11.1 per cent of total department store sales. It must be remembered that the sales of department stores include the sales of the mail-order offices and catalogue sales. If one were able to separate these sales from the store sales, the result would more positively indicate the growing importance of the suburban shopping centre branch in department store merchandising.

For retail trade as a whole, the trend towards larger-scale retail outlets continued during the 1950's. By 1961, there were 175,692 such outlets serving a population of 18,238,000—one store for every 103.8 persons. Average sales per store rose to $53,888 in constant dollars, a gain of 26.2 per cent over 1951. The number of outlets in the small-sales size (up to $19,999) continued to drop—only 28.7 per cent of the stores still remained in this category by 1961.

## 1961-1967

This period has witnessed the strengthening of some of the trends in merchandising which were becoming pronounced by the late 1950's, and a new development which was to cause more than a ripple in the merchandising sector—the discount department store.

**Discount Department Stores**—In 1960, the first discount department store outlet was opened for business in Toronto. Although discounting, as such, is by no means a unique phenomenon (it can still be found in the market place, bazaar or auction house), the establishment of large-scale outlets selling a wide variety of goods at prices usually lower than in competing outlets captured the imagination of many people. The technique employed by the modern discounter is to stock only fast-moving items and to eliminate all but the essential services, thereby making it possible to reduce prices to some extent.

The success of the discounter stems from many of the changes in merchandising which occurred in previous years. Gradually over the decades, both the consumer and the manufacturer have continuously assumed more and more of the selling functions of the retail merchant. For one thing, consumer buying habits have undergone considerable changes in recent years. The supermarket, with its concept of self-service, instilled in the consumer the confidence to buy goods directly from the shelves without resort to the merchant's advice or opinions. There has also been a trend, noticeable for more than a decade, for manufacturers to guarantee the satisfaction of their products—certainly in the case of brand-name goods. All of these developments created an environment suitable for the expansion of the self-service mode of merchandising from the food-market into other trades.

In 1962, the first year for which discount department store data are available, the sales registered by this type of merchandising development amounted to $106,000,000 or approximately one-half of one per cent of total retail sales; by 1964, sales had nearly doubled, to over one per cent of total retail trade in Canada. The growth of the discount department store group is even more impressive when viewed against the growth of traditional department stores. Between 1962 and 1964, sales of discount department stores increased by 94.2 per cent whereas the increase for traditional department stores amounted to only 15.3 per cent.

In the chain store field, the construction of large physical structures, which began with the early supermarkets, has continued, although this trend seems to be levelling off. The trend towards carrying an increased mix of commodities in chain grocery stores has continued also and will doubtless continue in the years to come. Many additional commodities will be in non-food lines, and will have the effect of completing, as one writer has put it, ". . . a full circle back to the general store of yesteryear".

Vertical integration in the chain store movement has increased significantly during the last several years—especially in the food field. It would seem inevitable that mass merchandisers will increase their investment or control in manufacturing plants producing not only their own private brands, but also products for sale to competitors. This period has also witnessed increased horizontal integration in retailing. For example, chain store organizations, especially in the food and variety trades, backed by their tremendous buying power and managerial talents, have moved into the discount department store field.

The increased use of scientific techniques for management decision-making, such as operations research, electronic computers and centralized data-processing centres has become more pronounced. These techniques as employed by merchandisers are still only in their infancy, but their importance should increase significantly in future.

The voluntary movement has continued to expand and prosper in the 1960's. In the food field, the aggressive attitude of the sponsoring wholesalers should enable the voluntary food retailers to capture at least 35 to 40 per cent of the total market in the foreseeable future. It is also probable that the voluntary movement will make stronger inroads in other than the food area in the future, especially in the hardware field. The growth of shopping centres has continued well into the 1960's but at a decreasing rate. If the trend continues, the rate of sales increase should level off at around 8 to 10 per cent per annum.

The vending industry has made significant gains during the past several years. By 1964, sales had increased to over $78,000,000, a gain of 75 per cent over 1961. There is no doubt that vending will play a large role in replacing or supplementing conventional selling methods, primarily in the distribution of low-price, low-profit merchandise. The automatic grocery store, for example, is closer to reality than ever before.

The changes which have occurred during the first part of this decade signal only the beginning of tremendous developments which will take place within the next decade or so.

## Conclusion

Canada has witnessed dramatic changes in the method of retailing goods during the past century. A number of retailing innovations stand out clearly: the department store and mail order, the chain store, the voluntary chain, the supermarket, the shopping centre and the discount department store. None of these developments completely replaced the existing retailing institutions of the day; instead, they served to reduce their former importance. The department store, for example, did not replace the general store—nor did the chain store replace the independent store.

A change in marketing institutions could occur only when the social and economic milieu of the country were favourable to its development. The establishment and success of the department store, for example, were made possible by the rapid growth of Canadian cities and the increased income available to the consumer.

The advent of the assembly line, bringing with it the ability to mass-produce goods at less cost, put pressure on existing retailing institutions to improve their methods of handling and disposing of goods. The chain store, in a sense, was the product of this pressure. The supermarket and the shopping centre were also by-products of the changes taking place in Canada's social and economic life. Without the increased use of motor vehicles, such developments could not have occurred.

With changes in retailing institutions have come changes in the performance of marketing functions. The manufacturer, over the past hundred years, has assumed more and more of the functions usually performed by the retailing sector; witness, for example, the tremendous importance of packaging and advertising undertaken at the manufacturing level.

The present century has also witnessed increased vertical and horizontal integration by retailers, with the result that the boundaries between retailing, wholesaling and manufacturing have become very hazy, indeed.

Even though retailing in Canada has undergone a dramatic evolution during the first hundred years of Confederation, there is no doubt that the second hundred years will witness even greater changes; retailing in the year 2067 will bear little resemblance to retailing in 1967.                                          (G. SNYDER)

The Winnipeg Grain Exchange, a voluntary unincorporated association, is the hub of the Canadian grain trade. Its trading floor is seldom silent. The head offices of the Canadian Wheat Board are situated in Winnipeg.

# Financial Institutions

In a developed economy such as Canada's, borrowing and lending assume very important roles. Almost every family, every active business and each level of government are involved as a borrower and lender of funds. The deposit of money in a bank, the purchase of a Government of Canada savings bond, the assumption of a mortgage, the repayment of a debt, are all common financial transactions in which there are exchanges of claims on money. Every financial claim represents an asset for the lender, and a liability for the borrower. For someone to borrow there must be a lender to buy the claim. The speed and ease with which the borrower and lender are brought together determine the quality of a financial system.

Much of the total borrowing and lending which takes place in Canada occurs directly among persons, non-financial business enterprises, governments and non-residents, without the intervention of financial intermediaries. Two examples are the sale of government bonds directly to persons, and advances by parent companies to their subsidiaries. This process works, however, only when someone with funds to invest can find someone who wishes to borrow, with conditions—size of loan, term of loan, security, etc.—satisfactory to both. The role played by the financial market is to furnish the meeting place for such borrowers and lenders.

The term, "financial institutions", embraces such institutions as banks, insurance companies and trust companies whose primary function is to deal in money and claims on money.

If these institutions did not exist, much of the credit which now flows from lenders to borrowers, would move only at higher interest rates if it moved at all. The time and expense involved would be very great if every borrower had to find a willing lender. The conception of new institutions, and the adaptation of old institutions to fit new needs are processes which are going on continuously. Recently, for example, there has been major emphasis on the setting up of provincial financial institutions for the purpose of facilitating the development of new industries in a province.

A recurring theme is the evolution from transactions directly between borrower and lender to transactions in which a financial institution acts as intermediary between borrower and lender. Less than 165 years ago there were in Canada no banks, no trust companies, no loan companies, no insurance companies. Even 100 years ago most small ventures were financed through individuals savings, and most large ventures were financed by British and United States capital. It was not until about 50 years ago, during World War I that the Canadian capital market became an effective instrument for channeling savings of Canadians into large-scale production and national resource activities.

Royal Commissions have studied the banking system on a number of occasions since 1867. The 1933 Commission, for example, made the recommendations which led to the formation of the Bank of Canada. The most recent Commission, whose report at time of writing had not been translated into legislative action, studied the operation of the financial system under four headings: the contribution the financial system might make in achieving economic goals; the changes in existing techniques which might be useful; the safeguards for the public; and the adequacy of the systems from the point of view of the borrower. The studies which the Commission made in its attempt to find answers to these problems are contributing to the rapidly-growing body of literature on the effective operation of financial systems.

## Classification of Financial Institutions

The description of financial institutions would be facilitated if they could be classified into homogeneous groupings, on the basis of the type of borrowing, the type of lending, the nature of the financial instruments used, or some other factor or factors. No completely satisfactory grouping is now available, but the classification recommended by the United Nations appears to be the most suitable one yet devised and is applied in the three groupings below.

**Monetary System**—The first major grouping is the monetary system, which includes the Central Bank, and institutions which accept deposits. In Canada, these institutions are the Bank of Canada, chartered banks, trust companies, mortgage loan companies, credit unions, the Quebec savings banks and provincial savings banks. Because these institutions are entrusted with the savings of a large part of the population, they have been traditionally subject to the greatest government control. At the federal (or national) level this control is exercised through the Inspector General of Banks and the Superintendent of Insurance; and the provinces also have regulatory bodies for institutions which come under provincial control.

**Insurance Companies and Pension Funds**—The second major grouping is that of insurance companies and pension funds. These institutions are peculiar in that their liabilities consist primarily of future claims for insurance and pensions. Life insurance companies, fire and casualty insurance companies and trusteed pension funds form most of this grouping. Life insurance companies rank second only to chartered banks in the size of their assets, and they are holders of an important proportion of government and corporation bonds.

**Other Financial Groups**—The third major grouping of financial institutions contains all the other companies which borrow funds through the issuance of debt or equity instruments and the proceeds to persons, business and government. Included here are sales finance companies, consumer loan companies, mutual and closed-end funds, business development companies, farm loan companies, Central Mortgage and Housing Corporation and other companies engaged in financing of persons, business and government.

The following table shows the condensed balance sheet for the major financial institutions. Where available, data are given for 1875, 1900, 1926, 1960 and 1964. Because there are differences in the way in which assets are valued, particularly for the early years and because of differences in definition and coverage, total assets should be taken only as indicative of size and growth.

## Total Assets of Selected Financial Institutions, Selected Years, 1875-1964
(Millions of dollars)

| Item | 1875 | 1900 | 1926 | 1960 | 1964 |
|---|---|---|---|---|---|
| **Banks and other deposit accepting institutions:** | | | | | |
| Bank of Canada............................. | — | — | — | 3,044 | 3,642 |
| Chartered banks ............................ | 183 | 314 | 2,940 | 14,263 | 18,661 |
| Quebec savings banks...................... | 8 | 21 | 76 | 311 | 403 |
| Government savings institutions.............. | 7 | 53 | 54 | 189 | 210 |
| Credit unions ............................. | — | — | 9 | 1,314 | 2,227 |
| Trust companies........................... | } 20 | 153 | { 117 | 1,274 | 2,789 |
| Mortgage loan companies.................. | | | 205 | 945 | 2,380 |
| **Total..................................** | **218** | **541** | **3,401** | **21,340** | **30,312** |
| **Insurance and pensions:** | | | | | |
| Life insurance............................. | n.a. | 60 | 919 | 8,007 | 10,638 |
| Trusteed pension funds...................... | — | — | n.a. | 3,616 | 5,820 |
| Fire and casualty insurance.................. | n.a. | 22 | 152 | 1,316 | 1,658 |
| **Total..................................** | **—** | **82** | **1,071** | **12,939** | **18,116** |
| **Other financial institutions:** | | | | | |
| Sales finance and consumer loan companies... | — | — | 24 | 2,177 | 3,700 |
| Mutual funds............................... | — | — | n.a. | 563 | 1,140 |
| Closed-end funds.......................... | — | n.a. | n.a. | n.a. | 442 |
| Investment dealers........................ | n.a. | n.a. | n.a. | n.a. | 619 |
| Central Mortgage and Housing Corporation.... | — | — | — | 1,642 | 2,280 |
| Alberta Municipal Financing Corporation...... | — | — | — | 161 | 336 |
| Export Credits Insurance Corporation.......... | — | — | — | 19 | 238 |
| Farm Credit Corporation (formerly Canadian Farm Loan Board) ..... | — | — | — | 164 | 458 |
| Industrial Development Bank................ | — | — | — | 107 | 229 |
| **Total..................................** | **—** | **—** | **—** | **—** | **9,442** |

n.a. = not available.      — = not yet in existence.

NOTE. The above table includes financial institutions believed to have approximately 99 per cent of the assets of all financial institutions. Omitted are fraternal societies, stockbrokers, some companies which specialize in financing business, and a number of relatively small government financial institutions. Total assets are not comparable from one period to the next, or between institutions. For example, life insurance totals for 1875, 1900 and 1926 include assets held on behalf of foreign policyholders while the later figures do not. Such discrepancies do not seriously affect the picture presented herein of the growth of financial institutions.

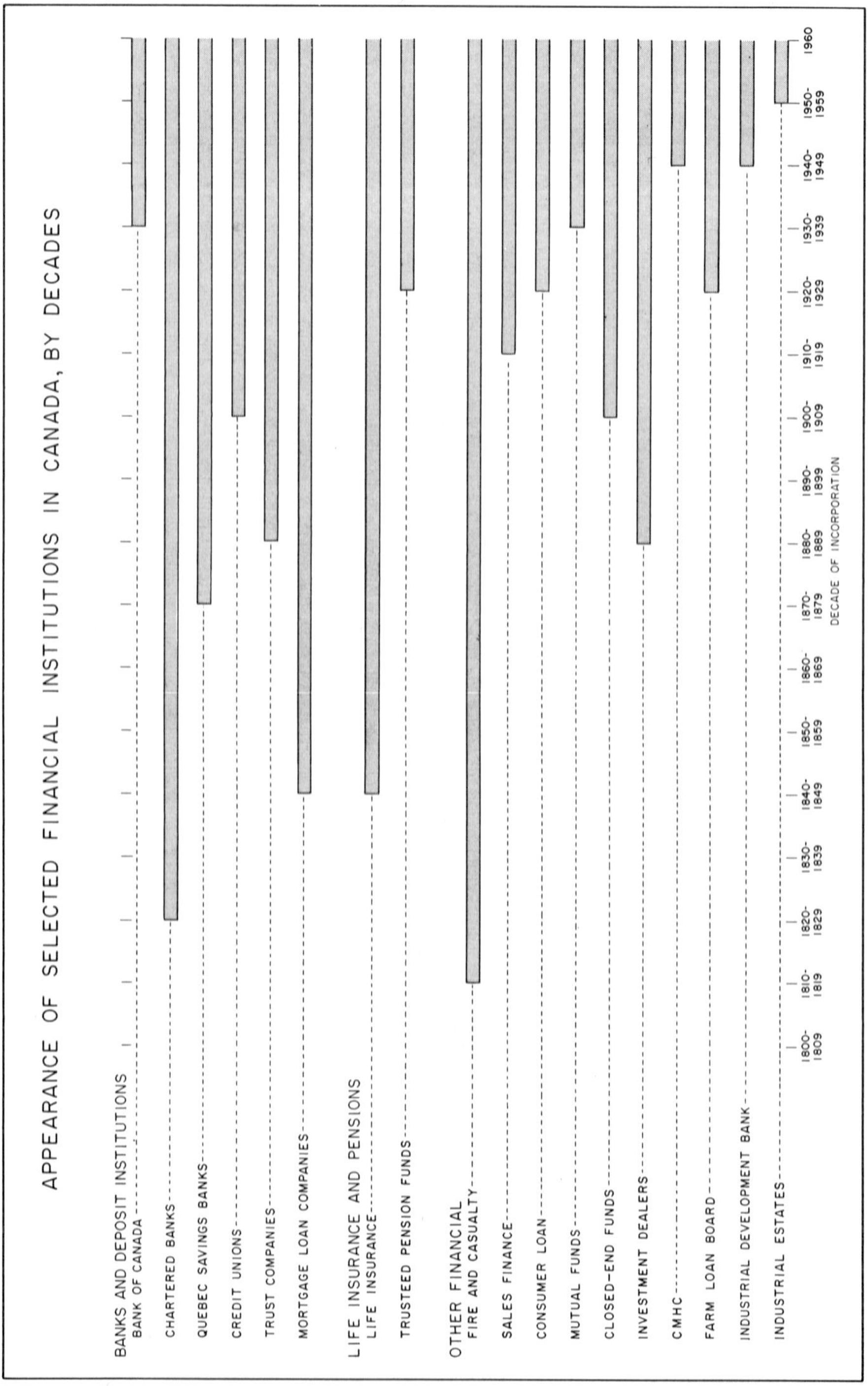

APPEARANCE OF SELECTED FINANCIAL INSTITUTIONS IN CANADA, BY DECADES

BANKS AND DEPOSIT INSTITUTIONS
BANK OF CANADA
CHARTERED BANKS
QUEBEC SAVINGS BANKS
CREDIT UNIONS
TRUST COMPANIES
MORTGAGE LOAN COMPANIES

LIFE INSURANCE AND PENSIONS
LIFE INSURANCE
TRUSTEED PENSION FUNDS

OTHER FINANCIAL
FIRE AND CASUALTY
SALES FINANCE
CONSUMER LOAN
MUTUAL FUNDS
CLOSED-END FUNDS
INVESTMENT DEALERS
CMHC
FARM LOAN BOARD
INDUSTRIAL DEVELOPMENT BANK
INDUSTRIAL ESTATES

1800-
1809
1810-
1819
1820-
1829
1830-
1839
1840-
1849
1850-
1859
1860-
1869
1870-
1879
1880-
1889
1890-
1899
1900-
1909
1910-
1919
1920-
1929
1930-
1939
1940-
1949
1950-
1959
1960

DECADE OF INCORPORATION

# History of Financial Institutions

Canadian financial institutions owe much to British and United States influences, modified by Canadian laws and customs. Canada's branch banking system evolved from the British System. The sales finance companies reflect the prior growth of similar institutions in the United States. Both Britain and the United States have more highly developed financial systems than has Canada, and it is to be expected that Canadians will continue to borrow procedures, instruments and institutions, modifying them to fit local requirements.

The chart p. 246 indicates the decade in which the more important financial institutions began operations. In general, the date given is that of incorporation, and this may be considerably later than the date when the activity first started. The origin of a number of financial institutions is found in a group of individuals gathering together to perform some function, and gradually formalizing the procedures until the corporate form was adopted. For example, in Montreal a group of brokers met regularly as early as 1832 to trade the shares of business and commercial enterprises of the day. Subsequently, a Board of Brokers was formed in 1866, and the Montreal Stock Exchange was incorporated in 1874. In general, the formal date of incorporation has been taken as the most important date.

# Currency and Banking before 1867

So long as trade remained in the hands of a few private traders, barter was the rule. Beads, blankets and other articles were traded directly to the Indians for furs. French currency was introduced during the seventeenth century, and in 1681 foreign coin was officially recognized, but it was stipulated by ordinance that it should pass by weight, and it was overvalued by one third, as compared with its value in the issuing country, in an attempt to keep it from being drained out of the country. Fiat paper money was introduced in 1685, largely as an expedient to meet government expenses, while awaiting Royal supplies. Later, however, paper money was issued without firm backing, and its chaotic history led to a distrust of paper currency, perhaps accounting for the lateness with which banks were introduced to Canada.

Following the period of military occupation (1759-1763), Spanish silver dollars became the medium of currency, although different valuations in Halifax, Quebec and Montreal led to trade problems. In 1775 Halifax currency became the official standard but was not generally adopted until 1821 when other currencies were deprived of legal recognition. To pay the expenses of the War of 1812, army bills were issued, and redeemed a few years later. They helped to pave the way for the first bank, the Bank of Montreal, which began business in 1817 as a private institution, and received a charter in 1822. However, the first chartered bank was the Bank of Upper Canada which received its charter in 1821. These early banks were organized by merchants for merchants, their chief function being to facilitate trade by issuing promissory notes payable to the bearer on demand. If the bank's credit was good, these notes passed from hand to hand and were the chief circulating media in Canada.

During the 1840's it was proposed that the provincial governments should issue notes which would replace those of the chartered banks. While this proposal was rejected, a financial crisis in 1848-49 forced the adoption of a policy which led to the withdrawal from the banks of the right to issue notes of lower denomination than five

As Toronto is the headquarters of the majority of the chartered banks, of several large insurance and trust companies and of numerous industrial concerns, a tremendous volume of business is transacted at the Toronto Stock Exchange. The mining stock exchange is a particularly busy place.

dollars. Between 1840 and 1867 the problem of establishing a uniform currency standard was also considered. The majority of Canadians favoured the United States decimal system, and it was adopted in the United Province of Canada in 1853 and 1858. In 1860 the official accounts of Nova Scotia and New Brunswick were kept according to the decimal system.

## Commercial Banking since 1867

At Confederation, jurisdiction over currency passed to the Federal Government. Dominion notes came into being as legal tender in 1870, circulating side by side with bank note issues which were not legal tender. The Bank Act of 1870, and the Banking Act of the Dominion in 1871 began the modern era in banking. These Acts, among other things, established the minimum size of banks, set the maximum interest or discount rate at seven per cent, made it simpler to loan on the security of warehouse receipts, provided for monthly statements, and contemplated regular decennial revisions. The Canadian banking system originated with the needs of merchants, and so the bank Acts put an emphasis on commercial banking. Lending, as far as possible, was short-term and self-liquidating with mortgage loans not permitted. It was not until the 1950's that the chartered banks emphasized personal lending.

Revisions to the Bank Act, which followed at intervals of approximately 10 years, made many changes in the details of reserve requirements, shareholders and director's responsibilities, statements to be prepared, etc.; but no fundamental changes were made until the sixth revision in 1934. The need for a central bank to regulate credit and currency became apparent during the 1920's and early 1930's and, following the recommendations of a parliamentary committee, the Bank of Canada Act was passed in 1934, and the Bank of Canada began operations in March 1935.

The Bank Act of 1934 gave the Bank of Canada the liability for all Dominion notes outstanding, and provided for partial replacement of chartered bank notes by Bank of Canada notes. The Bank Act of 1944 provided that chartered banks could not issue notes after 1945 and that remaining note liability of the chartered banks should be transferred to the Bank of Canada in 1950. The Bank of Canada, under its terms of responsibilities to regulate credit, is able to increase or decrease the total amount of cash reserves available to the chartered banks—in other words to regulate the money supply. The Bank Act requires that each chartered bank maintain a minimum amount of cash reserves in the form of Bank of Canada notes and deposits at the Bank of Canada. If the reserves increase, a bank can increase its deposits. If the reserves decrease, the bank must decrease its deposits. The chief method by which the Bank of Canada can affect the level of cash reserves of the chartered banks is by purchases and sales of government securities.

The Bank of Canada does not loan money on a regular basis. It has the power, however, to make short-term loans to the chartered banks, Quebec savings banks, money-market dealers, the Government of Canada and the provinces. In particular, the power to make loans to investment dealers means that these dealers can borrow large amounts of money on the market to finance short-term transactions in the knowledge that if credit conditions became very "tight" there is always a "last resort" from whom they can borrow. Traditionally the Bank of Canada has controlled the money supply through the chartered banks. This puts an indirect form of control on other deposit-accepting institutions, such as trust companies and credit unions. The extent to which direct controls are desirable on these near banks constitutes an interesting and important issue today.

## Credit Unions

The first credit union in Canada was founded in Levis in 1900 by M. Alphonse Desjardins. Its purpose was to promote thrift by encouraging saving and to provide loans to members who could not get credit elsewhere, or could get it only at high interest rates. At first growth was slow. In 1911, when the first figures were available, assets amounted to $2,000,000, and by 1940 they were only $20,000,000. Since that time there has been a spectacular increase, with assets of the Quebec credit union amounting to over $1,000,000,000 at the end of 1964. Growth came much later in the other provinces. The first legislation outside Quebec was in Nova Scotia in 1932, followed by provincial legislation in Manitoba and Saskatchewan in 1937, and Ontario and British Columbia in 1938. Although credit unions have not attained the same importance in these provinces as they have in Quebec, they follow the same principles of self-help.

Credit unions are under provincial legislation, with almost all local offices in each province belonging to provincial central credit unions, either directly or through regional unions. There is a considerable difference in the asset holding of credit unions in Quebec which have a large proportion of their investments in the form of mortgages and government bonds, as opposed to the other provinces which have much more in loans. Credit unions probably play their most important role in smaller communities where they may function to a large extent as local banks. However, they are growing rapidly in the cities, too, because the interest which they pay on shares and deposits is higher than that paid by most other financial institutions; while, because of their relatively low overhead, they charge comparatively lower rates on their loans.

## Trust Companies and Mortgage Loan Companies

Business such as that now transacted by mortgage loan and trust companies was first carried on by a company in Canada in 1844. In order to legalize and encourage such operations in Upper Canada, an Act was passed in 1845, followed by Acts in 1847 and 1849 in New Brunswick and Nova Scotia, respectively. These early companies were termed building societies, and their main function was to make loans to members on the security of real estate. An Act in 1859 gave them authority to "borrow money to a limited extent" while the Building Societies Act of 1874 gave them the additional authority to accept money on deposit and issue debentures.

The first known trust company was chartered by the province of Ontario in 1882. During the latter part of the nineteenth century the growth of trust companies, although considerable, was much less than that for mortgage loan companies. Trust companies however have an inherent advantage over mortgage loan companies in that their charters give them authority to carry out all the functions of mortgage loan companies in addition to their trust activities. During the first part of the twentieth century trust companies grew rapidly in importance, with some loan companies either changing their charters to trust company charters, or being absorbed by trust companies. The steady growth of the assets of loan and trust companies continued up to 1930 but, reflecting the depression and World War II, their assets changed very little between 1930 and 1945. Since 1945, however, their assets have grown very rapidly, reflecting such factors as the great expansion in the construction of buildings (with consequent mortgage debt), and the development of financial markets since 1945. As their name implies, mortgage loan companies concentrate on lending mortgage money, and hold other assets such as government bonds and short-term notes primarily to provide a sufficient degree of liquidity. Mortgages are also by far the largest single investment of trust companies, but trust companies are much more active than loan companies in the purchase of bonds and short term paper.

Trust company functions can be divided into three types—individual trusteeship, collective trusteeship and corporate trusteeship. Individual trusteeship relates to the management of estate, trust and agency funds. There are few statistics on the total assets administered by trust companies, but most of the resources of trust companies are devoted to individual trusteeship. Collective trusteeship where funds are provided by shareholders, depositors and purchases of certificates is the part normally covered by published statistics. Corporate trusteeship relates to the role of trust companies in assisting corporations by acting as trustee of the assets underlying secured borrowing. Trust companies may also act as receiver and manager in the reorganization or liquidation of a company and assist in the details of keeping shareholder records.

## Government and Other Savings Banks

The three types of savings banks in Canada are the Post Office Savings Bank, Provincial Government Banks in Ontario and Alberta, and two savings banks operating in Quebec, the Montreal City and District Savings Bank and La Banque d'Économie de Québec. The Post Office Savings Bank was established under the Post Office Act of 1867 in order, as the Act states, to "enlarge the facilities now available for the deposit of small savings, to make the Post Office available for that purpose, and to give the direct security of the Dominion to every depositor for repayment of all money deposited by him together with the interest due thereon". Deposits in the Post Office Savings Bank reached a peak of $48,000,000 in 1908 but, with the growth of other savings institutions, the deposits are now less than half this level and are declining year by year.

The Ontario and Alberta government savings banks were started in 1922 and 1939 respectively and have shown a steady growth. The two Quebec savings banks were incorporated under the Quebec Savings Bank Act which was passed in 1875. They accept deposits and invest the proceeds in a relatively restricted list of securities.

## Life Insurance

Life insurance business was developed first in the United Kingdom and the United States and introduced into Canada by companies from these countries. The first company was established in Canada in 1846, and it was followed by five more in the following five years. The main impetus to business came in the late 1860's and early 1870's when the formation of new life insurance companies, in Canada, England and elsewhere, proceeded at a very rapid pace. By 1875 there were at least 26 companies operating in Canada, including several purely Canadian companies. With this rapid growth in business the need for regulatory legislation was apparent, and the first Dominion Insurance Act was passed in 1868, followed by Acts in 1871, 1874, 1875 and in later years. Legislation showed the influences of British and United States experiences. A Royal Commission was appointed in 1906 to inquire into the conduct of life insurance business in Canada and a number of its recommendations were translated into law.

A decision of the Privy Council in 1931 established that companies formed or incorporated outside Canada must operate under Dominion regulation. The larger Canadian companies are also Dominion-registered, so that provincially-incorporated companies carry on a relatively small portion of total life insurance business. By agreement of the provinces, provincial legislation with respect to life insurance companies is parallel with the federal legislation.

Fraternal societies started operating in Canada at an early date. Although exempt from the Dominion Acts they followed most of the terms of these Acts. In 1919, when the Insurance Act was widened they were placed under direct supervision of this Act.

The life insurance industry is second in size of assets only to the chartered banks. At the end of 1963, life insurance companies held 10 per cent of outstanding provincial bonds, 14 per cent of municipal bonds, and 26 per cent of corporation bonds. They also held about 28 per cent of total outstanding mortgages. Their role in the financial markets is obviously a very important one.

## Pension Plans

During the past 25 years there has been a great increase in funds invested in pension plans as more and more companies have started to make provision for pensions for their employees, and as the assets of existing plans grew. Before 1939, a relatively small part of the working population was covered by pension schemes. With the advent of the Canada and Quebec Pension Plans in 1966, virtually all workers are contributing to a pension plan.

Prior to the initiation of the Canada Pension Plan, industrial pension plans took the form of trusteed pension plans, life insurance group annuities and Federal Government annuities. The Federal Government annuities were initiated in 1908 and now have well over a $1,000,000,000 in assets. They have been growing more slowly in recent years because of the increased popularity of trusteed pension plans, which now

The floor of the new Montreal and Canadian Stock Exchanges at Place Victoria, in the early moments of business.

rank third in size of total assets, after chartered banks and life insurance companies and are growing at a very rapid rate. At time of writing, it is too early to know the impact of the Canada Pension Plan and the Quebec Pension Plan on the financing of the economy. The funds collected by these plans will be available to the provinces to meet their requirements, and will undoubtedly have a considerable impact on provincial financing.

## Fire and Casualty Insurance Companies

Fire and casualty insurance in Canada was provided during the late eighteenth century by United Kingdom companies. In 1804 the first Canadian agency was established by a United Kingdom company, and the first purely Canadian company was founded in 1809 and received a charter in 1819. A number of other companies, including branches of United States companies, were chartered in the next decade. Today there are several hundred companies operating in Canada. Fire and casualty companies have as their main function the indemnity for financial losses suffered. Most of their business is in the area of fire and automobile insurance, but they also cover a great variety of other types of insurance such as hail insurance, sickness insurance, bonding, etc. Their liabilities thus consist largely of unearned premiums and unpaid claims so that in the process of insuring they have large sums of money temporarily in their possession. At the end of 1964 their investment portfolio was over $1,000,000,000, making these companies one of the major buying groups in the financial markets.

## Sales Finance Companies

The institutions we have been discussing so far were organized primarily for the financing of business, home ownership and the provision of security. There has always been a need, however, for loans to persons and small businesses which are temporarily in need of money. One important source of financing was, and is, the extension of credit by corner groceries, doctors, and other sellers of goods or services. Cash loans traditionally were made by friends and by individuals who specialized in this type of lending. With the rapid growth of the automobile industry, and the extension into Canada of United States small loan companies a large part of personal loans now are made by institutional lenders.

The primary function of sales finance companies is to extend wholesale and retail credit to persons and business. They finance the purchases of automobiles and durables by consumers and business, and they finance the inventories of automobile dealers and other wholesalers and retailers. Sales finance companies extend loans to consumers directly or, as in most cases, through subsidiaries. In addition, either directly or through subsidiaries, they make mortgage loans and capital loans to automobile dealers and other businesses, lease equipment, and provide insurance coverage on durable goods.

Sales finance companies owe their origin to the automobile. The development of a mass market for automobiles required a means of financing, since the cost of an automobile is often greater than the liquid assets of the purchaser. In contrast with most other industries where the manufacturer finances directly some of the inventories of wholesalers and retailers of its products, it has long been the custom of the automobile industry for the manufacturer to be paid promptly by the automobile dealers when they take delivery.

Various means of financing were used in the early years of the century. In 1916 the first of the present-day finance companies was established, and during the next ten years a number of these companies were formed. The industry grew rapidly until 1930, but the depression of the 1930's, the absence of cars from the consumer market during the latter part of the War, and the credit restrictions imposed during the War, retarded growth until 1946. Since that time growth has been very rapid, although in the last few years increased competition from other sources—particularly the chartered banks—has resulted in a drop in the proportion of consumer credit financed by sales finance companies.

Although sales finance companies engage in a variety of activities, most of their funds are employed in the retail financing of automobiles. An automobile dealer customarily has an arrangement with one of the sales finance companies whereby the finance company is prepared to finance the automobile from the time the dealer receives the car from the manufacturer until it is sold. At the retail level the dealer makes credit arrangements with his customer, and sells the customer's note to his finance company at a prearranged rate.

Any business which extends credit to its customers is carrying out a form of sales financing. Particularly when the sales financing activity of a company is separately incorporated it is difficult to draw a line between sales financing as a business and the extension of credit as a part of retail or wholesale trade. Subsidiaries of manufacturers and wholesale and retail dealers other than wholly-owned subsidiaries of automobile manufacturers are not considered as financial intermediaries.

## Consumer Loan Companies

Sales finance companies raise the money to finance their lending through issuing both short and long term debt, and through reserves and owner's equity. Finance company paper plays a very important role in the financial markets, providing an outlet for large amounts of short term funds. Consumer loan companies make cash loans directly to persons and businesses, thus differing from sales finance companies which finance consumer and business purchases.

Although there have always been small companies which loaned to individuals, the main impetus to the consumer loan field was given by the incorporation in Canada during the period from 1928 to 1933 of wholly-owned subsidiaries of United States small loan companies. This was followed by the incorporation of consumer loan subsidiaries by Canadian sales finance companies. At the present time about 60 per cent of the consumer loan business is done by wholly-owned subsidiaries of United States consumer loan companies, about 35 per cent by wholly-owned subsidiaries of Canadian incorporated sales finance companies, and about 5 per cent by other companies. With so much of the business carried on by wholly-owned subsidiaries, the financial statements of consumer loan companies are quite simple in form. Parent companies supply over 60 per cent of the required funds, and over 95 per cent of assets consists of consumer receivables.

Small loan companies are regulated by the Department of Insurance under the Small Loans Act. The Act states that the maximum rates of cost of a loan, including all charges, should not exceed two per cent per month on the unpaid balance of a loan under $300, one per cent per month on the portion of the balance between $300 and $1,000 and one half of one per cent of the balance between $1,000 and $1,500. No interest rate regulations exist on loans over $1,500. Unlicensed lenders must charge less than one per cent per month, or deal in amounts of more than $1,500.

## Farm Finance and Industrial Development Financing

There are a few non-government firms in this area, but because of the high risk involved

Seen under construction is Place Victoria which houses the Montreal and Canadian Stock Exchanges and a vast shopping complex. It is the highest building in the city.

they have not proved too profitable. Large firms can arrange for their financing through the market, while firms of all sizes have access to bank loans for short periods of time. The difficult financing area is that of relatively long term loans to small and medium size firms where the returns on investment are not sufficient to compensate for the risks involved.

The oldest of these types of institutions, historically, are those that lend to farmers. The Canadian Farm Loan Board was formed in 1927 and continued until 1959 when it was superseded by the Farm Credit Corporation. The Quebec Farm Credit Bureau and the Ontario Junior Farmers are among the provincial institutions which lend to farmers. Although these institutions are relatively small, they provide an important part of the mortgage money available to farmers. Much newer, but growing very rapidly in importance, are government owned or sponsored institutions providing loans to non-farm business. The oldest of these is the Industrial Development Bank which was incorporated by Act of Parliament in 1944 as a wholly-owned subsidiary of the Bank of Canada. It supplements the credit made available by other lenders, with small businesses as an area of particular interest. More recently, the provinces have been setting up institutions to aid business locating in the provinces. These institutions may provide assistance by constructing buildings and leasing them to business, by making loans or by providing share capital. They may be operated as wholly-owned government enterprises or as private companies such as the General Investment Corporation of Quebec which sold shares to the public.

## Investment Dealers

During the latter part of the nineteenth century, most businesses were small and made use of savings contributed directly by persons and other businesses while the financing of extensive ventures was largely done by the London market. The first Canadian dealers acted mainly as agents who sold Canadian municipal and other securities in London through their connections with the English banking houses.

By the turn of the century investment dealers were arranging capital issues for corporations, and this business grew steadily until the outbreak of war in 1914. The War had two main effects. First, the London markets were no longer able to supply funds to Canada. Second, the Government of Canada needed large amounts of money to finance the War, and the investment dealers organized to supply the need. Over $2,000,000,000 was raised domestically through bond issues, and a new stage of development of the financial markets had started.

During the 1920's there was a great upsurge of economic activity. The investment dealer industry grew very rapidly and developed the procedures and organization which distinguish it today. Investment dealers, through bringing buyers and sellers together, have played a dominant role in the money market since its start in 1954. Fourteen dealers, called the "money market dealers", have lines of credit with the Bank of Canada, and chartered banks also make day-to-day loans available to these investment dealers at relatively attractive rates. The dealers are therefore able to hold inventories of short-term securities to meet anticipated demands. Investment dealers underwrite new issues of securities and trade in existing issues. Normally they purchase the issue, making their profits from the difference between purchase and selling prices, as well as from fees charged for their services. A number of the larger dealers also act as brokers, through a special department, or a closely related stockbroking firm.

## Stockbrokers

In England and the United States stock markets were formally organized about 1800. In Canada, there were regular meetings of brokers during the 1830's. These gradually led to the incorporation of the Montreal Stock Exchange in 1874 and the Toronto Stock Exchange in 1878. At first, there were few listed companies and trading was light. The Montreal Stock Exchange traded 63 issues in 1874, the year of incorporation, as compared with 182 issues in 1914, and 760 issues in 1962. The number of shares traded had increased at a much faster rate. The Canadian stock markets play the important role of bringing buyers of securities together with sellers of securities. The brokers themselves, as the name implies, have relatively small holdings of securities in their own name.

The story of financial institutions in Canada is one of steadily growing complexity. Since 1950 Canada has been in a period of very rapid change, with a tremendous increase in the number of institutions and the types of financing they provide. It is difficult to imagine the world of 100 years ago when most ventures were still financed through individuals and syndicates. It is still harder to imagine the evolution of the next hundred years. (F. W. Emmerson)

# External Trade

Foreign trade is a large and integral part of Canada's economic life, and makes a major contribution to its standard of living. The spectacular upsurge in Canada's trade during the last 100 years, in relation to a world trade volume which was itself rapidly rising, is shown in the accompanying chart. In volume (after adjusting trade values to discount price rises) world exports multiplied about 18 times, while Canadian exports multiplied 37 times or twice as much between 1870 and 1965. This relationship was also roughly true for imports. In 1870, the value of Canadian exports was $65,000,000, and in 1965 some $8,523,000,000. Imports were $67,000,000 and $8,637,000,000 respectively.

## A Major Trading Country

Canada's rise to the status of a major trading country, the fifth largest in 1965, was part of world economic development. During the last century, economic growth and world trade were greatly stimulated by the achievements of the industrial revolution, by vast improvements in the efficiency of transportation, the linking of distant continents by cable, telegraph and radio, the spread of ideas, and the adoption of the latest technological processes. A feature of this revolution was the expansion of markets beyond national boundaries. World trade rose more rapidly than world production of goods and services, a process accompanied by rising incomes per capita in those countries whose trade grew most rapidly. Canada today is linked closely by trade ties to a dynamic, interdependent, international economy.

The flavour of the links between Canada's internal development and the outside world emerges powerfully in the following verse about the building of the first Canadian transcontinental railroad in the 1880's:

> "A cable started rolling mills in Europe:
> A tap of Morse sent hundreds to the bush,
> Where axes swung on spruce and the saws sang,
> Changing the timber into pyramids
> Of poles and sleepers"*

Especially in the decades around 1900, a large part of the savings of advanced countries flowed into new areas such as Canada, in the form of goods and services for investment. In turn, the growth of output here was oriented to a significant degree towards sales in the expanding markets of other countries.

Canada's rise as an industrial† nation in an industrializing world is associated with marked changes in trade during the last century. Its shifting foreign trade patterns reflect internal economic developments: the growth of waterways, railways, highways and airways; the emergence of new industries based on the seas, rivers, lands, forest and mineral wealth, and on the burgeoning industrial cities of the nation. Among

---

*Reprinted from *Towards the Last Spike* by E. J. Pratt, by permission of the estate of E. J. Pratt and The Macmillan Company of Canada Limited.

†The term "industrial" refers not only to the relatively great importance of manufacturing within a country, but also to the use of efficient industrial methods in the production of primary products. Many Canadian farmers, loggers, and miners are advanced producers in this sense.

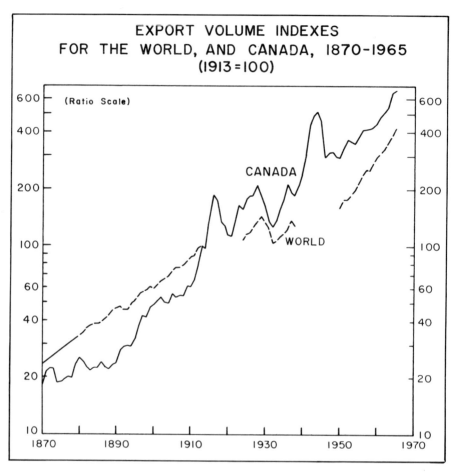

**EXPORT VOLUME INDEXES**
**FOR THE WORLD, AND CANADA, 1870-1965**
**(1913 = 100)**

Source: Based on data from the Dominion Bureau of Statistics adjusted to calendar-year basis, and from A. Maddison, "Growth and Fluctuation in the World Economy", *Review*, Banca Nazionale del Lavoro (Italy), June 1962, and on United Nations data.

fewer than 20 countries which could be classed as industrial today, Canada remains outstanding with its high ratio of natural resource assets in the economy. Yet Canada is also very much an industrial country like the others, with highly developed industry relying on modern technology and on expanding markets to sustain rising standards of living.

A century of dynamic change was not easy for the world or for Canada. Two world wars and a great depression played havoc with international economic affairs. In the long run, however, the remarkable fact which has emerged is the high capability for economic growth of advanced countries co-operating together and trading together. The devastating experiences of war and depression of the generation between 1914 and 1945 have led not to despair and withdrawal but rather to renewed international efforts to promote trade and economic growth. The world has created new and more effective institutions to facilitate trade, trade financing, and assistance to the poor countries which are striving to emulate the economic achievements of countries like Canada. These important adjustments were part of an ongoing process, which is still under way and in which international trade plays an indispensable role. It is against this tremendous backdrop of world growth, change and adaptation, that the growth of Canada's foreign trade and trade relations with other countries can best be understood.

## Changes in Foreign Trade since Confederation

The following table draws together the key figures which highlight changes in the pattern of Canada's foreign trade during the last century. Part 1 shows that Canada's share of world trade has approximately tripled since 1870, from about 1.4 per cent to 4.4 per cent of the value of imports and exports taken together. There were great upsurges after each war (and a decline in Canada's share during the 1930's), a conclusion which may also be reached by examining the chart. The two World Wars evoked a massive response from Canada in economic terms, accelerating the pace of change in internal and external economic affairs. Such a relative upsurge also occurred in peacetime, particularly from about 1890 to 1913, a reflection of the combined effects of relatively open international markets and rapidly rising Canadian capacity to produce, a situation in some ways not unlike that which exists in 1966.

Part 2 indicates the great changes which have occurred in the importance of particular products in Canadian exports. In the early days, staples such as fish and furs constituted the bulk of exports, followed at a later date by timber from Eastern Canada; the prominent rise of wheat exports between 1895 and 1930 reflects the integration of the hitherto untilled lands of Western Canada into the national framework. The large role of newsprint and pulp since the 1920's reflects intensified interest in and development of Canada's magnificent forest resource, one of the greatest such assets possessed by any state. Industrial development of the forest is proceeding apace in nearly all parts of the country today.

The historic significance of the forest to Canada emerges in the following lines:*

> "l'arbre et clou et croix
> croix de rail et de papier
> croix de construction" . . .

The rise in exports of metals, fuels, and other non-metallic minerals goes back to the early years of this century. Exploitation of these resources has contributed greatly to exports and to economic activity in the last 20 years as well. Canada has huge resources of this kind in the form of known reserves, and probably resources of great value yet to be discovered. Outlets far larger than the present size of the Canadian market are required for development of the potential of such assets, and the growth of trade will be a crucial factor in turning them into usable wealth. After a slump in the early 1960's, uranium exports are bound to rise again in line with world demands for energy for peaceful uses. Among present major mineral exports are iron, non-ferrous metals, oil and gas, potash, and sulphur.

---

*Reprinted by permission of the author M. Paul-M. Lapointe, whose poem *ARBRES* appears in *Anthologie de la poésie canadienne française*, (4eme édition, Beauchemin, Montréal, 1963).

# Key Features of Canada's Foreign Trade in Goods, 1870 to 1965

|  | 1870 | 1910 | 1930 | 1950 | 1960 | 1965 |
|---|---|---|---|---|---|---|

## Part 1 — Canada's Share of World Trade
### (Billions of Canadian dollars, or per cent)

|  | 1870 | 1910 | 1930 | 1950 | 1960 | 1965 |
|---|---|---|---|---|---|---|
| Value of World exports.................$ | 5.1 | 15.2 | 26.2 | 66.8 | 123.7 | 200.0 |
| Value of Canadian exports.............$ | 0.1[1] | 0.3 | 0.9 | 3.1 | 5.3 | 8.5 |
| Canada's share of World exports........% | 1.3 | 1.8 | 3.3 | 4.7 | 4.3 | 4.3 |
| Canada's share of World imports........% | 1.5 | 2.8 | 2.3 | 5.0 | 4.2 | 4.5 |

## Part 2 — Changing Composition:
### Principal products as a per cent of value of exports

|  | 1870 | 1910 | 1930 | 1950 | 1960 | 1965 |
|---|---|---|---|---|---|---|
| Wheat and flour...................... | 5 | 22 | 25 | 13 | 9 | 11 |
| Other agricultural items............... | 41 | 28 | 14 | 15 | 10 | 9 |
| Fish................................ | 5 | 6 | 7 | 4 | 3 | 2 |
| Timber and lumber.................... | 33 | 14 | 5 | 9 | 7 | 6 |
| Newsprint........................... | — | — | 15 | 16 | 14 | 10 |
| Woodpulp........................... | — | 2 | 4 | 7 | 6 | 6 |
| Iron ore, primary iron and steel......... | — | — | 1 | 2 | 6 | 5 |
| Non-ferrous metals and products........ | 2 | 12 | 13 | 14 | 17 | 16 |
| Uranium............................ | — | — | — | — | 5 | 1 |
| Oil and natural gas................... | — | — | — | — | 2 | 5 |
| Other non-metallic minerals and products. | 4 | 4 | 2 | 3 | 4 | 4 |
| Machinery and transport equipment..... | — | 2 | 5 | 7 | 6 | 11 |
| Chemicals........................... | — | 1 | 2 | 3 | 5 | 4 |
| Other............................... | 10 | 10 | 7 | 7 | 6 | 11 |
| **Total**........................ | **100** | **100** | **100** | **100** | **100** | **100** |

## Part 3 — Changing Composition:
### Principal products as a per cent of value of imports

|  | 1870 | 1910 | 1930 | 1950 | 1960 | 1965 |
|---|---|---|---|---|---|---|
| Textiles............................. | 24 | 17 | 15 | 12 | 8 | 7 |
| Agricultural and animal products........ | 41 | 24 | 25 | 18 | 15 | 11 |
| Coal................................ | — | 8 | 6 | 6 | 1 | 2 |
| Oil................................. | — | 1 | 7 | 10 | 7 | 5 |
| Iron and steel....................... | — | 5 | 6 | 5 | 5 | 5 |
| Machinery and transport equipment..... | — | 4 | 14 | 26 | 35 | 35 |
| Chemicals........................... | 3 | 3 | 4 | 5 | 7 | 6 |
| Other............................... | 32 | 38 | 25 | 19 | 22 | 29 |
| **Total**........................ | **100** | **100** | **100** | **100** | **100** | **100** |

## Part 4 — Changing Export Direction:
### Per cent of value of exports shipped to main destinations

| To: | 1870 | 1910 | 1930 | 1950 | 1960 | 1965 |
|---|---|---|---|---|---|---|
| Britain............................. | 38 | 50 | 27 | 15 | 17 | 14 |
| Other Commonwealth and Preferential... | 3 | 6 | 9 | 6 | 6 | 6 |
| United States........................ | 51 | 37 | 45 | 65 | 56 | 57 |
| Other............................... | 8 | 7 | 20 | 14 | 21 | 24 |
| **Total**........................ | **100** | **100** | **100** | **100** | **100** | **100** |

[1]Canada's exports in 1870 were $58,000,000 (U.S.) in value.

| | 1870 | 1910 | 1930 | 1950 | 1960 | 1965 |
|---|---|---|---|---|---|---|

## Part 5 — Changing Import Direction:
### Per cent of value of imports from main countries of origin

| From: | | | | | | |
|---|---|---|---|---|---|---|
| Britain........................... | 56 | 26 | 15 | 13 | 11 | 7 |
| Other Commonwealth and Preferential... | 2 | 4 | 6 | 8 | 5 | 4 |
| United States....................... | 32 | 59 | 62 | 67 | 67 | 70 |
| Other ........................... | 10 | 11 | 17 | 13 | 17 | 18 |
| **Total**........................... | **100** | **100** | **100** | **100** | **100** | **100** |

## Part 6 — Exports and imports as a per cent of Canada's Gross National Product

| | | | | | | |
|---|---|---|---|---|---|---|
| Exports............................ | 13 | 13 | 15 | 17 | 14 | 17 |
| Imports............................ | 15 | 17 | 18 | 18 | 15 | 16 |

## Part 7 — Per cent of value of exports accounted for by
### agricultural, primary, highly processed and manufactured products

| | 1899 | 1913 | 1929 | 1950 | 1960 | 1965 |
|---|---|---|---|---|---|---|
| Agriculture and fish.................... | 63 | 59 | 47 | 32 | 21 | 22 |
| Other primary........................ | 28 | 29 | 12 | 19 | 28 | 25 |
| Highly processed and manufactured[1]..... | 9 | 12 | 41 | 49 | 51 | 53 |

[1]Includes wood pulp, chemicals, machinery and transport equipment, newsprint and other highly-processed products identified by material of origin, and miscellaneous manufactures.

As early as the 1920's, Canada displayed considerable capabilities for a small country in exporting machinery and other highly-manufactured products. Since the early 1960's, Canadian exporters of these products have been turning in a dynamic performance. For the first time in history, highly-manufactured products have come to constitute a major export grouping. The value of these exports more than tripled between 1960 and 1965, from $411,000,000 to $1,300,000,000. Their share of Canadian exports roughly doubled in this period, from 7.8 per cent to 15.3 per cent.

Part 3 of the Table shows the changing importance over the century of selected commodities in Canadian imports. As an early frontier country, Canada has always imported a high proportion of manufactured products. But the emphasis on commodity imports has changed over time, towards machinery and transport equipment, and away from textiles and other soft consumer goods which were proportionately much more important a century ago. In Canada today, a significant proportion of imports is accounted for by investment goods destined to increase the capacity of the country to produce.

Parts 4 and 5 show the profound changes which have occurred during the century in the relative importance of other countries as direct trading partners of Canada. The United States has become by far Canada's largest customer and supplier. This fact reflects the high rate of economic growth of these two countries during the century, their proximity to one another across the width of a continent and along long reaches of coastline, and the close economic links between them. Although her relative importance has declined, Britain remains by far Canada's second largest trading partner. The United Kingdom, a large industrial country, is a major importer and a nation with which Canada's commercial channels of communication were well developed early in the life of this country.

A major change whose significance is sometimes overlooked is the long-term rise in the importance of third countries as direct trading partners of Canada. In addition to special ties with the United States and Britain, Canada's trade with all other countries has risen from under 12 per cent to over 25 per cent of its imports and exports combined, during the century. Much of this "third country" trade is with the industrial states of continental Europe and with Japan. One ought not, however, to overlook the potential role of the developing countries struggling towards higher living standards. Once these countries achieve the capacity for growth already reached by the industrial countries, the past century of change in world patterns of output and trade could conceivably appear merely as a prelude of greater things to come.

The world trading system in which Canada participates today is not, however, well described in terms of trade exchanges between pairs of countries. The efficiency of the system rests heavily on world-wide marketings and purchasing by the major trading countries, and on a multilateral balancing of import payments and export receipts for goods and services. Canada usually has a surplus of receipts with overseas countries combined, and a deficit with the United States.

Part 6 shows the relative importance of trade in relation to Canada's Gross National Product, the value of gross output of goods plus services. Canada has always been a trading country. The high and relatively stable ratio of trade to GNP indicates Canada's persistent dependence on trade as a factor in its economic growth. Exports and imports are today each equal to roughly 40 per cent of the value of goods output alone in Canada (excluding services). It is clear that trade continues to occupy a very large place indeed in the economic activity of the nation. This is, however, not an unusual position for an industrial country; there are many other countries today whose trade constitutes an even higher proportion of GNP. No country comparable in economic size to Canada has achieved a high standard of living without heavy participation in international trade.

Part 7 of the Table highlights the changing character of Canada's exports as the country grew and matured into an industrial state. At the turn of the century, more than 90 per cent of Canada's exports were agricultural, fish, or primary industrial products. By 1960, highly-processed and manufactured products accounted for more than half the value of exports. Meanwhile, the structure of employment in Canada was developing in a way more or less typical of an industrializing country. In 1891, 50 per cent of employment in Canada was located in the primary industries, 15 per cent in manu-facturing, and 35 per cent in government and other service industries. In 1963, only 13 per cent was in the primary industries, 25 per cent in manufacturing, and 62 per cent in other industries. By way of comparison, United States figures for 1963 were: primary 7 per cent, manufacturing 25 per cent, and other industries, 68 per cent.

It is clear that the structure of employment in Canada is related to changes in the pattern of external trade, as well as to developments within the domestic economy such as rising output per employee. One of the striking facts of recent years has been the close association between the growth of trade of the world's main commercial countries, and the rise in the efficiency of their employment of resources of labour, capital, and material supplies. Trade has risen most rapidly in those countries where the efficiency of output has risen most rapidly.

A unique application of plastic in the construction field is this housing unit which was originally designed for the Canadian climate but has since achieved popularity in warmer countries as motel units and homes. The buildings are made of fibreglass and polyurethane foam.

A shipment of live lobsters reaches Belgium.

These 6,500-horsepower synchronous motors manufactured in Hamilton, Ontario, are prepared for export to an oil refinery in Greece.

## Trade Relations since 1867

Commercial policy occupies a prominent place in Canada's history. Confederation removed tariffs between the then colonial territories of British North America. It created a customs union merging the import duties of Canada (roughly the St. Lawrence Valley) and the Maritimes into a single external tariff. The new Canadian state wavered between the commercial attractions of Britain and the United States. Confederation

Combines and windrowers from a Hamilton, Ontario, plant await shipment.

itself was, at least in part, a response to the U.S. abrogation of the Reciprocity Treaty of 1854-66, which had provided for free trade in primary products. That Treaty had been sought by the colonies as an offset to their earlier loss of preferences in the British market. It had been negotiated by Britain on their behalf in the belief that it would promote economic viability and help to avoid political union with the United States.

The ending of reciprocity had a considerable adverse influence on trade and investment in Canada, and the new state tried hard for better access to both major markets. In 1879, however, Canada adopted a policy then in vogue in most major trading countries other than Britain. The National Policy of higher tariffs aimed at fostering manufacturing in Canada and at increasing the flow of revenues to finance new transport facilities and general economic development. Since revenues then depended heavily on import duties there was a conflict between these objectives. The fact that internal development hinged significantly on a competitive export performance enhanced this basic conflict. Since that time, a major preoccupation of Canadian commercial policy has been to maintain the right "balance" between conflicting objectives.

Around the turn of the century, Canada unilaterally provided preferential duties favouring imports from Britain. At least partly for bargaining purposes, Canada in 1907 adopted a tariff which provided for three levels of duty—Preferential, Intermediate, and General. A renewed effort to obtain reciprocity in trade with the United States was turned down in the Canadian election of 1911.

After the crash in 1929, in the light of massive tariff increases in many countries and the serious international economic strains which were evident, Britain, Canada and other Commonwealth countries adopted a systematic, widespread system of tariff preferences. In 1937-38, in return for U.S. tariff reductions, Britain and Canada reduced tariffs and tariff preferences.

The breakdown of the world financial and trading system during the 1930's convinced many countries of the need for a fresh start. Canada strongly supported the General Agreement on Tariffs and Trade (or GATT) which came into force in 1948. About 80 countries today subscribe to the principles of the Agreement, which is both a trade treaty and an institution for trade negotiation, adaptation, and settling disputes.

The GATT, in effect, became Canada's main commercial treaty. It is no longer realistic, if it ever was, to consider Canada's commercial policy apart from the trends in the world trading community. The Agreement bans new preferences, outlaws import quotas except in specified circumstances, promotes non-discrimination in trade, and reductions of trade barriers in general. It also provides for regional free trade arrangements under conditions carefully specified so as to protect the interests of GATT members not participating in such arrangements.

Up to 1961, Canada took part in six multilateral tariff negotiations, leading to important reductions and undertakings to maintain stability both in Canadian and foreign tariffs. Postwar international trade relations have continued to evolve. Among the trade problems which Canada has encountered, the following may be listed: the problem of freer trade for agriculture; the level of protection to be adopted by countries participating in regional free trade; the problem of increasing mutually beneficial trade with the developing countries; and the problem of trading with the Communist countries where tariffs are not particularly meaningful commercial instruments.

A potential customer in the West Indies examines a Canadian-made stove.

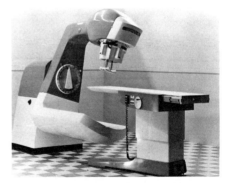

The Theratron 80 Cobalt 60 Teletherapy Unit, a product of Atomic Energy of Canada, Ltd., is used in the treatment of cancer. Similar Canadian units have been installed in some 45 different countries.

EXTERNAL TRADE

The United States and West Germany are major customers for these camera lenses, an increasingly important export commodity for Canada.

An ammonium-nitrate fertilizer plant was the first industry to be established in New Brunswick's 134-acre Westmorland Chemical Park, located near Moncton. A wharf to provide shipping facilities has been built. Initial costs of development and construction of the Park were paid by the New Brunswick Development Corporation. The plan is to have private enterprise own and operate plants on sites bought or leased from the corporation.

Port Arthur, on the northern shore of Lake Superior, is a busy city. Through this port are exported millions of tons of iron ore, millions of bushels of wheat. The city has large pulp and paper mills and the largest Canadian drydock on the Great Lakes.

266

Two important regional arrangements for free trade today are the European Economic Community (a customs union), and the European Free Trade Association which includes Britain. Much West European opinion holds that these two groups should merge, a course open to them under the terms of the GATT which sets out the conditions under which such a decision might be implemented, including safeguards for other GATT members. In the spring of 1966, a further round of multilateral tariff negotiations was under way. Canada has a considerable interest in promoting a steadily-effective international trading system, and participated in these negotiations. Efforts are being made within GATT, and within the framework of the United Nations, to improve the trading position of the developing countries. It is a sobering fact that by and large the rich countries have successfully expanded their trade while the poor countries have lagged behind.

The opportunities for beneficial trade with Communist countries have been approached bilaterally between them and other countries, and considerable trade has been conducted in this way. So far as can be foreseen, this is likely also to be the pattern in the years ahead. In the long-term future, it may perhaps be possible to obtain more of the efficiencies inherent in the western pattern of multilateral exchanges, though any attempt at assessing such possibilities would be speculative.

## Links with World Growth

It is clear that the growth of Canada's trade and national prosperity has been closely linked with the growth of the world economy, and with the emerging maturity of Canada as a viable industrial nation. Canadian policy has long aimed at fostering the rise of secondary industry, partly through protection. Yet the greater rise in Canadian manufacturing, and exports of highly manufactured products, took place in the last 20 years, when the national growth policies of the industrial countries were strong, when trade barriers were being reduced, and when international economic co-operation worked, if not smoothly, at least better than ever before.

The future of Canada's trade is bound up closely with the rate of improvement of the productive efficiency of the economy. This is a two-way street because rising productivity promotes greater output and trade, while expanding trade helps to promote rising productivity. Over much of the period since Confederation, high world demands for Canadian products brought about greater rises in prices for Canada's exports than for world trade in general. This was a considerable factor in the marked rise in Canada's share of world exports since 1870. The evidence of the last decade or so, however, has been that Canada can no longer count upon relatively rising export prices, but rather must strive for greater efficiency in production in order to maintain competitive prices. The real goal is rising productive efficiency; in other words, growing efficiency is closely associated with trade expansion.

The evidence of the last 20 years also indicates that the industrial countries can achieve high rates of economic growth which accompany trade expansion. In the overseas countries, recovery from wartime destruction has merged smoothly into a period of strong and steady growth and of rising trade. In North America, a period of slack in the late 1950's and early 1960's has been succeeded by a long sustained economic expansion and rising trade. The industrial countries together have agreed on a target for economic growth in the 1960's, that of raising their combined real income by 50

Transportation of products of inland areas is no problem when shipping on the St. Lawrence Seaway is so readily available.

per cent. The evidence of the past five years suggests that this target will be reached, or exceeded, by 1970, and this implies further expansion of world trade. This is a point of fundamental importance to Canada with one of the world's most rapidly-growing populations at the present time.

Loading iron ore at Sept Îles, Quebec.

An aluminum bridge is located at Arvida, Quebec, site of the largest aluminum smelter in the world. Canada ranks third in world aluminum production.

Beyond the industrial countries, the mass of the world's population is concentrated in developing lands which have not participated nearly enough in the rise of world output and trade. On a long view of the future, it must surely be in the interest of Canadians or, indeed, all "westerners", to devote more ingenuity and resources to the great problems and greater opportunities inherent in substantially expanding trade with these countries. (J. R. Downs)

EXTERNAL TRADE

# Labour Force: Growth and Change

At the time of Confederation there were some 3,500,000 people living in Canada. A hundred years later there are 20,000,000. The population has increased almost sixfold in a century.

Population growth has been generally rapid and persistent, though by no means uniform. In no intercensal decade of the period 1861-1961 does the official record show less than a 10 per cent increase, and in six of the ten decades the gains exceeded 15 per cent. Two, 1901-11 and 1951-61, displayed increases in excess of 30 per cent.

### Population Growth by Intercensal Decades, 1861-71 to 1951-61

|  | Increase | | | Increase | |
|---|---|---|---|---|---|
|  | '000 | % |  | '000 | % |
| 1861-1871............. | 459 | 14.2 | 1911-1921............. | 1,581 | 21.9 |
| 1871-1881............. | 636 | 17.2 | 1921-1931............. | 1,589 | 18.1 |
| 1881-1891............. | 508 | 11.7 | 1931-1941............. | 1,130 | 10.9 |
| 1891-1901............. | 538 | 11.1 | 1941-1951 [1]............. | 2,141 | 18.6 |
| 1901-1911............. | 1,835 | 34.2 | 1951-1961 [2]............. | 4,229 | 30.2 |

[1] Excluding Newfoundland throughout the period.   [2] Including Newfoundland.

The historical record of labour force growth is more difficult to compile. Information on the gainfully-occupied was collected in the Census of Canada as early as 1881. However, owing to changes in definitions and procedures from one census to another, and the difficulties of making adjustments because of the limited amounts of detail that were tabulated, only rough estimates are possible on a consistent basis for the earlier dates. Indeed, even in the present century it is not easy to construct a consistent series for the period prior to the advent of regular labour force surveys at the end of World War II. The limitations of the historical statistics are thus considerable, though probably not sufficient to distort significantly the broad outlines of labour force growth.

In general, it appears that the pattern of labour force growth is not markedly different from the pattern of population growth, although the rates in particular periods were by no means identical. Ten-year increases in the neighbourhood of 20 per cent in the 1870's and 1880's were followed by slower growth—something closer to 10 per cent— in the 1890's. Then, in the first decade of the twentieth century, with immigrants arriving at an unprecedented rate, the labour force grew by a spectacular 50 per cent. This period, or more correctly, if we abandon the framework of intercensal decades, the dozen or so years preceding the outbreak of World War I in 1914, was unquestionably the period of most rapid labour force growth, in percentage terms, since Confederation—and, indeed, for a long time before. Well over a million immigrants, predominantly adult males, entered the country in the three years, 1911-13, alone. Although for many Canada may have been merely a stepping stone to the United States, for many others it was a permanent home. In the single year 1913, some 400,000 immigrants arrived, by far the largest annual influx on record.

The labour force grew less dramatically but nevertheless substantially during the interwar period—more than 20 per cent in the 1920's and another 15 in the 1930's. At the outbreak of World War II it was approximately two and a half times what it had been at the beginning of the century.

With World War II came many changes. The Great Depression was at last a thing of the past. Chronic underutilization of human and other resources was replaced by intense pressure to expand output in furtherance of the war effort. Lingering prejudices about the employment of women were permanently weakened as large numbers of female workers took the place of men who had gone into the armed forces. The birth rate, which had reached the lowest point of a long-run decline towards the end of the 1930's, was now on the way up, presaging the postwar "baby boom". Advances in industrial techniques pointed the way to future peace-time applications and thus helped to sow the seeds of rising productivity and income levels in the years to come, with concomitant changes in the characteristics of employment.

The period after World War II is one of the most remarkable periods in the history of the Canadian labour force, remarkable to some extent for over-all growth but more so for changes in structure which will be discussed below. In total, the labour force increased by some 25 per cent in the 1950's, quite possibly the second most rapid rate since Confederation (certainty on this point is precluded by limitations of the statistics), though substantially below the rate attained in the immigration boom before World War I. The rate in the 1960's promises to be as great as that of the 1950's, and perhaps somewhat greater.

## Immigration as a Source of Growth

Immigration has been an important and highly variable factor in the growth of the Canadian labour force. Because of the high concentration in the active adult age groups, especially the age group under 35, the proportionate labour force content is appreciably higher for immigrants than for the population as a whole. However, it would be easy to overstate the quantitative effect of immigration.

**Gross and Net Immigration by Intercensal Decades, 1861-71 to 1951-61**

| | Immigration | | | Immigration | |
|---|---|---|---|---|---|
| Decade | Gross | Net | Decade | Gross | Net |
| | '000 | '000 | | '000 | '000 |
| 1861-1871............. | 187 | −192 | 1911-1921............. | 1,612 | 231 |
| 1871-1881............. | 353 | − 87 | 1921-1931............. | 1,203 | 229 |
| 1881-1891............. | 903 | −206 | 1931-1941............. | 150 | − 92 |
| 1891-1901............. | 326 | −180 | 1941-1951 [1]............. | 548 | 169 |
| 1901-1911............. | 1,759 | 716 | 1951-1961 [2]............. | 1,543 | 1,081 |

[1] Excluding Newfoundland throughout the period.   [2] Including Newfoundland.

In all periods, immigration has been offset in large measure by emigration, especially to the United States, and emigrants also tend to be concentrated in the younger adult age groups. *Net* immigration has been much less than *gross* immigration; in five of the ten decades between 1861 and 1961 it actually appears to have been negative, implying a net loss on the international exchange of population. As a consequence, natural increase has been by far the dominant source of population and labour force growth since Confederation and earlier. As Hood and Scott have shown, natural population increase in the period 1851-1951 totalled some 10,500,000, compared with gross immigration of about 7,200,000.* But estimated *net* immigration amounted to only

---

* Wm. C. Hood and Anthony Scott, "Output, Labour and Capital in the Canadian Economy", Royal Commission on Canada's Economic Prospects, 1957; Chapter 4.

a little over 700,000, a mere six or seven per cent of the total population increase.

**Natural Increase and Net Immigration by Intercensal Decades, 1861-71 to 1951-61**

| Decade | Natural Increase | Net Immigration | Decade | Natural Increase | Net Immigration |
|---|---|---|---|---|---|
| | '000 | '000 | | '000 | 000 |
| 1861-1871.......... | 651 | −192 | 1911-1921.......... | 1,350 | 231 |
| 1871-1881.......... | 723 | − 87 | 1921-1931.......... | 1,360 | 229 |
| 1881-1891.......... | 714 | −206 | 1931-1941.......... | 1,222 | − 92 |
| 1891-1901.......... | 718 | −180 | 1941-1951[1]......... | 1,972 | 169 |
| 1901-1911.......... | 1,120 | 716 | 1951-1961[2]......... | 3,148 | 1,081 |

[1] Excluding Newfoundland throughout the period.   [2] Including Newfoundland.

Because of data limitations, similar calculations have not been made for the labour force, as distinct from the total population. However, there is no doubt that the results would be substantially the same: by far the largest part of the hundred-year growth of the Canadian labour force would be found to have come from natural increase. In particular periods, however, immigration has been a major factor. One such period is the period prior to World War I discussed above. Another is the 1950's.

The decade of the 1950's was a time of rapid economic expansion in Canada. Roughly two thirds of labour force growth in the period 1950-55 came from net immigration and one third from domestic sources. In the period 1955-60 the positions were reversed: one third from net immigration, two thirds from domestic supply. But, for the decade as a whole, and more especially for the first half, it is evident that economic expansion would have proceeded at a much slower pace had it not been for substantial annual inflows of workers from abroad. The low birth rates of the 1930's were taking their toll in shortages of young people coming into the labour market and immigration offset these shortages.

The situation is different in the 1960's. No longer is the economy as dependent on immigration for its growth possibilities. The impact of the "baby boom" is being felt in the labour market, supplemented by the increased propensity of married women to take jobs outside the home. Roughly 85 or 90 per cent of labour force increase in the present decade is coming from domestic sources.

## Geographic Patterns of Growth and Distribution

The pattern of regional labour force and population change has shifted markedly over the decades. In this century, the pre-World War I period stands out as one of sudden growth and redistribution. This was the period of rapid settlement and agricultural development in Western Canada. More than three fifths of the total Canadian population increase in the decade, 1901-11, went into the Prairie and Pacific Coast regions. Saskatchewan and Alberta increased in population by over 400 per cent, British Columbia and Manitoba by 120 and 80 per cent, respectively.

British Columbia continued to experience rapid expansion in the following decades. In the Prairie Provinces, however, rapid growth gave way by the 1930's to comparatively small rates of increase and, in the case of Saskatchewan, to actual declines in the 1930's and 1940's. Throughout the period since 1900 the Maritime Provinces—Prince Edward Island, Nova Scotia, and New Brunswick—have consistently recorded relatively moderate gains if not actual declines. Ontario and Quebec have shown persistent and generally substantial rates of increase.

The period since World War II has been characterized by substantial and sustained growth in British Columbia and the Central Canadian provinces of Ontario and Quebec, and more moderate increases in the Maritimes and the Prairies, excluding Alberta. The latter province, with the fillip provided by a new and fast-growing oil industry, has shown rapid growth, indeed more rapid in terms of population than that of any other province.

As in the past, the labour force, like the population, is highly concentrated geographically. Almost two thirds are located in Ontario and Quebec, and the metropolitan areas of Montreal and Toronto alone account for a quarter of the Canadian total. The four Atlantic Provinces account for less than a tenth, and the same is true of British Columbia. About a sixth is located in the Prairie region.

### Regional Distribution of Population and Civilian Labour Force, 1965

| | Population (June 1) | | Civilian Labour Force (annual average) | |
|---|---|---|---|---|
| | '000 | Percentage of total | '000 | Percentage of total |
| Atlantic Region.......................... | 1,990 | 10.2 | 611 | 8.6 |
| Quebec.................................. | 5,657 | 29.0 | 2,022 | 28.3 |
| Ontario................................. | 6,731 | 34.5 | 2,614 | 36.6 |
| Prairie Region.......................... | 3,364 | 17.2 | 1,228 | 17.2 |
| British Columbia........................ | 1,789 | 9.2 | 666 | 9.3 |
| Canada[1]............................... | 19,531 | 100.0 | 7,141 | 100.0 |

1 Excludes Yukon and Northwest Territories with a combined population of 40,000.

## Urbanization and Changing Industrial Composition

At the beginning of the twentieth century, roughly three fifths of the people of Canada were living in rural areas and 40 per cent of the labour force were engaged in agricultural pursuits. Today, 70 per cent of the population are resident in urban areas and agriculture accounts for less than a tenth of the labour force.

The process of urbanization has continued with only minor interruption. In the 1930's, with severe shortages of industrial job opportunities, the off-the-farm flow was slowed or even halted for a time but the pattern was resumed in the following decades. Increased mechanization and other improvements in agricultural technology have combined with rapid expansion in non-farm sectors of the economy to produce a spectacular shift in the labour force since World War II. In 1950, farming still provided more than 20 per cent of total employment in Canada, but by the early 1960's the proportion had fallen to 10 per cent and the decline continues, albeit at a reduced rate. This off-the-farm movement, together with the high levels of immigration in the 1950's and increased labour force participation of married women, was one of the important factors in postwar economic growth. Whereas total employment increased by a little under 40 per cent between 1950 and 1965, *non-farm* employment increased by almost 60 per cent.

The decline of agricultural employment, both absolute and in relative terms, is one of the dominant features of the postwar period. Another is the expansion of the service sector. Service industries—retail and wholesale trade, finance, transportation, government, schools, hospitals, and so on—accounted for about 42 per cent of Canadian employment in 1950; in 1964 they accounted for 55 per cent. As noted below, this has been a major factor in the phenomenal increase in the number of working women.

### Percentage Distribution of Employment by Industry, 1950 and 1964

(annual averages)

|  | Percentage of Total including Agriculture | | Percentage of Total excluding Agriculture | |
|---|---|---|---|---|
|  | 1950 | 1964 | 1950 | 1964 |
| Agriculture. | 20.5 | 9.5 | — | — |
| Non-agricultural industries: |  |  |  |  |
| Total. | 79.5 | 90.5 | 100.0 | 100.0 |
| Goods-producing. | 37.0 | 35.5 | 46.6 | 39.3 |
| Service-producing. | 42.5 | 55.0 | 53.4 | 60.7 |
| Total, all industries. | 100.0 | 100.0 | — | — |

## Trends in Labour Force Participation

The over-all labour force participation rate—the ratio of labour force to population of working age—has exhibited remarkable stability over long periods of time. The available data do not permit reliable generalization for the earlier decades. However, the total labour force has been very close to 55 per cent of the population 14 years of age and over since at least 1921 and, in all likelihood, since the turn of the century. (Inmates of institutions are excluded from the population base in this calculation.)

The relative stability of the over-all participation rate is more remarkable when one considers the changes that have taken place in individual segments of the population. Among men, the average length of working life has contracted markedly. At one end, the tendency towards earlier retirement has reduced sharply the rate for older men: in 1921, roughly six out of every ten men over the age of sixty-five were still in the labour force, compared with less than three out of ten today, and the proportion is still falling. At the other end, the rise in the average school-leaving age has reduced the proportion of 14-19-year-old males in the labour force from about seven out of ten in 1921 to less than four in ten at the present time. The drop in the participation rate for young men has been especially rapid since the end of the 1940's.

### Civilian Labour Force Participation Rates, by Age and Sex, 1950 and 1965

(annual averages)

|  |  | 1950 % | 1965 % |
|---|---|---|---|
| Men | Total. | 84.0 | 77.9 |
|  | 14-19. | 55.9 | 38.7 |
|  | 20-24. | 93.0 | 87.6 |
|  | 25-64. | 95.3 | 95.2 |
|  | 65 and over. | 40.4 | 26.3 |
| Women | Total. | 23.2 | 31.3 |
|  | 14-19. | 33.0 | 30.2 |
|  | 20-24. | 46.4 | 52.6 |
|  | 25-64. | 20.2 | 32.7 |
|  | 65 and over. | 4.2 | 6.0 |

Contraction of the male working life and the associated reduction of participation rates for younger and older men have been offset by increases in the labour force participation of women. From something in the neighbourhood of 15 per cent at the turn of the century, the proportion of women 14 years of age and over in the labour force had risen to almost 25 per cent at the start of the 1950's; today it is well over 30 per cent. The increases in labour force participation of married women, especially since the early fifties, have been particularly dramatic. Further, the "profile" of work life of women has so radically altered that it is worthwhile elaborating these developments.

## Women in the Labour Force

As has just been observed there has been a remarkable rise in the labour force activity rate of women over the course of this century. In 1901, scarcely more than one out of every six or seven adult women in Canada was in the labour force: today that proportion has risen to nearly one out of three. No less remarkable than the increase in numbers of working women has been the change in the composition of the female labour force. In 1901, the typical urban working woman was young and single. One can surmise that the few who were married (a negligible two or three per cent of all married women in the country) were forced to venture into the labour market because of unfortunate personal circumstances or were in some way exceptional. Certainly prevailing mores and social attitudes were hardly conducive to such behaviour. Today

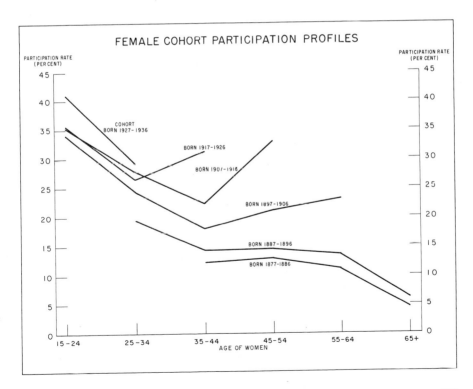

FEMALE COHORT PARTICIPATION PROFILES

almost one in four married women in Canada has some attachment to the labour force. Most of these women are over the age of 30 or 35 and a very substantial proportion of them have children who are still going to school. The working mother in a Canadian city today, while still not typical, is far from being the unfortunate creature or outlandish nonconformist of only a few decades ago.

While statistical information is too fragmentary to allow researchers to trace precisely these revolutionary changes, even the incomplete data available make quite clear the broad outline of their nature and timing. This may be seen from the chart depicting the "participation profiles"* of different cohorts or "generations" of Canadian women (groups of women born in the same time period).

Scarcely more than one out of ten women born just after Confederation would have entered the labour force before the turn of the century and, as may be seen in the chart depicted above and in the following table this proportion changed very little until these women reached their mid-fifties, after which their numbers in the working population declined. A similar pattern is observed for women born in the final decade of the last century, although the percentage of these women with some labour force attachment was consistently higher than that for the earlier generation. But the group of women who came of working age during and just after World War I (most of whom were born in the opening years of this century) behaved differently. After a phase of declining labour force participation which extended until their middle forties, some of these women decided to re-enter the labour market in later middle age during a decade, it should be noted, which straddled another major war. Most of them were married women whose children no longer required full-time care in the home. This "second phase" of women's work life is much more sharply in evidence in the next and subsequent "generations". It may be seen that as we move forward in time the re-entry phase occurs earlier in middle-life.

The emergence of the two-phase working life cycle of women depicted in the chart is one of the most significant labour force developments of the past 40 years. It has been accompanied by another phenomenon of equal significance. It may be noted from the chart that each successive "cohort profile" lies above that of the preceding one. In other words, a larger proportion of each new "generation" of women has entered the labour force and this early labour market experience has evidently influenced their behaviour in later years. We are witnessing an increased labour force participation of women at every age and, judging from the experience of other countries and particularly the United States, this trend is likely to continue for some time to come.

Just as this transformation in the working life pattern of women has profound and widespread economic and social implications, it is also the product of fundamental and pervasive socio-economic and demographic developments in Canada. The rapid growth of the service-producing industries and of white collar jobs in all sectors of the economy have opened up new work opportunities for women, opportunities to supplement family income in a society which places ever-greater emphasis on rising material standards of life. Improvements in "household technology", the development

---

* The term is used to describe a curve depicting participation rates of a group of individuals distributed by age.

of commercial substitutes for most household products, the reduction in working hours and the growth in part-time employment* have all combined to allow more and more women to take advantage of these opportunities by making it possible both to work and to maintain homes. Changes in the attitudes of employers, and in community attitudes generally, have favoured the increased participation of women as have a number of demographic developments, themselves related to these social and economic changes. Thus women are much more likely to work outside the home in urban than in rural areas† and the urbanization of Canada referred to above has been a factor of some importance in explaining the rise in female labour force participation. Changes in marital and fertility patterns have also exerted a significant influence. Women are marrying and starting their families earlier and they are younger when their last child enters school. Better educated than earlier generations, many of these women are less satisfied to stay at home than were their mothers and grand-mothers.‡

### Female Cohort Participation Rates, 1921-1961

| Date at which Cohort was: | | Percentage Participation Rate of Cohort in: | | | | |
| Born | 15-24 years | 1921 | 1931 | 1941 | 1951 | 1961 |
| --- | --- | --- | --- | --- | --- | --- |
| 1877-1886 . . . . . . . . . . . | 1901 | 12.2¹ | 12.9 | 11.1 | 4.6³ | |
| 1887-1896 . . . . . . . . . . . | 1911 | 19.5 | 14.3 | 14.5 | 13.5 | 6.2³ |
| 1897-1906 . . . . . . . . . . . | 1921 | 34.1² | 24.4 | 18.1 | 21.1 | 23.1 |
| 1907-1916 . . . . . . . . . . . | 1931 | | 35.3² | 27.9 | 22.4 | 32.9 |
| 1917-1926 . . . . . . . . . . . | 1941 | | | 35.6² | 25.5 | 31.2 |
| 1927-1936 . . . . . . . . . . . | 1951 | | | | 41.0² | 29.2 |
| 1937-1946 . . . . . . . . . . . | 1961 | | | | | 39.5² |

[1] Excludes a few Indians on reserves. Includes women 35-49 years. [2] Participation rate of women 14-24 years. Absence of age detail in earlier Censuses precluded removal of 14 year olds. [3] Participation rate of women 65 and over.

In this review of labour force trends in Canada we have so far concentrated on changes in *numbers* and changes in labour market *behaviour* but have made only passing

---

* Around the time of Confederation scattered evidence suggests that a typical work week in manufacturing industries was in the range of 60-65 hours. The history of change in working hours over the past century deserves to be the topic of a separate study: only the most severe limitations of space justify its relegation to a footnote. The shorter work week has, of course, economic and social implications far beyond the one suggested here in respect to female labour force participation. A more recent development, equally important in this regard, has been the growth in voluntary part-time employment among women. Almost one third of the increase in total employment over the 1954-64 decade was in part-time work, most of it voluntary, and concentrated in the service and trade industries. This has been a significant factor in drawing women into the labour market not only on a part-time but also a part-year basis.

† The jobs which have opened up in number for women—the white collar, trade and service jobs—are concentrated in urban centres while employment opportunities remain limited in rural areas. Other factors tend also to reduce the female participation rate in rural areas: more conservative social attitudes; high birth rate; lack of many household conveniences which increases the work load of women in the home.

‡ There is a very powerful and consistent positive association between educational level and participation for women. Part of the explanation lies in differential marital and fertility patterns: the more educated woman is more likely to marry later, if at all, and to have fewer children or, in many cases, none. But economic factors are of importance: more interesting, pleasant and remunerative work is available the more education a person has and, as a number of studies have shown, this "pull" factor has been important in explaining rising participation rates of women in recent decades. Further, as suggested in the text, education undoubtedly affects tastes and hence influences choice as between leisure, housework and work outside the home.

Women work as electronic assemblers at a radio engineering products plant in New Brunswick.

From more than 46,000,000 cwt. of potatoes produced annually in Canada come thousands of bags of potato chips.

reference to the very important changes in the *nature of the work* performed. The kind of work a person does—his occupation—not only determines his livelihood and therefore his mode and standard of life, it also strongly affects his social status. In more general terms there is a strong relationship between the occupational deployment of a nation's labour force and its stage of economic development and pattern of social organisation. The changes which occur in the occupational structure of the working population in the course of economic growth are the result of shifts in the industrial distribution of the labour force as well as modification of the occupational content of individual industries. The former reflect a wide complex of forces shaping the final demand for goods and services and hence the derived demand for labour. Within industries, occupational requirements respond to a great variety of pressures of which the most pervasive and compelling is technological change. There is, further, a continual interplay between changes in demand and changes in supply; in some periods independent developments on the supply side will occupy a major role in refashioning the pattern of labour force development. Over the long run the most important element on the side of supply has been the extension of public education which has increased the numbers of labour force entrants with both academic and technical qualifications relative to those capable only of unskilled manual exertion. It is evident that nothing short of a full-scale exposition of the economic and social development of Canada would suffice to "explain" the changing job content of this country over the past century. Our concern here is, of necessity, a much more modest one. Data restrictions preclude systematic analysis of the long-run changes in the *industrial* dimensions of labour force deployment and we must confine our attention to tracing the major shifts in the broad *occupational* pattern of the Canadian working population since the beginning of this century.

The full significance of the transformation of the Canadian labour force over this century is perhaps best grasped initially by visual means such as the bar diagram of the following Chart:

CANADA, 1867-1967

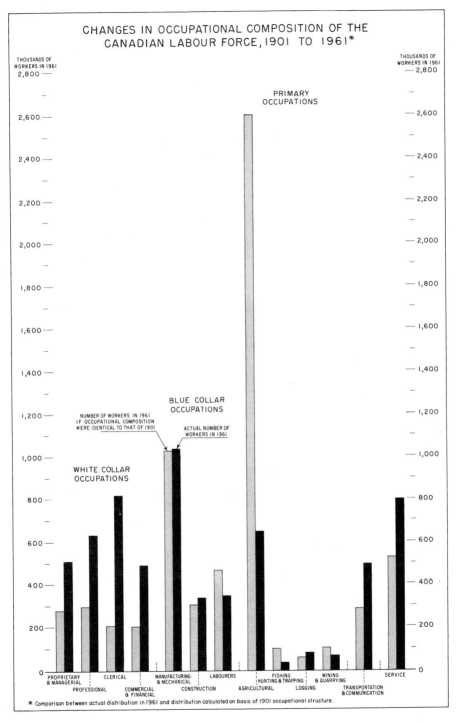

CHANGES IN OCCUPATIONAL COMPOSITION OF THE
CANADIAN LABOUR FORCE, 1901 TO 1961*

PRIMARY
OCCUPATIONS

THOUSANDS OF
WORKERS IN 1961

THOUSANDS OF
WORKERS IN 1961

BLUE COLLAR
OCCUPATIONS

NUMBER OF WORKERS IN 1961
IF OCCUPATIONAL COMPOSITION
WERE IDENTICAL TO THAT OF 1901

ACTUAL NUMBER OF
WORKERS IN 1961

WHITE COLLAR
OCCUPATIONS

PROPRIETARY
& MANAGERIAL
PROFESSIONAL
CLERICAL
COMMERCIAL
& FINANCIAL
MANUFACTURING
& MECHANICAL
CONSTRUCTION
LABOURERS
AGRICULTURAL
FISHING
HUNTING & TRAPPING
LOGGING
MINING
& QUARRYING
TRANSPORTATION
& COMMUNICATION
SERVICE

* Comparison between actual distribution in 1961 and distribution calculated on basis of 1901 occupational structure.

LABOUR FORCE                                                              279

Superimposed on the actual 1961 occupational distribution is the 1961 distribution as it would have been if the labour force had simply grown on the basis of the occupational configuration of the Canadian economy at the outset of the twentieth century. It is clear that the 1901 "mould" is no longer appropriate today. If the 1901 pattern had not altered, there would have been four times as many farmers and farm workers but well under half the number of white collar workers in Canada in 1961. Our growth in this century has been chiefly characterized, in other words, by two major occupational shifts; a marked shift away from agricultural pursuits and a decisive movement toward white collar jobs. The effect of long-run distributional changes on the numbers in blue collar occupations today has been virtually negligible.

Canada is not unique in this experience and the main reasons for these developments, which are well known in broad outline if not in precise detail and timing, need not be recapitulated here. What does need emphasizing, however, is that these occupational changes have not evolved in a smooth and steady fashion over the course of the past six decades. This is amply evident from the decade-by-decade distributions presented in the following table. It is apparent even in the case of the shift away from agriculture, the single most dramatic and persistent change in the deployment of the Canadian labour force during this century. Although each Census since 1901 recorded a decline in the labour force share of agricultural occupations, the numbers engaged in farming pursuits in this country continued to grow for the first three decades of this century. The much steeper fall of the agricultural share after 1941 reflects the combined effects of the relative and absolute decline of these occupations in Canada, a consequence of expanding job opportunities off the farm, at income levels well above those provided by farming, which siphoned off increasing numbers of the rural population made redundant by the enhanced pace of mechanization of farm production during those years. Over the 30-year period from 1901 to 1931, the great "wheat phase" of the Canadian economy, the numbers engaged in agriculture grew by just over 400,000: in the 30 years following, this growth was more than matched in size by a decline of 470,000 workers.

A pioneer Winnipeg manufacturer employs skilled labour in the production of grain elevator equipment, cereal grain processing machinery and screw conveyors.

## Numerical and Percentage Distribution of the Labour Force
### 15[1] Years of Age and Over, by Occupation
### Group for Canada,[2] 1901-1961 Censuses

|  | 1901 |  | 1911 |  |
| --- | --- | --- | --- | --- |
|  | No. | % | No. | % |
| All Occupations............................... | 1,782,832[3] | 100.0[3] | 2,698,481 | 100.0 |
| Proprietary and managerial........................ | 77,260 | 4.3 | 126,777 | 4.7 |
| Professional.................................... | 82,470 | 4.6 | 101,969 | 3.8 |
| Clerical....................................... | 57,231 | 3.2 | 102,950 | 3.8 |
| Agricultural.................................... | 718,281 | 40.3 | 928,336 | 34.4 |
| Fishing, hunting and trapping....................... | 27,184[3] | 1.5[3] | 34,430 | 1.3 |
| Logging....................................... | 16,055 | 0.9 | 41,396 | 1.5 |
| Mining and quarrying............................. | 27,905 | 1.6 | 60,926 | 2.3 |
| Manufacturing and mechanical[6].................... | 283,907 | 15.9 | 367,620 | 13.6 |
| Construction................................... | 83,933 | 4.7 | 128,458 | 4.8 |
| Transportation and communication.................. | 78,804 | 4.4 | 152,480 | 5.6 |
| Commercial.................................... | } 55,938[7] | 3.1[7] | { 119,083 | 4.4 |
| Financial...................................... |  |  | { 7,345 | 0.3 |
| Service....................................... | 145,561 | 8.2 | 204,803 | 7.6 |
| Personal service............................... | 139,251 | 7.8 | 198,226 | 7.3 |
| Labourers[8]................................... | 128,303 | 7.2 | 321,908 | 11.9 |
| Not stated.................................... | — | — | — | — |

|  | 1921 |  | 1931 |  |
| --- | --- | --- | --- | --- |
|  | No. | % | No. | % |
| All Occupations............................... | 3,143,603[5] | 100.0[5] | 3,908,117 | 100.0 |
| Proprietary and managerial........................ | 228,609 | 7.3 | 219,753 | 5.6 |
| Professional.................................... | 171,502 | 5.5 | 238,070 | 6.1 |
| Clerical....................................... | 216,685 | 6.9 | 260,564 | 6.7 |
| Agricultural.................................... | 1,025,358 | 32.6 | 1,118,342 | 28.6 |
| Fishing, hunting and trapping..................... | 28,916[5] | 0.9[5] | 47,457 | 1.2 |
| Logging....................................... | 36,602 | 1.2 | 42,030 | 1.1 |
| Mining and quarrying............................. | 46,366 | 1.5 | 57,320 | 1.5 |
| Manufacturing and mechanical[6].................... | 359,301 | 11.4 | 451,742 | 11.6 |
| Construction................................... | 147,119 | 4.7 | 183,519 | 4.7 |
| Transportation and communication.................. | 172,100 | 5.5 | 245,178 | 6.3 |
| Commercial.................................... | 159,453 | 5.1 | 211,031 | 5.4 |
| Financial...................................... | 18,588 | 0.6 | 28,228 | 0.7 |
| Service....................................... | 221,744 | 7.1 | 362,302 | 9.3 |
| Personal service............................... | 182,380 | 5.8 | 322,538 | 8.3 |
| Labourers[8]................................... | 304,151 | 9.7 | 440,932 | 11.3 |
| Not stated.................................... | 7,111 | 0.2 | 1,649 | [4] |

|  | 1941[9] |  | 1951[10] |  | 1961[10] |  |
| --- | --- | --- | --- | --- | --- | --- |
|  | No. | % | No. | % | No. | % |
| All Occupations................ | 4,183,557 | 100.0 | 5,276,639[5] | 100.0[5] | 6,458,156 | 100.0 |
| Proprietary and managerial........ | 225,551 | 5.4 | 392,896 | 7.4 | 500,911 | 7.8 |
| Professional.................... | 282,232 | 6.7 | 385,658 | 7.3 | 634,271 | 9.8 |
| Clerical....................... | 303,583 | 7.3 | 562,922 | 10.7 | 818,912 | 12.7 |
| Agricultural.................... | 1,074,904 | 25.7 | 826,093 | 15.7 | 648,910 | 10.0 |
| Fishing, hunting and trapping..... | 51,243 | 1.2 | 52,886[5] | 1.0[5] | 36,977 | 0.6 |
| Logging....................... | 78,710 | 1.9 | 101,169 | 1.9 | 79,682 | 1.2 |
| Mining and quarrying............ | 70,510 | 1.7 | 65,289 | 1.2 | 64,611 | 1.0 |
| Manufacturing and mechanical[6].... | 672,628 | 16.1 | 907,005 | 17.2 | 1,036,942 | 16.1 |
| Construction................... | 196,049 | 4.7 | 291,352 | 5.5 | 335,877 | 5.2 |
| Transportation and communication. | 266,057 | 6.4 | 412,379 | 7.8 | 496,823 | 7.7 |
| Commercial.................... | 223,875 | 5.4 | 315,268 | 6.0 | 439,672 | 6.8 |
| Financial...................... | 23,101 | 0.6 | 32,305 | 0.6 | 52,956 | 0.8 |
| Service....................... | 438,382 | 10.5 | 516,360 | 9.8 | 799,800 | 12.4 |
| Personal service.............. | 389,903 | 9.3 | 381,340 | 7.2 | 588,419 | 9.1 |
| Labourers[8]................... | 265,335 | 6.3 | 350,588 | 6.6 | 343,843 | 5.3 |
| Not stated.................... | 11,397 | 0.3 | 64,469 | 1.2 | 167,969 | 2.6 |

[1] 10 years and over in 1901.    [2] Not including Yukon and Northwest Territories.    [3] Does not include Indians.    [4] Less than 0.05 per cent.    [5] Does not include Indians living on reserves.    [6] Includes stationary enginemen and occupations associated with electric power production.    [7] Separate figures for "Commercial" and "Financial" not available for 1901.    [8] Labourers in all industries except those engaged in agricultural, fishing, logging or mining operations are included in this group.    [9] Not including persons on Active Service on June 2, 1941.    [10] Including Newfoundland.

Oil production and livestock-raising combine to increase the incomes of numerous Alberta farmers.

It should be noted that in the preceding table the "gainfully occupied" rather than the "labour force" concept was used prior to 1951 for determining the labour force status. The labour force figures exclude a few persons seeking work who have never been employed. Occupations for 1901, 1911, 1921, 1931, 1941 and 1961 were rearranged on the basis of the 1951 Classification though some adjustment of the 1951 grouping was necessary.

Just as was true in the case of agricultural occupations, the growth path of the white collar group has scarcely been smooth and steady. Very rapid expansion in numbers and increase in labour force share occurred between 1911 and 1921 and again between 1941 and 1961. In the middle period, however, between 1921 and 1941, the white collar occupation group as a whole barely sustained the same pace of growth as that of the total working population and their labour force share reached a plateau which was maintained until at least the early years of World War II. It may also be seen from the preceding table (although limitations of space preclude exposition here) that there was a good deal of similarity in the growth pattern of the component occupational groups, especially the large clerical group and the professional occupations. In both instances the pattern was marked by two phases of rapid expansion, one in the second decade of the century—which straddled World War I—and the more recent period, from 1941 to the present, which was initiated by World War II. The slowest-growing group of occupations within the white collar division is the commercial (sales) group. Although these occupations have increased their labour force share, their numbers have expanded much less rapidly than the white collar work force as a whole.

Among the blue collar occupations, only the construction group has grown steadily in step with the total labour force: the other two component groups, manufacturing and mechanical workers (the skilled and semi-skilled occupations) and unskilled labourers, exhibited marked variations in growth rates over the six-decade period. The unskilled were far the most rapidly growing occupational group in Canada in the opening decade of this century (increasing their share from just over 7 to almost 12 per cent) and it was not until 1941 that the Census recorded an absolute decline in their numbers, a decline which was halted temporarily by the wartime boom but resumed once more in the most recent intercensal decade. A reverse growth pattern was exhibited by the largest component group in the blue collar division, the skilled and semi-skilled manual workers (predominantly located in the manufacturing industries). A steady shrinkage in labour force share until 1931 was sharply reversed in the decade of the Great Depression and, in the years following 1941, this group of occupations has expanded at about the same pace as the total labour force. Finally, it may be noted that workers in transportation and communication occupations, after increasing their share of the labour force in earlier decades, have only just managed to keep step with over-all growth in the most recent decade. Service workers, on the other hand, decreased in importance in the earlier period but in the latest stages of growth have been increasing very rapidly.

These changes in occupational structure are sometimes cited as evidence of the changing quality of the work force. At best, they are equivocal in this respect and

The town of Asbestos, Quebec, owes its existence to the asbestos mines operated by the Canadian Johns-Manville Company Ltd. whose new mill is shown above.

difficult to appraise. A more direct means of evaluating changes in the "quality" of labour supply—or at least an important aspect of it—is through measures of the educational level of the working population. Although there is no reliable historical series on the educational attainment of the Canadian people, one can make use of current statistics in this area to give some notion of changes over time. In the following table the native-born* Canadian male population in selected age categories is distributed according to their present (February, 1965) level of education.† The native-born population living in Canada today is, of course, depleted by the mortality and emigration of earlier decades and for this reason at least‡ the use of current statistics as a substitute for historical data is not entirely satisfactory. None the less, each of the sex cohorts represented in the following table completed its education and entered the labour force at a different period in this century. Hence, the differences in level of education between successively younger cohorts provide a reasonably good guide

---

\* Includes a few immigrants who entered Canada before World War II, probably during the 1920's.
† Years of formal schooling.
‡ Mortality is probably not highly selective by educational level but the same is certainly not true of emigration and hence there is some understatement of the educational level of the older cohorts. Difficulties of recall and other types of response error are probably more acute for the older age groups as well.

### Improvement in Educational Level of Male Population,[1] Canada, Pre-1920 to Present

| Age of Cohort in Feb. 1965 | Period in which Cohort was born | Period in which most of Cohorts probably completed school | Percentage Increase in Median Years of Schooling of Successive Cohorts |
|---|---|---|---|
| 65 and over | 1900 or before | Before 1920 | |
| 55-64 | 1901-1910 | During 1920's | 3.9 |
| 45-54 | 1911-1920 | During 1930's | 5.0 |
| 35-44 | 1921-1930 | During 1940's | 9.5 |
| 25-34 | 1931-1940 | During 1950's | 4.4 |
| 20-24 | 1941-1945 | During 1960's | 9.4 |

[1] Excluding immigrants who entered Canada since World War II.

Automation has its effect on railway operations. Here, retarder operators in a dual control tower keep watch over freight cars rolling free to the classification tracks.

to the changing "quality" of labour supply over the past 50 years or so in Canada. As a rough measure of improvement in educational level we may use the percentage difference in median years of schooling as shown in the table on page 284.

It may be seen that while there has been consistent improvement in the "quality" of Canada's working population* over the past six decades or more, the rate of progress in this respect was very slow in the earlier part of the century and no doubt (it is a safe assumption) even slower before then. A more marked improvement may be observed for those unfortunate men who had to find their first jobs during the Great Depression (the cohort born between 1911 and 1920). But the greatest advance in educational levels was achieved by the men who completed their education in the 1940's, many of whom benefited from the Federal Government's assistance to returning war veterans (D.V.A. grants). The experience of the 1940's was not repeated in the following decade although the promise of the 1960's is brighter.

**Percentage Distribution of Male Population,[1]**
**20 Years of Age and Over, by Age, by Level of Education,**
**Canada, February 1965**

| Age | Level of education | | | | | | Median Years of Schooling |
|---|---|---|---|---|---|---|---|
| | Primary school | | High school | | University | | |
| | Some[2] | Finished | Some | Finished | Some | Degree | |
| 20-24 | 10.1 | 14.5 | 38.8 | 18.5 | 14.5 | 3.5 | 10.5 |
| 25-34 | 15.7 | 21.2 | 36.0 | 15.0 | 5.6 | 6.4 | 9.6 |
| 35-44 | 19.6 | 23.2 | 33.0 | 13.0 | 4.5 | 6.7 | 9.2 |
| 45-54 | 24.9 | 25.3 | 27.4 | 12.9 | 4.0 | 5.6 | 8.4 |
| 55-64 | 34.7 | 29.0 | 19.7 | 9.0 | 3.4 | 4.2 | 8.0 |
| 65 and over | 44.3 | 28.6 | 13.9 | 7.6 | 2.6 | 2.9 | 7.7 |

[1] Excluding immigrants who entered Canada since World War II. [2] Includes some persons with no formal schooling. **Note:** Median levels estimated in consultation with Education Division, D.B.S.

Finally, some notion of the full extent of change in the levels of schooling of the Canadian population over this century may be gauged from the last table. Over 70 per cent of Canadians born before 1900 failed to reach high school level: over 40 per cent did not even finish primary school. Today, almost 80 per cent of the young Canadians who enter the labour force have had at least some high school education. As we have seen, the progress in education has been halting and uneven from decade to decade, but the improvement in the "quality" of Canada's human resources has, none the less, been substantial.

(FRANK T. DENTON; SYLVIA OSTRY)

---

* These population figures are used to represent the "potential" labour supply in the older age categories. There is a strong (positive) association between education and participation among older men and hence use of current chronological cross-section *labour force* data for this type of historical analysis is inappropriate.

# Labour Organization and Legislation

The present structure and strength of the labour movement in Canada is in sharp contrast to the situation at the time of Confederation. A century ago the Canadian economy was largely agricultural, with few concentrations of population and industry. A few labour unions existed as early as the 1820's and 1830's, but little by way of broadening the base of organization beyond local units was evident until the latter half of the 19th century. Today union membership exceeds 1,500,000, and it is widely dispersed by industry, occupation and geography. About one in every four members of the labour force and about one in three non-agricultural paid workers in Canada belong to the union movement.

The legislative framework within which collective bargaining is carried on and which prescribes minimum standards and other forms of protection for workers has developed over almost the entire period of Canada's 100-year history. A starting point was the Trade Unions Act of 1872 which legalized trade unions, declaring that they were not to be regarded as criminal conspiracies subject to prosecution on the ground that they were in restraint of trade. This law gave unions freedom to develop and to pursue their goals which, in turn, led to further legislation.

## Development of Unions in Canada

Most unions currently operating in Canada are affiliated with one of the two central labour congresses. The larger of these, the Canadian Labour Congress, is comprised mainly of international unions with headquarters in the United States but also includes a number of national unions and directly chartered local unions. The total membership of CLC-affiliated unions in Canada at the beginning of 1965 was 1,181,000. The other central labour body, the Confederation of National Trade Unions, which operates almost exclusively in Quebec, had in affiliation at the same time 13 federations and a number of non-federated locals. Its total membership was 150,000.

The growth of the union movement in this country has been greatly influenced by events and developments in the United States. There were numbers of attempts in the past hundred years to "nationalize" the labour movement in Canada. However, with the notable exception of the portion of the labour movement represented by the CNTU and a few large national unions in the CLC, the international character of Canada's labour movement remains a unique feature.

In the decade preceding Confederation, unions which had been operating in the United States began to form locals in Upper Canada. This was the beginning of inter-national unionism in this country. The first attempt after Confederation to form a national federation of unions took place in 1873, when 30 local unions in Ontario formed the Canadian Labour Union. Conventions were held for several successive years but the organization failed to prosper. Meanwhile, the Knights of Labour, founded in the United States in 1869, organized a Canadian Assembly in 1881. The Knights attempted to organize workers regardless of skill or occupation and by the end of the 1880's claimed a membership of 16,000.

At a second convention of trade unions and Knights of Labour Assemblies in 1886, the Dominion Trades and Labour Congress was established. In 1893 this became the Trades and Labour Congress of Canada which retained its identity until 1956. (In April

The 15th Annual Convention of the Canadian Congress of Labour approved the agreement for the merger of the CCL (Canadian Congress of Labour) and the TLC (Trades and Labour Congress of Canada). Above are shown A. R. Mosher, CCL President and Claude Jodoin, TLC President.

1956 the Trades and Labour Congress of Canada and the Canadian Congress of Labour merged to form the Canadian Labour Congress.)

Just after the turn of the century, the international unions in the Trades and Labour Congress that held affiliation with the American Federation of Labour in the United States gained control of the Congress and measures were taken, by amending the Constitution, to eliminate "dual unionism" (more than one union in a trade or industry). There followed the expulsion of the District Trade Assemblies of the Knights of Labour and a number of purely Canadian unions in 1902. The expelled unions, together with others, thereafter formed a new federation, The National Trades and Labour Congress. This became the Canadian Federation of Labour in 1908.

Another schism in the Canadian labour movement, centred in the West, culminated in 1919 in the formation of an organization called the One Big Union. This organization sought to organize workers by industry rather than by trade and gained prominence following the Winnipeg General Strike in 1919. It claimed a membership of 41,500 at that time. However, due to internal conflicts, and opposition from the federal and provincial governments, as well as from the TLC, it soon began to decline.

Meanwhile, in the Province of Quebec, attempts were being made at federating the unions that had for a number of years been organizing in accordance with the social philosophy of the Roman Catholic Church. The origin of this development can be traced to a lock-out in Quebec City in 1900 involving a number of shoe manufacturers and three local unions. The Archbishop of Quebec was appointed to arbitrate the dispute and he recommended that the unions revise their constitutions in accordance with the social principles set forth in Pope Leo XIII's encyclical of 1891, *Rerum Novarum.* The Archbishop's suggestions called, among other things, for the appointment of chaplains to guide the deliberations of unions in accordance with the social teaching of the Church. In 1912 the first such union was formed among pulp and paper workers and soon units were organized among other occupational and industrial groups. In 1918, in Quebec City, these unions—or syndicates as they were called— united under the name National Central Trades Council. Later in the same year, a conference for the entire province was held, and at a founding convention in Hull in 1921, a permanent organization called the Canadian and Catholic Confederation of Labour was formed.

In 1927, dissident labour elements belonging to the Canadian Federation of Labour, the Canadian Brotherhood of Railway Employees and what remained of the One Big Union, united to form the All-Canadian Congress of Labour with the objective of achieving the complete independence of the Canadian union movement. However, the great depression of the 1930's brought its difficulties and both the All-Canadian Congress and the Trades and Labour Congress experienced declines in membership. Both these congresses also experienced dissatisfaction with leadership about this time, and the Workers' Unity League, formed by the Communist Party in Canada, had a short existence in the early thirties.

Following passage of the Wagner Act in the United States in 1935, with its clauses protecting labour's right to join unions and to bargain with employers, agitation began to grow for similar labour legislation in Canada. In the same year a number of unions within the AFL formed the Committee for Industrial Organization. These events sparked organizational activity in Canada in previously unorganized sectors with assistance from unions belonging to the Committee for Industrial Organization. In 1936 unions belonging to this Committee were suspended from the AFL for "dual unionism" and their expulsion a year later gave rise to the formation of the new federation in the United States, the Congress of Industrial Organizations. Under pressure from AFL-affiliated unions the TLC expelled the Canadian branches of CIO unions in 1939.

Although defections from the All-Canadian Congress of Labour had weakened this organization in the 1930's, it set new hope in policies of industrial unionism, political action and government intervention in economic affairs. The Canadian branches of the CIO unions joined the All-Canadian Congress of Labour at its 1940 Convention, the constitution was changed, and a new body, the Canadian Congress of Labour, came into being.

The period during and after World War II was one of rapid organizational gains for Canadian labour. Between 1939 and 1949 over-all membership grew from 359,000 to just over one million. This growth continued into the middle of the 1950's. Following the merger of the AFL and the CIO in the United States, the Trades and Labour Congress of Canada and the Canadian Congress of Labour at a joint Convention in

Toronto in April 1956 merged to become the Canadian Labour Congress.

Meanwhile, the Canadian and Catholic Confederation of Labour was undergoing significant changes in policy and viewpoint and it appeared in the late 1950's that merger with the Canadian Labour Congress might take place. However, this did not materialize. At its Convention in 1960, the CCCL changed its name to the Confederation of National Trade Unions. It also adopted a new statement of principles affirming adherence to Christian principles without referring specifically to the social doctrine of the Roman Catholic Church.

Today (1966) 85 per cent of all union members in Canada are in unions affiliated with one of the two central bodies, the CLC and the CNTU. Of the remaining union membership in Canada, about one per cent are in unions affiliated with the AFL-CIO only, while about seven per cent are found in unaffiliated international unions and a similar percentage in unaffiliated national unions and independent local organizations.

## Labour Legislation

Most employment in Canada involving an employer-employee relationship is carried on within a basic framework of labour laws which have grown up over a period of many years. Under labour relations Acts, workers and employers are guaranteed freedom of association and the right to organize. Upon the certification of a trade union as the exclusive bargaining agent of the employees of an employer in an appropriate bargaining unit, it is mandatory on the employer and the union to negotiate with the object of reaching a collective agreement. Should negotiations break down, Government conciliation services are available, and a strike or lockout is prohibited until the conciliation procedure has been completed. It is left to the parties to administer the agreement and to resolve any differences which may arise, by arbitration, if necessary. A strike or lockout is forbidden during this period. The Acts also make certain activities of employers, employees or trade unions "unfair labour practices", for which penalties may be imposed.

Government intervention in industrial disputes began in 1900 with the law which provided for a federal Department of Labour, the Conciliation Act. The Act provided for government conciliation which could be placed at the disposal of the parties to a dispute. The principle of compulsory conciliation was introduced in 1907 with the passage of the Industrial Disputes Investigation Act. This Act, which first applied to mines, transport, communication and public utilities but was later restricted in scope as a result of a court decision, provided for the appointment of a conciliation board in cases of dispute and added a new feature, the prohibition of a strike or lockout until after the legal requirements regarding conciliation had been complied with. Reports of conciliation boards were made public, with the aim of bringing the force of public opinion to bear on the settlement of the dispute. The I.D.I. Act and laws in the provinces embodying similar principles regulated the settlement of disputes until World War II.

A milestone in Canadian labour relations legislation was the enactment in 1944 by the Federal Government of PC 1003, known as the Wartime Labour Relations Regulations. This legislation, which was influenced by the Wagner Act in the United States and, under wartime emergency powers, was made applicable in all provinces, guaranteed workers the right to organize, provided for compulsory collective bargaining, and set up a Labour Relations Board to determine questions of union recognition. In the postwar era, when the provinces resumed their normal jurisdiction in labour matters, new legislation was enacted by Parliament and the provincial legislatures applying, with certain modifications, the national labour policy which had been established during the War.

The great majority of Canadian workers are subject to minimum standards of wages, hours, annual vacations and public holidays set by the Canada Labour (Standards) Code and corresponding provincial laws. While there are many exceptions, working hours are commonly limited to 8 in a day and to 40, 44 or 48 in a week or, if limits are not imposed, work beyond specified daily and weekly hours must be paid for at an overtime rate. For many workers in Quebec, wages and hours are fixed by decrees under the Collective Agreement Act. A similar system is in effect under industrial standards laws in several other provinces.

For workers under federal jurisdiction the minimum rate of pay to which they are entitled by law is $1.25 an hour. Under provincial minimum wage laws, rates in a majority of the provinces have reached or are approaching $1 an hour.

A two weeks' vacation is the usual standard set by law, and one province provides for a three weeks' vacation after five years' service. In three provinces workers are entitled to one week's vacation with pay. Under the federal law employers are obliged to give their employees eight paid holidays a year and, with some exceptions, to pay any employee required to work on a holiday at a premium rate. An increasing number of provinces have similar legislation.

Provincial regulation of minimum wages dates from the years following World War I and was a response to a demand for protection of women workers against exploitation. Six provinces had such laws by 1920. Minimum rates for men, although established in British Columbia in 1925, were not set in most provinces until the 1930's and it was not until the mid-1960's that they were put into effect in Ontario and Nova Scotia. Federal responsibility to regulate working conditions in certain industries was only clarified after World War II, and in 1965 the federal labour code fixed the first minimum rate for workers in federal industries. Thus, the process of setting minimum rates for workers of both sexes throughout the country has covered a span of 50 years.

The first hours of work Act in Canada, modelled on an International Labour Convention and restricting hours of male as well as female workers, was passed in British Columbia in 1923. Alberta followed British Columbia's example in 1936, and other provinces did likewise. Quebec began its regulation of wages and hours through the extension of collective agreements in 1934.

Annual vacation legislation was first enacted in Ontario in 1944, and within the next three years had been adopted in five other provinces. New Brunswick, Nova Scotia and federal legislation was enacted in the 1950's. Legal requirements regarding the observance of paid public holidays were first laid down in Saskatchewan in 1947.

With Canada's developing industrialization, a large body of laws designed to protect workers against the hazards of their working environment has grown up. These had their beginnings in the Ontario and Quebec factory Acts of 1884 and 1885 and in the five similar laws passed in other provinces before 1910. These not only fixed age limits for child workers and reduced the long working hours of women and children but also provided other safeguards for the health and safety of all workers in the factory. These laws, modernized and expanded, now cover many aspects of

Dosco's steel plant at Sydney, Nova Scotia, dominates the landscape. Canadian iron and steel mills employ almost 40,000 people.

employee safety. In some provinces they have been replaced by general industrial safety laws. Most provinces have special legislation to promote safe working conditions in the construction industry. Boiler, elevator, electrical, gas and oil and other types of mechanical inspection are carried out by specialized inspection staffs.

Under workmen's compensation laws, workers in most industries are protected against loss of earnings resulting from employment injury. To be entitled to benefits, a workman must be employed in an industry covered by the Act at the time of the injury. In some jurisdictions, however, compensation is not payable for injuries lasting less than a specified number of days, referred to as the "waiting period". A worker may also be disqualified if the injury is due to his own misconduct. Benefits for disability are based on 75 per cent of earnings, subject to an annual ceiling. Where disability is permanent, a life pension is paid, irrespective of future earnings. Medical benefits are provided without limitation, regardless of a waiting period. Where death results from an employment injury, fixed monthly payments are made to dependants.

The present system of workmen's compensation began in 1914, when Ontario passed a new law based on the report of a special commissioner, Sir William Meredith, now regarded as the "father of workmen's compensation" in Canada. This Act was based on several new principles. Under it the injured workman's right to bring an action for damages against his employer for negligence was taken away, and in return he was made eligible for compensation, regardless of his own negligence or that of his employer. In place of being personally liable for payment of compensation, employers came under a scheme of compulsory mutual insurance in a government-operated accident fund. All costs for compensation were to be borne by employers collectively. Claims were to be removed from the courts and decided by a largely autonomous Workmen's Compensation Board. The new system gradually spread throughout Canada. Prince Edward Island and Newfoundland were the last provinces to adopt it in 1949 and 1951, respectively.

Laws to guarantee workers equality of opportunity and treatment in employment, without discrimination on the basis of race, colour, religion or national origin are in force in most jurisdictions. These laws, which began with the Act of Ontario in 1951, had their inspiration in the Universal Declaration of Human Rights adopted by the United Nations. In recent years the grounds on which employment discrimination is prohibited have been extended. In Quebec, "discrimination" is defined to include any distinction based on sex. In British Columbia and Ontario, discrimination against older workers solely on grounds of age is forbidden. Equal pay laws in nine jurisdictions forbid discrimination in payment of wage rates solely on the basis of sex.

Laws in all provinces provide for government supervision of apprenticeship training. This program, which began in Ontario in 1928 but was not developed to any extent until the 1940's, involves an organized procedure of on-the-job and school instruction with a view to turning out skilled tradesmen, and is sometimes combined with trades-men's qualifications, under which certain classes of tradesmen are required to hold certificates in order to work at their trade. Costs of training are shared between the federal and provincial governments, except in Quebec, which has a somewhat different training program.

Since 1941 a compulsory contributory unemployment insurance plan has been in effect. It now covers about four fifths of all non-agricultural employees in Canada. It is financed by equal contributions from employers and employees, the amount depending on the weekly wages of the employee, plus a contribution from the Federal Government. To be eligible for benefit a person must have made the number of contributions required for entitlement, and must be capable of and available for work, but unable to obtain suitable employment. Benefits, varying with the earnings of the insured person, are payable for a period related to the length of the employee's contribution record, up to a maximum of one year.

The Unemployment Insurance Act was passed in 1940, following a constitutional amendment giving Parliament jurisdiction in this field. The Act provided for the appointment of the Unemployment Insurance Commission to administer the program. The public employment offices which had functioned under a joint federal-provincial arrangement since 1918 were replaced by a national employment service, which was operated by the Unemployment Insurance Commission until 1965. At the beginning of 1966 the national employment service became part of the government department dealing with manpower.

(Francis J. McKendy; Evelyn Woolner)

# Government Finance

One hundred years ago, government finance, as one knows it today, played a relatively unimportant role. Governments were mainly concerned with national defence, transportation and the development of natural resources. In addition, the federating provinces were faced with a relatively heavy burden of public debt. The motivational forces of Confederation were not without their financial characteristics.

Although Canada had been the "bread basket" of Great Britain since approximately 1815, the introduction of a British free trade policy in the 1840's had greatly reduced the British market for Canadian products. Efforts to make reciprocal arrangements with the United States for agricultural products had provided only temporary relief before the treaty was abrogated by the United States in the 1860's. Consequently, the loss of foreign markets coupled with an increasing, combined public debt and the growing threat of invasion from the south impressed upon the Fathers of Confederation the urgent need for domestic unity. They believed that the union would create a structure providing greater political, financial and commercial strength.*

## Financial Terms of Confederation

Under the terms of the British North America Act, and subsequent arrangements, the Federal Government was required to make annual payments to the provinces in the nature of allowances for government and legislature, allowances per head of population, other special grants, and interest on debt allowances. Each level of government was granted financial powers considered appropriate and adequate for their respective functions.

As described above, the Federal Government was charged with such responsibilities as defence, regulation of trade and commerce, coinage, currency, banking, administration of criminal law, postal and telegraph services, railways and canals. Relatively inexpensive functions, at that time, such as education, public welfare, administration of justice, and other matters of regional interest were entrusted to the provinces. The four provinces were given control over public lands and power to legislate with respect to property and civil rights.

---

*See pages 26 ff., describing Canada's Federal System of Government.

All income tax returns of Canadians are processed at the Department of National Revenue Taxation Data Centre. Information from returns is key-punched onto paper tapes, double-checked, then transferred to magnetic tapes for "memory storage" and feeding into the electric computer. One reel of magnetic tape can hold tax data on 100,000 Canadians.

Direct taxation was unpopular. None of the provincial governments and only a few municipalities in Ontario had ever used this form of taxation. It was commonly believed that direct taxation was uneconomic and subject to large-scale tax evasion, that it would inhibit individual and corporate initiative and, very likely, discourage immigration. Since all major sources of revenue were entrusted to the Federal Government there were only two alternative means of providing sufficient revenue sources to the provinces: transfer the right to levy certain indirect taxes, or provide a Federal Government system of subsidies. Apparently the Fathers of Confederation chose the latter course in order to maintain the fiscal supremacy of the Federal Government. Thus federal subsidies early became an important source of provincial revenue.

## Demands for "Better Terms"

During 1887 and again in 1902, provincial premiers held conferences demanding an upward revision of federal subsidies to provinces. At the turn of the century provincial demands for "better terms" became much stronger. In 1906 Sir Wilfrid Laurier called a conference of provincial premiers to revise the federal system of subsidies. The 1907 revisions brought substantial increases in federal transfers to provinces. Further increases were introduced in 1912.

During World War I there was little demand for additional federal aid but, following the War's end, provincial governments were again pressing for increases in the system of subsidies. Although most of Canada had emerged from the post-World War I depression, the Maritime Provinces were still facing difficulties that rekindled old feelings that Confederation had not been to their advantage. The "Maritime Rights" philosophy was launched seeking better terms. In order to investigate their grievances and economic hardships, the Federal Government appointed the Duncan Commission in 1926. In 1927 the Federal Government reduced certain freight rates under the Maritime Freight Rate Act by as much as 20 per cent, reimbursing the railways accordingly. The Duncan Commission also proposed that a special inquiry in depth be made concerning the financial problems of the Maritime Provinces. The White Commission, appointed in 1934, recommended that annual grants be further increased. These recommendations were accepted and became a permanent part of the federal, non-conditional subsidy system.

## Dominion-Provincial Relations

One of the more important problems underlying Federal-Provincial relations has been the division of financial responsibility. The Dominion-Provincial Conference of December 1936, marks the introduction of a series of such conferences dealing, for the most part, with financial considerations. In 1936 the Prairie Provinces were experiencing drought; the government of Alberta had gone into partial default on its outstanding debt; the governments of Saskatchewan and Manitoba made clear, at the 1936 conference, that in default of assistance they would be forced to take similar action. Consequently, the Bank of Canada was invited to undertake an examination of the financial situation existing in the Prairie Provinces. The Bank recommended a complete inquiry into the financial powers and responsibilities of Canadian governing bodies at all levels, pointing out that the burden of relief had proved completely beyond the capacity of all provincial and municipal governments.

Inuvik in the Mackenzie River delta with a population of 1,981 in 1966, is an administration Centre for Northern Affairs in the Mackenzie District of the Northwest
Territories.

As a direct consequence a Royal Commission on Dominion-Provincial Relations
was appointed in August 1937, generally referred to as the Rowell-Sirois Commission.
This Commission recommended important financial changes: (1) Exclusive federal
jurisdiction in income tax, corporation tax and succession duty fields. (2) Acceptance
by the Federal Government of responsibility for relief to able-bodied unemployed.
(3) Assumption by the Federal Government of net provincial debt charges. (4) Payment by the Federal Government of national adjustment grants designed to put each
provincial government in a position to provide average standards of services without
imposing higher than average rates of taxation.

Another Dominion-Provincial Conference was called, in January 1941, to consider
the Rowell-Sirois report but this Conference broke down on the second day in the
face of violent opposition from the Premiers of Ontario, British Columbia and Alberta.

## Introduction of Tax Rentals

Later in 1941 the Federal Government proposed that, as a war measure, provincial
governments and their municipalities should suspend imposition of income and
corporation taxes for the duration of World War II and be reimbursed by the Federal
Government on the basis of either the 1940 revenues of each province from these
sources or the amount of a province's net debt service less succession duty collections
in 1940. Agreements were negotiated and legislation passed in the spring of 1942

giving the Federal Government a free hand in the income and corporation tax fields. Immediately the Federal Government developed these sources of revenue very substantially as an aid in financing the war effort and combating inflation. While this wartime tax agreement was mooted as a temporary necessity, it turned out to be the first in a series of arrangements that have continued in force ever since, although the terms of these five-year contracts have been considerably revised over the years.

The next important conference on fiscal problems was held in 1945 when the Federal Government sought to obtain agreement concerning a number of prewar financial and constitutional problems. Primary stress was placed on the maintenance of a high and stable level of employment and income. The Federal Government proposed that the provinces should withdraw from the personal income tax, corporation tax, and succession duty fields in return for annual subsidies which would not fall below a guaranteed minimum and which would rise proportionally with population and increases in per capita Gross National Product. The Federal Government also proposed a substantial expansion in the program for natural resource development, conservation and public works, and a large increase in federal assistance to provincial government construction projects. The social security proposals made by the Federal Government were extensive. Family allowances had already been put into effect in 1945 and the Federal Government now proposed to increase substantially old age assistance, to make sizable contributions to provincially-administered health insurance schemes, to provide low interest rate loans for hospital construction and financial assistance for all unemployed employables. The provincial governments examined these proposals and made counter-proposals of their own. It was found that too wide a gap existed between the federal and provincial viewpoints to enable an agreement to be reached at that time. The Federal Government budget of June 1946 included proposals for a tax agreement which could be entered into by any individual province, and eventually agreements were concluded with all provincial governments.

Since 1945, tax rental arrangements have been negotiated every five years. During these last 20 years the negotiations have become progressively more complex. New features have been introduced and the economic studies prior to each Agreement have become much more comprehensive with the growing recognition and acceptance of the fact that the financial activities of all governments in Canada is a matter for mutual concern and co-operative development. A brief review of the latest agreement gives some idea of the changes that have taken place since 1945.

## Federal-Provincial Fiscal Arrangements Act, 1962-1967

The federal-provincial fiscal arrangements which came into effect on April 1, 1962, differ substantially from those of previous five-year periods. The "tax rental" system, in effect since 1942, was discontinued. The Federal Government partially withdrew from the personal income tax field. The amount of the withdrawal was 16 per cent of the federal tax in 1962 and, under the original arrangement, was to have increased by one additional percentage point each year to 1966, at which time the federal income tax would have been reduced by 20 per cent.

In April 1964, following the federal-provincial conference, the legislation was amended to increase the provincial abatement by two percentage points in 1965 and a further similar amount in 1966.

The provinces are not restricted to the rates of withdrawal from the income tax field and two provinces, Manitoba and Saskatchewan, during the tax years 1962, 1963 and 1964, each levied a personal income tax at a rate six percentage points higher than the rates of federal withdrawal. However, in 1965 Manitoba reduced its rate differential to five per cent and Saskatchewan made a similar reduction for 1966.

The Federal Government collects (free of charge) for all provinces which have signed a tax collection agreement, the amount of the federal withdrawal and any additional percentage of the federal tax which the provinces wish to impose. All provinces except Quebec have agreements with the Federal Government covering the collection of personal income taxes.

Under the federal-provincial fiscal arrangements for the 1962-66 tax years the Federal Government has made available in all provinces an abatement from federal corporation tax of nine per cent. The Federal Government, if so requested by a province, collects this percentage or any additional percentage on its behalf as a provincially-imposed tax. Six provinces have set their corporation tax at the basic nine per cent and four at higher rates. Quebec and Ontario are the only two provinces that continue to administer their own provincial corporation income taxes.

Since 1947, Ontario and Quebec have continued to impose their own succession duties and the Federal Government has allowed an abatement to avoid double taxation; on April 1, 1963, British Columbia re-entered this field.

Under the 1962-66 arrangements each province was to have received 50 per cent of the federal estate tax within its jurisdiction. At the federal-provincial conference of November 1963 the provinces' share was increased to 75 per cent. Under this five-year agreement, arrangements designed to equalize provincial revenue yields have been broadened to include 50 per cent of the revenues the provinces collect from natural resources. Once again there is a stabilization clause to provide a floor below which the payments will not be allowed to drop.

The Atlantic Provinces Adjustment Grants (introduced in 1958), are continued for the five-year period at the increased level of $35,000,000 per annum; $10,500,000 to each of Newfoundland, Nova Scotia and New Brunswick, and $3,500,000 to Prince Edward Island.

The provinces also continue to receive a share of the federal income tax collected from corporations whose main business is the distribution to, or generation for distribution to, the public of electric energy, gas or steam.

## Provincial-Municipal Relationship

While a great deal of thought has gone into the federal-provincial financial relationship, one must not overlook the remaining partner in Canada's three level system of government. Local governments in Canada are creatures of provincial governments. Provincial government administrative control is, for the most part, exercised through provincial Departments of Municipal Affairs. The control function is particularly evident with respect to finance. Municipal governments must obtain permission from the Department of Municipal Affairs or some other provincial agency before they proceed with long-term borrowing and subsequent expenditures of a capital nature. The reorganization of municipal government units is also subject to provincial government control.

In any examination of government finance in Canada one must not overlook the degree to which local government services are provided directly by provincial governments. Sizable land areas in Canada are not municipally organized. Nevertheless, while the population per square mile may be very light, local services such as schools, sanitation and waste removal, police and fire protection, must be provided. Where no local government organization exists, therefore, these services are met by provincial government funds. This situation creates all sorts of administrative, political and financial problems.

In recent years there have been a number of provincial government studies concerning the form of local government structure and provincial-municipal financial relationships. Some of these studies have resulted in considerable change with respect to both the nature of local government units and provincial-municipal financial arrangements. Perhaps the most controversial proposals were those submitted to the New Brunswick Provincial Legislature in 1966. The provincial government of New Brunswick was giving serious consideration to provincial government assumption of municipal responsibilities for education, social welfare, justice, public health, property assessment and tax collection. The motivation behind the recommendations being considered in New Brunswick was to provide minimum standards of essential services to all parts of the province regardless of the local taxpayers' ability to pay for those services. It raises, of course, many arguments concerning the advantages and disadvantages of centralization of government services and the financial considerations attached to these.

## Intergovernmental Money Transfers

Space will not permit a detailed reference to the huge sums involved in intergovernmental money transfers and the very rapid growth in these transactions in recent years. A wealth of information is available in various conference reports. Statistical data submitted to these conferences all serve to emphasize the tremendous growth in government revenue and expenditure as well as the flow of funds from federal to provincial to local governments. The tables following this commentary provide a condensed summary of the growing importance of government finance, the intergovernmental relationship, and evidence of the impact of government finance on the national economy.

A few figures taken at random will serve to emphasize the latter point. In 1952 total net expenditures of all governments in Canada were calculated to be in the neighbourhood of $6,300,000,000. In 1962 this figure had risen to $12,700,000,000. In per capita terms these amount to $436 in 1952 and $685 in 1962. As a percentage of personal income the 1952 expenditure figure represents a little over 36 per cent. The 1962 figure, on the other hand, amounts to over 41 per cent of personal income.

In 1962 the Federal Government paid over $1,000,000,000 to provincial and local governments in the form of conditional and unconditional subsidies plus payments under the federal-provincial tax-sharing arrangements. In the same year, provincial governments paid conditional and unconditional grants to local governments exceeding $1,000,000,000. In the years prior to 1952 the phenomenon of financial assistance flowing from federal to provincial to local governments grew in importance from a mere trickle prior to World War II to the immense sums involved today. The following tables show details of these transactions for the fiscal year ended March 31, 1964.

## Payments made by Federal Government to Provincial Governments, Territories and Municipal Corporations for Fiscal Year Ended March 31, 1964

| Function | Total |
|---|---|
| | $'000 |
| **Provincial Governments and Territories:** | |
| Federal-provincial fiscal arrangements.................................................... | 182,329 |
| Share of income tax on power utilities.................................................... | 9,868 |
| Subsidies.......................................................................................... | 66,525 |
| **Sub-total above three items** | **258,722** |
| | |
| Grants-in-aid and shared-cost contributions: | |
| Transportation: | |
| Road: | |
| Trans-Canada highway........................................................... | 39,240 |
| Roads leading to resources...................................................... | 8,132 |
| Railway grade crossing fund.................................................... | 4,560 |
| Other............................................................................... | 265 |
| Water................................................................................... | 8 |
| Other................................................................................... | — |
| **Total transportation**.............................................................. | **52,205** |
| | |
| Health: | |
| Hospital insurance and diagnostic services............................................ | 392,244 |
| Hospital construction....................................................................... | 22,300 |
| General health grants: | |
| General public health.............................................................. | 10,064 |
| Tuberculosis control................................................................ | 3,061 |
| Mental health........................................................................ | 8,331 |
| Professional training............................................................... | 1,743 |
| Cancer control....................................................................... | 2,810 |
| Public health research.............................................................. | 1,579 |
| Medical rehabilitation and crippled children............................... | 1,725 |
| Child and maternal health......................................................... | 1,204 |
| Other................................................................................... | 603 |
| **Total health**........................................................................ | **445,664** |
| | |
| Social welfare: | |
| Old age assistance......................................................................... | 39,208 |
| Blind persons' allowances................................................................ | 4,988 |
| Disabled persons' allowances........................................................... | 20,207 |
| Unemployment assistance................................................................ | 107,371 |
| Other.......................................................................................... | 819 |
| **Total social welfare**............................................................... | **172,593** |

Tape is fed into a computer at the Saskatchewan Wheat Pool.

## Payments made by Federal Government to Provincial Governments, Territories and Municipal Corporations for Fiscal Year Ended March 31, 1964—continued

| Function | Total |
|---|---:|
| | $'000 |
| Provincial Governments and Territories—continued | |
| Grants-in-aid and shared-cost contributions—continued | |
| Recreational and cultural services: | |
| Camp ground and picnic area development | 266 |
| Fitness and amateur sport | 249 |
| Other | 19 |
| **Total recreational and cultural services** | **534** |
| Education: | |
| Technical and vocational training: | |
| Capital assistance to trade schools | 102,038 |
| Vocational high school training | 2,765 |
| Technician training | 7,064 |
| Trade and other occupational training | 10,288 |
| Apprenticeship training | 2,335 |
| Assistance to students | 316 |
| Training of unemployed workers | 10,492 |
| Training of disabled persons | 605 |
| Other | 529 |
| Citizenship and language instruction for immigrants | 210 |
| Other | 219 |
| **Total education** | **136,861** |
| Natural resources: | |
| Fish and game: | |
| Registered traplines | 170 |
| Construction of vessels | 500 |
| Forests: | |
| Forest inventories, reforestation, forest fire protection and forest access road construction | 7,910 |
| Bud worm control | 138 |
| Forest stand improvement | 91 |
| Lands: Settlement and agriculture: | |
| Agricultural lime assistance | 1,596 |
| 4-H clubs | 145 |
| Transport of fodder, equipment and cattle | 41 |
| Farm labour agreements | 94 |
| Agriculture rehabilitation and development | 3,412 |
| Crop insurance | 429 |
| Other | 442 |
| Other | 7,638 |
| **Total natural resources** | **22,606** |

Paving the approach ramp to the Garden City Skyway, St. Catharines, Ontario.

So strategically situated is Saskatoon on the South Saskatchewan River with regard to railway, aeroplane, highway and river transportation services that it has become known as the Hub City. Centre of a large agricultural and industrial area, the city derives its name from the Cree word of an edible berry.

## Payments made by Federal Government to Provincial Governments, Territories and Municipal Corporations for Fiscal Year Ended March 31, 1964—concluded

| Function | Total |
|---|---|
| | $'000 |
| Provincial Governments and Territories—concluded | |
| Grants-in-aid and shared-cost contributions—concluded | |
| Other: | |
| Civil defence.......................................................... | 4,424 |
| Winter works projects in municipalities............................... | 26,644 |
| Grants to research councils........................................... | 188 |
| Other................................................................. | 870 |
| Total other ...................................................... | 32,126 |
| Total grants-in-aid and shared-cost contributions............... | 862,589 |
| Total amounts paid to provincial governments and territories........ | 1,121,311 |
| Municipal corporations: | |
| Grants in lieu of taxes on federal property........................... | 31,920 |
| Special grants........................................................ | 1,899 |
| Grants-in-aid and shared-cost contributions: | |
| Transportation: | |
| Air.................................................................. | 232 |
| Road................................................................ | 4,351 |
| Water............................................................... | 78 |
| Health.............................................................. | 7,900 |
| Schools operated by local authorities................................ | 1,977 |
| Slum clearance...................................................... | 3,840 |
| Other............................................................... | — |
| Total amounts paid to municipal corporations..................... | 52,197 |
| Grand total amounts paid to provincial governments, territories and municipal corporations........................ | 1,173,508 |

## Grants Paid to Local Governments by Provincial Governments
### Fiscal Year Ended March 31, 1964

| Function | Total |
|---|---|
| | $'000 |
| Unconditional grants: | |
| Shared-revenue contributions................................................... | 1,503 |
| Subsidies................................................................... | 73,693 |
| Grants in lieu of local taxes on provincial government property............... | 4,030 |
| **Total unconditional grants**............................................. | **79,226** |
| | |
| Grants-in-aid and shared-cost contributions (conditional): | |
| Protection of persons and property: | |
| Corrections............................................................... | 47 |
| Police protection......................................................... | 623 |
| Other—Fire protection..................................................... | 1,300 |
| Other................................................................. | 484 |
| | |
| Transportation and communications: | |
| Highways, roads and bridges............................................... | 112,822 |
| | |
| Health and social welfare: | |
| Public health............................................................. | 11,756 |
| Medical, dental and allied services........................................ | 158 |
| Hospital care............................................................. | 1,498 |
| Aid to aged persons (homes)............................................... | 8,123 |
| Aid to unemployed employables and unemployables........................... | 60,844 |
| Child welfare............................................................. | 5,075 |
| Other..................................................................... | 314 |
| | |
| Recreational and cultural services: | |
| Parks, beaches and other recreational areas............................... | 520 |
| Other..................................................................... | 644 |
| | |
| Education: | |
| Schools operated by local authorities..................................... | 767,476 |
| | |
| Natural resources and primary industries: | |
| Lands: Settlement and agriculture......................................... | 1,941 |
| Other..................................................................... | 1,606 |
| Local government planning and development................................. | 1,172 |
| | |
| Other expenditure: | |
| Civil defence............................................................. | 2,556 |
| Winter works projects..................................................... | 43,783 |
| Other..................................................................... | 5,482 |
| **Total grants-in-aid and shared-cost contributions**..................... | **1,028,224** |
| **Grand Total paid to local governments**................................. | **1,107,450** |

These intergovernmental transfers have had a very strong effect on the course of government finance. The amounts involved represent a high proportion of the total revenue of the provincial and municipal government recipients. One hundred years after Confederation the federal-provincial-municipal financial relationship presents a complex, challenging problem. Under the terms of the BNA Act, as they now stand, the claim is made that revenue fields open to provincial and municipal governments are not capable of producing the funds necessary to provide the services for which they are respectively responsible. Two suggestions are frequently put forward: (1) adjust responsibility for services, and (2) redistribute revenue fields so that responsibility for services and revenue-raising opportunities are more equal and intergovernmental aid is materially reduced.

Although the federal-provincial problem has received considerable attention, the same problems are present in the provincial-municipal relationship and the same proposition, namely, equating revenue opportunity to service responsibility, has been proposed. It has been implied that the property tax plus other available revenue sources cannot raise enough revenue to meet the costs of services traditionally provided at the local government level. Consequently, additional funds must be provided by senior governments in the form of conditional or unconditional aid to fill the gap. This point of view, however, has been challenged on two main grounds. First, it has been claimed that property tax rates could be justifiably increased by a considerable amount. Secondly, the present situation tends to create bad government. This latter viewpoint is based on the premise that any government should bear the political and financial responsibility for levying for the revenue it requires to pay for the services it provides and for which it claims credit. Supporters of this proposition maintain that the present scale of financial aid given to local governments by senior governments may encourage extravagance at the local level and frequently presents the taxpayer with a distorted feeling of injustice toward the taxation burden imposed by the senior levels of government. The problem seems to be that functions have spilled out over the political boundaries while authority to perform functions remains legally chained to the traditional units of local administration.

## In Retrospect

Assuming that government action reflects the wishes of the people in a democratic society, an examination of the financial transactions of governments in Canada demonstrates the desire for a progressively-accelerated participation by government in everyday affairs. One observes a marked increase in government revenues, in expenditures and in debt. On looking for a moment at government expenditures one finds large increases in social welfare, education and transportation services, in addition to an ominous expansion in public debt. In examining a few financial statistics one finds important changes in the financial relationship existing between the three levels of government. Matters concerning the public purse have been woven into every nook and cranny of Canada's economic and social way of life. In short, when one speaks of government finance one is, in a very real sense, discussing Canadian democracy.

Confederation began with only four provinces, Nova Scotia, New Brunswick, Quebec and Ontario, and an examination of the terms of the BNA Act relating to financial powers and responsibilities and the sums to be paid by the Federal Government to these provinces shows how much government has changed over the years both in size and complexity.

In the beginning, government finance as one knows it today played a very unimportant role. The Federal Government was mainly concerned with transportation, resource development, defence and the public debt and most revenue came from excise and customs import duties. In 1867 the Federal Government revenue and expenditure situation was briefly as follows:

## Federal Government Budgetary Revenue and Expenditure, 1867

| Revenue: | $'000,000 |
|---|---|
| Excise duties | 3.0 |
| Customs import duties | 8.6 |
| Return on investments | 2.1 |
| **Expenditure:** | |
| Defence | .8 |
| Social welfare | .3 |
| Transportation and communication | 1.8 |
| Resources development | 1.5 |
| Debt charges | 4.1 |
| Payments to provincial governments | 2.6 |
| Other expenditures | 2.6 |

In 1966 the revenue sources of the Government of Canada are estimated to be much greater and are derived from a much wider variety of sources. Also, the range of services has become far more extensive, as indicated below.

### Estimated Revenue and Expenditure—Fiscal Year Ending March 31, 1966

| | $'000,000 |
|---|---|
| **Revenue[1]:** | |
| Personal income tax | 2,150.0 |
| Corporate income tax | 1,610.0 |
| Estate tax | 106.8 |
| Non-resident tax | 170.0 |
| General sales tax | 1,385.0 |
| Excise duties and taxes | 734.0 |
| Customs duty | 676.0 |
| Other revenue[3] | 845.4 |
| **Total revenue[3]** | **7,677.2** |
| **Expenditure[2]:** | |
| Defence services and mutual aid | 1,578.7 |
| Veterans' pensions | 367.4 |
| Health and sanitation | 604.9 |
| Social welfare | 938.5 |
| Education | 298.2 |
| Transportation and communications | 578.9 |
| Natural resources and primary industries | 427.7 |
| Debt charges | 1,101.1 |
| Payments to provinces and municipalities | 409.5 |
| Other expenditure | 1,698.9 |
| **Total expenditure[3]** | **8,003.8** |

[1] Estimated revenue (Page 121, 1966-67 Budget papers).   [2] Estimated expenditure—based on a breakdown of expenditure by function as proposed in the 1966 estimates and supplementary estimates.   [3] Total expenditure and other revenue includes the estimated revenue of National Research Council and Canadian Broadcasting Corporation which were deducted in preparing the estimates. They amount to $4,200,000.

The story of provincial government finance is very closely related to finance at the local government level. Significant figures may be traced from about the year 1910 when provincial revenue ran to some $44,000,000 and the local government total was in the neighbourhood of $100,000,000. In that year, and apparently many years before, combined provincial-municipal government revenues exceeded those of the Federal Government. World War I reversed the situation and revenues of the Federal Government have more than equalled the provincial-municipal total ever since.

(G. A. WAGDIN)

CANADA, 1867-1967

The Chalk River Nuclear Laboratories of Atomic Energy of Canada, Ltd. Nuclear research reactors and other major research installations at Chalk River provide facilities for experiments in physics, chemistry, biology and for engineering and metallurgical programs directed toward development of nuclear power. CRNL is located on the Ottawa River 130 miles from Ottawa.

# Scientific and Industrial Research

Canada's large area and small population account for its two dominant long-term problems: transport and communication. In response to these challenges, Canada now has the two greatest railway systems in the world, and the longest television circuit—one that extends through seven time zones and embraces two languages. When the century began, in a land of farms, fish, and furs, the birch bark canoe was still important (we have never improved upon the design) and, at the end, Canada was a major exporter of the bush type of aircraft for hinterland flying.

The basic challenge is enormous—no other nation has attempted to establish an advanced industrial system in a country so vast but with such a small population. One result is that the pace has been a bit slow. Canada emerged from World War II with secondary industries at about the same stage of development as appeared in the U.S.A. and in Britain after World War I. Since then the gap has been closing very slowly. The current problem is to catch up and to keep up, both at the same time. By the end of World War II, it had become evident that the next frontier lay in scientific research. Canada could no longer depend on selling its enormous national resources in their simplest forms. The only way to upgrade them lay in technology.

# NRC Establishes Scholarships

Up to 50 years ago, Canada was entirely dependent on the U.S., Britain and Europe for postgraduate education. Research was rare in a Canadian university. Therefore, in 1917, the National Research Council of Canada initiated a system of scholarships for graduate students, and a system of grants in aid of research for professors. The idea was to ensure a flow of scientifically-educated people to deal with emerging technical and industrial problems. This is still the object, but the program today accounts for more than $30,000,000. The NRC tries to "throw the balls" just about as fast as "catchers" appear.

Through its various government agencies, Canada has invented and perfected a sharp scientific instrument called an associate committee. Members serve without pay other than for travelling and living expenses. Everybody in the country with a stake in a national technical problem (such as the St. Lawrence Seaway) is represented through members from industries, universities and governments. All are glad to serve, since this puts them on the "inside track" and gives them a say in how a problem should be tackled, who should do it, where and for how much. The moment a job is finished, the associate committee is disbanded. This low-cost mechanism has been widely admired.

At the beginning of the century, Canada was publishing three scientific and technical periodicals; at the end of the century, these had increased to a total of about 125. When the century opened, the primary industries held the stage. Each big government department that existed to service a primary industry—such as agriculture, mines, forestry, fisheries—had to find a spot somewhere for small and highly competent bands of scientific and technical workers. These fitted rather uneasily into the regulatory functions.

It so happens that a scientific person has to be independent-minded, or he isn't any good. He needs a great deal of freedom. A civil service is not the best place in which to put that kind of person, but it somehow had to be done. (This problem has not been solved in any country in the world; but Canada is doing as well as any.) Even while grumbling a bit about the low status, low pay, and red tape, these scientists did a superb job right from the start. When Canada's first great railway was pushed across the continent, men from the federal Department of Agriculture were dropping off at every measured mile to sow seeds, examine insects, check weeds, look for plant diseases, etc.

# Agricultural World Power

In 1903, Canada entered a new phase as an agricultural world power, because of the work of Sir Charles Saunders, Dominion Cerealist, and that of his co-workers. Their early-ripening Marquis wheat helped to open up the prairies. Ruby, Garnet and Reward wheats followed, each adapted to special prairie conditions. Department of Agriculture officers, assisted by such outstanding university scientists as Dr. W. P. Thompson, were leaders also in large-scale, systematic, government-sponsored studies on varieties resistant to rust.

The technical work associated with standards and with testing, and all the primary natural resources such as mining, forestry and fisheries—all this was done with unusual

306

devotion. It just couldn't have been for the money. Perhaps the federal scientists liked designing their way around the regulations that hampered them. In 1882, the first President of the Royal Society of Canada, Sir William Dawson, said: "We are sometimes told that the enterprise in which we are engaged is premature, that, like some tender plant too early exposed to the frost of our Canadian spring, it will be nipped and perish . . . unless this generation of Canadians is content, like those that have preceded it, to sow what others must reap in its full maturity, there will be little hope for our country . . . ." Few people are aware that Standard Time was invented in Canada. In 1884, Sir Sanford Fleming's system of international standard time measurements was adopted by the International Prime Meridian Conference held at Washington, D.C.

When the Canadian Pacific Railway was being pushed west, involving the enormous task of mapping the Rockies, Surveyor General E. G. Deville substantially eased the problem by using photographs. He climbed to the tops of mountains, panned around, measured angles, and plotted the formations shown. The birth of the aeroplane gave wings to the camera, and photogrammetry was on its way. Today, the Blachut group at NRC is one of the world's top teams in the photogrammetric research field, and includes U. V. Helava, who invented the Helava Plotter. The Plotter substitutes mathematical projection for the mechanical projection on which all other plotters rely.

## Aeronautical Research

Aeronautical research began in Canada, as elsewhere, at the turn of the century. The first Canadian pioneer of scientific aviation was Wallace Rupert Turnbull, who invented the controllable pitch propellor in the 1920's and built the first wind tunnel in Canada in 1902. Alexander Graham Bell, who was vitally interested in transport as well as in communication, hired two young engineers from the University of Toronto,

The 1960's have witnessed Canada's entry into the field of radio-astronomy. With a new 150-foot diameter radio telescope at the National Research Council's special observatory in Algonquin Park, Ontario, the nation has an excellent instrument for detailed and precise investigation. Added to such existing equipment as the 84-foot diameter radio telescope in British Columbia, the nation is now capable of scientific research across a massive segment of the universe. Shown here are 10-foot diameter reflectors for study of solar emission.

J. A. D. McCurdy and F. W. ("Casey") Baldwin. In 1909, McCurdy made the first powered aeroplane flight by a British subject in the British Empire. This was in the Silver Dart. One year later he transmitted by wireless the world's first aeroplane-to-ground communication. Casey Baldwin's work on the hydrofoil was remembered by the Canadian Navy in the 1960's, and they named a modern hydrofoil the KC-B in his honour.

John H. Parkin built the second wind tunnel in Canada, in 1918, at the University of Toronto. Later he built other wind tunnels at the National Research Council. The Council is currently adding to its extensive system of wind tunnels a so-called "low speed" wind tunnel with a wide aperture, to enable the Canadian aircraft industry (especially de Havilland) to retain the advanced position it holds in short take-off and landing aircraft (STOL).

The aircraft industry began in 1916 with a government-sponsored plant in Toronto. By the end of the War, it had produced 2,900 JN4 aircraft. Aircraft were produced for the RCAF by Canadian Vickers Limited beginning in 1924. United States and British firms set up branch plants in Canada about 1927. During World War II, Canadian companies produced over 16,000 aircraft.

## Industrial Research

The Steel Co. of Canada Ltd. had laboratories in Canada as early as 1903; Shawinigan Chemicals Ltd. had done the same by 1915; Northern Electric Co. by 1916; and Consolidated Mining and Smelting Co. of Canada Ltd. by 1917.

International Nickel Company of Canada Ltd. had laboratories going in 1922, and Canadian Industries Ltd. by 1929. In the early 1930's, large laboratory facilities were in use in Canadian Breweries Ltd.; Ayerst, McKenna and Harrison Ltd.; and Imperial Oil Limited. The early 1940's saw large-scale facilities for research opened by Aluminum Laboratories Ltd. near Kingston; by Dominion Rubber Co. Ltd. in Guelph; by British American Oil Co. Ltd. at Toronto; and Canada Packers Ltd. at Toronto.

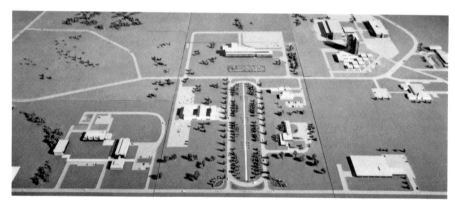

This is a model of Sheridan Park Research Community, which is located 15 miles west of Toronto. Construction began in 1963 and eight companies now occupy their own buildings and employ some 1,300 scientists and supporting personnel. It is expected that the full complement of 30 companies and 6,000 research workers will soon be reached. The Ontario Research Foundation, which does research and development for a multitude of large and small industrial firms, will soon move into its new building on the site.

An electric model heart, designed to reproduce all the electrical activity of the normal heart, was designed for study at the National Research Council. It is shown at the right, with recording equipment to the left.

## Medical Research

In 1921, Sir Frederick Banting, working in the laboratory of Dr. J. J. R. MacLeod, at the University of Toronto, and with the aid of Dr. Charles H. Best, succeeded in isolating insulin—one of the great medical discoveries of all time. In the following months, Dr. J. B. Collip found a means of purifying insulin. The resulting substance revolutionized the therapy of diabetes and led to greater understanding of carbohydrate metabolism.

## NRC Research

In 1932, Dr. L. M. Pidgeon, then a chemist at NRC and subsequently Head of the Department of Metallurgical Engineering, University of Toronto, developed a process for extracting magnesium metal from calcined dolomite, and ended Canada's dependence on foreign sources of magnesium.

In the 1930's all of the physical standards of Canada—mass, length, electricity, heat, light, ionizing radiations, time and frequency—were put in the hands of NRC scientists (now in the Division of Applied Physics) and were used to such effect that today Canada's standards are of a superior class, and a Canadian is President of the International Committee of Weights and Measures (Dr. L. E. Howlett of NRC).

During World War II, General A. G. L. McNaughton established Research Enterprises Limited for the rapid production of gun-sights, opticals, and about $300,000,000 worth of radar sets, designed and built in Canada. Out of its own evolving fabric, the NRC created the Defence Research Board in 1947, Atomic Energy of Canada Limited in 1952 and, in 1960, the Medical Research Council.

One application of Canada's nuclear reactor technology was the development of the Cobalt-60 cancer teletherapy unit. AECL has supplied these units for installation in hospitals all over the world.

In 1946, Dr. C. J. Mackenzie pointed out that: "There has never been any doubt of the State's responsibility in serving the individual farmer . . . I am inclined to believe that the small industry occupies a somewhat similar position . . . there is a public responsibility to see that provisions are made whereby the small industries may obtain the same type of non-secret scientific and technical knowledge that is available to the larger units in our country, and also have access to satisfactory research facilities."

RESEARCH

In the 1960's Canada is embarking on a new era of research and development to maintain and improve its position as one of the leading industrial nations of the world. Government research—federal and provincial—is leading the way, especially in the fields of nuclear technology, communications, transportation, geology, mineral processing, photogrammetry, agriculture, engineering and geophysics. Private industry across the country is meeting the challenge of competition from other countries in the manufacture of ultra-modern production. It is stepping up its own scientific and technical studies, with much of this increased effort based on Federal Government assistance. Until recently, little pure research was conducted in Canada by Canadian companies (with some notable exceptions). Many such companies are subsidiaries of United States or British companies and tended to rely on their parent bodies to conduct research. The result was the so-called "brain drain" of Canadian scientists to the United States.

## Research Centres

The Ontario Research Community at Sheridan Park is a virtual breakthrough for Canadian industry. At the opening of the Dunlop Research Building there, Ontario's Minister of Economics and Development said: "Dunlop is not merely investing in the future prosperity of their company but investing also in the people of Canada . . . particularly young Canadians . . . our leaders of tomorrow. Not only will centres like this one ensure that our industries remain competitive but, perhaps more important, will ensure that Canadian graduate students will find both challenge and creative opportunity at home."

Value of buildings already built or under construction at Sheridan Park is $27,000,000 with several sites still to be sold. Laboratories already opened include British American Research and Development Company's $4,000,000 project which includes in the building complex an analytical research and development building, an engine fuels

Whiteshell Nuclear Research Building at Pinawa on the Winnipeg River, Manitoba. This is one of a number of nuclear reactors installed by the Atomic Energy of Canada's new Nuclear Research Establishment.

The new Canadian Coast Guard
weather-oceanographic ship,
*Vancouver*, was put into service
in 1966.

and lubricants laboratory, a pilot plant, and an administration building. The first
infra-red spectrophotometer of its type to be used industrially in Canada is now being
used in BA's laboratories, to measure the infinitesimal electronic charges inside the
electron shells of atoms.

Other laboratories include Consolidated Mining and Smelting Co. of Canada's
$1,800,000 metal products laboratory; and Dunlop Research Centre's $1,500,000
project. Still under construction was a $5,500,000 energy research centre for Atomic
Energy of Canada Limited, to be completed by 1967; Abitibi Paper Company's
$1,800,000 project, International Nickel Company of Canada's $2,000,000 centre,
and Warner-Lambert Research and Development Company's $1,500,000 project were
completed in 1966. In addition, the provincial government's industry-supported
Ontario Research Foundation was building a $5,500,000 one-storey complex. ORF
employs about 200 scientists and carries out research projects for private companies
and government departments.

Officials at Sheridan Park expect that, in addition to self-interest, industry will be
encouraged to spend more on research because of new tax incentives and the possible
formation of research associations in industry similar to the Canadian Pulp and Paper
Association, where companies band together to pool expenditures on basic research
of use to all members in the industry. Nine universities in the area of Sheridan Park
provide scientists with a considerable talent pool from which to draw. Elsewhere, a
number of new research centres in industry were opened or were about to open.

New expanded research-development facilities for Nopco Chemical Canada Ltd.,
and its subsidiary, Canadian Aniline and Extract Co. Ltd., are planned for Hamilton.
The $200,000 installation will provide enlarged facilities for the two Canadian chemical
companies—backed by increased technical service for a wide range of Canadian
industries. The program of the laboratory will be scaled to meet the rapidly-growing
needs of Canada's expanding industrial economy. Imperial Oil will spend $1,000,000
on a new applications research and technical service laboratory to support the company's polyvinyl chloride resins operations at Sarnia, Ontario. Completion of the
laboratory is scheduled for the spring of 1966.

A new research group has been established by Canadian Liquid Air Ltd. to conduct applied research into the ultra-cold world of liquefied industrial gases and into new uses for these gases which are capable of generating some of the highest temperatures known to man. As the new Canadian research work gathers impetus it is planned to enlarge the company's existing laboratories in Montreal and have them complement other established research facilities in Canada.

Shawinigan Chemicals Ltd. will build a research and technical service centre on the western end of Montreal Island. This area is rapidly becoming a "research club", similar to Sheridan Park. Construction on the new site began in the spring of 1966. The Pulp and Paper Research Institute and Dominion Tar and Chemical already have research buildings there. The centre will house all of Shawinigan's centralized research and technical service functions. A special laboratory will be equipped to seek new applications in the vinyl plastic field.

## Federal Aid Program

The Industrial Research Assistance Program of the Federal Government rose from $1,600,000 in 1963-64 to an estimated $4,500,000 in 1966-67. Since this program began in 1962, an over-all industrial research effort has been initiated in industry amounting to more than $50,000,000, shared between company and government funding. The government program has coincided with a growing realization by many companies that they must get into research to compete with new foreign products or to avoid the alternative of selling out to a foreign company that can provide research support as a parent. Industrial research positions created by the program now total more than 800.

The government's involvement in scientific activities started with the formation of the Geological Survey of Canada shortly after Confederation. This was followed by early support to primary industries and agriculture through Federal Government

◀(Left) The Dominion Radio Astrophysical Observatory at Penticton, British Columbia, studies the emission of radio waves generated within our galaxy and in external sources.

(Below) NRC's long-beam cesium resonator.
▼

Inspecting ocean current meters at the Oceanographic Institute, Nova Scotia.

laboratories and experimental farms. Since 1916, there has been a steadily-growing, tangible, government-wide recognition of the need to encourage scientific research and related activities. (For a country that has so much of it, geography has received relatively little attention, with a few notable exceptions such as the current prodigious labours of Professor Trevor Lloyd of McGill.)

Federal Government expenditures on scientific activities in 1965-66 increased to an estimated $375,000,000, an amount representing about five per cent of total budgetary expenditures. The Department of Agriculture, Atomic Energy of Canada Limited, the National Research Council, the Medical Research Council, the Department of Energy, Mines and Resources, and the Department of National Defence account for about 80 per cent of all scientific expenditures of the Federal Government.

## Science Secretariat

The Federal Government's new Science Secretariat in the Privy Council Office expanded with the appointment of three deputy directors and an executive secretary. The Secretariat has the task of assembling, digesting, and analyzing information related to the Government's scientific and technological activities, including their interrelationships with university, industrial and provincial scientific establishments and of providing professional and administrative support to the Science Council of Canada.

The year 1965 saw the launching of PAIT—Program for the Advancement of Industrial Technology, sponsored by the federal Department of Industry. This complements the assistance programs of the Defence Research Board and the National Research Council, both of which support research. PAIT helps in developing products that result from applying such research. The plan is expected to triple the number of companies now taking advantage of government tax incentives for research and development spending.

The fact that Canada's area is nearly bisected by the auroral zone brings with it many special problems (mostly associated with disturbances in radio and telegraphic communication), but it also provides a facility, unique among the nations of the world, to investigate many of the current problems relating to outer space. These problems are being studied by federal agencies, in co-operation with a number of Canadian universities and industries—notably Bristol Aero-Industries Ltd., Winnipeg, makers of the Black Brant rockets.

Provincial governments are expanding their research activities to keep pace with the general expansion of the economy. The Quebec Provincial Government decided in principle to establish a scientific research council and an industrial research centre.

## University Research

A report to the Federal Government on "Financing Higher Education in Canada" recommended that federal grants for university research be increased in the 1966-67 fiscal year to more than $100,000,000 from $40,000,000 in 1965-66. "The scientists we met", reported the four-man commission headed by Dean Vincent Bladen of the University of Toronto, "impressed vigorously upon us that the security and the general welfare of the country urgently require further rapid and sustained growth of Canadian science. Science and technology are 'exploding' so fast that our efforts will have to be greatly increased if Canada is to keep up with the general momentum."

In the 1965-66 fiscal year, 17 federal departments and agencies spent an estimated $40,000,000 on university research projects. The Bladen Commission recommended basic grants of $75,000,000 for three agencies—$40,000,000 for NRC to finance projects in physical sciences, up from $21,600,000 in 1965-66; $20,000,000 for the Medical Research Council to aid medical schools and hospitals, up from $9,200,000; and $15,000,000 for the Canada Council for the arts, humanities and social sciences, up from an estimated $2,900,000.

The universities continued to be the country's main source of research in pure science and the main source of scientific manpower. Research activities continued to increase and much of this was made possible by federal grants. Dr. B. G. Ballard, President of NRC, summed up the Canadian scientific scene this way:

> "Canada is frequently accused of lack of initiative, but it is my firm conviction that there is no need to apologize for Canadian science in industry, in the government service, or in the universities. It has won acclaim both at home and abroad, despite the fact that Canadian per capita expenditures on science are lower than those of the other advanced countries. I suggest, however, that this should not be construed as an argument in favour of holding science expenditures at a low level. We must be alive to the need to compete with other countries not only for international markets, but even our own domestic market, but again, we do not need to apologize. We have the second highest per capita gross national product in the world, and while we should strive to have the highest, second place is not exactly a dishonour".

## "Alouettes"

The Canadian "Alouette I", launched in 1962, was the first international satellite to be completely designed and built by a nation other than the U.S. or the U.S.S.R. It was built by the Defence Research Board and fired by the U.S. It conducts three experiments for the Defence Research Board, to study the ionosphere; and one for the National Research Council, to observe cosmic rays.

A fabrication technique originated at NRC gave the spacecraft a unique feature—a 150-foot antenna, tip-to-tip. These are made of thin, heat-treated steel and are stored on drums until after the satellite is in orbit. Alouette II went up in 1965, with antenna extending 240 feet, tip-to-tip. The third and later Canadian satellites are to be called ISIS "A", "B", "C", etc., initials for "International Satellites for Ionospheric Studies".

In 1962 Dr. Neil Bartlett, at the University of British Columbia, achieved world fame by preparing the first true compound of the rare gas Xenon, thus overthrowing a number of theories on chemical bonding and opening up a new field of investigation.

In the late 1950's relocation of much of Aklavik to a new townsite, Inuvik, was the largest building-research and town-planning project ever undertaken in the Canadian North. The systematic studies connected with this undertaking revealed the extent to which permafrost can affect northern construction and the safeguard required to counteract the influence of permafrost.

In 1963, G. L. E. Jarlan, working in the NRC's hydraulics laboratory, invented the perforated breakwater. This design dissipates wave energy by a seaward vertical wall that is perforated with large-diameter holes, and backed by a wave chamber. The chamber reduces the wave action, thus providing a quiet harbour. The first full-scale structure was built at Baie Comeau on the St. Lawrence.

## Quebec Research

Science is popularized more vigorously in Quebec than in the rest of Canada, perhaps because of the generally stronger literary tradition. L'Association canadienne française pour l'avancement des sciences (ACFAS) was founded in 1923, and has produced a publication—*Le Jeune Scientifique*—so outstanding that it has been officially adopted by the Board of Education of Belgium.

Until sputnik, there wasn't a single science writer on the staff of any Canadian daily; today there are about a dozen.

## Spectacular Growth

It is evident that the build-up of industrial research in the major industrial countries of the world is spectacular. It is doubling every 10-15 years, with no sign yet of levelling off. Research is still one of the major factors influencing economic growth.

The scientific world of the 1920's was perhaps nearer to being a full-fledged international community than either before or later. Science has since become a matter of government policy and interest. E. W. R. Steacie, when he was President of NRC, said: "Public interest always means increased support, but also always means increased control and diminished freedom. The reconciliation of these two opposing factors in government, in industry, and even in universities, is the most important problem facing science in the next decade or two".

We humans have always teetered on a thousand knife-edges. The big thing about science in 1967 is this: Up till now, humans have always been in an extremely dangerous situation over which they had no control whatever. Now, there is one important exception: humans have the elements of control within their grasp, but *are too frightened to use them.*

# Famous Physicist

In a brief article, it is impossible to be just, or even merciful, to more than one man. A possible choice is J. C. McLennan, an irritable, difficult and important physicist who, among other virtues, had the grace to be born in the year 1867—the year of Confederation—at Ingersoll, Ontario. He died in 1935 in a railway carriage between Paris and Calais.

By 1915 he had achieved the considerable eminence necessary to be made a Fellow of the Royal Society of London, and ultimately became Vice-President of that body. In 1915, he had a good deal to do with setting up a meeting—held in the office of Sir George Foster, Minister of Trade and Commerce—a meeting which led directly to the founding of the National Research Council of Canada in 1916.

McLennan's apparently inexplicable influence on highly placed statesmen is easily explained: he had taught these future ministers, and several prime ministers, all that they knew about physics, mainly at the University of Toronto. These men remembered their irascible professor with respect and affection, and were disposed to listen to his advice, knowing well the heart and mind from which the words were springing.

In 1916, he became President of the Royal Canadian Institute, founded in 1849 by "our loving subjects in our Province of Canada" to advance the physical sciences, the arts, and manufactures. This Institute, because of McLennan—and the Canadian Manufacturers' Association—were both powerful influences in founding the NRC.

Another example of McLennan's influence has to do with a large telescope. In 1905, the Dominion Observatory, a handsome stone structure on the Experimental Farm at Ottawa, equipped with a 15-inch refractor, was officially opened. When the time was ripe for a second observatory, with a 72-inch reflecting telescope, this observatory was opened in 1918 in Victoria rather than in Ottawa, at the insistence (and that was what he always did; he unmistakably insisted) of Professor J. C. McLennan, that "this telescope be erected at the most suitable astronomical location in Canada". This was against the judgment of all the senior scientists involved who feared that the extra expense would cause the government to cancel the entire project. However, the Victoria establishment could and did do twice as much as was possible at Ottawa. McLennan had the uncomfortable habit of being right, as well as being listened to. And so, things often turned out as he advised. In 1924 McLennan was elected President of the Royal Society of Canada (founded in 1882).

It is pleasant to record that the knighthood, which he knew he had richly earned in World War I by his work as leading scientific adviser and director under the British Admiralty, finally came to him in 1935. A few months later, the man who died was styled "Sir John Cunningham McLennan".

In retrospect, McLennan's advice about science policy in Canada seems to have been forward-looking by half a century: the kind of over-all advisory committee that he recommended in 1917—one without operational responsibilities—was advanced again by the Glassco Commission in 1963, and is now being implemented in May, 1966, with the establishment of the Science Council of Canada under Dr. O. M. Solandt and Dr. Roger Gaudry as Chairman and Vice-Chairman respectively.

(M. W. Thistle)

The picturesque community of St. Jean de Matha, Quebec, lies north of the St. Lawrence River.

# A Century of Economic Growth

During the past century, the Canadian economy has been greatly dependent upon external forces. Waves of expansion and growth have tended to coincide with major periods of expansion elsewhere. Throughout this period of progressive development the most characteristic industries have been directed toward the export market. When these have thrived, the economy has thriven also.

While the Act of Confederation may have set the stage for a transcontinental expansion based in the St. Lawrence area, decades passed before this achievement was fully realized. Not until the new century dawned did a conjunction of favourable circumstances in world environment lead to attainment of earlier expectations. As the century progressed, closer relations with the United States economy became a major trend in an industrial age of mass production and consumption, in contrast to earlier east-west concentration on a few staple products for export to Europe.

External capital has always played a significant role in Canadian development. Indeed, scarcity of such capital has often put limits on the pace of Canada's expansion. In a country in which transportation facilities have been a major necessity, requiring large investments, it was natural that a considerable proportion of non-resident capital should have been used to finance canals, roads, railways, etc., and that securities represented borrowing for such purposes. Many productive pursuits carried out during the nineteenth century in small units, such as agriculture and small local industries with local markets, could be largely financed from the savings of individuals and other local sources. But, as industrial development advanced, non-resident capital played a progressively larger part in financing industrial and governmental enterprises.

This change became most evident in the twentieth century with the appearance of new industries, mines and sources of power requiring large investments of capital. Industries exploiting such Canadian resources as pulp and paper, non-ferrous smelting and refining, chemicals, petroleum and mining are all particularly capital-intensive and have drawn heavily upon non-resident sources of capital.

Other capital-intensive industries such as hydro-electric power, originally partly developed by private enterprise, have since become largely government-owned. Many of the secondary industries, for example, automobiles, rubber goods and electrical apparatus, have also been considerably influenced by non-resident capital. On the other hand, such secondary industries as iron and steel, textiles and beverages, are still mainly under Canadian control. Down the years an underlying trend has been to larger units and consolidations with a widening of markets and broader affiliations.

## Capital Inflows

Various periods of intensive investment and rapid growth in Canada have been highly dependent upon capital inflows. Some outstanding characteristics of these periods herein described, are largely in a context of capital investment and its sources and the external demands which made expansion possible. In the process of developing into a highly-industrialized economy, Canada has accumulated an exceptionally large balance of external indebtedness.

The total value of externally-owned investments in Canada at the beginning of Confederation was not great, compared with investments in subsequent periods of rapid Canadian expansion. However, such investments constituted a considerable burden for the size of the economy. The value of early non-resident investments is not known precisely, but even by 1900 the total was privately estimated at less than $1,250,000,000. Much of this total appears to have been accumulated during the first three decades following Confederation.

The Canadian provinces had experienced a period of heavy investment activity in the decade of the 1850's with the building of the Grand Trunk Railway which was financed by British capital and was at the centre of the expansion in that period. Other railways were also constructed before Confederation and were financed by capital both from Britain and the United States. Earlier construction of the various canal systems and other public works often had been made possible only by imports of capital from the sale of provincial bonds in London. Indeed, a number of canals, such as the Rideau system, had been constructed by the Imperial Government.

Investments by non-residents in Canadian industry in that early pre-Confederation period tended to be more limited, except for a few special types of activity where non-residents were major entrepreneurs as in the fur trade and in lumbering. The history of the Hudson's Bay Company alone is a record of Canadian development. In fact, one early objective—and result—of Confederation was Canadian Government purchase from the Hudson's Bay Company of Rupert's Land in order to open up the western prairies for settlement. Close business relations with Britain led to many partnerships and other business connections with that country.

In the period between Confederation and the turn of the century the greatest single influence on the rapid rise in non-resident investment in Canada was the building of the Canadian Pacific Railway. This major investment gave rise to a variety of other capital inflows, for example, agricultural and business opportunities and community development which followed the construction of an all-Canadian transcontinental railway. Financing of the railway itself, under construction from the 1870's to 1885, led to very substantial investments from the United Kingdom and, to a lesser extent, from continental Europe and the United States. Other railway construction of the period was also financed by non-resident investors and the Intercolonial Railway was completed in 1876.

Another aspect of National Policy, the introduction of a new tariff in 1879, was also an influence on industrial development and capital inflows. A number of new establishments in manufacturing and trade were set up in Canada in this period by American and other non-resident businesses. New mineral properties were acquired by non-residents and mining began in some areas, as well as operations in the pulp and paper industry. These industries did not yet play an important role in Canadian exports which were still mainly such primary products as lumber, fish, bacon, cheese, etc.

The great gold rush to the Yukon in the closing years of the nineteenth century brought a rush of prospectors from the outside world.

Even goats were pressed into service to transport supplies for foot-weary Klondike adventurers.

Through much of this post-Confederation period certain influences were pervasive in the general economic background of Canada. Among these were declining prices in Canada and elsewhere and large-scale emigration to the United States. Following the Civil War in the United States, settlement expanded westward and new industries sprang up to supply the growing markets.

The atmosphere of confidence with which the Canadian economy started the period soon changed with the depressive factors noted above which only receded towards the end of the century under the stimulus of an improving world environment with new gold discoveries, recovering exports and prices. It was only towards the end of the century that Prairie development accelerated although the export of prairie wheat had begun earlier on a relatively small scale.

## Accelerated Growth

It was not until the early part of the twentieth century that expansion of the Canadian economy on a more massive and concentrated scale occurred. Large infusions of both capital and immigrants provided a basis of rapid growth which was stimulated by rising prices for wheat and reduced costs of transportation as European industrialization created new markets.

This period of accelerated growth accompanying large investments, which came to a peak just before the outbreak of World War I, was rendered possible only by an infusion of foreign capital in unprecedented volume. In this way foreign resources were utilized to an unusually high degree to supplement domestic sources of capital in furthering the development of the Canadian economy. Again, the period was one in which railway construction was important in leading to capital inflows, with the building of two more transcontinental railways and many branch extensions of the main systems. These further reinforced the east-west movements of trade and contributed to the expansion of a transcontinental economy trading with the overseas world.

Much of the expansion accompanied the large and rapid population growth as immigration rose to new high levels and as population shifts within the country occurred with the opening up and development of Western Canada. This movement was encouraged by the growing scarcity of cheaper land in the United States. New borrowings abroad by governments and municipalities to assist in providing for the roads and other infrastructure for the wheat economy occurred in this period. British purchases of Canadian railway, government and municipal securities made up most of the capital inflows, with lesser amounts of Canadian securities being sold in the United States.

In the field of industry, direct investments in branches and subsidiaries controlled abroad continued to make up only a minor part of the totals, although this kind of investment was appearing more frequently than formerly as the economy became more industrialized with wider markets and placed less emphasis on production for local demands in smaller industrial establishments. Although information is incomplete, it has been estimated that, by the turn of the century, there were more than 100 instances of direct United States investments in Canada.

## World War I

By the beginning of World War I, apparently partly in response to Canadian tariffs, the number of these direct investments had tripled. In this period the value of Canadian manufacturing more than doubled as did the capital employed, with larger units necessary for developing new industries beginning to appear. Among these were new investments by United States concerns in pulp and paper plants, stimulated by opportunities for free entry into the United States market from 1911 onward, and by restrictions on exports of pulpwood.

Before the War there was also some expansion in non-resident-financed, non-ferrous metal industries. These primary industries, usually based in the Canadian Precambrian region, were to develop rapidly later with technological improvements, new sources of hydro-electric power, and with strong demands for their products in the United States and Europe. Other industries also first appeared in this period. The automobile industry is a significant example of an establishment designed to take advantage of preferential opportunities to export to Commonwealth markets.

World War I was a period of rising activity in both Canadian industry and agriculture. New demands created by the conflict led to full employment of many new facilities developed in the previous decade of rapid growth. War demands prevented readjustments from the preceding boom which had shown some hesitancy in the year before the War began. Canadian industry was able to expand rapidly into new kinds of production for the common Allied effort and to supply the rapidly-growing Canadian market which had been stimulated by new levels of consumption.

Prices also rose rapidly during, and immediately after, the War. Within a few years, exports had doubled in value and later trebled. Increases in shipments of food and war materials to Britain contributed much of this rise but sharp gains in exports to the United States were also very significant as the economy acquired closer links with that country. There was a notable acceleration in investments and in exports of the pulp and paper and non-ferrous metal industries, and a large merchant marine was constructed. Imports from Britain and continental Europe were curtailed, but they increased from the United States. As Canadian industry supplied more Canadian requirements, there was a widening of Canadian markets and an increasing interdependence between the economic regions of the country.

The United States had become a major source of capital and, during the short period of some four years, United States investments in Canada doubled. In contrast, little change occurred in British investments. At the same time, the high income of businesses and individuals in Canada were reflected in increased savings much of which were invested in Victory Bonds. The boom continued for several years after the War but came to an end in 1920 when prices were at their peak level—more than double the general level before the War. A sharp readjustment followed in 1921 with prices falling by about one third. It was not until 1922 and later that general economic recovery again began.

## Industrialization of 1920's

A revival of world trade with recovery and monetary stabilization in Europe, assisted by capital from the United States, again created a favourable environment for Canadian exports and development. Once more Canadian growth was outstanding. In the years from 1925 to 1929, exports were again close to the values of 1918-1920. As prices were much less in the later period, the volume of trade had risen to new peaks. Wheat prices and acreage under production rose once more with a very large crop in 1928.

Business investment, too, again became a source of strength. The Canadian economy was becoming more diversified with the rise to greater prominence of new industries such as pulp and paper, gold, non-ferrous metals, automobiles, electric light and power, and electrical apparatus. Consequently, agriculture decreased somewhat in importance as manufacturing and mining became relatively more important in the latter part of the decade and the service industries gained as well with the growing urbanization of Canada.

Capital exports from the United States to Canada were an important factor in this industrialization of the 1920's. There was a virtual doubling in the value of United States investments in Canada between 1918 and 1926, and a further rise of almost one half in the succeeding four years. This was particularly important in the new industries exploiting the wealth of the Precambrian Shield but it was also widespread in secondary manufacturing, trade and finance. New technologies were imported as well as capital, accelerating the process of industrialization and urbanization.

The new industries included some which were to bring distinction to Canada in the wider front of international industrialization as new metals and materials were required by the United States and other industrial nations. The rapid extensions in the use of electricity and motor transport were also to transform day-to-day life. These changes were the forerunners of even greater industrial transformations to come in later decades. While this influx of United States capital was taking place, Canadian investments abroad were also rising, particularly holdings of United States stocks, as well as Latin American and other foreign bonds.

## The 1930's

Canada was particularly vulnerable to the world-wide depression which set in during 1929 and 1930. Being highly dependent upon incomes from a few export staples, the decrease in world trade had far-reaching effects on the Canadian economy. The economic crisis of 1929 and the subsequent depression in the United States had widespread effects on world trade due to curtailments in capital lending. International dislocations were widespread and deep rooted being accompanied by currency readjustments and protective restrictions. In Canada every sector felt the downward pressure between 1929 and 1933 but none more so than did western agriculture. The depression and prolonged drought brought a rapid end to the extended wheat boom. Markets contracted and prices dropped to one quarter of the 1917-1920 peak but there was no corresponding drop in costs and overhead.

The impact of these changes forced readjustment that had been postponed by short-phased reactions earlier. Investment activity fell off rapidly, contracting to about one quarter of the 1929 level and was not again to reach that peak until the 1940's. Manufacturing activity was sharply reduced. Imports also contracted rapidly and were not to regain the levels of the more prosperous years until World War II, partly because of the low levels of investment in Canada in the 1930's.

Although world trade again began to increase after 1933, recovery in Canada tended to be slow and resources were under-utilized until World War II. The climate for some of Canada's primary products continued to be unfavourable because of surplus capacity and reduced world demand. Policies of autarchy in Europe, which lessened demand for wheat, are an example. But there was a rising demand for the products

322                                                                    CANADA, 1867-1967

of some mineral industries and the growth which occurred in this area became relatively more important.

A major gain occurred in the production and export of gold, stimulated by the higher prices offered since 1934. Exports of the leading non-ferrous metals also were stimulated by armament demands from overseas. Trade agreements between Canada and the United States signed in 1935 and 1938, combined with the general recovery, led to substantial increases in trade with that country in the years immediately before the War, although the short recession in the United States in 1938 was a restraining factor.

Another growing source of Canadian income was the trade from United States tourists as Canada's highways were developed. As imports gained relatively less than exports, there were sizable surpluses in Canada's external current account from 1934 on. These were available for reducing foreign holdings of Canadian securities.

The 1930's was the last period in which the traditional geographical distribution, the "triangular pattern" of Canada's balance of payments, was predominant, unimpeded by the type of international financial dislocations which were to become typical of the 1940's with the War and its aftermath. There were surpluses in Canada's balance of payments with Britain and overseas which could be freely converted to cover deficits with the United States. The unconvertibility of sterling which emerged with World War II meant that it was necessary to introduce new methods of financing Canada's external trade along more bilateral channels.

## World War II

The outbreak of World War II in 1939 brought to an end the long period of under-employment of resources. Once again the external environment was to become the determining factor in Canadian development. Soon, scarcity of resources was an over-riding element in the shaping of economic policy. Various official controls were introduced affecting production, prices and foreign exchange as well as general military and economic mobilization. Government expenditures as well as policy became increasingly prominent. New kinds of production were introduced and extended while other kinds were reduced by one factor or another. With a curtailment of imports to meet civilian purposes, new opportunities opened up for Canadian manufacturing. Some major industries, of which the automobile industry is an example, were diverted from production for civilian purposes in order to produce military equipment.

As a result of wartime mobilization, a great increase in the total of Canadian production to new high levels was achieved. Within several years, production had doubled in value and remained consistently above this level thereafter. Full employment became the characteristic situation in contrast to the unemployment which had prevailed for such a long period before the War. In the field of agriculture, production was diverted from wheat to dairy products and livestock in order to provide a wider range of food exports to Britain. In industry, production was greatly increased in many commodities which were to be exported—aluminum, nickel, other metals and materials, and in military equipment including aircraft, chemicals, electronic equipment and instruments, and ships. New investment during the period tended to be concentrated in industries producing war materials. By the end of the war, Canada had a much more rounded industrial development than formerly and many of the newest types of facilities.

## Gross National Product of Canada, 1926 - 1965

| Year | Millions of Current Dollars | Year | Millions of Current Dollars | Year | Millions of Current Dollars | Year | Millions of Current Dollars |
|------|------|------|------|------|------|------|------|
| 1926.... | 5,152 | 1936.... | 4,653 | 1946.... | 11,850 | 1956.... | 30,585 |
| 1927.... | 5,549 | 1937.... | 5,257 | 1947.... | 13,165 | 1957.... | 31,909 |
| 1928.... | 6,046 | 1938.... | 5,278 | 1948.... | 15,120 | 1958.... | 32,894 |
| 1929.... | 6,134 | 1939.... | 5,636 | 1949.... | 16,343 | 1959.... | 34,915 |
| 1930.... | 5,728 | 1940.... | 6,743 | 1950.... | 18,006 | 1960.... | 36,287 |
| 1931.... | 4,699 | 1941.... | 8,328 | 1951.... | 21,170 | 1961.... | 37,471 |
| 1932.... | 3,827 | 1942.... | 10,327 | 1952.... | 23,995 | 1962.... | 40,575 |
| 1933.... | 3,510 | 1943.... | 11,088 | 1953.... | 25,020 | 1963.... | 43,424 |
| 1934.... | 3,984 | 1944.... | 11,850 | 1954.... | 24,871 | 1964.... | 47,403 |
| 1935.... | 4,315 | 1945.... | 11,835 | 1955.... | 27,132 | 1965.... | 51,996 |

# Mutual Aid

The effect of this wartime economic mobilization was that Canada was able to export a record proportion of production to Britain and other Allied countries. In the latter years of the War, shipments on Britain's account alone were more than five times as high as exports to that country before the War. This was made possible by a variety of special arrangements including a $700,000,000 loan to the British Government to convert sterling balances accumulated by Canada early in the War. A contribution of $1,000,000,000 to Britain followed. Later, over $2,200,000,000 mutual aid was extended to Britain and other Allied countries. There was also a large-scale official repatriation of many Canadian bonds and other securities held in Britain. By the end of the War, virtually all of the Government of Canada and Canadian National Railway bonds held in Britain had been taken over by Canada. Canada's balance of indebtedness to Britain was considerably reduced, principally by the loan to Britain and the repatriation of securities there. In the same period, the Canadian Government had spent more than $2,500,000,000 on overseas military expense as well.

Commodity flows between Canada and the United States also rose to record proportions during the War, a major influence being the Hyde Park Agreement of April 1941. As a result, new sources of dollar receipts were developed which permitted Canada to specialize in the production of certain types of product required for the War. Sales of aluminum, ships and other war supplies to the United States were particularly large and demand for some civilian commodities expanded greatly. For example, grain shortages led to very large purchases of Canadian grains. Imports from the United States, although swollen by some heavy defence requirements, were curtailed by the prevailing shortages of the period and by the reduced levels of Canadian consumption brought about by temporary wartime restrictions on non-essential imports and by high taxes.

Long-term capital inflows from the United States continued and both portfolio and direct investments in Canada rose, the latter principally by retained earnings. Canada's reserves of United States dollars rose substantially in the latter part of the wartime period. The backlog of demands which had built up during the period of wartime curtailments in consumption was very great in Canada. This was supported by large accumulations of savings. Consequently, there was only a moderate fall in Canadian production in the transition from a wartime to a peacetime economy. Rising consumer expenditures and a revival of many types of business investment, including the accumulation of stocks, were factors of strength during the period in which government expenditures were being reduced and the composition of production and exports were undergoing alteration.

During 1946, the removal of price and other controls progressed, including the return in mid-year of the Canadian dollar to parity with the United States dollar. Prices rose substantially until the level stabilized temporarily during 1948 was reached. Further substantial rises were to follow in 1950 and thereafter under the world-wide impetus of price increases during the Korean war.

## Assistance Programs

Canada continued to extend generous assistance to the overseas world in the early postwar period. There were exceptionally heavy demands for commodities overseas but, to make high exports possible, financial aid was necessary. The early Canadian postwar program of assistance to overseas countries was greater than that of any other nation on a per capita basis. The postwar loan to Britain of $1,250,000,000 was a prominent part of this assistance which totalled over $1,800,000,000 including export credit loans to other countries.

Canadian financial assistance to overseas countries had the effect of reducing Canada's own capacity to cover Canadian external purchases concentrated in the United States. At first, imports dropped due to a world-wide scarcity of commodities in civilian demand and the end of trade in war materials, but by 1947 imports from the United States were rising rapidly. As there was less convertible exchange available because of the loans, Canada was able only to meet current expenditures in the United States, first by drawing heavily upon the official reserves accumulated in the wartime period, and later by introducing an emergency exchange conservation program.

## Oil Discovery

One of the most important economic events in Canada during the early postwar period was the discovery of oil at Leduc, Alberta. This ushered in a most significant development of a natural resource with many consequences for Canada's national income and balance of payments. It led to a long period of sustained investment activity arising from the exploration and development of petroleum and the increased diversification of the whole nation as well as the region in which the oil was discovered. Development

Mill Village, Nova Scotia, is the site of a satellite tracking station which will provide a link with a global satellite communication network now being established. Here a dacron radome, a giant balloon, looms over the countryside.

of this new, important source of energy was to sustain and accumulate capital inflows for investment in Canada, at first by United States companies, but later by overseas companies as well. Originally, the new production was used in Canada but later, with the construction of pipelines, it also became a major export to the United States in addition to natural gas, a by-product.

This development of a Canadian resource by United States capital is perhaps the best example of a whole series of new U.S. investments in Canada—a series which expanded greatly in the decade of the 1950's and drew Canada farther into the world of international corporate business. Many of these investments were for the purpose of supplementing United States resources of industrial materials by developing nearby Canadian resources as well, and required large imports of capital by international corporations. The cumulative effect of this type of activity and other forms of more domestically-oriented expansion led to the great investment boom in the 1950's.

## New Industries

In addition to petroleum and natural gas, the more outstanding new industries developed by international capital in this period included the massive investments in iron ore mining in Quebec and Labrador, the development of petrochemical and other chemical industries. Enlargements in such basic industries as aluminum, nickel and other non-ferrous metal mining and smelting and pulp and paper have also depended heavily upon foreign sources of capital.

The uranium industry was another major new mining development undertaken on a massive scale in response to United States needs, with some assistance from British capital. Investments in another source of energy, electric power, have also been out-standingly large, including large developments of power at the time of the construction of the St. Lawrence Seaway. Investments in many secondary industries during the 1950's and 1960's were also impressive. Characteristic industries of the period which grew rapidly were electronics, synthetic fabrics and materials. The capa-city of the iron and steel industry was expanded greatly with Canadian capital, making Canada much less dependent upon imports of steel than in the earlier part of the 1950's. The automobile industry and many others were expanded to supply a growing Canadian market as well as to meet the new opportunities for exporting which opened up in the 1960's.

## Increased Government Investment

Investments by governments have also been increasing substantially as the social capital needed to support a larger population stimulated by heavy immigration as well as natural increase, and a more industrial urban economy has been catching up with the private investment which was concentrated earlier. Such investments, too, have been partly financed by capital inflows, usually borrowings in the United States by junior governments and government enterprises.

Growth was rapid and sustained with few interruptions in most of the decade of the 1950's. In its rate, and in the extent to which it was supported by non-resident sources of capital, this period of growth had its nearest counterpart in the great expansion of the wheat economy before World War I. But it was more of an extension of the frontiers in depth bringing with it a much needed diversification to the Canadian economy as

This low temperature gas separation plant of Canadian Helium Limited is located near Swift Current, Saskatchewan. The plant made its first shipment of helium in 1964 and has since tripled its output. A second helium plant is under construction at Wood Mountain, some 60 miles from the site of the first plant.

Canada moved farther into the age of mass production and mass consumption with rising living standards.

Postwar developments have greatly increased the relationships between the Canadian and United States economies. Higher proportions of Canadian trade are now with the United States than in any earlier period. The capital markets of the two countries are more closely linked than ever before with increasing mobility of capital. The close corporate relations between so many of the business firms in the two countries have tended to draw Canadian business into the milieu of the neighbouring country. A wider use of imported technology is also increasing interdependence.

## U.S. Investment Capital

The United States has been the principal source of external investment capital for Canada since the 1920's and that country has a much larger investment stake in Canada than in any other country, with the total invested having more than doubled in less than a decade. United States investments in Canada are particularly prominent in industry. Close communications and transportation have also greatly increased contacts between the two countries. The complexity and interrelationships in the business environment have also been extended by the increasing size of business organizations and a tendency for large enterprises to grow and widen their spheres of activities.

The period of rapid growth was interrupted towards the end of the decade of the 1950's by a series of years of only modest over-all gains in output. These years were characterized by the apparent existence of a considerable degree of over-capacity in many industries which had been expanded so rapidly in the postwar years. The extent of under-utilized resources in the economy was most evident in the chronically high rate of unemployment which persisted until the early years of the 1960's. An anomaly of this period was the large current account deficits which continued after the period of rapid growth which extended up to 1956. Once again some of the difficulty could be traced to the external environment. This time the United States also was in a period of slow growth and to this was added an apparent decline in Canada's international competitive position with an exchange rate which was a deterrent to exporting at a time that supplies of many commodities exported by Canada were growing outside of Canada. This was a period during which the slow progress in North America contrasted with more rapid growth in economies elsewhere, particularly in continental Europe. In addition Canada experienced a financial crisis in 1962 which, being one of confidence, was short-lived.

# Increased Expansion

North American expansion again got under way in the early part of the decade and by the middle of the 1960's Canada, in common with the United States, had enjoyed over four years of expansion. This growth in Canada was at a somewhat higher rate than in the United States, with greater increases in exports accompanying the new exchange rate, established in May 1962, higher population increases, and a relatively larger volume of investment. With an apparently improved competitive position, Canada became less dependent upon the United States for capital than in the previous decade. The greatly-reduced current account imbalance of 1963 and 1964 was partly due to large sales of grain to Communist countries as well as to the improved international competitive position and the widespread expansionist environment in the principal industrial nations.

Investment activity in the mid-1960's has once more reached new peak levels both in the public and private categories. Among the more spectacular projects under way to meet external demands, and often with non-resident capital, are those in potash mining, and other chemicals, and new large expansions in non-ferrous metals, pulp, and electric power. An increasing amount of domestic capital is being invested in schools, universities and other institutions, and in housing.

The century of progress which has been briefly outlined here has revealed a transition in Canada from a relatively small economy still disunited, depending mainly on the production of agricultural and other primary staples for local consumption and export overseas into a highly-developed, increasingly-urban industrial nation with growing contacts with the United States and the rest of the world. First, a relatively simple transcontinental economy trading mainly with the overseas world became viable with the great rise in wheat production. This was followed by the development of a new range of large-scale industries based mainly on forest, mineral resources, and electric power supplying United States and other industrial countries with industrial materials, and the domestic industries producing for a growing internal market stimulated by mass consumption brought about by high living standards.

However, certain common factors have remained in the background throughout the century. The external environment continues to be a leading influence upon the health of the Canadian economy for, although Canadian production has all the diversity of an industrial nation, Canadian exports continue to be unusually concentrated in large portions of the production of a number of Canadian commodities. When external demand for Canada's surpluses which must be exported are strong and sustained, there is a reflection in Canadian activity, and when increased new capacity to meet the rising demands is needed on a large scale, expansion in the Canadian economy takes on dominating proportions. Examples of this type of growth occurred in the decade before World War I with the opening up of the West and, during the decade following World War II, with the development of mineral and power resources and rapid urbanization.

Other concentrations of rapid growth have occurred during the two world wartime periods during which the Canadian economy was fully employed, and the periods in the 1920's and 1960's when United States activity and world trade were rising strongly, and new facilities to meet rising demands, both internal and external, were being extended.

(C. D. BLYTH)

# The Social
# Milieu

# Canada's Industrial Society

A nation, if it is to deserve the term, must be more than a mere aggregate of individuals living within arbitrary political boundaries. Its inhabitants must share a sense of common identity and a body of historical experience that they feel to be particularly theirs. They must, in other words, have a sense of community, in terms of which they interpret their past and shape, as best they can, their future. If this sense of community is lacking, then, in spite of sophisticated political institutions or formidable weapons, the nation must remain a fictitious and artificial creation, and the odds against its survival are high.

A sense of nationality is not merely a lawyer's concept; it is necessary for survival, and will remain so as long as our world is organized into a system of autonomous and potentially hostile units. Canada has been slow in developing this sense of identity, for reasons which are not obscure. Canada's long experience of membership in the British Empire, its proximity to the United States, the constant movement of people and ideas to and fro across the continental boundary, its satellitic economic relationship, first to Great Britain and then to the United States, its internal cultural diversity, and above all else its geographic size and shape, have all militated against the facile development of a sense of common identity and common purpose. Nationality in Canada has been a seed slow to germinate.

## A Sense of Nationhood

The strategic decisions necessary for the creation of Canada as a nation were taken deliberately and self-consciously in the second half of the nineteenth century. Any inclination to date them more precisely—as for instance by reference to the passing of the British North America Act—must be resisted, for legislative measures provided no more than the constitutional skeleton (though, indeed, an indispensable one) around which the flesh and spirit of a nation might develop. Even to finance and construct an adequate transcontinental railroad system—one among the many items of social capital necessary for an industrial economy—required sustained effort by public and private interests over more than four decades. And the political evolution necessary for the development of a viable system of federal-provincial relations was likewise gradual.

Precise dates, if taken too seriously, obscure a vital truth: Canada as a nation was not and could not be created at any particular point in time. Its creation was, and remains today, a process, not an event.

## Productive Industrial Economy

In the course of this process of creation there has evolved in Canada an economic system which today ranks as one of the most productive in the world. The country's rich natural resources, its hospitality to capital, enterprise, and ideas from the rest of the world, its success in maintaining security for profits and property, and the energy and initiative of its inhabitants have all contributed largely to this achievement. Its very success in making the transition to modern industrialism, however, has transformed the nature of Canada as a society.

On balance, this transformation has probably reinforced Canada's sense of unity and identity. Economic development normally implies closer integration and greater interdependence of parts, and the vastly easier and more rapid mobility of people and products that accompanies industrialization makes geographic space a less formidable problem. But industrial transformation has also brought new problems, for the individual citizen and for government at all levels. It is largely through its efforts to meet these problems of social adjustment to rapid technological change and to the myriad forms of instability and insecurity that industrialism implies that Canada has attained a greater sense of what it is and what it wants to be. A mere rise in the average standard of living by itself does not contribute much to this end; it is through common efforts to solve common problems that a sense of community evolves.

The transformation that has made of Canada a highly productive industrial economy has been total, not merely economic. Indeed, it could not be otherwise. The hallmark of modern industrialism is not merely rapid technological change, but also the fact that technological change is cumulative. Each advance is an attempt to solve existing problems; to the extent that it successfully solves them, it creates new problems which call for further technological change. Thus, a progressive industrial economy is one that is continuously transforming itself by its own internal dynamics.

Under construction is Ontario Hydro's Lambton Generating Station on the St. Clair River, 14 miles south of Sarnia. Scheduled for completion in 1971 the four-unit thermal electric plant will have a capacity of 2,000,000 kilowatts.

One of the world's most modern rod mills came into operation at a large basic steel plant at Hamilton, Ont., in late 1966. The components of its complex control system have been miniaturized to fit snugly into an unusually compact area.

INDUSTRIAL SOCIETY

The Macdonald-Cartier Freeway which commemorates two of the principal architects of Confederation extends across Central Canada, linking its two major metropolitan centres, Toronto and Montreal.

An economy of this type cannot function and survive unless the society within which it exists is so organized as to generate the necessary skills and intelligence and to absorb without self-destructive stresses the tensions that continuous cumulative change in production and distribution imposes on it. Both of these problems—that of supplying the industrial economy with the type and quantity of human resources which it requires, and that of adapting to the new human relationships that technology imposes—require a social system of quite unusual flexibility. The capacity to absorb innovations must be at least as high as the capacity to generate them. This is one reason why so few societies have successfully achieved the transition to modern economic growth.

## Transition

Organizational change in every aspect of Canadian life, from the family to the Federal Government, has been the concomitant of the transition to a society capable of sustained growth. Industrialism, whether by its products (the social impact of the automobile on urban property values, birth rates, government capital formation, and a host of other variables has been the subject of much speculation and some rigorous analysis), or by the type of social relationships it engenders (for example, the problems of industrial morale, of strikes and mass unemployment) sets its imprint on all society.

For Canada the transition has not been without its difficulties, even though these have probably been less in the aggregate than for societies with a stronger heritage of feudal values. Some of the dimensions of the transformation stand out clearly when one considers the contrast between the Canada of the 1860's and the Canada of a century later.

Canada in the late 1860's was already a highly-commercialized economy, if indeed one may refer to it as a single economy. Descriptions of the pioneer agricultural community, isolated from the challenges and insecurities of the price system and relying on kinship ties to cope with personal and social emergencies, should be taken for the myths they are, not as representations of reality. There was no area of life in the Canadian colonies, from the wharves and shipyards of Quebec to the trading posts of Hudson Bay or the settlements in Red River and Vancouver, that was unaffected by the tides of international commerce, the movements of prices and interest rates, and the changing patterns of trade and investment. It was, however, a highly decentralized economy, both geographically and in terms of organizational structure. The provinces themselves were loosely integrated by commercial connections; most of them traded more with the outside world than they did with their partners in the new confederation. With the significant exception of a few large chartered companies, particularly in banking, the typical unit of enterprise, whether farm or factory, was small and based on locally-available raw materials. Short-term credit, extended through banks and mercantile houses and based in the last analysis on the resources of firms in England, financed the processing and shipment of goods. Long-term capital investments—Canada's hostages to fortune—were to be found principally in the canal and railroad system of the St. Lawrence lowlands and in the emerging cities of that area.

## Nineteenth Century Economy

An economy such as this, whose life blood is essentially the export trade in staples to more advanced areas, is often described as open or exposed, terms which suggest its vulnerability to movements in demand, prices, and technology over which it can exercise little or no control. Economic historians have made much of this aspect of the Canadian economy in the nineteenth century, and although one could wish for more comparative information (were fluctuations in prices and incomes really more severe in Canada than in, say, the United States or Great Britain?) there is little doubt that the pace of economic activity was very uneven. In general, the fact that upwards of 80 per cent of the labour force was engaged in agriculture, or in activities closely related to agriculture, provided a measure of protection against the extremes of economic distress. Unemployment or underemployment in agriculture can be a problem, but it is less of an obvious social problem than industrial unemployment in the cities. A measure of economic and psychological security was probably also to be found in the family system, although it is surely stretching the facts to think of the typical Canadian family of the 1860's, at least outside the Province of Quebec, as a tightly-knit kinship group of the type known to anthropologists in other cultures. Against seasonal and short-term cyclical fluctuations, these social arrangements gave the individual some sense of security; and, of course, if the future in Canada seemed unreasonably black or meaningless, there was always the deceptively easy recourse of emigration to the United States.

# Economic Changes

Technological change, in the form of cheap iron, the steam engine, and the railroad was already in the late 1860's influencing the potentials for Canada's development and the means available to realize those potentials. Reductions in transportation costs, both on the north Atlantic and in the St. Lawrence lowlands, helped to integrate Canadian communities with each other and to tie them ever more closely to markets in Britain and the United States. Diversification of economic activity increased as small-scale manufacturing developed in southern Ontario to supplement the old staple trades of timber, potash, and wheat. Most important of all, it was the new technology of the steam railroad that made Canadian confederation a realizable idea, for without low-cost overland transportation of bulk commodities the settlement of the Canadian West was impossible. Transcontinental confederation and transcontinental railroads were therefore inextricably linked together. Political integration of the British North American colonies depended on railroad construction, and the financing of railroad construction depended on the borrowing powers of the new Dominion.

Among the primary economic responsibilities of the new Federal Government was therefore the exploitation of the potentials of the new technology of the railroad to create an extensive frontier of settlement in Western Canada, to be based on low-cost production of cereals for the markets of industrial Europe. This was to remain a central concern of federal economic and social policy for the remainder of the nineteenth century and into the third decade of the twentieth. More was involved than just the creation of a new region of staple production, for the obverse of the new wheat and settlement frontier in Western Canada was the creation of a new urban industrial frontier in the east, the whole to form a simple linear structure of complementary regional specialization. What was being created, in short, was the Canada of today.

# Nation-Building

There is no need to dwell here on the difficulties and setbacks encountered in this first phase of Canadian nation-building. Two points, however, may be stressed. In the first place, the economic structure that was being developed, though it might be larger, more productive, and more viable than the old regional economies out of which it grew, did not in itself hold out much promise of greater economic or social stability. Precisely because of the high degree of regional specialization involved, vulnerability to external disturbance was probably increased. Efficiency, and the promise of higher incomes per head that efficiency held out, called for massive increases in scale and intimate involvement in the movements of prices on international markets. Thus an economy was being created in which the welfare of entire areas and very large numbers of people depended on the price of a single commodity.

The problems latent here were to become very real in the 1930's, and at that time were to call forth significant innovations in social policy. In the second place, although it occasioned less public discussion and lacked the drama of the new western frontier, the industrialization and urbanization of Central Canada was no less an integral part of the strategy of Canadian development than was the opening of the West. And in this area, too, problems for the future were being created of which there was little comprehension at the time. Contemporary discussion centred—as to a large extent

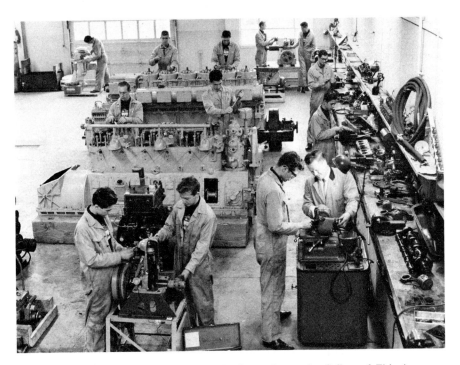

Future marine engineering officers receive instruction at the College of Fisheries, Navigation, Marine Engineering and Electronics.

it still does—on the tariff and railroad rate structures, and the degree to which they benefited certain regions and injured others.

What was not seen, or if seen was not conceived of as a potential set of problems, was that a new frontier was being created in Eastern Canada as well as in the West: a frontier of urban industrialism. This was a frontier of which Canadians, like their counterparts in the United States, had little experience. Indeed, they would have thought it nonsense to call it a frontier. Yet this intensive frontier of the city and the factory—a frontier not of sparse settlements and physical isolation but of dense agglomerations and psychological isolation—was to provide some of the major challenges to Canadian social policy in the mid-twentieth century, just as it was to provide some of the major sources of growth.

Whether social problems of the new urban industrial frontier are more intractable than those of the typical nineteenth-century raw-material-producing frontier may be an interesting question to debate, but for Canada the answer is irrelevant. Canada in the mid-twentieth century has both types of frontier and both types of human problem to deal with. The extensive frontier is now, to be sure, largely a highly-capitalized frontier of large resource development projects, but the problems of isolation, communications, and distance are not dissimilar to those encountered earlier in the country's history. This is a road Canada has travelled before. It is the problems of the urban frontier that are new and that present the greater challenge to creative imagination and intelligent policy. Canada is not, of course, alone in facing these

Niagara Falls is not only an historic source of industrial power but also an important tourist attraction. Now, with the addition of the $12,000,000 International Centre towering nearly 600 feet above the Falls, with a revolving dining room in the dome which rotates full circle each hour, diners have a panoramic view of this famous site.

problems, for in a sense they are the typical problems of a highly-developed industrialized society in the twentieth century. But it may be that Canada has special opportunities to assist in their solution.

What is involved is preservation of quality, individuality, and community in a society characterized by large organizations, intense occupational specialization, and very rapid technological change. The successful exploitation of technology has precipitated Canada into the world of modern industrialism—a world of large corporations and labour unions, ubiquitous government, mass distribution and consumption, extensive and increasing mechanization and, for the individual, insecurities and anxieties of a sort with which he finds it very difficult to cope. The appropriate guidelines for policy in this complex mosaic are not entirely clear, nor can they be until greater agreement emerges as to how much of the tremendous productivity of modern technology is to be devoted to improving the quality of human life and how much to increasing the measurable output of goods and services.     (HUGH G. J. AITKEN)

# Public Health

There is an old saying—Health is Wealth. If this is true, Canada today is a wealthy country, thanks to 100 years of progress made by workers in medical and other associated disciplines. Many interrelated forces and developments have shaped the course of health advances during the past century. Predominating factors were the great bacteriological discoveries, voluntary initiative, and increasing governmental responsibility in the provision of health services.

## 1867-1914

At the time of Confederation, the meagre references to health responsibilities among the powers delegated to the federal and provincial governments under the British North America Act reflected the limited concept of the role of government as regards organized action in public health and welfare. Thus, the Federal Government was assigned jurisdiction over "quarantine and the establishment and maintenance of marine hospitals", and the provinces were given powers relating to "the establishment, maintenance and management of hospitals, asylums, charities, and eleemosynary institutions". The basic idea was that regulatory measures in health matters needed only to be adopted in emergencies such as epidemics, or for purposes of ensuring elementary sanitation in urban municipalities. Such activities as were undertaken were almost wholly a function of local governments. Similarly, welfare was regarded as a local problem concerned with providing means of segregating destitute and disease-stricken persons and supplying their elemental needs; often the poorhouse was the only available facility.

Provincial governments concerned themselves only with a few special facilities beyond the capacities of local resources; for example, the confinement of the insane in poorhouses and common jails was considered unsatisfactory, and before Confederation efforts had been made in most provinces to provide separate accommodation. Mental asylums were the first special facilities to be set up under provincial control. Other examples were the establishment of the Ontario School for the Deaf in 1870, the Ontario School for the Blind in 1872, and the Orillia Asylum for the care of mental defectives in 1876. But the primary health problem of the day was the recurring epidemics of cholera, typhus, and smallpox; maritime quarantine was the only known control technique and this was a federal responsibility.

The bacteriological studies of Pasteur (1870) and Koch (1892) transformed the basis of public health work. The new knowledge led to the development of provincial regulatory measures and administrative machinery to control the spread of disease. The passage of public health regulations and the establishment of permanent provincial boards of health in Ontario in 1882, Quebec in 1886, and New Brunswick in 1887, permitted more effective control. The Ontario Public Health Act of 1884 gave authority to the provincial board to make regulations for the prevention or mitigation of disease and outlined the powers and responsibilities of local boards of health. The chief duties of provincial boards were to make investigations into the origins of disease and the effects of employment conditions, habits, etc., on the health of the people. The local boards were required to enforce quarantine, conduct disinfection, impose compulsory vaccination and obtain supplies of vaccine. When outbreaks of typhoid were traced to milk and water contamination, the area of inspection was extended to include dairies and meat supplies.

The inability of municipalities to administer adequately their mandatory functions dimmed the prospect of effective enforcement action. The usual approach was to employ a sanitary inspector without special training and a local physician as part-time health officer. At the turn of the century, leaders in public health began to urge the appointment of physicians qualified in public health who would devote their entire time to the administration of sanitary measures, and recommended that counties or districts be set up as administrative units in health matters.

At an early stage it was recognized that the new bacteriological knowledge could not be fully applied without the aid of public health laboratory facilities. The high prevalence of diphtheria was a stimulus for action. The establishment of the first provincial public health laboratory in Toronto in 1890 represented one of the earliest undertakings in public diagnostic bacteriology on the continent. Systematic examination of suspected diphtheria swabs and suspected typhoid fever gradually extended to analysis of water, food and milk.

The basic development of health services prior to World War I was largely a matter for private initiative, philanthropy, and voluntary development. Following in the tradition of the Hotel Dieu, founded in Quebec City in 1639, increasing numbers of hospitals were being established by religious and charitable organizations to help meet the desperate needs of the sick poor. The establishment of these facilities in centres of population helped to prepare the way for substantial advances in skilled medical and surgical attention and nursing care which began to emerge towards the end of the nineteenth century. Trained nurses and medical personnel were added to the hospital staffs, and the organization of hospital facilities was extended to include maternity departments, isolation rooms, and separate rooms for operations and anaesthetic purposes.

Approximately 362,000 refrigerators were produced in Canada in 1965. Rare is the household without one—or a youngster without a means of access to its contents.

CANADA, 1867-1967

Groups of citizens with common interests in certain health problems began to organize for a specific activity towards the end of the nineteenth century. The oldest of today's great national voluntary health organizations, the St. John Ambulance Association, was first established in Montreal in 1884, and the Canadian Red Cross Society in 1896. The Victorian Order of Nurses was founded in Canada in 1897 to bring into the home the new conception of nursing services. Tuberculosis prevention was built almost entirely on the basis of the work of voluntary associations. The National Sanatorium Association, founded in 1897, and the Canadian Association for the Prevention of Tuberculosis (subsequently known as the Canadian Tuberculosis Association), founded in 1900, succeeded in enlisting co-operation for the formation of societies to establish sanatoria, employ visiting nurses and conduct educational campaigns. Accordingly, by the beginning of World War I, more than 20 sanatoria had been built as a result of private initiative and philanthropy, while tuberculosis visiting was carried out under the auspices of the Victorian Order of Nurses, sanatoria and dispensaries.

## 1915-1944

The continuing advances in medical science and the accelerated rate of social change produced by World War I had important implications for the future status of public health. In the Connaught Laboratories of the University of Toronto, Canada had produced all the tetanus antitoxin required for her Armed Forces during the War. An historic event in the annals of medicine was the discovery of insulin by Dr. Frederick Banting and Charles H. Best in 1921, and the subsequent handing over of the product to the University of Toronto to be patented and produced at a minimal cost to the public. The introduction of a permanent protection against diphtheria through the use of toxoid developed by Ramon in 1923 at the Pasteur Institute, Paris, revolutionized techniques in communicable disease control. Canada was the first country outside France to initiate the use of this toxoid in the immunization of school children.

The growing demand for better conditions of social and economic life aroused governments to consider their role in providing more effective leadership in health and social welfare. Prior to 1919 federal health activities were divided mainly between the Departments of Agriculture, Marine and Fisheries and Inland Revenue, with additional functions assigned to the Conservation Commission.

In 1919 a federal Department of Health was established and the Dominion Council of Health was made the co-ordinating agency in federal and provincial health efforts. The introduction of conditional grants-in-aid to the provinces for the control of venereal disease, the establishment of a national public health laboratory and the passage of legislation requiring informative labelling in the sale of food and drugs were effected by 1921. At the same time, a major task of the Federal Government was the provision of pension benefits and the retraining and treatment services for disabled war veterans. In 1928 the federal Departments of Health and Soldiers' Civil Re-establishment were merged to form the Department of Pensions and National Health. In the provincial sphere, provincial boards of health were replaced gradually by departments of health as the chief executive agency. New Brunswick established the first Ministry of Health in 1918. The public health laboratory was one of the earliest provincial services developed to assist local public health departments. Provincial public health nursing services were developed, beginning in Manitoba in 1916, to assist municipalities to undertake local programs of immunization and child health protection. Certain specialized services, notably tuberculosis and venereal disease control, which were originally the responsibility of the local authorities were taken over for administrative purposes by some provincial governments. In the 1930's two additional special disease areas, cancer and poliomyelitis, began to claim attention, and provincial grants were allocated to permit designated hospitals to set up and equip specialized treatment facilities.

The Canadian Society for the Control of Cancer, subsequently named the Canadian Cancer Society, was organized in 1938. Severe epidemic occurrences of poliomyelitis in Western Canada led the government of Alberta in 1938 to adopt a program of free hospital, medical and surgical care to counter widespread paralytic effects of this disease.

The basic responsibility for implementing preventive programs, however, remained with the local boards of health, and the large centres of population alone could afford to support the full-time staff and organization necessary to conduct immunizations, school health inspection, sanitary inspection, as well as field surveillance in tuberculosis and venereal disease control. Voluntary organizations in many instances undertook

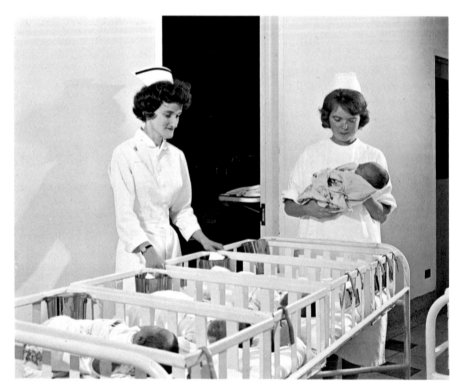

These infants, born in a Quebec hospital, helped Canada to attain a population of 20,000,000 in 1966.

CANADA, 1867-1967

Sunnybrook Hospital, Toronto, is a familiar name to veterans of the two World Wars. In 1965 the hospital was transferred to the University of Toronto but priority use of 1,200 beds was retained for veterans.

to set up child health immunization and home visiting services for the control of communicable disease. There are numerous examples of their pioneer work prior to the complete organization of provincial public health nursing services. The Victorian Order of Nurses and the Canadian Red Cross Society each helped to initiate child welfare and public health nursing programs, particularly in the eastern provinces. The Canadian Tuberculosis Association encouraged the formation of diagnostic clinics and organized the first chest diagnostic X-ray service beginning in the mid-1920's.

Various efforts were made to strengthen the position of local governments. Through the assistance of the Rockefeller Foundation, trial projects were initiated in seven provinces which demonstrated the effectiveness of grouped municipal areas (a county equivalent, in some provinces) as administrative units for the provision of full-time health services. In most instances, the provinces undertook to pay one half the cost of permanent operation.

Various co-operative systems were employed to overcome the problem of unequal distribution of medical services and hospital facilities in sparsely-settled areas of Western Canada. Legislation was passed in Saskatchewan (1916), Manitoba (1920), and Alberta (1929), permitting a municipal district to approve a scheme to engage the services of a physician, provided that a maximum salary rate was not exceeded. The plan was widely adopted by rural municipalities in Saskatchewan; by 1936 about one fifth of the rural population was covered. A similar type of co-operative planning was utilized in Manitoba, Saskatchewan and Alberta in the construction and operation of union and municipal hospitals.

The impact of the depression and the drought made the problem of providing health services more complicated. Despite federal-provincial financial aid, municipalities were obliged to assume an increasingly heavy burden of unemployment relief, as well as the major portion of the cost of hospital and medical services for indigent patients.

Although provincial governments had assumed a large part of the cost of mental hospital care and were providing larger grants for tuberculosis care as well as statutory per diem grants to public hospitals for paying and non-paying patients, the total cost to the municipalities of various types of hospitalization was beyond their ability to pay, with the result that, in poorer provinces especially, municipalities frequently refused to guarantee payment of indigent hospital care unless a patient's condition was deemed to require emergency treatment. Non-payment of medical fees was also a source of acute embarrassment to municipal governments.

The position in which municipalities were placed forced upon provincial and federal governments the urgency of consideration of unemployment insurance, medical and nursing care and other social legislation. In several provinces health insurance plans were the subject of special studies. Health insurance legislation was passed in Alberta in 1935, and in British Columbia in 1936, but lack of success in negotiating terms on which to base the programs prevented the measures from being put into effect. In Ontario the provincial government and medical profession entered into a co-operative arrangement in 1935 whereby indigent persons would be served, and the profession would receive at least partial remuneration, expenditures being shared two thirds by the province and one third by the municipality. In Newfoundland the depression produced the earliest government-sponsored plan (1935) to provide prepaid medical care to large numbers of population. Through a chain of small, widely-distributed "cottage hospitals", hospital service and domiciliary medical care were made available for a small annual fee to residents of remote outports.

The financial collapse of local governments in the face of unprecedented welfare needs and the further evidence that provincial revenues were not sufficient to rescue municipalities from their plight led to the setting up of the Royal Commission on Dominion-Provincial Relations in 1937. Expressions of the need for federal financial aid to assist and stimulate provincial programs of health, hospital and medical care

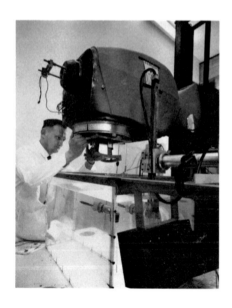

The gamma ray beam in the head of this cancer therapy machine is tested before final assembly. The therapy units service more than 200,000 cancer patients annually in many countries throughout the world.

came not only from the report of the Commission but also from the Dominion Council of Health and representatives of medical and other organizations.

Following the outbreak of World War II, an advisory Committee on Health Insurance was set up by the Federal Government in February 1942. In a report to the House of Commons Committee on Social Security in 1943, it endorsed the principle of national health insurance and emphasized that preventive services should form an essential part of such a program. Included in the Committee's report was a draft bill providing for health insurance on a nation-wide basis under provincial administration, and proposing a health insurance grant together with a series of public health grants to the provinces. The series of studies for the Special Committee on Social Security also included a report on *Social Security for Canada* (Marsh Report). To effect co-ordination in the postwar planning of comprehensive social measures and to carry on established federal health functions, legislation was passed in 1944 setting up the Department of National Health and Welfare. A separate department of veterans affairs was also formed at this time to deal exclusively with war veterans' measures.

## 1945-1967

In 1945, a Dominion-Provincial Conference on Reconstruction was convened to discuss postwar economic and social development. Influenced by a growing tendency on the part of the provinces to support the adoption of a health insurance program in progressive stages, the federal health proposals, while endorsing a flexible plan of health insurance, gave emphasis to a program of increased grants to the provinces to develop a solid base of hospital and public health services on which a national insurance scheme might be built.

The National Health Grants Program introduced in 1948 provided for ten categories of assistance related to health surveys (basic studies of health needs and resources of all the provinces), hospital construction, professional training for health personnel, public health research, general public health, mental health, tuberculosis, cancer, venereal disease, and crippling conditions in children. Three new grants were added in 1953—child and maternal health, medical rehabilitation, and laboratory and diagnostic services. In 1961 a consolidation was effected in certain grant categories: the laboratory and radiological services grant and the venereal disease control grant were absorbed into the general public health grant, and the medical rehabilitation and crippled children grants were combined. Initially the annual outlay for these grants was $30,000,000; for the fiscal year 1966-67 the appropriation was more than $67,000,000.

Aided materially by the national health grants, the provinces undertook a planned expansion of their health services. Increased provincial budgets lightened the burden of financial responsibility of local governments, e.g., municipal payments to tuberculosis sanatoria and mental hospital care were eliminated in most provinces. Centralized programs to combat tuberculosis, mental illness, venereal disease, cancer and other diseases were further developed under the aegis of departments of health or through subsidies to special agencies.

The scope and availability of preventive services was greatly extended. By 1952, with the assistance of national health grants, the use of a triple antigen in immunization (H. pertussis, tetanus toxoid and diphtheria toxoid) had become general throughout Canada. Similar assistance was given to extend the use of antimicrobial drugs, in

Marsh Lake, one of the many scenic spots of the Yukon Territory, is yearly attracting an increasing number of tourists.

particular to make supplies of streptomycin readily available for distribution to tuberculosis patients who might benefit from this form of therapy. About the same time Canadian scientists were engaged in the development of a process which was to play an important part in the successful production of Salk vaccine. The Connaught Laboratories developed a medium suitable for the growing of poliomyelitis virus and for a number of years supplied a large part of the culture fluids which were used by pharmaceutical manufacturers in the United States in the preparation of the vaccine. Beginning in 1945, controlled experiments were undertaken in three Ontario communities, in co-operation with federal and provincial health departments, to study the effect of mechanically-fluoridated drinking water on dental health. The positive results of the project led to the widespread use of water fluoridation, which now covers more than 4,000,000 people in Canada.

With the enormous decline in the incidence of communicable disease, the magnitude of the problems of chronic disability and degenerative diseases claimed public attention. Pioneer rehabilitation programs had been worked out for recipients of workmen's compensation and war disability pensions. In 1951 a National Conference on Rehabilitation was convened, and in subsequent years medical and vocational services for civilian disabled persons were developed in the provinces, supported partly by assistance from national health grants, and the federal Department of Labour. In 1955 provision was made for a federal-provincial income maintenance program for permanently and totally disabled persons. New national voluntary societies, formed to voice the special health needs of patients suffering from particular forms of chronic disease or disability, called for programs of research, public education and medical rehabilitation.

344

Among the national voluntary agencies founded in the postwar period were the Canadian Paraplegic Association (1945), Canadian Arthritis and Rheumatism Society (1948), Canadian Foundation for Poliomyelitis (1948), Multiple Sclerosis Society of Canada (1948), Canadian Diabetic Association (1953), The Canadian Council for Crippled Children (1953), Muscular Dystrophy Association (1954), and the Canadian Heart Foundation (1956). Physical rehabilitation centres, specialized hospitals to treat the handicapped child, and hospital departments for physical medicine were organized under voluntary auspices.

Organized services for the mentally ill, who had suffered from lack of resources and public apathy throughout the first half of the century, were affected by several important postwar developments. Dramatic changes in mental hospital treatment methods followed the advent of drug therapy in the early 1950's. The "day hospital" was first introduced in 1946 as an experimental form of hospitalization for psychiatric patients at the Allan Memorial Institute of Psychiatry in Montreal. The growth of psychiatric units in general hospitals contributed new resources to the treatment of mental illness and, by 1966, the annual number of admissions was approaching the number admitted to mental hospitals. The growing emphasis given to the role of the community and its resources in treatment and rehabilitation of the mentally ill and the mentally retarded owes much to the work of groups of voluntary citizens* whose efforts have contributed to the setting up of such projects as day care centres, sheltered workshops, boarding home care and social centres for discharged patients.

In the realm of active-treatment hospital care, various provincial governments were subsidizing hospital care for some specific diseases, assisting in paying the cost of care directly for various indigent groups and were providing regular maintenance grants to hospitals. Comprehensive, public prepaid hospital care plans for the whole population had been introduced by Saskatchewan in 1947 and British Columbia in 1949, while Alberta and Newfoundland operated insurance plans covering a portion of the population. It was in this setting that a federal offer to assist in the establishment of a nation-wide hospital insurance program through grants-in-aid was made to the provinces in January 1956, and that the Hospital Insurance and Diagnostic Services Act was enacted the following year. Five provinces participated when the national program commenced on July 1, 1958, and all the remaining provinces and territories had joined the program by January 1, 1961.

Under the hospital insurance legislation, the Federal Government pays approximately 50 per cent of the national sharable cost of active and chronic hospital care. Participating provinces are required to ensure that certain basic hospital services (public ward care and other specified inpatient services, including laboratory and diagnostic procedures), are universally available as insured benefits to all residents. Outpatient services, although not mandatory, are included in the program. More than 98 per cent of the Canadian population is now insured for hospital care benefits under this program.

Provincial personal health care programs for specified groups of public assistance recipients have developed in seven provinces: Newfoundland, Nova Scotia, Ontario, Manitoba, Saskatchewan, Alberta, and British Columbia. The Federal Government

---

*Organized under the auspices of the Canadian Mental Health Association (formerly the National Committee for Mental Hygiene, and reconstituted under its present title in 1950) and the Canadian Association for Retarded Children (founded in 1958).

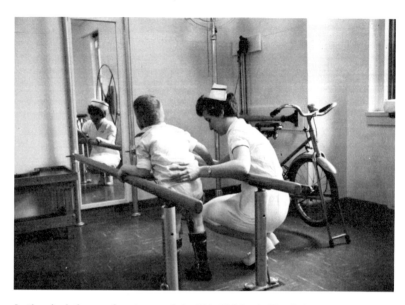

In the physiotherapy department of the Sick Children's Hospital, Toronto, a young patient tries out his braces. In 1965 there were 1,452 public, private and federal hospitals operating in Canada.

supplies such care to recipients of war veterans' allowances, and an expanded program of health care for Indians and Eskimos has been developed in the postwar period under the auspices of the Department of National Health and Welfare. For the general population, there has been a vast development of voluntary health insurance programs by commercial and voluntary non-profit insurance agencies. In 1962, the first insurance plan to provide a comprehensive range of physicians' services to the entire population of a province was introduced in Saskatchewan. Recent programs in Alberta (1963), British Columbia (1965), and Ontario (1966), are all designed to make physicians' services insurance available on a voluntary basis and include provision to subsidize premium payments for persons with little or no taxable income.

During 1964-65, the federally-appointed Royal Commission on Health Services published the results of its inquiry into the status of health services in Canada. The core of its recommendations was contained in its declaration "for the nation to achieve its health goals, a universal, comprehensive health service program should be available to all Canadians". In response to this report the Federal Government proposed in 1965 that a comprehensive medical care program be introduced in 1967. As an interim measure, it was proposed that health care for public assistance recipients should be included as part of the Canada Assistance Plan to be launched in 1966. In anticipation of expanding health services, the Federal Government announced its intention to introduce legislation at the 1966 session of Parliament to set up a $500,000,000 health resources fund to assist in capital expansion of medical, dental, nursing and related training and research facilities in the next fifteen years.

Because of its many dedicated public servants and its thousands of voluntary workers Canada may well look back with pride on its record in the field of public health and look forward to advances even more sweeping in the century ahead.

(Prepared under the direction of Dr. J. N. Crawford.)

# Social Welfare

Social welfare in Canada during the country's early development was shaped by practices which had prevailed in France and England when the colonies were established. In Lower Canada, the home of the majority of French-speaking Canadians, the tradition of Catholic charity nurtured by religious orders was transplanted, while settlers in Nova Scotia and New Brunswick brought with them the philosophy and practice of the Elizabethan poor law. Upper Canada, though first settled in large part by English-speaking United Empire Loyalists, rejected the English poor law, and introduced instead a variety of public and voluntary measures. By the middle of the nineteenth century arrangements to meet some of the most pressing social welfare needs had been made in most of the settled areas, either through public or voluntary action, and some initiative was being taken at the provincial level.

When Canada became a self-governing federal state in 1867 social security programs in the modern sense were not envisaged or anticipated, and therefore the respective areas of jurisdiction of federal and provincial governments in the field of social security were not made explicit in the British North America Act. However, charities and charitable institutions were assigned to the provinces, and penitentiaries to the Federal Government. While social welfare in Quebec and the Maritime Provinces continued to develop gradually along previously-established lines, new types of measures were taken in Ontario, notably in the field of child welfare. These were influential in the formation of programs in other parts of Canada, particularly in the western provinces where the emphasis on public programs was especially marked.

From the turn of the present century onwards the social services were extended and consolidated. The provinces strengthened existing programs and established new ones—workmen's compensation, measures on behalf of neglected and dependent children and of widowed mothers. The Federal Government established pensions for veterans of World War I and their survivors, old age pensions in 1927, pensions for the blind in 1937, and unemployment relief measures and social assistance to war veterans in the 1930's.

The transformation of Canada from a predominantly rural-agricultural to an urban-industrial society, the limited financial resources of some provinces to provide minimum standards of social welfare, and the inadequacies of the voluntary and public service programs, exposed so dramatically during the depression of the 1930's, resulted in persistent demands for a nation-wide system of social security. Traditionally, welfare services developed under local and provincial auspices, and the interpretation of the British North America Act with regard to income maintenance programs left the question of federal jurisdiction in doubt.

Demands to introduce social insurance and social assistance programs on a national basis mounted over the years in Parliament. In the light of this situation, three different approaches were used to meet the constitutional problem. One was the establishment of federal grants-in-aid; the first major step was the legislation for the aged and blind, designed to establish a nation-wide federal-provincial system of pensions. This method was also used extensively in the depression of the 1930's for unemployment aid. The second involved amending the British North America Act with the agreement of the provinces to give the Federal Government authority in specific areas such as unemployment insurance and old age pensions. The third approach was the establishment of family allowances and veterans' programs which required no constitutional amendment.

The continued development and improvement of social welfare programs were being shaped by the impact of massive and pervading social and economic change: by the experience of the depression and of World War II; by the rapid industrialization and urban concentration that followed; and by an increasing awareness of the interdependence of social and economic measures. Comprehensive nation-wide social security programs for postwar Canada were set out in the Marsh Report on Social Security in 1943 and in the federal proposals of 1945 to the Dominion-Provincial Conference on Reconstruction.

The design of Canadian social security has been fashioned with considerable flexibility by historical and constitutional influences, in response to evolving and increasing social needs. At the same time, Canada's social welfare system has had a rather piecemeal development. It could be expected that a growing demand for integration of social security programs would emerge. Such a reform is now in process, signalized by a co-ordinated social insurance system—the Canada and Quebec Pension Plans—complemented by a comprehensive social assistance program—the Canada Assistance Plan.

The dynamic development of Canadian social welfare has been marked, particularly in the past three or four decades, by an increasing intervention of the Federal Government in both the operation and the financing of welfare programs. An index of the increasing financial role of the Federal Government is reflected in the shift in welfare expenditures from local to provincial government and from local and provincial to the federal level of government. In 1926 public welfare expenditures were about $86,000,000 of which $49,000,000 were federal and the balance shared equally by the provinces and the municipalities. In the fiscal year 1964-65 expenditures totalled $2,894,000,000, of which 82 per cent was federal, 16 per cent provincial, and 2 per cent municipal.

Quebec has, in recent years, broadened the scope of its activities and has indicated its desire to operate and finance its own social welfare programs. A provincial schooling allowance program was established in 1961 and the Quebec Pension Plan in 1965. Quebec governments have indicated their desire to contract out of shared-cost programs and have worked out arrangements with the Federal Government to this end.

A more significant partnership between the federal and provincial governments has been developing in the sixties in the formulation and administration of welfare programs. This is assisted by more frequent federal-provincial welfare conferences of Ministers, Deputy Ministers and officials. The National Council of Welfare, established in 1963, comprising the ten provincial Deputy Ministers of Welfare and ten non-government representatives with the federal Deputy Minister of Welfare as Chairman, brings together representatives of public and private welfare in Canada to advise the Minister of National Health and Welfare.

## Private Agencies

Throughout Canada's history it has been the private welfare agencies that have pioneered in the development of social welfare services. The first children's aid society was established in Toronto in 1891, and the first prisoner's aid society in Montreal in 1892. The first Canadian Conference of Charities and Corrections, a forerunner of the Canadian Conference on Social Work, was held in Montreal in 1898. In 1899 the first family agency, now the Family Welfare Association, was established; and the first probation service was organized in Ottawa in 1906 by the Ottawa Children's Aid

Murray Harbour, a typically charming community of Prince Edward Island, was Eskwadek, or "the fishing place", of the native Micmac Indians. The harbour and river of the same name are still popular with anglers and tourists.

Society. In 1914, the first graduate school of social work was organized in Toronto. The first community chest was established in Montreal in 1917 while 40 years later the United Appeal was instituted in Toronto, marking a trend away from the community chest approach.

Many of the advances in social welfare initiated and operated by private institutions have received government encouragement and financial support. In Quebec, private institutions assisted by public funds operate essential services which elsewhere are provided publicly. By supplementing government social welfare measures, stimulating interest and promoting action on welfare, private agencies constitute one of the most vital components of the social welfare system.

The Canadian Welfare Council, established in 1920, is the voluntary agency clearinghouse and the medium for co-operative welfare planning and action. Through its divisions of child and family welfare, chests and councils, public welfare, research and special projects, and corrections, the Council serves also as the headquarters of local agencies in these fields. A provincial welfare council, established in Ontario, carries on similar functions in that province. Local community chests and councils play a key role in co-ordinating, planning and developing welfare services in the community.

SOCIAL WELFARE                                                                            349

A national welfare forum for many years has been the Canadian Conference on Social Welfare. Other conferences are now providing specialized forums. In 1960 Canada's first National Conference on Children was convened; a second was held in 1965. A National Conference on the Family, held in 1964, was followed in 1965 by the establishment of the Vanier Institute of the Family. The first Canadian Conference on Aging was held in 1966.

Social welfare in Canada has developed through three main streams or approaches: social assistance and welfare services; social insurance; universal payments. The rationale of each of these courses and the specific directions taken are worthy of note.

## Social Assistance and Welfare Services

**Child Welfare Services**—For years provincial child welfare programs developed and provided services for the protection of neglected and dependent children, services for the unmarried mother and her child, adoption services, and foster home care. The program may be administered by the provincial authority or the administration may be delegated to specified voluntary agencies, including religious organizations. Children's aid societies, to which authority is delegated in five provinces, are voluntary agencies with local boards of directors, chartered, supervised, and generally assisted financially by provincial departments. Services are operated provincially in Saskatchewan, Prince Edward Island, Newfoundland, and Alberta. In Ontario and New Brunswick, services are administered by a network of children's aid societies and in British Columbia, Manitoba, and Nova Scotia, by children's aid societies in the more populated areas, and by the province elsewhere. In Quebec, substantial financial aid is given by the province to a variety of recognized voluntary agencies and institutions caring for children, for preventive and rehabilitative work among neglected and dependent children, and for youth protection schools. Thus, as the nature and scope of these services have increased and as the amount of provincial financial support has likewise increased the extent of provincial involvement has also grown.

Institutional services for children have been developed under the auspices of provincial authorities or voluntary agencies. Among current trends are the increasing use of small specialized institutions for emotionally-disturbed children and the development of group foster homes for children who find it difficult to adjust to the requirements of foster family living. Continued emphasis is being placed upon the early adoption placement of children, and several provinces have developed a province-wide clearance service, particularly for children difficult to place because of age, physical handicaps, or other reasons.

One of the most important developments in providing income support for widowed mothers with dependent children occurred during World War I when the Province of Manitoba introduced in 1916 its Mothers' Allowances legislation. Subsequently, during the war and postwar period, other provinces followed this approach and before long a network of provincial programs was developed across Canada.

**Assistance and Services to the Aged**—In the first decade of the 20th century there was discussion in the Federal Parliament concerning some type of legislation to give income support to older people in need. It was decided in 1908, however, that government legislation in this field should be restricted to providing government annuities through which people could contribute during their working life in order to make provision for their old age. Old age pension legislation was not introduced until 1926, but

Housing for the elderly and needy is tailored to suit the needs of the various communities throughout Canada. This is Island Lodge, Ottawa, which was opened recently.

the Bill was defeated in the Senate. A year later, following a general election, a new Bill providing old age assistance of $20 a month for all persons of age 70 and over, based on tests of means and residence, was passed by Parliament. The Federal Government would contribute 50 per cent of the cost of pension payments made by provincial governments. British Columbia was the first province to enter the program. During the depression, when it became apparent that the cost to the provinces would be so onerous that some would not participate, the federal share was increased from 50 to 75 per cent. By 1936 all provinces and the Northwest Territories were part of the federal-provincial system of pensions. In 1949 Newfoundland entered Confederation and joined the program, and that year the Yukon initiated payments, making the program effective in all parts of Canada.

In 1950 the Joint Committee of the House of Commons and Senate on Old Age Security recommended a universal flat-rate payment for persons 70 years of age and over to replace the Old Age Pension legislation and a new Old Age Assistance program for persons 65 to 69 based on a means test. These proposals were implemented through federal legislation in 1951 and the provinces put into effect new Old Age Assistance legislation.

Some special conditions of present-day living—such as automation and early retirement, increase of life expectancy, problems of urbanization, and lack of adequate housing—have focused social concern upon services and housing and living arrangements for the aged. With the development of income maintenance programs, visiting homemaker services and organized home care programs, and the extension of visiting nurse services, greater numbers of elderly persons are now able to continue living independently in their own homes. The availability of long-term loans through the Central Mortgage and Housing Corporation has brought about some progress in the provision of self-contained living accommodation for elderly persons. Institutional care for those requiring such arrangements has been increasing and standards for such care are being improved. Over the past few years provincial assistance to homes for the aged and nursing homes in the form of capital grants, maintenance grants, or both, has increased. Local community recreation and social programs for older adults are being developed. Clubs for senior citizens have been widely organized; in some larger communities senior citizens' centres have been established.

Senior citizens' apartment tower, located in the midst of a federal-provincial low-rental housing project, Toronto, typifies the national interest in housing for elderly and low-income families.

Yet much remains to be done. This was apparent from the Report of the Special Committee on Aging in 1966, which made a thorough assessment of the welfare, health, recreational, housing and income security needs of the aged, and submitted recommendations.

**Disability Allowances and Rehabilitation Services**—The first program designed to provide public assistance to disabled persons was introduced by the Federal Government in 1937 when the Old Age Pensions Act was amended to provide pensions for blind persons. Separate legislation, the Blind Persons Act, was passed with respect to allowances for blind persons in 1951. Initially the age of eligibility was 40, but this was eventually lowered to 18.

A number of the provinces became interested in developing programs for disabled persons not covered by the blind persons legislation. The provinces of Ontario and Alberta introduced such programs, and this was followed in 1954 by the Federal Government's enactment of the Disabled Persons Act which made provision for allowances for totally and permanently disabled persons 18 years of age and over. Within a short period of time all provinces were participating in this federal-provincial program.

Significant advances in the development of rehabilitation services have been made, particularly in the postwar years. The Ontario Workmen's Compensation Board was

352

one of the pioneers in Canada and the world to demonstrate the value of a specialized program to rehabilitate injured workmen and to prevent disability. The Rehabilitation Institute and the Occupational Therapy and Rehabilitation Centre in Montreal, the G. F. Strong Rehabilitation Centre in Vancouver, and Lyndhurst Lodge for paraplegics, the Ontario Crippled Children's Centre and Bakerwood of the Canadian National Institute for the Blind, all in Toronto, are a few of the centres developed by voluntary agencies. The national vocational rehabilitation program begun in the 1950's and now administered by the Department of Manpower and Immigration provides federal sharing of the costs of assessment and other rehabilitation services. Since 1954, the medical rehabilitation grant and other grants under the National Health Grant Program and the hospital insurance program have assisted provincial health departments, teaching hospitals, rehabilitation centres and voluntary agencies to extend their rehabilitation services and to train rehabilitation personnel. The National Employment Service developed special placement services for the handicapped, while vocational training of the disabled has been assisted through the federal-provincial Technical and Vocational Training Program. National Welfare Grants and the Canada Assistance Plan are contributing to social rehabilitation measures.

With the support of provincial and local bodies, national agencies have become increasingly active in stimulating interest in broadening services for the handicapped. The Canadian Rehabilitation Council for the Disabled, established in 1962, co-ordinates voluntary rehabilitation activities.

**Unemployment and General Assistance**—Depression years were difficult as the numbers of unemployed steadily increased. Local governments found the burden of relief payments far heavier than they could cope with. They sought aid from their respective provincial governments who, in turn, appealed to the Federal Government. During this period the Federal Government became involved in sharing the cost of relief payments and relief works projects with provincial and municipal governments.

During the 1950's there were pockets of unemployment and representations were made to the Federal Government to provide protection beyond that of the federal unemployment insurance program introduced in 1940. Remedial action was taken in two ways. Unemployment insurance was extended to assist persons whose benefits were being exhausted because of seasonal unemployment. Also, a federal program of unemployment assistance was introduced in 1956, under which the Federal Government shared half the cost of provincial assistance payments above a threshold designed to leave the full cost of assistance for unemployables with the provinces. The legislation was amended in 1957 to remove this threshold and from then on, federal sharing included the costs of all general assistance payments of provinces and municipalities except those for provincial mothers' allowances programs.

**The Canada Assistance Plan**—The Canada Assistance Plan introduced in 1966 provides a basis for the co-ordination of all federal-provincial public assistance programs. Where there were formerly four federal-provincial assistance programs—for the aged, the blind, the disabled, and the unemployed—the provinces may at their option under the Canada Assistance Plan combine all into one single program. Assistance under the Plan is on the basis of an individual's or family's budgetary requirements, as well as available income.

The Plan puts greater emphasis on developing and improving services designed to lessen the amount of dependency. It provides support for the administration of public assistance programs and associated welfare services. Provision is made for special programs to help improve the motivation and work capacity of persons who have unusual difficulty in securing or retaining employment.

Federal aid is given for child and youth welfare services. For the first time there is federal sharing of costs of provincial mothers' allowances programs for needy mothers and their dependent children. For the first time also, the Federal Government contributes to the cost of health care services to assistance recipients. The plan provides for supplementary payments if on the basis of individual or family need other social insurance or social assistance benefits are insufficient.

**Corrections**—The responsibility for correctional service for adults is shared between the federal and provincial governments. The federal penitentiaries system, administered by the Commissioner of Penitentiaries, receives all offenders sentenced by the courts to two years or more. The National Parole Board automatically reviews all sentences of two years or more, and has power to grant, refuse, revoke or suspend parole, and to revoke or suspend any sentence of whipping.

Institutions for offenders serving sentences of less than two years and adult probation services are a provincial responsibility. Seven provinces now have public probation services and their introduction is being planned in others. Voluntary welfare agencies provide after-care services and also some parole supervision.

Correctional services for juveniles are under the jurisdiction of the provinces. Institutions for juvenile delinquents are operated by the provincial authorities or with provincial supervision, by voluntary organizations. During recent years the areas served by juvenile courts have been extended and probation services for juveniles are being developed and extended.

**Welfare Manpower**—There has been an expansion of training facilities since the early 1960's. Enrolment has been increased at the eight existing schools—at Universities of Laval, Montreal, McGill, Ottawa, Toronto, Manitoba and British Columbia and at the Maritime School of Social Work—and new schools are being established at Waterloo Lutheran University and the University of Alberta at Calgary. All provide a two-year graduate course for the Master's degree in social work; McGill and Toronto offer a third year, while the latter has a doctoral program.

Courses leading to the B.A. degree with a major in welfare are offered by Sir George Williams University, Montreal, and Memorial University, St. John's. This type of educational program is being established in other universities.

Vocational training at the post-secondary level for welfare employment is being provided at technological institutes in Toronto, Brandon and Vancouver and active planning of comparable courses is under way at other similar institutions. A wide variety of in-service training programs has been developed by both public and private welfare agencies. A national focal point for the consideration of welfare manpower problems has been the Commission on Education and Personnel for the Social Services established in 1960.

**National Welfare Grants**—These grants, administered by the Department of National Health and Welfare, are designed to develop and strengthen welfare services, to increase the number of trained welfare personnel, and to support welfare research. The program established in 1962 entered its fourth year of operation with an appropriation of $2,000,000 in 1966-67. In some instances projects are aided entirely by the Federal Government while in others federal contributions match those of the provinces.

A broad range of demonstration and other projects designed to assist both public and voluntary welfare services within the provinces are supported. Priority is given to those projects holding promise of making significant steps forward in the organization, co-ordination and staffing of welfare services now being provided, and in the development of new services focused on meeting welfare needs and on the prevention of welfare problems in dependency.

Staff development grants are provided for a variety of staff training programs for welfare personnel in both public and voluntary welfare agencies on direct service, supervisory and administrative levels, where this can be justified as a means of achieving more effective and efficient administration. Financial contributions are made for additional staff in Canadian schools of social work and in field instruction posts thereby making possible a higher enrolment. Welfare bursaries and welfare training grants made by the provinces for students attending schools of social work are assisted. Welfare scholarships and postgraduate fellowships are awarded on a national competitive basis.

**Recreation**—During the postwar years, provincial and local governments together with recreational and sports bodies have done much to develop and extend recreational programs across Canada. With the steady increase in urbanization and with more and more leisure time from industrialization and automation, the growing need for the expansion of recreational activities has long been apparent. After a limited venture into this field under the National Physical Fitness Act of 1943 which was rescinded a decade later, the Fitness and Amateur Sports program of 1961 administered by the Department of National Health and Welfare has added federal support for recreational programs in Canada.

Prospective home-owners have the opportunity to purchase fully-serviced residential building lots at reasonable cost through joint co-operation between federal, provincial and municipal governments. This land assembly project, Corner Brook, Newfoundland, offers an outstanding view of the heart of the city and its environs.

Fully-serviced suburban subdivisions with excellent housing mixtures and attractive landscaping offer quiet family living on the outskirts of Canadian cities. National Housing Act mortgage loans for new dwellings in NHA-approved subdivisions, as above in Barrie, Ontario, enable Canadians to build within their financial capacity and according to their individual needs.

## Social Insurance

Whereas social assistance progressed from poor relief toward the concept of mutual aid, social insurance in somewhat parallel fashion has moved from early concepts of private insurance to public contributory programs having a concept of benefits which include some recognition of need. The development of social insurance programs has been in the direction of extending protection to a more complete coverage of the population and to a wider range of risks. In this development the emphasis is on social adequacy of benefits rather than on actuarial equity.

**Workmen's Compensation**—The first steps in the development of a Canadian system of social security were in the field of workmen's compensation. A workmen's compensation law, adopted in the Province of Ontario in 1914, created a new design for workmen's compensation in Canada and set a legislative pattern for the other provinces. This law embodied two main principles: collective liability and state insurance. Since that date similar measures have been passed by all other provinces and provision has been made for employees of the Federal Government through the federal Department of Labour.

Workmen's compensation provides income support to employees injured by accident on the job, or disabled by a prescribed industrial disease. Benefits also include medical services, hospitalization, rehabilitation and in case of death, benefits for surviving dependants. Compensation is payable as a matter of right and questions of fault or negligence are not relevant. The coverage of the legislation is extensive. The

356

Upgrading of Canada's rental housing stock continues apace as the nation's home builders seek to meet the growing demand for good accommodation. This new apartment in Hamilton, Ontario, financed under the National Housing Act, is typical of such developments.

principal hazardous industries, and practically all those involving manual labour (excluding farming), are covered in each province. A considerable number of non-industrial occupations are also covered.

Contributions are paid entirely by employers in the covered industries. An employer's annual contribution is determined by the size of his payroll and the accident experience of the class of his industry. All compensation costs including administration costs are paid from the Compensation Fund. Workmen's compensation is administered by provincial Workmen's Compensation Boards with exclusive and final jurisdiction for compensation. In some provinces, the Workmen's Compensation Board has wide authority for accident protection, while in others industrial safety is promoted by associations of employers organized under the legislation.

**Unemployment Insurance**—The depression of the 1930's emphasized the need for some type of income maintenance program for unemployed persons and the nation-wide scope of unemployment indicated clearly the need for a national approach. Parliament passed unemployment insurance legislation in 1935, but it was declared *ultra vires* in 1937. A constitutional amendment agreed to by all the provinces brought this matter under federal jurisdiction in 1940, and it was followed by the passage of the federal Unemployment Insurance Act.

Unemployment insurance protects a person's income during temporary loss of employment and is related to earnings prior to unemployment. Coverage extends to about 77 per cent of the non-agricultural labour force. The legislation has been amended periodically to extend coverage and to increase contributions and protection.

The Unemployment Insurance Fund is financed by equal employee and employer contributions, the Federal Government paying 20 per cent of their aggregate contributions and the cost of administration. The program is administered by the Unemployment Insurance Commission. The Unemployment Insurance Act also established a National Employment Service replacing the federal-provincial service which had developed over the years under the Employment Offices Co-ordination Act of 1918. Operated by the Commission for 25 years, the National Employment Service is now administered by the Department of Manpower and Immigration.

**Canada and Quebec Pension Plans**—It was not until 1965 that a comprehensive contributory program of old age, survivors and disability insurance was introduced in Canada. Federal activity in this field is governed by the 1951 amendment to the British North America Act which authorizes Parliament to make laws in relation to old age pensions in Canada, so long as the federal law does not affect the operation of any provincial old age pension legislation, present or future. A further amendment in 1964 extended the scope of this provision to survivors and disability benefits.

The Canada Pension Plan, passed by Parliament in 1965, provided that it would not be applicable in respect of any province taking action to establish a comparable comprehensive pension plan and the Province of Quebec decided to introduce such a program. The Canada and Quebec Plans are co-ordinated thereby providing one nation-wide system of contributory pensions. The Plan provides comprehensive compulsory coverage of the labour force. The contribution rate is 1.8 per cent each from employer and employee and a combined rate of 3.6 per cent from self-employed persons. Initially the upper limit for contributory earnings is set at $5,000 a year and earnings up to $600 a year are exempt.

The Plan includes retirement pensions, disability benefits, survivors benefits for widows and orphans and a lump sum death benefit. The Plan features the automatic adjustment of pensions to changes in wage levels and of benefits-in-pay to increases in the cost of living.

Contributions not needed for benefit and administrative expenses are credited to an Investment Fund and invested in provincial securities. Contributions are collected by the Department of National Revenue and benefits are paid by the Department of National Health and Welfare. The Quebec Plan is administered by the Quebec Pension Board.

## Universal Payments

The third support to the tripod of Canadian income security is the system of universal payments. These programs are universal in that they provide benefit payments for virtually all persons either below or above a specified age. They redistribute income in favour of families with children and of senior citizens. In the fiscal year, 1966-67, these payments amounted to $1,662,000,000.

**Family and Youth Allowances**—In the midst of the unsettling effects of war conditions Canada, by instituting a system of family allowances in 1945, took a significant step in assisting children in low income families and in ensuring a buoyancy of consumer expenditure of particular importance in the postwar readjustment period. The program is a companion measure to other income maintenance schemes in which little or no provision is made in their structure of benefits for the needs of dependent children of recipients.

Family allowances are paid by the Department of National Health and Welfare to mothers for every child under the age of 16, born in Canada or resident in Canada for one year. A family assistance program provides similar payments on behalf of children of immigrants or of Canadians resettling in Canada who do not meet the one year residence requirement. Payments are to be spent on the care and education of the child, and are not payable for any child who fails to comply with provincial school regulations. Some adjustments in the rate structure have been made since 1945, the last being in 1957 when the allowance was raised to $6 a month on behalf of children under 10 and $8 a month for those 10 and up to 16 years of age.

Youth allowances were introduced in September 1964 to encourage young people to continue their education beyond the usual school-leaving age. Payments are made at the monthly rate of $10 on behalf of dependent youths ages 16 and 17 attending school or who cannot attend because of disability. Quebec had already introduced,

A boy and his dog have many mutual interests—including a feeling for music.

in 1961, schooling allowances for children in this age group so that federal payments have not been made in Quebec; instead, federal fiscal compensation has been provided to that province for the payment it makes.

**Old Age Security Pensions**—When the federal old age security program came into effect on January 1, 1952, it was up to that time the most ambitious of Canada's ventures into the social security field. Administered by the National Health and Welfare Department through its regional offices, the flat-rate pension initially was payable to all persons 70 years of age and over, subject only to a residence qualification. In 1965 an amendment provided for the lowering of the eligible age by one year each year, beginning in 1966 and continuing until 1970 when some 1,600,000 persons 65 years and over will be receiving the pension. Another amendment provided for adjustment of the pension in line with increases in the cost of living.

Since the inception of the program considerable attention has been focused on the adequacy of the pension. At the outset in 1952 a rate of $40 a month was paid, but on a number of occasions the amount was increased and by 1963 it was $75 a month. Discussion of the need for a more adequate benefit has continued. As Canada approached its centennial year this question had become one of the most contentious issues in the field of social security. One proposal has been to increase old age security from $75 to $100 a month. Another put forward in the Senate Committee's Report on Aging is to provide a guaranteed minimum income initially of $1,260 for a single person and $2,220 for a married couple based on an income test; subsequently these amounts would be replaced by socially-acceptable minimum budgets developed by a technically-competent body. In July 1966, the Federal Government announced that it proposed to introduce later in the year supplementary benefits for those old age security recipients who were not being assisted or for those who would only be assisted to a limited extent by the Canada Pension Plan.

## Social Welfare in Retrospect and Prospect

Over the past one hundred years the design of Canadian social welfare, especially at the critical stages, has, in Browning's phrase, decomposed only to recompose in response to the changing conditions of the Canadian environment and the basic needs of the Canadian people. The century has been marked by an increasing collaboration between the federal and provincial governments, and between public and private bodies in the welfare field. While these developments have involved persistent problems, a comprehensive and co-ordinated system of social welfare programs is now emerging.

Just as Canada seems to be within reach of establishing a full range of income security measures, attention has been directed to a basically-new approach to income maintenance, the guaranteed minimum income. This technique at once offers a more universal approach to income security and an effective anti-poverty measure. In a dynamic and increasingly complex society, with changing views on the respective roles of the federal and provincial governments in welfare matters and with the effects of automation and other socio-economic developments, one of Canada's greatest needs as it enters its second century of nationhood will be a willingness to change and adapt its existing welfare, fiscal and constitutional arrangements to meet the onrush of social welfare problems.

(JOSEPH W. WILLARD)

The Gairdner Fine Arts Building, erected on the campus of Mount Allison University, Sackville, New Brunswick, reflects the millions of dollars which have been spent on expansion of educational facilities in postwar years. The building will accommodate 50 students and faculty.

# Education

Within the last hundred years, education in Canada has advanced from the privilege of the few to the right of the many, from log schoolhouses to multi-million dollar establishments. Before Confederation only a few hundred pupils were receiving instruction at the secondary level; by 1867 high school attendance was beginning to improve, and by 1900 it had increased appreciably. Today the tremendous growth of the school population has involved the provinces and nation in the expenditure of hundreds of millions of dollars for new and expanded educational facilities and improved teachers' salaries.

## Pioneer Schooling

In the sixties of the last century, the public schools were primitive and diverse in philosophical outlook. Ontario's system was patterned on the reforms advocated by Egerton Ryerson. Quebec schools were, for the most part, modelled on the French schools of the eighteenth century. In both provinces, programs provided a deep-rooted sense of religion in addition to the fundamentals of reading, writing, and arithmetic.

In the Atlantic area, a Free School Act was passed in Prince Edward Island in 1852; in Nova Scotia in 1864; and in New Brunswick in 1871. By Confederation, Prince Edward Island had a few district schools, a classical academy, and a college. In Newfoundland (not a part of Canada until 1949) education was provided by missions of various denominations.

The first schools in the West and on the Pacific coast were established under religious auspices and by the Hudson's Bay Company. Following the immigration of thousands of homesteaders to the prairies, local responsibility began to be patterned on the Ontario system. In British Columbia, the Common School Act of 1865 established a general board of education headed by a superintendent empowered to establish schools, prescribe courses of study and textbooks, and inaugurate inspection services.

## Education in the BNA Act

Confederation did not alter the provincial education structures: education remained the responsibility of the provinces. Under the British North America Act of 1867, sovereign powers over education were granted to the various provincial legislatures by Section 93. However, the Federal Government was given responsibility for the education of Canadians living outside the provinces, and for Eskimos and Indians within or outside the provinces. Section 93 deserves quoting in full:

93. In and for each Province the Legislature may exclusively make laws in relation to Education, subject and according to the following Provisions:—

(1) Nothing in any such Law shall prejudicially affect any Right or Privilege with respect to Denominational Schools which any Class of Persons have by Law in the Province at the Union:

(2) All the Powers, Privileges, and Duties at the Union by Law conferred and imposed in Upper Canada on the Separate Schools and School Trustees of the Queen's Roman Catholic Subjects shall be and the same are hereby extended to the Dissentient Schools of the Queen's Protestant and Roman Catholic Subjects in Quebec:

(3) Where in any Province a System of Separate or Dissentient Schools exists by Law at the Union or is thereafter established by the Legislature of the Province, an Appeal shall lie to the Governor General in Council from any Act or Decision of any Provincial Authority affecting any Right or Privilege of the Protestant or Roman Catholic Minority of the Queen's Subjects in relation to Education:

(4) In case any such Provincial Law as from Time to Time seems to the Governor General in Council requisite for the due Execution of the Provisions of this Section is not made, or in case any Decision of the Governor General in Council or any Appeal under this Section is not duly executed by the proper Provincial Authority in that Behalf, then and in every such Case, and as far only as the Circumstances of each Case require, the Parliament of Canada make remedial Laws for the due Execution of the Provisions of this Section and of any Decision of the Governor General in Council under this section.

Today Canada has ten provincial education systems. Although they have much in common, some have unique features. Newfoundland retains a denominational organization under a single Department of Education. Quebec has two branches under the same Department—one essentially French-language and Roman Catholic; the other, English-language and Protestant. The system in the Yukon Territory is patterned largely on the structure in British Columbia. In the Northwest Territories, the Federal Government is the operative agency. The federal Department of Indian Affairs and Northern Development co-operates with provincial departments of education in enrolling Indian children in local schools, or provides special schools on reserves when expedient.

## Organization and Administration

Each province designates a Cabinet member to serve as Minister of Education. Under him the Deputy Minister, a civil servant and senior professional educationist, administers the Department and advises the Minister on policy.

Each Department of Education undertakes: (1) the training and certification of teachers; (2) inspection services directed towards maintaining specified standards;

(3) to provide financial assistance to the schools through grants and services; (4) to prescribe courses of study and textbooks; and (5) to set out rules and regulations for the guidance of trustees and teachers. Each Department requires regular reports from the schools.

Department personnel usually include: a chief inspector of schools; high school and elementary school inspectors or superintendents; directors or supervisors of curricula, technical education, teacher training, home economics, guidance, physical education, audio-visual education, correspondence instruction, adult education, a limited number of other services; technical personnel and clerks. In Newfoundland there is a superintendent for each of the five denominations recognized by the school Act; and in Quebec there are two deputies, one in charge of the French-language system, the other in charge of the English-language system.

Recent provincial Royal Commissions on Education recommended basic changes. In New Brunswick the provincial Department is taking over functions previously exercised by county boards; British Columbia has established new institutions of higher education; and Ontario has established a Department of University Affairs under the Minister of Education.

Far-reaching changes have occurred in the Province of Quebec. Designated as "Operation 55", a reorganization of the administration of secondary education into larger units was started in 1964 and concluded early in 1966. Selected members of several hundred French-language Roman Catholic local boards formed 55 Regional School Boards for secondary grades, while the local boards continued with elementary grades. A similar operation reorganized English-language Protestant trustees into nine Regional Boards. In addition to the Boards, 64 Regional Planning Committees were created, and 64 Regional Plans for over-all education facilities were outlined.

## Local Units of Administration

In all provinces local boards of trustees function as corporations and operate under their provincial School Act and Regulations. They establish and maintain schools, select qualified teachers, prepare budgets for annual meetings and present them to municipal authorities. The original boards were of three members, but, as towns and cities grew, provision was made for larger elected, or appointed, boards. In some school districts there are different boards for elementary and secondary schools as well as for separate schools.

The movement towards larger units of administration gained momentum after World War II. In the rural areas original school districts were generally four miles square. After the War two main topics plagued the trustees: severe shortages of teachers and inequality in financial ability to support the schools. It was hoped that larger units would correct these problems and bring better facilities to more school children. Larger units were introduced by Acts of the legislatures of Alberta and British Columbia and by similar Acts with provision for local option in Saskatchewan and in the Atlantic Provinces. Manitoba introduced legislation making it beneficial for areas to organize larger secondary units. Quebec's "Operation 55" placed secondary and vocational education under larger units of administration. Ontario has recently established five new areas around three northern and two southern cities, and others will follow. Each area embraces six or more counties or several northern districts. Alberta, in some regions, established county school areas coterminous with municipal units; and in these a committee from the municipal council administers the schools, with authority and power normally exercised by the unit board.

## Enrolment and School Organization

In 1964-65 there were 4,732,476 pupils enrolled in elementary and secondary levels in the public and separate schools, 198,902 pupils in private academic schools, and 30,668 in private business schools. There were 20,105 enrolled full-time in post-secondary courses at institutes of technology, some 200,000 in vocational courses at the high school level, and about 127,000 young adults in full-time vocational courses operating under the Federal-Provincial Agreements, including apprenticeship training.

Higher education institutions enrolled 178,238 full-time students of whom 13,797 were in the graduate division, and 63,824 in part-time courses of university standard. More than 7,000 others were enrolled in teacher training. Adult education activities involved an additional 250,000 or more. In 1964-65, 33,497 bachelor or first degrees and equivalent diplomas were granted. Of these 17,357 were in arts and science to form the largest group, followed by 5,204 in education, 2,256 in engineering, and 1,627 in commerce and business administration. For the same academic year there were granted 4,095 master's degrees and licences, 569 doctorates, and 258 honorary degrees.

The 8-4 plan (8 elementary grades, 4 secondary) covering schooling from the first year to university entrance was for many years the basic frame for organizing the curriculum and schools, other than the Quebec Catholic schools. This plan is still found in some rural and village areas but has generally been modified by the addition of one or two kindergarten years at the beginning or the addition of an extra year at the end. Thus, in addition to the original 8-4 plan there are 6-3-3, 6-3-4, 7-3-3, and 7-4-2 plans, the middle number referring to junior high grades. Post-secondary institutions are increasing in number. These include junior colleges, institutes of technology, and community colleges. Quebec is preparing to introduce a two-year "Institute" between secondary education and university.

In all provinces, increasing provision is being made for children in need of special programs. There are six schools for the blind in Canada, 13 for the deaf, and several special classes in regular schools for the hard-of-hearing and those with poor vision. Taking enrolments at all levels of formal education together, more than one quarter of the total Canadian population is attending full-time in schools, colleges, and universities.

## Financing Canadian Education

The percentage of Canada's gross national product directed to education rose from 1.5 in 1944 to an estimated 6.0 in 1964. In 1962, 29.8 per cent of municipal, 29 per cent of the provincial, and 4.7 per cent of federal expenditure went for formal education. The estimated cost of formal education in 1964 was $2,677,100,000. The Federal Government makes grants for provincial trade and technical schooling, university education, and for a variety of manpower programs. The provincial governments have provided either flat or incentive grants and special grants. Recently, several have adopted some sort of foundation program under which a minimum level

(Right) A hospital-school for retarded children at Lancaster, New Brunswick, aids the handicapped to obtain a suitable education.

Typical of modern school construction are these institutions, (centre) at Taber, Alberta and (below) at Cobourg, Ontario.

EDUCATION                                                365

of services is guaranteed after local authorities have applied the proceeds from a tax on an equalized assessment, the province making up the balance. A district may levy to provide additional services.

Universities and colleges at present receive about 25 per cent of their operating monies from student fees, 22.2 per cent from Federal Government grants, 39.8 per cent from the provincial governments, and the remainder from endowments, religious organizations, gifts, and other sources.

## Professional Staffs

Teachers comprise four per cent of Canada's work force. In times of prosperity there has generally been a shortage of teachers, the shortage in the 1960's being mainly in specialists at the secondary level and in university professors. The trend is towards raising the requirements for certification, extending the length of training, and moving all teacher training to university campuses. In the western provinces, combined arts, science and education courses leading to degrees are given, with the provision that students may withdraw from courses after two years to begin teaching. The majority of high school teachers are university graduates with one year of professional training, and elementary school teachers have high school completion or better, plus a year of professional training. Training is also provided for teachers of vocational subjects and of special subjects. During 1964-65 there were 204,305 teachers and principals in the public elementary and secondary schools. Of these, some 64 per cent were women, 56 per cent of whom were married.

In the colleges and universities the basis of selection is mainly academic record, knowledge of research, and personal suitability. For higher ranks, publication may be a factor in promotion. In 1963-64, 44.4 per cent of university teachers held a doctorate, 34.6 per cent a master's degree, 19.5 per cent a bachelor's degree or better, and 1.5 per cent held no university degree.

## Pre-School Education

Day nurseries are for pre-school children, aged one-and-a-half to five years. About two thirds of the establishments are conducted by public or private welfare agencies. Some 1,200 nursery schools, most of them private or co-operative institutions, provide care and some instruction for children aged three to five who usually attend for a half-day. Most large urban centres provide one year of kindergarten in their elementary school systems. These are mainly for five-year-olds, although some admit children aged four. The Canadian Broadcasting Corporation provides a 15-minute radio program "Kindergarten of the Air" five days a week, from autumn to spring.

## Regular School Program

In September of each year the six-year-olds enter the first year of elementary school to remain for from six to eight years before entering a "junior high" section. The junior high, usually grades 7, 8, and 9, may be in the same building as the elementary, in a school by itself, or part of one of the various high schools: academic, commercial, vocational, or composite.

At the secondary level, the number of subjects and options has been increased considerably, especially in Alberta and British Columbia, and pupils have a wide

Deaf students learn to speak with the aid of microphones and an oscilloscope at the Montreal Oral School for the Deaf.

Special telecasts enrich the curriculum of many Canadian schools. They include programs on the United Nations, world news, science, literature and oceanography.

choice to suit their interests and abilities. Pupils are generally encouraged to develop qualities of good citizenship and a desire to continue learning after graduation. Some emphasis is placed on music, art, physical education, and guidance, to complement the instruction in the basic subjects. Extra-curricular activities cover many fields ranging from orchestras and glee clubs to recreation and hobby clubs. Elected student councils assist in planning and administering sports and recreational programs.

## Vocational Education

For many years Canada did little to provide vocational training for students below the university level, and most of the training that was provided during the early years of the 20th century was oriented towards agriculture. However, this situation changed rapidly after World War II as the country's industrial capacity developed and Canada changed largely from a rural to an urban economy. Vocational training received further impetus in the late 1950's as the supply of technically-trained European immigrants decreased.

An important milestone in vocational education in Canada was the passing by Parliament of the Technical and Vocational Training Assistance Act (SC 1960-61, c. 6), effective April 1, 1961 replacing the Vocational Training Co-ordination Act of 1942. The objectives of the new Act are: to provide assistance for the training of Canada's labour force; to develop skilled manpower from domestic sources to meet future requirements; to reduce the number of unemployed persons by providing them with a skill required to gain and progress in employment; and to develop manpower efficiency.

The Nova Scotia Institute of Technology, Halifax, Nova Scotia, provides a new program for training of technicians in the mechanical, electronic and electrical fields and in medical laboratory technology, as well as classes for apprentices.

The Minister of Labour, who administers the Act, was authorized to enter into some ten different types of agreement with any province for up to six years, that is, until April 1, 1967, covering the provision of financial support for building and equipping vocational schools, training persons for employment, and upgrading workers. Under these agreements 737 projects were approved to 1965, and an additional 251,451 student places were provided. New construction included 17 institutes of technology, 60 trade schools, and 353 vocational high schools; also there were 193 major and 114 minor additions or alterations to existing schools. The total estimated cost of these projects was $801,087,000 of which the estimated federal contribution was $471,377,000.

The numbers of students enrolled in and graduating from the various fields of vocational training is increasing year by year at a rate greater than the normal population growth. In 1964-65 the total full-time enrolment in post-secondary courses at institutes of technology was 20,105. Forty institutes offered this type of training and some 30 provincial trade schools provided partial or complete courses at the technician level. Some 200,000 secondary school pupils were enrolled in vocational courses. For persons who had left the regular school system, some 36,500 were enrolled full-time in trade or other occupational courses at provincial trade schools, about 60,000 in courses for the unemployed in Canada, and about 21,000 received training as indentured apprentices. A few thousand more were enrolled in vocational courses under other government-sponsored programs for training disabled persons, employees of the Federal Government and its agencies, and some others. An additional 30,000 were enrolled full-time at private trade schools and business colleges. Thus, the total full-time enrolment in vocational courses under these various programs and types of training was in excess of 350,000. In addition, many thousands more took vocational courses in evening or other part-time classes.

## Universities and Colleges

In older provinces, university establishment began with the founding of Church of England or Roman Catholic institutions, followed by those of dissenting and other groups. Later, the denominational characteristics of the original foundations were reduced. However, because of early sectarian rivalry there were more institutions than the small population warranted. In Nova Scotia alone, for example, King's College opened in 1790, Dalhousie in 1838, Acadia in 1839, St. Mary's in 1841, St. Francis Xavier in 1853, and Collège Sainte Anne in 1890. In 1896 these six institutions had a total staff of 82, a student body of 533, and conferred 124 degrees.

The western provinces were aware of the early sectarian rivalry and multiplicity of institutions, and they were influenced by the 1906 Royal Commission Report that resulted in the reorganization of the University of Toronto. Consequently, they established non-sectarian universities, although they accepted theological colleges on campus as affiliated, or federated, institutions. In 1964-65 Canada had some 400 institutions of higher learning. All forecasts indicate that university enrolment will increase for many years, possibly doubling during the next decade. Many existing institutions are expanding their facilities, and new institutions are being established. Because of an increasing demand for post-secondary courses, there have arisen junior and community colleges which provide another avenue to the universities in addition to terminal courses.

Two newly-established postwar universities are (above) Simon Fraser University, British Columbia, and (bottom) Laurentian University, Sudbury, Ontario. (Centre) Expanded facilities of the University of Ottawa.

Changes made during the 1964-65 academic year included: Prince of Wales College at Charlottetown, P.E.I., which became a degree-conferring institution; St. Thomas University, affiliated to the University of New Brunswick, which moved from Chatham to Fredericton, N.B.; l'Université d'Ottawa which became a non-denominational institution; Thorneloe University which opened in Sudbury in federation with Laurentian University; Trent University which opened in Peterborough, Brock University in St. Catharines, and Simon Fraser University in Burnaby. A new college of Veterinary Medicine was also organized as a part of the University of Saskatchewan, Saskatoon.

Multimillion dollar projects also mark an unprecedented expansion of university facilities. Completed in 1966 were: a $27,000,000 all-purpose building for Sir George Williams University, Montreal; a 14-storey, $6,000,000 social science building at the University of Alberta; seven buildings at an estimated cost of $11,000,000 at Memorial University, Newfoundland; an $8,500,000 medical building at Dalhousie University; a $10,500,000 library at McGill University; a $4,000,000 sports centre and a $14,000,000 nuclear physics laboratory at the University of Montreal; a new $9,000,000 college (Scarborough), a $10,000,000 research library in the humanities and social sciences, and a $12,000,000 physics building, at the University of Toronto. Carleton University, Ottawa, opened a new chemistry building, two new residences, a third engineering block, a physics building, and expects shortly to construct another arts building. Several projects are under construction in the West and on the Pacific coast. These include a new $3,500,000 arts building at the University of Manitoba; a $3,500,000 seven-storey library and a $6,000,000 biological sciences, oceanography, and fisheries complex at the University of British Columbia.

## Education Changes

Canadian education is undergoing change in response to social, economic, and political pressures. It is involved in economic advance and social change through the full development and utilization of manpower. Emphasis is directed towards keeping young people in school longer and in having them complete a vocational or academic course.

There are also both quantitative and qualitative changes. Although the birth rate is again falling, the absolute numbers entering all levels of education will increase, with the numbers entering university accelerating most rapidly during the next decade at least. At the same time an "explosion" in new knowledge has raised many problems at all levels. A variety of visual and auditory aids have been introduced into the classroom: television, the overhead projector, programmed instruction by machines, and language laboratories. Increasing use is being made of computers for marking papers, preparing reports, processing attendance and other reports, and for scheduling classes.

Interest in research in education is growing, although neither the amount spent nor the numbers involved appear adequate when compared with efforts at research and development in other areas. Research is needed at all levels and for all types of education. Recognizing this, Quebec has established a Bureau of Planning in connection with the Department of Education. In Ontario, the new Institute for Studies in Education will undertake a wide variety of research and conduct a graduate education program. There is a concerted effort to prepare more tradesmen and technicians; to

Convocation is a happy and impressive occasion. At Carleton University, Ottawa, ceremonies are held in the university quadrangle.

provide suitable vocational courses for retraining and upgrading. The new institutes of technology are well-designed structures and are achieving notable status. At the university level, in addition to expanding facilities and provision of more graduate courses, many of the new institutions are organizing around somewhat different concepts: operating twelve months a year and offering combined alternate work and study periods.

Library facilities have expanded greatly in Canada in postwar years. The interior of the Regina Public Library, Saskatchewan, is typical of the increased emphasis being placed on such services.

Canadian institutions provide training not only for Canadians but also for more than 10,000 foreign university students from some 150 countries. These constitute about 6 per cent of the university enrolment. Canada's External Aid Office is responsible for the operation and administration of foreign assistance programs.

While education remains a provincial responsibility, circumstances have forced federal authorities to take a financial interest in its operations. This is expressed in grants to universities and in payments for vocational and technical education; in the Canada Student Loan Plan; in research grants through the National Research Council, the Medical Research Council, and the Canada Council; and in the scholarships and fellowships awarded by numerous Federal Departments.

The Department of National Defence operates Collège Militaire Royale, Royal Military College, and Royal Roads, for the training of officers. There are also schools and courses for enlisted men. Schools for dependants of Armed Services personnel include 65 on Crown lands in Canada (under provincial jurisdiction) and over a dozen in Europe on NATO bases. Training programs and adult education projects are provided for enlisted men and their families.

Other departments of the Federal Government concerned with particular aspects of education include: the Department of Manpower and Immigration which provides financial assistance to the provinces for trade and technical schools and vocational classes, and which conducts related research projects; the Department of Finance which channels government funds for university grants and loans to students; and the Dominion Bureau of Statistics with an Education Division which compiles, analyses, and publishes data at all education levels for all Canada.          (F. E. WHITWORTH)

Canadians famous in the annals of journalism have been commemorated in stained glass windows of the Men's Press Club, Moncton, New Brunswick. (Below) A town crier disseminates the news. In the days when Canada was young and communications facilities were scarce, he performed an important service.

The news room of a daily newspaper is a sensitive and busy centre. In this typical scene at the Montreal Star reporters and editors prepare copy.

press. The Federal Government and the provinces passed libel laws, making life somewhat easier for the editor who had to decide what could be published within the law.

As the country grew, newspapers followed population to the West and to the North. The first newspaper in the West appeared in Victoria in 1858, followed by newspapers in Manitoba in 1859, Saskatchewan in 1878 and Alberta in 1880. In 1898, two newspapers were launched within the year in Dawson City, Yukon Territory.

In the West the traditional combination of journalism and politics continued. Amor de Cosmos was the romantic name adopted by William Alexander Smith for a career that was both flamboyant and effective. De Cosmos founded a newspaper in Victoria and played a leading part in the battle for responsible government in British Columbia. To name only a few additional examples of journalists in politics, Frank Oliver, founder of a newspaper in Edmonton sat in the House of Commons and became Minister of the Interior. Nicholas Flood Davin established his newspaper in Regina and also became a parliamentarian. William A. Buchanan founded a paper in Lethbridge and, after a number of years in the Commons, was appointed to the Senate. Charles Bishop, the "dean of the parliamentary press gallery", also became a senator.

COMMUNICATIONS                                                    377

A dominating figure of the present century was John Wesley Dafoe who, as editor of the Winnipeg *Free Press* from 1901 to 1944, achieved a position of influence in the life of Canada that earned him the title, "editor-statesman". Dafoe thought and wrote with clarity and fought constantly for the achievement of full national status for Canada. He had deep knowledge of, and interest in, international affairs and attended the Peace Conference in Paris at the close of World War I. Between the Wars he raised his voice against the failure of the democracies to oppose the rise of Hitler. His memory is honoured in the J. W. Dafoe Foundation which provides scholarships to journalists and students of international affairs.

Of many French-Canadian journalists of stature in this century, there emerges the dominating figure of Henri Bourassa, a co-founder of *Le Devoir*, which continues as an influential newspaper. Bourassa served as a member of Parliament and was a leading figure in Quebec nationalist ranks. Associated with Bourassa in founding *Le Devoir* was Olivar Asselin who in the course of a distinguished journalistic career also served *Le Nationaliste* and *Le Canada*.

## Magazines

There are many thriving magazines in Canada, but they serve mainly business, farming, academic and other specialized interest. In the general magazine field a national figure was the gifted writer, B. K. Sandwell, who edited *Saturday Night* from 1932 to 1951. *Saturday Night*, which has undergone many transformations, and *Maclean's*, which appears in English and French editions, are among the few survivors in the general magazine field. Most of the general magazines which dominate Canadian news-stands are from the United States. *Time* and *Reader's Digest* provide special editions printed in Canada for Canadians. The problem of United States competition in the general magazine field has led to a royal commission inquiry and to consideration by Parliament of the difficult question of providing protection to Canadian publications without interfering with the traditional freedom of the press.

## News Agencies

In 1967, The Canadian Press, the co-operative news agency serving most of Canada's daily newspapers, marks its 50th anniversary. This busy organization gathers news from across Canada and around the world and distributes it to the more than 100 daily newspapers that own and operate it. From small beginnings it has grown into a $4,000,000 a year enterprise employing some 400 editors, correspondents and teleprinter operators in a dozen offices across Canada, in New York and London.

Until early in the present century, Canadian newspapers were dependent for news from outside their own community on the mails and on a telegraph news service provided by the railways. Objecting to both the rates and the control of news by others, the newspapers began to organize their own news service. Shortly after, the railways decided to retire from the news field. By 1917 the urgent need to report the progress of the War promptly to all Canadians made the time opportune to combine the various regional agencies into a national co-operative organization, The Canadian Press. The government provided an annual subsidy of $50,000 to help bridge the gaps between Canada's main cities with telegraph links. The grant continued until 1924 when the newspapers decided to pay the entire bill to avoid the possibility, or even the suspicion of, government influence.

A major part of the CP's budget, amounting to some 10 per cent of the total, is paid out for the leasing of the 40,000 miles of wire required to speed the news to and from its member dailies in all parts of Canada. Most of the Canadian news is contributed to CP by its member newspapers, with additions by its own reporters and by CP representatives in the Press Gallery of the House of Commons, Ottawa. World news comes mainly through exchange arrangements with the Associated Press and Reuters, with additional material provided by CP overseas staff and roving foreign correspondents. Since 1951, The Canadian Press has provided a complete service in French to the 10 French-language member papers.

The annual cost of operating The Canadian Press is shared out among the member daily newspapers on a pro rata basis, according to circulation. In the control of the organization and the election of directors, each newspaper, large or small, has an equal vote. Through subsidiary operations, The Canadian Press is also the chief source of news for broadcasting stations and networks. News for the Canadian Broadcasting Corporation is provided through Press News Limited. A separate company, Broadcast News Limited, with direction shared between The Canadian Press and the private broadcasters, serves more than 265 private radio and television stations. Canadian news for world distribution is also provided by a private company, United Press International, formerly known as British United Press.

Today's newspaper serves the public well. It delivers a factual, objective account of local, Canadian and world news swiftly and at modest expense. The age of personal journalism and violent political partisanship has disappeared. The press has played a proud role in winning freedom of speech and of the printed word for Canadians, in assisting them along the difficult path to responsible government, Confederation, and complete Canadian autonomy. The press continues to play an important role, a role transformed to meet the needs of a different age. To serve properly millions of readers with the latest news, to offer colour and photography in both daily newspapers and periodicals, to inform and entertain, the modern publication must necessarily be big business.

## Broadcasting

In broadcasting and receiving equipment, coverage, quality and variety of programs, Canada ranks among the half-dozen leading countries in the world. Radio reaches 98 per cent of the people; television reaches 94 per cent. Since 1958, the official body for the regulation of broadcasting matters has been the Board of Broadcast Governors. The BBG, composed of three full-time members and 12 part-time members, reports to Parliament through the Secretary of State. In granting new licences, the Department of Transport must approve technical plans and the BBG examines the program plans of the applicant. The recommendations of these two bodies are submitted to the Governor General in Council (that is, the Federal Cabinet) for final decision.

Canadians are served by a "mixed system" of broadcasting composed of the Canadian Broadcasting Corporation, owned by the Canadian people and largely supported out of public funds, and a private sector composed of individually owned radio and television stations licensed by the government. The debate on the merits of public versus private broadcasting continues, but the fire of the argument has largely been extinguished by the evidence of history: to serve Canadians well, both public and private sectors are necessary.

From the beginning, almost 50 years ago, broadcasting has been a contentious subject. Over the years it has been examined by a series of parliamentary committees, by federal commissions and committees. In general, these official inquiries have affirmed the need for the public service provided by the CBC. In the words of the 1965 Report of the Committee on Broadcasting headed by R. M. Fowler: " . . . the CBC is the *essential* element of the Canadian broadcasting system and the most important single instrument available for the development and maintenance of the unity of Canada."

At the same time there has come widespread acceptance of the fact that the private stations have a permanent and useful role to play. In the Fowler Report, quoted above, one also reads: ". . . private radio and television stations are an integral and valued part of the Canadian broadcasting system".

It is not possible to draw a clear line between public and private broadcasting, for a number of the private stations serve as affiliates of the CBC and, by agreement, carry a certain number of hours daily of CBC network programs. If private stations supplement the CBC in certain areas, in other areas they are in open competition for audiences and for dollars, since the CBC obtains about 25 per cent of its annual income from advertising.

The financial stake of the audience in broadcasting is often overlooked. Yet, it far exceeds that of the broadcasters. In the 10-year period from 1953 to 1962, the sales of Canadian-made radio and television receivers exceeded $1,000,000,000, an amount far greater than the investment in studios and transmitters. The income of the broadcasting system from advertising and from government grants is of the order of $200,000,000 annually, whereas the annual cost of operating all the radio and television receivers in the country—including depreciation, repairs and electric current—has been estimated at more than $400,000,000.

In 1963, the entire broadcasting system had revenues of $218,000,000. Of this amount the income of the private stations, derived entirely from advertising, was $111,000,000. The income of the CBC was $107,000,000, of which about 25 per cent was derived from advertising and 75 per cent from public funds voted by Parliament. Of the 16,000 people with full-time jobs in broadcasting, about half worked for the CBC and half for the private stations.

In 1965, there were 396 stations, plus 264 repeater transmitters. In television there were 75 stations, made up of 16 CBC stations, 44 private stations affiliated with the CBC, 11 stations affiliated with the private English-language CTV network and four unaffiliated private stations. There were 262 AM radio stations; of these 31 were CBC, 84 were private stations affiliated with the CBC, and 147 were private stations with no network affiliation. There were 54 FM radio stations, of which five were CBC and the rest private. There were five shortwave transmitters operated by the International Service of the CBC.

The large number of transmitters is related to the numerous services provided and the fact that the main services must be broadcast in English and French. In addition to national network programs for both radio and television, there are regional programs to serve the five main regions of Canada, plus local broadcasts for both urban and rural audiences. Programs in other languages are provided by a number of stations for the benefit of newly-arrived Canadians. There are broadcasts to the Canadian North in several Eskimo and Indian languages. The complexity of the

Canadian broadcasting system stems from the vast and varied geography of the country, and from the diverse origins and interests of its people.

**Radio's Early Years**—The first test transmissions went out in 1918 from the Marconi station XWA in Montreal, and the first licence for regular broadcasting was issued to this station in 1920. During the first decade, growth was haphazard. Licences issued were for low-power stations and these were heavily concentrated in the Montreal and Toronto areas. A number of these pioneer stations had links with United States networks from which they drew many of their programs. In centres of population close to the border there was competition with U.S. stations for frequencies, audiences, and advertising revenue.

In an effort to attract more passengers, the Canadian National Railway established a Radio Department, equipped a number of its cars with radio receivers and earphones, and set up a chain of stations to provide entertainment. The first network programs to be broadcast in Canada were arranged by the Radio Department of the CNR and broadcast over its stations.

Radio was in its infancy in the 1920's, but a number of far-sighted Canadians had visions of its future importance. Two young men, Alan Plaunt and Graham Spry, organized the Canadian Radio League and sought nation-wide support for a system of public broadcasting. The private stations organized the Canadian Association of Broadcasters. The government appointed a Royal Commission and the result was the Aird Report (1929), which favoured a public system of broadcasting supported by licence fees to be paid by radio set owners.

## Broadcasting Commission

Legislation was delayed by the economic problems of the depression and by the constitutional question of whether broadcasting was the responsibility of the National Government or of the individual provinces. In 1932 the legal question was decided in favour of the Federal Government, which then passed legislation establishing the first publicly-owned broadcasting organization, the Canadian Radio Broadcasting Commission.

With the country still deep in depression, the proposal of the Aird Report that the government should buy up all private stations was not economically feasible. The result was a mixed system which included a public broadcasting body and private stations. This remains the basic pattern of broadcasting in Canada. The broadcasting Commission took over the stations, equipment and staff of the CN's Radio Department and set to work on the difficult task of providing the country with radio broadcasting in both English and French, and of controlling all broadcasting, both public and private.

With Hector Charlesworth as Chairman, the CRBC began with seven stations, with added coverage provided by 47 private stations affiliated with the national network. At the time there were some 600,000 radio receivers in use, and only 40 per cent of the population was within range of a radio station. It started with a modest two hours per week of network broadcasting in 1933. By 1936 it had increased this to 48 hours per week, and the number of Canadians within range of a radio station increased to 49 per cent. In its short but active life, the Commission presented symphony broadcasts, established the Northern Messenger service and set up powerful receiving equipment for transmitting programs from Europe. The CRBC was supported by a $2.00 licence fee on every radio receiver, a system of finance that was later abandoned in favour of direct annual grants by Parliament.

## Canadian Broadcasting Corporation

In 1936, legislation was passed creating the Canadian Broadcasting Corporation, which took over the stations and a staff of 130 from the Canadian Radio Broadcasting Commission.

This is the CBC's mandate:

1. *To be a complete service*, covering in fair proportion the whole range of programming; bringing things of interest, value and entertainment to people of all tastes, ages and interests;

2. *To link all parts of the country* through programs which include a wide variety of national and common interests, and by using its physical resources to bring the national program service to as many Canadians—in remote as well as in urban areas—as finances will allow;

3. *To be predominantly Canadian in content and character*, serving Canadian needs, bringing together the widely-scattered population, and contributing to national unity;

4. *To serve equitably* the two main language groups and cultures, and the special needs of Canada's various geographic regions.

In addition to meeting these heavy responsibilities, the CBC was also to control the stations in the private sector. The first Chairman of the Board of the CBC was Leonard Brockington; general manager was Gladstone Murray, who had acquired considerable experience with the British Broadcasting Corporation.

The war years were a testing time for the CBC. Despite shortages the CBC established a series of high-power stations and by 1942 was within reach of 96 per cent of homes with radios. Writers, musicians and actors were discovered. The Farm Department presented many services to rural Canada; the Canadian Farm Radio Forum, with its unique approach to group listening and to a two-way flow between broadcasters and audience, later became a model for conveying information to farmers in developing countries. In 1941, the CBC established its own news service. Headquarters for the CBC was Ottawa. The majority of programs for "Radio Canada", the French language network, originated in Montreal. Toronto was the source of most English language network programs. Educational broadcasting became a regular service, despite the fact that authority in educational matters rests with the provinces, and success meant close team-work with provincial education departments. Time for political broadcasts was not sold, but was distributed proportionally among the parties. In radio drama and in reporting the news the CBC began to acquire an international reputation for excellence.

Despite the stress and strain of the war years, the CBC emerged as the strongest single communication link for bringing Canadians together, and for keeping them informed about national and international developments. The CBC was not without its critics, particularly among the private broadcasters, who considered it unjust that the CBC was both a competitor and the authority for controlling the private stations. Long and persistent campaigning finally led to the Broadcasting Act of 1958 which established a control authority quite separate from the CBC, the Board of Broadcast Governors.

**Television**—In the years following the War the CBC continued to extend coverage and consolidate its position. Also, it was preparing for the new era of television. During the period from 1945 to 1958, the CBC was headed by Chairman of the Board A. Davidson Dunton. In 1958 Mr. Dunton resigned and was succeeded by J. Alphonse Ouimet, who made his way to the top from the engineering side of broadcasting.

According to the Massey Report* of 1951, the CBC was to be first in the field of television, with its own stations and with private affiliates. Only then were second television station licences to be issued in those cities which could support two stations. Television began in Toronto and Montreal in the fall of 1952. Growth was rapid. From 150,000 in 1952, the number of television receivers mounted to close to 5,000,000 by 1965. All attention was focused on television; radio became the neglected member of the broadcasting family.

Of CBC expenditures on production of $103,000,000 in 1965, television accounted for $83,000,000 and radio for $20,000,000. In 1963, 229 private radio stations reported operating expenditures of $54,000,000; 61 private television stations reported expenditures of $48,000,000.

From the beginning, competition from United States stations has been a spur to Canadian broadcasting. Despite the great increase in the number and power of Canadian stations, stations located in the United States claim an important part of the audience in cities close to the international border. Now the cycle is about to be repeated for colour television. If a free choice were possible, the introduction of colour TV could be put off, and money and effort devoted to improving the content of radio and black-and-white television. But some of the private stations argue that they must be allowed to meet border competition. Canadian manufacturers are anxious to get into the production and sale of colour sets, and with every colour TV set sold to a Canadian, the argument in favour of colour mounts. The decision has been to introduce television in colour in 1967, both at the Canadian Universal and International Exhibition in Montreal and across the country.

The members of the Engineering Department of the CBC keep a close watch on developments in the field of satellite communication. Within a short time it may be possible to link stations across Canada more efficiently by this method than by microwave and cable. A ground station for space communication has been completed by the Department of Transport at Mill Village, Nova Scotia, for commercial telecommunications and broadcasting.

For each of its regular services—French and English—television, AM radio and FM radio—national, regional and local—the CBC strives to provide a balanced schedule of high quality programs. It must use Canadian talent wherever possible so that a minimum of 50 per cent of the programs will have Canadian content. The CBC must concern itself with news, drama, politics, music, religion, sport, education for schools and information for its listeners and viewers. Members of interest groups keep a constant watch and are quick to protest if they consider that the CBC has failed to achieve a balanced approach to trade unions, farmers, industry and commerce, women, religion, etc.

---

*Report, Royal Commission on National Development in the Arts, Letters and Sciences, Ottawa, Queen's Printer, 1951.

A production of Shakespeare's Macbeth was presented on Canadian School Telecasts of the CBC by members of the National Theatre School of Canada.

Orchestral and solo presentations are equally popular live or televised.

In addition to its many regular services, the CBC renders special services in the field of international broadcasting, and in services to the Canadian North and to the Canadian Armed Forces. The International Service of the CBC began operations in 1945. By short-wave it carries news and information abroad to make Canada better known, and to help achieve the country's trade and immigration goals. In 1965, the International Service reported a staff of 150 and a budget of $1,800,000. It broadcasts in 11 languages for a total of 90 hours per week. Most broadcasts originate in Montreal and are transmitted through short-wave transmitters located at Sackville, New Brunswick. In addition to the short-wave broadcasts, the International Service ships transcriptions and tapes to many lands. It has also made a start in television with a monthly 15-minute program called "Canada Magazine". Guidance in policy matters is provided by the Department of External Affairs, and there is a separate parliamentary grant to meet the expenses of the International Service.

One of the oldest broadcasts on the CBC is a message service which began in 1932 to Canadians in the Far North. The "Northern Service" was established in 1958 to provide CBC service to listeners in the Yukon and Northwest Territories, and to settlements in those provinces that extend into the thinly-populated Arctic. The CBC Northern Service has a staff of 75, and an annual budget of $1,200,000. It operates 21 medium-wave units; six manned stations and 15 unmanned relay transmitters. The facilities of the International Service are used for broadcasts to the North for nine hours daily. Its schedule includes programs in Eskimo and Indian languages. The per capita cost is high to reach a small, scattered population, but the Northern Service does help to reduce the sense of isolation and is a factor in the more rapid development of the Canadian North.

"The Armed Forces Service" of the CBC helps to provide Canadian troops abroad with broadcasting from home. It is based on an arrangement by which the CBC provides programs and key personnel and the Department of National Defence bears the cost of the service. CBC programs reach the members of the Armed Forces in several ways. Direct broadcasts to Europe go by short-wave from the Sackville transmitters for from two to three hours daily. Program material in English and French is provided to two FM transmitters operated by the Armed Forces in Europe. Recorded programs are provided to Canadian troops in such remote areas as the Arctic, the Congo, Cyprus and the Gaza Strip. This service is another example of the diverse tasks performed by the Canadian Broadcasting Corporation.

### Films

The National Film Board is Canada's unique contribution to the development of public communication. In 1964, when the National Film Board celebrated its 25th anniversary, its place in the life of Canada was firmly established. It was the best known spokesman for Canada in the world at large, and it was recognized in film circles as a leader in the realm of the documentary film.

The earliest commercial film showing is reported to have taken place in Ottawa, in 1894. Making use of Edison equipment, Andrew M. Holland presented film entertainment in his Kinetoscope Parlor with success. The charge was 25 cents per person and revenue for opening night was reported as $120.

The development of cinemas, for the pleasure of the public and the profit of the exhibitor, followed closely that in the United States. From one-night showings in empty stores and warehouses, there developed regular showings in specially-built cinema mansions. The pattern of growth continued until the appearance in 1952 of a serious rival, television. Since 1952, there has been a steady decline in the number of cinemas and of their revenues. In 1963, there were some 1,500 movie houses, with annual receipts of close to $72,000,000.

The growth of the new entertainment industry depended on the product, film. The need was supplied by a mushroom growth of film studios, first in New York, later in Hollywood. There was, in 1965, no industry in Canada for the production of feature-length entertainment films. From time to time a feature film is produced, but few have achieved critical acclaim and far from producing profits, the revenues have rarely covered the costs of production. Cinemas in Canada show much the same films as do their counterparts in the United States. There is a somewhat higher proportion of films from Europe, particularly in French-speaking areas, where films from France are an important part of the program.

There are a number of companies engaged in the production of film, concentrated heavily in Toronto and Montreal, with one important company located in Ottawa.

They are principally engaged in producing documentaries for industry and commercials for television.

Attention is concentrated here on the National Film Board because of its distinctive contribution to Canadian life, and to its projection of the image of Canada abroad.

**Early Days of Film Production**—Film-making in Canada dates from about 1914 and from the outset the government took the initiative. To promote trade and encourage immigration the government turned to the new medium, the film, to portray life in Canada with particular emphasis on the beauties of nature and the rich resources. The railway companies were also pioneers in film-making, with parallel interest in increasing Canada's population and trade.

As a number of departments of government became active in the making and distribution of films, the Federal Government decided to co-ordinate these activities and, in 1921, the Canadian Government Motion Picture Bureau was established. The Bureau was responsible for films and photographs required by all government departments. During the 1920's, the Bureau gained the reputation of a leader in the making of documentary films. Because of depression economies it was not until 1934 that money was supplied for sound equipment, and by this time the Bureau had slipped from its position of leadership.

The National Film Board is sometimes considered a product of the Second World War, because it was during the war years that many Canadians first became acquainted with films produced by the Board. In fact, however, the National Film Board Act was passed in May 1939, several months before the outbreak of the War.

The chain of events which led to the establishment of the National Film Board was set in motion when a member of the Canadian High Commissioner's staff in London, Ross McLean, submitted a report which expressed dissatisfaction with Canadian Government films sent for presentation in Britain. This led to an invitation to John Grierson, director of the Film Unit of the General Post Office in Britain, who had a number of distinguished documentary films to his credit. Mr. Grierson was invited to visit Canada, examine the state of film-making and advise on future policy in the making and distribution of Canadian informational films.

**The National Film Board**—The report submitted by John Grierson had two important consequences: the passing of the memorable National Film Board Act, and Grierson's appointment, in October 1939, as Canada's first Government Film Commissioner. The original plans called for the continuation of the Canadian Government Motion Picture Bureau as the producing body, with the newly-created National Film Board serving as a planning body, to advise the government on film matters. But, by mid-1941, the new Board absorbed the old Bureau, and became the single body responsible for both planning and production.

John Grierson gathered about him a small group of experienced film-makers, mainly from Britain. Their objective was to attract a staff of bright young Canadians eager to learn an exciting new *métier*, and to train them to operate a truly Canadian documentary film centre. Their formula was an abundance of hard work and a great deal of freedom. Canada is indebted to Grierson both for the idea of the Film Board and for inspiring and instructing a first generation of documentary film-makers.

The main activities of the National Film Board are: production, technical operation, distribution and administration. There is a never-ending struggle to maintain harmony and reasonable balance between these four main activities. But, from the outset the principle was recognized that it is not enough to create documentary films of great merit; it is equally important to build an audience for these films. The Second World War put the newly-established National Film Board to the test. Suddenly, every government department had need of films: to train aircrew, to increase the output of industry, to explain rationing, to sell war bonds.

The purpose of the National Film Board was to produce and distribute films in the national interest, films that would interpret Canada to Canadians and to other nations. The Board also had the right to assign the making of some films to others. In early years most of the staff were young and inexperienced. It grew from 55 persons in 1941 to 780 in the fall of 1945. In those years equipment was limited and the demand so great that frequently it was in use around the clock. In recent years films from the National Film Board have regularly captured from 30 to 50 awards annually in world film festivals and competitions. In 1964, the number of awards to films, film-strips and photographs created by the National Film Board was 83.

For a quarter of a century the cameras of the National Film Board have focused on the history of Canada, on the Canadian scene, urban and rural, in all seasons and on the Canadian people at work and enjoying their leisure. Practically every technique has been tried, and a number of new methods and technical advances originated at the National Film Board. Techniques developed by Norman McLaren to produce animation and sound by applying paint direct to film stock have won world renown for him and his employer. The long list of awards given in honour of McLaren's films includes the "Oscar" presented in 1952 by the Hollywood Academy of Motion Picture Arts and Sciences for the best documentary short of the year. In that year McLaren's work received a similar award from the British Film Academy. To interpret the events of the War, and to describe Canada's role to Canadians and to others, the National Film Board produced regular editions of "Canada Carries On" and "World In Action". High in quality and in general interest, these short films were booked into theatres in Canada, the United States and abroad.

Recognizing that it could not depend entirely on commercial distribution, the National Film Board developed its own distribution system within Canada and abroad. Basically, the non-commercial showing of films is achieved through voluntary groups which have an interest in seeing films that are enjoyable to watch, and convey useful information. During war years, the National Film Board set up rural circuits and circuits which covered factories and trade unions. It established film libraries throughout the country and encouraged schools and universities, public libraries, church groups and service clubs to borrow and show its films. To serve the circuits, representatives of the National Film Board travelled far and wide with films and projection equipment and arranged showings. In the cities the establishment of Community Film Councils was encouraged. These linked together community groups interested in the regular showing of NFB films. To secure distribution outside Canada, the Board opened offices in 1943 in London, New York and Chicago; others later in San Francisco, Paris, New Delhi and Buenos Aires. These NFB offices abroad supplement the work of Canadian embassies and commercial offices in arranging the showing of NFB films.

In 1964, the 25th anniversary of its founding, the National Film Board reported for the year (1964-65) 437,418 showings of 16mm. films to local groups in Canada.

Millions abroad also viewed these films. In the same year, the National Film Board announced the successful launching in commercial theatres of its first two feature length films: *Drylanders*, a story of the opening of the West, and *Pour la suite du monde*, a view of life in l'Île-aux-Coudres. These films used the documentary approach, a medium in which NFB film-makers have developed much skill and experience over the years. Theatrical income for the year was about $50,000, of which half was earned in Canada, 10 per cent in the United States and the remainder in other countries.

Television has become important both as a channel of distribution and source of income. In 1964, the National Film Board earned more than $750,000 from television showings of its films, both old and new; of this total more than half a million dollars came from Canadian television and the balance was divided between sales in the United States and in other countries. The output of the National Film Board in 1964 included 81 original films, 172 versions and revisions (including versions in 34 languages), plus many news reels, news clips, film-strips and still photographs. The number of completed productions for the year totalled 508.

In October 1945, John Grierson resigned from the post of Film Commissioner and returned to Britain. He was later succeeded by Ross McLean. A decline from the wartime peak of activity was inevitable. Between 1945 and 1950 the number of films produced and the number of employees declined each year. Fortunately, the government realized that an institution of great value to the country had been created, and that it must be maintained. A study of the operations of the Board was made by a firm of management consultants. New legislation followed their report.

Under the National Film Act of 1950, the National Film Board once again moved forward. Previously, the responsible Minister had served as Chairman of the Board. Now, the Film Commissioner is Chairman of the Board and chief executive officer. Membership on the Board was increased to include five citizens from the main geographic areas and four members from government service. The purpose of the Board was re-affirmed: to produce, distribute and promote films designed to interpret Canada to Canadians and to the people of other nations. The Board's third Film Commissioner, first under the new Act, was W. Arthur Irwin who was succeeded by Dr. A. W. Trueman. Since 1957 the National Film Board has been headed by Film Commissioner Guy Roberge.

During the period of postwar adjustment, when production and personnel figures were dropping, figures for distribution continued to increase. The years of effort by field representatives began to pay dividends. Volunteers had been trained to serve as projectionists. Film libraries and Film Councils had been established. By 1950, Film Councils numbered 250, some with as many as 200 member organizations. Interest in documentary films had been developed to the point that, when contraction of field staff was necessary, voluntary effort more than took up the slack.

Evidence of the world-wide respect in which the National Film Board is held is shown in the number of requests received from abroad each year for the training of film-makers. Norman McLaren has travelled to mainland China and to India to instruct in the art of film animation. At the request of a number of countries, key personnel have travelled abroad to set up film organizations and to train personnel. Each year, under Canada's program of external aid, or under international programs of technical assistance, students arrive from many parts of the world for on-the-job training at the National Film Board.

In 1956, after a number of years of planning, the National Film Board moved from Ottawa to a headquarters building in Montreal, which had large studios and excellent equipment. An office is maintained in Ottawa for contact with government departments, which remain the Board's principal clients, and also for the Still Photograph Division which continues its long-standing role as official photographer for the government. Constant research by the Technical Division has contributed to the Board's reputation as a leader in the making of documentary films. One example is the combination of microscope and camera to produce motion pictures or still photographs with magnification up to 1,000 times. Another product of Board research is the "Sprocketape" machine, a light weight, low cost sound recording system.

There is a movement on the part of the government to encourage the production of feature films in Canada by private producers, with the National Film Board an active partner in these efforts. A co-production agreement has been signed with France and similar agreements with other countries are being considered.

Whatever developments in film-making the future may unfold, the National Film Board of Canada, with more than a quarter century of experience and distinguished achievement, is certain to play a leading role.

## The Post Office

The Canada Post Office came into being with the establishment of the nation. Before Confederation, the Post Office had historical links with the postal services of the United States and Britain. The first post office in Canada was established at Halifax in 1755. After the American revolution, postal services in British North America were administered from London by the Postmaster General of the United Kingdom. In 1851, the Canadian colonies took over their own postal services. With Confederation, the Post Office became the responsibility of the Federal Government for both domestic and international mail.

Canada is served by more than 11,000 post offices and by some 40,000 employees, of whom more than 9,000 are uniformed carriers. In recent years business done by the Post Office has exceeded $200,000,000 per year, and there has been a steady increase in its annual revenues. The value of postal money orders issued annually is close to $1,000,000,000. Among numerous services provided by the Post Office is the postal savings department.

In 1918, the first experiment in transporting mail by air was carried out in flights between Toronto and Montreal. Thirty years later, in 1948, the Canada Post Office pioneered with an "all-up" mail service which in effect provides that all first class letters within the country will be carried by air. In its effort to get mail to the receiver swiftly and at low cost the Post Office uses every available type of transport, from truck and train to boat and plane.

Considerable use is made of Railway Mail Service in which a railway car serves as a sorting and distributing centre while the mail is en route. This has its marine counterpart in an Atlantic Coastal Service with mail clerks sorting mail aboard a coastal steamer between ports of call. Another phase of operations is the Canadian Postal Corps which serves the Armed Forces. Contact with other countries is regulated through membership in the Universal Postal Union. This body, which meets at five-year intervals, held its 1957 conference in Ottawa.

A modern facer-canceller machine showing a close-up of cancelling dies and stackers is in contrast with the primitive delivery of mail at Tagish Post during the gold rush days of the late nineteenth century.

RECEIVING MAIL AT TAGISH POST – 1898

## Telecommunications

Canadians are provided with telegraph and cable services by nine companies operating more than half a million miles of wire, plus thousands of miles of undersea cable which link Canada with every part of the world. The Canadian National and the Canadian Pacific, in addition to providing the extensive communications required by their rail services, supply the main service to the public for sending telegrams and cables.

There is an apparent paradox in the fact that the number of telegrams transmitted declined steadily from 20,000,000 in 1954 to 12,738,652 in 1964 while during the same period operating revenues of the telegraph companies more than doubled. The explanation is provided by the increase in the volume and variety of services provided to

390                                                    CANADA, 1867-1967

business, such as the transmission of data, radio and television networks, facsimile and wire photo services. One example is Telex which links some 6,000 Canadian companies, and through a world-wide network, subscribers in 84 other countries.

In addition to land-line and cable, considerable use is made of microwave. The Canadian National and the Canadian Pacific co-operated in construction of a microwave system from Montreal to Vancouver which was completed in 1963. Additional microwave links provide communication with the Atlantic Provinces.

Telegraph and telephone links between Canada and the rest of the world by cable and by radio are provided by the Canadian Overseas Telecommunication Corporation, established in 1950. Internal and external communication facilities are being constantly extended, particularly in the North.

Canadians are well provided with telephone facilities and make heavy use of them. In 1963, there were 6,656,613 telephones in use; of these 1,910,178 were business telephones and 4,746,435 were residential telephones. In that year Canadians made more than 11,000,000,000 local calls and 257,000,000 long distance calls. The average number of telephone calls per capita was 593.

To supply this service there were 2,296 separate telephone systems. However, a major part of the $787,000,000 annual revenue was earned by a small number of large

(Above) The new electronic push-button telephone is now in use in a number of Canadian cities. (Right) A telephone used by subscribers to Canada's first telephone exchange which opened at Hamilton, Ontario, in July 1878. The bell was used for signalling and the wooden gadget below for talking and listening.

Information for the Department of Transport weather map service is transmitted by CN-CP telecommunications.

companies. The Bell Telephone Company of Canada, founded in 1880, operating in Ontario, Quebec, Newfoundland and the Northwest Territories, served 61 per cent of all telephones in Canada. The British Columbia Telephone Company which, like the Bell Company, is shareholder-owned, served 9.4 per cent. In each Prairie Province— Manitoba, Saskatchewan and Alberta—the telephone system is owned and operated by the provincial government. There are three main companies serving the Maritime Provinces. These eight leading companies make up the Trans-Canada Telephone System which provides a transcontinental microwave system for telephone, data, and other communication services. The big eight, along with three other telephone companies, co-operate in the Telephone Association of Canada.

Smaller companies, which number more than 2,250, join forces in a number of provincial and regional associations. For long distance calls, the individual company participates in arrangements which make it possible to provide two-way service with other telephone systems. Telephone companies which have national incorporation are subject to the rulings of the Board of Transport Commissioners. Smaller companies which operate within one province are responsible to a provincial regulatory body.

Telephone activity in Canada dates back to 1876 when Alexander Graham Bell carried out the first "long distance" voice communication in a call from Brantford to Paris, Ontario.

Wire, cable and microwave are among the means used to link Canada's 6,300,000 telephone subscribers with one another, and with telephone systems around the world. A total of some 30,000,000 miles of wire is used. A microwave system stretches 3,900 miles from Atlantic to Pacific. Thousands of miles of cable link Canada with almost every country where the telephone is in use. Constant efforts aim at improving existing equipment and extending the service to remote areas. Among the services introduced in recent years are Direct Distance Dialing, Data-Phone for transmission of business statistics and TWX by means of which subscribers can exchange typed messages, statistics and drawings. To provide telephone service to settlements which are separated by great distance and difficult terrain, use is made of a variety of electronic methods, including microwave, tropospheric scatter and high frequency transmission.

392

Gander, Newfoundland, has one of the world's largest airports. During the Second World War it was an important Atlantic patrol base. In the foreground is the airport, a few miles distant the new townsite.

Reference has been made to microwave links operated by telegraph and telephone companies. These facilities are leased for a number of uses, including the CBC and CTV television networks. The needs of some companies, such as a number of hydro-electric companies, are so great that they operate their own microwave networks.

In addition to the microwave networks which link the country from the Atlantic to Pacific, an ever-increasing number of microwave systems provide links between the densely-settled areas and the distant settlements in the northern reaches of the provinces, and in the Territories.

## Department of Transport

In the field of telecommunications, the authority is the Telecommunications and Electronics Branch of the Department of Transport. This department is the licensing authority for radio and television stations; since 1958 all applications to establish or modify radio and television stations must be referred to the Board of Broadcast Governors. In effect, the Department of Transport examines the technical plans of the applicant, the Board of Broadcast Governors, the program plans.

In addition to providing licences for radio and television stations, the Department of Transport issues some 100,000 radio licences annually for boats, aircraft, automobiles, taxis and trucks and for communications systems serving highway safety, police and forest protection and weather reporting. As an example, the Meteorological Branch of the federal Department of Transport is an important user of both land-line and radio services. This branch uses 55,800 miles of teletype serving 355 offices; for the transmission of weather charts it uses 14,500 miles of facsimile circuits serving 80 offices.

In 1966, the Department of Transport completed, at Mill Village, Nova Scotia, a ground station for communication by satellite with other nations. This station is available to the Canadian Overseas Telecommunication Corporation for participation in an international commercial satellite system. Important aids to navigation for Canadian ships and planes, and for those of other nations, are also provided by the Department of Transport. Besides issuing licences for a wide range of telecommunication and electronic purposes, the Department of Transport operates a series of monitoring stations to ensure that the conditions of these licences are respected. The monitoring stations, plus a fleet of automobiles equipped to locate and measure sources of interference, help to keep the air channels clear. (ALBERT A. SHEA)

# The Fine and Lively Arts

What is frequently termed the 'cultural pattern' of a nation is a mosaic of many intricately adjusted parts touching almost every aspect of the "way of life" of a people, but common usage associates the word 'culture' chiefly with the arts—the fine arts and the lively arts. Strict definitions of "the fine arts" and "the lively arts", or attempts to establish distinctions between them, are impossible and useless. Often the fine arts are lively and equally often the lively arts are fine. So, let it be understood that hereafter we are referring to music, painting, drama, literature, the dance, sculpture, architecture, handcrafts, "cinema", opera, drawing, engraving, and television broadcasting when reference is made to the cultural pattern.

## Historical Background

Canada's cultural development, marked by alternating periods of drag and spurt throughout a period of more than 200 years, has been exceptionally complex. Most of its stimuli and main influences have not come from within but from without and the general pattern of the arts has been notably imitative. This was true, more or less, for other North American countries but in Canada special historical circumstances prolonged immaturity and imitation far beyond the early-growth stages and well into the current century. Only since the early 1950's have there been country-wide signs of the emergence of vigorous, ambitious and original powers within the community of Canadian creative and performing artists; a development which has prospered in an atmosphere of public approval and support hitherto unknown in Canada. To generalize: prior to 1950 Canada's cultural development was a long, dull, earnest and imitative business, whereas the succeeding years have brought forth a cultural explosion of genuine validity and far-reaching promise.

Today—with notable qualifications—the Canadian cultural stream is predominantly Anglo-Saxon; and strong, sometimes seemingly excessive influences from the United States and Britain are evident in almost every aspect of the thinking and actions of the Canadian people. Dominant in the province of Quebec and extending in many ways beyond the province's borders is the French Canadian culture with distinctive qualities based firmly on three centuries of self-development in the New World. A third power in the Canadian cultural stream is the abundant and pervasive influence of citizens whose roots reach back, perhaps immediately or perhaps through three generations, to the ethnic sensibilities and artistic wealth of many European fatherlands. These three major influences which are so obvious today have been effective throughout the years of Canada's growth; and Canada's development in the arts cannot be understood unless one bears in mind the fact that the three distinctive cultural powers have been and still are at work—the Anglo-Saxon Power, the French-Canadian Power and the Third Power. (The term "Anglo-Saxon" has been sanctified by prolonged careless usage by scholars and journalists but for our purposes the expression "Anglo-American" would be more meaningful.)

The contemporary culture of Canada on the eve of the country's centennial gives a superficial impression of merely mirroring the artistic life and thought of the United States; and critics who tend to deplore what they term the Americanization of Canada do not lack solid evidence when they look from Newfoundland to British Columbia and cry despairingly: "American movies! American magazines! American music! American architecture! American decor! American books! American television!" Fortunately, however, there is more to it than the superficial view, and those who are genuinely eager to find more "Canadian content" in the cultural pattern do not have to scratch far below the surface.

No one would deny that among the influences which impinge upon Canadian cultural development those from the United States are by all odds the most numerous and the most pervasive. They are projected incessantly, and often unintentionally, across more,than 3,000 miles of international border. Hollywood movies, the shock troops of American culture, with their incredible mixture of the refined and the shoddy, set many fashions for Canadians to follow. Even in rural Quebec, where other non-French influences have failed to make substantial headway, the Hollywood film with French-language adaptations has a dependable clientele. The American motion picture impact has been greatly expanded in recent years by the fact that virtually every television station in English-speaking Canada favours its audience with one or more "old movies" daily. Much of the contemporary literary fare of Canadians is provided by the hundreds of American magazines which are bought eagerly in every part of English-language Canada. Specialized journals of the arts, art columns in the popular magazines, book-review sections in American week-end newspapers; these all help Canadians to become saturated with the cultural likes and dislikes of the United States. American books crowd the shelves of Canadian bookstores and thousands of Canadians subscribe to American clubs which supply one book per month. A never-ending influx of seemingly prosperous United States tourists suggests to many Canadians some sort of enviable excellence of the American cultural environment. Perhaps most impressive of all is the fact that every television screen in Canada presents, in either immediate or delayed broadcast, every day of the week, a program heavily loaded with "American content".

A superficial impression which is created by this massive dosage is that the average English-language community in Canada must be a pale imitation of its United States counterpart culturally. But this is an illusion which is dissipated by a deeper consideration of the facts. For a period of a century and a half prior to World War I, Canada—with the exception of Quebec—was thoroughly impregnated with the British cultural tradition and this is the bedrock upon which all contemporary cultural influences must strive to flourish—be they imported from other lands or based upon a Canadian national desire of indigenous self-expression. Generations of British colonial officials and soldiers brought the tastes and preferences and prejudices of England and Scotland to British North America and established firm and lasting foundations in aesthetic and intellectual matters. British-trained schoolmasters frequently guided the tastes of young Canadians and exercised notable influence in community development; Scottish clergymen for the Presbyterian Church in Canada and English clergymen for the Church of England in Canada aided materially as well as spiritually in developing among Canadians a fundamentalist concept of "good taste" in cultural matters. A wave of middle-to-upper-class English colonial families (the historic United Empire Loyalists), unwilling to remain in the revolutionary United States, settled in Upper Canada and the Maritimes following 1775 and had a profound influence upon the cultural development of their new land. Preferential trade arrangements gave British publishers exceptional opportunities to dominate the

Night illumines the Stratford Theatre where various presentations—plays, ballet and musical productions—attract an increasing number of patrons. The Stratford Shakespearean Festival has been held here since 1953. The building was opened in 1957.

Canadian market for books, magazines and imported newspapers. At the beginning of the 20th century British literature, theatre, music and art were firmly established as Canadian preferences; bearing in mind that, with some exception for cosmopolitan Montreal, the province of Quebec plotted its own cultural course.

About one third of the people of Canada are of French ethnic and cultural background; reared in the French language and thoroughly attached to French Canadian customs and likes and dislikes in the arts. Through more than three centuries they have proudly maintained a special and separate cultural identity within the broad Canadian framework and have consciously resisted temptations to become assimilated with the Anglo-American majority. The province of Quebec is the homeland of French Canadian culture but important French-language communities are found elsewhere in Canada, notably in New Brunswick, Ontario, Saskatchewan and Alberta; and in recent years the means of cultural communication among these widely scattered fragments have assumed real importance. Most French Canadians who live in the larger centres of Quebec, and nearly all those living in the outside-Quebec communities, are bilingual and their resistance to the gigantic Anglo-American cultural wave is a matter of thoughtful and competent perception and discrimination. Although in recent years French Canada has deliberately stimulated a program of cultural exchanges with France her earlier ties with Paris were unsubstantial and the development of a distinctive French Canadian culture has been a do-it-yourself phenomenon of notable character.

But the British and French Canadian underpinning of contemporary Canadian cultural tendencies do not provide the complete story. Canada's massive immigration program during the past century brought to the new land an admixture of European cultures which contributed vitally rich, profound and sensitive variety to the Canadian cultural pattern. Hanoverian Germans settled in Nova Scotia two centuries ago. Pennsylvania Dutch trekked to what is now western Ontario following the American Revolution. In the great migration between 1885 and 1914 hundreds of thousands of European families—German, Polish, Ukrainian, Belgian, Scandinavian, Hungarian, Italian, Russian, Greek—brought their deep-rooted national customs, music, literature, dances and handcrafts and contributed them generously to the artistic life of their new home. The importance of this European influence, added to the British and the French Canadian, cannot be over-emphasized when assessing the Canadian cultural pattern of today.

These complications—the penetrating influence of "the three powers" in the foundation stages and the superficial influence of the United States in recent years—have made the Canadian cultural pattern difficult to understand and appreciate. Nevertheless, the story of what has been achieved against considerable odds in the field of the fine arts and the lively arts is one to generate Canadian pride—at the centennial point in the country's growth. In literature, in music, in theatre, in painting and in the other cultural forms, achievements of the earlier days were solid and real and Canadian participation in the international contemporary cultural scene is becoming more satisfying to even the hard-bitten critics.

## Literature

Pre-Confederation Canadians were engaged mainly with the great physical task of transforming a vast, rugged and unknown land into a modern community; but, nevertheless, they found time and opportunity to produce a surprising amount of indigenous literature. The first truly Canadian literary works were written in French by explorers, missionaries and settlers, and many of them became the inspiration for subsequent writings. Replete with impressive and skilful descriptions of life in the newly-discovered land and embellished with excellent literary expositions of faith and idealism, some of the early works were notable literature. Justly renowned are Champlain's accounts of his explorations in New France. *Les Relations*, remarkable records of the French Jesuit missionaries, have served as source material for scholars during the past 300 years. Marc Lescarbot's *Histoire de la Nouvelle France*, first published in Paris in 1609, is a world classic of historical writing. Comparable records and memoirs by English-language explorers and adventurers, such as Samuel Hearne's *Journey from Prince of Wales Fort* and Alexander Mackenzie's *Voyages from Montreal ... to the Frozen and Pacific Oceans*, have lasted through the years not only as delightful reading-matter but also as mines of information for historical writers. In the maritime regions, in Quebec, in Upper Canada and even in the Far West men and women of literary inclinations wrote about the new land—books of adventure, religion, education, pioneer life, fiction, poetry, travel, nature. Books by the hundreds dealing with what is now known as Canada poured from the publishing houses of London,

Edinburgh, Paris, Boston and New York; and by July 1, 1867 there was a sizable collection of what could properly be termed 'Canadiana'.

The fact of Confederation in 1867 and the early subsequent accessions of Prince Edward Island and Manitoba stimulated a sense of real or imaginary identity and mutual interests and led to the beginning of a Canadian national spirit, and this development was of particular importance in the field of writing. In the years 1867-1900 a considerable body of distinctively Canadian literature appeared. Not much of it was of broad literary importance or free from the sins of self-conscious imitation of the styles and themes of foreign writing; but some of it, in both English and French, was commendable and lasting. In 1877 William Kirby's *The Golden Dog* was praised by critics at home and abroad and it has remained as a Canadian classic. Two of Sir Gilbert Parker's historical romances, *When Valmond Came to Pontiac* (1895) and *The Seats of the Mighty* (1896), based on the Canadian scene, became immediate best-sellers in Great Britain and the United States as well as in Canada and remain highly regarded to this day. Ralph Connor's popular series of Canadian novels commenced in 1898 with *Black Rock* and held a spot in the long-term best-seller lists for many years. *Beautiful Joe*, written in 1894 by Margaret Marshall Saunders has been translated into at least 14 languages and has been one of the all-time most popular animal stories written in English. The records show that up to 1880 Canadian fiction writers produced 250 volumes, with two thirds of the total appearing in the 1860's and the 1870's. Stories of nature and wild animals by Canadian writers have enjoyed high rating throughout the world and some of the most successful of these authors had met with success prior to the turn of 1900. The first of the animal stories by Sir Charles G. D. Roberts appeared in 1895, Ernest Thompson Seton published his famous *Wild Animals I Have Known* in 1898, and Catherine Paar Traill's noted nature books appeared in 1894 and 1895.

Poetry came into its own as a Canadian phenomenon in the decades immediately following Confederation and has never lost speed since; although the contemporary poets are less enamoured with the patriotic and naturalist themes. Isabella Valancy Crawford published, in 1884, a volume of poems which depicted the wilderness of

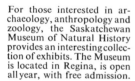

For those interested in archaeology, anthropology and zoology, the Saskatchewan Museum of Natural History provides an interesting collection of exhibits. The Museum is located in Regina, is open all year, with free admission.

Canada with the spirit and attachment which later inspired the Group of Seven to do their intense visual tributes to their country; but the names which still stand out as the bell-wethers of Canadian verse are those of The Big Four: Charles G. D. Roberts, Archibald Lampman, Duncan Campbell Scott and Bliss Carman. Inspired by the vastness and beauty and potential greatness of Canada, and encouraging and supporting each other like musketeers, these four produced an amazing quantity of verse and won favourable attention from literary critics both at home and abroad. Their influence upon English-language letters did not abate until well into the present century. In French Canada the great poet, Emile Nelligan, whose first volume was published in 1896, was linked with Nérée Beauchemin (*Patrie Intime*) and Guy Delahaye (*Phases*) to constitute a trio commanding respect in Paris and popular affection at home. Personal memoirs of political figures and public servants appeared in great number in the post-Confederation period and added considerably to the existing quantity of Canadian literature. Even though the writing was not great writing, or even competent in some instances, the recorded facts concerning the times have since proved to be a rich treasure for Canadian and other writers.

The period 1900-1940 was a prolific one for Canadian writers, particularly novelists, but the literary output of the times was, with notable exceptions, parochial, narcissistic, missionary, earnest and unexciting. Regional novels were the rule of the period. Norman Duncan wrote of the harsh Atlantic coast (*Doctor Luke of Labrador*), Pierre Coalfleet (*Solo*) was inspired by the Maritime Provinces' countryside, J. G. Symes (*Our Little Life*) was intrigued by the city life of Montreal; but Robert W. Service's *Trail of '98* was the only truly successful novel of the genre. The experiences of immigrants to Canada were a compelling theme for a number of Canadian writers of the period: *Hansen*, by Augustus Bridle, *Painted Fires* by Nellie McClung, *Wild Geese* by Martha Ostenso, *The Viking Heart* by Laura Goodman Salverson, *Settlers of the Marsh* by Frederick Philip Grove and *The Foreigner* by Ralph Connor. The physical and psychological stresses involved in the opening of the West to settlement were also a driving theme for many writers: W. A. Fraser's *Bulldog Carney*, Douglas Durkin's *The Heart of Cherry McBain*, Ralph Connor's *The Sky Pilot*, Robert Stead's *The Cowpuncher*, Nellie McClung's *Purple Springs*, Isabel Patterson's *The Shadow Riders* and Robert Watson's *Gordon of the Lost Lagoon*. The critics both at home and abroad found little for admiration in most of these novels, the general complaint being that grand and vivid situations were peopled by pale and minor characters. Many Canadian writers were stirred by the excitement and challenge of the times but lacked the literary competence to portray good enough characters to embellish the plots.

Fiction of the 1920's tended to be dominated by two dissimilar authors, Frederick Philip Grove and Mazo de la Roche. Grove's stark realism was far in advance of the work of his contemporaries but his heavy-handed style won him few friends among the critics and book buyers of his day. His *A Search for America* (1927), *Our Daily Bread* (1928), *The Yoke of Life* (1930) and *Fruits of the Earth* (1933) have worn well with the passage of time and command more admiration today than they did during the lifetime of the dour author. Miss de la Roche achieved world-wide favourable recognition for her long series of *Jalna* novels, commenced in 1927 and continuing popular into contemporary times through numerous reprint editions, magazine serialization, translations and motion picture adaptations. Her real, vivid, sympathetic and highly personal development of fiction people frequently resulted in her being pointed out by critics as the Canadian writer who really understood how to do it. Morley Callaghan's earliest stories were written in the late 1920's but his best-known novels and the ones which, in time, gave him international recognition were written in the 1930's: *Such is My Beloved* (1934), *They Shall Inherit the Earth* (1935) and *More Joy in Heaven* (1937). Callaghan's reputation has grown with the years and he is now regarded by many as the first of Canada's school of modern novelists. Other noteworthy Canadian novelists of the 1930's whose work tends to be well regarded by contemporary critics are Frederick Niven (*The Flying Years* and *Mine Inheritance*), Philip Child (*The Village of Souls* and *God's Sparrows*) and W. George Hardy (*Father Abraham* and *Turn Back the River*). It is interesting and enlightening to note that Child's *God's Sparrows* is practically the only successful Canadian novel dealing with World War I, although Canada's sacrifices in men and materials in that conflict were astonishing.

In French Canada the problems of the writer were considerable. A real sense of isolation (from both English-speaking Canada and the French-speaking world), an overpowering propriety-compulsion stemming from strict Roman Catholicism, a very small and relatively unsophisticated reader-market and a tendency to favour academic and formal literary themes and styles—all these tended to put the brakes on natural and vigorous French Canadian writing and it was not until after World War I that a break-through became evident. From 1867 until well into the 20th century the bulk of good Quebec writing was concerned with history, politics and religion; but in these limited areas some notable good writing did appear. Stirring political pamphlets with magnificently stated French Canadian nationalist sentiments flowed from the pens of Henri Bourassa, Olivar Asselin and Jacques Fournier. Sir Thomas Chapais (*Cours d'Histoire du Canada*) and Joseph Edmund Roy (*Histoire du Notariat au Canada*) were notably literate and successful historians of their day. Edmond de Nevers' *L'Avenir du Peuple canadien-français* was admired throughout the French-speaking world as a long essay of extraordinary literary merit and the religious work *Droit publique de l'Eglise*, by the Canadian priest Louis Adolphe Paquet, was an important literary work. In the field of philosophical writing the French Canadian names of Rev. Louis Lachance, Rev. Louis-Marie Régis, Charles De Kroninck and François Hertel achieved international eminence. The historical works of Canon Lionel Groulx (*La Découverte du Canada* and *Histoire du Canada français*) were not only notably competent in literary style but also exceptionally effective in the stimulation of national spirit among French Canadians. During the 1920's and the 1930's literary criticism in Quebec was especially vigorous and searching, in the forms of books and periodical writing, and the names of Albert Pelletier, Jean Charles Harvey, Louis Dantin, Jean Chauvin and Pierre Daviault stand out brilliantly in this field. The novel form of writing was notably late in developing in Quebec and it was not really until after World War I that signs of vigour and competence appeared. Jean Charles Harvey's *Les Demi-Civilisés*, Ringuet's *Trente Arpents*, Claude Henri Grignon's *Un Homme et son Péché* and Felix Antoine Savard's *La Minuit* were able precursors of the French Canadian novel which appeared with both power and sensitivity at the end of World War II.

The decade of the 1940's, marked by great human participation in great events, brought forth a particularly rich harvest of Canadian writing. In some ways it appeared that shackles had been removed, and Canadian novelists were moved to tackle universal themes for the first time. Although the settings of stories might be within Canadian boundaries, problems and plots were concerned with the world-man. This period saw the emergence of Canada's first-rank writers. With *Barometer Rising* (1941), *Two Solitudes* (1945) and *The Precipice* (1948), Hugh MacLennan, of Montreal, established himself as a writer of international importance. Sinclair Ross (*As for Me and My House*), Gwethalyn Graham (*Earth and High Heaven*), William O. Mitchell (*Who has seen the Wind*) and Edward McCourt (*Music at the Close*) were in the crop of new Canadian novelists inspired by an understanding of man and able to write with genuine skill. Joyce Marshall's *Presently Tomorrow* (1946) and Henry Kreisel's *The Rich Man* (1948) have stood up well to critical appraisal. Thomas Raddall of Nova Scotia established himself in the 1940's as an outstanding Canadian historical novelist with *His Majesty's Yankees*, *Roger Sudden* and *Pride's Fancy*.

Since 1950 the Canadian literary scene has been one of intense excitement and fruitfulness, with new writers emerging faster than the reading public's ability to keep up and with established writers turning their talents to new forms and new styles with notable success. The roster of good writing of the period involves a very large number of books and only a few of the highlights can be indicated in a brief survey. Ethel Wilson, of Vancouver, received international plaudits for *Hetty Dorval* (1947), *The Innocent Traveller* (1949), *The Equations of Love* (1952), *Swamp Angel* (1954) and *Love and Salt Water* (1956); a notable achievement for a new writer. David Walker achieved prominence with his *Digby* (1953) and *Geordie* (1950), while Robertson Davies pleased the critics and the public with his *Tempest-Tost*, *Leaven of Malice* and *A Mixture of Frailties*. Ernest Buckler's *The Mountain and the Valley* and Charles Bruce's *The Channel Shore*, both Nova Scotia based, were works of outstanding literary merit, while Adele Wiseman's story of a Winnipeg Jewish family, *The Sacrifice*, received the Governor General's fiction award for 1956 and high praise in New York and London. Another chronicler, in fiction, of Canadian Jewish family life, Mordecai Richler, has proved to international critics that he is a satirist of great power, with his *Son of a Small Hero*, *A Choice of Enemies* and *The Apprenticeship of Duddy Kravitz*. Douglas LePan's first novel, *The Deserter* (Governor General's fiction award winner for 1964), and Henry Kreisel's second novel, *The Betrayal*, are both courageous and sensitive exposures of World War II themes.

In French Canada the post-1950 period has also been a rewarding one for novelists and poets. Gabrielle Roy's penetrating novel of urban realism, *Bonheur d'Occasion*, received the Governor General's fiction award for 1947 for its English translation *The Tin Flute*. *Le Survenant*, by Germaine Guèvremont, placed its author in the forefront of French-language novelists, in both Montreal and Paris, while Roger Lemelin's *Au Pied de la Pente Douce* and *Les Plouffes* brought fame to their young Quebec author. The French Canadian novel, long bogged down in sentimentality and stilted prose, leaped into and beyond the stage of hard realism with surprising gusto and is at present largely concerned with a deep probing of men's minds—the strange psychological fiction form. Current examples are: Robert Elie's *La Fin des Songes*, André Langevin's *Poussière sur la Ville*, Jean Vaillancourt's *Les Canadiens errants* and Yves Thériault's *La Fille Laide*. Anne Hébert, although best known as a poet, has written a novel *Les Chambres des Bois* and a volume of short stories *Le Torrent* which are both characterized by a probing for human motives. And a very young Montreal writer, Claire Blais, has recently published two psychological novels, *La Belle Bête* and *Tête*

*Blanche*, which have both shocked and delighted the literary worlds of Canada, France and the United States. Winners of the Governor General's awards in recent years for French-language fiction were: André Giroux's *Malgré tout, la Joie* (1959), Yves Thériault's *Ashini* (1961), Jacques Ferron's *Contes du Pays Incertain* (1962), Jean-Paul Pinsonneault's *Les Terres sèches* (1964) and Gérard Bessette's *L'Incubation* (1965).

Although the growth of competent novel writing was the main feature of Canada's literary scene after World War I the period saw marked changes in the work of Canadian poets. Colonel John McCrae's *In Flanders Fields* was the only important Canadian verse related to the 1914-1918 conflict, but it is among the best-known and best-loved of all Canadian poems. In the between-wars period E. J. Pratt easily attained recognition as Canada's leading poet in the English language, showing notable power in the field of narrative verse based on major events in contemporary human affairs: *Titans, The Roosevelt and the Antinoe, The Titanic, Brébeuf and his Brethren, The Last Spike, Dunkirk*. He twice won the Governor General's Award for Poetry and in 1940 was awarded the Lorne Pierce Gold Medal by the Royal Society of Canada. Noteworthy as Pratt's poetry contemporaries were Arthur S. Bourinot, Anne Marriott and Dorothy Livesay, all of whom wrote strong, vigorous verse which foreshadowed the work of a new, young school of poetry realists. Earle Birney, of Vancouver, displayed a highly personal style of writing which won him two Governor General's Awards for poetry, *David and Other Poems* (1942) and *Now is Time* (1945). A Montreal-based group, Frank Scott, A. J. M. Smith, Leo Kennedy and Abraham Klein, became the most interesting Canadian poets of the 1940's in some respects, writing extremely well but deliberately stirring controversy to attract public attention to their work and themselves. In recent years a strong academic tradition in Canadian poetry has been marked by the work of Roy Daniells, Robert Finch, Louis Mackay, James Reaney and George Johnston. The 1960's brought into prominence Irving Layton, Louis Dudek, Raymond Souster and Alfred Purdy in English-language Canada and Anne Hébert (*Poèmes*), Jacques Languirand (*Les insolites*), Gatien Lapointe (*Ode au Saint-Laurent*), Pierre Perrault (*Au Coeur de la Rose*) and Gilles Vigneault (*Quand les Bateaux s'en vont*) in French-language Canada.

In many ways the development of Canadian creative writing from the early days, through the Confederation period and into modern times has been a wearying and frustrating business; but there is no doubt that Canadian writing has now "arrived". Independence, vigour, imagination, courage and writing skill are the demands made upon the Canadian writer of today, because he is living in a compact world with instant communications and he knows that every writer is more or less in competition with every other writer. Canada is still a young country in world affairs and its modern spirit of enterprise and ambition is a driving force for its writers as they share in the excitement of a nation's 100th anniversary.

## Visual Arts

The visual arts in Canada today present a scene of unprecedented activity; with public interest and professional involvement at high levels in every part of the country. Art schools are jammed with students and the demand for new teaching facilities is insistent. Fine arts departments of universities are hard-pressed to find staff and facilities to develop the corps of art historians and teachers sought by institutions in all provinces. Adult courses in painting are swamped with applications. Awards and scholarships for painters and sculptors are multiplying. Exhibitions are frequent and well patronized. Sales of canvases, at good prices, are better than they have ever been before. The daily and periodical press are providing increasingly good coverage for art events. Governments at all levels are opening the public purse to encourage painters. There is widespread involvement of the public in art matters. As Canadian artists stand at the country's centennial point, looking back over the years and forward into the promising future, they cannot help remarking that "things look good".

In some ways painting has been the most successful of all the arts in the expression of our national personality for within its general circumference there is a small recognizable arc which is identifiably Canadian. The catalogue of the National Gallery of Canada contains a major section which describes works of the "Canadian School" —a bold attitude for Canadian officialdom to take, but a just and necessary one. It is not suggested that Canadian artists have devised novel methods or that they have set fashions for non-Canadians to follow; but it is believed that some Canadian painting has a specific content not found elsewhere, a manner of portraying locale and atmosphere, which marks it apart. Most of this specific content appeared during the period 1910 to 1930, when the Group of Seven and their immediate predecessors and immediate successors painted what they saw and what they felt with unrestrained enthusiasm and depth of feeling. The history of painting in Canada, from the early days, into the Confederation period, through two great wars and their in-between term and into the contemporary scene, must use the Group of Seven as its bench-mark and basis for comparison. It is the opinion of many Canadians that our early paintings were dull and uninspiring in comparison with the verve and personal impact of the Group's work, and not because of formal international standards of art appreciation; and that our modern painting is exciting and powerful because it respects the basic colour and composition factors employed by the Seven, and not because of favourable comparison with the works of New York and Paris.

The earliest paintings in Canada were the work of untutored, unambitious and unimaginative French settlers who, sponsored by their Church, produced works of religious and moral value and little artistic merit. The early works by English artists were mainly reportorial drawings and topographical paintings by military men and land surveyors; fastidiously correct portrayals of what stood before the eyes. The first Canadian painters to gain personal recognition were Paul Kane, who came from Ireland as a young boy to settle in what is now Toronto, and Cornelius Krieghoff, who was born in either Amsterdam or Dusseldorf and came to Canada as a mature young man. Kane's painting talents flourished between 1845 and 1860 when he became noted mainly for his faithful but sensitive paintings of the native Indians in all parts of Canada. Krieghoff was a prolific painter from 1845 to 1865 and his portraiture and genre paintings based mainly on the joys and tragedies of French Canadian life, particularly rural, were in keen demand at good prices. Works of both men are considered desirable collectors' items on both sides of the Atlantic today, with public and private patrons paying thousands of dollars for small canvases. There was a pattern of procedure for young English-area Canadians with ambitions to become painters in the pre-Confederation era and well into the latter part of the 19th century. At the studio of the local art teacher he studied to gain technical skills then proceeded to England or the Continent for advanced training in artistic mannerisms and fashions.

The province of Quebec has long been noted for its devotion to cultural pursuits.
There the arts flourish and even such functional structures as this rehabilitation
centre in the province's capital has an artistic décor.

He absorbed the attitudes of European teachers and then returned to Canada to paint
the Canadian scene through European glasses. A few went to New England art schools
where they learned the European approach second-hand. Much of the work of these
early painters was technically good, much of it was inept, but practically none of it
breathed any spirit of Canada's youth and strength while almost all of it reflected the
maturity and weariness of Europe. During this period "amateur" painters in both
French Canada and English Canada were numerous and active and they produced
many honest and local works of folk art: portraits, family groups, scenes and votive
pictures. It would not be unjust to make the generalization that during the whole
period prior to the approach of the 20th century painting in Canada was imitative,
purposeless and insignificant; but then it is necessary to mention the names of some
painters who did rise above the average and whose works are rated as the beginnings of
the "Canadian School", and some of whom worked into the early 1920's with genuine
success.

The topographer, *W. H. Bartlett* (b. 1809), a meticulous delineator of the Upper
Canada scene, has lasted well and reproductions of "Bartlett Prints" have enjoyed
respect and wide popularity into contemporary times. *François Beaucourt* (b. 1740)
of Montreal is remembered with appreciation through his "Portrait of a Negro Slave"
now in the McCord Museum of McGill University. *Joseph Légaré* (b. 1795) of

Quebec was a pioneer painter and collector and the teacher of *Antoine Plamondon* (b. 1804), the most impressive French Canadian portrait painter of his times. *Daniel Fowler* (b. 1810), who worked near Kingston, was a water-colourist of notable talent and one of the charter members of the Royal Canadian Academy. *John Arthur Fraser* (b. 1838), a landscape painter, produced a remarkable series of Rocky Mountain paintings under commission from the Canadian Pacific Railway. *Otto Jacobi* (b. 1812), German-taught and widely travelled, who lived the last 40 years of his long life in Canada, was a landscape painter of note and President of the R.C.A. from 1890 to 1893. *Lucius R. O'Brien* (b. 1832), a native Canadian who was one of the earliest artists to show a passionate interest in the landscapes of Western Canada, was an Upper Canada architect and civil engineer before turning to painting. He was the first president of the Royal Canadian Academy. *Paul Peel* (b. 1860), Canadian-born son of a marble cutter and drawing teacher, was chiefly active in France but also worked in Toronto and London (Canada) and achieved wide critical admiration for his academic figure studies. In Nova Scotia *Robert Field* (b. 1769), and *William Valentine* (b. 1798) were portraitists of sufficient merit to win acceptances by museums and art galleries in Canada and New England.

By 1900 in Toronto and Montreal a small number of painters sensed and talked about the beginnings of a definite artistic national feeling. *William Cruikshank, Robert Holmes, Charles Jefferys* and *Fred Brigden*, all established painters and teachers, were boldly advocating a new attitude "suited to the Canadian scene"; while in Montreal a number of followers of the distinguished *Maurice Cullen*, and admirers of the successful *James W. Morrice*, were becoming provocative advocates of a "Canadian Manner" in painting. The critics and the collectors and patrons did not appear to sense or share the burgeoning attitude, but an incipient "Canadian Art Movement" was simmering in the early years of the 20th century. Strongly imbued with it were the younger painters of the day who were not inspired by European painting, and gratefully tolerant of it were many of the middle-age group of Canadians who had become art teachers and found that their own training and experience provided them with little inspiration for young Canadians. This latter group were most important in the gradual change from the old to the new in Canadian art concepts. Among them were these honoured painters: *J. W. Beatty, F. M. Bell-Smith, Franklin Brownell, William Brymner, Franklin Carmichael, William Cruikshank, Maurice Cullen, Clarence Gagnon, Robert Harris, Robert Holmes, Franz Johnston, Ozias Leduc, J. E. H. MacDonald, J. W. Morrice, George Reid, Fred Verner, Horatio Walker* and *Homer Watson.*

The conventionality of Canadian painting received its first effective challenge in 1913 when a small group of Toronto painters, led by J. E. H. MacDonald, inspired by the remarkable personality of Tom Thomson and subsidized by Dr. J. M. McCallum, began to work together with the specific aim of depicting the glories of Canada's northland in a manner suited to the times and the subject. The group's feverish eagerness received a solid setback by the outbreak of World War I but, immediately after the war, the painters came together again, minus Thomson who had died in 1917. Concentrating on the Algoma country and the north shore of Lake Superior, the group painted a magnificently eloquent and bold collection of canvases which shocked and dismayed the standard critics. The name, "Group of Seven", was adopted in 1920 by *Frank Carmichael, Lawren Harris, Alexander Jackson, Franz Johnston, Arthur Lismer,*

*J. E. H. MacDonald* and *Frederick Varley*, and in May they held their first public exhibition at the Art Gallery of Toronto. Reaction to the show was immediate, violent and disapproving. Canada's first band of art revolutionaries were anathema to the conventional critics and to the unsophisticated public of Toronto. Scorn and abuse were rained upon the painters, individually and as a group, and according to all the rules of the normal art world their first exhibition should also have been their last. However, the open-minded directorate of the National Gallery of Canada stood by the Group of Seven against bitter opposition, bought some of the canvases and helped arrange an exhibition under important auspices in London. Unexpectedly favourable and mature comments came from many of Britain's most respected art critics. The art fraternity of Paris—painters, critics, dealers and patrons—looked at the Group's powerful paintings and openly admired them. Several of the leading art opinion leaders in the United States troubled to look at the Group's work and said they liked what they saw. Praise was not universal, of course, but it came from many important critics. Such praise could not be ignored by Canadians, and during the five years following the first exciting exhibition a gradual, almost reluctant, acceptance of the Group of Seven came about. This was the greatest happening in Canadian art history.

The Group of Seven as an entity lasted through ten vigorous and eventful years, with some changes in personnel during the period. Franz Johnston resigned in 1922. *A. J. Casson, Edwin Holgate* and *L. L. Fitzgerald* joined the Group in 1926, 1931 and 1932 respectively. It seems unlikely that the influence of the Group upon Canada's cultural life will ever be forgotten, even though changing times and changing fashions may label their formidable canvases anachronisms. During its few active years the Group inspired many young painters to attempt to tell the true story of Canada on canvas, broke down forever in Canada the colonial rigidities of art appreciation which had stood firm for a hundred years, and let fresh air into the whole concept of what Canada's participation in the world of art should be. Some cynical and crotchety critics now complain that the work of the Group of Seven has become, as a result of over-exposure to a gullible public, synonymous with "Canadian art" and that the world has labelled Canadians only as painters of solemn vistas, tortured pines and endless snows. But this is a senseless comment. Already the direct impact of the Group upon young and maturing Canadian painters has dwindled and there is no thoughtless imitation of the Group's manner in any of the contemporary exhibitions. The Canadian School of today is open-minded and receptive as well as strongly creative and is willing to consider all manner of influences, be they native or foreign, and is not afraid of the critics; and for much of this they should be grateful to the Group of Seven for "busting the thing wide open".

A number of painters who worked or flourished simultaneously with the Group of Seven but were not associated with it are entitled to recognition and respect in any review of the Canadian art story; because they, like the Group members, were men and women of spiritual and artistic independence who provided substantial inspiration to younger Canadian painters. In Quebec the names of *Clarence Gagnon, Albert Robinson, Lilias Torrance Newton* and *John Lyman* stand out, as do those of the British Columbia genius *Emily Carr* and Ontario's *David Milne*.

The 1930's, 1940's and 1950's brought mounting excitement and change and controversy to Canada's art world, through periods of representational painting, regional painting, rebellious painting, abstract painting, non-objective painting—right up to

The Group of Seven (and Barker Fairley) are shown at the Arts and Letters Club, Toronto. From left to right: A. Y. Jackson, Frederick Varley, Lawren Harris, (Barker Fairley), Franz Johnston, Arthur Lismer, J. E. H. MacDonald.

A. Y. Jackson is photographed with one of his latest masterpieces.

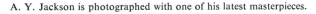

the very edges of "pop and op". On the West Coast a strictly nonconformist Vancouver School was led by the distinguished painter and teacher, *Jack Shadbolt*, whose influence upon young artists is now observed in all parts of Canada. Other West Coasters whose names stand out and whose works continue to wear well are *B. C. Binning*, *Bruno* and *Molly Bobak*, *Gordon Smith* and *Lionel Thomas*. A flourishing Prairie Provinces art movement has brought to prominence the names of *Joe Plaskett*, *Takao Tanabe*, *Kenneth Lochhead*, *Roy Kiyooka*, *Janet Mitchell* and *Roloff Beny*. In the Atlantic Provinces recent decades have enabled *Alex Colville, Jack Humphrey, Lawren Harris, Jr.* and *Robert Annand* to win their way to the top grouping of Canadian contemporary painters.

The hard-hitting, tempestuous Montreal School headed by *Alfred Pellan* was the most interesting Canadian art happening during the 1940's and early 1950's, particularly if one includes in the School the radical Automatistes headed by *Paul-Emile Borduas*. Followers of Pellan who have risen to eminence are numerous, three of the best-known being *Jacques de Tonnancour*, one of the most versatile painters of our time, *Léon Bellefleur* and *Robert La Palme*. The eminently successful non-objectivist, who smashed his way into European favour in the mid-1950's, *Jean-Paul Riopelle*, was a Borduas follower. *Goodridge Roberts* and *Stanley Cosgrove*, both on the fringes of, if not actually within, the Montreal School, have become notable elder statesmen.

During the period 1930-1950-plus Toronto's excellent facilities for teaching, exhibiting, criticising, understanding and selling art found themselves fully occupied, but in a rather stodgy way. Not much of the feverish excitement which marked the art world elsewhere seemed to influence what might be termed the Toronto School, although a great deal of good and forward-looking work was completed by top-ranking artists like *George Pepper, Will Ogilvie, Jack Nichols, Carl Schaefer, L. A. C. Panton* and *Charles Comfort*. In Ottawa *Henri Masson* painted genre works and landscapes in a vigorously personal manner during the period and as a teacher influenced a large number of young painters. *Gerald Trottier*, a native Ottawan who has since won distinction for his liturgical paintings, was a promising neophyte in the early 1950's. *André Biéler*, a strong painter and a masterly teacher, went to Queen's University in Kingston as resident artist in 1936 and for the following 25 years was a progressive force in the Canadian painting world.

The years since 1955, when the National Gallery of Canada held its first Biennial Exhibition, are extremely difficult to cope with in a review. They have been crowded with new developments, new trends, new organizations, new patrons and, above all, new artists. An astonishing awakening of public interest in the visual arts, engendered largely by improved communications and exchanges in tune with economic affluence, has resulted in unprecedented encouragement for artists. Multiple new opportunities to exhibit and to sell have brought forth a new batch of fledgling painters with new ideas and new techniques, and new youthful bravado. They have been ready and willing to compete on equal terms with their elders for the approval of critics and patrons; and in many instances the elders have turned their hands to the new "isms". Some of the new names appearing most frequently in the exhibition catalogues, critical reviews and honours lists during the past ten years are: *Harold Town, Jean McEwen, Guido Molinari, Graham Coughtry, Michael Snow, Peter Daglish, Pierre Gendron, Arthur McKay, Christopher Pratt, Tony Urquhart, Jacques Hurtubise*. There are many more.

Art classes for children at the National Art Gallery, Ottawa, are popular occasions with young people. The originality and diversity of their work is particularly noteworthy.

Although painting has received most of the attention in the art world of Canada, sculpture and the handcrafts have been in evidence since the earliest times. Sculpture has been publicly ignored and neglected and only in the past ten years has this art "rated" in Canadian eyes. In the pioneer days of French Canada wood carving, mainly for church embellishment, was a notable form of artistic expression and the influence of the early, self-taught carvers has persisted through the years. A select group of Canadian sculptors produced standard works in stone for parks and public buildings in the years succeeding Confederation, but it was not until the 1930's that some vigour and excitement in sculpture were noted. During the past quarter-century there has been a closer association of architects and builders and sculptors, and today sculpture works in stone, metals, wood and synthetic materials are normally included in plans for all public buildings. Governments and Big Business have become eager patrons of the sculptors. Exhibitions of sculptors' work are normal art happenings today and the general public is now able to take in its stride the "way-out", non-objective production of the latest generation of Canadian sculptors. Prominent in contemporary sculpture

Les Feux Follets have already won international acclaim for their dynamic choreography based upon folk dances of Canadians of many ethnic origins. Here the theme is Eskimo.

exhibitions are the stone carvings of the Eskimo people of Canada's eastern Arctic region, while among the most interesting and most respected of museum-guarded sculptures are the totem pole carvings of the Pacific Coast Indians. *Jean-Baptiste Coté* and *Louis Jobin* are the best-remembered of the pre-Confederation wood carvers of Quebec, while sculptors most eminent in the years on both sides of 1900 are *Philippe Hébert* and his son, *Henri Hébert, Aurèle de Foy Suzor-Coté, R. Tait McKenzie* and *Alfred LaLiberté*. Distinguished Canadian sculptors, whose work as carvers and teachers helped bridge the gap between the modern school and the awakening era following World War I, included *Emanuel Hahn, Florence Loring, Florence Wyle, Elizabeth Wyn Wood, Sylvia Daoust* and *Louis Archambault*. The frequent contemporary sculpture exhibitions have brought forth the work of many little-known artists who will undoubtedly become well-known with the passage of time. Meanwhile, names most frequently encountered in the sculpture scene of today include *Dora de Pedery Hunt, Armand Vaillancourt, Arthur Price, Yves Trudeau, E. B. Cox, Ulysse Comptois, Victor Tolgesy, Gord Smith, John Chambers* and *Claude Roussel*.

Until very recent times the term handcrafts was a "catch-all" to include a considerable variety of local folkcraft, traditional fine craftsmanship and some esoteric art forms; but since 1960 a definite category of fine crafts has received recognition in Canadian art circles and is now attracting some of Canada's most able creative artists. In Quebec this is not a new development because the French Canadians have been craft-minded always; but the elevation of the crafts to a fine arts status is recent. Contemporary recognition and respect for the fine crafts, officially and in the public mind, has resulted from a number of factors including: the influence of foreign countries, encouragement from provincial governments, the work of the Canadian Handicrafts Guild and the recently-incorporated Canadian Craftsmen's Association. Among the great number of professional fine crafts workers in Canada some of those whose work has attracted international attention are: *Micheline Beauchemin* (tapestry), *Helga Palko* (enamels and precious metals), *Merton Chambers* (ceramics), *Charlotte Lindgren* (weaving), *F. Desrochers-Drolet* (enamels), *Adolph Schwenk* (pottery), *Krystyna Sadowska* (multiple), *Mariette Rousseau-Vermette* (tapestry), *Marc-André Beaudin* (goldsmith), *Barbara Richardson* (stained glass) and *Gail Lamarche* (batiks). There are many more.

Over the years institutions as well as individuals have been vital elements in the development of the visual arts in Canada. Some have been big, some small; some

A presentation of *Cavalleria Rusticana* at the O'Keefe Centre, Toronto.

have been long-lived, some have grown, flourished and withered in a brief space of time. Some have been national, most have been local. Some have been subsidized by the public treasury, some have flowed from the philanthropy of individuals, some have been entirely the creations of artists. But all have contributed to the picture, even though only a few can be remembered. The Church was the earliest patron and promoter of art in Canada and today it is still encouraging every form of visual art. Among the lay institutions of greatest importance have been the National Gallery of Canada, the Royal Canadian Academy of Arts, the Quebec Government, the Art Gallery of Ontario, the Montreal Museum of Fine Arts. Artists societies of notable influence included the Canadian Group of Painters, Canadian Society of Painters in Water-colour, Canadian Society of Painter-Etchers and Engravers, Sculptors' Society of Canada, Canadian Guild of Potters, Association Professionnelle des Artisans du Québec, the Ontario Society of Artists and the Toronto Art Students League. The two most influential schools in Canadian art history are Toronto's Ontario College of Art and L'École des Beaux Arts in Montreal. Art galleries in smaller centres, such as London, Quebec, Hamilton, Vancouver, Saskatoon, Winnipeg and Fredericton, have—in spite of great financial difficulties — played a vital rôle. In recent years Canadian universities have assumed important responsibility by engaging resident artists, offering credit

THE FINE AND LIVELY ARTS

411

courses in the history of art, establishing their own art galleries, promoting public interest through exhibitions and summer courses and commissioning important mural paintings, sculptored works and fine craft décor. Communication between artists and between the various sectors of the patron-public has improved immeasurably in the past two decades and in Canada this has been noted particularly in radio and television programming, in art film distribution and in the growth of Canada's two chief art journals, *Canadian Art* and *Vie des Arts*. Direct support for the arts in a substantial way has recently been forthcoming from several of the provincial governments. Finally, the most important shot-in-the-arm for the visual arts in Canada has come from the Canada Council, inaugurated by the Federal Government in 1957 and performing miracles and good works continuously since.

## Music

Musically, Canada is relatively underdeveloped in some ways and thoroughly mature and advanced in others.

It has been pointed out that among French Canadians there is an instinctive, light-hearted and uninhibited turning to music to express both individual and group emotions, that in parts of Canada the basic folk music of continental Europe plays an important part in individual, family and community life, and that the dominant group of Canadian life is fundamentally influenced by Anglo-Saxon reticence and does not easily find an emotional outlet in musical expression. (The final part of the above statement might be modified in view of the experiences of England's "Beatles!") Be that as it may, the over-all pattern of musical development in Canada is a relatively simple one: many years of dull, parochial and fruitless musical isolation followed by a period of eager and competent participation in the life of the broad musical world. The turning point was reached by 1940. The main factors involved in a country's musical development are: appreciation (listening to music); composition (creating musical pieces); performance (making musical sounds) and education (providing musical understanding); and in each of these areas Canada's early story was mediocre whereas its contemporary activity is significant and exciting.

The Toronto Symphony Orchestra has won international acclaim under its talented young Japanese-born conductor, Seiji Ozawa.

From the earliest times simple musical activity was a part of the Canadian story. In 1535 when Cartier first met with the native people at Hochelaga he "ordered the trumpets and other musical instruments to be sounded, whereat the Indians were much delighted"; and while there was really no Canadian content to this musical episode other than the geographical factor it was a starting point for Canadian musical historians. The musical life of New France was not insignificant, in an inward-looking sense, because it added a modicum of joyousness and local refinement to times burdened by hard work and frequent despair. Traditional songs of Old France, with many new variations, were sung with naturalness and spontaneity in the home, in the school and on festive occasions. Sacred music was cherished and exploited with dedication and success by the early Church in the new world, and a love for good music was stimulated by priests and nuns of French musical training. Musical education, especially in the form of singing, was a prime responsibility of the early convents — with settlers' children and native Indian children being equally enthusiastic pupils. From the earliest times through to the contemporary scene French Canada has always taken an official (through the Church and the provincial government) attitude of responsibility for promotion of musical activity among French Canadians; and today Quebec is well advanced in musical appreciation, musical performance, musical composition and musical education.

In non-French Canada in the century preceding Confederation there was no guided musical development in any substantial sense. In the Atlantic areas a memorable body of folk music was created and enjoyed; some of it directly inspired by English, Scottish and New England songs and themes, but much of it of purely local genesis. The fishing people and the pioneering farmers found a full complement of cultural enjoyment in their folksongs and standard hymns, while in Halifax, Yarmouth and other seaport towns the arrival of ships with travellers from the cities of Europe and the English Colonies created a desire for more sophisticated music. In Upper Canada the early settlers had little time or inclination for indulgence in music and there was no real stimulation of musical interest beyond the influence of British military bands garrisoned in Canadian towns. The bands fitted into local life in many ways: at concerts, dances, religious observances, festivals and ceremonials. They inspired the formation of local orchestral groups and Canada's early march music was composed by British army bandsmen. At the same time the musical influence of the British Colonies to the south was felt increasingly. The Colonies (United States after 1783) had outstripped Canada in cultural growth in every respect and when thousands of United Empire Loyalists chose Canada as their new home they brought with them musical tastes and sophistication. Between 1770 and 1820 more than 300,000 immigrants came to Canada, from Europe, the British Isles and the United States, and brought with them an eagerness for musical activity unknown to the early Canadians.

By Confederation the musical life of Canada was at a stage where it contained a bit of everything except virtuosity. The urban centres of the several colonies and provinces had conservatories and orchestras and chamber groups and choral societies, even a few opera companies; vocal and instrumental soloists of professional calibre; a small musical-instrument industry; and well organized liturgical music activities. Many rural areas had developed amateur music activity as a local cultural embellishment, and the importation of big-city music for one-night presentations began. Over the years the musical life of the Canadian community had grown in size and complexity, between the beginning days and Confederation times, but there had not been a comparable development in Canadian musical taste, musical performance or musical ambition. Importation and imitation were the order of the day and there seemed little promise of musical creations or performances which might reflect the stirring times and challenging conditions of life in Canada.

But Confederation did do something to Canadian music. Excitement and public interest, almost for the first time, plunged across local and parochial borders and the uplifting prospect of a united country was a pervasive influence. The conferences and meetings, the debates, the comings and goings of political leaders, the verbal fury of newspaper editors, the stern warnings of clergymen, the sense of involvement felt by farmers and workers and scholars; the thought that all the people north of the United

*Aida*, as staged by the Montreal Symphony Orchestra in La Grande Salle of La Place des Arts.

CANADA, 1867-1967

States border might form a single nation; the hope that Canadians of French culture and other Canadians might become brothers in fact; the belief that the future would be challenging and bright: all this created an atmosphere which stimulated artistic people in Canada and, in the field of music the stimulation was most obvious. The several decades following Confederation brought developments which lifted Canada from her musical rut and paved the way for solid growth in the early 1900's.

In Toronto a deeply felt attachment to the British tradition of choral music was the key to musical development. In 1872 the Philharmonic Society launched a career which continued successfully, mainly under the direction of Frederick Torrington, for more than 20 years, and Toronto's reputation for superiority in oratorio performance has lasted into the present time. Numerous small orchestras and chamber music groups and brass bands emerged in the 1870-90 period; none of them of lasting character but all contributing to a general enlargement of public enthusiasm for musical life. In 1886 the Toronto Conservatory was founded and was a substantial enterprise from the start and the opening of Massey Music Hall in 1894 provided a long needed focal point for musical activity. In French Canada the Mendelssohn Choir (1864) and the Philharmonic Society (1877) flourished and provided inspiration for many minor musical groups of excellent quality such as the Société Musicale des Montagnards Canadiens, Les Orphéonistes, Société Ste-Cécile, Société des Symphonistes and the Septuor Haydn. Some of the first "big names" of Canadian music were active at this time: Arthur Lavigne, Joseph Vézina, Frantz Jehin-Prume, Guillaume Couture and Calixa Lavallée (the brilliant composer of "O, Canada"), John Bayley, Edward Fisher, Arthur Fisher, Theodore Zoellner, W. J. Birks, C. A. Sippi, Gustave Smith and Charles Henry Porter. In Halifax, Ottawa, Peterborough, Saint John, London and Berlin (now Kitchener) musical growth was notable between Confederation and the turn of the century—in the sense of involving more and more people, rather than in the sense of creative achievement. The musicality of Canadians was still overburdened with imitation and derivation, but the way was being prepared for a new era, commencing early in the 1900's, when Canada would show some initiative in speaking in its own musical voice.

Although the years prior to 1900 were marked by musical mediocrity their importance lay in the preparatory steps for advancement which occurred between 1900 and 1940, and the exciting musical activity which followed World War II. Factors which entered into the new development included massive immigration, improvement of travel, new devices for communication, better education facilities and more congenial economic conditions. Among the tens of thousands of newcomers to Canada were many musically well-educated men and women who gave long needed leadership. There developed an important two-way traffic in musicians—international celebrities appearing before Canadian audiences and Canadians travelling to Europe and the United States to perform or to pursue advanced studies. Books, journals, sheet-music, gramophone records, lectures, films and, eventually, radio brought a musical harvest to every part of Canada. The availability of good music educators resulted in a great multiplication of public and private musical schooling opportunities. And the new relative affluence enabled the people to spend money, privately and through taxation, on the promotion of every form of musical activity. By this time, too, the vast prairie region had been opened, was prospering, and effective railway communication had brought British Columbia intimately into the Canadian musical family.

In the early decades of the present century a music-conscious Canada saw progress and enlargement of the music community in every sense. In all areas of performance and public participation there was multiplication, improvement, ferment and a forward-looking eagerness. Only in the field of composition was there a lack of evidence of the new spirit of the times. Although the number of Canadian composers and their works increased substantially, a persistent European tradition of style and manner seemed to inspire most of their work, and it was not until close to mid-century that the spell was broken. Some of the musical organizations which showed great enterprise in the early years of our century have continued until today. Many succumbed, especially during the 1914-1919 period. But all were relatively important in the development of Canada's musical life. Mention of a few highlights indicates the geographical spread and musical variety. The Mendelssohn Choir of Toronto, under the leadership of Augustus Vogt, was internationally respected. Toronto's fame for choral music was also enhanced by The National Chorus, under Albert Ham, the Oratorio Society and the Schubert Choir. The Orpheus Club in Halifax, the Festival Chorus of New Brunswick, the Elgar Choir in Hamilton, Winnipeg's Oratorio Society, the Edmonton Male Chorus, the Apollo Singers in Calgary, and first-class vocal groups in Vancouver, Victoria, Lethbridge and Truro emphasized the persistence of Canada's first musical love. In Quebec province superb choral performance was provided by Montreal's St-Louis de France choir and the Union Musicale in the capital city. The Montreal Opera Company was a notably ambitious undertaking from 1910 to 1913. In 1908 the first Toronto Symphony Orchestra was launched. The Governor General's Award for Orchestra Playing was won in 1907 by the celebrated Société Symphonique de Québec and in 1908 by the Ottawa Symphony Orchestra. Halifax, Vancouver, Regina, Edmonton, Hamilton and Calgary were among the Canadian cities developing orchestral groups. In 1908 the burgeoning city of Edmonton gave Canada its first competitive musical festival.

The years of the great economic depression and World War II immediately following brought disruption and distress to Canada's musical life, but also a breaking-away from musical shackles of the past and introduction of a new, vigorous, independent attitude toward musical creation and performance. The past 25 years have seen Canada gradually move into the world stream of music with composers speaking out in global terms, artists regarding themselves as international professionals, and the musical public demanding exposure to the music of today and tomorrow in all forms. The most notable change has been in composition with the new successful modernists seeming to be in no way related to their Canadian predecessors of three decades earlier. However, a small number of extremely important middlemen did, in fact, serve as a link between the two musical generations. These were the highly competent, personally dedicated musician-teachers including Sir Ernest MacMillan, Healey Willan, Claude Champagne, Alfred Laliberté and Edwin Collins. Also important in providing theme material for the new composers were the assiduous collectors of early Canadian folk songs, chief among them being Marius Barbeau and Hector Gratton. The new school of Canadian composers cannot be labelled as conforming to any style or method. Undoubtedly they are impressed by the vigour and daring of outstanding European and American modernists but at the same time they show no hesitation about attempting new and unproven musical manners and devices. Extensive travel, the success-story of musical recordings and the encouragement offered by

radio broadcasting agencies have helped young Canadian composers to taste the honey of success at home and to participate in the great new world-wide brotherhood of music. Among the most prominent of the new school of Canadian composers are the following: John Weinzweig (influential teacher and prime mover of the important Canadian League of Composers), Barbara Pentland (b.1912), Alexander Brott (b.1915), Harry Somers (b.1925), Maurice Blackburn (b.1914), Jean Coulthard (b.1908), Jean Vallerand (b.1915), Jean Papineau-Couture (b.1916), Violet Archer (b.1913), Clermont Pépin (b.1926), Pierre Mercure (b.1927), Oscar Morawetz (b.1917), Roger Matton (b.1929), Louis Applebaum (b.1918), Maurice Dela (b.1919) and Harry Freedman (b.1922).

Musical performance since 1940 has expanded and improved immeasurably, in keeping with the affluence of the times in Canada and in harmony with a contemporary world-wide upsurge of musical interest. In every part of the country every aspect of musical activity has been prospering. It would be unwise to attempt to indicate the number of active orchestras, chamber groups, bands, choral groups and other musical organizations; they are legion. A hint is contained in the 1964-65 annual report of the Canada Council which lists substantial grants to the Canadian Music Council, Canadian Music Educators Association, Les Jeunesses Musicales du Canada, National

and small
from Engla
for almost
school-hous
came enlarg
theatres and
theatres equ
and opera h
Saint John,
fare provide
Canadian au
this theatrica
had swarmed
motion pictu
theatre creat
appeared fro

Meanwhile
cultural fabr
activity whic
any integratic
themselves a
Ottawa Dran
completely a
ten-night sta
successful Ur
University of
In many othe
it was natural
has become o

THE FINE AN

A presentation of *Salome* was a feature of the recent opera season in Toronto.

Manitoba Theatre Centre performances have become a major attraction during the winter season in Winnipeg, and include a wide variety of plays.

Yo
syp
To
as
nu
To
bec
Ha
pia
hav
ther
and
ope
Mau

W
mus
prim
toda
gene
diver
of M
Cons
Deep
has t
and r
unlike
witho
castin

**The**

Until
with a
seemed
fession
never s
tinuous
playwri

In th
instinct
earliest
for the
of the t
there is
migratic
an unso
and by

strong enough to resist possible undermining by the movies and by the attractions of television and the renaissance of professional theatre. A national festival, climax of a series of regional competitive festivals, is held each year in a different Canadian city. Plays in English and in French, three-act plays and one-act plays, plays by Canadian playwrights and plays by foreigners, all produced and performed by amateurs, have met head-on in furious competition in this most Canadian of all festivals. The little theatre movement and the Dominion Drama Festival have inspired a knowledgeable and appreciative theatre audience throughout Canada and have provided the basic training for a surprising number of successful actors playing in professional ranks beyond Canadian borders as well as at home.

The professional theatre story of today is one of great enterprise, excitement and promise, with the Stratford Shakespearean Festival commanding most of the spotlight. Launched in 1953 as the impossible dream of a small Ontario town the Stratford venture has become the great legend of Canadian theatre. Its first season, in a great circus-type tent, saw the production of two Shakespearean works and a number of afternoon concerts. Its 14th season in 1966, in a magnificent 2,200-seat modern theatre, offered three works of Shakespeare, two modern plays, one opera, one ballet performance and numerous concerts, throughout a season extending from June 6 to October 8. The enthusiasm and excitement engendered by the success of the Stratford venture sparked a new Canadian determination to have professional theatre on a regular and nation-wide scale, and the gradual realization of this ambition is what Canadians are experiencing today. It would be an error, however, to believe that the contemporary Canadian professional theatre had sprung full-fledged from the Stratford inspiration. A long line of summer theatre ventures, most of them of professional excellence and financial shakiness, provided Canadians with good theatre fare during the 1935-65 period. Some of those deserving permanent salutation are: the John Holden Players of Winnipeg and Bala, the Brae Manor Theatre at Knowlton, P.Q., Montreal's Mountain Playhouse, the summer players at Peterborough, Niagara Falls and Vineland, the Straw Hat Players at Port Carling, the Red Barn Players at Jackson's Point and the Theatre Under the Stars in Vancouver. Year-round repertory groups worthy of note included Les Compagnons du Saint Laurent, Canadian Reper-

418

CANADA, 1867-1967

tory Theatre (Ottawa), International Players (Kingston), Totem Theatre (Vancouver) and the New Play Society (Toronto).

The contemporary Canadian professional theatre is by no means living on Easy Street, but the indications are that it is here to stay and that there is a bright and promising future for young Canadians prepared to devote themselves to the theatre. Financial help for professional theatre is now coming from federal, provincial and municipal authorities, from foundations, from arts councils and from individual philanthropists. Box office support is massive and dependable. Supplementary income from television and movies is available. Universities are beginning to accept responsibility for scholarly studies and research in the drama field. The Canadian Theatre Centre and the Canadian Theatre School are gaining in experience and competence. The Canada Council and other agencies are seriously committed to the encouragement of Canadian playwrights. New playhouses of the most up-to-date design are appearing in Canadian cities. Scholarships and travel grants for individual actors, directors and producers are rapidly multiplying. Company tours in Canada and abroad are now being realized by most Canadian professional companies. It seems that good times are just beginning for distinguished Canadian professional companies such as: La Comédie canadienne, the Canadian Players-Crest Theatre group, the Manitoba Theatre Centre, Théâtre du Rideau Vert, the Neptune Theatre and Théâtre de l'Égrégore. And it also seems that competent amateur theatre will continue to be supported liberally by the people of Canada to complete an intelligent, well-rounded and satisfying national theatre complex.

# Architecture

Architecture, one of the classical fine arts, has not enjoyed any special consideration in Canada, either as a folk art in early times or as a specialized modern profession. The planning of areas and structures and making the best use of available materials to suit the environment, i.e. architecture, led to the primitive ice block igloo of the Eskimo peoples, to the hide-covered wigwam of the wandering Indian tribes, to the log cabins of early white-man settlements and to the sod shanties of the prairie pioneers. The farm houses of developing Quebec and Ontario and the Maritime areas were functional and effective and a tribute to the common sense of the do-it-yourself folk architects of the times. Early public structures provided other examples of form and location dictated by purpose and materials. The old forts, schools, churches and inns, built of local logs and stones were as effective as the circumstances would permit and employed architecture as a basic, elemental art. From Confederation to the 1920's much of the building in Canada was in the "Victorian tradition", with picturesqueness a prime aim. Bank buildings and railway stations were often adapted from classical Greek design and many hotels were made to resemble European châteaux. In some of the more elegant structures imitation of pure Gothic style was pursued with diligence. Between the two World Wars reaction against Victorian mannerisms occurred and was followed by a preference for "modernism", emphasizing space, light and function, and greatly influenced by the architecture profession in the United States. This is the architectural fashion of contemporary Canada, as it is, in fact, throughout the western world. Residences, office buildings, schools, churches, prisons, hospitals— throughout Canada today these are all planned and designed and built in the modern,

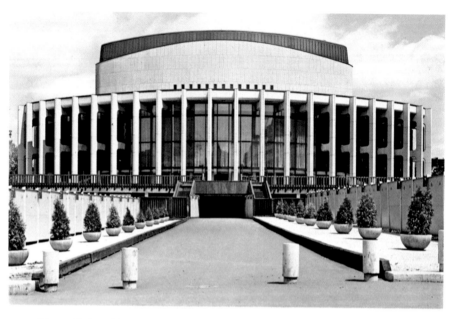

Montreal's beautiful La Place des Arts is host to many cultural events during the artistic season.

universal manner. Some observers, especially journalists, are inclined to refer to the country and terminal grain storage elevators of the prairies and the seaports as "distinctively Canadian architecture", a comment not properly referring to architectural origin but to geographical frequency. Architecture as a vocation and career is well organized in Canada and excellent teaching is provided at seven institutions at the university level. The Central Mortgage and Housing Corporation, an agency of the Federal Government, gives substantial encouragement to the architecture profession.

## Ballet

Ballet, juniormost among the arts in Canada, has been a matter of public interest only since the 1930's; but today three top-ranking professional companies, the Royal Winnipeg Ballet, the National Ballet Company, of Toronto, and Les Grands Ballets Canadiens, of Montreal, are genuinely noteworthy and these are backed up by many small groups, amateur and semi-professional, throughout Canada. Public appreciation of ballet is still relatively limited but is increasing rapidly, thanks to the respect paid to the art in the popular mass media—movies and television. Between 1948 and 1954 ballet festivals were held in Winnipeg, Toronto and Ottawa, bringing together the dance and choreography of ten Canadian companies, playing to sell-out audiences and receiving extensive press coverage. For economic reasons these national festivals have been discontinued but it is now customary for Canadian companies to participate in festivals held in neighboring parts of the United States. In 1965 the Northeastern International Ballet Festival was held in Ottawa with great success. The Royal Winnipeg Ballet, pioneered by Gweneth Lloyd and Betty Farrally, the National Ballet

Company, directed by Celia Franca, and Les Grands Ballets Canadiens, under Ludmilla Chiriaeff, are thoroughly professional companies, with schools attached. They have toured widely abroad, in Europe, South America and the United States, and make frequent appearances in the main Canadian cities and on television programs. A recent newcomer to the scene, Montreal's Les Feux Follets, has already won international favour for its dynamic and high-spirited choreography based upon folk dances of Canadians of many ethnic origins. There is a notable exchange of dancers between the Canadian companies and foreign companies, and the names of some of Canada's leading choreographers have become well known in the international ballet community. Financial help from the public treasury and from private purses in Canada is becoming increasingly generous, as Canadian ballet people continue to demonstrate their ability to win international recognition and approval. In many ways the art of the ballet seems unsuited to the Canadian scene and temperament, but it appears that ballet may, sooner or later, develop into one of this country's most popular cultural activities.

Ballet is performed against a backdrop of the Expo insignia.

The Royal Winnipeg Ballet owes its origin to Gweneth Lloyd of England who created over thirty original ballets for the company which is renowned for its sprightly presentations.

A Canadian Indian motif serves as background for the happy group of Les Feux Follets

# Religion

Freedom of religion has always been a prerogative of Canadian people. From earliest days Indians and Eskimos practised their ceremonial rites as in subsequent eras newcomers of many other races likewise observed their religious practices.

In 1960 these rights were confirmed by the passage in Parliament of "An Act for the Recognition and Protection of Human Rights and Fundamental Freedoms". It contained this provision:

"It is hereby recognized and declared that in Canada there have existed and shall continue to exist without discrimination by reason of race, national origin, colour, religion or sex, the following human rights and fundamental freedoms, namely, . . .

    (c) freedom of religion. . . ."

The rich diversity of religious denominations, as recorded in the 1961 Census and set out in the following official compilation, is a tribute to Canada's religious freedom:

| | |
|---|---:|
| Canadian Population | 18,238,247 |
| Adventist | 25,999 |
| Anglican Church of Canada | 2,409,068 |
| Baptist | 593,553 |
| Brethren in Christ | 16,256 |
| Buddhist | 11,611 |
| Christian and Missionary Alliance | 18,006 |
| Christian Reformed | 62,257 |
| Christian Science | 19,466 |
| Churches of Christ Disciples | 19,512 |
| Church of the Nazarene | 13,412 |
| Confucian | 5,089 |
| Doukhobor | 13,234 |
| Evangelical United Brethren | 27,079 |
| Free Methodist Church of Canada | 14,245 |
| Greek Orthodox | 239,766 |
| Jehovah's Witnesses | 68,018 |
| Jewish | 254,368 |
| Lutheran | 662,744 |
| Mennonite | 152,452 |
| Mormon | 50,016 |
| Pentecostal | 143,877 |
| Plymouth Brethren | 12,326 |
| Presbyterian | 818,558 |
| Roman Catholic | 8,342,826 |
| Salvation Army | 92,054 |
| Ukrainian (Greek) Catholic | 189,653 |
| Unitarian | 15,062 |
| United Church of Canada | 3,664,008 |
| Other | 283,732 |

Mormon Temple, Alberta. According to the Census of 1961, more than 50,000 Canadians follow the Mormon tradition. The Church of Jesus Christ of Latter Day Saints was founded in 1830. The faith was introduced into Canada by four United States elders at Ernestown, Upper Canada, in 1832.

Notre Dame des Champs, Roman Catholic Church, Repentigny, Quebec. According to the Census of 1961, more than 8,300,000 Canadians are Roman Catholics.

Beth Ora Synagogue, St. Laurent, Quebec— an ancient faith in a new sanctuary. Adherents of the Jewish faith in Canada number more than 254,000 (1961 Census). In 1959 Canadians of Jewish origin celebrated the 200th anniversary of their permanent settlement in Canada.

St. Paul's Chapel of the Mohawks, Brantford, Ontario. Early in the eighteenth century, Queen Anne sent a valuable sacramental service of plate, a communion cloth and Bible to the church.

Ukrainian Catholic Church, St. Catharines, Ontario. Members number some 190,000 and are settled in every province of Canada.

Riverview United Church, Calgary, Alberta. Almost 3,700,000 Canadians are members of the United Church of Canada, the second largest denomination in the country.

RELIGION

429

# Recreation

"A cottage at the lake", a "summer home by the ocean", a "tent pitched in a grassy plot" . . . these reflect the joy of the outdoors which is part of Canada's traditional heritage. Nowhere is there such a variety and multiplicity of seasonal pastimes available as in Canada; nowhere more beauty of landscape or seascape.

## Pioneer Activities

In early days, however, Canadian waters were commercial freeways and critical factors in the economic and commercial development of the country. Horseback riding, canoeing, hunting, fishing, and camping, however pleasant, were typical work activities for many Canadians. Free time was a scarce commodity during much of the 19th century. Nor was it ordinarily available in blocks of time such as two and three weeks annual vacations, or regular two-day weekends which are standard today— although full advantage was taken of every official holiday.

The customs of the times involved fairs and exhibitions, contests and displays, sports and social events. Many recreational activities were closely related to work activities. There was horse racing in summer or snowshoe racing in winter; exhibitions of farm produce in the fall, or a barn-raising when required.

Throughout the 19th century, and well into the 20th, demonstrations of work skills and competitions between workers were popular forms of recreation and amusement. Thus, plowing matches, sawing competitions, log hurling, and nail-driving contests were, and continue to be, popular events at picnics, fairs and outings. During the later 19th century, track and field sports were pursued in the larger population centres and soccer was played as a team sport. Yacht racing flourished on both coasts and on inland waters.

Lacrosse, adopted as Canada's national game at the time of Confederation, was played by Indians in all parts of the country, and was soon adopted by settlers. By 1867 definite rules had been established and play was organized into leagues. The rules have subsequently been changed radically and today Box Lacrosse, an indoor version of the game, is popular in several Ontario communities; the Winnipeg area of Manitoba; in Vancouver and Vancouver Island, British Columbia. The older outdoor game also flourishes in eastern United States universities, particularly in those of the "Ivy League".

## Ice Sports

Ice hockey, Canada's most popular sport, was in its early organizational stages at the time of Confederation. The game is believed to have originated on the Chain Lakes, Dartmouth in 1828. By 1890 there were organized leagues in most centres of population. In 1893 the Governor General, Lord Stanley, offered a cup for senior competition. The first winners were the Montreal Canadien Athletic Association; in 1965, the professional Montreal Canadiens Team. Since 1912 only professional teams have competed for the Stanley Cup and since 1926 it has been the trophy of the National Hockey League.

Pleasure skating has been, and continues to be, tremendously popular as a form of recreation. Most Canadian children learn to skate before they start to school. Natural ice is annually available in all parts of the country with the exception of southern British Columbia and the extreme south of Ontario. Thousands of rinks are flooded by municipal authorities in towns and cities throughout the land. Pleasure skating is an activity that leads quite naturally to special interest in ice hockey or figure skating.

As a participant sport, figure skating rivals ice hockey in the number of devotees. As a competitive sport, it has produced a significant number of Canadian international champions in recent years. While the vast majority of the participants in figure skating are female, Canadian males also have achieved considerable success in international competition.

The Canadian record in international hockey competition is outstanding. Other nations are learning however. In recent years Canadian "amateur" teams have not been the "sure winners" in international events they used to be.

## Recreational Influences

Recreational developments in English-speaking Canada have been influenced by the sport interests of Britain and the United States. Thus, cricket and baseball; lawn bowling, curling and ten-pins; golf, rugby, soccer and football; tennis and badminton; volleyball and basketball, all flourish in Canada.

For recreation—and excitement—the track at Mosport, Ontario provides interesting results.

The continuous increase in the number of trailers on the roads of Canada has led to the provision of special trailer parks equipped to meet the needs of such vehicles and their owners. This is a trailer campsite in the beautiful environs of Waterton Lakes National Park, Alberta.

After 1900 the influence of the United States is shown in baseball. Football, as developed in Canada from Rugby, has also been continuously changing in form as a direct result of influence from the United States. Professional hockey has modified its rules and organization to appeal to the American spectator. The organization of minor team sports has followed the concept of the "farm" system first developed in professional baseball.

The development of radio during the 1920's and of network broadcasting during the 1930's gave tremendous impetus to the influence of the United States on Canadian patterns of recreation. Radio itself, and subsequently television, became major media of recreation. The height of American influence was, perhaps, the declaration by the Canadian Broadcasting Corporation in 1963 that the so-called World Series was an event of national importance in Canada. Broadcast of this event was regarded as constituting a program of "Canadian" content!

An important trend of the postwar years bodes well for recreation. Canadians appear to have come to terms with their geography. While many agencies have operated summer camps, and playground programs during an eight-week summer season, they have, in the past, tended to focus unduly on indoor activities during the long winter season. More recently, however, winter camping has been initiated, skiing has flourished, and skating and toboganning parties are becoming increasingly popular. Indicative of this trend is the fact that in recent international competition Canadian bob sledders and skiers have achieved impressive records.

Prince Edward Island is famous for its long miles of smooth sandy beaches. Paved roads, an equitable climate and a variety of modern accommodations have added to the Island's lure.

With a touch of nostalgia, a stern-wheel steamer, especially designed for the tourist trade, plies the waters of the Red River, Manitoba.

RECREATION

Young Alberta students on a Centennial exchange are seen with hostesses on the Citadel in Halifax, Nova Scotia. In the background is the famous Old Town Clock.

The Trans-Canada Highway west of Banff lures visitors into an area famous for its snow-capped mountain peaks and its intriguing tree-shadowed lakes.

Canada is a land of contrasts and every season has its charms. Whether it is fishing in the summertime, skiing or snowmobiling in the winter, or even bending over the chessboard indoors, Canadians have a wide variety of interesting pursuits from which to choose.

## Year-Round Activity

Canada now appears to be developing year-round recreational programs compatible with both its history and geography. The flow of traffic from centres of population to ski resorts, ice fishing grounds, and winter resorts, during the winter months is beginning to approach the massive proportions of summer traffic to the cottage, camp, or summer resort during the summer months. Within most Canadian communities winter activities are no longer severely limited to hockey, skating, and indoor gymnasium and swimming programs. Rather, there is a vast increase in such participant sports as curling, skiing and skidooing. Family clubs, offering a wide range of activities throughout the year, are springing up around major cities. Golf, curling, swimming, tennis, skiing and bowling, are typical of the range of activities offered by such clubs.

The patterns of recreation in Canada have always been subject to outside influence. It is only in recent years that Canadians have been appreciably influenced by nations with a similar climate. However, although the international achievements of Canadians in recreation have been modest, interests have been varied. Probably no other nation has as wide a variety of participant activities with such a significant number of devotees. For example, four types of football are played in Canada; Association Football, Rugby Football, American Football and Canadian Football. Association is, perhaps, the international sport; Rugby Football is a British game; American Football is a uniquely American game; while Canadian Football is an indigenous development. That all four forms of the game thrive is indicative of the richness of Canada's recreational programs—and reflective of the various influences that have affected Canada's recreational pursuits.                                        (JOHN FARINA)

# Emergence of Canada as a Power in International Affairs

# Canada in World Affairs

In the hundred years since the union of British North America, the changing place of Canada in world affairs has been broadly consistent with the needs and capacity of the developing country. Originally, the Dominion was rich in territory but small in population. Of some 3,500,000 people, not more than 100,000 lived west of Ontario, while the great northern area was virtually unpeopled and barely explored. There were many pressing domestic tasks: to put into operation the provisions of the British North America Act, to fulfill the commitments of railways to east and west coasts, to enlarge the canals in the central provinces, to encourage industry.

Canada was in the world scene as part of the British Empire. The Fathers of Confederation had neither desired nor asked for any direct responsibility in international relations. It was true that Canadians of the day thought in general terms that their country would assume a greater stature than had been possible for the component colonies: in due time, perhaps, become a sovereign state. Such expectations, however, were not expressed in constitutional terms and in the eyes of the rest of the world Canada was a colony, albeit one that was self-governing within its own frontiers.

Factors that have mainly influenced the external relationships of Canada can be deduced from its origin, economic structure, and environment. Its people were, for the most part, and particularly in the first few decades, of French or British extraction, inheriting the traditions of two great European civilizations. Politically it was the British influence that was dominant. The British system of government had been applied in modified form to each colony as it came under the Crown, and proved acceptable to those of French as well as of British origin.

With the institutions came the concepts of political and civil liberty. That Canada was an integral part of the British Empire meant to those of British race a continued connection with their motherland; but to the French-speaking community it was a tie which had no such inherited meaning, and was accepted out of necessity and because, on the whole, the new rule was tolerant of French-Canadian traditions. Britain's involvement in foreign wars was viewed differently by the two races. In other respects, too, the racial composition of the population affected external policy.

If the sources of Canada were in Europe its place in North America was next to a country older and stronger than itself, and this juxtaposition of a small and a great power remained a main element in Canadian history. At the time of the union of the provinces, Canadians believed that there was real danger of a further invasion from the south. Indeed, the provision of military defence was a major argument in favour of Confederation. Almost a century after the operations against Montreal and Quebec in 1775 a lasting settlement was effected.

Trade was another vital factor. Canada was a producer of staples—fish, lumber, grain—and purchaser of manufactured goods. More than in most countries external trade was a necessity of life, and without it the standard of living could not be maintained. Even later when the economy became more diversified and manufacturing blossomed, external trade remained a basic element.

In 1870 exports accounted for 17.2 per cent of the gross national product. The highest percentage thereafter was 32.03 in 1926. In the past ten years the average has been a little over 20 per cent. Related to this was the need for imported capital for public works, mainly canals and railways, and for the private sector. Thus, economically Canada was inescapably part of a larger world.

In the first 40 years or so after Confederation many of the principal issues in external relations came up for decision. Relations with Britain and the United States involved major questions for the future of Canada, and were themselves mixtures of the political and economic. The concept of the Dominion was of a continental state whose economic viability required immigrants, internal communications, development of resources, domestic and external trade.

Political unity assumed, amongst other things, that what at first could be no more than a narrow east-west belt would be maintained against the pull of the north-south axis. To some extent the answer was within Canadian initiative, but for long there was a shadow of absorption by the United States, whether by force, peaceful agreement, or commercial domination. The first faded with the over-all British-American settlement in the Treaty of Washington (1871), which, while disappointing to Canadians in some respects, did begin a period of more normal relations. As to the second there had been intermittent and localized movements for annexation long before Confederation and there were to be others later.

Like England, Canada had a stake in external trade but, unlike the mother country, believed that it was in no position to adopt free trade. The tariff was variously known as revenue or protective but was, in fact, intended for both purposes. There was a difference in degree between the political parties, the Liberals inclining toward lower rates and the Conservatives toward higher.

The "National Policy" adopted by the Conservatives in 1878 was frankly protectionist, introduced at a time of depression and intended to help the infant industries to survive. Certainly it had appeal as an election plank, and was claimed to have been an aid in the economic improvement which took place. When the Liberals secured office in 1896 they made few changes in the tariff, having previously been rebuffed in their support of unrestricted reciprocity with the United States.

## Reciprocity Debated

In principle, both parties and most Canadians believed in reciprocity. Since 1854 it had been a substitute for the British preference, terminated as a result of the adoption of free trade in England. The Reciprocity Treaty of 1854 was not renewed by the United States and the expectation that it would not be renewed was an argument in favour of the union of the provinces as an alternative. It was still hoped, however, that reciprocity could be revived, and both Conservative and Liberal Governments took soundings in Washington.

Around 1887 a particular proposition came to be widely discussed both in Canada and the United States. It was variously known as unrestricted reciprocity and commercial union. There was considerable confusion between the two. The first would have left each country free in its arrangements with third parties while the second would have built a common wall against the rest of the world. One significant difference was that commercial union would have left no room for Canadian reciprocal agreements with Britain, but a more common objection was that it would draw Canada completely into the American orbit, politically as well as economically.

Officially, Liberals fought the election of 1891 on unrestricted reciprocity although some of them tended to use "commercial union" in their letters and speeches. The Conservatives (who were in office) for the most part disregarded the distinction and emphasized the more radical and objectionable of the two propositions. It was a heated election in which Liberal newspapers and politicians pointed to the continuing depression, claiming that reciprocity would greatly stimulate trade. Tacitly admitting that Canadian manufacturing might be hurt, one editor asked if "the millions shall be kept back for the benefit of the score or the hundreds."

The anti-reciprocity campaign has been criticized as sentimental and misleading. Certainly it had an emotional side. Commercial union was labelled as "veiled treason" and the Prime Minister averred that he would die, as he had been born, a British subject. Some denounced the opponents of reciprocity as friends of the "vested interests", careless of the lot of the ordinary man, while opponents of reciprocity called the sponsors traitors who were leading the country into annexation by the United States.

There was, however, more substance on each side of the debate. The Liberals were doing no more than pushing to its limits a proposition which had always been popular in itself, that trade could be improved, to the general advantage, by reciprocal arrangements with the United States. The Conservative case, stripped of oratory, was that the whole future of Canada depended on the maintenance of the east-west axis; that much effort—and certainly much money—had been spent on giving reality to that program—and that the Liberal policy would destroy all hope of a diversified economy. If allowed free play the strong north-south pull would, in fact, break the Canadian fabric into pieces. During these years of argument the Union Jack was prominently displayed, literally and metaphorically, reminding Canadians of their other external pole. Some of those who most vigorously waved the flag in their attacks on commercial union were at the same time worried by the fact that Canada had still no more than colonial status. They were ardent believers in empire but thought that Canada should have in it a place more consonant with its growing maturity.

## Imperial Integration vs. Nationalism

The Imperial Federation League was founded in London, in 1884; in Canada, in 1885. For nearly forty years Canada had been more imperially-minded than the metropolitan power itself, but this was increasingly combined with nationalism. To the imperial federationists in Canada the two were not contradictory but related. While a limited number of those who supported the League would commit themselves to federalism, and some of them even opposed it, the objective as seen in Canada was some form of imperial reorganization which would allow Canadians to participate in any imperial policy that was likely to affect them. The League was never widely supported in Canada and, indeed, was regarded by many people with suspicion. In England its chief achievement was the first Colonial Conference in 1887; in Canada it was a focus for those who saw in commercial union a threat to the future of Canada, either to its continued place in the empire or as independent of the United States.

A photograph of Queen Victoria
taken in 1867.

The Queen's Scarf of Honour, won 67 years ago by Private Richard Rowland Thompson in the South African War, was returned to Canada on permanent loan in 1965. The scarf was one of eight personally crocheted by Queen Victoria and awarded for conspicuous gallantry under fire.

In the years from the 1880's to 1914 some basic issues were discussed with Britain and often with the other colonies. One practical problem, for which only temporary solutions could be found, was the method of negotiation with foreign countries on matters which, in whole or in part, directly affected Canada. Since Canada was not a sovereign state any such negotiation had to be conducted, at least nominally, by

British representatives. One compromise device that was employed is illustrated in the case of the Treaty of Washington. Because there were important Canadian interests involved, Prime Minister Macdonald was appointed a member of the British team, known as a High Commission and, like his colleagues, was a plenipotentiary receiving his instructions from the Foreign Office. Macdonald claimed that the other commissioners gave insufficient support to Canadian demands while, for his part, he seemed to feel no responsibility for anything else. In the opinion of Canadians this method worked inefficiently in the case of the dispute over the boundaries of Alaska. A tribunal of six was established. It was to make a judicial decision on questions submitted to "impartial jurists of repute". But, as the Americans appointed were known partisans, and were supported by a determined president, the scheme was stillborn. The British appointees, one English and two Canadians, met the requirements of the treaty which set up the tribunal but the proceedings did not have the intended detached tone. There was bitter complaint in Canada that the British member, Lord Alverstone, had not supported his Canadian colleagues. Whether he was influenced by the evidence or by the political motive of terminating a quarrel with the United States remains a moot point.

A more common and more satisfactory procedure, one used in dealing with reciprocity, fisheries, and commercial agreements, was to send a Canadian Minister or the High Commissioner in London to a foreign capital where the British Ambassador would assist him and act as the formal negotiator. Through several experiments in the 1880's and 1890's the process was worked out, the British ambassador taking a decreasing part in the procedure.

In a tradition older than Confederation it was frequently asserted that British diplomacy in matters affecting Canada was far from satisfactory, the various boundary settlements being offered as proof. There were remarks, in the House of Commons and elsewhere, that Canada would do better to conduct its own negotiations, but they are to be taken as indications of displeasure rather than statements of intent. It would seem that the creation of a Department of External Affairs in 1909 was a step toward providing specialized knowledge of foreign affairs and diplomacy but, in fact, it was not intended at the time to be a foreign office or in any way to replace the British structure; rather, it had the modest purpose of handling tidily the incoming and outgoing communications between Ottawa and London. Meanwhile, a series of Colonial Conferences followed the first held in 1887. Major subjects of discussion were: whether the empire should be reorganized; its military defence; and the enlargement of intra-imperial trade by means of preferential tariffs.

The story of the last is long on the record but brief in result. The Canadians believing that they would benefit by imperial preference, urged its adoption, and introduced unilateral preference in 1897. The British could not agree since they believed in free trade. More words, and considerably more emotion, were used up in debate on whether the empire should have centralized institutions. Here the roles were reversed. The proposals for change came from the British side, with talk of federalism or of an imperial council. Sir Wilfrid Laurier, who was Prime Minister through all the conferences except the first, was hostile to any form of imperial integration. He drew attention to the growing nationalism in all the colonies but concluded that to Canada the existing arrangements were temporarily satisfactory. The discussion never progressed beyond majority acceptance of that view.

The primary purpose of an imperial parliament or council would be to discuss, and presumably to direct, the position of the Empire in respect to foreign countries, recognizing the inescapable connection between foreign policy, defence, and war. However, when there was found no generally acceptable plan for political co-ordination, the questions of peace and war, and the related military planning, were left without a political base. But they could not be ignored. The threat to British sea-power caused by German naval building, colonial rivalry, and the developing system of alliances in Europe combined to weaken the relative military power of Britain and therefore of the Empire.

That this situation was recognized in Canada was shown by participation in the Boer War and again by agreement in principle on the need for some kind of naval program. The decision of the Liberal Government to send to South Africa a substantial force of volunteers met with wide popular approval and, indeed, had been demanded in the English-speaking provinces; but it created vigorous opposition in Quebec. Henri Bourassa denounced British "imperialism" and Canada's association with it, a point of view which was to have important repercussions on the naval question, and again in the War of 1914-18.

Although the political parties recognized a need for naval defence, nothing more was done under the Liberal legislation providing for a Canadian navy than to acquire two ageing cruisers, one of which was run on a rock and the other retired to Esquimalt for want of officers and men. Nor did anything come of the Conservative proposal that there should be in addition an emergency grant to the British navy. In the general election of 1911 the dominating subject in Quebec was the navy. The Nationalists attacked all plans, whether for a Canadian navy or for a contribution to British expenses, one objection being that it would involve Canada in the results of a British foreign policy in which it had no voice. Although the Conservative leader, R. L. Borden, continued to advocate a naval program he, too, was disturbed that a share in imperial defence should be divorced from a share in policy.

## World War I

If Laurier had successfully fended off the proposals for imperial integration he had found no substitute; and neither he nor any other Canadian could, by abstaining from consultation, change the course of British policy and of world events. Thus it was that when England was at war in 1914 Canada legally was at war, too. A policy of no commitments had left open the way for the greatest commitment of all. There remained freedom of action on the degree and form of Canadian participation, the question before the government and parliament in the summer of 1914.

In the early years and months of the War the Canadian people were virtually unanimous in their determination to play a full part and no thought was given to the theoretical alternative of avoiding participation. The attitude that was general then, though less so later, was that the whole resources of the country should be thrown into the struggle against German domination; and, indeed, they continued to be, even when there were minority protests against the scale of the operation. With the exception of the production of food, many resources were still to be developed. There was some industrial capacity, but direct experience of the manufacture of munitions had not extended beyond small arms. The professional army was a nucleus of some 3,000 men, though the militia had, in the previous two or three years, been built up to nearly 60,000. The Navy, with its two inactive cruisers, was handicapped.

**War Effort**—In the First as in the Second World War, the Canadian effort was large-scale and sustained. Early in August the cruiser *Rainbow*, with half the proper crew and no high-explosive shells, set out to counter the powerful German cruisers on the Pacific coast. Happily it missed them—and certain destruction. Two recently-constructed submarines were acquired and numerous small craft were gradually added. Many were used against submarines in the Atlantic. Total naval personnel rose to some 10,000. There was no Canadian air force, but some 22,000 Canadians served with the British air forces, many distinguishing themselves as fighter pilots. The large Canadian contribution was in land forces. Of a total of 619,636 men on active service, 424,148 went overseas. An additional 3,079 Canadians enlisted in Britain. The first contingent sailed for England in October 1914, and others followed. One of the great defensive battles in which Canadian troops fought was the second battle of Ypres in which gas was first used in combat. Canadians became well known, too, as shock troops in offensive operations. In general, their operations on the ground were recognized to be carefully planned and vigorously carried out.

Hardly less striking were the advances in the production of food, munitions, and the financial structure on which they rested. The recession of 1913-1914 was overcome by the demands created by the War. By the end of hostilities the acreage under wheat in the prairie provinces was nearly 80 per cent above that of 1913, and exports of other foodstuffs rose quickly. The demand for munitions similarly stimulated the industrial structure which had been in trouble immediately before the War. Factories were converted to the manufacture of munitions, with the result that about one third of the Canadian industrial capacity was diverted to war orders.

Finance also showed remarkable resilience. Deprived of the possibility of borrowing in London or New York, the Canadian Government turned to domestic taxes, including the first federal income tax, and to borrowing from its own people. The early effects of rapid economic development and financial change were mixed. On the one hand the economy was becoming more varied, and more self-sufficient; on the other there were severe social dislocations. The economic upsurge brought increased wealth to a limited number of people and employment rose, but rising prices hit those of modest means in town and country. Discontent and pressure against the existing régime were expressed in the Winnipeg strike of 1919 and in the growth of new political parties intended to represent the interests of farmers and labour.

The great military effort, in itself a remarkable achievement, had indirect results both good and bad. It created a proper pride and a new sense of Canadian nationalism. It established a valid claim to a greater place for Canada in the international community. The experience gained in the War led to little change in Canadian military policy but did establish a military tradition and a group of skilled officers whose value was seen in the interwar period and more especially in the Second World War. On the liability side was the serious divergence between Quebec and the other provinces which developed in the second year of the War and reached a dangerous height with the imposition of compulsory military service in 1917.

In the early part of the War the cause of England and France was fully accepted by the people of Quebec with hardly a suggestion of opposition from the nationalists who had opposed participation in the South African War; but, quite early, doubts were expressed that Canada should supply as many soldiers as the Government proposed. As the demands for manpower increased, opinion within Canada became more divided, and even before conscription was decided on there was a strong element which opposed further participation.

The adoption of conscription brought on riots in Quebec, and a bitter battle of words between French-speaking and English-speaking Canadians over Ontario schools. The War finally broke the unity that had once been so striking. It is obvious now— as it was to a few people at the time—that too little attention was paid to the direct Canadian stake in winning the War; that is, to judge it from Canadian interest rather than as assistance to Britain and France.

On the political side, one result of the War was the assumption by the Government, with parliamentary authority, of greater powers over individual citizens, in the area of rights sometimes disputed with the provinces, and over the economy. Another result, arising out of the dispute over conscription, was to distort the normal pattern of political parties. Conscription, in the view of the Conservative Government, was a measure that should rest on the shoulders of a coalition government; but when a coalition was formed and sought the support of the electors it secured only three seats in Quebec and elsewhere lost only twenty to the Liberal opposition. The unhappy effect was virtually to create for a short time English-speaking and French-speaking parties.

As Canadian participation in the War, military and economic, grew out of all proportion to what had been anticipated, it became evident that the failure to design either imperial institutions or else an organized intra-imperial relationship left a gap that was wholly unsatisfactory to the Canadian Government. Borden had long spoken in general terms of the necessary relationship of foreign affairs and war. Now his increasing dissatisfaction with Canadian ministers being treated as "toy automata", and with the British conduct of the War itself, found a ready listener in Lloyd George. The Imperial War Cabinet could hardly be called a Canadian invention but it, together with the appointment of a Canadian officer to command the Canadian Corps, and the presence in London of a Minister of Overseas Military Forces, combined to Canadianize the corps itself and to allow a Canadian voice in higher direction and strategy. Equally, the Canadian Government was determined to have a part in a peace settlement following a war in which the country had played a significant role. The War was a wholly practical problem, lasting for a limited period; and the reason for the Canadian demand for participation in its direction came not from theory but from function.

## Peace Conference

The approach to the Peace Conference, on the other hand, was mixed. The Canadian ministers who attended it were impressed with the substantive problems raised, but in Parliament and the press the main interest was in "status" rather than in the attempt to solve a series of complicated international problems for the future. Canada was represented at the Paris Peace Conference in two ways: as a member of the British Empire Delegation, which meant access to the inner circle; and, as a minor power, which meant recognition of international status but little else. That great realist, Clemenceau, who ordinarily paid little attention to smaller countries, had a weakness for the dominions because of their fighting capacity, which is a good illustration of the functional principle.

The debate in the House of Commons on the treaties of peace was turgid and unilluminating. No one would guess from it that more than 600,000 Canadians had fought to achieve a better world. Throughout the debate almost the only subject raised in response to ministers' statements on the work of the conference was whether the settlement had enhanced the international status of Canada.

## Post-1919 Policy

When hostilities were over, and the treaties of peace signed, the way was open for Canadians to assess their interests and commitments and to design external policy. There could, of course, be no simple and instantaneous answer, but the broad lines of policy that were followed can be detected, mainly from the responses to particular situations. First, however, a glance at the general outlook of the country.

The atmosphere in 1919 and in the years immediately following was coloured by the assumption that a war to end war had been won. It seemed reasonable, then, to look forward to an era in which aggression no longer threatened; to a world in which democracy was assured, international trade encouraged, and military preparedness could be kept to a minimum. While it had been shown that Canadians would fight when they thought it necessary, they had much to do at home in developing the country and in meeting the financial burdens that directly or indirectly resulted from the War. Far from seeking new territory Canada was fully engrossed in peopling and equipping its already wide acres.

Canada is, geographically, a North American country which meant that it was considered to be relatively insulated from the complications and dangers of European rivalries (the War of 1914 presumably being an exception), and was neighbour to the United States by which it was influenced in a number of ways.

In spite of friction in the past and of a Canadian tendency to be over-sensitive to any supposed American pressure, the two peoples had much in common, although Canada was more conscious of its powerful neighbour than the latter was of Canada. Crisscross of population, similar social conditions, and labour affiliations were capped by a trade which had become increasingly vital. Though Canadian foreign policy was far from being a slavish copy of that of the United States and, indeed, in these years was very different, there remained a desire to ensure that there be no serious divergence between British and American policies. Latin America made little impact on Canada, less than the British West Indies which had been well known to the commercial men of the Atlantic Provinces.

**Mother Countries**—Outside the Americas the chief connection was with Britain, the mother country for the majority of Canadians, one of Canada's principal trading partners and the channel between Canada and foreign countries. The whole imperial structure was open to revision, as had been agreed during the War. In regard to foreign affairs the Imperial War Conference of 1917 had resolved that any readjustment "should recognize the right of the Dominions and India to an adequate voice in foreign policy and in foreign relations, and should provide effective arrangements for continuous consultation in all important matters of common Imperial concern, and for such necessary concerted action, founded on consultation, as the several governments may determine". That resolution while laying down a broad principle, left the way open for alternative courses. It was drafted mainly by Borden and Smuts.

Toward France, the other mother country, the Canadian attitude was more complex. In the early part of the War French Canadians had emphasized the common cause with their country of origin but, over the years, their sense of identity had been in the cultural rather than in the political field. They were essentially *Canadiens* and felt little sympathy for the secularism and rationalism of contemporary France, or compulsion to support French foreign policy. To Canadians generally Europe was familiar ground, and the more so now that hundreds of thousands of them had served, and many had died, there. But whether such a general familiarity was to be translated into terms of policy remained to be seen. These were the areas of prime concern.

**In the League of Nations**—There was also the question of Canadian policy in the League of Nations. The purpose of the League as seen by those who designed and endorsed the covenant was to introduce order into international relations, filling a conspicuous gap evident in the prewar world. While the League was much discussed and generally approved in Canada the delegation at the Peace Conference had endeavoured to limit the commitments to be undertaken by members and especially by the smaller powers. In particular, objection was taken to Article X, which read:

"The members of the League undertake to respect and preserve as against external aggression the territorial integrity and existing political independence of all members of the League. In case of any such aggression or in case of any threat or danger of such aggression, the Council shall advise upon the means by which this obligation shall be fulfilled".

This article, together with XVI which provided for sanctions, was the main expression of the doctrine of collective security. The Canadian objections to Article X were many, but essentially they were directed against a universal guarantee of the *status quo* by a minor power. Efforts to have the Article eliminated or amended were unsuccessful. There were, of course, many other aspects of the League to which, with the International Labour Organization, Canadian approval was given; but the core of the League was the attempt to replace what had been styled "international anarchy" with solid barriers against war as a means of settling international disputes.

The magnitude of the Canadian effort in the War had overtaken not only Canadian status in the empire and the world—and that was subject to remedy—but also the knowledge of, and experience in, international affairs on the part of the civil government. In the 1920's and 1930's there was ample opportunity to remedy that situation. For the first stage after the War Canadian foreign policy was conducted within the framework of imperial policy, that being a practice unknown—though dreamed of—before the War, and resulting now from the experience of the Imperial War Cabinet. It was virtually this body which had appeared in Paris as the British Empire Delegation to the Peace Conference; and in its next existence it dealt, in two stages, with the problems of the Far East.

**Anglo-Japanese Treaty**—The question of the renewal of the Anglo-Japanese Treaty was to come up at the Conference of Prime Ministers in 1921. Before it met, the Canadian Prime Minister, Arthur Meighen, telegraphed to Lloyd George his opinion that the alliance should not be renewed but that, instead, the Far Eastern questions should come before a conference of the British Empire, the United States, China, and Japan. In London he continued to argue strongly against renewal, contrary to the view of Britain, Australia, and New Zealand. The last three were concerned with security in the Pacific.

The Canadian case seems to have been based entirely on the fact that the United States was hostile to the Treaty, and there is no indication that the Government made any study of the Far Eastern question as such. After a vigorous debate in London a compromise decision was reached that there should be a conference of the powers but that abrogation of the Treaty should be conditional on that conference's success. Thereupon the imperial statesmen packed their bags again and set out, as a delegation, for an international conference at Washington. The conference was successful in that a number of treaties and agreements were signed. Whether it had more effect in stabilizing the Far East than a renewed alliance would have had is speculation. Certainly it did meet the Canadian demand in that the old Treaty was terminated; and so far as is known the common delegation was satisfactory to Sir Robert Borden, the Canadian member.

Thus far the device of a co-operative imperial policy had worked well, but the cases so far had had certain characteristics: they were on subjects of general interest in the Empire, and they were not urgent and so could be discussed personally in advance. Without those conditions imperial policy was much less workable, the more so because at the Prime Ministers' Meeting in 1921 they had, while paying lip-service to the principle of consultation, done little to provide means to make it more effective, or, indeed, that it would take place at all.

**Chanak**—This became painfully apparent in the Middle Eastern crisis of 1922. When the Canadian Government, together with others in the Empire and outside it, was invited to support British policy in face of the emergency at Chanak there had been no previous consultation; and, to make matters worse, the British communication, precipitate enough, was delayed at Ottawa. The particular case, while arising out of a treaty to which Canada was a party, proved to be one test of the range of area and subject in which Canada was prepared to take responsibility. Since the crisis itself faded, a conclusion on the Canadian position cannot be final, but the obvious distaste for intervention and the refusal to make a firm decision indicated a limitation of Canadian commitments.

The questions arising in connection with the League of Nations were more clear-cut. Since Canada had expressed a dislike for agreement to take automatic action against future aggression, it could have been predicted that its government would not subscribe to the various proposals for strengthening the collective system made in 1922-25. So it proved with the Draft Treaty of Mutual Assistance and the Geneva Protocol for the Pacific Settlement of International Disputes. The Canadian objection was to the "rigid provisions for application of economic and military sanctions in practically every future war", a response consistent with the attitude toward Article X and in particular with the developing doctrine that such major decisions should not be made by an international body, in so far as Canada was concerned, without the approval of Parliament.

It is appropriate to note, however, that Canada was far from being alone in rejecting the two agreements. All Empire governments, among others, turned them down. When the Europeans moved to regional security it appears that Britain did not consult the dominions; and equally it seems evident that the Canadian Government felt no resentment in not being offered a place in the treaties of Locarno.

**Halibut Treaty**—Meanwhile there were developments in procedure as well as in substance. In 1923 the Halibut Treaty with the United States was signed, with British agreement, by a Canadian plenipotentiary alone. Also in 1923 an Imperial Conference laid down general rules on the negotiation and signature of treaties. Broadly it was envisaged that countries of the Empire might, according to circumstances, act individually, in groups, or as a whole (i.e., continue to pursue an Empire policy). In the case of the first, other Empire governments should be kept in touch if their interests were involved. The Imperial Conference of 1926 still retained, as one alternative in negotiation, the use of a British Empire delegation; but, in practice, this procedure was almost obsolete.

As a national policy was developing, a body of specialists was needed in this as in other aspects of government. The Department of External Affairs grew slowly and the conspicuous advance was in offices abroad. After the War there were still only the High Commissioner in London and the Commissioner-General in Paris, but in 1925 an "advisory officer" was sent to Geneva to keep in touch with League affairs and to advise delegates to international conferences. In 1927 diplomatic representation in foreign capitals began with the accreditation of a minister plenipotentiary to the United States and in the next two years legations were established in Paris and Tokyo. It was, perhaps, a modest beginning but it was, nevertheless, the nucleus of a Canadian foreign service.

## "Security" in the 1930's

Before 1930 the foreign policy of Canada was being worked out in a relatively peaceful and prosperous world. Planning against aggression was influenced, not only in Canada but in many other countries, by a sense of unreality. As in most periods, thought on the subject was distorted rather than aided by the human weakness for phrases. Those countries, such as France and Poland, which had reason to fear inroads on the settlement of 1919-20 were described as "consumers of security" while others, like Canada, being less directly affected, were called "producers of security". It was a form of nonsense that was to be tragically dispelled in 1939, but is none the less understandable in its setting. For Canada important elements of the picture were the largely common ground with other countries of the Empire and the isolationism of the United States.

In the 1930's the world switched from postwar to threatened and actual hostilities which might, or might not, remain localized. The transition was accompanied and influenced by a collapse, or near collapse, of the whole economic structure. For Canada this spelled a disastrous curtailment of the foreign markets on which it depended so much. Demand went down steeply and with it prices. In 1933 the average of Canadian export prices was 60 per cent of the 1929 figure, while one main component, wheat, was down to 45 per cent. The Conservative Government which came into office in 1930 sought to secure what trade it could by raising the tariff to a new height and then by a series of bilateral agreements for preferential trade in the Imperial Economic Conference of 1932. While economic conditions improved in some degree in the later 1930's, the depression came to an end only when it was overtaken by the demands of another war.

Whether the Second World War could have been prevented by a tight and widely-supported system of collective security will never be known; but at least it is evident that the process of separate concession and compromise in the face of aggression was a disastrous failure. During the 1920's Canada, with many other states, had resisted the various efforts to set up protective measures; and in the 1930's it was no more and no less willing than the average country to make a stand.

**Manchuria**—The active moves against the peace settlement began with the Japanese seizure of Manchuria in 1931-32. When questioned in the House, the Prime Minister pleaded "slight knowledge" of the situation and continued to refuse to be drawn; and only when a proposal for non-recognition of "Manchukuo" came before the League Assembly did the Government show its hand by voting in favour. Meanwhile, at the Conference for the Reduction and Limitation of Armaments in Geneva the Canadian representative protested against sanctions and developing the League into a "super-state".

**Ethiopia**—By the early autumn of 1935 the pressing question was the Italian invasion of Ethiopia. The first Canadian member of a small committee of the League Assembly appointed to examine the matter demanded that the League should show that "it meant business" and that "when a breach of the Covenant took place it proposed to deal with the aggression in the proper way". What that way was, was not defined, but when the alternate delegate, W. A. Riddell, proposed, on his own authority, to extend the list of sanctions to oil and other compelling items, the succeeding Liberal Government stated that his views were not those of the Canadian Government.

Canada had implemented such sanctions as had so far been agreed but was not prepared to be in the van. There was a case for leaving the initiation of drastic moves to the great powers which would have borne the brunt of any military reaction to crippling economic sanctions. Hitler broke the treaties of Versailles and Locarno by re-occupying the Rhineland in March 1936. Japan, Italy and Germany all defied those countries which sought to preserve the *status quo* and the international atmosphere was tense.

# World War II

As the situation grew steadily worse the Government maintained its position that automatic sanctions were unacceptable, and that Parliament must decide the appropriate action in particular circumstances. This, however, should not be interpreted as wholly negative since Mackenzie King warned Parliament, as he did Hitler in private conversation, that Canadians would not be idle if England were attacked.

By 1937 comprehensive plans for rearmament began to come into effect. Particular attention was paid to the Air Force and (to a lesser extent) to the Navy, both of which had been sadly neglected. Increased capacity was developed for the manufacture of munitions and aircraft. While the program on the whole was on a modest scale, Canada was substantially more ready for military operations than had been the case 25 years before.

**Canada Declares War**—In 1939 Canada declared war with the approval of the House without division and of the Senate unanimously. Its government and Parliament had had what opportunities were open to a small power to influence the course of

North Nova Scotia Highlanders embark during World War II.

Royal Winnipeg Rifles and support troops head for the Normandy beaches for assault landings, June 6, 1944.

Evacuation over the causeway of the Zuider Zee, The Netherlands, May 29, 1945.

A discussion centres around the formal surrender of all German forces still in The Netherlands.

events, and now, as a sovereign state, it decided to take up the sword again in the cause of the liberty which was a cardinal belief.

Canada's part in the Second World War was no less striking than in the First, but necessarily in a form adjusted to the altered character of warfare. Fortunately the preparations which have been mentioned provided a base, if not an adequate one, from which to start. The army overseas was numerically slightly smaller than in the War of 1914 and circumstances did not allow it to be in combat at such an early stage. Compared with World War I, the Navy in the Second was ten times larger in personnel and was supplied with vessels which enabled it to play a major part in the Battle of the Atlantic. The Royal Canadian Air Force was, of course, new to warfare and, fortunately, as the nature of the War showed, had been given priority in the prewar planning. The total of personnel was 249,624 of whom 95,166 served overseas. Canadians took a large share in the Royal Air Force Bomber Command in which nearly 10,000 lost their lives. Under the British Commonwealth Air Training Plan 131,583 men from some 14 countries were trained in Canada.

Response to the War in the economic field was as effective as in the military. The Government quickly assumed wide powers over money, prices, and production through taxation, the Foreign Exchange Control Board, the Wartime Prices and Trade Board, and the Department of Munitions and Supply. War industries were conjured out of almost nothing, promoting general industrialization and diversification of the economy. By 1943 more than half the net value of Canadian production was in manufactured goods. Already by 1940 the unemployment and excess capacity of the depression years were being absorbed, so that by 1944 employment had increased by nearly 60 per cent. Yet, in spite of this swelling activity, the cost of living rose by only 20 per cent during the War. The Second World War, like the First, greatly accelerated the process by which Canada was moving from a producer of a limited number of staples to a more balanced economy.

## Postwar Status of "Middle Powers"

The Canadian economic and military roles in the War were for a time in the setting of the Commonwealth fighting alone against the German advance, with western Europe overrun, the Soviet Union still allied with Germany for the pursuit of spoils, and the United States neutral. It did not need any late survival of the search for status for its own sake to suggest the need of some equation between the substantive part that Canada was playing and its place in international councils.

When the Soviet Union was forced into the War by Germany in June 1941, and the United States by Japan in December, the great-power pattern reappeared in the alliance and the Canadian position was relatively, though not absolutely, less important. Whereas during the First World War the Canadian Government had sought, and found, a place in imperial policy-making, it had in the Second World War, as the Government of a sovereign state, to fit as best it could into a relationship with foreign great powers. It was under these circumstances that there was evolved the formula which, it was considered in Ottawa, would define the appropriate position for Canada either in the wartime alliance or in the larger community that would follow after peace was established. The particular application was made in relation to the United Nations, the successor to the League of Nations.

The doctrine, described in 1943 and 1944, denied the validity of a simple division between great and small powers. There should be a recognition of the existence of "middle powers", those which were already making important contributions to the War and could similarly contribute to the maintenance of peace. It was not claimed or desired that Canada should compete for the lead with the great powers, but rather that its voice should be heard in proportion to a capacity proven in the War and anticipated for the postwar period.

Not during the War in relation to the main allied agencies, in the procedure for treaties of peace, or in the character of postwar organizations did the Canadian doctrine work out with mathematical precision. The Canadian Government was openly displeased with the arrangements for making treaties with the enemy states in Europe. The conference at Paris in 1946 was called so that the lesser states might comment on drafts drawn up by the great powers, a retrograde step in comparison with arrangements of 1919. In 1947 the Government was invited to submit in writing its views on the character of the settlement with Germany and Austria. In doing so it again protested that opportunity for discussion was not provided.

The San Francisco Conference on the charter of the United Nations came only after the great powers had drafted a plan at Dumbarton Oaks. Canada, with the lesser powers, was active enough in the drafting at San Francisco, but the resulting document still provided a primary position for the great powers. A similar distinction was made for the North Atlantic Treaty Organization.

It need not be concluded that Canada had found victory or defeat in the attempt to apply a formula that, at the height of its considerable effort in the War, had seemed reasonable. No such plan could, indeed, be exact, nor could it be assumed that it would necessarily seem to the great powers to be wholly suitable. Furthermore, the pattern of international organization and relationships that was emerging from the War was one that, on the one hand, was to take unexpected turns, and, on the other, offered wide opportunities for useful and sometimes effective intervention by a country which was prepared to accept a measure of responsibility for the peace and well-being of the world.

In no respect was the effect of the War more evident than in the radical alterations in Canadian foreign policy. That very change, however, can be magnified or misunderstood if it is not seen against the background of an attitude on the part of allies wholly different from that of 1918, and also of adverse developments which had no counterpart in the dozen years after the First World War. The starting-point for thinking on postwar planning was similar—the necessity of establishing an international organization, the primary purpose of which would be to maintain peace by collective action. In the 1940's, however, there was none of the assurance of future peace that had earlier been one of the factors working against a recognition of the actual need for security. The prevailing feeling was relief that the destructive hostilities had ceased, but without any sense of finality, and with a consciousness that a damaged world must be nursed back to health politically and economically. Whereas in 1920 Canada's Commonwealth partners had, in varying degrees, shared their distaste for commitments, and the United States had withdrawn into chilly isolation, now all of their closest friends accepted the principle that a price had to be paid for peace and order.

Across a Korean valley a Princess Patricia Canadian Light Infantry company moves in single file toward enemy positions.

It is with this background, together with a realization of Canada's greater strength and experience, that its changed policy should be examined. In the years between the Wars, Canadian activity in international affairs had been restricted by two conditions: a limitation of geographical area of responsibility and caution about commitment to future action. Neither, of course, was completely discarded by Canada (or, indeed, by many other countries, if any), but the difference in degree was so great that it can be regarded as a new policy.

Canada had no wild delusions of being a great power but was prepared to participate in, and take responsibility for, international questions in most parts of the world, and its spokesmen explicitly (and without protest from Parliament or public) drew attention to the wide-flung obligations which resulted from full acceptance of the spirit and letter of the United Nations charter. Foreign policy being more than good intentions, it was necessary to provide in the postwar period the civil and military structure needed for the support of the policy as it developed.

Several departments of government—such as Finance, Agriculture, Fisheries, and Trade and Commerce—had always been concerned with aspects of foreign affairs and, of course, continued to be. Since the present discussion is on the main lines of policy it will be sufficient to add a word on the position, after the War, of National Defence and External Affairs, the departments mainly affected. While the heaviest responsibilities of the first had been during the period of hostilities it later took on important duties in the enforcement or maintenance of peace as well as in the defence of the country.

## Integration of Armed Services

Two principal changes may be noted. Shortly after the War a Defence Research Board was created—in effect a fourth service, responsible for the co-ordination of research and development to meet the requirements of the Army, Navy, and Air Force. Several years later a more comprehensive plan of integration was undertaken. The principle adopted was to integrate the Armed Forces under a single Chief of Defence Staff and a Defence Staff, to whom would fall control of all planning and operations, thus creating not only a stronger force but also substantial savings which could be diverted to the purchase of capital equipment. The second significant postwar factor was that provision was made for much larger and better equipped services than had existed in previous periods of peace.

Before the outbreak of war in 1939 the regular strength of the three services was about 8,000 officers and men. In 1954 (after the Korean increase) it was about 112,000. It was this great increase in the regular establishment that enabled Canada to accept responsibilities for peace-keeping.

## Increased Representation

The Department of External Affairs which, with its foreign service, has a general responsibility for relations with other countries, was forced into rapid expansion during and after the War. Regular recruiting multiplied the officer strength by ten up to 1951; and by 1964 that had been doubled again. More conspicuous as an indication of widening interest in world affairs was the growth in representation abroad. The first moves in 1939 and 1940 were to send high commissioners to Commonwealth countries: Australia, New Zealand, Ireland, and South Africa (and Newfoundland in 1941)—primarily to meet practical needs arising out of the War.

Wartime conditions limited general expansion, particularly in Europe but, by 1945, Canadian representation covered six Commonwealth countries, seven European countries, six in Latin America, one in the Far East, and one in the United States. In 1964 there were diplomatic representatives accredited to 70 foreign states; there were 17 high commissioners and commissioners in the Commonwealth, 8 missions to international organizations, 9 consular offices, and the military mission to Berlin. At that time the number of officers serving abroad was 273.

It was wholly in the Canadian interest—and Canadians believed it to be in the general interest—to co-operate in a variety of organizations and undertakings designed to bring closer a world that was orderly, peaceful, and prosperous, one in which the concepts of civil and political liberty and of the rule of law would take the maximum place. Much of the Canadian energy in foreign affairs was devoted to this formidable task, but that was not the only preoccupation; there were also important bilateral questions, particularly in the economic and military fields. The network of relations with individual countries was broadening, as is reflected in the growing list of diplomatic missions.

The Passport Office of the Department of External Affairs is a busy place in the tourist season.

It would be superfluous to recall the many common interests and the frequent consultations with the British government. That Canadians continued to value the links with Britain was illustrated by the concern with which many of them viewed the possible results of Britain's joining the European Economic Community, thinking not only in terms of trade (and on that there was disagreement whether a loss to Canada would finally result) but of a re-orientation toward Europe and away from the Commonwealth.

In the days of the Empire and even of the early Commonwealth, Canadians tended to equate the whole with Britain alone. From the time of the War there was much more consciousness of the Commonwealth as a whole. Because of the events that came to a head during and immediately after the War it was becoming a new kind of Commonwealth. In the interwar years the statesmen of Britain and the dominions had thought out and developed a relationship between the component parts that was in conformity with the stature of the former colonies. There was no constitution and no legal obligations but largely common interests.

During the War the question was raised of reviving the Imperial War Cabinet of the First World War, but Mackenzie King and the majority of other Commonwealth Prime Ministers were opposed. As a long list of colonies became sovereign, the Commonwealth had to adjust itself to contain the strong nationalism of a series of new states in Asia, Africa, the Caribbean, and the Mediterranean.

## Commonwealth Relations

The Commonwealth remained one of the main poles of Canadian external policy. Its position in world affairs, however, took on a different character. Instead of a small group of states with, for the most part, similar interests and policies, the Commonwealth was now marked by diversity, both as between cultures and in foreign policies. It was the very fact that the members brought together all continents, many races, and a host of outlooks that afforded an opportunity to compensate for the centrifugal forces so generally apparent in the world. It was, it was true, many years since the Commonwealth had acted as a unit in international relations, but for a longer time it had been a group of states with similar objectives. In the 1950's and 1960's, however, only a few of the members were attached to alliances while the majority were unaligned. The main forum for the exchange of views, the periodic meetings of prime ministers, became so large as to threaten to be unwieldy but, on the other hand, they opened to Canadians a wide circle of world opinion.

## Relations with the United States

Relationships with the United States became no less important but took some new turns. After the Second World War, as contrasted with the First, there was a large area of common foreign interest. There was room for difference as, for example, in the attitudes toward Cuba; but in the east-west division and in continental defence there was agreement. Bilaterally, too, there were some important steps. The project of the common development of the St. Lawrence, long marked by more talk than action, at last came into effect for electrical power in 1958 and for the seaway in 1959. The Columbia River Treaty became effective in 1964, a dramatic example of the joint use of water and water power.

Some aspects of the economic relationship gave cause for alarm as well as satisfaction. The balance of trade improved in the 15 years after the War, but there was concern over the extent and results of American capital investment. No one seriously questioned the need for imported capital, or that the bulk of it must now come largely from the United States; but the growing ownership of Canadian companies and resources stirred the old apprehension that Canada would be "taken over" by the United States.

## External Aid

In the international economic field the Canadian interest in foreign trade as a necessary element in the country's welfare was consistent with the rehabilitation of countries damaged during hostilities and assistance to underdeveloped areas. Canada participated in the United Nations Relief and Rehabilitation Administration and made reconstruction loans to European countries. In addition to these temporary plans, it was associated from the beginning with the General Agreement on Tariffs and Trade, the International Bank for Reconstruction and Development, the International Monetary Fund, and the International Development Association. Since 1951, too, Canada has followed an increasingly diversified and extensive program of aid to developing countries.

Beginning on a modest scale some 16 years ago, Canadian external aid, in various forms, has become a major aspect of the country's participation in world affairs. Some indication of this will be seen from the fact that in 1951 the first parliamentary appropriation was for $400,000 while in 1964 the amount made available to developing countries was $226,000,000, extended to 63 countries. Aid is funnelled, in part, through agencies of the United Nations, and in part through multilateral organizations such as the Colombo Plan and the Commonwealth plans, but even under collective schemes

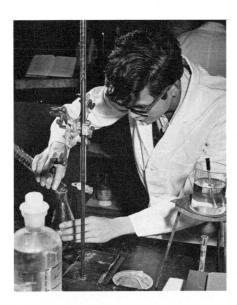

(Left) Through Canada's External Aid Program, a student from Malaysia studies chemical technology at the Southern Alberta Institute of Technology, Calgary.

Under the Colombo Plan, a Singapore fireman toured Canada studying the adaptability of Canadian industrial fire fighting methods to conditions in his own country. In Ottawa he examines the circuitry of an industrial fire alarm system. He is shown here with the Dominion Fire Commissioner.

A typing class is conducted in this Educational Training Centre, Siblin, Lebanon, which was built with Canadian funds.

The Canadian High Commissioner in Tanzania presents books from the Overseas Institute of Canada to the Chief Education Officer.

the actual relationship is largely bilateral. Consultation makes it possible for the priorities of the developing countries to be observed, and effective co-operative arrangements draw on the respective resources of the partners in such enterprises.

Assistance can be in the form of grants or in long-term interest-free loans and has made possible the development of power (hydro-electric and thermal), of transport facilities, natural resources, educational facilities, and supply of foodstuffs. Canadians have gone to many countries to give expert advice and assistance in a wide variety of fields; in 1964, for example, 550 Canadians—teachers and advisers—went abroad under aid programs. These human links have been complemented by the presence in Canada of students and trainees from other countries. In 1956 the total of such persons was 370. In 1964 it was 1,820, of whom 953 came from South and Southeast Asia, 189 from the Caribbean, and 358 from Africa.

## Canada in the United Nations

The United Nations bulked large in Canadian external policy and action. With its complex network of committees, councils, and specialized agencies it covered most of the field of human endeavour, offering many avenues for concerted action. It gave to the lesser powers opportunities for exerting influence by ideas and patient diplomacy far beyond their capacity if measured by population, wealth, or military strength.

Israel—Particularly in the first decade of the United Nations, when the membership was comparatively small and deliberate negotiation and compromise more the rule, Canadian delegations, with those of a few other middle powers, earned a reputation as constructive intermediaries in controversial questions. One such, in which Canadians played a recognized role, was the negotiation leading up to the establishment of the State of Israel.

458

**Kashmir**—Another, with a less conclusive ending, was the mediation between India and Pakistan over Kashmir undertaken in 1949 by the Canadian president of the Security Council at the Council's request. There are many others, some apparent in committees, and others unrecorded in the endless conversations in corridors. Perhaps the best known and one of the most fruitful interventions was in the Middle Eastern crisis of 1956-57. Here the Canadian initiative and readiness to accept responsibility, seen in contrast to the crisis of 1922 in the same area, afford a good example of the change through which Canadian policy had gone, and of the opportunities occasionally open to a middle power.

**Egypt**—At the end of October 1956, following the nationalization by Egypt of the Suez Canal Company, British and French forces took military action against Egypt, which in turn led to the calling of a special session of the General Assembly of the United Nations. The Canadian delegation abstained on a resolution which, amongst other things, called for a cease-fire and withdrawal of forces, explaining that it had done so because the resolution did not go on to measures to re-establish peace in the area. The Secretary of State for External Affairs then suggested the formation of a

A lonely desert patrol is enlivened by a meeting with bedouins and their camels. Canadian soldiers have served with the United Nations Emergency Force for many years.

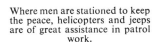

Where men are stationed to keep the peace, helicopters and jeeps are of great assistance in patrol work.

The Canadian Prime Minister and the Minister for External Affairs represent Canada at a meeting of the North Atlantic Treaty Organization, whose headquarters were originally in Paris and have now been moved to Brussels.

United Nations force to guard against hostilities while a political settlement was being made. Two days later a Canadian resolution formally proposing such a force was adopted, and before long the United Nations Emergency Force was in operation.

**Korea**—When the charter of the United Nations was drawn up, provision was made for the use of military force if that were needed to meet breaches of the peace, but only on one occasion, and because of fortuitous circumstances, could such action be taken. The North Korean attack on the Republic of Korea in June 1950 led the Security Council to recommend that member states contribute military forces to assist the republic and restore peace. To this the Canadian Government responded by sending three destroyers, RCAF transport aircraft, and an infantry brigade group. Already, however, it had become evident that the division between east and west would normally prevent the United Nations from acting as a unit, while apprehension of aggression by the Soviet Union and its allies suggested the need of collective security against that threat. As early as 1946 the Canadian Government had expressed concern with the failure to provide for military co-operation in the United Nations, and welcomed the Treaty of Brussels as a development which "deserves our full support".

## North Atlantic Treaty Organization

Government spokesmen gave clear warning of the need for mutual protection against Communist aggression, and Canadians participated in the discussions in Washington in 1948 on the project of a regional security arrangement. The North Atlantic Treaty, signed in April 1949, was the result of these discussions and became

In 1966 the first air transport agreement linking Montreal and Moscow was signed by Prime Minister Pearson and Mr. D. Polyansky, first Deputy Chairman of the Council of Ministers of the U.S.S.R.

one of the foundations of Canadian foreign policy. It was a return to the concept of regional security as attempted in the 1920's. Canada took its part in the formation of the alliance and in the planning which followed, and contributed Armed Forces consisting of an air division, an infantry brigade group, and naval support on a stand-by basis.

Greatly as Canadian foreign policy had widened, the move in that direction was not unlimited. Indeed policy after the Second World War was not intended to have universal application in the sense of involvement in every enterprise in every area. Canadians were slow to associate themselves with the problems and interests of Latin America. Close as it was, it made not the immediate impact that Europe did, or even to a degree the Far East.

On the other hand, defence of North America was immediate. The Permanent Joint Board on Defence, established in the summer of 1940, continued as a medium for consultation. In 1957 provisionally, and in 1958 formally, there came into existence the North American Air Defence Command. There was to be an integrated headquarters (at Colorado Springs), with an American commander-in-chief, a Canadian deputy, and staff officers from both countries. The starting-point was that the air defence of North America was a single problem and, under the arrangement, there was created a single operational control over forces supplied by both countries.

## A "Middle Power"

"Canada's position in the world," wrote the Secretary of State for External Affairs in the preface to his Department's report in 1964, "is that of a middle power. This involves some limitations upon the conduct of Canadian foreign policy. But it also provides Canada with opportunities for action . . . Canada's activities in the peace-keeping field . . . are a good illustration of what I have in mind. Canada has participated in every peace-keeping operation mounted by the United Nations since 1948."

Mention has already been made of the Emergency Force for the Middle East. To it Canada contributed more than a thousand men, one-sixth of the total. Already, however, there had been experience in peace-keeping, first in observers on the cease-fire line in Kashmir. This, too, was a United Nations undertaking, but that in Indochina was by invitation of the Geneva Conference of 1954, to serve with two other countries on International Control Commissions for Laos, Vietnam, and Cambodia. For this task (which, with most of the others, is still being carried out) both civil and military personnel were needed. The others required service personnel.

In the same year Canada agreed to provide a chief of staff and a group of staff officers for the United Nations Truce Supervision Organization in Palestine. Other peace-keeping tasks followed: in Lebanon in 1958, in the Congo, in West New Guinea, and on a large scale in Cyprus. The Canadian Government believes that there should be a permanent international force ready and prepared for such duties.

"Peace-keeping" is a phrase coined to describe the international groups sent to prevent actual or incipient hostilities from spreading to dangerous proportions. Another and related approach to the prevention of at least major warfare has been the traditional one of the reduction and limitation of armaments. This, too, has been a matter of deep concern to Canadian governments. The effort to achieve results has been at least as difficult as in the interwar years, but given additional stimulus by the appalling prospect of nuclear war. Canada, like other members of the United Nations, was on its disarmament commission, the committee of ten, and the committee of eighteen. Its representatives laboured consistently to find some formula for an agreement between the great powers of west and east.

Such progress as was actually made was through a treaty which came into effect in 1963 between the Soviet Union, the United States, and Britain banning nuclear tests other than those underground. It was at least a step on a main avenue to the international peace which has been the principal objective of Canadian foreign policy.

(G. DE T. GLAZEBROOK)

The Russian luxury liner "Alexander Pushkin", which inaugurated the first passenger liner service between the U.S.S.R. and North America, in 1966, received a vociferous welcome on her arrival in Montreal.

# The Centennial
# of Canadian
# Confederation

# Centennial Celebrations

Canadians throughout 1967 are giving a long, joyous and thankful salute to their land and its people for what has been accomplished in the first century of Confederation. They are dedicating themselves to the job of making the second century as good, as fruitful and as admirable as the first. This has been the constant goal of the Centennial Commission and its staff for nearly four years and of countless other Canadians to a lesser degree for an even longer period. Now one may see and experience the results of all this planning and dreaming.

There is something for everyone in the Centennial Year programs—unlimited varieties of celebration and observances which the Commission had no hand in planning —the innumerable activities of purely private organizations and individuals.

The Dominion of Canada came into formal existence on July 1, 1867, with the union of what are now the provinces of Ontario, Quebec, New Brunswick and Nova Scotia. Success of that union in achieving the hopes of its Fathers must be apparent in the remarkable story of Canada's growth and development portrayed in the foregoing pages.

Canada is a widely-respected country, rich in its various racial sources, in its material blessings and with almost unbounded room for growth and worthy achievement as a nation. It was because of these circumstances that many thoughtful Canadians in

Some 1,000 spectators will be provided with seating accommodation at Nepean Point, Ottawa, to view the "Son et Lumière" program staged on the site of the Parliament Buildings during the Centennial celebrations.

The story of Canada from its earliest history to today's exciting growth in an age of science will be dramatized for Canadians visiting any of these eight motorized caravans during Centennial Year. The vehicles expect to cover more than 25,000 miles, and to make hundreds of stops throughout the country.

recent years talked and wrote of the desirability of a Canadian plan for a huge, combined birthday and thanksgiving party for 1967.

In 1960 a large group of public-spirited citizens organized the Canadian Centenary Council—a private organization for the promotion of the idea of a fitting Centennial Year observance. In 1961 the Federal Government took definite action and obtained passage of "An Act Respecting the Observance of the Centennial of Confederation". In January 1963, the government created the Centennial Commission, and instructed it to promote interest in and plan programs so that the Centennial might be observed throughout Canada in a manner in keeping with its national and historic significance.

The Act empowered the Commission to administer funds to be appropriated by the federal treasury to be spent on purely federal projects and on joint projects with the provinces. Provision was made for the widest participation by the provinces through membership in the National Committee and the National Conference, both composed of citizens from across Canada meeting periodically with the Commission and its board of directors.

Centennial planning has involved erection of numerous structures, initiation and support of cultural movements of a lasting nature, and many spectacles on a grand scale designed to bring Canada's history to life. (The Centennial Commission, however, has no formal or official affiliation with the organization staging Expo 67—the colossal world exhibition project at Montreal which will be a universal centre of attraction during the summer of Centennial Year.)

CENTENNIAL CELEBRATIONS

A major feature of the Commission's projects is the Confederation Train—a 15-car special with eight exhibition cars which are travelling back and forth across Canada during most of 1967 taking a unique presentation of Canada's past and present to some 83 rail centres in the mainland provinces. There are also eight trailer-truck caravans, each with eight vehicles containing the same type of actual and symbolic representations of Canada's history, visiting close to 700 sites in all the provinces and the territories. Thus an important part of the Centennial spectacle is being carried to the people.

A 3,500 mile canoe race between crews representing the provinces and territories, in replicas of the canoes used by the voyageurs who opened Canada to settlement and trade, and wearing voyageur costumes and following their routes, will take paddlers from the Rocky Mountains to a grand finish in Montreal late in the summer. With numerous stops at waterway points made famous by the voyageurs, this 100-day spectacle also will bring a part of the Centennial to people unable to travel to large centres.

Train-loads of specially trained service personnel from the Department of National Defence are carrying the famed military tattoo to some 40 Canadian points. There are also the best of Canadian and foreign talent engaged in performing arts presentations across Canada, and original Canadian Centennial plays in both English and French for special presentations under Commission sponsorship and free use by theatrical organizations everywhere in Canada.

The Centennial Flame, located on the main walk to the House of Commons on Parliament Hill, was set alight on January 1, 1967. The Flame is surrounded by a moat and bordered by plaques displaying the armorial bearings of the ten provinces and the territories.

John Fisher, Commissioner and Chairman of the Board of Directors of the Centennial Commission, has generated both enthusiasm and interest in the various projects. To recapture a colourful chapter of Canada's past, a Voyageur Canoe Pageant was designed to follow the original route of explorers and fur traders from Edmonton to Expo 67, Montreal.

Almost all these activities are being carried out in co-operation with the provinces. A shared-cost arrangement will result in every provincial capital having some sort of cultural structure costing $5,000,000 or more as lasting and useful Centennial memorials. Under another shared-cost program some 2,000 projects, mostly involving construction of cultural and recreational buildings, will blossom out all across the nation. In addition, there is a constant and important relationship between Canada's program of rejoicing, a spiritual appreciation of a people's blessings, and its humble thanks to a kind Providence. At the invitation of the Commission, a Canadian Inter-Faith Conference has been actively working on plans to ensure that all religious faiths play a part in the observances of the Centennial.

It is anticipated that during 1967 there will be a vast movement of Canadian people to and fro in Canada, and a great inflow of visitors from abroad. But perhaps the most useful kind of travel will be the result of one of the Centennial Commission's most interesting and potentially valuable operations: the youth travel movement which, in co-operation with the provinces and numerous public organizations in several seasons of experiments, has already seen thousands of school-age boys and girls travel across Canada to spend some time in the homes of other Canadian teenagers. This youth travel movement, reaching a high level of activity in 1967, is certain to bring about a deeper understanding in the minds of the nation's most important citizens, the young, who will be Canada's leaders tomorrow.

A solid knitting of Canadians in a common pride in their country and a determination to make it greater and more united essentially depends upon the friendly understanding of peoples divided by great distances and, in some cases, by language.

(JOHN FISHER)

CENTENNIAL CELEBRATIONS                                        467

Princess Canada for 1966-67, was named at the sixth annual meeting of the National Indian Council. She is Miss Marlene Jackson, the former Princess Manitoba. During Centennial Year Miss Jackson will travel throughout Canada speaking on behalf of her people.

A cowhide scroll bearing the signatures of the people of St. Paul, Alberta, was exchanged in Ottawa for a similar scroll with the signatures of the 265 Members of Parliament. Shown from left to right are: Roland Rocque, President of the Chamber of Commerce, St. Paul; Hon. John Diefenbaker, Leader of the Opposition in the House Commons and former Prime Minister; John Lagassé, Chairman of the St. Paul Centennial Committee; Frederick J. J. Bigg, Member for Athabasca, and Hugh Fuller, lawyer, St. Paul.

The Centennial Building, Fredericton, New Brunswick, will house government offices. It is shown (above) under construction and (below) completed.

Edmonton, Alberta, chose a public library as its Centennial project.

The newly-completed National Library and Archives Building, on Wellington Street, Ottawa, viewed from the Garden of the Provinces.

Students from Yellowknife, Northwest Territories, visit Prime Minister Pearson and R. J. Orange, Member of Parliament for the Northwest Territories.

The Sir Charles Tupper Confederation Memorial Building is for the study of medical science at Dalhousie University, Halifax, Nova Scotia. The building commemorates one of the Fathers of Confederation and former Prime Minister of Canada.

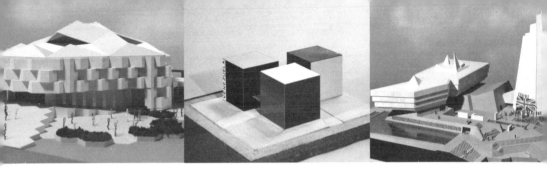

Israel          Venezuela          Britain

## Canadian Universal and Int

Officially associated with Canada's Confederation celebrations is Expo 67, the first exhibition sanctioned by the International Bureau of Exhibitions as a First Category Exhibition to be held in North America. The over-all theme is Man and His World; the site, two islands in the St. Lawrence River.

Mexico          U.S.S.R.          India

Africa

Germany

Japan

# ational Exhibition, Montreal

In keeping with this theme, the Canadian Pavilion reflects the people of Canada, its development, and its relationships with other countries—many of whose national pavilions are also illustrated. Every continent is represented as well as major industries. Visitors will be transported to and from the exhibition grounds on the Expo Express, a fully-automated, rapid transit system, and by three secondary transportation systems of the monorail type.

United States

Australia

Czechoslovakia

# Retrospect and Prospect

*"Fix your eyes on the greatness of your country as you have it before you day by day, fall in love with her, and when you feel her great, remember that her greatness was won by men with courage, with knowledge of their duty, and with a sense of honour in action, who, even if they failed in some venture, would not think of depriving the country of their powers but laid them at her feet as their fairest offering."*

*—Pericles*

Here, then, in capsule form is the 'Face of Canada' as it evolved through its first hundred years as a federal state, as a new political nationality.

The physical size of modern Canada was realized with unprecedented speed and un-remitting effort: within seven years (1867-1873), the new Confederation had attained an east-west dominion, *a mari usque ad mare*, and in another seven (1880) had acquired a vast Arctic domain extending to the Pole.

Canada holds a strategic position geographically within the Northern Hemisphere and opens four doors to the world. The northern salient, formed by the Arctic Archipelago, makes Canada neighbour to the Union of Soviet Socialist Republics, while the southern salient of peninsular Ontario thrusts deep into the United States of America and makes Canada and its southern neighbour co-partners in the industrial heartland of a continent. On the east, the salient of Labrador and Newfoundland (which joined Confederation in 1949) faces Europe and commands the shortest crossing of the North Atlantic. In the west, the broad arc of land comprising British Columbia and the Yukon provides terminal points for the shortest routes across the North Pacific to the peoples of the Far East. Canada thus lies at the crossroads of aerial and water navigation linking it with the most powerful nations and some of the most populous areas of the world. Moreover, across its Arctic frontier Canada shares with the Soviet Union, the United States (through Alaska), Denmark, Iceland and Norway, in close and vital interrelationships, the future of this newly realized central mediterranean position of the Arctic in the world community.

Canada's transcontinental dimensions in the northern half of the North American continent emphasize its vast expanse. Its generous share of such physiographical features as the Precambrian Shield, the plains, the mountains, and the countless lakes and rivers help to explain its varied, yet well-balanced economy; its geographical location provides the benefits of both insularity and universality—removal from the major devastations of Old World struggles but neighbour to western European, eastern Asiatic, trans-Arctic and American peoples. From such universal contacts Canadians derive rich and increasing economic, social and cultural benefits. All these factors together with Canada's unsurpassed combination of natural resources, widely distributed within such vast domain of country, truly provide unlimited horizons for its people.

Within these pages one has seen unfold the thrilling development of isolated pioneer colonial economies into one of the most productive and prosperous of modern industrialisms, possessing an exceedingly rich endowment of physical and human resources. One has witnessed, so to speak, the exploitation of a nation's bountiful resources

Canada, blessed as few others with natural and human resources and with an industrial aggressiveness nourished by its own increasing prosperity, moves confidently from a hundred years of growth and building into the exciting modern world of technological-scientific progress. The rising generation, working on the foundations of the past, have before them the challenging task of keeping this magnificent country in the forefront of world progress and of making it an increasingly potent force for betterment in the evolution of mankind.

of forest, land, minerals, fisheries, and the harnessing of a multiplicity of energy resources in the service of man; the opening of the Canadian West and the explosion of prairie settlement in one of history's swiftest and most dramatic population movements, with the transformation of the virgin land into vast oceans of golden grain, scattered farmsteads and towering grain elevators in market towns extending along thousands of miles of railway and telegraph lines; the attainment of industrial maturity by the 1950's and 1960's through the transformation of the glacially-eroded Canadian Shield from the role of forbidding barrier to east-west economic alignment to that of bridge, source of power, and site of tremendous mineral and forest wealth; the rapid expansion of productive and manufacturing capacity and capital investment in such basic resource industries as pulp and paper and metal refining, in the burgeoning oil, gas and chemical industries, and in a multiplicity of secondary industries rendering all the requirements of an affluent modern society. Indeed, the health of Canada's modern industrialism is indicative of the abundance of its heritage, human and physical—the availability of cheap hydro-electric power, the economies of proximity to abundant raw materials, the locational advantage of large and expanding markets particularly to the south, the application of modern technological methods in resource development, and the dependence of the prosperity of these major industries and the health of the Canadian economy upon tariff policies and fluctuations in demand in foreign countries.

Moreover, one will have observed the entry of the Canadian economy during the past two decades upon its most remarkable era of industrial expansion; the staggering investments in the discovery and development of Western Canada's oil and gas fields, in crude petroleum production and refining, in oil and gas pipeline construction, in the spectacular production of uranium ores which have placed Canada in the forefront as a world source of uranium concentrate—thereby freeing the nation from its erstwhile deficiencies in some of the traditionally basic elements of industrial development. One will have become more consciously aware of a highly significant concomitant of this increased industrial diversification of the Canadian economy, particularly applicable to basic industries. Such capital-intensive industries have drawn heavily upon non-resident sources of investment capital, thereby bringing Canada further into the world of international corporate business—and making Canadians somewhat fearful of the extent to which their nation's extractive resources and industrial production have come under the ownership and control of United States and other foreign corporations.

Although it will be recalled that during the 1960's numerous Canadian industries, particularly pulp and paper, primary iron and steel, industrial machinery, petrochemicals, and textiles have "achieved positions of great strength" and proved themselves competitive with United States prices, he will find in the following digest of remarks by the Prime Minister of Canada to the American Society of Newspaper Editors (Montreal, May 19, 1966) much that may tend to assuage his preoccupation with the far-reaching effects of Canada-United States economic relations on his country's future economic and political independence:

"All Canada's postwar international policies testify to its Government's belief in the concept of interdependence and internationalism—economic and political. We have consciously preferred multilateral to regional arrangements . . . . We need the

Yellowknife, largest and most developed community in Canada's North with a population of over 3,600, famous as a major gold-mining centre since 1935, was created a town in 1963 and in 1966 was recommended as the future capital by the Advisory Commission on the Development of Government in the Northwest Territories.

maximum of international contacts in the widest possible world—thereby diffusing pressures in wider international arrangements and groupings.

"We shall continue to encourage, by positive action, greater Canadian control and ownership of Canadian resources and production; ensure that our financial system and communications media remain essentially Canadian; insist that subsidiaries of foreign corporations in Canada should act as good Canadian citizens . . . become Canadian in their operations and outlook; and encourage a higher rate of domestic savings and their investment in the exploitation of our wealth of resources through utilization of our national advantages and most modern industrial techniques."

Other significant characterizations of Canadian development which this volume has sketched in broad strokes include the immensely important arteries of commerce and communications which have enabled a sparsely-populated, transcontinental entity to develop into a leading industrial nation. These include the Canadian Pacific and Canadian National railway systems; the St. Lawrence Seaway which extends into the heart of the continent; the jet-propelled airways in which government ownership and private ownership compete in serving Canadians and linking them in commerce with the world at large; Canada's great public and privately owned transcontinental radio, television, telephone and interrelated telecommunication systems which contribute to the dissolution of regionalism and to the growth of national unity and consciousness; and the response of scientific and industrial research to the challenges of the nation and the times.

One will have observed that Canada, which ranked fifth in 1965 among the world's major trading countries, has long striven to promote international economic co-operation through foreign trade, in the realization that its own national prosperity is closely bound up in world economic growth and change. Indeed, trade is its very life blood; trading and commercial relationships, based upon mutuality of self-interest, are among the most durable and beneficial means of reaching distant peoples, of sharing scientific knowledge, and identifying potential areas for joint ventures or collaboration—thereby, as a priceless by-product, increasing the body of shared experiences and contacts through which mutual tolerance, understanding and goodwill may flourish. The currently increased opportunities for mutually beneficial trade with the Communist countries, which the governments of Canada and these countries have been developing bilaterally, and Canada's recently expanded External Aid Program for underdeveloped nations (with whom its own developing resources and nationalistic sensitivities make it more attuned) constitute the latest affirmation of its belief in the inestimable benefits to be derived from international economic co-operation.

Here, then, is a miniature portrait of the land and the people and the ultra-modern industrial society that is Canada: a land so vast and richly endowed with Nature's gifts as to thrill the heart of every Canadian with the potentialities of his country; a people who, from colonial times, have been English-speaking or French-speaking and who subsequently have grown to include a multiplicity of other tongues representative of diverse ethnic origins, creeds and colour. Thus, the Canadian cultural stream, enriched by a sensitive heritage of artistic endeavours, is producing, in the concluding years of Canada's first century, a cultural renaissance of far-reaching promise.

Treasuring such priceless cultural and institutional heritages, believing in a federalism which harmonizes cultural diversities within the framework of wider co-operation, the Canadian democratic concept of "unity in diversity" has developed from Canada's pragmatic experience with forces and events during the first century of nationhood. It is well at the beginning of Canada's second century to reflect upon its many treasures and upon the things that unite rather than divide us as a people. For, are we not truly one nation—"a body of people who have done great things together in the past" and whose minds and hearts are "moved by dreams of the great things that we may yet do together in the future"?*

(C. Cecil Lingard)

*Frank H. Underhill, *The Image of Confederation*, Canadian Broadcasting Corporation, 1963, pp. 58 and 70.

# Bibliography

# Some Books About Canada

This list of books about Canada, compiled by the National Library (July 1966), includes a selection of 180 titles of publications grouped alphabetically by author and arranged under broad subject classifications matching the major divisions of this centennial volume: Canadian Nation Building, the Canadian People, the Economy, the Social Milieu, Canada in World Affairs, and concluding with basic Reference Books. The selection emphasizes the latest editions of books published within the past ten years, often reprint editions in such series as "Carleton Library" and "Canadian University Paperbooks", and includes titles issued in either or both English and French, accompanied by the publisher's address. For additional titles, the reader should consult one or more of the bibliographical collections listed below under the heading "Reference Books", including the monthly or annual editions of *Canadiana* published by the National Library.

## Canadian Nation Building

### Confederation and after:

BOLGER, F. W. P. *Prince Edward Island and confederation, 1863-1873.* Charlottetown, St. Dunstan's University Press, 1964. 308 p.

BROWN, R. C., and PRANG, M. E., eds. *Confederation to 1949.* Scarborough, Ont., Prentice-Hall, 1966. 334 p. (Canadian historical documents series, v. 3).

CARD, B. Y. *The Canadian prairie provinces from 1870 to 1950; a sociological introduction.* Toronto, Dent, 1960. 46 p.

COWAN, John. *Canada's Governors-General, Lord Monck to General Vanier.* Centennial ed. Toronto, York, 1965. 260 p.

CREIGHTON, D. G..*John A. Macdonald.* Toronto, Macmillan, 1966. 2 v.

CREIGHTON, D. G. *The road to confederation; the emergence of Canada, 1863-1867.* Toronto, Macmillan, 1964. 489 p.

CRÉPEAU, P.-A., and MACPHERSON, C. B., eds. *The future of Canadian federalism. L'avenir du fédéralisme canadien.* Toronto, University of Toronto Press; Montréal, Presses de l'Université de Montréal, 1965. 188 p.

EGGLESTON, Wilfrid. *Choix de la Reine; étude sur la capitale du Canada.* Ottawa, Imprimeur de la Reine, 1961. 342 p.

EGGLESTON, Wilfrid. *The Queen's choice; a story of Canada's capital.* Ottawa, Queen's Printer, 1961. 325 p.

FARIBAULT, Marcel, et FOWLER, R. M. *Dix pour un; ou, Le pari confédératif.* Montréal, Presses de l'Université de Montréal, 1965. 163 p.

FARIBAULT, Marcel, and FOWLER, R. M. *Ten to one; the confederation wager.* Toronto, McClelland and Stewart, 1965. 150 p.

MACDONALD, R. S., ed. *The Arctic frontier.* Toronto, University of Toronto Press, 1966. 311 p.

MASSEY, Vincent. *Confederation on the march; views on major Canadian issues during the sixties.* Toronto, Macmillan, 1965. 101 p.

MORTON, W. L. *The critical years; the union of British North America, 1857-1873.* Toronto, McClelland and Stewart, 1964. 322 p. (The Canadian centenary series, 12).

MORTON, W. L. *Manitoba; a history.* Toronto, University of Toronto Press, 1957. 519 p.

O'HEARN, P. J. T. *Peace, order and good government; a new constitution for Canada.* Toronto, Macmillan, 1964. 325 p.

OLLIVIER, Maurice. *Actes de l'Amérique du Nord Britannique et statuts connexes, 1867-1962.* Ottawa, Imprimeur de la Reine, 1962. 675 p.

OLLIVIER, Maurice. *British North America Acts and selected statutes, 1867-1962.* Ottawa, Queen's Printer, 1962. 662 p.

OLLIVIER, Maurice. *Problems of Canadian sovereignty from the British North America Act, 1867 to the Statute of Westminster, 1931.* Toronto, Canada Law Book Company, 1945. 491 p.

ORMSBY, Margaret A. *British Columbia; a history.* Toronto, Macmillan, 1958. 558 p.

SKELTON, O. D. *Life and times of Sir Alexander Tilloch Galt.* Toronto, McClelland and Stewart, 1966. 293 p. (Carleton library, no. 26).

STANLEY, G. F. G. *The birth of western Canada; a history of the Riel rebellions.* Toronto, University of Toronto Press, 1963. 475 p. (Canadian university paperbooks, 10).

STANLEY, G. F. G. *Louis Riel.* Toronto, Ryerson Press, 1963. 433 p.

UNIVERSITY LEAGUE FOR SOCIAL REFORM. *The prospects of change; proposals for Canada's future,* edited by Abraham ROTSTEIN. Toronto, McGraw-Hill, 1965. 361 p.

WAITE, P. B., ed. *The confederation debates in the province of Canada, 1865; a selection.* Toronto, McClelland and Stewart, 1963. 157 p. (Carleton library, no. 2).

WAITE, P. B. *The life and times of confederation, 1864-1867.* Toronto, University of Toronto Press, 1962. 379 p.

WRIGHT, J. F. C. *Saskatchewan; the history of a province.* Toronto, McClelland and Stewart, 1955. 292 p.

### Canadian government and politics:

AITCHISON, J. H., ed. *The political process in Canada; essays in honour of R. M. Dawson.* Toronto, University of Toronto Press, 1963. 193 p.

ASHLEY, C. A., and SMAILS, R. G. H. *Canadian crown corporations; some aspects of their administration and control.* Toronto, Macmillan, 1965. 360 p.

BEAL, J. R. *The Pearson phenomenon.* Toronto, Longmans, 1964. 210 p.

COHEN, R. I. *Quebec votes; the how and why of Quebec voting in every federal election since confederation.* Montreal, Saje Publications, 1965. 128 p.

COHEN, R. I. *Le vote au Québec; les "pourquoi" et "comment" du vote fédéral au Québec depuis la confédération.* Montréal, Saje Publications, 1965. 128 p.

COOK, G. R. *The politics of John W. Dafoe and the Free Press.* Toronto, University of Toronto Press, 1963. 305 p.

CORBETT, D. C. *Canada's immigration policy; a critique.* Toronto, University of Toronto Press, 1957. 215 p.

CORRY, J. A., and HODGETTS, J. E. *Democratic government and politics.* 3d ed. Toronto, University of Toronto Press, 1959. 691 p. (Canadian government series, 1).

DAWSON, R. M., ed. *The development of Dominion status, 1900-1936.* London, Cass, 1965. 466 p.

DAWSON, R. M. *The government of Canada.* 4th ed. Rev. by Norman WARD. Toronto, University of Toronto Press, 1963. 610 p.

DAWSON, R. M. *William Lyon Mackenzie King; a political biography.* Vol. 1, 1874-1923. Vol. 2, 1924-1932 by H. Blair NEATBY. Toronto, University of Toronto Press, 1958-63. 2 v.

GRAHAM, W. R. *Arthur Meighen; a biography.* Toronto, Clarke, Irwin, 1960-65. 3 v.

GREASON, G. K., and KING, R. C. *Canadian democracy at work.* Rev. ed. Toronto, Macmillan, 1966. 116 p.

HUTCHISON, Bruce. *Mr. Prime Minister, 1867-1964.* Toronto, Longmans, 1964. 394 p.

IRVING, J. A. *The Social Credit movement in Alberta.* Toronto, University of Toronto Press, 1959. 369 p.

KILBOURN, W. M. *The making of the nation; a century of challenge.* Text for picture albums by Pierre BERTON and Ken LEFOLLII. Toronto, Canadian Centennial Pub. Co., 1965. 127 p. (The Canadian centennial library).

KNOWLES, Stanley. *The New Party.* Toronto, McClelland and Stewart, 1961. 136 p.

KNOWLES, Stanley. *Le Nouveau Parti.* Montréal, Éditions du Jour, 1961. 159 p.

KUNZ, F. A. *The modern senate of Canada, 1925-1963; a re-appraisal.* Toronto, University of Toronto Press, 1965. 395 p. (Canadian government series, 15).

McNAUGHT, K. W. K. *A prophet in politics; a biography of J. W. Woodsworth.* Toronto, University of Toronto Press, 1963. 339 p. (Canadian university paperbooks, 17).

MACPHERSON, C. B. *Democracy in Alberta; Social Credit and the party system.* 2d ed. Toronto, University of Toronto Press, 1962. 258 p. (Canadian university paperbooks, 9).

MASSEY, Vincent. *What's past is prologue; memoirs.* Toronto, Macmillan, 1963. 540 p.

NEWMAN, P. C. *Renegade in power; the Diefenbaker years.* Toronto, McClelland and Stewart, 1963. 411 p.

PICKERSGILL, J. W. *The Mackenzie King record.* Vol. 1, 1939-44. Toronto, University of Toronto Press, 1960. 723 p.

POPE, Sir Joseph. *Public servant; the memoirs of Sir Joseph Pope.* Edited and completed by Maurice POPE. Toronto, Oxford University Press, 1960. 312 p.

RUSSELL, P. H., ed. *Leading constitutional decisions; cases on the British North America Act.* Toronto, McClelland and Stewart, 1965. 234 p. (Carleton library, no. 23).

SCHULL, J. J. *Laurier: the first Canadian.* Toronto, Macmillan, 1965. 658 p.

SCOTT, F. R., and OLIVER, Michael, eds. *Quebec states her case; speeches and articles from Quebec in the years of unrest.* Toronto, Macmillan, 1964. 165 p.

SKELTON, O. D. *Life and letters of Sir Wilfrid Laurier.* Ed. by D. M. L. FARR. (Abridged ed.). Toronto, McClelland and Stewart, 1965. 2 v. (Carleton library, no. 21-22).

STANLEY, G. F. G. *The story of Canada's flag; a historical sketch.* Toronto, Ryerson Press, 1965. 96 p.

THOMSON, D. C. *Alexander Mackenzie, clear grit.* Toronto, Macmillan, 1960. 436 p.

VARCOE, F. P. *The constitution of Canada.* 2d ed. Toronto, Carswell, 1965. 314 p.

WARD, Norman. *The Canadian House of Commons; representation.* Toronto, University of Toronto Press, 1950. 307 p. (Canadian government series, 4).

WARD, Norman. *The public purse; a study in Canadian democracy.* Toronto, University of Toronto Press, 1962. 334 p. (Canadian government series, 11).

WATKINS, Ernest. *R. B. Bennett, a biography.* Toronto, Kingswood House, 1963. 271 p.

# The Canadian People

ARSENAULT, Bona. *Histoire et généalogie des Acadiens.* Québec, Conseil de la vie française en Amérique, 1965. 2 v.

BOULIZON, Guy, et ADAMS, Geoffrey. *Canada, 20ème siècle—20th century.* Texte français de Guy BOULIZON. English text by Geoffrey ADAMS. Paris, Éditions de la Pensée moderne; Montréal, Beauchemin, 1964. 1 v.

GARIGUE, Philippe. *La vie familiale des Canadiens français.* Montréal, Presses de l'Université de Montréal, 1962. 142 p.

HOLT, Simma. *Terror in the name of God; the story of the Sons of Freedom Doukhobors.* Toronto, McClelland and Stewart, 1964. 312 p.

HONIGMANN, J. J., and HONIGMANN, Irma. *Eskimo townsmen.* Ottawa, Canadian Research Centre for Anthropology, University of Ottawa, 1965. 278 p.

IGLAUER, Edith. *The new people; the Eskimo's journey into our time.* Garden City, N.Y., Doubleday, 1966. 205 p. (About Canadian Eskimos.)

JENNESS, Diamond. *The Indians of Canada.* 5th ed. Ottawa, Queen's Printer, 1960.

JENNESS, Diamond. *People of the twilight (Eskimos).* Chicago, University of Chicago Press, 1959. 250 p. (Phoenix books).

KOSA, John. *Land of choice; the Hungarians in Canada.* Toronto, University of Toronto Press, 1957. 104 p.

KRISTJANSON, Wilhelm. *The Icelandic people in Manitoba; a Manitoba saga.* Winnipeg, Wallingford Press, 1965. 557 p.

REAMAN, G. E. *The trail of the black walnut.* Toronto, McClelland and Stewart, 1957. 256 p. (The Pennsylvania Germans in Ontario.)

ROSS, M. M., ed. *Our sense of identity.* Toronto, Ryerson Press, 1954. 346 p.

SACK, B. G. *History of the Jews in Canada.* Rev. ed. Translated by Ralph NOVEK. Montreal, Harvest House, 1965. 299 p.

VLASSIS, G. D. *The Greeks in Canada.* Ottawa, 1953. 364 p.

WADE, Mason, ed. *Canadian dualism; studies of French-English relations.* Toronto, University of Toronto Press; Québec, Presses de l'Université Laval, 1960. 427 p.

WADE, Mason, éd. *La dualité canadienne; essais sur les relations entre Canadiens français et Canadiens anglais.* Québec, Presses de l'Université Laval; Toronto, University of Toronto Press, 1960. 427 p.

YUZIK, Paul. *The Ukrainians in Manitoba; a social history.* Toronto, University of Toronto Press, 1953. 232 p.

## The Economy

ANDERSON, W. J. *Canadian wheat in relation to the world's food production and distribution.* Saskatoon, Modern Press, 1964. 100 p.

ASHLEY, C. A. *The first twenty-five years; a study of Trans-Canada Air Lines.* Toronto, Macmillan, 1963. 72 p.

BRITNELL, G. E., and FOWKE, V. C. *Canadian agriculture in war and peace, 1935-1950.* Stanford, Calif., Stanford University Press, 1962. 502 p.

CAIRNS, J. P., and BINHAMMER, H., eds. *Canadian banking & monetary policy, recent readings.* Toronto, McGraw-Hill, 1965. 377 p.

CAMU, Pierre, WEEKS, E. P., and SAMETZ, Z. W. *Economic geography of Canada.* Toronto, Macmillan, 1964. 393 p.

CARROTHERS, A. W. R. *Collective bargaining law in Canada.* Toronto, Butterworths, 1965. 553 p.

CORBETT, D. C. *Politics and the airlines.* Toronto, University of Toronto Press, 1965. 350 p.

CURRIE, A. W. *Economics of Canadian transportation.* 2d ed. Toronto, University of Toronto Press, 1959. 735 p.

EASTERBROOK, W. T., and AITKEN, H. G. J. *Canadian economic history.* Toronto, Macmillan, 1956. 606 p.

GALBRAITH, J. A. *The economics of banking operations; a Canadian study.* Montreal, McGill University Press, 1963. 510 p.

GLAZEBROOK, G. P. de T. *A history of transportation in Canada.* New ed. Toronto, McClelland and Stewart, 1964. 2 v. (Carleton library, no. 11-12).

JAMIESON, A. B. *Chartered banking in Canada.* Rev. ed. Toronto, Ryerson Press, 1955. 448 p.

JAMIESON, S. M. *Industrial relations in Canada.* Toronto, Macmillan, 1957. 144 p. (Studies in international labor.)

LEONARD, W. G. *Financial management in Canadian business.* Toronto, McGraw-Hill, 1965. 235 p.

MCIVOR, R. C. *Canadian monetary, banking and fiscal development.* Toronto, Macmillan, 1958. 263 p.

MACKINTOSH, W. A. *The economic background of dominion-provincial relations; Appendix III of the Royal Commission report on dominion-provincial relations.* Toronto, McClelland and Stewart, 1964. 191 p. (Carleton library, no. 13).

NEUFELD, E. P., ed. *Money and banking in Canada; historical documents and commentary.* Toronto, McClelland and Stewart, 1964. 369 p. (Carleton library, no. 17).

PARKIN, J. H. *Bell and Baldwin; their development of aerodromes at Baddeck, Nova Scotia.* Toronto, University of Toronto Press, 1964. 555 p.

PEITCHINIS, S. G. *The economics of labour; employment and wages in Canada.* Toronto, McGraw-Hill, 1965. 412 p.

POTTER, C. C. *Finance and business administration in Canada.* Scarborough, Ont., Prentice-Hall, 1966. 578 p.

STEVENS, G. R. *Canadian National Railways.* Toronto, Clarke, Irwin, 1960-62. 2 v.

WOODS, H. D., and OSTRY, Sylvia. *Labour policy and labour economics in Canada.* Toronto, Macmillan, 1962. 534 p.

## The Social Milieu

BABBITT, J. D., ed. *Science in Canada. Selections from the speeches of E. W. R. Steacie.* Toronto, University of Toronto Press, 1965. 198 p.

BISSELL, C. T., comp. *Great Canadian writing; a century of imagination.* Toronto, Canadian Centennial Pub. Co., 1966. 127 p. (The Canadian centennial library).

BROWN, Florence M. *Breaking barriers; Eric Brown and the National Gallery.* Ottawa, Society for Art Publications, 1964. 113 p.

CANADA. DEPARTMENT OF CITIZENSHIP AND IMMIGRATION. *The Arts in Canada.* Ottawa, Queen's Printer, 1957. 120 p. (Canadian citizenship series, 6).

CANADA. MINISTÈRE DE LA CITOYENNETÉ ET DE L'IMMIGRATION. *Les arts au Canada.* Ottawa, Imprimeur de la Reine, 1958. 120 p. (Cahiers de la citoyenneté canadienne, 6).

*Canadian writers. Ecrivains canadiens. A biographical dictionary edited by—un dictionnaire biographique rédigé par*—Guy SYLVESTRE, Brandon CONRON, and C. F. KLINCK. Toronto, Ryerson Press, 1964. 163 p. (Articles on French language authors are in French.)

CARELESS, J. M. S. *Brown of the Globe.* Toronto, Macmillan, 1959-63. 2 v.

CLARK, S. D. *Church and sect in Canada.* Toronto, University of Toronto Press, 1948. 458 p.

CLARK, S. D. *The developing Canadian community.* Toronto, University of Toronto Press, 1962. 248 p.

EGGLESTON, Wilfrid. *Canada's nuclear story.* Toronto, Clarke, Irwin, 1965. 368 p.

ELKIN, Frederick. *La famille au Canada; données, recherches et lacunes du savoir sur les familles au Canada.* Ottawa, Congrès canadien de la famille, 1964. 208 p.

ELKIN, Frederick. *The family in Canada; an account of present knowledge and gaps in knowledge about Canadian families.* Ottawa, Canadian Conference on the Family, 1964. 192 p.

ELLIS, F. H. *Canada's flying heritage.* 2d ed. Toronto, University of Toronto Press, 1961. 398 p.

FOWKE, Edith M., and MILLS, Alan, (pseud.) *Canada's story in song.* Rev. ed. Toronto, Gage, 1965. 230 p. (Songs accompanied by explanatory text.)

GOWANS, Alan. *Looking at architecture in Canada.* Toronto, Oxford University Press, 1958. 232 p.

*Great Canadians; a century of achievement.* Selected by Vincent MASSEY and others. Toronto, Canadian Centennial Pub. Co., 1965. 122 p. (The Canadian centennial library).

HAMELIN, Jean. *Le renouveau du théâtre au Canada français.* Montréal, Éditions du Jour, 1962. 160 p. (Les Idées du jour, D4).

HUBBARD, R. H. *The development of Canadian art.* Ottawa, Queen's Printer, 1963. 137 p.

HUBBARD, R. H. *L'évolution de l'art au Canada.* Ottawa, Imprimeur de la Reine, 1963. 137 p.

INNIS, D. Q. *Canada; a geographic study.* Toronto, McGraw-Hill, 1966. 423 p.

IRVING, J. A., ed. *Mass media in Canada.* Toronto, Ryerson Press, 1962. 236 p.

KALLMANN, Helmut. *A history of music in Canada 1534-1914.* Toronto, University of Toronto Press, 1960. 311 p.

KEMP, V. A. M. *Scarlet and stetson; the Royal North-West Mounted Police on the prairies.* Toronto, Ryerson Press, 1964. 280 p.

KERR, D. G. G., ed. *Historical atlas of Canada.* Toronto, Nelson, 1960. 120 p.

KLINCK, C. F. et al, eds. *Literary history of Canada; Canadian literature in English.* Toronto, University of Toronto Press, 1965. 945 p.

LASKIN, R. J., ed. *Social problems; a Canadian profile.* Toronto, McGraw-Hill, 1964. 472 p.

*Livres et auteurs canadiens; panorama de la production littéraire* . . . Montréal, Éditions Jumonville. Annuel.

PACEY, Desmond. *Creative writing in Canada; a short history of English Canadian literature.* 2d ed. Toronto, Ryerson Press, 1961. 314 p.

PALARDY, Jean. *The early furniture of French Canada.* 2d ed. Toronto, Macmillan, 1965. 413 p.

PALARDY, Jean. *Les meubles anciens du Canada français.* Nouv. éd. Paris, Arts et Métiers graphiques, 1965. 192 p.

PORTER, J. A. *The vertical mosaic; an analysis of social class and power in Canada.* Toronto, University of Toronto Press, 1965. 626 p. (Studies in the structure of power; decision-making in Canada, 2).

ROSS, Malcolm, ed. *Poets of the confederation.* Toronto, McClelland and Stewart, 1960. 130 p. (A New Canadian library original, 91).

ROYAL SOCIETY OF CANADA. *Higher education in a changing Canada; symposium presented . . . in 1965. L'enseignement supérieur dans un Canada en évolution; colloque présenté . . . en 1965.* Edited by J. E. HODGETTS. Toronto, Published for the Society by University of Toronto Press, 1966. 90 p. ("Studia varia" series, 8).

ROYAL SOCIETY OF CANADA. *Pioneers of Canadian science; symposium presented . . . in 1964. Les pionniers de la science canadienne; colloque présenté . . . en 1964.* Ed. by G. F. G. STANLEY. Toronto, Published for the Society by University of Toronto Press, 1966. 146 p. ("Studia varia" series, 9).

SCHMEISER, D. A. *Civil liberties in Canada.* London, Oxford University Press, 1964. 302 p.

SISSONS, C. B. *Church and state in Canadian education; an historical study.* Toronto, Ryerson Press, 1959. 414 p.

SMITH, A. J. M. *The book of Canadian prose.* v. 1. *Early beginnings to Confederation.* Toronto, Gage, 1965.

SMITH, A. J. M., ed. *The Oxford book of Canadian verse in English and French.* Toronto, Oxford University Press, 1960. 445 p.

SOCIÉTÉ ROYALE DU CANADA. *Structures sociales du Canada français; études des membres de la Section I* . . . éditées par Guy SYLVESTRE. Québec, Toronto. Publié pour le compte de la Société par les Presses de l'Université Laval et University of Toronto Press, 1966. 120 p.

STRATFORD SHAKESPEAREAN FESTIVAL FOUNDATION OF CANADA. *The Stratford Festival story, 1953-1964.* Stratford, Ont., 1964. 28 p.

SWINTON, George. *Eskimo sculpture. Sculpture esquimaude.* Toronto, McClelland and Stewart, 1965. 224 p. (Text bilingual.)

SYLVESTRE, Guy, éd. *Anthologie de la poésie canadienne-française.* 4e éd. Montréal, Beauchemin, 1964. 376 p.

TOUGAS, Gérard. *Histoire de la littérature canadienne-française.* 2e éd. Paris, Presses Universitaires de France, 1964. 312 p.

TOUGAS, Gérard. *History of French-Canadian literature.* Translation by Alta Lind COOK. 2d ed. Toronto, Ryerson Press, 1966. 301 p.

TURNER, J. P. *The North-West Mounted Police, 1873-1893.* Ottawa, King's Printer, 1950. 2 v.

WEIR, E. A. *The struggle for national broadcasting in Canada.* Toronto, McClelland and Stewart, 1965. 477 p.

## Canada in World Affairs

BANFF CONFERENCE ON WORLD DEVELOPMENT. 3d, Banff, Alta., 1965. *Canada's role as a middle power; papers given at third annual Banff Conference on World Development, August 1965.* Ed. by J. King GORDON. Toronto, Canadian Institute of International Affairs, 1966. 212 p. (Contemporary affairs, no. 35).

CADIEUX, Marcel. *The Canadian diplomat; an essay in definition.* Trans. by Archibald DAY. Toronto, University of Toronto Press, 1963. 113 p.

CADIEUX, Marcel. *Le diplomate canadien; éléments d'une définition.* Montréal, Fides, 1962. 127 p. (Bibliothèque économique et sociale).

CANADA. ARMY. *Official history of the Canadian army in the Second World War.* Ottawa, Queen's Printer, 1955-1960. 3 v.
   v. 1. *Six years of war; the army in Canada, Britain and the Pacific,* by C. P. STACEY.
   v. 2. *The Canadians in Italy, 1943-1945,* by G. W. L. NICHOLSON.
   v. 3. *The victory campaign; the operations in north-west Europe, 1944-1945,* by C. P. STACEY.

CANADA. ARMÉE. *Histoire officielle de la participation de l'Armée canadienne à la Seconde Guerre mondiale.* Ottawa, Imprimeur de la Reine, 1957-1960. 3 v.
   v. 1. *Six années de guerre; l'Armée au Canada, en Grande-Bretagne et dans le Pacifique,* par C. P. STACEY.
   v. 2. *Les Canadiens en Italie, 1943-1945,* par G. W. L. NICHOLSON.
   v. 3. *La campagne de la victoire; les opérations dans le nord-ouest de l'Europe, 1944-1945,* par C. P. STACEY.

*Canada in world affairs.* Toronto, Oxford University Press, 1941:
   v. 1 and 2 out of print.
   v. 3. *September 1941-May 1944,* by C. C. LINGARD and R. G. TROTTER. 1950. 332 p.
   v. 4. *From Normandy to Paris, 1944-46,* by F. H. SOWARD. 1950. 372 p.
   v. 5. *From U.N. to NATO, 1946-49,* by R. A. SPENCER, 1959. 460 p.
   v. 6. *1949 to 1950,* by W. E. C. HARRISON. 1957. 382 p.
   v. 7. *September, 1951 to October, 1953,* by B. S. KEIRSTEAD. 1956. 280 p.
   v. 8. *1953 to 1955,* by D. C. MASTERS. 1965. 223 p. (An Oxford in Canada paperback, OCP4).
   v. 9. *October 1955 to June 1957,* by James EAYRS. 1965. 291 p. (An Oxford in Canada paperback, OCP5).
   v. 10. not yet published.
   v. 11. *1959-1961,* by R. A. PRESTON. 1965. 300 p.

CLASSEN, H. G. *Thrust and counterthrust. The genesis of the Canada-United States boundary.* Don Mills, Ont., Longmans, 1965. 386 p.

EAYRS, J. G. *The art of the possible; government and foreign policy in Canada.* Toronto, University of Toronto Press, 1961. 232 p.

EAYRS, J. G. *In defence of Canada.* v. 1. *From the Great War to the great depression.*
   v. 2. *Appeasement and rearmament.* Toronto, University of Toronto Press, 1964-65. 2 v. (Studies in the structure of power; decision-making in Canada, 1, 3.)

GLAZEBROOK, G. P. de T. *A history of Canadian external relations.* Rev. ed. Toronto, McClelland and Stewart, 1966. 2 v. (Carleton library, no. 27-28).

MINIFIE, J. M. *Open at the top; reflections on U.S.-Canada relations.* Toronto, McClelland and Stewart, 1964. 104 p.

NICHOLSON, G. W. L. *Canadian Expeditionary Force, 1914-1919.* Ottawa, Queen's Printer, 1962. 621 p.

NICHOLSON, G. W. L. *Le Corps expéditionnaire canadien, 1914-1919.* Ottawa, Imprimeur de la Reine, 1963. 671 p.

PENLINGTON, Norman. *Canada and imperialism, 1896-1899.* Toronto, University of Toronto Press, 1965. 288 p.

RIDDELL, W. A., ed. *Documents on Canadian foreign policy, 1917-1939.* Toronto, Oxford University Press, 1962. 806 p.

ROUSSIN, Marcel. *Le Canada et le système interaméricain.* Ottawa, Éditions de l'Université d'Ottawa, 1959. 285 p. (Les publications sériées de l'Université d'Ottawa, 59).

SCHULL, Joseph. *The far distant ships; an official account of Canadian naval operations in the Second World War.* Ottawa, Queen's Printer, 1961. 527 p.

SCHULL, Joseph. *Lointains navires; compte rendu officiel des opérations de la Marine canadienne au cours de la seconde Grande Guerre.* Ottawa, Imprimeur de la Reine, 1953. 605 p.

SPICER, J. K. *A samaritan state? External aid in Canada's foreign policy.* Toronto, University of Toronto Press, 1966. 272 p.

STANLEY, G. F. G. *Canada's soldiers; the military history of an unmilitary people.* Rev. ed. Toronto, Macmillan, 1960. 449 p.

## Reference Books

ASSOCIATION DES ÉDITEURS CANADIENS. *Catalogue de l'édition au Canada français.* 3e éd. Montréal, 1965. 278 p. (4e éd. paraîtra prochainement.)

CANADA. DOMINION BUREAU OF STATISTICS. *Canada; official handbook of present conditions and recent progress.* Ottawa, Queen's Printer. Annual.

CANADA. BUREAU FÉDÉRAL DE LA STATISTIQUE. *Canada; revue officielle de la situation actuelle et des progrès récents.* Ottawa, Imprimeur de la Reine. Annuel.

CANADA. DOMINION BUREAU OF STATISTICS. *Canada year book.* Ottawa, Queen's Printer. Annual.

CANADA. BUREAU FÉDÉRAL DE LA STATISTIQUE. *Annuaire du Canada.* Ottawa, Imprimeur de la Reine. Annuel.

CANADA. DOMINION BUREAU OF STATISTICS. *Publications of the Dominion Bureau of Statistics. Bureau fédéral de la statistique, publications.* Ottawa, Queen's Printer.

CANADA. NATIONAL LIBRARY. *Canadiana; publications of Canadian interest noted by the National Library.* Ottawa, Queen's Printer. Monthly, with annual cumulation.

CANADA. BIBLIOTHÈQUE NATIONALE. *Canadiana; publications se rapportant au Canada notées par la Bibliothèque nationale.* Ottawa, Imprimeur de la Reine. Mensuel, avec refonte annuelle.

*Canadian almanac and directory.* Toronto, Copp Clark. Annual.

*Canadian annual review.* Toronto, University of Toronto Press.

*Canadian periodical index. Index de périodiques canadiens.* Ottawa, Canadian Library Association. Association canadienne des bibliothèques. Monthly. Mensuel.

*Encyclopedia Canadiana.* Rev. ed. Ottawa, Grolier of Canada Limited, 1966. 10 v.

*Slavica Canadiana.* Winnipeg, Canadian Association of Slavists. Annual.

TANGHE, Raymond. *Bibliography of Canadian bibliographies.* Toronto, University of Toronto Press, 1960. 206 p. With biennial supplements.

TANGHE, Raymond. *Bibliographie des bibliographies canadiennes.* Toronto, University of Toronto Press, 1960. 206 p. Avec suppléments biennaux.

WATTERS, R. E., comp. *A check list of Canadian literature, and background material, 1628-1950.* Toronto, University of Toronto Press, 1960. 789 p.

(NATIONAL LIBRARY)

# Acknowledgements
## Notes on Contributing Writers

AGNEW, W. H. (*The Canadian Mosaic*) who was born in Albany, U.S.A., received his B.A. and M.A. degrees from Queen's University, and is chief of the Programmes and Materials Division of the Canadian Citizenship Branch of the Secretary of State Department. Mr. Agnew is the author of *Guide to Government in Canada*.

AITKEN, HUGH G. J. (*Canada's Industrial Society*) was born at Deal, England, served in the R.A.F. (1942-46), and is a professor at Amherst College, U.S.A. He received an M.A. Honours degree from St. Andrews University, an M.A. from the University of Toronto, and a Ph.D. from Harvard University. Among his major publications are: *The Welland Canal Company, Canadian Economic History* (with W. T. Easterbrook), *American Capital and Canadian Resources* and *Taylorism at Watertown Arsenal*. Dr. Aitken is editor of "The State and Economic Growth" and "Explorations in Enterprise".

BAIRD, IRENE (*The Eskimos in Canada*) who was born at Carlisle, England, is the first woman to be appointed to head an Information Service of the Federal Government. Mrs. Baird, a newspaperwoman, joined the National Film Board in 1942 and while stationed in Mexico opened that Board's first office in a Spanish-speaking country. She combined her Film Board duties with those of Press Officer to the Canadian Embassy. Mrs. Baird has served as consultant to the United Nations on the press and information needs of Technical Assistance Missions in the field, and was on the Government's Public Relations Committee at the NATO ministerial meeting held in Ottawa in 1963. She is the author of three novels: *John, Waste Heritage* and *He Rides the Sky*.

BATTLE, ROBERT F. (*Indians in Transition*) was born in Delia, Alberta and joined the Indian Affairs Branch following his return from overseas in 1945. Subsequently, he was appointed Regional Supervisor of Indian Agencies for Alberta and the Northwest Territories. He came to Ottawa in 1960 as Chief of the Branch's new Economic Development Division and in 1963 became Assistant Director of Indian Affairs in charge of Operations Services. In 1964, Mr. Battle was appointed Director of Indian Affairs, a position which later was elevated to that of Assistant Deputy Minister.

BLYTH, C. D. (*A Century of Economic Growth*) who was born in Ottawa, received his B.A. degree from the University of Toronto. Mr. Blyth has been successively a statistician with the Internal Trade Branch of the Dominion Bureau of Statistics, Acting Chief of the Statistics and Research Section, Chief of the Balance of Payments Section, Director of the International Trade Division and, since 1962, the Director of National Accounts and Balance of Payments Division.

BOOTH, JOHN F. (*Agriculture*) was born in Chicago, Illinois, of Canadian parents, and is an economic consultant. He received a B.S.A. from the University of

Saskatchewan, M.Sc. and Ph.D. degrees from Cornell University. Dr. Booth has been the Senior Economist, Bureau of Agricultural Economy, Washington; the Commissioner of Agricultural Economy, Department of Agriculture, Ottawa; Director, Economics Division and Special Adviser to the Department; member of the Wartime Agricultural Food Board, and the Agricultural Prices Support Board.

BORDEN, R. L. (*Energy Resources*) is a native of Saskatchewan, a graduate of the Universities of Alberta and Western Ontario and holds the degrees of M.Sc. and M.B.A. Mr. Borden worked for oil companies, for the (then) Department of Mines and Technical Surveys, and is now Chief of the Energy Statistics Section of the Dominion Bureau of Statistics. Mr. Borden has written numerous articles on geological and energy economics and is a lecturer in the field of mineral economics at Carleton University.

BROWN, A. L. and E. T. STEEVES (*Transportation*). Mr. Brown is a native of Charlottetown, Prince Edward Island. After five years' wartime service with the Canadian Army, he entered the University of Western Ontario and received an Honour B.A. in Business Administration. He is the Assistant Director, Governments and Transportation Division, Dominion Bureau of Statistics.

Mr. E. T. Steeves, a native of Moncton, New Brunswick, received a B.A. *magna cum laude* from St. Francis Xavier University, Antigonish, Nova Scotia, and an M.A. from Clark University, U.S.A. Mr. Steeves was Assistant Transport Economist with the Railway Association of Canada, Transport Economist with the Maritime Transportation Commission, and is now Chief of the Transportation and Public Utilities Section, Governments and Transportation Division, Dominion Bureau of Statistics.

CHAMPION, HELEN, (*Introducing Canada, Expansion* "... *from Sea to Sea* ...." and *Canadian Citizenship*) is a native of Prince Edward Island, and holds the degrees of B.A. (Dist.), Dalhousie University, Halifax, Nova Scotia; M.A., University of London, Eng.; and D.P.A., Carleton University. After historical research in Europe and Australia, teaching in India, editorial work with the Halifax Chronicle-Herald, and information for the (then) Department of Citizenship and Immigration, Miss Champion became editor of *Canada* (Handbook). Her publications include: *Over on the Island* and *Indian Education*.

CRAWFORD, J. N. (*Public Health*—prepared under Dr. Crawford's direction). Dr. Crawford was born in Winnipeg, Manitoba. He received an M.D. from the University of Manitoba and engaged in postgraduate study in the United States. After World War II, in which he served, Dr. Crawford was Deputy Director of General Medical Services; Brigadier and Executive Staff Officer, Canadian Forces Medical Council. He is now Deputy Minister of National Health.

DEMPSEY, H. V. (*Fisheries*) is a native of Alberta. Mr. Dempsey engaged in biological survey work in Fisheries before joining the Federal Department of Fisheries in 1945 at Winnipeg. Mr. Dempsey is now the Director of Inspection Service, Department of Fisheries.

ACKNOWLEDGEMENTS

DENTON, FRANK T. and SYLVIA OSTRY (*Labour Force: Growth and Change*). Mr. Denton, who was born in Toronto and received his B.A. and M.A. degrees from the University of Toronto, is Senior Adviser, Research and Econometrics at the Dominion Bureau of Statistics and acts as a part-time research consultant to the Economic Council of Canada. Previously he worked as a research economist for the Senate Committee on Manpower and Employment. His published work has appeared in leading economic, political science and statistical journals.

Dr. Ostry was born in Winnipeg and is Assistant Director of the Labour Division, of the Dominion Bureau of Statistics. She received an M.A. degree from McGill University and a Ph.D. with residence at Cambridge University and McGill. Dr. Ostry has been a Research Officer at the University of Oxford Institute of Statistics, an Assistant Professor at McGill University, and an Associate Professor of Economics at the University of Montreal. Her published works include *Labour Policy and Labour Economics in Canada* (with H. D. Woods) and *The Economic Status of the Aging* (with Miss J. Podoluk).

DOWNS, J. R. (*External Trade*) received an M.A. from the University of Saskatchewan and spent a year at the London School of Economics on a fellowship granted by his university. Mr. Downs was employed with the Department of Trade and Commerce and, in 1964, joined the staff of the newly formed Economic Council of Canada. He is the author of several articles on trade and international trade relations including *Export Projections to 1970* which is Staff Study No. 8 of the Economic Council of Canada.

EMMERSON, F. W. (*Financial Institutions*) was born in Abernethy, Saskatchewan. He received his B.A. degree from the University of Saskatchewan and his M.B.A. from the University of Chicago. Since graduation he has been with the Dominion Bureau of Statistics, and is co-ordinator, Financial Statistics.

ENGLISH, H. E. (*Manufacturing*) was born in Victoria, British Columbia, and is Professor of Economics at Carleton University, Ottawa. He received a B.A. from the University of British Columbia, a Ph.D. from the University of California. Dr. English has been Director of Research of the Canadian Trade Committee of the Private Planning Association of Canada and Secretary of the Private Planning Association. He is the author of *Industrial Structure in Canada's International Competitive Position*, Canadian Trade Committee, 1964, and several chapters in *Canadian Economic Policy*.

FARINA, ALFRED J. O. (*Recreation*) was born in Vancouver, British Columbia, and is Associate Professor, University of Toronto School of Social Work. He received B.A., B.S.W. and M.S.W. degrees from the University of British Columbia, and a D.S.W. from Washington University, U.S.A. Dr. Farina has served as Superintendent, City of Edmonton Recreation Commission; as Secretary, Group Work and Recreation Division, Canadian Welfare Council, Ottawa, and has written extensively on recreational subjects.

FISHER, JOHN W. (*Centennial Celebrations*) was born in Sackville, New Brunswick. He received his LL.D. from the University of Western Ontario, a D.Litt. from the University of St. Joseph, a D.Univ. from the University of Montreal. He has served as Commentator with the Canadian Broadcasting Corporation, Executive Director of the Canadian Tourist Association, as Special Assistant to the Prime Minister, and has been, since 1963, Commissioner of the National Centennial Administration.

GLAZEBROOK, GEORGE PARKIN DE T. (*Canada in World Affairs*) was born in London, Ontario. He received a B.A. from the University of Toronto and an M.A. from Oxford University. Formerly he was Professor of History, University of Toronto, Minister to Washington, and Assistant Under-Secretary of State for External Affairs, and is now Special Lecturer in History at the University of Toronto. He is the author of *Sir Charles Bagot in Canada*, *A Short History of Canada*, *History of Canadian External Relations*, and *A History of Transportation in Canada*.

HARRISON, J. D. B. (*Forestry*) was born in Edmonton, Alberta and received B.Sc.F., and M.Sc.F. degrees and, later, an honorary LL.D. from the University of New Brunswick. He was also awarded the Distinguished Conduct Medal for his service in World War I. Dr. Harrison conducted the first general economic study of Canadian forests and forest industries, "The Economic Aspects of the Forests and Forest Industries of Canada", was later chief of the forestry economics section of the Food and Agriculture Organization in Washington, and chairman of the North American Forestry Commission. Dr. Harrison, who became Canada's Deputy Minister of Forestry, retired in 1962.

HERBERT, WALTER B. (*The Fine and Lively Arts*) was born in Philadelphia of Canadian parents. From the University of Alberta he received his B.A., LL.B., and LL.D. degrees. Dr. Herbert is Executive Director of the Canada Foundation; member of the Senate, Carleton University; Director, Canadian Cultural Information Centre; chairman, Canadian Film Awards; and Seminar leader, School of Journalism, Carleton University. In 1958 Dr. Herbert received the Canadian Arts Council Diplôme d'Honneur; in 1962, the National Medal and President's Medal of the Canadian Public Relations Society; and in 1965 the Canada Council Medal.

LAGASSÉ, JEAN H. (*The Two Founding Peoples*) was born in Gravelbourg, Saskatchewan. He received a B.A. from the University of Manitoba and an M.A. from Columbia University. He was the Director of the Social and Economic Research Office, Department of Agriculture, Manitoba; subsequently, Director of the Community Development Services, Department of Welfare, Manitoba, and has been for some years Director of the Citizenship Branch, Department of the Secretary of State. Among his publications are *The People of Indian Ancestry in Manitoba*.

LANDRY, J.-MAURICE (*The National Capital*) is a native of Ottawa. Mr. Landry served in the Second World War, attended the University of Ottawa and the London School of Languages, and joined the federal civil service as a translator. In 1960 Mr. Landry was appointed Assistant Director of the Information and Historical Division of the National Capital Commission. Three years later he became Director of that Division.

LINGARD, C. CECIL (*Canada's Federal System of Government*, *Attainment of National Sovereignty* and *Retrospect and Prospect*) was born in Saskatchewan. He received a B.A. (Hon.) and M.A. from Queen's University and a Ph.D. from the University of Chicago. From 1945 to 1950 he was Editor of *International Journal* and Research Secretary of the Canadian Institute of International Affairs. In 1951 Dr. Lingard became Editor of the Canada Year Book and is now Director of the Canada Year Book, Handbook and Library Division of the Dominion Bureau of Statistics. His publications include: *Territorial Government in Canada, Canada in World Affairs 1941-44* (with R. G. Trotter), "Administration of the Northland", in *The New Northwest* and numerous articles in learned journals and encyclopaedias. The present volume was planned, edited and produced by Dr. Lingard, with the assistance of Miss Helen Champion.

LOWER, A. R. M. ("*British North America*" *in the 1860's* and *Factors in Confederation*) was born in Barrie, Ontario. He received B.A. and M.A. degrees from the University of Toronto, A.M. and Ph.D. degrees from Harvard University. He was also awarded LL.D. and D.Litt. degrees. Dr. Lower has served on the staff of Tufts College, Harvard University, the University of Toronto, and as Professor of History at the University of Manitoba and Queen's University. He has been President of the Royal Society of Canada, and a Senior Fellow of the Canada Council. Dr. Lower has twice won the Governor General's medal. His published works include: *Colony to Nation*; *A History of Canada*; *This Most Famous Stream*; and *Canadians in the Making*.

McKENDY, FRANCIS J. (*Labour Organization*) and MISS EVELYN WOOLNER (*Labour Legislation*). Mr. McKendy was born in Bathurst, New Brunswick. He received a B.A. degree from St. Thomas University, Chatham, New Brunswick and has studied at the University of Ottawa. He is Head, Labour Organizations and Labour Disputes Section, Economics and Research Branch, Department of Labour.

Miss Woolner was born at North Rustico, Prince Edward Island. She received a B.A. (Hon.) from Acadia University, and an M.A. from McGill University. She is on the staff of the Legislation Branch of the Department of Labour and is responsible for the annual publications, "Provincial Labour Standards" and "Workmen's Compensation in Canada".

MONAGHAN, WILLIAM A. (*Construction and Capital Investment*) was born in Halifax, Nova Scotia. He received a B.A. degree in Political Science and an M.A. in Political Economy from the University of Toronto and was employed with the Provincial Bank of Canada, Central Mortgage and Housing Corporation, Defence Research Board, Department of Trade and Commerce, Department of Northern Affairs and National Resources, and the Dominion Bureau of Statistics, until his appointment in 1965 to the External Aid Office.

OSTRY, S. (See page 490)

SHEA, ALBERT A. (*Communications*), a graduate of the University of Toronto who later taught political science at that university, and at the University of Manitoba, conducted research for the 1965 Committee on Broadcasting, and undertook commercial research, with special interest in Communications. Among his publications are: *World Communications* (Unesco), *Broadcasting the Canadian Way*, and *Canada, 1980*. Mr. Shea is with the Department of Mass Communications, UNESCO, Paris.

STEEVES, E. T. (See page 489)

STEWART, K. J. (See below)

SNYDER, GERALD (*Retail Trade*) was born in Ottawa, Ontario. He received a B. Com. degree from Carleton University, majoring in Economics, and undertook postgraduate work at the University of Ottawa. Mr. Snyder is now Chief of Current Statistics, Merchandising and Services Division, Dominion Bureau of Statistics.

THISTLE, MELVILLE W. (*Scientific and Industrial Research*) was born in St. John's, Newfoundland. He received B.Sc. and M.A. degrees from Mount Allison University, New Brunswick. He is the author of *Peter the Sea Trout*, and *The Inner Ring*, an early history of the National Research Council. Mr. Thistle is Manager, Public Relations Office, National Research Council.

TOOMBS, R. B. and STEWART, K. J. (*Mines and Minerals*). Mr. Toombs was born in Vancouver, British Columbia and received the degrees of B.A., B.A.Sc., and M.Sc. from the University of British Columbia. Mr. Stewart is a native of Charlottetown, Prince Edward Island, and received the degrees of B.Sc. and M.Sc. from the University of New Brunswick.

Mr. Toombs is Assistant Chief of the Mineral Resources Division, Department of Energy, Mines and Resources. Mr. Stewart is employed in the Research and Special Projects Section of the Mineral Resources Division. Their work includes analyses of Canada's mineral economy and the preparation of reports for government use and general distribution. Both were employed in the Canadian mineral industry in engineering and geological capacities prior to their entering government service.

WAGDIN, GEORGE A. (*Government Finance*) was born in Toronto, has a C.A. degree and is Director, Governments and Transportation Division, Dominion Bureau of Statistics. Prior to his arrival at DBS, Mr. Wagdin was a member of the Ontario Bureau of Statistics and Research. Mr. Wagdin was successively statistician in charge of provincial finance, and Chief of Federal and Provincial Finance Section, Public Finance Division, before he received his present appointment.

WHITWORTH, F. E. (*Education*) was born in Winnipeg. He received his M.A. degree from the University of California and his Ph.D. from the University of California, and was for some years on the staff of Carleton University. Dr. Whitworth developed the UNESCO statistical program and, until his recent retirement from the Public Service, was Director of the Education Division of the Dominion Bureau of Statistics. He is now the Director of the Canadian Council for Research in Education.

ACKNOWLEDGEMENTS                                                              493

WILLARD, JOSEPH W. (*Social Welfare*) who was born in Hamilton, Ontario, is the Deputy Minister of National Welfare, Department of National Health and Welfare. Dr. Willard received B.A. (Hon.) and M.A. degrees from the University of Toronto; M.P.A., A.M., and Ph.D. degrees from Harvard University, and joined the staff of National Health and Welfare in 1947. While Director of the Research and Statistics Division he played an important role in the development of the Department's programs. Dr. Willard has participated extensively in international health and welfare activities. He has been Canadian Representative on the Board of UNICEF, consultant to Health and Welfare Planning Commission of the Commonwealth of Puerto Rico, and in Medical Economics to the Jamaican Government.

WOOLNER, EVELYN F. (See page 492)

# Art and Photography

The art work for the cover was executed by Mr. Len Verhoeven of Brigdens Limited, Toronto. The assistance of Mr. J. D. Shaw, Mr. I. Young and Mr. R. Reck, respectively Production Manager, Chief of Planning, and Chief of Art and Illustrations, Publishing Production Division, Public Printing and Stationery, Ottawa, in various aspects of layout of the volume is gratefully acknowledged. The contributions of Mr. L. Tessier, Drafting Unit, DBS, in the preparation of the charts and of the Surveys and Mapping Branch, Department of Energy, Mines and Resources in compiling and drawing the maps are greatly appreciated.

Grateful acknowledgement is also made to the following governmental and commercial sources for assistance in supplying photographic material:

## Colour Transparencies

Alberta Government, Department of Industry and Development
Buckley, Anthony, London, England
Canadian Broadcasting Corporation
Canadian Government Participation Expo 67
Canadian Government Travel Bureau
Canadian Universal and International Exhibition, Montreal
Cholette, Paul, Managing Editor, *Montréal '66*
Department of National Defence, Ottawa
Department of Veterans Affairs, Ottawa
Ellefsen Photographe Inc.
Hunter, George, Toronto
Malak of Ottawa

Manitoba Department of Industry and Commerce
Moncton Men's Press Club
National Ballet of Canada
National Capital Commission
National Film Board
Nova Scotia Information Service
Office du Film du Québec
Onoszko, A. R., Ottawa
Ontario Department of Tourism and Information
Prince Edward Island Travel Bureau
St. Lawrence Seaway Authority

## Black and White Photographs

Alberta Government Department of Industry and Development
Atomic Energy of Canada Limited
Canada Cement Company Limited
Canadian Broadcasting Corporation
Canadian Government Travel Bureau
Canadian National Railways
Canadian Opera Company
Canadian Pacific Railway Company
Centennial Commission, Ottawa
Central Mortgage and Housing Corporation
Cobourg Public Schools
Department of Agriculture, Ottawa
Department of Energy, Mines and Resources, Ottawa
Department of External Affairs, Ottawa
Department of Fisheries, Ottawa
Department of Indian Affairs and Northern Development, Ottawa
Department of Manpower and Immigration, Ottawa
Department of National Defence, Ottawa
Department of National Health and Welfare, Ottawa

Department of National Revenue, Ottawa
Department of Public Works, Ottawa
Department of Trade and Commerce, Ottawa
Department of Transport, Ottawa
Deuterium of Canada Limited
Dominion Wide Photographs Limited
Edmonton Public Library
Engineered Buildings, Limited
General Motors of Canada Limited
Globe and Mail, Toronto
Harrington, Richard, Toronto
Hunter, George, Toronto
The Hydro-Electric Power Commission of Ontario
Industrial Canada
Industrial Development Board of Greater Winnipeg
Labour Gazette, Ottawa
Malak of Ottawa
Manitoba Department of Industry and Commerce
Moncton Publishing Company
Mount Allison University

National Film Board
National Research Council
New Brunswick Central News Bureau
New Brunswick Electric Power Commission
Nova Scotia Information Service
Office du Film du Québec
Onoszko, A. R., Ottawa
Ontario Department of Tourism and
  Information
Ontario Editorial Bureau
Ontario Research Foundation
Overseas Institute of Canada

Post Office Department, Ottawa
Prince Edward Island Travel Bureau
Public Archives, Ottawa
Regina Public Library
Rolly Ford Photo Publications Limited
St. Lawrence Seaway Authority
Saskatchewan Department of Industry
  and Information
Sherritt Gordon Mines Limited
Steel Company of Canada Limited
Toronto Art Gallery
United Press International

# Index

# Notes

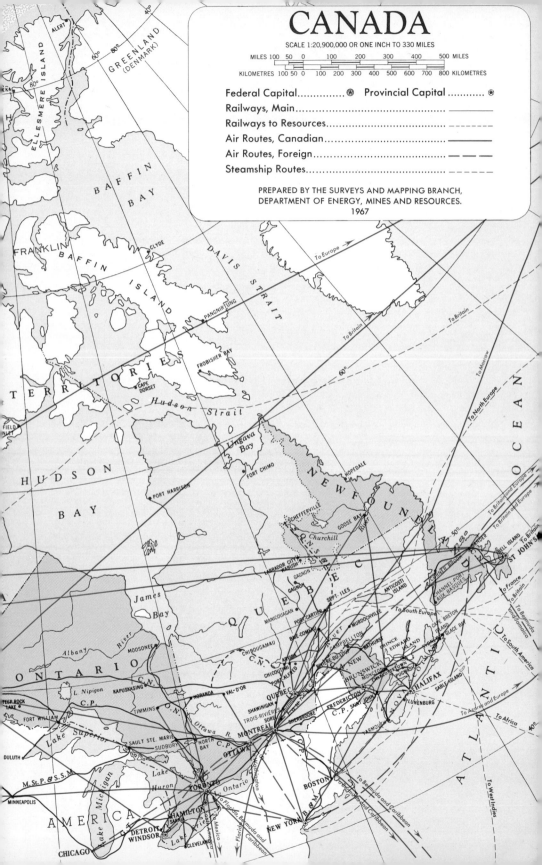

# CANADA

SCALE 1:20,900,000 OR ONE INCH TO 330 MILES

MILES 100 50 0 100 200 300 400 500 MILES

KILOMETRES 100 50 0 100 200 300 400 500 600 700 800 KILOMETRES

Federal Capital............... ⊛  Provincial Capital ............ ✦

Railways, Main.........................................................

Railways to Resources.............................................

Air Routes, Canadian...............................................

Air Routes, Foreign..................................................

Steamship Routes....................................................

PREPARED BY THE SURVEYS AND MAPPING BRANCH,
DEPARTMENT OF ENERGY, MINES AND RESOURCES.
1967